German Grammar and Usage

German Grammar and Usage

A E Hammer

 Edward Arnold

© A. E. Hammer 1971

First published 1971
by Edward Arnold (Publishers) Ltd.,
25 Hill Street,
London W1X 8LL

First published as a paperback 1973
Reprinted with corrections 1974
Reprinted with corrections 1976
Reprinted with extensive corrections 1977

Cloth ISBN: 0 7131 5985 5
Paper ISBN: 0 7131 5699 6

Printed in Great Britain by
Whitstable Litho Ltd., Whitstable, Kent

PREFACE

This book is intended as a reference grammar for sixth form and university use, while teachers may also find it helpful. I have sought to test traditional rules and forms by current German practice, to avoid smoothing over the complications and vagaries of a living language and at the same time to present its complexities in as handy a form as possible. I hope the user may find that the book answers a good many of the questions.

No one writing a book on German grammar at this point of time starts from scratch or can avoid indebtedness to earlier workers in the field. My own great and principal debt is to the Dudenverlag in Mannheim and to the grey volumes of 'Der große Duden'. Volume 4, *Grammatik* (1966), has been invaluable as a sheer guide for the ground to be covered, as a reminder of many details which might have escaped inclusion (the paragraphs on the uses of the subjunctive may serve as an example) and for its exhaustive lists (e.g. of nouns with double genders, of adjectives used with the dative and of verbs with prepositional constructions). In the case of particularly helpful and perceptive sections of Duden, I have given specific references; factually, my chapter on word formation owes most to the *Grammatik*. Where I have used examples from Duden, I have frequently mentioned the fact, and always where the example is a quotation. I should, however, say that I have never accepted Duden as infallible, have frequently checked his rulings by reference to the layman and sometimes reached different conclusions. Exceptions to this are the chapters on orthography and punctuation, which are based more or less unquestioningly on the *Duden-Taschenbücher* listed in the Bibliography and especially on vol. 3, from which my examples are largely taken. Finally, I cannot forbear mentioning a magic week's work, in August 1967, at the 'Sprachberatungsstelle' of the Dudenverlag in Mannheim, with Dr. Wolfgang Mentrup as my untiring guide, philosopher and friend; he has been equally untiring in answering queries by letter.

My book owes much, too, to the Anglo-German dictionary of Muret-Sanders and to *Cassell's New German Dictionary* by Dr. H. T. Betteridge, who very kindly gave me permission to draw on his admirable examples without individual acknowledgement, which, in the event, I have only sometimes presumed to do.

My indebtedness to the other items of the Bibliography has everywhere been specifically indicated. Beyond that, I owe something to the sound competence of F. R. H. McLellan's book and to J. A. Corbett's very full treatment of prepositions, while my section on the rendering of English prepositions in further contexts goes back to paragraph 296 in H. S. Beresford-Webb's *Practical German Grammar*; I also owe something to the treatment of prefixes in that book.

Some of my illustrative quotations are taken from papers set at Advanced Level by the Oxford and Cambridge Schools Examination Board and for Cambridge Scholarship Examinations; some of these come from works that I have not read.

I acknowledge with pleasure and sincere gratitude my debt to countless Germans of every age and calling, some of them complete strangers, who have willingly submitted to linguistic interrogations and have furthered my attempt to make this book at least an approximate reflection of current German usage. (As the late Professor Boyanus once observed, 'the native is always right'.) Even those who have, in addition, meticulously answered many pages of queries by letter are too numerous to mention by name. I must, however, make an exception in the case of my friend Dr. Günther Deitenbeck, of the Zeppelin-Gymnasium, Lüdenscheid, and his family, who have helped me indefatigably over so many years.

Among those on this side of the North Sea who have kindly helped me in various ways, I would particularly like to thank Dr. C. H. Good, of the University of East Anglia, who read the manuscript, correcting many points of detail and suggesting numerous, in some cases far-reaching improvements; Mr. C. W. Oakley, Head of the Modern Languages Department, Selhurst Grammar School for Boys, Croydon, who checked the proofs and suggested various clarifications; and Mr. J. A. Towers, sometime Senior Mathematics Master at Sedbergh School, who supplied the material from which 'some contemporary mathematical terms' (paragraph 259) were selected.

Finally, I gratefully remember the late Dr. S. H. Steinberg and his ever ready collaboration in the production of a privately printed booklet of German Grammar Notes that formed the nucleus of the present volume.

A.E.H.

London
June, 1971

POINTS FOR THE USER

1. Lists of words are in general alphabetical, though occasionally a deviation from this has seemed more helpful.
2. Where required, a noun is followed by a bracket containing its nominative plural in abbreviated form, e.g. das Lager (–) = die Lager; der Hut (–e) = die Hüte; (–en, –en) and (–n, –n) indicate that the noun has those endings except in the nominative singular, e.g. der Affe (–n, –n).
3. A separable prefix is indicated by a hyphen, but where this factor is of no immediate relevance, the hyphen is often omitted in the interests of clarity.
4. Where required, a stressed word is indicated by italics, a stressed syllable by a grave accent, e.g. Ich habe die Birne *ihr* gegeben; der Dòktor, die Doktòren.
5. All numbers refer to paragraphs, unless preceded by p. or pp., when they refer to pages.
6. For time phrases, the user should go to Chapter X; they have been kept to a minimum in the chapter on prepositions.
7. North German, rather than South German, has been taken as standard.

CONTENTS[1]

[1] The numbers following the sections of each chapter refer to paragraphs, not pages.

[1] For Subordinating Conjunctions not included in E—I, see D.

BIBLIOGRAPHY

Agricola, Erhard, *Wörter und Wendungen*, Leipzig, 1968
Bech, Gunnar, *Studien über das deutsche Verbum Infinitum*, Copenhagen, 1955 and 1957
Beresford-Webb, H. S., *A Practical German Grammar*, Longmans, 1914
Betteridge, H. T., *Cassell's New German Dictionary*, 1957
Carstensen, Broder, *Englische Einflüsse auf die deutsche Sprache nach 1945*, Heidelberg, 1965
Collinson, W. E., *The German Language Today*, Hutchinson's University Library, 1968
Corbett, J. A., *Essentials of Modern German Grammar*, Harrap, 1948
Der Große Duden, Dudenverlag, Mannheim

  1 *Rechtschreibung*, 1967
  2 *Stilwörterbuch*, 1963
  4 *Grammatik*, 1966
  8 *Synonymwörterbuch*, 1964
  9 *Hauptschwierigkeiten*, 1965

Duden-Taschenbücher

  1 *Komma, Punkt und alle anderen Satzzeichen*, 1968, by Dieter Berger
  3 *Die Regeln der deutschen Rechtschreibung*, 1968, by Wolfgang Mentrup
  6 *Wann schreibt man groß, wann schreibt man klein?* 1969, by Wolfgang Mentrup and others

Eggeling, H. F., *A Dictionary of Modern German Prose Usage*, Oxford, Clarendon Press, 1961
Erben, Johannes, *Abriß der deutschen Grammatik*, Darmstadt, 1963
Es geht weiter, Everyday German by Radio, B.B.C., 1965
Fleischer, Wolfgang, *Wortbildung der deutschen Gegenwartssprache*, Leipzig, 1969
Grubačić, Emilija, *Untersuchungen zur Frage der Wortstellung in der deutschen Prosadichtung der letzten Jahrzehnte*, Zagreb, 1965
Mater, Erich, *Rückläufiges Wörterbuch der deutschen Gegenwartssprache*, Leipzig, 1965
McLellan, F. R. H., *A School Grammar of Modern German*, Cambridge University Press, 1938
Möller, Georg, *Deutsch von Heute*, Leipzig, 1962
Muret-Sanders, *Enzyklopädisches englisch-deutsches und deutsch-englisches Wörterbuch*, Berlin, 1910
Schulz-Griesbach, *Grammatik der deutschen Sprache*, Longmans-Hueber, 1965
Stopp, F. J., *A Manual of Modern German*, University Tutorial Press, 1960
Wahrig, Gerhard, *Deutsches Wörterbuch*, Gütersloh, 1968

Articles from periodicals are mentioned at the relevant place in the text.

List of main authors and journals quoted

Vicki Baum	Gerd Gaiser	Thomas Mann
Heinrich Böll	Albrecht Goes	Theodor Plievier
Hermann Broch	Michael Horbach	Thomas Valentin
Hans Fallada	Annette Kolb	Ingeborg Wendt
Max Frisch	Elisabeth Langgässer	Carl Zuckmayer

Also numerous authors included in the anthology *Erfundene Wahrheit, Deutsche Ge-schichten seit 1945*, herausgegeben von Marcel Reich-Ranicki, München, 1965

Frankfurter Allgemeine Zeitung   *Der Spiegel*
Hamburger Abendblatt   *Süddeutsche Zeitung*
                                                Die Zeit

ABBREVIATIONS

A., acc.	accusative	m., masc.	masculine
adj.	adjective(s)	MHG	Middle High German
adv.	adverb	misc.	miscellaneous
attrib.	attributive	N.	Note; Nominative
ch., chap.	chapter	n., ncut.	neuter
cl.	clause	neg.	negative
coll.	colloquial	nom.	nominative
compar.	comparative	obj.	object
condit.	conditional	obs.	obsolete
conj.	conjunction	OHG	Old High German
D., dat.	dative	o.s.	oneself
decl.	declension, declined	part.	participle
def. art.	definite article	perf.	perfect
demonstr.	demonstrative	pers.	person
dimin.	diminutive	phr.	phrase(s)
dir.	direct	pl., plur.	plural
elev.	elevated style	pluperf.	pluperfect
exc.	except, exception(s)	possess.	possessive
f., fem.	feminine	prep.	preposition, prepositional
fig.	figurative(ly)	pres.	present
Fr.	French	pron.	pronoun; pronounced
fut.	future	refl.	reflexive
G., gen.	genitive	rel.	relative
Gn.	German	(s)	conjugated with 'sein'
Gr.	Group	s.o.	someone
(h)	conjugated with 'haben'	s.th.	something
imperf.	imperfect	sep.	separable
impers.	impersonal	sing.	singular
indecl.	indeclinable	sl.	slang
indef. (art.)	indefinite (article)	str.	strong
indic.	indicative	sub. cl.	subordinate clause
indir.	indirect	subj.	subjunctive
inf., infin.	infinitive	subst.	substantive, substantival
insep.	inseparable	superl.	superlative
interrog.	interrogative	tr.	transitive
intr.	intransitive	uninfl.	uninflected
lit.	literal(ly)	wk.	weak

The five volumes of *Der große Duden* listed in the Bibliography are respectively referred to as:

Du. Rechtschreibung   Du. Synonymwörterbuch
Du. Stil.   Du. Haupt.
Du. Gram.

Newspapers:

FAZ = *Frankfurter Allgemeine Zeitung*

Hbg. Abendblatt = *Hamburger Abendblatt*

Spiegel = *Der Spiegel*

SZ = *Süddeutsche Zeitung*

Zeit = *Die Zeit*

I NOUNS

A. GENDER RULES

1. German nouns are masculine, feminine or neuter, e.g. der Tisch *table*, die Blume *flower*, das Buch *book*.
There are a certain number of useful gender rules, but it is all-important to learn all nouns with their definite article. With growing familiarity with the language, the ear becomes increasingly helpful for determining the gender of a noun not covered by rules, e.g. 'der Schrank' sounds right; 'die Schrank' and 'das Schrank' sound wrong. The Plural Lists (20 ff.) are also a mine of gender information.
Only those gender rules are here given, which, in the author's view and experience, are of practical use.

2. Masculine by meaning are:

(a) **Names of male persons and animals** (but see 8):
der Vater, der Arzt, der Tischler *carpenter*, der Löwe, der Hengst *stallion*.

Note:
i The species may be masc., fem. or neut., e.g. der Fisch, die Ratte, das Pferd.
ii In the absence of a current specific term, the male or female of any species of animal or bird, irrespective of size, may be indicated by 'das Männchen' or 'das Weibchen', e.g. das Zebramännchen, das Weibchen des Elefanten.
iii The terms for the young (human and animal) are neuter (see 6(a)).

(b) **A picture by such-and-such an artist:** Er will seinen Rembrandt verkaufen.

(c) **Most instruments or inanimate agents in -er:** der Computer, der Wagenheber *jack*, der Wecker *alarm-clock*.
They are masculine by analogy with animate agents (der Bäcker, der Maler); in other words, they are personified. In some cases the same word may denote an animate and an inanimate agent: der Anhänger 1. *adherent* 2. *trailer*; der Hörer 1. *listener* 2. *receiver, headphone*.

(d) **Makes of cars** ('der Wagen' being understood): der Mercedes, der Opel, der Rolls-Royce.

(e) **Seasons, months, days of week, points of compass:** der Frühling, der Januar, der Montag, der Norden.

3. **Masculine by form are:**

(a) **Nouns in -ich, -ig, -ing, -ling:** der Teppich, der Honig, der Hering, der Liebling.

(b) **Foreign nouns in -ant, -ast, -ismus, -or:** der Konsonant, der Kontrast, der Idealismus, der Regulator.

Some further foreign suffixes mainly denote male persons: der Ingenieur, der Offizier, der Optimist (male or female), der Student.

(c) **Most nouns 'formed from strong verb stems to which nothing has been added'**[1] (cf. 714): der Biß *bite*, der Fall *fall; case*, der Wurf *throw* (BUT: die Falle *trap*, die Flucht *flight*).
Common exceptions are: das Band *bond; ribbon*, das Grab *grave*, das Leid *harm; sorrow, care*, das Maß *measurement*, das Schloß *lock; castle*, das Verbot *prohibition*.

4. **Feminine by meaning are:**

(a) **Names of female persons and animals** (but see 8): die Mutter, die Ärztin, die Löwin, die Stute *mare*.

Note:
i The commonest way of forming nouns denoting females is to add -in to the masculine form, often with Umlaut (cf. 715(c)).
ii All diminutives in -chen, -lein etc. are neuter (see 7(b)); therefore: das Mädchen, das Fräulein.

(b) **Most makes of aeroplanes** ('die Maschine' being understood): eine Boeing 727, die Comet, eine Junker (eine Ju) 52, BUT: der PAN-AM Clipper, der Starfighter.

(c) **Ships named after countries or towns** (die Deutschland, die Bremen) **and many others** (e.g. die Bismarck, die Graf Spee).

(d) **German rivers:** die Donau, die Mosel, die Ruhr. Exc. der Rhein, der Main, der Neckar, der Inn, der Lech.
Non-German rivers are mainly masculine, e.g. der Ganges, der Nil, der Severn, but those ending in -a or -e are feminine, e.g. die Wolga, die Loire, die Themse.

(e) **Cardinal numbers:** eine Null (0), eine Fünf; ich habe für den Aufsatz eine Eins[2] bekommen.
Hundert and Tausend are feminine when they denote 'the numerical symbol, but neuter when used substantivally as a unit of quantity (cf. 245(b)). Thus: Unter die Tausend schrieb er eine Hundert. BUT: das erste Tausend Soldaten.

[1] from Corbett, op. cit., 62(c).
[2] the best of the six grades (Noten) used in German schools.

5. **Feminine by form are:**

(a) **Most nouns in -e:** die Blume, die Garage, die Wärme.

EXCEPTIONS:

i Names of male persons and animals: der Junge, der Lotse *pilot* (of ship), der Riese, der Löwe.
ii 7 masculines in Group 1, usually without -n in nom. sing., e.g. der Name (see 20).
iii der Käse (see 50).
iv Most nouns with prefix Ge- (see 27), these being mainly neuter: das Gebäude, das Gelaufe *running about, bustle.*
v das Auge, das Ende, das Erbe *inheritance,* das Interesse.

(b) **Nouns with the suffixes -ei, -heit, -keit, -schaft, -ung:** die Schmeichelei, die Kindheit, die Ehrlichkeit, die Freundschaft, die Landung.
Exc. das Petschaft *seal, signet.*[1]

(c) **Foreign nouns in -a**[2], **-anz, -enz, -ie, -ik, -ion, -tät, -ur:** die Kamera, die Eleganz, die Existenz, die Biologie, die Musik, die Explosion, die Qualität, die Natur.
Exc. der Atlantik, der Pazifik, der Spion; das Genie *genius,* das Stadion *stadium.*

6. **Neuter by meaning are:**

(a) **Most terms for the young (human and animal):** das Baby, das Kind, das Mündel *ward, minor;* das Ferkel *young pig,* das Füllen *foal,* das Kalb, das Küken *chick,* das Lamm.

Note: In the absence of a specific term, the substantival adjective das Junge (ein Junges) is used, e.g. das Junge des Leoparden.

(b) **Continents, countries, towns:** das gärende Afrika *Africa in ferment;* das schöne Italien; Paris—ich liebe es!

EXCEPTIONS:

MASCULINE, generally used with definite article: (der) Irak, (der) Iran, der Jemen, der Kongo, der Libanon, der Sudan; der Haag *The Hague.*

FEMININE, always used with definite article:
i die Schweiz   ii countries in -ei: die Tschechoslowakei   iii die Bundesrepublik Deutschland (die BRD), die Deutsche Demokratische Republik (die DDR), die Sowjetunion (die UdSSR).

N.B. UdSSR = Union der Sozialistischen Sowjetrepubliken.
USSR = Ukrainische Sozialistische Sowjetrepublik.

PLURAL: die Niederlande, die Vereinigten Staaten (von Amerika), die US(A). While officially die USA is plural, in conversation it is generally treated as fem. sing.: die USA hat (haben) noch nicht geantwortet; in der (den) USA.

For the gender of names of regions (der Balkan, die Arktis, das Elsaß)

[1] of Czech origin; MHG petschat; the f crept in by analogy.
[2] but not in -ma (see 31(b)ii).

consult a dictionary. The 11 Länder of the German Federal Republic are all neuter, e.g. das eigenwillige Bayern.

(c) **Metals:** das Eisen, das Kupfer.
Exc. der Stahl, die Bronze.

(d) **Other parts of speech used as nouns:** das Schwimmen, ein zartes Blau, das vertraute Du, sein ewiges Nein, das Für und Wider, das Jenseits *the next world*, das Ach (cf. 639).
Exc. der Rechtsaußen *outside right*, der Linksinnen, and Cardinals (see 4(e)).

(e) **Onomatopoeic words:** das Kikeriki *cock-a-doodle-doo*, das Tucktuck-tuck des Motors.
The numerous masculine exceptions are generally well established words, some of which have further, derived meanings:
der Klaps (–e) *smack, slap*; *'screw loose'* (sl.)
der Klatsch (–e) *smack, crack* (of whip); *gossip*
der Krach (–e) *crash*; *noise, din*; *quarrel*; *bankruptcy*
der Puff (⁒e) *puff, bang*; *blow, nudge*
Also e.g. der Bums, der Plumps, der Schwaps.

(f) **Letters of the alphabet:** ein großes M, das hohe C.

(g) **Fractions:** das Fünftel.   Exc. die Hälfte.

7. **Neuter by form are:**

(a) **Most nouns with the prefix Ge-;** see 27.

(b) **Diminutives in -chen, -el, -erl, -le, -lein and -li:** das Bäumchen, das Mädel, das Fräulein (cf. 715(b), but see also 672(b)iii).

(c) **Nouns in -nis:** das Ereignis, das Gefängnis, das Geheimnis.
The five commonest fem. exceptions are: die Erlaubnis, die Ersparnis *saving*, die Finsternis, die Kenntnis, die Wildnis.

(d) **Nouns in -tum:** das Christentum *Christianity*. das Eigentum *property*.
Exc. der Irrtum *error*, der Reichtum *wealth*.

(e) **Foreign nouns in -at, -ett, -fon (older: -phon), -ma, -ment, -um, -ium:** das Internat *boarding-school*, das Ballett, das Telefon, das Klima *climate*, das Experiment, das Album, das Stadium *stage, phase*.
Exc. die Firma, der Zement.

B. MISCELLANEOUS GENDER POINTS

8. **Some anomalous genders of names of human beings**

die Memme *coward* (commoner: der Feigling)
die Ordonnanz *orderly*
die Person *person*
die Wache *guard, sentry*
die Waise *orphan* (m. or f.)
(BUT: zum Waisen machen *to orphan*)

das Genie *genius* (creative power + person)
das Haupt *head* (e.g. of family, the state) cf. das Staatsoberhaupt
das Individuum *individual*
das Mitglied *member*
das Weib *woman, wife* (archaic, elev. or pejorative)

9. Teil *part, share* is generally masc. in modern German: dieser Teil von Deutschland; er behielt den größeren Teil. It is neut. in certain fixed phrases, e.g. du hast dein Teil getan, ich für mein Teil; see dictionary. Compounds of 'Teil' (they all add -e to form plural):
DER Anteil, Hinterteil *back part*; stern.
DAS Abteil, Erbteil, Gegenteil, Hinterteil *buttocks, crupper*, Oberteil, Vorderteil.

10. Meter and its compounds:
Meter, Millimeter and Zentimeter are officially neuter, but colloquially they are often masculine; in Switzerland they are officially masc.
Kilometer and Gasometer are masculine.
Barometer and Thermometer are neuter.

11. Fußball is masculine, both for the ball and the game.

12. Compound nouns have the gender of the last component: der Pflaumenbaum, die Bushaltestelle, das Seebad.

EXCEPTIONS:
i Compounds of 'der Mut': about half are feminine:
DER Edelmut, Freimut, Gleichmut, Hochmut, Kleinmut, Mißmut, Übermut, Unmut, Wankelmut.
DIE Anmut, Demut, Großmut, Langmut, Sanftmut, Schwermut, Wehmut.
(die Armut *poverty* is not a compound of 'Mut'.)
ii die Scheu *timidity* BUT: der Abscheu *abhorrence*.
iii das Wort *word* BUT: die Antwort *answer*.

13. The gender of abbreviations is determined by the basic word, e.g. die CDU (die Christlich-Demokratische Union), die NATO (die Organisation). (See also 6(b): Exceptions) Cf. colloquial abbreviations: der Krimi (der Kriminalroman), die Kripo (die Kriminalpolizei), die Uni (die Universität), das Labor (das Laboratorium).

14. The gender of foreign loan-words in German[1] (See also 3(b), 5(c), 7(e).)

(a) **Greek and Latin loan-words** normally retain their original gender: der Planet, der Zirkus; die Dosis, die Kamera; das Symptom, das Album.

(b) **French masc. nouns:**
i all animates are masc. in German: der Ingenieur, der Kadett.
ii nouns in -ant are masc. in German: der Konsonant ['nant]
iii nouns in -age are fem. in German: die Etage (pron. as 3 syllables).
iv nouns in -et and -ment are neut. in German: das Ballett, das Instrument, das Abonnement; exc. der Zement.
v the remainder are partly masc. and partly neut. in German: der Karton, der Likör; das Bonbon, das Café, das Restaurant ['rã:]

Words derived from French fem. nouns are fem. in German; -tät corresponds to French -té: die Existenz, die Fassade, die Nation, die Qualität.

[1] cf. Corbett, op. cit., 65.

(c) **English (and American) words** are mainly masc. (der Boom, der Job, der Slogan, der Streik, der Trend) or neut. (das Hobby, das Image, das Make-up, das Quiz, das Understatement).[1] Sometimes an analogous German or French word decides the gender; where the English word is fem. in German, this is almost always the case. Thus:

der Container (cf. 2(c))	die Story (die Historie)
der Hit (der Schlager)	das Dumping (corresponds to a
die City (la cité)	Germ. infin. used as a noun)
die Party (die Partie)	das Festival (das Fest)

15. **Nouns with varying genders:** there are very many of these; the following list is selected from Du. Gram. 1385, with the gender most commonly used:

der Abscheu *abhorrence*	das Match *match, game*
der Barock *Baroque*	der Meteor *meteor*
der Chor *choir; chancel*	das Pendel *pendulum*
der Dschungel *jungle*	das Radar *radar*
das Gelee *jelly*	das Radio *radio*
der Kehricht *sweepings, refuse*	das Taxi *taxi* (commoner: die Taxe)
der Keks *biscuit*	das (Vogel)bauer *bird-cage*
der Knäuel *skein, tangle*	das Willkommen *welcome*
der Kompromiß *compromise*	das Zepter *sceptre*
der Liter *litre*	das Zubehör *accessories*

16. For lists of **double genders with different meanings,** see 39.

C. PLURAL FORMATION

17. **Note on the Plural Groups in 18:**

i In the way in which they form the plural, German nouns fall into 7 main groups.

ii The plural groups supersede the older terminology of strong, weak and mixed declensions; a scheme similar to that given in 18 is used in Schulz-Griesbach, op. cit., C 101.

iii The following vowels can have Umlaut (modification): a, o, u, au; in the case of Groups 4 and 5, (⸚e) and (⸚er) imply 'with Umlaut where possible'.

iv (–(e)n), in Groups 6 and 7, means that -n is added to nouns ending in -e, in unstressed vowel + l or in unstressed vowel + r; otherwise -en is added. E.g.

Nom. Sing.	Nom. Plur.	Nom. Sing.	Nom. Plur.
die Schule	die Schulen	die Uhr	die Uhren
die Tafel	die Tafeln	der Pfau	die Pfauen
der Nachbar	die Nachbarn		

v Where two examples are followed by 'etc.', this means that they are the first two nouns of the corresponding list; these lists follow in 20–26.

[1] Regarding the spread and influence of English and American words, see articles by D.V. White, Estelle Morgan and David Heard in *Modern Languages*, June 1959, June 1965 and December 1970 respectively; Du. Haupt.: Amerikanismen/Anglizismen; and Carstensen, op. cit. in Bibliography.

vi For the plural of Ge- nouns, see 27.
vii For the plural of foreign nouns, see 28–31.

18. Plural Groups

1 (–) Most masc. and all but one neut. in {-el: der Onkel / -en: der Schatten / -er: das Ufer}
(see Group 2)
Neut. in -chen and -lein: Mädchen, Fräulein

2 (⸚) 22 masc. in -el, -en, -er: Acker, Apfel etc.
2 fem.: Mutter, Tochter
1 neut.: Kloster

3 (–e) 57 masc.: Aal, Abend etc.
56 neut. monosyllabics: Beet, Beil etc.
nouns in -nis (–nisse): das Ereignis, die Ersparnis

4 (⸚e) **Most masc.**: Stuhl, Vorhang
33 fem. monosyllabics: Angst, Axt etc.
1 neut.: Floß

5 (⸚er) **Most neut.**: Buch, Eigentum
12 masc.: Geist, Gott etc.

6 (–(e)n) **Most fem.**: Schule, Uhr, Lehrerin (–innen)
18 masc.: Ahn, Dorn etc.
5 neut.: Auge, Bett etc.

7 (–(e)n) (thus in plur. and also in acc., gen. and dat. sing.)
Masc. in -e: Affe, Russe
33 masc. not in -e: Asiat, Bär etc.

19. Survey of plural formation according to gender

MASCULINE
MOSTLY Group 4: der Stuhl (⸚e)
Those in -el, -en, -er:
  mainly Gr. 1 (–): der Onkel, der Schatten, der Lehrer
  22 in Gr. 2 (⸚): Acker, Apfel etc.
57 in Gr. 3 (–e): Aal, Abend etc.
12 in Gr. 5 (⸚er): Geist, Gott etc.
18 in Gr. 6 (–(e)n): Ahn, Dorn etc.
Those in -e ⎫ Gr. 7 (–(e)n ⎰ der Affe
33 not in -e ⎭ except in nom. sing.) ⎱ Asiat, Bär etc.

FEMININE
MOSTLY Group 6: die Schule (–n)
2 in Gr. 2 (⸚): Mutter, Tochter
Those in -nis: Gr. 3 (–e): die Ersparnis (–se)
33 monosyllabics in Gr. 4 (⸚e): Angst, Axt etc.

NEUTER
MOSTLY Group 5: das Buch (⸚er)
Those in -el, -en, -er, -chen, -lein: Gr. 1 (–):
    das Segel, das Kissen, das Ufer, das Mädchen, das Fräulein
    One exception: das Kloster (⸚)
56 monosyllabics }: Gr. 3 (–e) { Beet, Beil etc.
Those in -nis }   { das Ereignis (–se)
1 in Gr. 4 (⸚e): das Floß
5 in Gr. 6 (–(e)n): Auge, Bett etc.

D. PLURAL LISTS

(These lists are not 100% complete, but include all nouns normally required and
which are used in the plural.)

20. Group 1 (–): 7 masc. are usually without -n in nom. sing.

Buchstabe[1] *letter of alphabet*
Friede *peace*
Funke *spark*
Gedanke *thought*
Glaube *belief*
Name *name*
Wille *will*

Example:
N. der Name
A. den Namen
G. des Namens
D. dem Namen
Plur. die Namen etc.

21. Group 2 (⸚): 22 masc. in -el, -en, -er

Acker *ploughed field*
Apfel *apple*
Boden *floor; attic*
Bogen[2] *arch, curve, arc*
Bruder *brother*
Faden *thread*
Garten *garden*
Graben *ditch*
Hafen *harbour*
Hammer *hammer*
Kasten *(wooden) box*

Laden *shop; shutter*
Magen *stomach*
Mangel *lack, deficiency*
Mantel *overcoat*
Nagel *nail*
Ofen *oven, stove*
Sattel *saddle*
Schnabel *beak*
Schwager *brother-in-law*
Vater *father*
Vogel *bird*

Note: das Lager (–) *camp; couch* sometimes has plur. die Läger, especially when
used in the sense of supplies in store (commercialese).

22. Group 3 (–e): 57 masc.

Aal *eel*
Abend *evening*
Ahorn *maple*
Akt *act* (of play); *nude* (art)
Amboß *anvil*
Arm *arm*
Besuch *visit*
Dachs *badger*
Dolch *dagger*
Dom *cathedral*

Erfolg *success*
Forst *forest* (as part of afforestation)
Fund *find*
Gau *district* (elev., obs.)
Grad *degree*
Gurt *girth, belt*
Halm *blade, stalk*
Horst *eyrie; air-station; shrubbery*
Huf *hoof*
Hund *dog*

---
[1] never: der Buchstaben.
[2] BUT: der Rundbogen (–), der Spitzbogen (–).

Knall *bang, report*
Kobold *goblin*
Kork *cork*
Kuckuck *cuckoo*
Lachs *salmon*
Laut *sound*
Leichnam *corpse*
Luchs *lynx*
Molch *salamander*
Monat *month*
Mond *moon; month* (elev.)
Mord *murder*
Ort *place; town, village*
Pfad *path*
Pol *pole* (astronomy, magnetism); *terminal* (electricity)
Puls *pulse*
Punkt *point, dot*
Raufbold *rowdy*

Ruck *jolt, jerk*
Ruf *call, cry; reputation*
Salm *salmon*
Schalk *rogue*
Schlot *factory chimney*
Schuft *scoundrel*
Schuh *shoe*
Spalt *crack, cleft*
Sproß *shoot; offspring*
Star *starling*
Stoff *material*
Strand *shore*
Tag *day*
Takt *tact; beat, bar* (music)
Thron *throne*
Trunkenbold *drunkard*
Verlag *(firm of) publishers*
Verlust *loss*
Versuch *attempt*

Group 3 (–e): 56 neut. monosyllabics

Beet *flower-bed*
Beil *hatchet*
Bein *leg*
Bier *beer*
Boot *boat*
Bord *shelf*
Brot *bread, loaf*
Bund *bundle*
Ding[1] *thing*
Erz *ore*
Fell *hide, skin*
Fest *festival*
Garn *yarn*
Gas *gas*
Gift *poison*
Gleis *rails, track*
Haar *hair*
Heer *army*
Heft *exercise book*
Heim *home*
Jahr *year*
Kinn *chin*
Knie[2] *knee*
Kreuz *cross*
Los *lot, fate; lottery ticket*
Mal *time[3]; sign, mark[4]*
Maß *measure(ment)*
Meer *sea*

Moor *moor, bog*
Moos *moss*
Netz *net*
Öl *oil*
Paar *pair*
Pferd *horse*
Pfund *pound*
Pult *desk*
Recht *right*
Reh *roe*
Reich *realm, empire*
Rohr *reed, cane; pipe, tube; barrel* (of gun)
Roß *steed*
Salz *salt*
Schaf *sheep*
Schiff *ship*
Schwein *pig*
Seil *rope*
Spiel *game*
Stück *piece*
Tau *rope, cable*
Tier *animal*
Tor *gate; goal* (in games)
Vlies *fleece*
Werk *work* (of art)
Zelt *tent*
Zeug *stuff*
Ziel *aim, goal*

---

[1] plur. also die Dinger (coll. and pejorative).
[2] Plur. is written 'die Knie, auf den Knien', and pronounced either as one or as two syllables.
[3] e.g. die ersten paar Male (see 255).
[4] Commoner in compounds, where plur. varies, e.g. die Merkmale *characteristic features*, die Denkmäler *monuments*.

23. Group 4 (–e): 33 fem. monosyllabics

Angst *fear, anxiety*
Axt *axe*
Bank *bench*
Braut *fiancée*; *bride*
Brust *breast, chest*
Faust *fist*
Frucht *fruit*[1]
Gans *goose*
Gruft *vault, tomb*
Hand *hand*
Haut *skin*
Kluft *cleft*
Kraft *strength*
Kuh *cow*
Kunst *art*
Laus *louse*
Luft *air*; Pl. *air* (elev.), *breezes*
Lust *pleasure*; *desire*[2]

Macht *might*
Magd *maid*
Maus *mouse*
Nacht *night*
Naht *seam, join*
Not *need, distress, difficulty*[3]; *necessity*
Nuß *nut*
Sau *sow*
Schnur *string*
Stadt[4] *town, city*
Wand *wall* (of room, of rock)
Wurst *sausage*
Zunft *guild*

compounds of -flucht, e.g.
   Ausflucht *excuse*
compounds of -kunft, e.g.
   Auskunft *information*

24. Group 5 (–er): 12 masc.

Geist *spirit*
Gott *God*
Irrtum *error*
Leib *body*[5]
Mann *man*
Mund[6] *mouth*

Rand *edge*
Reichtum *wealth*
Strauch[7] *shrub*
Vormund[8] *guardian*
Wald *forest*
Wurm *worm*[9]

25. Group 6 (-(e)n): 18 masc.

Ahn *ancestor*
Dorn *thorn*
Fasan *pheasant*
Lorbeer *laurel*
Mast *mast*
Muskel *muscle*
Pantoffel *slipper*
Papagei *parrot*
Pfau *peacock*

Schmerz *pain; grief*
See[10] *lake*
Sporn (Pl. Sporen) *spur*
Staat *state* (country)
Stachel *prickle*
Strahl *ray*
Untertan *subject* (of ruler)
Vetter *cousin* (m.)
Zeh[11] *toe*

5 neut.

Auge *eye*
Bett *bed*
Ende *end*[12]

Hemd *shirt*
Ohr *ear*

[1] das Obst (sing. only)=fruit (collective).
[2] plur. e.g. die Lüste des Fleisches.
[3] plur. e.g. in Nöten sein (commoner: in Not sein).
[4] plur. often pronounced with long ä.
[5] more serviceable: der Körper.
[6] plur. also: Munde.
[7] plur. also: Sträuche.
[8] plur. also: Vormunde.
[9] BUT: *das* arme Wurm (the poor little mite).
[10] Plur. is written 'Seen', but pronounced 'See-en'; see also 39(a).
[11] or: die Zehe(-n).
[12] BUT: das Westend.

26. Group 7: (–(e)n) in all cases except nom. sing.

33 masc. not in -e

Asiàt (–en, –en) *Asian*
Bär (–en, –en) *bear*
Bauer (–n, –n) *peasant, farmer*
Bayer (–n, –n) *Bavarian*
Bub (–en, –en) *boy* (S. Gn., Austr.)
Bursch (–en, –en) *lad*[1]
Christ (–en, –en) *Christian*
Elf (–en, –en) *elf*
Fels (–en, –en)[2] *rock*
Fink (–en, –en) *finch*
Fürst (–en, –en) *sovereign*
Geck (–en, –en) *fop*
Graf (–en, –en) *count*
Held (–en, –en) *hero*
Herr (**–n, –en**)[3] *gentleman*
Hirt (–en, –en) *herdsman*
Kosàk (–en, –en) *Cossack*

Lump (–en, –en) *scamp*
Mensch (–en, –en) *human being*
Mohr (–en, –en) *Moor*
Nachbar (–n, –n) *neighbour*
Narr (–en, –en) *fool*
Nerv (–en, –en) *nerve*
Oberst (–en, –en) *colonel*
Ochs (–cn, –cn) *ox*
Pommer (–n, –n) *Pomeranian*[4]
Prinz (–en, –en) *prince*
Spatz (–en, –en) *sparrow*
Steinmetz (–en, –en) *stone-mason*
Ta(r)tàr (–en, –en) *Ta(r)tar*
Tor (–en, –en) *fool*
Ùngar (–n, –n) *Hungarian*
Vorfahr (–en, –en) *ancestor*

Note: There is a fairly strong tendency to treat some masc. Group 7 nouns as Group 6 nouns, either (a) in acc., gen. and dat. sing. or (b) in acc. and dat. sing. Of the nouns in the above list, der Bär and der Narr are prone to deviation (a): den Bär, des Bärs, dem Bär, and the following to deviation (b): der Bub, der Fink, der Kurfürst *Elector*, der Nerv, der Oberst, der Spatz: ich sprach mit dem Bub; ich sah den Oberst. (See also 57(a) and 63(d).)

E. Ge- NOUNS: GENDER AND PLURAL

27. It is convenient to treat **nouns beginning with Ge-** separately. The following lists classify them as regards gender and plural. Some have no plural by meaning. (Cf. Word Formation 716(a).)

MASCULINE	FEMININE
Names of male persons, e.g.	**Names of female persons,** e.g.

der Gehilfe (–n, –n) *assistant*	die Gehilfin (–nen) *assistant*
der Gemahl (–e) *husband*	die Gemahlin (–nen) *wife*
der Genosse (–n, –n) *companion, comrade*	
der Gevatter (–n)[5] *godfather*	

11 others: Group 4 (–̈e), unless indicated.	**11 others:** Group 6 (–(e)n), unless indicated.

der Gebrauch *use*	die Gebärde *gesture*
der Gedanke[6] *thought*	die Gebühr *fee*

---

[1] 'der Bursch' is a regional form of 'der Bursche', which also means 'fellow'.
[2] or: der Felsen (Group 1).
[3] Plur. is often pronounced 'Herrn'.
[4] Pomeranian dog: der Spitz (–e).
[5] old-fashioned; current usage: der (Tauf)pate.
[6] see 20.

der Gefallen (–) *favour*[1]
der Gehalt (–e) *content, capacity*[2]
der Gehorsam *obedience*
der Genuß *enjoyment*
der Geruch *smell*
der Gesang *singing*
der Geschmack *taste*
der Gestank *stink*
der Gewinn *profit*

die Geburt *birth*
die Geduld *patience*
die Gefahr *danger*
die Gemeinde *congregation*
die Geschichte *history, story*
die Geschwulst (–̈e) *swelling, tumour*
die Gestalt *figure*
die Gewähr *security, guarantee*
die Gewalt *force*

NEUTER: all others

Group 1 (–): those in -e, -el, -er

das Gebäude[3] *building*
das Gebirge[3] *mountain-chain*
das Gemurmel *murmuring*
das Geländer *railing*

Group 3 (–e): MOST
das Gebot *commandment*
das Gebüsch *shrubbery*
das Gedicht *poem*
das Gespräch *conversation*

Group 5 (–̈er): 7

das Gehalt *salary*
das Gemach *room* (elev.)
das Gemüt *temperament*;[4] *heart, mind*;[5]
    soulfulness, feeling[6]
das Geschlecht *family, stock, line*; *sex,*
    gender; *generation*
das Gesicht *face*
das Gespenst *ghost*
das Gewand *robe*

F. PLURAL OF FOREIGN NOUNS

**Note: Most foreign nouns are stressed on the last syllable; in
what follows, the stressed syllable is indicated when it is not
the last.**

28. Masculine foreign nouns

Group 1: those in -er: der Minìster (–), der Revòlver.
    Exc. der Charàkter, die Charaktère.

Group 3: MOST: der Boß (Bosse), der Frisör, der General, der Roman,
der Triumph.

Group 4, e.g. der Abt (–̈e), der Altar, der Baß (Bässe), der Bischof, der
Choral, der Kanal, der Kardinal, der Palast, der Tenor.

Group 5: der Ski (–er) only; also spelt and always pronounced 'Schi'.

Group 6
i Nouns in -or with the stress on the penultimate syllable; note the shift
of stress in the plural: der Dòktor, die Doktòren; der Profèssor, die
Professòren.

[1] e.g. jemandem einen Gefallen tun.
[2] The normal word for 'contents' is 'der Inhalt'.
[3] declined like 'der Käse' in 50.
[4] Er hat ein heiteres Gemüt.
[5] Die Nachricht verwirrte die Gemüter (men's minds).
[6] Er ist ganz ohne Gemüt. 'Gemüt' is a German monopoly: 'cette vie intime, cette poésie
de l'âme', as Madame de Staël called it.

der Mòtor conforms to the above type, with an alternative: der Motòr, die Motòre (Group 3).

der Pastor may be stressed on either syllable in the sing.; the plur. is die Pastòren, but regionally also Pastòre and Pastōre.

ii A few others: der Kònsul (–n), der Dämòn (Dämònen), der Partisan (–en), der Psalm[1], der Typ.[2]

Group 7

i Nouns in -e: der Sklàve (–n, –n), der Stratège *strategist*.

ii Nouns in -t denoting persons: der Fabrikant (–en, –en), der Komponist, der Rekrut, der Student.

iii Nouns in:

-ant	der Diamant (–en, –en)
-aph	der Paragraph (–en, –en)
-oph	der Philosoph (–en, –en)
-arch	der Monarch (–en, –en)
-nom	der Astronom (–en, –en)
-og(e)	der Psychologe[1] (–n, –n)

Note on foreign nouns in -og(e): The form with -e is preferred; cf. der Biologe, der Demagoge, der Theologe. Foreign nouns in -og denoting inanimates have no alternative form in -oge and belong to Group 3: der Katalog (–e), der Monolog (–e).

iv Many others, e.g.:

der Barbar (–en, –en)	der Kamerad	der Lakai	der Planet
der Chirurg	der Katholik	der Leopard[4]	der Tyrann
der Elefant[3]	der Komet	der Magnet	der Zar

29. Feminine foreign nouns

Group 6: ALL: die Armee,[5] die Krìse, die Nation, die Tour.
Exc.: die Ànanas *pineapple* has plur. Ànanas or Ànanasse.

30. Neuter foreign nouns

Group 1: those in -en, -er: das Exàmen (–), das Theàter.

Group 3: MOST: das Grammophon (–e), das Ideal, das Konzert, das Produkt, das Symptom, das Telegramm.

Note:
i das As *ace* (1. at cards 2. champion) doubles the s before an ending.
ii das Regime (–) is pronounced as a bisyllabic in the sing. and as a trisyllabic in the plur.; it may therefore be assigned to Gr. 3.

Group 5: Two nouns only: das Hospital (¨er), das Regiment.

Group 6: a few, e.g. das Insekt (–en), das Interèsse, das Juwel, das Statut, das Verb (–en) BUT: das Adverb (–ien).

---

[1] pronounced p + s.
[2] or: der Typus (gen. sing.: des Typus, nom. plur.: die Typen).
[3] also: den Elefant, dem Elefant.
[4] also Group 6.
[5] plur. written 'Armeen', pronounced: Armee-en.

31. Some special types of foreign nouns

(a) **Foreign nouns in -us (all masc.)**

i The commoner and more concrete have plur. in -usse: die (Aùto)-busse, Bònusse, Zìrkusse.

ii The more abstract and all those in -ismus have plur. in -en: der Gènius, die Gènien *guardian-angel*; der Rhỳthmus, die Rhỳthmen; der Organìsmus, die Organìsmen.

iii Note the following analogies and deviations:

der Àtlas, die Atlànten   der Kàsus, die Kàsus
der Kàktus, die Kaktèen[1]   der Kùrsus, die Kùrse

(b) **The following neuter foreign nouns have plur. in -en or -ien:**

i Those in -um, e.g. das Àlbum, die Àlben[2]; das Indivìduum, die Indivìduen; das Ministèrium, die Ministèrien; das Musèum, die Musèen[3]; das Zèntrum, die Zèntren.

ii Those in -ma, e.g. das Dògma (die Dògmen), das Dràma, das Thèma. Cf. one fem.: die Fìrma.
Exc. das Kòmma, die Kòmmas; das Schèma, die Schèmata.[4]

iii Some in -al and -il, e.g. das Material, die Materialien; das Reptil, die Reptilien; BUT: die Minerale (commoner than 'Mineralien'), die Portale, die Ventile *air-valves, vents*.

iv das Èpos, die Èpen   das Rìsiko, die Rìsiken[6]
das Mỳthos, die Mỳthen   das Prinzip, die Prinzipien
das Kònto *account* (financial),
   die Kònten[5]

(c) **A large number of foreign nouns have not been assimilated to German and end in -s throughout the plural.** They have a normal singular, e.g. der Klub, den Klub, des Klubs, dem Klub. They include all foreign nouns in -o. Examples:

der Balkon (–s)	der Israèli	der Park	der Waggon *railway-*
der Bankier	der Jòckei[7]	der Scheck	*carriage; goods truck*
der Chef	der Klub	der Streik	
der Èskimo	der Lèutnant[8]	der Tee[9]	

die Couch (–es), die Pàrty (die Pàrtys, Pàrties)

[1] pronounced: Kaktèe-en.
[2] also: die Àlbums.
[3] pronounced: Musèe-en.
[4] also: die Schèmas.
[5] also: die Kòntos.
[6] also: die Rìsikos.
[7] pron. as in Engl., but also [jɔkɪ] or [jɔkaɪ].
[8] plur. also: die Lèutnante.
[9] die Tees = tea-parties; die Tees or die Teesorten = types of tea; cf. die Kaffeesorten, die Obstsorten, die Fleischarten.

das Arrangement	das Detail	das Hòbby	das Niveau *level, standard*
das Àuto	das Ècho	das Hotel	das Pendant *counterpart*
das Bonbon	das Èxtra	das Klischee	das Restaurant
das Café	das Genie	das Lèxikon[1]	das Tèmpo[2]

Note: Where the sing. of an unassimilated noun ends in a mute s, the form of the noun remains unchanged throughout, but the final s is pronounced in the gen. sing. and throughout the plur., e.g. der Kommis, *clerk*, der Korps *army corps*.

G. NOTES ON PLURALS

32. Nouns in -sal, fem. or neut., are mainly Group 3; few are in common use, e.g.

die Mühsal (–e) *toil, trouble*	das Scheusal (–e) *monster*
die Trübsal (–e) *sorrow*	das Schicksal (–e) *fate*

33. A few Germanic 'Nordseewörter' and German abbreviated words generally have -s throughout the plural: der Kai *quay*, das Deck, das Dock, das Wrack *wreck* (pron. Vrack); der Krimi, der Vati, die Mutti. (For foreign nouns with plur. in -s, see 31(c).)

34. The following have a colloquial plural in -s in addition to the orthodox form: der Bengel *rascal*, der Junge (die Jungens, die Jungs), der Kerl, der Onkel, das Fräulein, das Mädel.

35. Other parts of speech used as nouns (see 6(d)): most of these, if used in the plural, remain unchanged: diese vielen Wenn und Aber; er schreibt sich mit zwei M (he spells his name with double M).

EXCEPTIONS:
i Some infinitives: see 713.
ii The cardinals have plural in -en: drei Nullen, Einsen; die Fünfen sind schlecht geschrieben. (See also 4(e), 244, 245(b).)
iii Plural of colours: colloquial usage: add -s: die verschiedenen Blaus, Rots; literary usage generally prefers a circumlocution: die verschiedenen blauen/roten Töne.
iv Interjections ending in a vowel or vowel+h add s: die Bravos, die Pfuis, die Ohs; the rest remain unchanged: die Ach, die Pst.
v Masc. onomatopoeic words add e in plur.; der Puff also modifies (see 6(e)).

36. Plural of 'Mann' and its compounds

i Normal: der Mann, die Männer *man, husband*.

ii Archaic and poetic (or facetious): die Mannen *vassals*.

iii After cardinals, generally with reference to troops: dreitausend Mann (stark); cf. Alle Mann an Deck! Unser Chor ist 70 Mann stark (may be used of a mixed choir).

---

[1] plur. better: die Lèxika.
[2] plur. 'die Tèmpi' is common in discussing music.

iv Compounds of 'Mann' generally form plur. with 'Leute,' e.g.

der Hauptmann	die Hauptleute	*captain* (army)
der Kaufmann	die Kaufleute	*merchant*
der Landsmann	die Landsleute	*fellow-countryman*

Exc. Ehemänner *husbands* (BUT: Eheleute *married couples*), Ehrenmänner, Ersatzmänner *substitutes*, Feuerwehrmänner, Lebemänner *men of the world*, Milchmänner, Schneemänner, Seemänner (individual) *sailors* (BUT: Seeleute *sailors* (in general)), Staatsmänner, Steuermänner *helmsmen*, Strohmänner *figure-heads*, *dummies* (also at cards).

37. Leute and Menschen

Frequently either may be used, but while 'Menschen' suggests individuals, however numerous, 'Leute' suggests a vague or impersonal mass or group:

Was werden die Leute dazu sagen?	*What will people say?*
Vier Leute (or: Vier Menschen) kamen ins Wirtshaus	*Four people entered the inn*
Die Stadt wimmelte von Menschen (more vivid than: von Leuten)	*The town was swarming with people*
Alle Menschen müssen sterben	*All men must die*

'Herr und Frau Müller sind sehr nette Leute' is a colourless compliment; 'Herr und Frau Müller sind sehr liebe Menschen' is warmer, more personal.

38. Some nouns have two plurals with different meanings

das Band *bond; ribbon*	die Bande *bonds* die Bänder *ribbons*
die Bank *bench; bank* (financial)	die Bänke *benches* die Banken *banks*
der Bau *building; burrow, earth*[1]	die Bauten[2] *buildings* die Baue *burrows, earths*
der Block i *block, bulky piece* ii *group, alliance* iii *pad of paper* iv *block of houses, flats*, etc.	der Felsblock, die Felsblöcke der Militärblock, die Militärblöcke der Notizblock, die Notizblocks der Wohnblock, die Wohnblocks

der Druck (–e)[3] *print* (cf. drucken); cf. Neudrucke *reprints*, Sonderabdrucke *off-prints*
der Druck (–e)[3] *pressure* (cf. drücken); cf. Dampfdrücke *steam-pressures*, Fingerabdrücke *finger-prints*

das Gesicht *apparition; face*	die Gesichte *apparitions* die Gesichter *faces*
das Land *land, country*	die Lande *lands, regions* (elev.) die Niederlande *Netherlands* die Länder *lands, countries*
die Mutter *mother; (screw-)nut*	die Mütter *mothers* die Muttern *nuts*

[1] cf. der Fuchsbau (–e) *foxes' hole*.
[2] rare except in a few compounds e.g. die Neubauten; otherwise use 'die Gebäude' (plur. of 'das Gebäude').
[3] cf. Du. Haupt.: Druck.

der Rat *council*; *councillor*;   die Räte *councils*; *councillors*
     counsel, advice   die Ratschläge *counsels*

der Strauß *ostrich*; *bunch of*   die Strauße *ostriches*
     flowers; fight (elev.)   die Sträuße *bunches; fights* (elev.)

das Tuch *cloth*: die Tuche: *cloths, kinds of cloth*
     die Tücher: *cloths, tea-cloths*, and in all compounds:
         Handtücher, Taschentücher etc.

das Wort *word*: die Worte: connected words, cf. geflügelte Worte *familiar quotations*
     die Wörter: unconnected words, cf. Hauptwörter *nouns*, Zeitwörter
     verbs, but also Sprichwörter *proverbs*

der Zoll *customs (duty)*; *inch*   die Zölle *customs duties*
     drei Zoll *three inches*

39. Double genders with different meanings (cf. Du. Gram. 1390 ff.).

(a) Related words

der Band (¨e) *volume, book*   das Band (–e) *bond*[1]
     das Band (¨er) *ribbon*

der Bund (¨e) *waistband; union*   das Bund (–e) *bundle* (e.g.of hay)
der Erbe (–n, –n) *heir*   das Erbe[2] *inheritance*
der Flur (–e) *entrance-hall, passage*   die Flur (–en) *fields, plain* (elev.)
der Gehalt (–e) *content, capacity*   das Gehalt (¨er) *salary*
der Gummi (–s) *india-rubber eraser*   das Gummi *rubber*
der Hut (¨e) *hat*   die Hut *protection, guard*[3]
der Kunde (–n, –n) *customer*   die Kunde *news, tidings*
der Militär (–s) (coll.) *military*   das Militär *the military, soldiery, army*
     man, professional officer
der Moment (–e) *moment*   das Moment (–e) (determining) *factor*[4]
der Pack (¨e) *package, bundle*   das Pack *mob, rabble*
der Schild (e) *shield*   das Schild (–er) *signboard*
der See (–n) *lake*   die See (–n) *sea*
die Steuer (–n) *tax*   das Steuer (–) *rudder, helm*
der Stift (–e) i *peg*   das Stift (–e) *foundation, home* (for old
         ii *stripling* (coll.)   people)
der Verdienst *earnings*   das Verdienst (–e) *service, merit*

(b) Unrelated words

der Heide (–n, –n) *heathen*   die Heide (–n) *heath*
der Kiefer (–) *jaw*   die Kiefer (–n) *pine*
der Laster (–) (coll.) *motor-lorry*   das Laster (–) *vice, depravity*
der Leiter (–) *manager*   die Leiter (–n) *ladder*
der Mangel (¨) *lack, deficiency*   die Mangel (–n) *mangle*
die Mark i *mark* (coin)   das Mark *marrow* (of bone)
         ii *border-country*[5]
der Messer (–) *surveyor*; *gauge*[6]   das Messer (–) *knife*
der Tau (–e) *dew*   das Tau (–e) *rope, cable*
der Tor (–en, –en) *fool*   das Tor (–e) *gate*; *goal* (in games)

---

[1] also distinguish: die Bande *band, gang* (die Räuberbande).
[2] gen.: des Erbes; for plur. use 'die Erbschaften'.
[3] e.g. auf der Hut sein *to be on one's guard.*
[4] e.g. Dies ist ein wichtiges Moment in unsrer Außenpolitik.
[5] e.g. die Mark (Brandenburg): the Brandenburg Marches.
[6] cf. der Landmesser *surveyor*, der Höhenmesser *altimeter*, der Durchmesser *diameter*.

40. Nouns with special plurals

SINGULAR	PLURAL	MEANING
der Saal	die Säle[1]	*large room, hall*
der Streit	die Streite	*dispute*
	die Streitigkeiten	
der Betrug	die Betrügereien	*deception, fraud*
der Zank	die Zänkereien	*quarrel*
das Bestreben	die Bestrebungen	*effort, endeavour*
die Furcht	die Befürchtungen	*fear*
das Unternehmen	die Unternehmungen[2]	*enterprise*
das Versprechen	die Versprechungen[2]	*promise*
der Atem	die Atemzüge	*breath*
der Glaube	die Glaubensartikel	*belief*[3]
	die Glaubenssätze	
der Kohl	die Kohlköpfe	*cabbage*[4]
das Lob	die Lobsprüche	*praise*
der Luxus	die Luxusartikel	*luxury*
der Schmuck	die Schmucksachen[5]	*jewellery*; pl.: *pieces of jewellery*
das Spielzeug	die Spielsachen	*toy*
der Raub	die Raubfälle	*robbery*
der Tod	die Todesfälle	*death*
das Unglück	die Unglücksfälle	*misfortune* (in sing. only[6]), *accident*

41. Some nouns are plural only and take a plural verb; most of these correspond to plural nouns in English, e.g. die Eltern *parents*, die Ferien *holidays*,[7] die Lebensmittel *provisions*, die Leute *people*, die Trümmer *ruins*. To be noted are die Händel[8] *quarrel(s)* and die Noten[9] (*books of*) *music*.

The following nouns are mainly used in the plural:

(der Gewissensbiß)	die Gewissensbisse	*pangs of conscience*
(das Möbel)[10]	die Möbel	*furniture*
(die Vergnügung)	die Vergnügungen	*pleasures, amusements*[11]
(der Zins)	die Zinsen	*interest* (e.g. 5%)

42. Weihnachten, Ostern, Pfingsten
These are generally treated as plurals, e.g. Fröhliche (but also: Fröhliches) Weihnachten! Haben Sie schöne Weihnachten gehabt? Er besuchte uns letzte Ostern; but as subjects they are followed by a singular verb, e.g. Weihnachten steht vor der Tür.

---

[1] cf. 727(d).
[2] cf. 713.
[3] What are your beliefs? Woran glauben Sie?
[4] BUT: der Blumenkohl (-e) *cauliflower*.
[5] also, less common, die Schmuckstücke.
[6] after all these misfortunes: nach all diesen Mißgeschicken.
[7] a short holiday = kurze Ferien or ein kurzer Urlaub.
[8] der Handel (sing.) = trade.
[9] die Note (sing.) = i note (musical or diplomatic) ii grade, mark (at school); 'die Noten' also denotes the plur. of these.
[10] for 'piece of furniture,' 'das Möbelstück' is commoner than 'das Möbel'.
[11] pleasure (sing.) = das Vergnügen.

43. The following nouns are singular in German and plural in English:

die Asche *ashes*
der Bodensatz *dregs, lees*
die Brille *(pair of) glasses*
der Dank *thanks*
  Vielen Dank! *Many thanks!*
die Dynamik *dynamics*
das Feuerwerk *fireworks*
der Hafer *oats*
das Hauptquartier *headquarters*
der Hopfen *hops*
die Hose *(pair of) trousers*[1]
der Inhalt *contents*
die Kaserne *barracks*
der Lohn *wages*
die Mathematik *mathematics*
das Mittelalter *the Middle Ages*
  im Mittelalter *in the Middle Ages*

der Mohn *poppies*[2]
die Nachricht *(piece of) news*
die Physik *physics*
das Quartier *quarters*
im Rückstand (m.) *in arrears*
der Schadenersatz *damages, compensation*
die Schere *(pair of) scissors*
die Statistik *statistics* (science of)
die Treppe *(flight of) stairs*
die Umgebung *surroundings*
die Umgegend *surroundings, neighbourhood*
das Unkraut *weed, weeds*
das Werk *works, factory*
das Stahlwerk *steel-works*
die Zange *(pair of) tongs*

Note:

i Clearly, many of the above German nouns may also be used in the plural, e.g.

Die meisten Löhne sind erhöht worden   *Most wages have been raised*
Er erhielt von beiden gute Nachrichten   *He received good news from both of them*
Er wohnt zwei Treppen hoch   *He lives on the second floor*

ii The following nouns are virtually singular only:

der Kummer *care, sorrow*   der Verdacht *suspicion*
die Sehnsucht *longing*   der Verdienst *earnings*

H. DECLENSION OF NOUNS

44. Paradigms of declensions

Note:

i Allowing for the differences in the formation of the plural between the various groups, the first three paradigms respectively stand for any masculine, feminine and neuter noun in Groups 1–6.

ii The fourth paradigm represents the exceptional Group 7, whose nouns end in -(e)n in all cases except the nom. sing.

		MASC.		FEM.		NEUT.	
SING.	N.	der	Onkel	die	Schule	das	Buch
	A.	den	——	die	——	das	——
	G.	des	——s	der	——	des	——es
	D.	dem	——	der	——	dem	——(e)
PLUR.	N.	die	Onkel	die	Schulen	die	Bücher
	A.	die	——	die	——	die	——
	G.	der	——	der	——	der	——
	D.	den	——n	den	——	den	——n

[1] plur. also possible: Er trug eine graue Hose *or* graue Hosen.
[2] a poppy = eine Mohnblume.

Group 7

SING.			PLUR.		
N.	der	Affe	N.	die	Affen
A.	den	——n	A.	die	——
G.	des	——n	G.	der	——
D.	dem	——n	D.	den	——

I. NOTES ON THE DECLENSION OF NOUNS

45. Masc. and neut. gen. sing.: -es or -s?

-es must be added:
i to nouns ending in a sibilant: des Krebses, des Busches;
ii to the word 'Gott': die Wege Gottes;
iii to German (not to foreign) monosyllabics, or polysyllabics ending in a stressed syllable, if used as a preceding attributive genitive (the Saxon Genitive): des Tages Hitze, des Geschenkes Wert, BUT: des Chefs Tochter.

-s is added:
i generally to nouns ending in a vowel (des Baus) or in vowel+h (des Viehs);
ii generally to polysyllabics ending in an unstressed syllable: des Bahnhofs, des Christentums; where the last syllable is el, em, en, er, chen, lein, only s can be added: des Atems, des Vaters, des Mädchens;
iii to proper names: J. S. Bachs Kantaten;
iv to most foreign nouns: des Klubs, des Hotels.

Otherwise, it is a question of style, rhythm and ease of pronunciation, the ending -s being favoured, especially in conversation.

46. Neut. nouns in -nis have gen. sing. -nisses, e.g. das Ereignis, des Ereignisses.

Foreign nouns in -as, -os, -us have no ending in the gen. sing., e.g. der Atlas (des Atlas), das Epos, der Zirkus.
Exc. das As, des Asses; der (Auto)bus, des (Auto)busses.

47. Masc. and neut. dat. sing.: add e?

This again is a question of style and rhythm. Except in certain fixed phrases, the e is never essential and is, in fact, dying out.
It is mainly added to monosyllabics: auf dem Pulte.
It is rarely added to polysyllabics ending in an unstressed syllable: am Bahnhof.

It is **not** added in the following cases:

i to nouns ending in -el, -em, -en, -er, -chen, -lein: auf dem Boden, mit dem Kätzchen;
ii to nouns ending in a vowel (mit einem Ei) or in vowel+h (mit dem Schuh);
iii to a noun used immediately after a preposition or a genitive: aus Holz; in dessen Haus; dies hat Bismarcks Ruf geschadet;

iv in phrases denoting quantity: mit einem Glas Wein, mit einem Stück
Seife;

v to geographical names (am Main) and names of months and days (im
März, am Montag);

vi to foreign nouns: in dem Klub.

The -e is generally added in certain fixed phrases, e.g.: bei Hofe, unter
Tage arbeiten *to work below ground*, hierzulande *in this country*, jemanden
zu Rate ziehen *to consult s.o.*, sich zu Tode arbeiten. (In spoken German, nach/zu Haus are at least as common as nach/zu Hause.)

48. Feminine nouns remain unchanged throughout the singular

EXCEPTIONS:

i Sui generis is 'boredom': die Langweile or, more commonly, die
Langeweile; mainly in literary language, the first part of the latter
form is declined as an adjective, e.g. wegen der Langenweile, aus
Langerweile.

ii Mutters Kleid, Tantes Hut: see 51(f).

49. All German nouns end in -(e)n in the dative plural

EXCEPTIONS:

i a few German nouns with -s throughout plur.: see 33–4.

ii unassimilated foreign nouns with -s throughout plur.: see 31(c).

iii proper names, e.g. bei Müllers: see 54.

50. Two special cases:

der Käse, den Käse, des Käses, dem Käse; die Käse, der Käse, den
Käsen.

das Herz, des Herzens, dem Herzen; die Herzen etc.

J. DECLENSION OF PROPER NAMES AND TITLES

51. Genitive singular of proper names without titles and of geographical names

(a) Proper names (other than those ending in a sibilant: see 51(g)) take -s
in the gen. sing.: **Heinrichs Mantel,** Annas Kind, Goethes Werke,
die Werke Goethes, die Ermordung Cäsars, Johann Sebastian Bachs
Werke, die Werke Johann Sebastian Bachs, die Werke Heinrich von
Kleists, der Tod Friedrichs des Großen, der Tod Friedrich Wilhelms
III. (des Dritten), **Deutschlands Städte,** die Städte Deutschlands,
Nürnbergs Kirchen, die Kirchen Nürnbergs.

Note: 'die Kirchen von Nürnberg' is also common usage, but not 'die
Städte von Deutschland'. In the majority of the examples in 51(a) (d)
(e), 'von' could be used; it is colloquial, but frequently sounds ineffec-
tive, e.g. die Siege von dem großen Napoleon.

(b) A colloquial variant for the gen. of proper names is illustrated by the
following (bad German): Dem Wenter sein Krecht (H. Broch);

Huck Finn (dat.) sein Vater (A. Andersch), the speaker being a ship's boy; Else (dat.) ihr Bruder ist krank (cf. end of 61).

(c) After some prepositions taking the genitive, proper names drop the -s, e.g. statt Müller, trotz Wagner, unweit Frankfurt, wegen Heinrich, BUT: hinsichtlich Berlins, um Hermanns willen, von seiten Karls, zugunsten Roberts.
With außerhalb, oberhalb, diesseits and their opposites, von+dat. is colloquially more usual than the gen.: innerhalb von Frankreich (innerhalb Frankreichs), diesseits von Nürnberg.

(d) If they are preceded by a def. art.,[1] demonstrative or possessive, proper names of persons have no -s in the gen.: die Rolle des Egmont, die Werke des Johann Sebastian Bach, die Siege des großen Napoleon, die Briefe dieses Schmidt, die Krankheit unsres Peter. (N.B. Goethe's title 'Die Leiden des jungen Werthers' is archaic.)

(e) Geographical names 1. used after the def. art. (i.e. when limited by an attributive adjective, cf. 84(c)) or 2. of which the def. art. forms a part (e.g. der Nil, der Balkan) frequently drop the -s of the genitive; in the second category, German names tend to retain the s. E.g.
1. die Probleme des heutigen Deutschland, die Einwohner des geteilten Berlin.
2. des Kreml, das Problem des Kongo, an den Ufern des Nil, auf dem Gipfel des Brocken, BUT: an den Ufern des Rheins.

Note: Compounds formed with -berg, -gebirge, -wald etc. always have the -s of the genitive (cf. Du. Gram. 1940): auf dem Gipfel des Feldbergs, die Täler des Schwarzwalds.

(f) The generic names of members of the family are colloquially treated like proper names: Vaters Anzug, Mutters Kleid, Tantes Hut (cf. Annas Kind).

(g) **Gen. sing. of proper names ending in a sibilant: s, ß, x, z, tz.**

i Fem. Christian names: use 'von' or an apostrophe: die Schwester von Agnes, Agnes' Schwester.

ii Masc. Christian names, surnames and classical names: four possibilities:
1. an apostrophe (mainly confined to writing, where the apostrophe is perceptible): Fritz' Handschuhe, bei Klaus' Hochzeit, Marx' Einfluß, Sophokles' Tragödien.
2. von (the commonest): die Handschuhe von Fritz, der Einfluß von Marx, die Operetten von Johann Strauß.
3. add the ending -ens (old-fashioned): Fritzens Handschuhe, Vossens Homerübersetzungen.
4. def. art., with classical names only: die Tragödien des Sophokles.

iii Geographical names: use 'von' (or an adjective, if available): die Straßen von Paris or die Pariser Straßen.
Where the def. art. forms part of a geographical name, the gen. is used

[1] normally when limited by an attributive adjective (cf. 84(c)); the first two examples in 51(d) are less common variants of 'die Rolle Egmonts' and 'die Werke Johann Sebastian Bachs'. (Never: die Werke des Bach, des Goethe.)

with -es or, more frequently, uninflected: die Gipfel des Harzes, die Dörfer des Elsaß, die Städte des Peloponnes.

52. Proper names do not change in the dative, but, of course: nach Friedrich dem Großen; see also 81 N.

53. Declension of proper names with titles

(a) **Title + name:** only the name is declined, the combination being regarded as a unit: König Heinrichs Politik, die Politik König Heinrichs, Onkel Roberts Haus, die Gründung Kloster Beurons, die Regierungszeit König Ludwigs XIV. (des Vierzehnten), ich hörte gestern Präsident Heinemann (not: Präsidenten), ich ging zu Kollege Müller (not: Kollegen).

Two exceptions:
i 'Herr' is always declined: Herrn Müllers Söhne; (Herrn) Professor (Doktor) Kramers Vortrag (*lecture*).
ii After some prepositions taking the gen., neither title nor name is declined, e.g. statt, trotz, wegen König Heinrich, BUT: um König Heinrichs willen; hinsichtlich, von seiten, zugunsten Professor Naumanns.

(b) **Article (demonstrative, possessive) (+ adj.) + title + name**

i Official usage is to decline the title: die Siege des (mächtigen) Kaisers Karl, die Rede des Präsidenten Heinemann, die Söhne dieses Herrn Müller; cf. die Werke des (berühmten) Philosophen Kant, die Hauptstadt des Landes Niedersachsen.

ii Provided the title is not a Group 7 noun, it is now commoner to decline neither title nor name: der Vortrag des Professor Klein, das Haus unseres (alten) Onkel Robert, die Schwester des Leutnant(s) Schmidt.

iii 'Doktor' and 'Fräulein' are not declined: die Erfolge unseres Doktor Meyer, die Mutter dieses Fräulein Lehmann.

54. Proper names in the plural

(a) **Masc. Christian names**
i names with Group 1 endings: same in plur.
die zwei Peter, die zwei Hänschen.
ii names ending in a sibilant: same in plur. or add -e
die zwei Fritz/Fritze.
iii names ending in other consonants: add -e or, more colloquially, add -s: die zwei Heinriche/Heinrichs.
iv names ending in a vowel: add -s: die zwei Ottos.

(b) **Fem. Christian names**
i diminutives in -chen and -el: same in plur.
die zwei Gretchen, die zwei Bärbel.
ii names ending in a sibilant: same in plur.
die zwei Agnes.

iii names ending in other consonants: add -s
   die zwei Gertruds.
iv names ending in -e: add -n: die zwei Luisen.
v names ending in other vowels: add -s
   die zwei Klaras.

(c) **Surnames**
   i They mostly add -s:
     Müllers sind heute bei Schlegels; Müllers' neues Haus.
   ii Those ending in a sibilant add -ens and are sometimes used with the
      def. art.: (Die) Benzens und (die) Straußens kommen heute.

(d) **Names of countries and towns:** no ending or add -s: die zwei
   Deutschland, die beiden Berlin (U. Johnson), die zwei Chinas.

55. **Titles of poems, plays etc. and names of journals, hotels etc.
   are declined:** in der letzten Strophe des 'Erlkönigs'; ein Zitat aus
   Schillers 'Räubern'; haben Sie 'Nathan den Weisen' gelesen?; ich
   wohne im 'Goldenen Anker'; in der neusten Nummer des 'Spiegels',
   BUT: in der Zeitschrift 'Der Spiegel'.
   Note: short titles preceded by the def. art. sometimes drop the -s of the
   masc. gen.: der Dichter des 'Faust'.

K. NOUNS OF WEIGHT, MEASURE AND VALUE

56. **Nouns of weight, measure and value**

(a) Nouns denoting weight, measure or value, preceded by a cardinal or
   by an adjective indicating number, do not take the form of the plural;
   the noun denoting the thing measured is in apposition to the noun
   of measurement and not in the genitive:

   Ich kaufte zwei Pfund[1] Kirschen und zwei Sack Kartoffeln; er trank ein Glas
   Bier; er trank zwei Glas (Bier); er trank mehrere Glas Bier; mit zwei Glas
   Bier; ich bestellte drei Dutzend Eier; zwei Paar Schuhe.

ein paar Schluck (Kaffee)	*a few mouthfuls (of coffee)*
Wir hatten fünf Grad Kälte	*We had five degrees of frost*
zehn Schritt	*ten paces*
3 Schuß—50 Pfennig!	*3 shots for 50 Pfennig!*
Mit zwanzig Mark komm' ich nicht aus	*I can't make do with twenty marks*

Note:
i Particularly when shopping, the word 'Stück' is much used to indicate
  the number of articles required, from writing-pads to electric bulbs
  and from peaches to handkerchiefs: Diese hier sind gerade das
  richtige; geben Sie mir bitte drei Stück!

ii Time units take the form of the plural, but a noun following them is
   generally in apposition: sechs Jahre Krieg; die ersten Monate
   Parlamentserfahrung (*Zeit*); nach einer Stunde Warten (*Zeit*).

[1] an English pound=450 grams; a German pound=500 grams; butter, cheese, sausage,
meat, fruit and vegetables are usually bought by the 'Pfund'.

iii Feminine nouns of measurement etc., other than 'die Mark', take the plural form: zehn Flaschen Wein, zwei Ladungen Holz.

iv After 'viele', practice varies: Er trank viele Glas/Gläser Bier.

(b) Beyond the recognized nouns of measurement illustrated in 56(a), there are numerous words denoting quantity which are followed by a noun in apposition, e.g. zwei Gruppen Schulkinder, eine Menge Schallplatten, zwei Pakete Lebensmittel, eine Schar Schulkinder, mehrere Sträuße Nelken.

Used in the plural without a preceding cardinal or adjective denoting number, they are followed by 'von': große Mengen von Schallplatten, Pakete von Lebensmitteln (or: Lebensmittelpakete), Schwärme von Bremsen *swarms of horseflies* (E. Jünger).

The following are almost always followed by 'von': eine Sammlung, eine Ansammlung *accumulation*, eine Versammlung *gathering*, eine Serie; after eine Reihe, 'von' is safer.

(c) kind, type, make of

i die Sorte and die Art are generally followed by a noun in apposition: zwei Sorten Äpfel; eine neue Art (von) Religion; es ist eine Art (von) Museum.

ii der Typ either forms a compound noun (Er schildert einen neuen Menschentyp) or is followed by a genitive (ein neuer Typ des Mercedes) or by von (see 555(c)ii).

iii die Marke forms a compound noun: diese Automarke.

(d) When a masc. or neut. noun of measurement is in the gen. sing. and is followed by a masc. or neut. noun denoting the thing measured, normal usage is to inflect the latter, but not the former; ('von' is commoner when practicable):

der Preis eines Pfund Fleisches/von einem Pfund Fleisch	*the price of a pound of meat*
der Geschmack dieses Stück Kuchens/ von diesem Stück Kuchen	*the taste of this piece of cake*
jenes Blättchen Papiers (A. Goes)	*of that slip of paper*
anstatt eines Glas Weins	*instead of a glass of wine*

Where the thing measured is fem.:

der Preis eines Pfundes Butter (or: von einem Pfund Butter)	*the price of a pound of butter*
anstatt eines Glases Milch	*instead of a glass of milk*

Where the noun of measurement is fem.:

der Preis (von) einer Flasche Wein/Milch	*the price of a bottle of wine/milk*
statt einer Tasse Kaffee/Milch	*instead of a cup of coffee/milk*

(e) When the noun of measurement is in the dative (sing. or plur.), the noun denoting the thing measured, if plur., is often given the inflection of the dat. plur., though practice varies:

mit einem Haufen Butterbrote(n)	*with a pile of sandwiches*
mit vielen Haufen Butterbrote(n)	*with many piles of sandwiches*
mit einem Dutzend Kühe(n)	*with a dozen cows*

(f) Nouns of measurement have the plural inflection if they are viewed as concrete individual objects. (Only 'Mark' never changes.) E.g.

Auf dem Hof lagen zehn Fässer	*In the yard there were ten barrels*
Ich gab ihm meine letzten zehn Pfennige	*I gave him my last ten pfennigs*

(g) Note the following restaurant usage:

Drei Erdbeereis, bitte!	*Three strawberry-ices, please*
Noch zwei Bier, bitte!	*Two more beers, please*

(h) For normal usage if the noun denoting the thing measured is preceded by an adjective, see 99 ff., e.g. Ich trank zwei Tassen starken Kaffee (Apposition).

(i) If the noun denoting the thing measured is preceded by the def. art., a demonstrative or a possessive, it goes into the genitive, with 'von' as a common alternative: zwei Glas des besten Weins (vom besten Wein), von diesem Wein, von unserm Wein.

L. SOME FURTHER INSTANCES OF NON-INFLECTION[1]

57. There are a number of instances, apart from nouns of measurement, in which nouns are not inflected:

(a) A Group 7 noun has no -en in acc. or dat. sing.:

   i when used, without a qualifying word, after a preposition (the inflected -en form might be sing. or plur.):

das Verhältnis zwischen Fürst und Volk	*the relationship between sovereign and people*
Er war ohne Kamerad[2]	*He was without a comrade*

   ii when it is, as it were, quoted: Was ist die Bedeutung von 'Astronom'?

(b) The genitive of nouns denoting languages: der Stil des modernen Englisch.

(c) The genitive of the names of months frequently drops the -s, by analogy with proper names; the months in -er tend to retain it: am Morgen des zehnten Juni; in den ersten Tagen des Oktobers.
None of the months are inflected when in apposition to 'des Monats' (in den letzten Tagen des Monats Oktober) nor after Anfang, Mitte, Ende (Anfang Dezember) (see 329).

(d) In the genitive of the names of the days of the week, practice varies: am Morgen des folgenden Mittwoch(s); mit Ausnahme des (kommenden) Donnerstag(s).

(e) 1. Certain foreign nouns (especially modern loan words) and 2. certain German nouns frequently drop the -s of the gen. sing. Duden (Gram. 2020) cites for instance:
der Barock (des Barock), der Dativ, der Dynamo, das Establishment, der Gulasch, das Interesse, der Islam, das Parlament, das Parterre *back stalls* (theatre), das Radar, der Test.

---

[1] cf. Du. Gram. 1980 (2), 1990 f., 2005 f., 2020.
[2] Regarding the omission of 'einen', see 563.

der Heilige Abend (des Heiligen Abend), der Gründonnerstag, der Karfreitag, der Ostersonntag, der Biedermeier (Early Victorian Style), der Hanswurst *clown*. der Holunder *elder*, der Löwenzahn *dandelion*. (These are all in the nature of proper names.)

(f) In the genitive of some other parts of speech used as nouns practice varies: ein Stück des eignen Ich(s); eines klaren Entweder-Oder; meines Gegenüber(s); seines ewigen Nein(s); des grauen Einerlei(s); anstatt eines A.

(g) **The declension of abbreviations,** e.g.
    der LKW: der Lastkraftwagen *motor lorry*
    die GmbH: die Gesellschaft mit beschränkter Haftung *limited liability company*

    gen. sing.:   des LKW(s)   der GmbH
    (nom.) plur.: die LKW(s) die GmbH(s)
    In conversation, the form with -s is commoner.

(h) See also 51(c)(d)(e)(g), 53(b), 63(d) and 581.

M. THE MAIN USES OF THE CASES

Note: Only those uses which seem to demand it and which are not dealt with elsewhere are here treated at any length.

58. **The nominative case** is used for the subject, for the person or thing addressed and for the complement of sein, werden, bleiben, heißen, scheinen, sich betrachten als *to regard o.s. as*, sich dünken *to imagine o.s. to be* (archaic or facetious), sich erweisen als *to prove to be*, sich fühlen als *to feel o.s. to be* and of nennen *to name, call* used in the passive. E.g.
Karl bleibt mein bester Freund; er dünkt sich ein großer Künstler; er erwies sich als der Mörder; er wird immer der Faulenzer genannt.

59. **The accusative case** is used for the direct object, after certain prepositions (558 ff., 566 ff.), in certain time-phases (315 f., 319 f.) and:

(a) for the complement of nennen, heißen *to call*, schelten *to call* (chidingly), ansehen als *to look upon as*, bezeichnen als *to designate as* etc.: Er nennt sich einen Optimisten; er schalt mich einen Taugenichts; ich sehe Sie als meinen Freund an.

(b) as an **adverbial accusative,** to denote weight, measure, value, space traversed: Der Sack wog einen Zentner *a hundredweight* (or: war einen Zentner schwer); der Tisch ist ein Meter breit; einen Schilling wert; wir gingen noch einen Kilometer; ich bin den ganzen Weg zu Fuß gegangen.

(c) for **absolute phrases,** where these may be regarded as the object of a suppressed transitive present participle, e.g. haltend or habend:

Den Hut in der Hand [haltend],   *Hat in hand, he entered the room*
kam er ins Zimmer
und sagte, gemäßigten Vorwurf in der   *and said, with mild reproach in his voice*: ...
Stimme [habend]: ... (A. Goes)

(Genuine absolute accusatives are rare, e.g.

Seinen üblichen Eifer vorausgesetzt, wird er sicher Erfolg haben	*Assuming his usual keenness, he's sure to succeed*)

Otherwise, absolute phrases go into the nominative, being regarded as the subject of intr. pres. participles, e.g. liegend or seiend:

Er saß am Feuer, der Hund zu seinen Füßen [liegend]	*He sat by the fire, the dog at his feet*
Holmes saß schweigend und gefaßt, . . . aber jeder Nerv gespannt [seiend]	*Holmes sat silent and composed, . . . but every sense on the alert* (Conan Doyle)

Both the acc. and the nom. construction are frequently replaced by mit + dat.: Mit dem Hut in der Hand, . . .; mit dem Hund zu seinen Füßen.

60. The genitive case is, in conversation, felt to be somewhat stilted and there is a strong tendency to avoid it, mainly by using von + dat. This tendency is referred to in 51(a) N.(c), 56(d) (i), 63(a), 101, 113 (b)N, 152, 172, 181, 207(e) ii 2, 212(b), 227 ff., 498, 555(c) v2 and vi, 578, 715(b) N.i.

In line with this tendency is the dropping of the -s of the masc. and neut. gen. sing. by proper names in certain circumstances (see 51(c)(d)(e) (g), 53(b)) and by some other nouns (see 57(b)–(g))[1]

With the above proviso, the genitive is used to express possession, partitively (die Hälfte des Kuchens, manche meiner Freunde, but see 555(c)i, 56, 99 ff.), as a subjective or objective genitive (die Abfahrt des Zuges, der Umbau des Hauses), to define a preceding generic word (die seltene Tugend der Bescheidenheit *the rare virtue of modesty*), after certain prepositions (574 ff.), after certain verbs (498 ff.), with certain adjectives (118), to denote indefinite or habitual time (317) and as an adverbial genitive.

Only the first and last of these uses need further comment here:

(a) to express possession:

Das ist das Haus meines Bruders	*That is the house of my brother*
Das ist meines Bruders Haus	*That is my brother's house*

The latter order, the so-called **Saxon genitive,** is normal with proper names: Goethes Gedichte, Karls Handschuhe; apart from this, it is mainly literary and is not much used in conversation, especially not with fem., plur. and Group 7 nouns; thus always: die Wohnung meiner Schwester, die Eltern des Studenten. Examples of Saxon Genitive:

seiner Vorfahren großes altes Haus (Th. Mann)	*the large old house of his ancestors*
Nicht ohne Schauder greift des Menschen Hand In des Geschicks geheimnisvolle Urne (Schiller)	*Not without awe does the hand of man plunge into the dark urn of Fate*

(b) examples of **adverbial genitive:**

meines Erachtens (m. E.)	*in my view*
leichten/schweren Herzens	*with a light/heavy heart*
Er fährt erster Klasse	*He travels first class*
schlimmstenfalls	*if the worst comes to the worst*

---

[1] For a full treatment of the decline of the genitive in modern German, see Winfried Weser: Der Genitiv im neuesten Deutsch (*Muttersprache*, Juli/August and September 1968).

61. The dative case is used for the indirect object (654), as a dative of advantage or disadvantage (83, 489 f.), instead of a possess. adj. with parts of the body (82(b)-(f)), after certain prepositions (547 ff., 566 ff., 576 ff.), after many verbs (486 ff.), in various impersonal expressions (373 ff.) and with certain adjectives (117).

Two further uses require illustration here:

(a) **The ethic dative** (of the person indirectly interested, emotionally involved) (cf. Erben, op. cit., 221):

Du bist mir ein schöner Schwindler!	*You're a nice fraud*
Falle mir ja nicht hin!	*Now be sure you don't fall*
Karl, rühr' mir den Bub nicht an!	*Karl, don't you touch the boy*
(H. Weis)	

(b) a colloquial use, with a possess. adj., to indicate possession (bad German) (cf. 51(b)):

Das ist meiner Mutter ihr Hut	*That's my mother's hat*
Unserm Onkel sein Garten ist ganz groß	*Our uncle's garden is quite big*

N. APPOSITION

62. Basic rule for apposition: a noun in apposition has the same case as the noun or pronoun to which it refers:

Ich sah meinen Freund, den Pfarrer	*I saw my friend, the parson*
	I knew him as a boy
Ich kannte ihn als Junge[1]	= *when I was a boy*
Ich kannte ihn als Jungen[1]	= *when he was a boy*
Es gibt nichts Schlimmeres als einen Betrunkenen (cf. Du. Haupt.: Apposition II)	*There is nothing worse than a drunken man*
in Michelstadt, einem Städtchen im Odenwald	*in Michelstadt, a little town in the Odenwald*

cf. der Fall Hamlets, des Dänen, dieses typischen Literaten (Th. Mann).

63. Main deviations from the apposition rule given in 62:

(a) Especially in conversation, there is a strong **tendency to avoid an appositional genitive singular,** using instead one of the following: 1. von+dat. 2. a relative clause 3. the nominative (Weser, loc. cit., p. 227, draws attention to the clearer, more emphatic effect of the nominative, as opposed to the appositional genitive.)

　1. der Sohn von meinem Freund, dem Pfarrer.

　2. or 3. nach dem Tod meines Onkels, der früher der Bürgermeister unsrer Stadt war/der frühere Bürgermeister unsrer Stadt.

　3. mit der Hilfe meines Freundes, Professor Kretschmar; die Verantwortung meines Bruders, als ältester Sohn.

(b) **Appositional phrases with 'als' *as* referring to a noun or pronoun in the dative.** Orthodox version:

Er sprach mit ihr als ältester Tochter　*He spoke with her as the eldest daughter*
Colloquially, three alternatives occur:

---

[1] Regarding the absence of an article, see 85(h).

1. Provided there is no ambiguity, the appositional phrase is put in the nominative: Er sprach mit ihr als älteste Tochter.
2. The dative is used, but the adj. is given the weak ending -en (cf. Du. Gram. 2185): Er sprach mit ihr als ältesten Tochter.
3. The rather cramped sentence is loosened up: Er sprach mit ihr, weil sie die älteste Tochter ist.

(c) For **comparative phrases introduced by 'wie'** *like* normal usage is the nominative, here justified as the subject of a truncated clause, e.g., in Zeiten wie die heutigen [es sind]; in einem Fall wie dieser (or: diesem) (Du. Gram. 5825); zwischen zwei Männern wie du und ich (Du. Haupt.: Apposition II); ich fühlte mich wie ein Fremder.

(d) **Group 7 nouns** used in apposition often remain uninflected: Ich schrieb an Herrn Schulze, Präsident (not: Präsidenten) des Gesang-vereins; mir als Tourist war dies einerlei.

64. Miscellaneous types and uses of apposition

(a) die Ära Adenauer, der Fall Lehmann *the Lehmann case*, im Monat Mai, die Stadt Bremen, die Universität Heidelberg, BUT: die Schlacht bei Leipzig (see also 84(f)).

(b) in der Zeitschrift 'Der Spiegel'; in dem Drama 'Die Räuber'; im Hotel 'Deutscher Hof'.

(c) See also 51(a), 53, 56, 99 ff., 109, 115, 313(b).

II SOME SPECIAL USES AND OMISSIONS OF THE ARTICLES

A. DECLENSION OF THE ARTICLES

65. Declension of the definite article ('the')

	MASC.	FEM.	NEUT.	PLURAL (all genders)
N.	der	die	das	die
A.	den	die	das	die
G.	des	der	des	der
D.	dem	der	dem	den

66. Declension of the indefinite article ('a')

	MASC.	FEM.	NEUT.	
N.	ein	eine	ein	No
A.	einen	eine	ein	Plural
G.	eines	einer	eines	
D.	einem	einer	einem	

B. USE OF THE DEFINITE ARTICLE WITH ABSTRACT NOUNS

67. Note: The use of the def. art. with abstract nouns is one of the most elusive parts of German grammar and usage and some 'Sprachgefühl' is essential. Brackets indicate that the article may be used or omitted, for German practice varies considerably. If in doubt, it is on the whole safer to put in the def. art.

68. Abstract nouns may here be divided into two groups. (Purists may query whether some of the nouns in Group A are abstract.)

Group A: the names of features and forms of human life and thought

EXAMPLES:

das Alter *old age*   die Arbeit *work*[1]
das Altertum *antiquity*   das Christentum *Christianity*

---

[1] Included here in the general sense: 'application of effort to some purpose' (C.O.D.).

die Dämmerung *dawn; dusk*
die Ehe *marriage, married life*
die Einsamkeit *solitude*
das Elend *misery*
die Forschung *research*
die Freiheit *freedom*
die Gesellschaft *society*
das Glück *fortune, fate; luck; happiness*
der Handel *trade*
die Industrie *industry* (manufacture)
die Jugend *youth*
der Kommunismus *Communism*
der Krieg *war*

das Leben *life*
die Menschheit *humanity*
die Nacht *night*
die Nachwelt *posterity*
die Natur *nature*
die Not *need, want, distress*
die Politik *politics*
das Schicksal *fate*
der Schlaf *sleep*
die Sklaverei *slavery*
der Tod *death*
die Wahrheit *truth*
die Zeit *time*

Group B: human qualities and emotions

EXAMPLES:

die Angst *fear*
die Beliebtheit *popularity*
der Ehrgeiz *ambition*
die Eifersucht *jealousy*
die Eitelkeit *vanity*
die Faulheit *laziness*
die Geduld *patience*
die Gerechtigkeit *justice*
die Gesundheit *health*
die Größe *greatness*
der Haß *hatred*
die Liebe *love*
die Menschlichkeit *humaneness*
das Mißtrauen *distrust, suspicion*

die Müdigkeit *tiredness*
der Mut *courage*
die Schönheit *beauty*
die Sehnsucht *longing*
der Stolz *pride*
das Talent *talent*
die Treue *faithfulness*
die Tugend *virtue*
die Vernunft *reason, good sense*
der Verrat *treason, treachery*
die Verschwendung *wastefulness, extravagance*
das Vertrauen *confidence*

69. Nouns in Group A are distinctive and familiar phenomena and are almost always used with the def. art.:

Er fürchtet das Alter
Er liebte die Demokratie (Kl. Mann)
... daß die Ehe ein Wagestück sei (C. Zuckmayer)
Wir hängen von der Industrie ab
Der Krieg brach aus[1]
Ich interessiere mich für (die) Politik
Der Schlaf kam über ihn
Die Zeit vergeht

He is afraid of old age
He loved democracy
... that marriage is a risk
We depend on industry
War broke out
I'm interested in politics
Sleep came upon him
Time passes

In the same way, numerous non-abstract nouns, used in the plural in a general sense, have the def. art. where there is, or need be, none in English. E.g.

Die Beschwerden vermehren sich
Die Geschmäcke sind verschieden
Die Maßstäbe sind heutzutage strenger
Die Preise sind gestiegen
Die Steuern waren drückend (B. Brecht)

Complaints are increasing
Tastes differ
Standards are higher nowadays
Prices have gone up
Taxes were oppressive

[1] All the more arresting is Heinrich Böll's unorthodox: Krieg kam.

70. Nouns in Group B are generally used with the def. art. when the quality as a whole, as an individualized and familiar concept, is referred to or envisaged; they are then the equivalent of Group A nouns:

Ich bewundere den Ehrgeiz	*I admire ambition*
eine Schwäche wie die Eitelkeit	*a weakness such as vanity*
Die Erfahrung lehrte ihn, daß dies die Liebe sei. Aber obgleich er genau wußte, daß die Liebe ihm viel Schmerz ... bringen müsse, ... (Th. Mann)	*Experience taught him that this was love. But although he knew very well that love must cause him much suffering, ...*
Er war die Liebenswürdigkeit selbst	*He was amiability personified*
Die Vernunft gebietet, daß du das tust	*Reason demands that you should do this*

Group B nouns may similarly be used with the def. art. in a more circumscribed context, especially when the presence of the quality in question is already known to the reader or listener, e.g.

Im Heer sinkt der Mut	*Courage is sinking in the army*
Das Mißtrauen wächst unter seinen Anhängern	*Distrust is increasing among his adherents*

To appreciate that the courage is sinking and the distrust increasing we must know, or be expected to assume, that they already existed. In the second example 'the distrust' would be possible in English.

Contrast with these two examples the sentence:

Unter seinen Anhängern entstand Mißtrauen	*Distrust arose among his followers*

Here distrust comes as something new and 'das Mißtrauen' would be impossible.

In some contexts the def. art. is used with Group B nouns with the sense of a possessive adjective:

Du mußt versuchen, die Angst (= deine Angst) zu überwinden	*You must try to overcome your fear*
Ich werde ihm die Faulheit austreiben (from Du. Stil.)	*I'll rid him of his laziness*
Er verlor den Mut	*He lost his courage*

71. Nouns in Group B are generally used without the def. art. when the quality is referred to, not as an entity, but in an indefinite and often partial sense. This is almost always the case where the quality or emotion, as the object, is the essential completion of the sense of the verb, e.g. Angst haben, Geduld lernen, Mut fassen, Vertrauen erwecken.

Das klingt wie Eitelkeit	*That sounds like vanity*
Er fühlte Liebe für sie	*He felt love for her*
Zu dieser Aufgabe gehört Mut	*This task demands courage*
Unentschlossenheit wäre jetzt verhängnisvoll	*Indecision would now be fatal*
Er versucht es mit Untertänigkeit (H. Fallada)	*He [a salesman] tries humility*
Ich habe ihm Vernunft gepredigt (from Du. Stil.)	*I urged him to be reasonable*

Es war nicht das erstemal, daß Verrat seinen Lebensweg gekreuzt hatte (S. Hermlin)	*It was not the first time that treachery had crossed his path*

72. Similarly, **some group A nouns** may be used in an indefinite or partial sense or as the essential completion of the sense of the verb; they are then used without the def. art.

Er hat mir Arbeit gegeben	*He took me on*
Dieses Gemälde hat Leben	*This painting has life*
Gibt es Leben auf anderen Planeten?	*Is there life on other planets?*
Ich brauche (nichts als) Schlaf	*I need (nothing but) sleep*
Hast du heute Zeit für mich?	*Have you any time for me today?*

Arbeit suchen *to look for work*	Not haben *to have difficulty*
Glück haben *to be lucky*	Ich hatte Not, ein Zimmer zu
Handel treiben *to trade*	finden
Deutschland treibt mit vielen	Not leiden *to suffer want*
Ländern Handel	Zeit sparen *to save time*
Krieg führen *to wage war*	

73. **Infinitives used as nouns and denoting an activity are in general treated like Group B nouns:**

(a) with def. art. when the activity as a whole is referred to:

Das Kaffeetrinken kam im 17. Jht. nach Europa (*Der Volksbrockhaus* (1956))	*Coffee-drinking came to Europe in the 17th century*
Vermeide das Spekulieren!	*Avoid speculating*

(b) without def. art. when they are used in an indefinite and partial sense:

Spekulieren war sein Verhängnis	*Speculating was his undoing*
Diese Sache verlangt Nachdenken	*This matter demands reflection*
Sein Hobby ist (das) Schreinern	*His hobby is carpentry*

74. **Some modifications of the guide-lines for Group A and Group B nouns**

(a) **after some prepositions** (see also 78):

außer *except*: Group B nouns are better used with def. art.:

Er hat keine Schwächen außer dem Stolz[1]	*He has no weaknesses except pride*

durch: some Group A nouns may be used without def. art.:

durch Arbeit, Forschung, Handel, Krieg	*through/by means of work, research, trade, war*

Group B nouns almost always without def. art.:

Durch Feigheit kann man alles verlieren	*Through cowardice one can lose everything*

---

[1] Without 'dem', 'Stolz' is accusative: cf. 549(b)N.

gegen: Group B nouns tend to be used without the def. art. even when the quality as a whole is referred to:

Ich bin nicht gegen (die) Freiheit	*I'm not against freedom*
Ich bin gegen (das) Spekulieren	*I'm against speculating*

in + dat. always has the def. art. except in certain types of phrase (see (b) below and 78) and in pairs of words (see 79):

im Krieg	*in wartime*
im Vertrauen	*in confidence*
Mein Haß gegen ihn wurzelte in der Furcht	*My hatred towards him was rooted in fear*
Die Gefahr liegt im Zögern	*The danger lies in hesitating*

in + acc.: generally without def. art. with Group B nouns and occasionally with certain Group A nouns:

Er geriet in Wut	*He flew into a rage*
Sein Glück verwandelte sich in Elend	*His happiness was transformed into misery*
Die Dämmerung ging allmählich in Nacht über	*Dusk gradually passed over into night*

ohne is preponderantly used without the def. art., even with many Group A nouns:

Es schien eine Stadt ohne Jugend und ohne Leben zu sein	*It seemed to be a town without youth and without life*
Ohne (den) Kommunismus sähe die Welt anders aus	*Without Communism the world would look different*
ohne Arbeit, Glück, Handel, Not, Schlaf, Wahrheit	*without work, happiness, trade, want, sleep, truth*

über *about, concerning:* Group B nouns tend to be used without the def. art. even when the quality as a whole is referred to:

Seine Ansichten über (die) Freiheit	*his views on freedom*
Wir sprachen über (die) Gesundheit	*We spoke about health*
ein Aufsatz über den Ehrgeiz	BUT: *an essay on ambition*

zu is almost always used with the def. art.:

Ich brachte ihn zur Vernunft	*I brought him to reason*
Er neigt zur Verschwendung	*He is prone to extravagance*
der Weg zum Erfolg	*the road to success*
Ich komme wenig zum Lesen	*I have little time for reading*

(b) **Set phrases,** mainly with prepositions, in which nouns from both groups are used without an article:

bei Nacht	*by night*
Ist er in Arbeit?	*Is he in a job?*
sich in Geduld üben	*to practise patience*
in Not sein	*to be in distress*
in Wahrheit	*in fact*
in Wirklichkeit	*in reality*
Da können Sie von Glück sagen	*You can count yourself lucky*
von Jugend auf	*from (his) youth upward*
Er ist von Natur aus bescheiden	*He is by nature modest*
Er hat sich zu Tode gearbeitet	*He has worked himself to death*
wenn Not an den Mann geht	*when help is needed*

(c) **When Group B nouns are preceded by an adjective,** the def. art. tends to drop away or to be replaced by the indef. art.:

Ich verachte kleinliche Eifersucht	*I scorn petty jealousy*
Im Heere wuchs (ein) neuer Mut	*In the army a new courage was growing*
Er neigt zu unnötiger Ver- schwendung	*He is prone to unnecessary extravagance*

The same applies to a number of Group A nouns, e.g. Arbeit, Elend, Forschung, Freiheit, Glück *happiness*, Not, Wahrheit:

anstrengende Arbeit	*strenuous work*
politische Freiheit	*political liberty*
ungetrübtes Glück	*unclouded happiness*
Sie bekämpfen schwere Not	*They are combating great distress*
wissenschaftliche Wahrheit	*scientific truth*

(d) **Straightforward necessity for def. art.** when an abstract noun is particularized by a gen. sing., a relative clause or by some other means: Er zeigte den Mut eines Helden; das ist die Tugend, die ich am meisten bewundere; er hatte die Unverschämtheit, das zu behaupten.

(e) **No article in many recognized proverbs or comparable statements:**

Alter schützt vor Torheit nicht	*Age is not proof against folly*
Not kennt kein Gebot	*Necessity knows no law*
Stolz ist keine Tugend	*Pride is no virtue*

(f) For the omission of an article in pairs of words and enumerations, which applies to abstract as to other nouns, see 79.

(g) For the use of the def. art. to indicate the genitive or dative case, with abstract as with other nouns, see 80 f.

C. USE OF THE DEFINITE ARTICLE WITH NOUNS DENOTING ARTS, SCIENCES AND SPORTS

75. With nouns denoting arts, sciences and sports the def. art. is, for the most part, used or omitted as with abstract nouns. The following examples will serve as guide-lines and ear-training:

Die Literatur ist etwas Wunderbares	*Literature is something wonderful*
Ich erwartete von der Literatur mehr Anregung als vom Leben (Günter Grass)	*I expected more stimulus from literature than from life*
Es wird großes Interesse für Literatur gezeigt	*There is great interest in literature*
Die deutsche Literatur ist im ganzen ernst	*German literature is on the whole serious*
Gute Literatur ist heutzutage selten	*Good literature is rare today*
Wir sprachen über (deutsche) Literatur	*We talked about (German) literature*
Darüber schweigt die Geschichte (from Du. Stil.)	*History is silent about that*
Geschichte ist sein Hauptfach	*History is his main subject*

Er studiert (deutsche) Geschichte	*He is studying (German) history*
die Kunst fördern	*to promote art*
Ich interessiere mich für Kunst	*I am interested in art*
In der Kunst ist der Stil alles	*In art style is everything*
(die) abstrakte Kunst	*abstract art*
Es klang wie Musik	*It sounded like music*
Musik treiben	*to go in for music*
Die Physik wird immer schwerer	*Physics is becoming more and more difficult*
Ich kann Physik nicht verstehen	*I can't understand physics*
Ich kann die moderne Physik nicht verstehen	*I can't understand modern physics*
(Der) Sport ist gesund	*Sport is healthy*
Er hat sich beim Fußball verletzt	*He got hurt at football*

D. USE OF THE DEFINITE ARTICLE WITH NAMES OF SPECIES AND SUBSTANCES

76. The use of the def. art. with the names of species

(a) The def. art. is always used with 'Mensch', and any other species, in the singular:

Der Mensch ist ein seltsames Geschöpf	*Man is a strange creature*
Der Tiger ist ein Raubtier	*The tiger is a beast of prey*

(b) Before a species in the plural, the def. art. is generally omitted; the fourth is a counter-example; the last example is a fixed usage:

(Die) Menschen sind seltsame Geschöpfe	*Men are strange creatures*
Hunde sind mir sympathischer als Katzen	*I prefer dogs to cats*
Ich interessiere mich für Flugzeuge	*I am interested in aeroplanes*
Woran man sieht, daß es auch bei den Schiedsrichtern Charakterunterschiede gibt (*Zeit*)	*From which one can see that referees too differ in character*
N.B. Die Leute meinten, er sei verrückt	*People thought he was mad*

(c) No def. art. when a species in the plural is used partitively:

Menschen haben dies getan, nicht Tiere	*Men did this, not animals*
In dem Wildpark kann man Hirsche und Bisamtiere sehen	*In the game-preserve one can see stags and musk-deer*

77. The use of the def. art. with the names of substances

(a) The def. art. is generally omitted, e.g. some quotations from *De Volksbrockhaus* (1956):

Gold hat hohe Politurfähigkeit; Kaffee wird in fast allen tropischen Länder angebaut; Elektrizität wurde früher als ein unwägbares Etwas (*an imponderabl something*) angesehen; Seife entsteht, wenn . . . cf. Bier ist erfrischender als Wein

(b) No def. art. when the name of the substance is used partitively:

Wir aßen Brot mit Käse	*We ate bread and cheese*
Wir importieren Kaffee aus Afrika	*We import coffee from Africa*
Holz hacken	*to chop wood*

(c) The def. art. is used before the names of substances in the following cases (in addition to those where it would likewise be used in English):

i Especially in conversation, it brings out the familiar character of the substance in question:

Die Butter kostet drei Mark das Pfund	*Butter costs three marks a pound*
Der Wein war sein Verderben	*Wine was his undoing*
Die Steuern waren drückend, und das Brot hatte erst kürzlich wieder aufgeschlagen (B. Brecht)	*Taxes were heavy and only recently the price of bread had gone up again*

cf. the book-title *Du und die Elektrizität*

Similarly, in an encyclopaedia article, after the name of the substance has been introduced without the def. art., at a later mention it often has the def. art.

ii Occasionally the def. art. has demonstrative force (as in English):

Trinkst du noch ein Glas?—Nein, ich mag den Wein nicht	*Are you having another glass?—No, I don't care for the wine*

iii The def. art. is often used before the name of a substance in the accusative where it is used in a general and not in a partitive sense:

Wer hat den Kaffee in Europa eingeführt?	*Who introduced coffee into Europe?*
Faraday hat die Elektrizität erforscht	*Faraday investigated electricity*

iv to indicate case (cf. 80 f.):

der Alkoholgehalt des Weines	*the alcoholic content of wine*

v a few special cases:

im Wasser leben	*to live in water*
beim Bier sitzen	*to sit over a glass of beer*
Das steht nur auf dem Papier	*That is only on paper*
Am Bahnhof trank ich einen Kaffee	*At the station I had a cup of coffee*

E. PREPOSITIONAL PHRASES WITHOUT AN ARTICLE

78. Prepositional phrases without an article[1]

(a) **Set phrases,** e.g. auf Wache *on guard*, auf Wunsch *on request*, bei Tisch *at table*, nach Kriegsende *after the end of the war*, nach Wunsch *as desired*, von Beruf *by profession*, über Erwarten *beyond expectation*.
See also 74(b), 79 and 620 ff.; for phrases of the type 'seit Anfang Januar', see 329 N.ii.

(b) **Preposition + a noun formed from a verb + a genitive** (often officialese):

bei Ausbruch des Ersten Weltkriegs	*at the outbreak of the First World War*
in Anerkennung seiner Verdienste	*in recognition of his services*
nach Empfang Ihres Briefes	*after receiving your letter*
zwei Monate vor Ablauf seiner Amtszeit (*FAZ*)	*two months before the expiration of his term of office*

---

[1] See also the examples of some figurative uses of: an + dat., 597(a); auf + acc., 600(c); aus, 601 (a); nach, 604(a)(b); vor + dat., 612(a).

(c) Preposition + adjective/participle + noun

This is a crisp and effective combination; English will generally have the indef. art.; Duden frowns on the insertion of the indef. art. in German (Du. Haupt., p. 185: ein (Artikel): 1).

i adjectival

... einen Virtuosen mit italienischem Namen (Th. Mann)	*a virtuoso with an Italian name*
ein Anzug von altmodischem Schnitt	*a suit of old-fashioned cut*

ii adverbial

in endloser Kette	*in an endless chain*
mit letzter Anstrengung (G. Gaiser)	*with a final effort*
nach kurzer Pause	*after a short pause*
auf eigne Kosten	*at my (his etc.) own expense*
auch bei bester Organisation	*even with the best organization*
nach bestandener Prüfung	*after passing his exam*

F. OMISSION OF ARTICLE IN PAIRS OF WORDS AND ENUMERATIONS

79. The article is frequently omitted in pairs of words, with or without a preposition, and in enumerations. The first group of examples are set phrases.

(in) Form und Inhalt	*(in) form and content*
in Hülle und Fülle	*in plenty*
in Krieg und Frieden	*in war and peace*
(BUT: im Krieg)	*in wartime)*
mit Müh und Not	*with great difficulty, only just*
mit Rat und Tat	*by word and deed*
Es geht um Leben und Tod	*It's a matter of life and death*
der Unterschied zwischen Stolz und Hochmut	*the difference between pride and arrogance*
Er haßt Lesen und Schreiben	*He hates reading and writing*

Sie biß in eine von den Bananen und ließ Schale und Rest im Eßzimmer liegen (V. Baum)
Eine mehrstündige Militärparade auf dem Roten Platz demonstrierte... Geschichte und heutige Stärke der Roten Armee (*Zeit.*)

Example of an enumeration:
... die alten menschlichen Werte (*values*)—ich möchte hier nur Pflicht, Gehorsam, Anstand (*good manners*), Autorität, Ordnung nennen (Th. Valentin)

G. USE OF THE DEFINITE ARTICLE TO INDICATE CASE

80. The def. art. may be used to indicate a genitive

(a) With the exceptions noted below, no German noun can be given a genitive inflection without a preceding article or a possessive, demonstrative or ordinary adjective. Thus 'the smell of seaweed' is 'der

Geruch des Seetangs' (or 'der Geruch von Seetang'); 'an expression of astonishment' is 'ein Ausdruck des Erstaunens'.

EXCEPTIONS:

i proper names: Peters Buch, Nürnbergs Kirchen.
ii generic names of members of the family: Vaters Anzug.
iii after some prepositions + gen.: wegen Menschenraubs.
iv sometimes after a word of quantity: voll Hasses; hinter Stürzen Wassers (H. Mann).

(b) For the use of 'von' in place of the genitive, see 555(c) and (c) below.

(c) With abstract nouns and infinitives used as nouns, the use of 'von', with or without the def. art., instead of the gen. sing., is not to be recommended; it is generally poor style and frequently wrong. Therefore: die Bande der Freundschaft, ein Gefühl der Verzweiflung, die Wichtigkeit des Stils, die Kunst des Fechtens *the art of fencing*.

EXCEPTIONS:

i ein Mann von Erfahrung *a man of experience*, eine Frau von Geschmack *a woman of taste* and the like.
ii 'von' is used before two or more abstract nouns of different genders, to avoid repeating the article, e.g.

der Abgrund von Ironie, Unglaube,	*the gulf of irony, scepticism, opposition,*
Opposition, Erkenntnis, Gefühl,	*perception and feeling that separates you*
der Sie von den Menschen trennt . . .	*from others*
(Th. Mann)	

81. The def. art. may be used to indicate a dative

Ich ziehe Kaffee dem Tee vor	*I prefer coffee to tea*
Dieses Metall gleicht dem Gold	*This metal resembles gold*
Er hat sich der Physik gewidmet	*He has devoted himself to physics*
(BUT: Er studiert Physik	*He is studying physics*)

Note: With proper names and generic names of members of the family, the insertion of a clarifying def. art. is possible but not usual: (Dem) Karl scheint es zu riskiert zu sein. Wir müssen (dem) Lehmann mal wieder was schicken. Das will ich (der) Mutter sagen.

H. USE OF DEFINITE ARTICLE WITH PARTS OF BODY AND ARTICLES OF CLOTHING

82. The def. art. is generally used instead of the possess. adj. when speaking of parts of the body and articles of clothing

(a) Where there is no contrary indication, the def. art. refers back to the subject:

Er machte die Augen auf	*He opened his eyes*
Er hob den Arm	*He raised his arm*
Er steckte die Hand in die Tasche	*He put his hand in his pocket*
Er zog den Mantel aus	*He took off his coat*
Er hielt den Hut in der Hand	*He held his hat in his hand*

Das Mädchen . . . zog den rötlichen Kamm aus dem Haar, nahm ihn in den Mund und fing an, mit den Fingern die Frisur zurechtzuzupfen (H. Böll) (. . . *and began to put her hair right by plucking it with her fingers.*)

(b) With actions which are slightly more complex, the def. art., even though it obviously refers back to the subject, is reinforced by a reflexive pronoun in the dative (a kind of dative of advantage or disadvantage). 'Sprachgefühl' may have to decide whether the addition of the reflexive sounds convincing or not, for it is rarely optional.

Ich wusch mir die Hände	*I washed my hands*
Er wischte sich den Schweiß von der Stirn	*He wiped the sweat from his forehead*
Er kratzte sich den Kopf	*He scratched his head*
Ich habe mir die Haare schneiden lassen	*I had my hair cut*
Ich habe mir den Fuß verstaucht	*I've sprained my ankle*
Ich habe mir in den Finger geschnitten	*I've cut my finger*

(c) Where the def. art. does not refer back to the subject, a dative is essential to show who is involved:

Er trat mir auf den Fuß	*He trod on my foot*
Das Blut schoß ihm ins Gesicht	*The blood rushed to his face*

(d) Even where the question of avoiding the possess. adj. does not arise, the dative of advantage is generally preferred to a genitive:

Die Mutter wusch dem Kind die Hände	*The mother washed the child's hands*
Wir zogen dem Verletzten die Jacke aus	*We took off the injured man's jacket*

BUT, significantly:

Sie wuschen die Beine des Toten[1]	*They washed the dead man's legs*

(e) The def. art. cannot be used when the part of the body or the article of clothing is the subject and the sentence is purely descriptive (cf. Kolisko and Yuill: *Practice in German Prose*, p. 31):

Ein Fremder erschien; seine Stirn glänzte; sein Anzug war altmodisch	*A stranger appeared; his forehead glistened; his suit was old-fashioned*
Die Augen taten ihr weh	BUT: *Her eyes hurt*
Der Finger juckt mich (or: Mein Finger juckt)	*My finger itches*

(f) Apart from the exception noted in 82(e), the use of the def. art. instead of the possess. adj. with parts of the body and articles of clothing is usual, but not sacrosanct; the first two examples are taken from modern novels:

Sie legte ihre Hand auf seine Hand (I. Wendt)	*She laid her hand on his hand*
Groenewold nahm die Brille ab, preßte die Lider zusammen und rieb seine Schläfen (Th. Valentin)	*Groenewold took off his glasses, pressed his eyelids together and rubbed his temples*
Zieh lieber deinen Mantel an!	*You'd better put on your coat*

In some instances, the use of the possess. adj. is inevitable:

Er blickte hinab; dicht bei seinen Füßen lag ein Ring	*He glanced down; close to his feet lay a ring*

[1] From Weser, loc. cit. in 60(footnote), p. 223.

('dicht bei den Füßen lag ihm ein Ring' would be impossible, while 'bei den Füßen' alone would not refer back to 'Er'.)

Ich sah eine Wespe auf meinem Ärmel   *I saw a wasp on my sleeve*
(On *whose* sleeve must be specified, and 'mir auf dem Ärmel' would be impossible; contrast 'Ich hatte eine Wespe auf dem Ärmel', which is un-ambiguous.)

83. The use of the def. art., coupled with a dative of advantage or disadvantage, is found in other contexts, e.g.

Er füllte meinem Vater das Glas	*He filled my father's glass*
Er ebnete mir den Weg	*He smoothed my path*
Er trug ihr den Koffer zur Bahn	*He carried her bag to the station*
Der Appetit ist mir vergangen	*I've lost my appetite*
Er versauert mir das Leben	*He spoils my whole life*
Wir kamen ihm auf die Spur	*We got onto his track*
Dem Alten ist gerade die Frau gestorben (J. Ziem)	*The old man's wife has just died*

I. USE OF DEFINITE ARTICLE BEFORE GEOGRAPHICAL AND PROPER NAMES

84. Before geographical and proper names, the def. art. is used in German as in English with the following main exceptions. (A few further cases will be found in 51(d)(g), 55) It is used:

(a) before masc. and fem. countries and regions (see 6(b)): der Libanon, die Normandie, die Schweiz. But no article in addresses: Hotel X., Kandersteg, Schweiz.

(b) before a few neuter regions, e.g. das Elsaß *Alsace*.

(c) before all geographical and proper names if preceded by an adjective: das schöne Italien, das betriebsame Frankfurt (*busy Frankfurt*), der junge Heinrich, der alte (Doktor) Schulze.

(d) in the following and analogous cases:
der Bodensee *Lake Constance*   der Jupiter *Jupiter* (planet)
der Montblanc *Mont Blanc*   Er spielt den Brutus *He plays Brutus*
die Königstraße *the Königstrasse*

(e) before the names of persons:
  i occasionally to clarify case; see 81N.
  ii before the surnames of women where nothing else indicates the sex: Ich habe eben mit der Rupp (BUT: mit Anna Rupp) gesprochen.
  iii familiarly, in Central and South Germany: Ich habe den Rudolf gesehen. Ich bin bei der Frau Schmidt gewesen.
  iv to individualize the person concerned more strongly: Ich hätte den Klaus sofort wiedererkannt. Der Lehmann hat vorzüglich geredet.
  v in the rural formula 'die Sabest Minna' (H. Broch) = Minna Sabest.

(f) No def. art. in German for Emperors (Kaiser Karl V., the Emperor Charles V) nor in names of the following type (where German has apposition): Schloß Sanssouci *the Palace of Sanssouci*, Kloster Beuron *the Monastery of Beuron*.

J. MISCELLANEOUS USES AND OMISSIONS OF THE ARTICLES

85. (a) **The def. art. is generally used before the names of seasons, months and meals**

Der Sommer ist zu Ende; der Juli war sehr warm; im Sommer, im Juli; BUT: Es war Sommer/Juli; das Wetter war kühl für Juli; vor, nach, seit Juli

Das Frühstück war reichlich (*plentiful*); vor dem/zum/beim Frühstück; BUT: Ich habe (das) Frühstück bestellt; wann bekommen wir Frühstück?

(b) **Further common nouns and phrases where English has no article and German has the def. art.**

im Bett *in bed*	das Parlament *parliament*
(BUT: Ich ging zu Bett)	im Parlament *in parliament*
beim Fußball *at football*	mit der Post *by post*
im Gefängnis *in prison*	Die Schule ist gut für ihn *School is*
der Himmel *heaven*	*good for him*
die Hölle *hell*	vor der Schule *before school*
in der Kirche *at church*	in der Stadt *in town*
zum Markt *to market*	mit dem Zug (Schiff etc.) *by train*
das Paradies *paradise*	(*boat etc.*)

(c) **The def. art. is always used before 'meist'**

Er hat das meiste Geld	*He has most money*
das meiste davon	*most of it*
die meisten Jungen	*most boys; most of the boys*
die meisten meiner Freunde	*most of my friends*
der größere Teil unserer Triebkraft/ des Kuchens	N.B. *most of our industrial energy/of the cake*

(d) **The def. art. is used with the sense of 'each' as an alternative to 'pro':** Die Butter kostet drei Mark das Pfund; wir fuhren 80 Kilometer die Stunde; sie kommt zweimal die Woche (or: in der Woche); er verdient 1000 Mark im Monat (also: den Monat (coll.)).

(e) **No article before professions and other broad classes, used as the complement of sein, werden or bleiben:** Er ist Arzt; er wurde Arzt; ihr Mann ist Franzose/Deutscher; er ist Katholik, Oberleutnant; er blieb Junggeselle *a bachelor*.

BUT: Er ist ein bekannter Arzt, ein Schwindler, ein Narr, (ein) Fanatiker.

(f) **Omission of article in officialese** (cf. Du. Gram. 1490), as in: Beklagter hat zugegeben ... *The accused has admitted* ... Überbringer *the bearer*, Unterzeichneter *the undersigned*.

(g) **Other idiomatic instances of complement or real subject without an article:**

Das ist Geschmacksache	*That is a matter of taste*
Es ist Mode (geworden)	*It is (has become) the fashion*
Das ist hier Sitte	*That is the custom here*
Donnerstags ist Sitzung[1]	*On Thursdays there is (always) a meeting*

[1] From Erben, op. cit., p. 93.

Es ist Tatsache, daß ...	*It is a fact that ...*
Tatsache ist, daß ...	
Es ist Sache der Soziologie, diesem Konflikt nachzuspüren (*Hbg. Abendblatt*)	*It is the business of sociology to investigate this conflict*
Grund meines Schreibens ist der Artikel 'Unser Garten' (Letter in *Hbg. Abendblatt*)	*The reason for my writing is the article 'Our Garden'*

(h) **No article after 'als' meaning 'as'** (in the capacity of, by way of, as being)

Er sprach als Franzose	*He spoke as a Frenchman*
Er sprach wie ein Franzose	BUT: *He spoke like a Frenchman*
Er gab mir dies als Belohnung	*He gave me this as a reward*
Als (überzeugter) Demokrat, kann ich das nicht gutheißen	*As a (convinced) democrat, I can't approve of that*
Als erstes kaufte ich mir eine Zeitung	*The first thing I did was to buy a paper*
Er gilt als guter Chirurg	*He is considered [as being] a good surgeon*
Er gilt als der beste Chirurg	BUT: *He is considered the best surgeon*

(i) **The article is often omitted, in literary and journalistic German, before a substantival phrase in apposition to the subject**

Westfale von Geburt, lebte er jetzt in Bayern	*A Westphalian by birth, he was now living in Bavaria*
Bei aller Geschäftigkeit hat dieses Zürich, Treffpunkt der Kaufleute, etwas Kurorthaftes (M. Frisch)	*For all its bustle, this Zürich, the meeting-place of businessmen, has something of a spa about it*
Neil Armstrong, amerikanischer Astronaut, betrat als erster Mensch den Mond (*Zeit*)	*Neil Armstrong, the American astronaut, was the first man to set foot on the moon.*

(j) **The article (mainly the def. art.) is sometimes omitted before an attributive adjective.** This can be an effective and often arresting literary device, demanding a good deal of 'Sprachgefühl', though the first three examples represent almost fixed usage:

Beigefügter Zeitungsausschnitt dürfte Sie interessieren	*The enclosed cutting might interest you*
folgendes Beispiel	*the following example*
Das ist beschlossene Sache	*That's definitely arranged*
Jüngstes Mitglied der Regierung ist X.	*The youngest member of the government is X*
Gleicher Doppelsinn ... lauert im Titel (from a book review in *FAZ*)	*A similar ambiguity lurks in the title*
Im Straßengraben grünte erstes Unkraut (H. Broch)	*The first weeds sprouted in the roadside ditch*

Sie erschrak oft, wenn ihr klar wurde, wie vernünftig er war: genauer Rechner, scharfer Kalkulator, ... : kühles Hirn, scheues Gesicht ... (H. Böll)

(k) **No article in the adverbial genitive,** e.g. schweren Herzens *with a heavy heart*: see end of 60.

(l) i **The names of indispositions and illnesses are generally used without an article:** Er hat Kopfschmerzen, Husten, Grippe, (eine) Lungenentzündung *pneumonia*, (die) Gelbsucht *jaundice*
EXCEPTIONS: Er hat eine Erkältung, einen Schnupfen *a cold in the head*,

den Schluckauf *hiccups*

ii With actual illnesses denoted by a plural noun, the def. art. is frequently used and is never wrong: Er hat (die) Masern *measles*, (die) Röteln *German measles*

iii Examples of indispositions and illnesses limited by adjectives:

Er hat schlimme Masern	*He's got measles badly*
Ich habe ekligen Rheumatismus	*I've got nasty rheumatism*
Er hat einen schlimmen Husten	*He has a bad cough*
Ich hatte eine langwierige Grippe	*I had a lengthy bout of flu*
Er hat eine leichte Lungenentzündung	*He has slight pneumonia*

(m) **Articles are often omitted in newspaper headlines and advertisements**

Verbrechen gestanden. Münchner Kaufmann von Geschäftspartner erschlagen (*Hbg. Abendblatt*)	*Crime admitted. Munich business-man killed by partner*
Möglichst nahe Stadtmitte (*Hbg. Abendblatt*)	(accommodation required) *as near as possible to town-centre*

III ADJECTIVES

A. UNINFLECTED AND INFLECTED USE OF ADJECTIVES

86. Uninflected use of adjectives: used non-attributively, German adjectives are not inflected: Sie waren fleißig. Vor dem Haus stand ein Mann, kahl, blaß und mager.[1] Optimistisch wie immer, ließ sie sich von ihrem Vorhaben nicht abhalten.

The exceptional instances of attributive adjectives being uninflected are treated in 116.

87. Inflected use of adjectives: used attributively, i.e. when they limit a following noun, German adjectives are inflected, being declined in three different ways: the weak declension, the mixed declension and the strong declension. (Logically, the strong declension should be treated first, but in view of its more protracted commentary, it has seemed preferable to place it last.)

The adjective endings are presented schematically at the beginning of each of the three declensions.

B. WEAK DECLENSION

88. Weak declension: der (dieser etc.) + adj. + noun

---

[1] Only where there are two or more adjectives can they be placed after the noun; the effect is rather literary.

Sing.

N. der gute Wein	die gute Suppe	das gute Brot
A. den guten Wein	die gute Suppe	das gute Brot
G. des guten Weines	der guten Suppe	des guten Brotes
D. dem guten Wein	der guten Suppe	dem guten Brot

Plur. N.	die guten Suppen
A.	die guten Suppen
G.	der guten Suppen
D.	den guten Suppen

Sing.

N. dieser gute Wein	diese gute Suppe	dieses gute Brot
A. diesen guten Wein	diese gute Suppe	dieses gute Brot
G. dieses guten Weines	dieser guten Suppe	dieses guten Brotes
D. diesem guten Wein	dieser guten Suppe	diesem guten Brot

Plur. N.	diese guten Suppen
A.	diese guten Suppen
G.	dieser guten Suppen
D.	diesen guten Suppen

89. The weak declension is used after the def. art. and after the following:

aller *all*	jeglicher (obsolescent) *each, every*
beide *both, two* (plur. only)	jener *that*
dieser *this*	mancher sing.: *many a*
irgendwelcher *some (or other)*, *any*	plur.: *some, many*
(*whatsoever*)	sämtlicher *all, complete*
jeder *each, every*	solcher *such*
jedweder (archaic) *each, every*	welcher? *which?*

These words are all declined like 'dieser' (with the deviation given in N.i below); the paradigms in 88 show that the endings of 'dieser' are identical with those of 'der' except in the nom. and acc. fem., neut. and plur., where they are similar: the weak declension is therefore used after 'der' and words declined like it. (One deviation from this is given in N.ii below and a few others are noted in Chap. VI Sect. B where the words listed above are treated in detail; see Index.)

Note:
i Masc. and neut. gen. sing.: a variation: the declension of der, dieser and jener is fixed, but all the other words listed above, apart from beide, may have the ending -en before the gen. sing. of a masc. or neut. noun other than a Group 7 noun or a substantival adjective (see 106 ff.); the ending of the attributive adjective is not affected:

Das war der Ursprung alles/allen späteren Fortschritts	*That was the origin of all later progress*
ein Beweis solchen starken Glaubens	*a proof of such strong faith*
	BUT:
jedes guten Christen (Gr. 7)	*of every good Christian*
der Genuß manches Schönen (subst. adj.)	*the enjoyment of many things of beauty*

This masc. and neut. gen. in -en, as circumscribed above, is found:

occasionally in the case of jeder and welcher.
frequently in the case of aller, mancher, solcher.
always in the case of irgendwelcher, jedweder, jeglicher, sämtlicher.

The above variation is largely determined by ear; if in doubt, it is safer to use the gen. in -es.

ii dieser + mein (dein etc.) + adj. + noun: the declension of 'mein' is fixed and the adjective has the mixed declension (see 90): dieser mein jüngster Sohn; mit diesem meinem jüngsten Sohn.

C. MIXED DECLENSION

90. Mixed declension:[1] ein (kein, mein etc.) + adj + noun

SING.
N. ein guter Wein	eine gute Suppe	ein gutes Brot
A. einen guten Wein	eine gute Suppe	ein gutes Brot
G. eines guten Weines	einer guten Suppe	eines guten Brotes
D. einem guten Wein	einer guten Suppe	einem guten Brot

N. ihr guter Wein	ihre gute Suppe	ihr gutes Brot
A. ihren guten Wein	ihre gute Suppe	ihr gutes Brot
G. ihres guten Weines	ihrer guten Suppe	ihres guten Brotes
D. ihrem guten Wein	ihrer guten Suppe	ihrem guten Brot

PLUR. N. ihre guten Suppen
A. ihre guten Suppen
G. ihrer guten Suppen
D. ihren guten Suppen

Here the adjective indicates the case in the masc. nom. and the neut. nom. and acc., where ein (kein, mein etc.) have no ending and, incidentally, in the fem. nom. and acc.

91. The mixed declension is used after the indef. art. and after the words which, in the sing., are declined like it, viz.

---

[1] The convenient term 'mixed declension' is used in some German grammars written in English, but German grammarians do not normally use an equivalent term.

irgendein *some (or other)*, *any (whatsoever)*, kein *no* and the possessive adjectives:

mein *my*	unser *our*
dein *your* (familiar sing.)	euer *your* (familiar plur.)
sein *his, its*	ihr *their*
ihr *her, its*	Ihr *your* (polite)

In the plural:
i ein drops away, leaving adj.+noun (strong declension).
ii kein, mein etc. are declined like dieser and the adjective ends in -en throughout; the plural of irgendein is irgendwelche (see 207(e)i).

92. Note:

(a) **A warning:** through their ending in -(e)r, a common error is to bring the masc. nom. and the neut. nom. and acc. of unser, euer and ihr into line with those of dieser and to write or say 'ihrer Vater' instead of 'ihr Vater', 'unseres Haus' instead of 'unser Haus'. The thing to remember is that all the possessive adjectives are declined like ein; therefore where ein has no ending, unser, euer and ihr have no ending.

(b) **Spelling of inflected unser and euer:** wherever unser and euer have an ending, the unstressed e of the stem is frequently dropped, especially in spoken German. In the masc. acc., the masc. and neut. dat. and the dat. plur. the alternative possibility of dropping the e of the ending is commoner. (It is not wrong to retain both e's.) E.g. das Dach unsres Hauses, in unsrer Stadt, die Namen eurer Kinder, in unserm/unsrem Garten, mit unsern/unsren Eltern.

(c) **The titular Euer:** an uninflected Euer is an alternative in the four singular cases of feminine titular words, e.g. Euer (commoner: Eure) Majestät, mit Euer (commoner: Eurer) Exzellenz; the written abbreviation of any of these is Ew. A declined Ihr will also be accepted.

D. STRONG DECLENSION

93. Strong declension: adj.+noun

er	e	es
en	e	es
en	er	**en**
em	er	em

e
e
er
en

SING.

N. guter Wein	gute Suppe	gutes Brot
A. guten Wein	gute Suppe	gutes Brot
G. guten Weines	guter Suppe	guten Brotes
D. gutem Wein	guter Suppe	gutem Brot

PLUR. N. gute Suppen
      A. gute Suppen
      G. guter Suppen
      D. guten Suppen

94. **Here the adjective does the work of indicating the case** (thence, no doubt, the 'strong' declension), having the endings of dieser, except in the masc. and neut. gen. where the -(e)s ending of the noun indicates the case and the adjective ends in -en.

In two instances, however, the adjective must end in -es in the masc. and neut. gen., viz. before a Group 7 noun and before a substantival adjective (see 106ff.), neither of which has a distinctive genitive ending. As most Group 7 nouns denote persons, the combination adj. + Group 7 in the gen. sing. is negligibly rare. In a pseudo-Schillerian drama, the following stirring iambic might conceivably occur:

     Das nenn' ich edles Helden kühnen Mut.

Quite normal, of course, is the combination miscellaneous adj. + Group 7 (sing.); miscellaneous adjectives with a tendency to end in -en in the masc. and neut. gen. must end in -es before Group 7 (cf. 89 N.i), e.g.

     Er kannte den Namen jedes/jeden neuen Schülers BUT: jedes Studenten.

Note: The terms 'strong declension' and 'strong endings' as used in this book imply -en in the masc. and neut. gen. sing., while 'the endings of dieser' is used to indicate -es in masc. and neut. gen. sing.

95. **The simplest form of the strong declension is adj. + noun** (mit neuem Mut, das hohe Niveau französischer Filme); **it is also used when adj. + noun** are immediately preceded by, and **form a unit with, a word or phrase that does not indicate their case.** Such are:

(a) the following uninflected forms:

     manch *many a, many*: manch reichen Landes.
     solch *such*: bei solch gutem Wetter.
     viel *much, many*: viel indischer Tee.
     welch! *what (a)!*: Welch herrliches Wetter!
     wenig *little, few*: wenig deutsche Bücher.
     (See Chap. VI for the detailed treatment of these words.)

(b) indeclinable words and phrases denoting quantity or range, e.g.

ein bißchen *a little*	derlei *suchlike*
ein wenig *a little*	keinerlei *of no sort, not any*
ein paar *a few*	mancherlei *various*
etwas *some, any* (sing. only)	mehrerlei *various*
lauter *nothing but, a whole lot of*	solcherlei *suchlike*
mehr *more*	vielerlei *many kinds of*
weniger *less, fewer*	welcherlei *what kind of; whatever*
	wievielerlei? *how many kinds of?*
was für . . .?[1] *what (kind of)?*	zweierlei *two kinds of*
was für . . .![1] *what!*	dreierlei etc. *three kinds of*
allerhand ⎫ *all kinds of, various* allerlei ⎭	

---

[1] plur. of was für ein, but also used in sing. without ein (see 175(a)ii).

etwas frisches Obst	*some fresh fruit*
lauter wertvolle Bilder	*a whole lot of valuable pictures*
Er trank noch mehr starken Kaffee mit ein bißchen braunem Zucker	*He drank some more strong coffee with a little brown sugar*
Er redete allerlei dummes Zeug	*He talked a lot of nonsense*
Er nannte mir die Namen zweierlei englischer Äpfel	*He gave me the names of two kinds of English apples*

(c) cardinal numbers (other than 'one'):

zwei schöne Pfirsiche	*two fine peaches*
Da standen an siebenhundert deutsche Kriegsgefangene (Th. Plievier)	*Getting on for seven hundred German prisoners of war were standing there*
	BUT:
die zwei schönen Pfirsiche	*the two fine peaches*
seine zwei jungen Söhne	*his two young sons*

See also 242(a)

(d) genitives denoting possession:

Karls unermüdlicher Eifer	*Karl's indefatigable zeal*
in meines Vaters kleinem Arbeitszimmer	*in my father's little study*
Mein Freund, dessen ältester Sohn krank ist, . . .	*My friend, whose eldest son is ill, . . .*

in den . . . Gartensalon hinab, hinter dessen hoher Glastür die Terrasse lag (Th. Mann).

96. The adjective is still used attributively, and inflected, if the following noun is understood, being represented by 'one' in English:

Welcher Junge ist das? Es ist der dumme	*Which boy is that? It's the stupid one*
Ich habe mein Taschenmesser verloren; ich muß mir ein neues kaufen	*I've lost my penknife; I must buy a new one*
Englische Äpfel sind besser als deutsche	*English apples are better than German ones*

E. ADJECTIVAL USE OF PARTICIPLES

97. The following types of participle may be used as attributive adjectives, being declined exactly as adjectives are:

(a) all present participles, though 'seiend' and 'habend' may be excluded.

ein lachendes Kind	*a laughing child*
lachende Kinder	*laughing children*

(b) the past participle of transitive verbs:

mein verlorener Schirm	*my lost umbrella*

(c) the past participle of intransitive verbs conjugated with sein and signifying a completed action:

die angekommenen Gäste	*the guests who had arrived*
nach der geglückten Generalprobe gegen Frankreich (*Die Zeit* on football)	*after the successful dress-rehearsal against France*

der hereingelaufene Junge	*the boy who had run in*
der Junge, der gelaufen war,	BUT: *the boy who had been running* (stress on duration, not on completion)

98. Adjectival participles: many present participles, and many past participles (when they are not being used to form compound tenses), have come to be felt as adjectives rather than participles, e.g.

angreifend *tiring, trying*	angegriffen *worn, ill*
auffallend *striking, conspicuous*	aufgeregt *excited*
aufregend *exciting*	erfahren *experienced*
empörend *shocking*	gelehrt *learned*
reizend *charming*	verrückt *deranged, insane*

F. NOUN OF MEASUREMENT + ADJECTIVE + NOUN

99. Noun of measurement + adj. + noun denoting the thing measured: the noun denoting the thing measured may be put in the genitive, but, since the gen. of adj. + noun—and especially the gen. sing.—has a somewhat stilted ring, the case in apposition is generally preferred, especially in conversation:[1]

Eine Tasse starker Kaffee würde mir gut tun	*A cup of strong coffee would do me good*
. . . und beschloß, mir noch zwei Tassen echten Kaffee zu bereiten (A. Goes)	*. . . and decided, before going ahead, to make myself two cups of real coffee*
Er kam mit einer Tasse starkem Kaffee	*He came with a cup of strong coffee*
Ich aß ein Stück frisches Brot	*I ate a piece of fresh bread*

NOTE: As Duden rightly observes (Gram. 2185), in the dative the adjective preceding the second noun is frequently given the weak ending -en:

mit einem Stück brüchigen Eisen (W. Raabe) (Duden's example)	*with a piece of cracked iron*
Ich bestrafe Sie mit drei Wochen geschärften Arrest (A. Goes)	*I'm giving you three weeks' close arrest*

Examples of literary usage; genitive instead of apposition:

eine bedeutende Fläche sumpfigen Wiesenlandes (Storm)	*a considerable area of marshy meadow-land*
ein Stück frostigen Winterhimmels (Th. Plievier)	*a piece of frosty winter sky*

100. When the noun denoting the thing measured, preceded by an adjective, is plural, the following is the commonest practice:

(a) After a specific noun of weight or quantity, use the case in apposition:

zwei Dutzend frische Eier	*two dozen fresh eggs*
Er kam mit einem Paar braunen Schuhen	*He came with a pair of brown shoes*

---

[1] For usage where there is no adj., see 56.

(b) After a vaguer, more general word of quantity, use gen. or von:

Er saß hinter einem Berg neuer Bücher (or: von neuen Büchern)	*He was sitting behind a pile of new books*
eine Menge nützlicher Anregungen (*S.Z.*)	*a number of useful suggestions*
eine Gruppe müder Reisender	*a group of tired travellers*

(c) After ein Korb, ein Kasten and analogous words, use mit: ein Korb mit süßen Äpfeln.

101. **If both nouns are in the gen. sing. and the second is preceded by an adjective,** official usage is to put both into the genitive. Normal usage conforms to this if one of the two nouns is fem., but, if both are masc. or neut., uses von instead of the first gen.; whereupon the second becomes dative, in apposition, its adjective possibly having the weak ending -en (cf. 99 N.):

der Preis	*the price*
eines Liters frischer Milch	*of a litre of fresh milk*
eines Pfundes gekochten Schinkens/von einem Pfund gekochtem (or: gekochten) Schinken	*of a pound of boiled ham*

102. **After 'die Sorte' the genitive is used, after 'die Art' the case in apposition**: diese Sorte englischer Äpfel; diese Art englische Rose; mit einer Art zornigen Unschuld (E. Langgässer).[1]

G. SPELLING OF CERTAIN ADJECTIVES

103. **Spelling of adjectives in -el, -en, -er and of 'hoch', when inflected**

(a) Those in -el always drop the e of the stem, e.g. ein dunkler Wald, eine respektable Leistung (Duden's example: Haupt: Adjektiv 10).

(b) Those in -en sometimes do so: Er hat einen seltenen (seltnen) Schmetterling gefangen.
This may also apply, in speech but hardly in writing, to the past participle of strong verbs: in der gegebnen Situation; zerrißnes Papier (But only 'die Geschworenen' *the jury*).

(c) Those in -er: foreign adjectives in -er (e.g. makaber) always drop the e of the stem: eine makabre Geschichte (Du. Haupt. Adjektiv 10); others sometimes do so, especially where the e of the stem is preceded by a diphthong (e.g. teuer): mit teuren Weinen; mit munteren (or: muntren) Studenten.

(d) Note:
  i The -er of comparatives is usually retained: see 121 N.B.
  ii ander: see 190(c).
  iii The e of an internal -el or -er is also frequently dropped: neb(e)lig, wäss(e)rig.

[1] see 99 N.

(e) hoch drops the c when inflected: Dieser Berg ist hoch, BUT: ein hoher Berg.

104. Adjectives spelt with or without a final e

e.g. Er ist feig or feige *cowardly*; both have the same inflected forms: der feige Junge, ein feiger Junge etc.
The following list of these adjectives gives what is probably the commoner of the two forms: blöd, böse, fade *insipid; dull, trite*, feige, irre *confused*, leise, mild, müde, öde, träge *indolent, sluggish*, trübe, vage, zäh.

Note:
i Adverbially, only the forms böse, fade, leise, öde, vage are usual, but either form of the remaining words may be used.
ii Colloquially, the adj. and adv. allein often adds an e.
iii dick and dünn add an e in two slang phrases:

Du mußt es ja sehr dicke haben	*You must be rolling in money*
Ich habe mich dünne gemacht	*I made myself scarce*

H. INFLECTION OF A SERIES OF ADJECTIVES[1]

105. In all three declensions, two or more adjectives have the same ending: dieser schöne, große Garten; mein lieber alter Vater; gutes bayrisches Bier; die Lösung wichtiger politischer Probleme.

Note: There is **one occasional deviation** in the strong declension: in the masc. and neut. dat. there is a tendency to give the second (and subsequent) adjectives the weak ending -en, especially where the second adjective forms a conceptual unit with the noun, such that the two adjectives are not separated by commas and could not be joined by 'und', as in the second and third examples below:

Nach langem, beunruhigenden Schweigen ließ er wieder von sich hören	*After a long disquieting silence he wrote again*[2]
mit dunklem bayrischen Bier	*with dark Bavarian beer*
mit hohem steifen Kragen (Arno Schmidt)	*with a high stiff collar*[2]

I. SUBSTANTIVAL ADJECTIVES AND PARTICIPLES

106. All adjectives and all those participles which may be used as attributive adjectives (see 97) can be used as nouns. In the masc., fem. and plur. they mainly denote persons; in the neut. they mainly denote abstract or collective concepts. They are written with a capital letter (with the exceptions noted in 110 and 732) and are inflected as if they were followed by Mann, Frau, Menschen and e.g. Element (neut.) respectively, e.g.
MASC.: der Fremde *the stranger*, ein Fremder, ich fragte einen Deutschen.
FEM.: eine Angestellte *employee*, die Antwort der Angestellten.

---

[1] for punctuation see 743(i).
[2] Regarding the absence of the indef. art. in the German, see 78(c).

PLUR.: Fremde, die Angestellten.

NEUT.: Das Wahre ist wichtiger als das Schöne; das Hervorragende (*the outstanding thing*) an diesem Film; Schöneres habe ich nie gesehen.

N.B. Hereafter the term 'substantival adjective' will be used to include both adjectives and participles used substantivally, unless specifically stated.

107. Notes on substantival adjectives

(a) **They are rarely used alone in the gen. plur.**; thus in the phrase 'mit der Hilfe Verwandter' normal usage would substitute 'von Verwandten'.

(b) **der Beamte** *the official* was formed from an old participle 'beam(p)t' *entrusted with an office* (Du. Haupt. p. 103), which, in the form 'beamtet', is little used today.

(c) **der Junge** *boy* is declined as a Group 7 noun, **die Brünette** and **die Kokette** *coquette* as Group 6 nouns, and not according to the adj. declensions: Er ist ein netter Junge; ich sprach mit der Brünette.

(d) **Some substantival adjectives have special meanings,** e.g.
die Rechte 1. *right hand* 2. *the Right* (in politics) (cf. die Linke)
die Gerade 1. *straight line* (geom.) 2. *the straight* (on a racecourse) 3. eine rechte Gerade *a straight right* (boxing)
die Elektrische *tram* (from 'die elektrische Bahn')
das Junge *young* (of animals), *cub* etc.
Wir gingen ins Freie *We went into the open*
Wir schliefen im Freien *We slept in the open*
die Schwarzen 1. *negroes* 2. *Roman Catholics* (as a political force, a clerical party)

(e) **A substantival adjective may be limited by an adverb:**
das typisch Deutsche an seiner Rede   *the typically German thing about his speech*

108. Declension of substantival adjectives when preceded by an attributive adjective

In the weak and mixed declensions regularity prevails: with the one exception noted below, the attrib. adj. and the subst. adj. are inflected identically throughout: der arme Fremde, ein armer Fremder

EXCEPTION: In the neut. nom. and acc. of the mixed declension, Äußere, Innere, Ganze are generally given the weak ending (cf. Du. Gram. 2260). E.g.
sein schlichtes Äußere ·   *his plain outward appearance*
ein einheitliches Ganze(s)   *a uniform whole*

In the strong declension:

(a) Attrib. adj. and subst. adj. have the same endings (e.g. Karls alter Bekannter; arme Alte!) except:
i in the dat. sing.: here the subst. adj. ends in -en:
Ich sprach mit Karls altem   *I spoke to Karl's old acquaintance*
Bekannten

ii in the nom. and acc. plur. after a gen. expressing possession: here the
subst. adj. ends in -en:

Vaters alte Bekannten[1]   *father's old acquaintances*
                                        BUT:
lauter alte Bekannte   *a whole lot of old acquaintances*

(b) The gen. sing. is not used, 'von' being substituted.

(c) The gen. plur. is somewhat stilted:[2] die Erlebnisse mancherlei armer
   Heimatloser/vier junger Deutscher.
   Normal usage is 'von': die Erlebnisse von vier jungen Deutschen/von
   ein paar jungen Deutschen.
   Coupled with a gen. expressing possession, 'von' **must** be used:

die Erlebnisse von Karls alten   *the experiences of Karl's old acquain-*
   Bekannten   *tances*

(d) The neut. nom., acc. and dat. are in practice rare, e.g.

Neues Aufregendes ist geschehen   *New exciting events have occurred*

109. The substantival adjective in apposition: Herr Müller, der neue
Angestellte; Heinrich Schulze, Geschäftsreisender, 35 Jahre alt; das
hat uns, als junge Deutsche, interessiert.

There are two deviations from orthodoxy:
i Where the noun to which the subst. adj. refers is in the gen. sing.; see
   63(a).
ii In the dat. sing. of the strong declension, the commonest practice is to
   give the substantival adjective the weak ending (–en), but a preceding
   attributive adjective the strong ending (–em or –er) (see also 115):

Der Chef sprach mit ihm, als   *The director spoke to him as the oldest*
   ältestem Angestellten   *employee*

**110. Substantival adjectives are written with a small letter in many
set phrases,** e.g.

auf dem laufenden bleiben   *to be acquainted with what is going on*
Es bleibt beim alten   *Things remain as they were; we carry on*
                                          as before
bei weitem   *by far*
Er ging bis ins kleinste   *He went into the smallest details*
Ich fragte den ersten besten   *I asked the first person I met*
den kürzeren ziehen   *to get the worst of it*
im allgemeinen   *in general*
im (großen und) ganzen   *on the whole*
im stillen   *on the quiet*
im trüben fischen   *to fish in troubled waters*
jemanden zum besten haben   *to make a fool of someone*
(BUT: zum Besten der Armen   *for the benefit of the poor*)

Note:
i See also 116(h) and 732, Exc. (b).

---

[1] It is thus distinguished from the fem. sing. Vaters alte Bekannte.
[2] To be sure, a letter recently received contained: Ich komme zum Besuch guter Bekannter
für ein paar Tage nach London.

ii With few deviations, the indefinite adjectives (see 112(b)) have a small letter when used substantivally (cf. 732, Exc. (c)):

| Ich habe noch verschiedenes zu tun | *I've still got various things to do* |
| Jetzt sind viele dagegen | *Now many people are against it* |

iii Von allen Tieren ist der Hund das treueste: here 'das treueste', standing for 'das treueste Tier', is not a substantival adjective in the true sense; thence the small letter. Contrast: Alice könnte überall die Schönste, die Erste und Einzige sein (H. Mann); here there is no noun, elsewhere in the sentence, that is understood after the three adjectives.

J. NICHTS NEUES and ALLES NEUE

111. (a) When linked up with a preceding indeclinable or uninflected word, the neuter adjective has the strong endings,[1] but the genitive case is generally avoided.

(b) When linked up with a preceding inflected word, the neuter adjective has the weak endings.

In both cases it often has a collective connotation, that can only be rendered by a plural in English.

The neuter adjective has a capital letter, except for most of the indefinite adjectives (see 732, Exc. (c)).

This gives the following two types:

(a)	(b)
N.A. **nichts Neues** *nothing new*	**alles Neue** *everything new*
G. (nichts Neuen)	alles[2] Neuen
D. nichts Neuem	allem Neuen

Further instances of type (a):

allerhand/allerlei Neues	*all kinds of new things, various new things*
etwas ganz Neues	*something quite new*
ganz was Neues (coll.)	
genug Neues	*enough new things*
lauter Neues	*nothing but new things; a whole lot of new things*
eine Liste von mancherlei Neuem (avoiding gen.)	*a list of various new things*
was für Neues?	*what new things?*

Further instances of type (b):

folgendes Neue	*the following new matter*
der Einkauf verschiedenes Unnötigen	*the purchase of various unnecessary things*
weiteres Neue	*further new things*

N.B. Distinguish:

| alles Mögliche | *everything possible* |
| alles mögliche | *all kinds of things* (idiomatic) |

---

[1] Historically, Neues was a gen. sing. ('nothing of the new'): cf. Weser loc. cit. in 60 (footnote), p. 226.

[2] Miscellaneous adjectives with a tendency to end in -en in the masc. and neut. gen. sing. (cf. 89, N.i) must end in -es in this context.

K. DECLENSION OF ADJECTIVES AFTER AN INDEFINITE ADJECTIVE

112. Indefinite adjectives

(a) The declension of adjectives after a number of words to which the term 'indefinite adjective' woüld be applicable has been treated in 89 (irgendwelcher, mancher) and 95(b) (e.g. allerhand, allerlei, mancherlei etc., ein bißchen, etwas *some, any*, lauter, mehr, weniger); ₂this will not be repeated here.

After irgendein *some (or other)*, *any (whatsoever)* the mixed declension is used.

(b) The term 'indefinite adjective' is traditionally and conveniently applied to the following. (An asterisk denotes that the word is fully treated in Chap. VI B.):

ähnlich *similar*	obig *above-mentioned*
ander* *other*	sogenannt *so-called*
besagt *aforesaid*	sonstig *other, remaining*
bestimmt *certain*	übrig *other, remaining*
derartig *suchlike, such*	unzählbar *innumerable*
einige* *some, a few*	unzählig *innumerable*
einzeln *single, individual*	verschiedene *various, several*
etliche[1] *some, several, a few*	vieler,[2] viele* *much, many*
etwaig *possible, potential*	weiter *further, additional*
folgend *the following*	weniger,[2] wenige* *little, few*
genannt *aforenamed*	zahllos *innumerable*
gewiß *certain*	zahlreich *numerous*
mehrere *several*	

(c) These indefinite adjectives have strong, weak or mixed endings like any other adjective: ähnlicher Wein; die Wirkung derartigen Mutes; dieser ähnliche Wein; sein übriges Leben.

113. The declension of attributive and substantival adjectives in the following combinations:

indef. adj.＋attrib. adj.＋noun

indef. adj. (＋attrib. adj.)＋subst. adj.

(a) **in the singular**:

i For ander, einige, viel and wenig, see 190(b)ii, 205(a), 228, 230.

ii After folgend, weak endings predominate:

folgender neue Plan	*the following new plan*
folgendes unglaubliche Ergebnis	*the following incredible result*
mit folgender nachdrücklichen Warnung	*with the following emphatic warning*

iii With most of the remainder, the above combinations rarely occur in the singular; where they do, the attrib. adj. normally has the strong

---

[1] has a somewhat archaic flavour, but is by no means rare.
[2] After the uninflected forms viel and wenig, an attrib. adj. has the strong endings (see 228).

endings, though the weak ending is often used in the masc. and neut. dat.:

obiger griechischer Philosoph	*the above-mentioned Greek philosopher*
weiteres dummes Gerede	*further foolish talk*
nach weiterem dummem (or: dummen) Gerede	*after further foolish talk*

iv In neuter collective phrases of the type alles Neue *everything new*, mehreres Neue *several new things*, the second component has the weak endings: see 111, type (b).

(b) **in the plural:**
Commonest usage: strong endings for all the adjectival components in all cases.

EXAMPLES: *many big rooms* — *several (young) Germans*

N.	viele große Zimmer	mehrere (junge) Deutsche
A.	viele große Zimmer	mehrere (junge) Deutsche
G.	vieler großer Zimmer	mehrerer (junger) Deutscher
D.	vielen großen Zimmern	mehreren (jungen) Deutschen

Note: In the gen., some Germans give the attrib. and subst. adjectives the weak ending -en, e.g. vieler großen Zimmer, vieler Reisenden, mehrerer (jungen) Deutschen. Colloquially, von + dat. is preferred.

114. **If the indefinite adjective is preceded by one of the words after which the weak or mixed declension is regularly used** (e.g. der, dieser, aller etc. or ein, kein, mein etc.), then the indef. adj., the attrib. adj. (and a subst. adj.) all and always have the weak or mixed endings as the case may be. E.g.

aller ähnliche französische Wein	*all similar French wine*
kein weiteres wichtiges Problem	*no further important problem*
unsere vielen neuen Angestellten	*our many new employees*

L. INFLECTION OF ATTRIBUTIVE AND SUBSTANTIVAL ADJECTIVES IN APPOSITION TO A PERSONAL PRONOUN

115. On the whole, **this construction is not much used**; instead of 'Ich gab ihm armem Kranken die Hand', the German will normally say: 'Ich gab ihm die Hand, als er krank dalag'.
The following should cover all practical needs. The little used gen. of the personal pron. is never followed by a phrase in apposition. (Str. and wk. refer to the inflection of the attrib. and subst. adj.)

N. SING.: str.: ich einsamer Fremder, du dummer Kerl, Sie Ärmster!
A. SING.: str.: für ihn als einsamen Fremden.
D. SING.: masc.: generally str.: Er hat sein Geld mir, als Ältestem, vermacht; fem.: wk.: mir alten Frau.
N. PLUR.: generally wk.: wir früheren Kollegen, wir (jungen) Deutschen (also: wir (junge) Deutsche).
A. PLUR.: str.: uns frühere Kollegen, uns (junge) Deutsche.
D. PLUR.: uns (jungen) Deutschen.

M. INSTANCES OF UNINFLECTED ATTRIBUTIVE ADJECTIVES

116. Attributive adjectives are uninflected in the following instances:

(a) before a nom. or acc. neut. noun (cf. Du. Gram. 2200 and 2210)

i in certain set phrases and uses:

Ich bekam ein gut Teil[1] vom Geld	*I got a good part of the money*
ein gut Stück	*a good amount* (e.g. of work), *a good way* (distance)
ein gehörig (or: tüchtig) Stück Kuchen	*a substantial piece of cake*
etwas auf gut Glück tun	*to take a chance*
ruhig Blut bewahren	*to keep calm*
Er will sich lieb Kind bei mir machen	*He is trying to ingratiate himself with me*
groß A	*capital A*

N.B. one masc. and one fem. instance:

Wir sind wieder gut Freund	*We're friends again*
römisch III	*Roman figure III*

ii in some proverbs and in archaic and poetic style, e.g. Gut Ding will Weile haben (Du. Gram. 2210) *Nothing good is done in a hurry.*

iii sometimes, in conversation, outside the set phrases given in 116(a)i: ein einzig Wort, ihr eigen Kind, wir haben unser ander Haus verkauft, ein wunderbar Glas Bier. (In none of these would the inflected form be wrong.)

(b) einzig is often left uninflected before adj.+noun, where it refers primarily to the adjective, e.g.: Er war der einzig zufriedene Mensch *He was the only contented person*; die einzig mögliche Lösung; mein einzig anständiges Paar Schuhe.

cf. einzig before a substantival adjective: das einzig Gute *the one good thing*; das einzig Wahre an der Geschichte; er als einzig Überlebender.

(c) halb and ganz before the names of continents, countries (other than those used with the def. art.)[2] and towns, e.g.: halb Europa, in ganz München BUT: die ganze Schweiz, im ganzen Kongo.

(d) the names of the inhabitants of towns, used adjectivally, but retaining their capital letter: Frankfurter Würstchen, des Kölner Doms, auf den Londoner Straßen.

Note:

i The origin of e.g. 'Frankfurter Würstchen' was 'die Würstchen der Frankfurter'.

ii For deviations from the type Frankfurt: Frankfurter, see 715(a)-er:1; the adjective of Hannover is hannoversch (declined).

iii der Kölner Dom, Hauptbahnhof etc., BUT: Kölnisch Wasser *eau-de-cologne*; Die Kölnische Zeitung.

iv Uninflected adjectives of the above type are also formed from die Schweiz and from the names of a number of provinces and regions,

---

[1] 'Teil' is here neut.; see 9.
[2] see 84(a) and (b) and 6(b).

where they are again identical with the name of the inhabitants.
E.g.

Kärntener *Carinthian* (Kärnten is an Austrian Bundesland.)

Pfälzer *of the Palatinate*

Rheingauer *of the Rheingau* (a wine-growing district west of Wiesbaden)

v Less common than the forms in -er are the inflected forms with the suffix -isch, which are used attributively or predicatively and mainly in contexts conveying the ethos of the place:

Er hat einen echt frankfurterischen (or: Frankfurter) Humor.

Sein Humor ist echt frankfurterisch (münchnerisch, düsseldorferisch etc., BUT: kölnisch).

(e) a number of adjectives of colour, foreign loan-words, of which the commonest are rosa *pink* and lila *lilac* (cf. prima *first-rate*). Colloquially, 'rosan' and 'lilan' (inflected) are used attributively. Thus:

mit rosa (or: rosanen) Bändern *with pink ribbons*.

For 'orange' normal usage is e.g. ein orangenes Halstuch.

(f) the first of two adjectives of colour.

Duden (Gram. 2195) distinguishes between:

ein blau-grünes Kleid	*a blue and green dress*
ein blaugrünes Kleid	*a bluey-green dress*

In spoken German, the former is normally 'ein blau und grünes Kleid'.

(g) Certain miscellaneous adjectives have alternative uninflected forms: all (see 187(b)), manch (217(c)), solch (222(b)), viel (226 ff.), welch (174(e)), wenig (226 ff.).

(h) Substantival adjectives are uninflected in set phrases often involving opposites (Du. Gram. 2275): Alt und jung, arm und reich,[1] strömten aus der Stadt; bei arm und reich; jenseits von Gut und Böse *beyond good and evil*.

N. ADJECTIVES USED WITH THE DATIVE CASE

117. Many adjectives are used with the dative case, mostly corresponding to 'to' in English

Note:

i These adjectives normally follow the dative noun or pronoun dependent on them, but the following may also precede it: ähnlich, gleich, nahe, treu, ungleich, untreu, e.g. Treu seinen Grundsätzen, hat er sein Amt sofort niedergelegt.

ii Where indicated, the adjective may alternatively be used with 'fur' (but never with 'zu', a not uncommon error). The 'für' construction is slightly more colloquial. The 'für' phrase generally precedes, but may follow, the adjective. Thus:

Dieses Instrument ist mir sehr nützlich.

Dieses Instrument ist für mich sehr nützlich.

Dieses Instrument ist sehr nützlich für mich.

---

[1] These phrases have small letters, being the equivalent of jedermann (cf. Du. Taschenbücher 3: R 286).

iii Those marked with an asterisk are only used predicatively, e.g.

Das Glück war ihm hold	*Fortune favoured him*

The common ones are the following (mainly selected from Du. Gram. 5425):

ähnlich	*similar to*
Er ist (sieht) seinem Bruder sehr ähnlich	*He is (looks) very much like his brother*
angenehm (or für)	*agreeable to*
begreiflich	*comprehensible to*
behilflich	*helpful to*
Er war mir beim Umzug behilflich	*He helped me when I was moving*
bekannt	*known, familiar to*
dankbar	*grateful to*
eigen, eigentümlich	*peculiar to*
Er hatte das mit der ihm eigenen griesgrämigen Fröhlichkeit gesagt (H. Broch)	*He had said that with the surly cheerfulness that was peculiar to him*
ergeben	*devoted, attached to*
feind*	*hostile to*
fremd	*unknown to; alien to*
gehorsam (or with gegenüber)	*obedient to*
gemeinsam	*common to*
gesinnt	*disposed towards*
Er ist mir gutgesinnt, übelgesinnt, freundlich (feindlich) gesinnt.	
gewogen (rather literary)	*well disposed towards*
gleich	*a matter of indifference to, all the same to*
Es ist mir ganz gleich (gleichgültig, einerlei, egal, piepe (sl.), Wurst (sl.), Wurscht (sl.), Schnuppe (sl.)), ob er kommt oder nicht	*It's all the same to me whether he comes or not*
gram*	*angry with, bearing a grudge against*
hold* (elev.)	*favourably disposed towards*
lästig (or für)	*troublesome, a nuisance to*
leicht (or für)	*easy for*
nah, nahe	*near to*
Sie war dem Weinen/dem Tode nahe	*She was near to tears/to death*[1]
nützlich (or für)	*useful to*
peinlich (or für)	*embarrassing for*
schädlich (or für)	*injurious to*
schuldig	*owing*
Du bist mir 3 Mark schuldig	*You owe me 3 marks*
schwer (or für)	*difficult for*
treu	*faithful, loyal to*
überlegen	*superior to*
Er ist mir an Schlagfertigkeit überlegen	*He surpasses me at repartee*
unangenehm (or für)	*disagreeable for*
unbegreiflich (or für)	*incomprehensible to*
unbekannt	*unknown, unfamiliar to*
unentbehrlich (or für)	*indispensable to*
unmöglich (or für)	*impossible for*

---

[1] In literal, spatial contexts, 'near to' is usually nah(e) bei or in der Nähe von; nahe forms the sep. prefix of a number of verbs taking the dat., e.g. Sein Tod ist mir nahegegangen *I felt his death keenly.*

unterlegen	*inferior to*
untreu	*unfaithful, disloyal to*
unzugänglich (or für)	*inaccessible to*
verhaßt	*hateful to*
wichtig (or für)	*important to*
willkommen	*welcome to (someone)*
zugänglich (or für)	*accessible to*
zugetan*	*well-disposed towards, attached to*
zuwider*	1. *contrary to* (e.g. the law)
	2. *repugnant to*

Note:

iv An adjective or adverb limited by 'zu' or 'genug' is used with a preceding dative of the person interested. This construction is neater than the use of für; with the latter, the adjective may precede or follow the für phrase.

Diese Uhr ist mir zu teuer/ist zu teuer für mich	*This watch is too expensive for me*
... eines Mörders, dem keine Lüge zu frech ist (*Zeit*)	*of a murderer for whom no lie is too brazen*
Du gehst mir zu schnell	*You walk too fast for me*
Dieser Mantel ist mir nicht warm genug	*This coat is not warm enough for me*

O. ADJECTIVES USED WITH THE GENITIVE CASE

118. A certain number of adjectives are used with the genitive case, mostly corresponding to 'of' in English. Except for 'bar', they follow the genitive noun or pronoun dependent on them. The resultant phrases tend to have a somewhat stilted or literary ring and are not much used in ordinary conversation. **The commoner ones are the following** (selected from Du. Gram. 5445):

bar	*devoid of*
Seine Handlungsweise war bar aller Vernunft	*His mode of action was devoid of all reason*
bedürftig	*in need of*
bewußt	*conscious of*
Ich war mir meines Irrtums bewußt	*I was conscious of my error*
fähig (also: zu)	*capable of*
Er ist einer solchen Tat (or: zu einer solchen Tat) nicht fähig	*He is not capable of such a deed*
Er ist zu allem fähig	*He's capable of anything*
gewiß	*certain of*
Ich bin seiner Zustimmung gewiß	*I am certain of his consent*
kundig (elev.)	*versed in*
ledig	*free from* (e.g. an anxiety, a duty)
mächtig	*master of*
Sie ist des Deutschen absolut mächtig	*She has a complete command of German*
schuldig	*guilty of*
sicher	*sure of*
Du kannst seiner Freundschaft sicher sein	*You can be sure of his friendship*
überdrüssig (coll. also with acc.)	*tired of, sick of*
wert 1. with gen.	*worth* (worthy of)

Es ist nicht der Mühe wert   *It's not worth the trouble*
2. with acc.   *worth* (in value), also fig., e.g.
Er ist keinen Schuß Pulver wert   *He's not worth a cent*
würdig   *worthy of*

An example from officialese:
Er ist der Bürgerrechte für verlustig   *He has been deprived of his civic rights*
erklärt worden

P. FULL OF

119. full of: the alternatives in normal use are covered by the following examples:

i   *He brought a basket full of fruit*
    Er brachte einen Korb voll Obst, voller Obst

ii   *He brought a basket full of apples*
    Er brachte einen Korb voll Äpfel, voller Äpfel

iii   *He brought a basket full of lovely fruit*
    Er brachte einen Korb voll herrlichen Obstes (elev.)
    Er brachte einen Korb voll herrlichem Obst
    Er brachte einen Korb voll von (or: voll mit) herrlichem Obst

iv   *He brought a basket full of lovely apples*
    Er brachte einen Korb voll herrlicher Äpfel
    Er brachte einen Korb voll von (or: voll mit) herrlichen Äpfeln
    Er brachte einen Korb voller herrlicher Äpfel

Note:
1. The indeclinable 'voller' cannot be used attributively and is never used with von or mit.
2. full of it: voll davon (voll damit)
    full of them (persons): voll von ihnen.
                    (things): voll von ihnen, voll davon (voll damit)

Some literary examples:

Augen voll Ernst und Schwärmerei   *eyes full of seriousness and rapture*
(Th. Mann)
Er erhielt ein Eßgeschirr voll   *He was given a mess-tin full of hot water*
heißen Wassers (Th. Plievier)
Die Luft war voller Vogellaut, voll   *The air was full of the sound of birds,*
zierlich-innigem und süßem   *full of a sweet, a delicate and moving*
Flöten, Zwitschern . . . und   *fluting, twittering and sobbing*
Schluchzen (Th. Mann)
aus Bunkern voller Sterbender   *from pill-boxes full of dying men*
(Th. Plievier)

N.B. Adjectives used with prepositions are treated in Chap. XIII.

IV COMPARISON OF ADJECTIVES AND ADVERBS

A. FORMATION AND DECLENSION OF COMPARATIVE AND SUPERLATIVE

120. The normal rule for the formation of the comparative and superlative is as follows:

(a) **Adjectives**: the comparative and superlative are formed by adding -er and -st to the simple form:

| voll | voller | der vollste[1] |
| langsam | langsamer | der langsamste[1] |

The same rule is followed for polysyllabics (in contrast to English usage):

unwiderstehlich   unwiderstehlicher   der unwiderstehlichste

(b) **Adverbs**: the comparative is the same as that of the adjective; the main superlative is formed with 'am':

Hans läuft schneller als ich	*Hans runs quicker than I*
Heinrich läuft am schnellsten	*Heinrich runs quickest*
die am schlechtesten bezahlten Arbeiter	*the worst paid workers*
Das hasse ich an den Schulmeistern am meisten (Th. Valentin)	*That's what I hate most about school-masters*
Er war am leichtesten zu überreden	*He was the easiest to persuade*

121. Comparative of adjectives in -el, -en, -er (their superl. is normal)

Those in -el regularly drop the e of the stem:
dunkel, dunkler, der dunkelste.

Those in -en and -er may drop the e of the stem when inflected (to avoid three consecutive unstressed e's):
selten *rare*: die seltneren (or selteneren) Schmetterlinge.
bitter: ein bittrerer (or bittererer) Geschmack.
    BUT:
Diese Schmetterlinge sind seltener; diese Orangen sind bitterer.

---

[1] As the use of the uninflected superl. is limited to one type of adverbial superlative (see 137), der vollste, der langsamste etc. has been chosen as the stock superlative form, ready for use in e.g. Der vollste Korb stand auf dem Boden; von allen Zügen nach Köln ist dies der langsamste.

Those ending in diphthong + er generally drop the e even when unin-flected: teuer: Die Butter ist teurer geworden.

N.B. In the comparative of all adjectives, the e of the -er with which the comparative is formed and the e of the flexional endings -e, -em, -en, -es are both retained in written German and, preponderantly, in spoken German:

Wärmere Tage werden kommen	*Warmer days will come*
Er hat ein netteres Zimmer	*He's got a nicer room*

122. The superlative is formed by adding -est after the following:

(a) s, ß, x, z.

hilflos, der hilfloseste	fix (*quick, nimble*), der fixeste
süß, der süßeste	stolz, der stolzeste

Occasional deviations may be heard, determined by individual ease of pronunciation: der fixte Schüler, der stolze Kerl.

(b) after sch, d and t: 1. in monosyllabics 2. if the last syllable of the simple form is accented and 3. with the suffix -haft:

rasch, der rascheste	verhaßt, der verhaßteste
gesund, der gesündeste	boshaft *malicious*, der boshafteste
sanft, der sanfteste	

BUT:

kòmisch, der komischste	gefürchtet, der gefürchtetste
pàssend, der passendste	

Occasional deviations may be heard, e.g. die frischsten Brötchen, der aufgeregteste Junge.

(c) generally after a diphthong or a diphthong + h, sometimes after a vowel + h: Er ist mein treuester Freund; der früh(e)ste Zug.

(d) Individual taste occasionally adds -est to endings other than those listed above, e.g. die dumpfesten Töne *the most muffled sounds*.

123. Eighteen common monosyllabics modify in the compar. and superl. (e.g. alt, älter, der älteste), as do three of the irregulars in 124 (groß, hoch, nah):

alt	stark	warm	arg *bad*[1]	krank
jung	schwach	kalt	arm	oft[2]
lang	klug		grob *coarse, rude*	scharf
kurz	dumm		hart	schwarz

Among those that fluctuate between modifying and not modifying the fol-lowing are the commonest, the modified form being preferred in conversation, except for 'blaß': blaß, fromm, gesund, glatt, naß, rot, schmal.

---

[1] e.g. Es war die ärgste Enttäuschung; es könnte nichts Ärgeres geschehen.
[2] häufiger *more frequently* is often used instead of öfter, while am häufigsten is commoner than am öftesten.

124. Nine irregulars

bald	eher	am chesten	*soon*
gern[1]	lieber[1]	am liebsten[1]	*willingly, gladly*
groß	größer	der größte	*big*
gut	besser	der beste	*good*
hoch	höher	der höchste	*high*
nah	näher	der nächste	*near*[2]
ungern,[1] noch weniger gern, am wenigsten gern *unwillingly*			
viel	mehr[3]	der meiste	*much, many*
wenig	weniger[3]	der wenigste	*little, few*

Colloquially one may occasionally hear 'bälder' and 'am ungernsten'.

125. The following 8 adjectives, only used attributively, are comparative in form; they form a superlative:

der äußere *outer, external*	der äußerste *outermost, utmost*
der innere *inner, internal*	der innerste *innermost*
der obere *upper*	der oberste *uppermost, top(most)*
der untere *lower*	der unterste *lowest, bottom*
der vordere *front*	der vorderste *foremost, front*
der hintere *back*	der hinterste *back(most)*
der mittlere *central, middle; medium*	der mittlerste *central, middle*
der niedere *low, inferior* (mainly of social rank)	der niederste *lowest*

EXAMPLES:

seine äußere Erscheinung	*his external appearance*
mit der äußersten Höflichkeit	*with the utmost politeness*
seine innersten Gedanken	*his innermost thoughts*
die untere Schicht	*the lower layer*
Wir saßen in der vorderen (or vordersten) Reihe	*We sat in the front row*

Note: When 'external' and 'internal' are used predicatively or adverbially, 'äußerlich' and 'innerlich' are available:

Seine Verletzungen sind nicht äußerlich, sondern innerlich	*His injuries are not external, but internal*
Äußerlich blieb er ganz ruhig	*Externally he remained quite calm*

126. The comparison of compound adjectives and participles.
Duden (Gram. 2470) gives the following guide-lines:

(a) If, in the simple form, both components have retained their original meaning, the first should be compared:

schwerverständlich	*difficult to understand, abstruse*
schwerer verständlich	-comparative
am schwersten verständlich	-superlative
dichtbevölkert	*densely populated*
tiefblickend[4]	*perceptive*
tiefgehend[4]	1. *profound, far-reaching* (e.g. difference)
eine viel tiefer gehende Skepsis (*Zeit*)	*a much deeper scepticism*
	2. *profound, penetrating* (e.g. investigation)

---

[1] for the use of these, see 277 ff.
[2] see also 550.
[3] not declined; see also 234.
[4] absolute superlative: tiefstblickend, tiefstgehend

(b) If, in the simple form, the combination forms a single concept, especially with a new and figurative meaning, the second component is compared; in other words, the compound is regarded as an indissoluble single word and is compared as such:

hochfliegend	*lofty, ambitious* (e.g. plans)
hochfliegender	-comparative
der hochfliegendste	-superlative
vielversprechend	*promising, full of promise*
weittragend	*far-reaching* (e.g. consequences)
zartfühlend	*sensitive, tactful*

Note:

i Some compounds fluctuate between (a) and (b), e.g. schwerwiegend *weighty* (e.g. reasons), weitgehend *extensive* (e.g. support). In such cases, and if in doubt, method (b) is recommended as the neater and more convincing.

ii naheliegend *obvious* (e.g. reasons) rather surprisingly belongs to type (a): näherliegend, nächstliegend.

127. Declension of the compar. and superl. of the adjective used attributively: they are declined like the simple form (cf. 88, 90, 93):

der alte/ältere/älteste Lehrer; ich sah den ältesten Lehrer; mein junger/jüngerer/jüngster Bruder; meine jüngeren Brüder; jüngere Brüder.

B. LESS, FEWER, LESSER AND LEAST

128. The rendering of less, fewer, lesser and least (In what follows, alternative versions are deliberately limited.)

(a) less and fewer are rendered by weniger (indeclinable).[1]

Er war weniger optimistisch als sein Bruder	*He was less optimistic than his brother*
Er hat weniger Geld (weniger Freunde) als ich	*He has less money (fewer friends) than I*
Er kann das Rauchen nicht reduzieren, viel weniger aufgeben	*He can't reduce his smoking, much less give it up*
Er war mehr oder weniger (or: mehr oder minder) zufrieden	*He was more or less satisfied*

In three instances 'less' is not rendered by 'weniger':

Seine Chancen sind geringer als meine	*His chances are less* (predic. adj.) *than mine*
kein Geringerer als	*no less a person than*
Es ist schon fast ein Wunder	*It's little less than a miracle*

(b) lesser.

das kleinere (or: geringere) Übel	*the lesser evil*
ihre geringeren Forderungen	*their lesser demands*

(c) least (adjectival) = slightest: mindest or geringst.

Er hat nicht die mindeste/geringste Chance	*He hasn't the least chance*

[1] see also 234.

least (adjectival) = smallest amount of: wenigst or am wenigsten.

Von allen Anwesenden zeigte er das wenigste/am wenigsten Interesse	*Of all those present, he showed least interest*
Er machte die wenigsten/am wenigsten Fehler	*He made the least (or fewest) mistakes*
N.B. Das wissen die wenigsten Hausfrauen	*Very few housewives know that*

the least (substantival).

Das ist das mindeste (das Geringste, das wenigste), was man erwarten kann	*That is the least one can expect*
gelinde gesagt	*to say the least of it (putting it mildly)*

least (adverbial): am wenigsten.

Von allen Gästen sprach er am wenigsten	*Of all the guests he spoke least*
am allerwenigsten	*least of all*
Seine Rede war am wenigsten interessant (or: die wenigst interessante)	*His speech was the least interesting*
Er arbeitet am wenigsten gut	*He works least well*

(d) at least: wenigstens is always correct; there are varying alternatives:

Das Buch kostet wenigstens (or: mindestens) 20 Mark	*The book costs at least 20 marks*
Er wird mir das Geld leihen, wenigstens (or: zumindest) hoffe ich es	*He will lend me the money, at least I hope so*
Wenn er wenigstens angerufen hätte!	*If at least he had rung up!*

(e) not least: nicht am wenigsten, nicht zum mindesten.

Alles interessierte sie, nicht zum mindesten die Frisuren	*Everything interested her, not least the hair-styles*

(f) not in the least: nicht im mindesten, nicht im geringsten.

Er war nicht im mindesten beleidigt	*He wasn't in the least offended*

C. THE ABSOLUTE COMPARATIVE

129. The absolute comparative does not imply comparison with other persons or things, but merely a fair degree of the quality in question: ein älterer Herr *an elderly gentleman*.

Only a limited number of comparatives can be used thus, e.g.

alt	groß	lang	dick	hell	neu
jung	klein	kurz	dünn	dunkel	bekannt

EXAMPLES:

in jeder größeren Stadt	*in every town of any size*
seit längerer Zeit	*for quite a time now*
irgendein hellerer Stoff	*some fairly light material*
ein bekannterer Schriftsteller	*quite a well-known author*

A predicative comparative and the comparative of an adverb may have this same meaning:

Mein Onkel ist schon älter	*My uncle is elderly*
Er hat uns öfter (or: öfters)[1] besucht	*He visited us quite often*

[1] a colloquial alternative, peculiar to oft; a more literary alternative is des öfteren.

D. TYPES OF PREDICATIVE AND ADVERBIAL COMPARISON

130. Equality

(a) main type: as old as: so alt wie.
Er ist so alt wie ich; er arbeitet so fleißig wie ich; er besucht uns so gut wie nie.

Note: In certain set phrases, the 'so' may be omitted (cf. Du. Gram. 2315): Er ist (so) hart wie Stahl; er ist (so) schlau wie ein Fuchs.

(b) In spoken German, a faulty 'als' is frequently used instead of 'wie'; it has become an accepted alternative in the following cases:
i as well as (=and also): sowohl Karl wie (auch)/als (auch) Hans.
ii as little as: Fritz wollte so wenig wie/als ich Tennis spielen.
iii before 'möglich': so bald wie/als möglich.

(c) just as
Er ist ebenso (geradeso, genauso)   *He is just as old as I am*
   alt wie ich

(d) (just) as much (indicating degree)
Die Brücke ist ebensosehr ein Teil der   *The bridge is as much a part of the*
   Landschaft wie der Fluß   *landscape as the river*
Ich habe dich ebensosehr beneidet   *I envied you just as much as I admired*
   wie bewundert   *you*

(e) To convey two attributes possessed in equal measure by the same or, respectively, by two different persons: ebenso . . . wie.
Er ist ebenso fleißig wie geschickt   *He is as industrious as he is skilful*
Cf. Er arbeitet ebenso fleißig wie   *He works as industriously as he does*
   geschickt   *skilfully*
Er ist ebenso faul, wie sein Bruder   *He is as lazy as his brother is industrious*
   fleißig ist

131. Superiority

(a) main type: older than: älter als.
Er ist älter als ich; er arbeitet fleißiger als ich; er arbeitet fleißiger, als du glaubst.

(b) Mainly colloquially, 'wie' is so frequently used instead of 'als' that it can barely be called wrong. ('als wie' is also to be heard but should not be imitated.)

(c) Note the sequence of cases in the following:
Ich kenne faulere Jungen als ihn   *I know lazier boys than him*
Ich habe nie einem besseren Spieler   *I have never watched a better player than*
   zugesehen als ihm   *him*

(d) The use of 'denn' for 'than':
i to avoid 'als als' for 1. *than as* 2. *than when*; the far commoner solution is to use 'wie' for 'than' in 1. and for 'when' in 2., e.g.
Er ist als Kritiker bekannter denn   1. *He is better known as a critic than as a*
   als (or: wie als) Dichter   *poet*
Er sieht besser aus, denn als (or: 2. *He's looking better than when I saw*
   als wie) ich ihn zuletzt sah   *him last*

ii in the set phrase 'denn je' *than ever*, though 'als je' is perfectly idiomatic.

iii not infrequently in literary style, e.g.

der eher einem Bäcker denn einem Landwirt ähnelt (H. Broch)	*who looks like a baker rather than a farmer*

(e) Degree of difference is expressed by um+acc. or, more commonly, simply by the acc.:

Er ist (um) drei Jahre älter als ich	*He is three years older than I am*

(f) Comparing two qualities of the same person or thing, or two adverbs: this is done with 'mehr' or, more delicately, with 'eher' (cf. 292(b)):

Er ist mehr faul als dumm	*He is more lazy than stupid*
Er sprach eher geistreich als überzeugend	*He spoke wittily rather than convincingly*

(g) twice as, three times as etc.

Er ist zweimal (or: doppelt) so alt wie ich	*He is twice as old as I am*

132. Inferiority (less than)

Er ist weniger optimistisch als ich; er ist nicht so optimistisch wie ich; er arbeitet weniger fleißig als ich; er ist nicht so sehr dumm wie faul *He is not so much stupid as lazy*

133. Progression (faster and faster)

Er lief immer schneller (or: schneller und schneller)	*He ran faster and faster*
Meine Arbeit wird immer schwerer (or: schwerer und schwerer)	*My work is getting harder and harder*

Note:
i The bracketed alternative is rather less common and is virtually limited to monosyllabics.
ii A further alternative is to place 'mehr und mehr' before the simple adj. or adv.: Er arbeitet mehr und mehr intensiv. This is rare with monosyllabics.

134. Proportion (the more ..., the more ...)

Je länger man Deutsch lernt, um so/ desto/je leichter wird es (The second 'je' is uncommon in modern usage.)	*The longer you learn German, the easier it becomes*
Je älter er wird, desto witzigere Reden hält er	*The older he gets, the wittier are the speeches he gives*

The reverse order of clauses is possible, though less usual; 'um so' could then be omitted or replaced by 'desto', but not by 'je':

Er hält (um so) witzigere Reden, je älter er wird	*He gives wittier speeches the older he gets*

Further examples and applications:

Je besser das Wetter, um so mehr können wir wandern	*The better the weather, the more we can go hiking*
je eher, desto besser	*the sooner, the better*
je länger, je lieber	*the longer, the better* (set phrase)

Dies machte meine Lage um so schwieriger	*This made my situation all the more difficult*
um so/desto besser	*all the better (for that)*
um so mehr, als/da/weil	*all the more because*
um so weniger, als/da/weil	*even less as*

E. THE PREDICATIVE SUPERLATIVE

135. (a) **When a person or thing is compared with other persons or things:**

> i if their common denominator, their distinctive group, is stated, or implied (3rd example), either the form with 'am' or the form with the def. art. may be used, but with 'best' only the latter (4th example):

Von den drei Brüdern ist Karl am gescheitesten/der gescheiteste	*Of the three brothers, Karl is the most intelligent (one)*
Diese Blume ist am schönsten/die schönste	*This flower is the most beautiful*
Wer (von euch) ist am stärksten/der stärkste?	*Which of you is the strongest?*
Von all seinen Werken ist dieses das beste	*Of all his works this is the best*

> ii if their common denominator, the group to which they belong, is not stated, the form with 'am' is used:

Für meinen Geschmack ist eine Nelke schöner als eine Tulpe, aber eine Rose ist am schönsten	*For my taste a carnation is more beautiful than a tulip, but a rose is the most beautiful*
Ein Mercedes ist am teuersten	*A Mercedes is the dearest*

(b) **When a person or thing is compared with himself or itself in different circumstances,** the form with 'am' is used:

Ich bin montags am faulsten	*I'm (at my) laziest on Mondays*
Der Rhein ist hier am romantischsten	*The Rhine is (at its) most romantic here*

(c) **Where the subject is, or refers to, not a specific person or thing, but a course of action,** the form with 'am' is generally used (cf. Erben, op. cit., 169):

Es würde am einfachsten sein, seinen Brief unbeantwortet zu lassen (or: wenn du es ihm sagtest)	*It would be simplest to leave his letter unanswered* (or: *if you were to tell him*)

F. THE ABSOLUTE SUPERLATIVE

136. (a) **The absolute superlative does not imply comparison with other persons or things, but merely a high degree of the quality in question:**

Ich schließe immer sehr vorsichtig ab	*I always lock up most* (= very) *carefully*
Er war äußerst dankbar	*He was most* (= extremely) *grateful*

(b) Further adverbs available to form the absolute superlative:
außerordentlich *extraordinarily*, höchst *extremely, in the highest degree*, überaus *exceedingly*.

(c) 'höchst' is **not** used before most monosyllabic adjectives and adverbs, nor before numerous others, e.g. billig, dunkel, durstig, fröhlich, glänzend, glücklich, großartig, herrlich, hungrig, langsam, plötzlich, schrecklich, teuer, traurig, wenig, wunderbar.

Some examples of the use of 'höchst':
höchst anständig *respectable*, bemerkenswert *noteworthy*, erstaunt, günstig, leichtsinnig *thoughtless*, notwendig *necessary*, sonderbar *strange*, unangenehm, ungern, ungesund, ungünstig, unwillkommen

The following are written as one word: höchstwahrscheinlich, höchstpersönlich *in his own person* (generally facetious), der Höchstbietende *the highest bidder*.

(d) An attributive superlative frequently has absolute and not comparative force:

Meine liebste Mutter!	*My dearest mother, . . .* (letter)
Ich habe den ehrlichsten Respekt vor ihm	*I have the most genuine respect for him*
Es herrschte das rauheste Wetter	*The weather was extremely raw*
Modernste Kureinrichtungen stehen zu Ihrer Verfügung (Advert. for Baden-Baden in *FAZ*)	*You have the use of the most up-to-date curative equipment*

137. **Two somewhat stilted types of adverbial absolute superlative**: Ich danke dir (a) **herzlichst** (b) **aufs herzlichste.** *I thank you most cordially.*

Type (a) is mainly found with a number of adverbs formed from adjectives in -ig and -lich and is characteristically used in commercialese. Thus:

Sie werden höflichst gebeten, diesen Irrtum zu berichtigen	*You are politely requested to rectify this error*

cf.: baldigst *as soon as possible*, freundlichst *kindly*, gefälligst, gütigst *obligingly*, *kindly*, schleunigst *as promptly as possible*, sorgfältigst *most carefully*

gefälligst may have a sharper edge (cf. Betteridge op. cit.), e.g. Sie werden gefälligst davon schweigen *You will kindly not speak about it.*

Type (b): Examples:

Ich war aufs angenehmste überrascht	*I was most pleasantly surprised* (set phrase)
man versteht sich aufs beste (Th. Mann)	(at a social gathering:) *everyone is getting on very well together*
aufs genaueste	*most exactly, accurately*
Der Vorfall hat mich aufs peinlichste berührt	*The incident made a most painful impression on me*

G. MISCELLANEOUS POINTS CONNECTED WITH COMPARATIVE AND SUPERLATIVE

138. (a) **Adjectives which are only used predicatively** (e.g. those marked with an asterisk in 117) **and participles that are not felt as adjectives** (contrast those exemplified in 98) **are compared by placing 'mehr' and 'am meisten' in front of them** Used

attributively, passive past participles may alternatively form a superlative with a prefixed 'meist-'.

Er ist mir noch mehr zuwider als sein Bruder	*He is still more repugnant to me than his brother*
Von den beiden ist dies das mehr gelesene Buch	*Of the two, this book is read more*
der meistgekaufte Geschirr-spülautomat Deutschlands (advert. in *Die Zeit*)	*The most popular washing-up machine in Germany*

(b) **ersterer ... letzterer *the former* ... *the latter*,** with strong
   endings: Da sind Karl und Wilhelm; ich habe mit ersterem Tennis
   und mit letzterem Federball gespielt.

Note:
i For the gen. sing. use des (or der) ersteren/letzteren.
ii An alternative rendering is jener *the former* ... dieser *the latter*, not used in
gen. sing.: see 166(a).

(c) **The adverbial superlative 'am meisten' is used colloquially
   in the sense of 'most, the greatest amount or number of',
   applied to the object:** Mein ältester Bruder hat am meisten/das
   meiste Geld; er hat am meisten/die meisten Fehler gemacht.

(d) **A group of frequently needed adverbial superlatives in -ens:**

höchstens *at the most*	spätestens *at the latest*
wenigstens *at least*	nächstens *shortly, soon*
frühstens *at the earliest*	

Further instances shown in a context:

Ich danke (Ihnen) bestens	*Thank you very much*
Ich stehe meistens[1] früh auf	*I mostly get up early*
Die Einwohner sind meistens[1] Katholiken	*The inhabitants are mostly Catholics*
Grüßen Sie ihn schönstens von mir	*Give him my kindest regards*
strengstens verboten	*strictly prohibited*
Ich kann das Buch wärmstens empfehlen	*I can recommend the book most warmly*

(e) **'möglichst' is used as follows** (never after the def. art.):

Du mußt einen möglichst guten Eindruck machen	*You must make the best possible impression*
Komme möglichst früh (so früh wie möglich)	*come as early as possible*
Gib ihm möglichst viel Geld (so viel Geld wie möglich)	*Give him as much money as possible*
Er hat sein möglichstes getan	*He has done his utmost*

(f) **'möglich' may be adjoined to the superlative forms best,
   größt, höchst, kleinst, kürzest** (little used in conversation):

die bestmögliche Lösung	*the best possible solution*
der größtmögliche Schaden (*Spiegel*)	*the greatest possible damage*

[1] also meist (more literary)

V THE PERSONAL PRONOUN

A. DECLENSION

139.	*I*	*you* (familiar sing.)	*he*	*she*	*it*
N.	ich	du	er	sie	es
A.	mich	dich	ihn	sie	es
D.	mir	dir	ihm	ihr	ihm

	we	*you* (familiar plur.)	*they*	*you* (polite: sing. & plur.)
N.	wir	ihr	sie	Sie
A.	uns	euch	sie	Sie
D.	uns	euch	ihnen	Ihnen

For the genitive case, see 151.

B. THE USE OF 'DU' AND 'IHR'

140. The familiar 2nd person du (plur. ihr) is used as follows:

i in addressing relatives, intimate friends, children (up to about 16 years of age), animals and inanimate objects (du, mein treuer Regenschirm!).

ii among all schoolchildren; their teachers call boys Sie in the top three forms of secondary schools, girls in the top four forms.

iii among workmen, privates, N.C.O.'s of the same rank, students and athletes.

iv to address the reader: Lies Goethes, . . . Rilkes Briefe—und du begreifst . . . (A. Goes). Vermeide Mißverstandnisse! (Duden). But also: Lesen Sie weiter auf Seite 30 (*Zeit-Magazin*).

v in poetry and proverbs.   vi the Deity is always Du.

Note:

i In a letter Du (Dein), Ihr (Euer) etc. are written with a capital (cf. 731(b)).

ii Note the verbs duzen (Fr. tutoyer) and, less used, Siezen.

iii For a short sketch of the history of the pronouns used as forms of address, see Corbett, op. cit., 45 (c), 46.

C. THE 3RD PERSON

141. The personal pronoun of the 3rd pers. sing. agrees in gender with the noun for which it stands

Leih mir deinen Bleistift!	*Lend me your pencil*
Ach, ich hab' ihn verloren; eben lag er auf dem Tisch; er ist rot	*—Oh. I've lost it; just now it was lying on the table; it's red*
Er hörte meine Meinung und stimmte ihr bei	*He heard my opinion and expressed agreement with it*

Regarding personal pronouns standing for neuter diminutives referring to persons (e.g. das Mädchen, das Söhnchen), see 672 (b).

142. The personal pronoun of the 3rd pers. is used in comparative clauses introduced by wie *such as* to repeat, in the grammatical context of the clause, the person or thing to which the clause refers:

Hier gibt es keine Wälder, wie man sie in Deutschland findet	*Here there are no forests such as you find in Germany*
Ein Kuchen, wie ihn Ihre Mutter backt, ist etwas Besonderes	*A cake such as your mother makes is something special*
Es war ein Auto, wie ich es noch nie (or: wie ich noch keins) gesehen hatte	*It was a car such as I had never seen before*

In a comparative clause introduced by 'as (good) as', 'ein' or 'kein' is used with the same function as the personal pron. above:

Sie hatte eine so leckere Torte gebacken, wie ich noch nie eine gegessen habe	*She had made as delicious a flan as I have ever eaten*
Der Film war so spannend, wie ich noch keinen gesehen habe	*The film was as exciting a one as I have ever seen*

In an 'als' clause (*than*), 'es' is sometimes introduced to represent the preceding main clause:

Er arbeitet viel besser, als ich (es) erwartet hatte	*He works much better than I had expected*

D. SOME SPECIAL USES OF 'ES'[1]

143. (a) 'es' is used as complement and demonstrative with the verb 'sein':

Wer ist es? Wer ist's?	*Who is it?*
Bist du es? Bist du's? Sind Sie es?	*Is it you?*
Ich bin es. Ich bin's	*It's me*
Wir sind es. Wir sind's	*It's us*
Es ist meine Mutter	*It's my mother*
Es sind meine Brüder	*It's my brothers*
Was sind es?	*What are they?*
Sind es Ihre Handschuhe?	*Are they your gloves?*

Note: Was ist es? Was sind es? but only: Wer ist es?

[1] See also 372 ff., 382 ff. and 512 ff.

(b) **It was he who . . ., It was then that . . . etc.**

  i In German 'he' comes first:

Er war es, der es mir sagte	*It was he who told me*
Du warst es also, der es getan hat	*So it was you who did it*

  ii With a noun, either order is possible:

Es war mein Vetter (Mein Vetter war es), der es mir erzählte	*It was my cousin who told me*

  iii Except with relative clauses this formula is less common in German, where the item to be emphasized is placed first followed by inversion:

In diesem Augenblick trat mein Vater ins Zimmer	*It was at this moment that my father entered the room*
Aus diesem Grunde habe ich nichts gesagt	*It was for this reason that I said nothing*

(c) **It is used to avoid repeating the complement of 'sein'** where in English nothing equivalent is required:

Er soll zuverlässig sein, und ich bin sicher, daß er es ist	*He is said to be reliable and I am sure he is*
Er ist immer so argwöhnisch.—Und warum ist er's?	*He is always so suspicious.—And why is he?*
Wir sind nie so erfolgreich, wie wir (es) sein möchten	*We are never as successful as we would like to be*

In the same type of context 'es' may correspond to English 'so':

Wer jetzt allein ist, wird es lange bleiben (Rilke: *Herbsttag*)	*He who is now alone will long remain so*

(d) **It corresponds to English 'so' used as the object of to say and to do:**

Er hat es gesagt	*He said so*
Warum hast du es getan?	*Why did you do so?*

With to think and to hope, 'es' is not generally used:

Kommt er heute?	*Is he coming today?*
—Ja, ich glaube (Ja, ich hoffe)	*—Yes, I think so/hope so*
Das will ich meinen!	N.B. *I should think so!*

(e) **It is used as an introductory subject,** only in normal order and when the real subject is a noun; its most usual effect, apart from purely rhythmical considerations, is to give greater emphasis to the real subject. This construction is widely used in German; in English, it may sometimes be rendered by 'there':

Es saß eine alte Frau am Fenster	*There was an old woman sitting at the window*
Es erhoben sich die Anwesenden	*Those present rose to their feet*
Es stieg ein kalter Nebel	*There was a cold mist rising*

cf. Es zeigte sich ein großer Unterschied; es wird dies nicht das letzte Mal sein.

(f) **It is used to denote a subject that is vague,** often conveying the feeling of an impersonal force at work:

bar jeglicher Ordnung, wie von einem Trichterwirbel erfaßt, strudelte es zähflüssig dieser Toreinfahrt zu (H. Broch)	*without a semblance of order, as though seized by a whirlpool, the crowd swirled in a thick mass towards this gateway*

Es drängte mich, ihm alles zu sagen	*I felt an urge to tell him everything*
Plötzlich schüttelt es ihn in einem wilden Krampf (A. Goes)	*Suddenly a fierce spasm shakes him*

(g) **It is used as an indeterminate object in certain set phrases,** e.g.

es gut haben	*to be fortunate*
es besser haben (als)	*to be luckier, to be better off (than)*
es gut meinen	*to mean well*
es sich (dat.) bequem machen	*to make oneself comfortable*
es weit bringen	*to go far* (fig.)
Er hat es zum Generaldirektor gebracht	*He has attained the post of Director General*
Er hat es mit mir zu tun	*He has me to deal with*

(h) **The 'es' which appears to be used as the object of a number of adjectival phrases with the verb 'sein' is really an old genitive,** e.g. Ich bin es los *I'm rid of it*; ich bin es satt *I'm sick of it.*[1]

E. THE USE OF DAMIT, DARAUF ETC.

144. After the following prepositions, the personal pronouns of the 3rd person acc. and dat. are normally used only with reference to persons; if they refer to things, the usual form is da+preposition, e.g. damit *with it*; if the preposition begins with a vowel, an 'r' is inserted, e.g. darauf *on it*, darüber *above it, about (concerning) it*; colloquially these often become drauf, drüber etc.

preps.+dat.: aus, bei, mit, nach, von, zu
preps.+acc.: durch, für, gegen, um
the 9 preps.+dat. or acc.: an, auf, hinter, in, neben, über, unter, vor, zwischen

(The above list comprises all the common prepositions except außer, gegenüber, seit; bis, ohne; and those taking the genitive.)

Leih mir dein Messer. Ich will das Paket damit öffnen	*Lend me your knife; I want to open the parcel with it*
Ich erkannte das Haus mit der großen Eiche daneben	*I recognized the house with the big oak next to it*

Colloquially, these forms are sometimes divided: Da hab' ich (nichts) von gewußt. Da will ich nichts mit zu tun haben (G. Gaiser).

145. Compounded with da, some prepositions are restricted in sense

(a) **aus, durch, nach and zu** do not usually have their literal sense of motion from, through or to a place, but connotations such as the following:

Er kaufte sich Holz und machte einen Schrank daraus	*He bought some wood and made a cupboard out of it*
Dàdurch ist alles so schwierig geworden	*Through that, everything has become so difficult*
danach	1. *after that* 2. *according to that*

For dazu, see 288.

[1] cf. Eggeling, op. cit., es 1 and 2

Note: dàraus (stressed thus) may have its literal sense:

Ich habe das Geld dàraus genommen   *I took the money from there* (i.e. out of
                                      that drawer)

(b) **darin** means 'in it', but not 'into it'

(c) **daran** may mean 'on it' or 'on to it' (the wall) but not 'by it' or
    'up to it' (the door, the blackboard):

Diese kahle Wand!   *This bare wall*:
  Früher hingen Bilder daran   *there used to be pictures on it*
  Ich will ein paar Bilder daran   *I'll hang a few pictures on it*
  hängen

(d) To express motion, the da- compounds of an, aus, durch, in, nach
    and zu are best replaced by separable prefixes:

hin *to it*   hinein, herein *into it*
hinaus, heraus *out of it*   durch, hindurch *through it*

Endlich fand ich den Schalter und   *At last I found the booking office and went*
  ging hin   *to it*
Der Hund kam zur Hütte und lief   *The dog came to the hut and ran into it*
  hinein
Wir kamen an einen langen Gang   *We came to a long passage and hurried*
  und eilten hindurch   *through it*

146. Usage with prepositions that are not compounded with da

(a) For the main prepositions+gen., see 153(a)ii.
(b) With gegenüber and ohne, the ordinary personal pronoun may be
    used or, more commonly, omitted:

Dies ist ein vorzügliches Wörterbuch;   *This is an excellent dictionary; I can't get*
  ohne (es) kann ich nicht fertig   *on without it*
  werden

(c) außer: use one of the adverbs außerdem or sonst.
(d) When in doubt, use derselbe (see 168), which, though cumbersome, is
    generally possible:

Seine Ankunft verursachte eine gewisse   *His arrival caused a certain restlessness;*
  Unruhe; dank derselben (better: *thanks to it I was able to steal away*
  infolgedessen) konnte ich mich
  wegstehlen

**147. da+prep. is the more usual and the safer form with reference
to things, but, as the following examples show, it is by no
means sacrosanct, particularly when referring to a plural noun:**

In der Nähe standen drei Eichen; ein Weg führte um sie herum.
Man spürt es an der Luft ganzer Städte, ob der Schmied oder der Weber in ihnen
  regiert (E. Jünger).
Er hatte ihn [den Wagen] erst seit einigen Wochen und war sehr zufrieden mit ihm
  (I. Wendt) (here 'mit ihm' harmonizes better with 'ihn' than would 'damit').

N.B.: darunter, in the sense of 'among them', is frequently used with
reference to persons, e.g. Ich erwarte zehn Gäste, darunter meine zwei
ältesten Freunde.

148. with it, with that, with this

with it, in it etc.	=damit, darin etc., with a slight stress on the preposition.
with that, in that etc.	=dàmit, dàrin etc., with a strong stress on da.
with this, in this etc.	=hiermit, hierin etc., with a slight stress on the prep. unless 'this' is to be emphasized.

Dàmit kann ich die Büchse nicht öffnen	*I can't open the tin with that*
Dàrüber sprechen wir nie	*We never talk about that*
ein Beispiel hiervon	*an example of this*
Kann man etwas hiergegen machen?	*Can one do anything against this?*

149. The form da + prep. is never used as the antecedent of a relative clause:

Ich richtete meine ganze Aufmerksam-keit auf das (*not*: darauf), was er erklärte	*I focused my whole attention on what he was explaining*

150. The many idiomatic uses of these compounds are not included in this chapter,[1] e.g.

Ich kann nichts dafür	*I can't help it*
Es liegt mir viel daran	*I attach great importance to it*

F. THE GENITIVE OF THE PERSONAL PRONOUN

151. The forms of the genitive

Nom.	Gen.	Nom.	Gen.
ich	meiner (mein)	wir	unser
du	deiner (dein)	ihr	euer
er	seiner (sein)	sie *they*	ihrer (ihr)
sie *she*	ihrer	Sie	Ihrer
es	seiner (sein)		

The bracketed forms are archaic and poetic, e.g.
> So oft der Mond mag scheinen,
> Gedenk ich dein allein, . . . (Brentano: *Der Spinnerin Lied*)

152. Outside a few contexts, the gen. of the personal pronoun sounds stilted and literary and its use is very limited in modern colloquial German. It is used:

(a) after a few verbs + gen. which have no alternative construction:

Er hat sich meiner angenommen	*He befriended me*

(b) with a few adjectives used with the genitive:

Ich bin seiner nicht sicher	*I'm not sure of him* (i.e. if I can count on him)
Er ist ihrer nicht würdig	*He's not worthy of her*

(c) in the phrases:

Das ist unser aller Wunsch	*That is the wish of all of us*
Das ist unser beider Wunsch	*That is the wish of both of us*

[1] for dabei and dazu see 287 f.

153. How the use of the gen. of the personal pronoun is avoided

(a) preps. + gen.

    i referring to persons:

1. the prepositions wegen, um . . . willen and . . . halber have special forms: meinetwegen etc., (um) meinetwillen, meinethalben (see 582(b), 586(b)(d)).
2. the prepositions wegen, statt and trotz are colloquially often used with the dative: wegen mir, statt ihm.
3. in the case of the remaining relevant prepositions + gen. there is always an alternative possibility. E.g.
    with regard to him: was ihn betrifft, or: in bezug auf ihn (not: hinsichtlich seiner).
    including you: Wir sind alle eingeladen, du mit eingeschlossen, or: auch du (not: einschließlich deiner).

    ii referring to things:

1. adverbs or adverb phrases may be used: deswegen *because of it*, trotzdem *in spite of it*, außerhalb, draußen *outside* (*it*), diesseits, auf dieser Seite *on this side* (*of it*), statt dessen *instead* (*of it*).
2. in the case of preps. + gen. which are often used with von (see 576(b)), davon may be used, e.g. auf Grund davon *on the strength of it*.

(b) verbs + gen.: the alternative construction or a different verb is used, e.g.

Erinnern Sie sich an mich? Ich schämte mich für ihn (though not all Germans would eschew: Erinnern Sie sich meiner? Ich schämte mich seiner).

Gib mir jetzt deinen Rat; ich brauche ihn (not: ich bedarf seiner).

(c) adjectives used with gen. (referring to things): use dessen *of that, of it*; for fem. and plur. use derselben:

Ich war mir dessen bewußt	*I was conscious of it*
Eine solche Ehre? Er ist derselben (but also: ihrer) nicht würdig	*Such an honour? He's not worthy of it*

VI MISCELLANEOUS ADJECTIVES AND PRONOUNS

A. REFLEXIVE AND RECIPROCAL PRONOUNS

154. Forms of the reflexive pronoun

(a) The personal pronouns are used as reflexive pronouns except for the acc. and dat. of the 3rd person and of the polite 2nd person, which are 'sich'. The refl. pron. is sometimes strengthened with 'selbst' (cf. 159); this is especially so in the genitive[1] (cf. 155).

(b) Present tense of sich setzen *to sit down*

REFL. PRON.: ACCUSATIVE

ich setze mich
du setzt dich
er setzt sich
wir setzen uns
ihr setzt euch
sie setzen sich
Sie setzen sich

Pres. of sich erlauben (etwas zu tun) *to allow oneself (to do something)*

REFL. PRON.: DATIVE

ich erlaube mir
du erlaubst dir
er erlaubt sich
wir erlauben uns
ihr erlaubt euch
sie erlauben sich
Sie erlauben sich

155. The genitive of the refl. pron. is barely used except in conjunction with one or two adjectives:

Er ist seiner selbst sicher
Er war seiner selbst nicht mehr mächtig

He is sure of himself
He had lost control of himself

156. Care must be taken to use the reflexive form for a pronoun following a preposition, when the pronoun refers back to the subject:

Er hatte kein Geld bei sich
Sie schlossen die Tür hinter sich

He had no money on him
They closed the door behind them

An exception must be made in certain contexts, to avoid producing ambiguity or the wrong sense. E.g.

Karl fand Walter mit einem Bericht über sich
Karl fand Walter mit einem Bericht über ihn

Karl found Walter with a report about himself (i.e. about Walter)
Karl found Walter with a report about him (i.e. about Karl)

---

[1] cf. Schulz-Griesbach, op. cit., D 108.

157. After verbs followed by a plain infinitive without 'zu', especially sehen, hören, lassen, the refl. pron. normally refers to the object and the personal pron. is used to refer to the subject:

Er sah seinen Sohn ihm entgegenkommen	*He saw his son coming to meet him*
Er hörte seinen Freund sich tadeln	*He heard his friend blaming himself*
Er hörte seinen Freund ihn tadeln	*He heard his friend blaming him*

But after a preposition, the refl. pron. refers to the subject:

Er sah seinen Freund vor sich hergehen	*He saw his friend walking along in front of him*
Er ließ den Tiger auf sich zukommen	*He let the tiger come towards him*
Er fühlte Mariannes Blick auf sich ruhen (V. Baum)	*He felt Marianne's gaze resting on him*

158. The dative of the refl. pron. is used idiomatically in a good many contexts as a kind of dative of advantage (or disadvantage)

Ich muß (mir) einen neuen Füller kaufen	*I must buy (myself) a new fountain-pen*
Er will sich das Haus ansehen	*He's going to have a look at the house*
Mein Versuch ist mir mißglückt	*My attempt has failed*
Er steckte sich eine Zigarette an	*He lit a cigarette*
Ich will mir bald Urlaub nehmen	*I'm soon going to take a holiday*
Ich habe es mir notiert	*I've made a note of it*
Ich habe (mir) oft gedacht, daß . . .	*I often thought (to myself) that . . .*

159. (a) **The emphatic 'myself', 'yourself' etc. is rendered by 'selbst' or 'selber' (invariable)**
Note:
i selbst and selber follow the noun or pronoun to which they refer, though not always immediately;
ii they are always stressed;
iii selber is the more colloquial of the two.

Ich habe selbst mit dem Minister darüber gesprochen	*I have spoken to the minister about it myself*
Ich habe mit dem Minister selbst darüber gesprochen	*I have spoken to the minister himself about it*
Ich habe selber den Brief gelesen	*I have read the letter myself*
Ich habe den Brief selber gelesen	

In the last example, both positions of 'selber' are equally idiomatic; the second version clearly could convey 'the letter itself', but in practice the context generally obviates such theoretical ambiguities.

(b) **selbst (unstressed) can also mean 'even' (cf. sogar).**
Selbst mein alter *Vater* ist dafür; man wußte selbst in *Berlin* nichts davon.

160. The reciprocal pronoun (*each other*) is rendered either by the plural forms of the reflexive pronoun or by 'einander' (invariable); the former are preferred in conversation, except after a preposition, where only 'einander' can be used; prep. + einander is written as one word.

Sie sahen sich (or einander) oft	*They often saw each other*
Wir gehen uns aus dem Wege	*We evade each other*
Wir verlassen uns aufeinander	*We rely on each other*
Fünf Autos standen hintereinander	*Five cars were standing behind one another*

Where the refl. pron. might be ambiguous, 'selbst' may be added to give the reflexive sense and 'gegenseitig' *mutually* to give the reciprocal sense:

Sie bewunderten sich selbst	*They admired themselves*
Sie bewunderten sich gegenseitig	*They admired each other*
(or: Sie bewunderten einander)	

B. THE POSSESSIVE PRONOUN[1]

161. The possessive pronoun has three forms:

(a) **meiner** – meine – mein(e)s *mine*   uns(e)rer *ours*
      deiner *yours*   eu(e)rer *yours*
      seiner *his, its*   ihrer *theirs*
      ihrer *hers, its*   Ihrer *yours*

Note:

i This form has the endings of dieser; it is therefore identical with the possess. adj. (see declension of 'ihr' in 90) except in the masc. nom. and the neut. nom. and acc.

ii In the neut. nom. and acc., the forms meins, deins, seins, ihrs and Ihrs are generally used, especially in conversation; 'unseres' and 'eueres' are fairly common alongside 'unsers' and 'euers'.

iii In the remaining cases, unserer and euerer frequently drop the unstressed e of the stem, especially in spoken German. In the masc. acc., the masc. and neut. dat. and the dat. plur. there is the alternative possibility of dropping the e of the ending. It is not wrong to retain both e's. E.g. Wir sprachen mit seinem Vater und er sprach mit unsrem (unserm, unserem).

(b) **der meinige** – die meinige – das meinige *mine*, der deinige *yours* etc.
Note:
i meinige, deinige etc. have the weak endings (cf. 88).
ii der uns(e)rige, der eu(e)rige: the bracketed e is generally dropped in spoken German, but frequently retained in writing.

(c) **der meine** – die meine – das meine *mine*, der deine *yours* etc.
Note:
i meine, deine etc. have the weak endings (cf. 88).
ii der uns(e)re, der eu(e)re: the bracketed e is frequently dropped, especially in spoken German; alternatively, in all cases other than the nom. sing. and the fem. and neut. acc. sing., the e of the ending may be dropped, e.g. den unsren or den unsern.

Of the three forms, (a), (b) and (c):
   (a) is the neatest and the most used, except in the gen. sing. and gen. plur.;
   (b) is cumbersome but not uncommon;
   (c) is somewhat literary.

Unser Garten ist größer als ihrer (der ihrige, der ihre).
Er sprach mit meinen Eltern, ich sprach mit seinen (den seinigen, den seinen).
Das ist die Unterschrift deines Lehrers, und dies ist die Unterschrift des meinigen (des meinen) (commoner: von meinem).

---

[1] for the possessive adjective, see 90–92.

162. **mein, dein, sein, unser, euer** (but not 'ihr' or 'Ihr') **are used predicatively, uninflected, to express possession,** but never after 'es ist' or 'das ist'. Historically, these forms are genitives of the personal pron. This usage is archaic and literary. E.g.

Mein ist der Helm, und mir gehört er zu (Schiller)
Die Stadt ist unser (normal version: ist in unseren Händen)

163. **Note the following:**

die Meinigen, die Meinen	*my people, my family*
Grüße auch die Deinigen (die Deinen)!	*And give my kind regards to your people*
Ich habe das Meinige getan	*I have done my part*
ein Freund von mir	*a friend of mine*
einer meiner Freunde	
einer von meinen Freunden	
Freunde von mir	*friends of mine*
verschiedene meiner Freunde	*several friends of mine*
(von meinen Freunden)	

C. DEMONSTRATIVE ADJECTIVES AND PRONOUNS

164. **The form der – die – das**

(a) **As a demonstrative adj., it is declined like the def. art.**, but it is stressed and is sometimes italicized; if strengthened with 'da' or 'hier', it can, but need not, be stressed. It is not used in the genitive.

Mit *dem* Lehrer habe ich wenig zu tun	*I don't have much to do with that master*
just in *dem* Moment (Th. Plievier)	*just at that moment*
Das Bild da gefällt mir gut	*I like that picture*

(b) **As a demonstrative pronoun it is declined as follows:**

	MASC.	FEM.	NEUT.	PLUR.
N.	der	die	das	die
A.	den	die	das	die
G.	dessen	deren	dessen	deren
		(derer)		(derer)
	(des)	(der)	(des)	(der)
D.	dem	der	dem	denen

For the use of bracketed forms of the gen., see Notes vi and vii in 165.

165. **Notes on the demonstrative pronoun der – die – das**

i Except as used in Notes iii, v, and ix, it is always stressed, even when strengthened with 'da' or 'hier'.

ii **Typical uses:**

mein Wagen und der meines Bruders	*my car and my brother's*
Die Sache ist nämlich die: er ist schon verheiratet	*You see the thing is this: he's married already*
Diesen Schulze, den kann ich nicht leiden	*This chap Schulze, I can't stand him*
Den (da) kann ich nicht leiden	*I can't stand that chap*

Diese Seife ist besser als die, die ich gebrauche	*This soap is better than the one I use*
Wohl dem, der . . .	*Happy is he who . . .*
Die im Wartezimmer reden. Denen wird die Zeit auch lang (H. Fallada)	*The people in the waiting-room are talking. They too find time hanging heavily*

iii It is frequently used, unstressed, with virtually no demonstrative force:

Müllers? Ich glaub', die sind verreist	*The Müllers? I think they're away*
Von den Töchtern—es sind deren fünf—hat die älteste . . . (A. Kolb)	*Of the daughters—there are five of them— the eldest . . .*

iv A 't' is added to dessen and deren when they are compounded with halben, wegen, willen:

Derentwegen hat er keinen Finger gerührt	*He didn't raise a finger to help that lot (or: to help her)*

v **A particular use of the genitive is to replace the possessive adj. when the latter might be ambiguous**

Karl sprach zuerst mit Heinrich, dann mit seiner Schwester(= with his (Karl's) sister)/dann mit dessen Schwester(= with his (Heinrich's) sister)

Sie [unsere Partei] hat den Menschen nichts als deren eigene objektive Interessen verständlich gemacht (*Neues Deutschland*)	*Our Party has made clear to people nothing but their own objective interests*

vi As antecedent to a relative clause, the fem. and plur. genitives are derer. (The fem. gen. is rarely used thus):

auf der Seite derer, die unter die Räder gekommen sind (A. Goes)	*on the side of those who have been crushed by life*

vii The short forms of the genitive (des, der, des, der) are archaic and poetic, except before a genitive; here only they can be used (3rd and 4th examples):

Des freuet sich der Engel Schar (Martin Luther)	*Thereat rejoices the angelic host*
Wes Brot ich ess', des Lied ich sing' (Proverb)	*Never quarrel with your bread and butter*[1]
Infolge meiner Rede und der meines Kollegen wurde der Antrag angenommen	*As the result of my speech and that of my colleague the motion was carried*
Die Interessen meiner Kinder und der meines Bruders sind sehr verschieden	*The interests of my children and of my brother's (children) are very different*

viii Before ist and sind (war, waren etc.), 'das' is used irrespective of the gender and number of the person or thing indicated:

Das ist mein Bleistift, meine Mutter, ihr Kind; das sind die jungen Deutschen; das waren glückliche Tage

ix das is used, mainly pejoratively, meaning 'they' or 'such people':

Das hat an allem etwas auszusetzen	*Such people find fault with everything*

x **such-and-such (a one)**

Er nannte mir die und die Adresse	*He gave me such-and-such an address*
Er sagte, der und der hätte es getan	*He said such-and-such a one had done it*

[1] Betteridge's rendering: op. cit. Lied.

166. dieser *this* **and jener** *that* **are used adjectivally and pronominally**

(a) **Declension**: see 88; the masc. and neut. gen. sing. dieses and jenes are rarely used pronominally.

EXAMPLES:

Dieser Stuhl ist bequemer als jener (commoner: als der da)	*This chair is more comfortable than that one*
Karl und Hans sind beide auf Urlaub; jener ist in Frankreich, dieser in der Schweiz	*Karl and Hans are both on holiday; the former is in France, the latter in Switzerland*[1]
Ich habe mit diesem und jenem gesprochen	*I talked with one or another*

(b) **The form dies** is often used in place of the neut. nom. or acc. dieses, mainly pronominally; cf. 166(c). E.g. Dies geschieht nicht oft; gerade dies hatte ich vergessen; hast du dieses/dies Buch gelesen?

(c) Before 'ist' and 'sind', **dies** is used irrespective of the gender and number of the person or thing indicated (cf. 165 viii): Dies sind meine Schwestern *These are my sisters*.

(d) **jener** is mainly used:
i when contrasted with dieser, as in the examples in (a) above.
ii when speaking of something remote in time or space:[2]
In jenen glücklichen Tagen hatte er nie gedacht, daß ihm so etwas passieren könnte.

Otherwise jener has something stilted and is relatively little used. Thus:

Dieser Junge (or: Der Junge da) arbeitet gut	*That boy works well*

N.B. dieser can never be used, in place of jener, adjectivally in 'that/ those . . . who, which' or pronominally in 'those who':

Er zeigte wiederum jene Aggressivität, die ihm so oft geschadet hatte	*Once again he displayed that aggressiveness which had so often done him harm*
Er sprach von jenen/denen/ denjenigen, die ihm geholfen hatten	*He spoke of those who had helped him*

(e) **Preposition+pronominal 'this' or 'that'** is most commonly rendered by stressed hier or da+prep. (cf. 144 and 148):

Stelle den Topf hìerauf, nicht dàrauf!	*Put the saucepan on this, not on that*

167. derjenige *that*

(a) Declension (cf. 88)

	MASC.	FEM.	NEUT.	PLUR.
N.	derjenige	diejenige	dasjenige	diejenigen
A.	denjenigen	diejenige	dasjenige	diejenigen
G.	desjenigen	derjenigen	desjenigen	derjenigen
D.	demjenigen	derjenigen	demjenigen	denjenigen

---

[1] It is logical that dieser (this one) refers to the second or closer noun (i.e. Hans). See also 138(b).
[2] cf. Schulz-Griesbach, op. cit., D 450.

(b) A cumbersome and ugly form, derjenige should be used sparingly.

i Used pronominally, it is followed by a relative clause, a genitive or a prepositional phrase:

Er sprach oft von denjenigen (better: von denen or jenen), die ihm geholfen hatten.

Mein Haus ist größer als dasjenige meines Bruders. (Commoner and better: als das von meinem Bruder or als meines Bruders).

Diejenigen (better: Die) in den hinteren Reihen konnten nichts sehen.

ii Used adjectivally, it is followed by noun + relative clause:

Er gab mir diejenigen Bücher, die er selber gelesen hatte.

N.B. It is *not* used thus: Ich habe dieses Buch lieber als dasjenige; this should be: als das da or als jenes.

(c) Note the facetious 'derjenige, welcher':

Sie sind wohl derjenige, welcher!   *I suppose you're the one (who did it)*

168. derselbe – dieselbe – dasselbe *the same*[1]

(a) Declension: like 'derjenige' (see 167(a)), but with 'derselbe' a contraction of preposition + def. art. is possible.

EXAMPLES:

Er gab mir dieselbe Antwort	*He gave me the same answer*
Er gab mir diese selbe Antwort	*He gave me this same answer*
Es läuft auf (eins und) dasselbe hinaus	*It comes to (one and) the same thing*
Sind das dieselben?	*Are those the same ones?*
Ich wohne im selben Haus wie mein Chef	*I live in the same house as my boss*
Er geht aufs selbe Gymnasium wie sein Bruder	*He goes to the same grammar school as his brother*

Note:

i it may be strengthened by prefixing 'eben':

an ebendemselben Tag   *on the very same day*

ii the forms 'derselbige' and 'selbiger' are archaic.

(b) 'derselbe' is sometimes used pronominally in place of a personal pronoun or a possessive adjective, but this use is cumbersome and should be avoided:

Ich erhielt seinen Brief mit der ersten Post; erst später las ich denselben (say: ihn); der Inhalt desselben (say: sein Inhalt) erstaunte mich.

169. For **solcher** *such*, see 222.

D. THE INTERROGATIVE PRONOUN

170. Declension of the interrogative pronoun

N.	wer? *who?*	was? *what?*	
A.	wen?	was?	
G.	wessen? (archaic: wes)	wessen? (archaic: wes)	
D.	wem?	—	

[1] Purists distinguish between derselbe *the same* and der gleiche *the same, a similar*; e.g. Er trug den gleichen (not: denselben) Hut wie ich.

The above are singular in form, but may be singular or plural in meaning. As subject, 'wer' and 'was' take a singular verb, but they can be the complement of a plural verb; where the subject is the demonstrative 'es' or 'das', this applies only to 'was' (cf. 143(a)N.).

Wer hat diesen Brief geschrieben?	*Who wrote this letter?*
Wer sind diese Leute?	*Who are these people?*
Wessen Mäntel sind diese?	*Whose coats are these?*
(commoner: Wem gehören diese Mäntel?)[1]	
Was sind diese Dinge?	*What are these things?*
Was sind das?	

Note:

i For a colloquial means of indicating that 'wer' and 'was' are plural in meaning, see 173(b).

ii The archaic genitive 'wes' still occurs in the compounds weshalb? and weswegen? *why? wherefore?* and in the set phrase 'Wes Geistes Kind ist er?' *What kind of a fellow is he?*

171. When the interrog. pron., referring to a thing, is used with one of the following prepositions, the usual form is wo+prep., e.g. womit? *with what?*; if the preposition begins with a vowel, an r is inserted, e.g. worauf? *on what?*

an, auf, aus, bei, durch, für, gegen, hinter, in, mit, nach, über, um, unter, von, vor, zu

Womit schreibst du?	*What are you writing with?*
Ich wußte nicht, worauf ich mich setzen sollte	*I didn't know what to sit down on*

Note:

i Compounded with 'wo', durch, nach, von and zu do not generally express motion:

Wodurch weißt du das?	*How is it that you know that?*
Wonach sehnst du dich?	*What are you longing for?*
Wonach soll man die Lage beurteilen?	*By what is one to judge the situation?*
Wovon sprachen wir?	*What were we talking about?*
Wozu gebrauchst du dieses Instrument?	*What do you use this instrument for?*

To express motion, the following renderings may be used: durch: durch was? von: von wo? woher? *from where?* nach and zu: wohin? *where to?*

ii Colloquially, prep.+was is also used, even with prepositions taking the dative:

Von was lebt er?	*What does he live on?*
'Biste fertig oder machste weiter?'	*'Have you finished or are you going on?'*
'Mit was?' 'Schreiben.' (J. Rehn)	*'With what?' 'Writing.'*

iii In practice, prepositions not compounded with 'wo' are rarely required before the neut. interrog. pron.; because of what?=weswegen? or, coll. and emphatic, wegen was?

[1] cf. Collinson, op. cit., p. 49.

172. The genitive and dative of 'was'

(a) The neut. gen. 'wessen' sounds stilted and is avoided. Thus normal usage is: Worauf lautet die Anklage? (Not: Wessen ist er angeklagt?) Warum (not: Wessen) schämst du dich?

In other contexts 'of what?' may be rendered by 'wovon?' or turned more freely, e.g.

Wozu gehört diese Schraube?   *Of what is this screw a part?*

(b) For the non-existent dative of 'was', a serviceable substitute is 'welcher' followed by a suitable noun:

Welcher Konstruktion ähnelt Ihre Erfindung?   *What does your invention resemble?*

Welcher Ursache kann man seinen Erfolg zuschreiben?   *To what can one ascribe his success?*

173. Miscellaneous points connected with the interrogative pronoun

(a) **wer and was may be used exclamatorily:**

Wer hätte so was erwartet! (a rhetorical question)   *Who would have expected such a thing!*

Was *haben* wir gelacht!   *How we laughed!*

Compare some of the examples in 173(b)

(b) **Colloquially an uninflected 'alles' may be added to (though generally separated from) wer, was, etc. (and also to wo, wohin, woher) to show that more than one person, thing or place is referred to:**

Wer kommt denn alles?   *What people are coming?*

Was hat er alles gefragt?   *What were the things that he asked?*

Du weißt ja, was sie alles durchgemacht hat (H. Böll)   *Of course you know everything that she's been through*

Wofür ist diese Salbe alles gut?   *What are the things that this ointment is good for?*

Wem *hat* er nicht alles geholfen!   *Whom hasn't he helped!*

Was er nicht alles tut!   *The things he does!*

Wo bist du in den Ferien alles gewesen?[1]   *What places have you been to in the holidays?*

(c) **Neuter collective substantival adjectives are used in apposition to the interrogative was,** but are separated from it:

Was haben sie Wichtiges besprochen?[2]   *What important matter* (or *matters*) *did they discuss?*

Was ist Komisches daran?   *What is there funny about it?*

Was gibt es Neues?   *What's the news?*

Was könnt ihr hier anderes erwarten? (H. Fallada)   *What else can you expect here?*

(d) **The regional use of wer in the sense of someone, anyone** (not used in gen.) should be recognized but not imitated, e.g. Es ist wer an der Tür. Hast du wen gesehen? Er wird schon wen finden, den er mit seinem Geschwätz glücklich machen kann (H. Broch).

---

[1] from Eggeling op. cit.: all (German) 6(b).
[2] Historically, Wichtiges was a partitive gen.: 'What of the important did they discuss?' The same applies to the other examples. Cf. Eggeling op. cit.: was (interrogative) 4(a).

(e) **Some phrases and idioms**

Was stößt du mich immer? (coll.)	*Why do you keep nudging me?*
Wie ist der Name, bitte?	*What is your name?*
Wie ist das Buch?	*What's the book like?*
Wie (bitte)?	*What did you say? I beg your pardon?*
Du kommst doch, was? (or wie?) (coll.)	*You are coming, aren't you?*

E. THE INTERROGATIVE ADJECTIVE

174. The interrogative adjective welcher? welche? welches? plur. welche? *which? what?*

(a) Declension

It is declined like dieser, except for a fluctuation in the masc. and neut. gen. sing.: see 89 N.i; in practice the genitive is rare, 'von' being preferred.

(b) It may be used pronominally:

Hier sind zwei gute Romane: welchen willst du lesen?	*Here are two good novels: which one do you want to read?*

(c) Before ist, sind (war, waren), the neuter welches may be used irrespective of the gender and number of the person or thing to which it refers: Welches ist die jüngere Schwester? Welches sind die besten Zeitungen? ('Welche', respectively fem. and plur., would also be correct.)

(d) welcher may be used exclamatorily, though was für (ein) is commoner (see 175(d)): Welcher Unterschied! *What a difference!* Welche Überraschung! *What a surprise!*

(e) An **undeclined welch** is used, mainly exclamatorily, before ein or before an attributive adjective, which has the strong endings: Welch ein Pedant! Welch herrliches Wetter! (Was für (ein) is commoner)

(f) For the use of welcher as an indefinite pronoun (some, any), see 237.

175. The interrogative adjective was für ein *what kind of (a)? what (a)?*

(a) Declension

    i was für is invariable and does not affect the case.

    ii ein is declined like the indef. art.; it is, of course, absent in the plural and generally in the singular before nouns denoting materials and substances. Where there is no ein, an attributive adjective has the strong endings.

Aus was für einer Familie stammt er?	*From what kind of family does he come?*
Sie können sich denken, in was für einer schwierigen Lage ich mich befand	*You can imagine in what an awkward situation I found myself*
Was für ausländische Marken haben Sie?	*What kinds of foreign stamps have you got?*
Was für Käse soll ich kaufen?	*What kind of cheese shall I buy?*

(b) Colloquially, was für ein is sometimes used instead of welcher, without any ingredient of 'what kind of?':

Was für deutsche Dramen haben Sie gelesen? *What German plays have you read?*

(c) 'was für ein' may be used pronominally: masc. nom.: was für einer? neut. nom. and acc.: was für eins? plur.: was für welche?

Er hat sich ein Auto gekauft.—Was für eins? *What kind of one?*
Ich habe ihr Blumen gebracht.—Was für welche? *What kind?*

(d) It may be used exclamatorily:

Was für eine Chance! *What a chance!*
Was für herrliche Blumen! *What lovely flowers!*
Er ist ein Schauspieler und was für einer! *He's an actor and what an actor!*

(e) In the nom. and acc. was is frequently, though never necessarily, separated from für (ein): Was hast du denn für ein Buch gekauft? Was sind das für herrliche Blumen!

F. THE RELATIVE PRONOUN

176. The relative pronoun has two forms:

(a)	MASC.	FEM.	NEUT.	PLUR.
N.	der	die	das	die
A.	den	die	das	die
G.	dessen (des)	deren	dessen (des)	deren
D.	dem	der	dem	denen

Note:
i The two bracketed forms are archaic and poetic.
ii When 'dessen' and 'deren' are compounded with 'halben', 'wegen', and 'willen', a 't' is inserted: dessenthalben, dessentwegen, (um) dessentwillen *for whose sake, because of which.*

(b)	MASC.	FEM.	NEUT.	PLUR.
N.	welcher	welche	welches	welche
A.	welchen	welche	welches	welche
G.	—	—	—	—
D.	welchem	welcher	welchem	welchen

It will be noted that form (a) is identical with the def. art. except for the four genitives and the dat. plur. and that form (b) is identical with the interrog. adj. welcher? but is not used in the genitive.

177. The use of the two forms

i 'der' is used far more than 'welcher' and **must** be used when the antecedent is a personal pronoun (see 184) or a non-neuter indefinite pronoun (e.g. jemand, niemand, jedermann).
ii 'welcher' is sometimes preferred for reasons of rhythm and style.
iii 'welcher' can be used adjectivally before a noun referring to part or the whole of the main clause:

Er wurde zum Stadtdirektor ernannt, welches Amt er gewissenhaft verwaltete	*He was appointed town-clerk, which office he conscientiously administered*
Er will sich zunächst an seinen Onkel um Geld wenden, mit welchem Plan ich einverstanden bin (better: ein Plan, mit dem ich einverstanden bin)	*He intends in the first place applying to his uncle for money, of which plan I approve*

178. Agreement of relative pronoun: as in Latin, the rel. pron. agrees with its antecedent in gender and number, but takes its case from its function in the relative clause:

Ich kannte den Rechtsanwalt, der gestern gestorben ist	*I knew the barrister who died yesterday*

179. The relative pronoun is never omitted in German

Das Buch, das ich lese, ist recht interessant	*The book I'm reading is very interesting*

180. whose eldest son etc.: see 95(d).

whose one son: 'ein' here has the endings of dieser; colloquial usage would favour 'von': Mein Freund, dessen einer Sohn (von dem der eine Sohn) krank ist, . . .

181. Where 'of which' would be used in English, the normal genitive of the relative pronoun is used in German:

Wir kamen an die Straße, an deren anderem Ende er wohnt	*We came to the street, at the other end of which he lives*
die . . . Dialekte . . ., deren Studium ich mich einmal . . . gewidmet hatte (G. Hartlaub) ('Studium' is dat.)	*the dialects, to the study of which I had once devoted myself*

This does not apply to phrases of the type 'one of whom', 'some of which', 'most of whom'; here 'von denen einer', 'von denen manche', 'von denen die meisten' are normal usage (e.g. Seine Bücher, von denen ich drei gelesen habe), while 'deren einer' etc. is distinctly literary.

Note:

i Dieser Schriftsteller, drei von dessen Büchern ich gelesen habe, . . . (smoother: von dem ich drei Bücher gelesen habe)	*This author, three of whose books I have read, . . .*

ii For the translation of 'all of which' etc., see 189.

182. 'was' is used as a rel. pron. with the following antecedents:

(a) **neuter indefinites**, e.g. allerhand, allerlei, alles, das (demonstrative), das bißchen, dasjenige, einiges, etwas, folgendes, mancherlei, manches, nichts, vieles, weniges.

Nichts, was er sagte, war mir neu	*Nothing that he said was new to me*
Ich bin mit allem, was er tut, zufrieden	*I am satisfied with everything that he does*

. . . ein eifriger Leser dessen, was neu auf den Markt kommt (*Zeit*)	. . . *a keen reader of what is new on the market*

Note:

i In the genitive, 'dessen' (and not 'wessen') is normal usage:

Ich dachte an so manches, dessen ich mich schäme	*I thought of many things of which I am ashamed*

ii After 'etwas' (and occasionally after some of the others) there is a tendency to use 'das' where 'etwas' represents something sharply specific:

Gerade in diesem Moment fiel ihr etwas ein, das sie erstarren ließ. Die Gasrechnung (V. Baum)	*Just then she remembered something that paralysed her; the gas bill*
irgend etwas, was ich nicht verstand (H. Böll)	BUT: *something or other that I did not understand*

iii When these indefinites are coupled with an adjective used substantivally, a following rel. pron. is generally 'was'; 'das' is sometimes used, bringing out the individual nature of what is referred to.

Der alte Seemann lehrte mich manches Nützliche, was ich seitdem vergessen habe	*The old seaman taught me many useful things that I have since forgotten*
vieles Interessante, was (or das) er erzählte	*many interesting things that he related*
Ich erinnere mich an etwas Merkwürdiges, das er sagte	*I remember something strange that he said*

(b) **a neuter substantival adjective**

After this type of antecedent, there is some fluctuation between 'das' and 'was'; 'was' is more usual, especially when the adjective is a superlative or a superlative equivalent (das erste, das letzte, das einzige); 'das' is used if the thing in question is envisaged as, or associated with, something definite and specific (last example):

Das Richtige, was man sich ansehen müßte, finden wir nie (H. Fallada)	*The right things* [in museums], *that one ought to look at, we never find*
Das Beste, was du tun kannst, ist nach Hause zu gehen	*The best thing that you can do is to go home*
Das erste, was Evelyn sah, waren Mariannes Augen (V. Baum)	*The first thing that Evelyn saw was Marianne's eyes*
Das Gute, das er getan hat, wird ihn überdauern	*The good that he has done will outlive him*

(c) **a clause**

Er hat sein Examen bestanden, was mich sehr erstaunt	*He has passed his examination, which very much surprises me*
Seine Frau kann das Klima nicht ertragen, weswegen sie umziehen werden	*His wife can't stand the climate, for which reason they are going to move*

Note: **The relative 'was' is not used after a preposition**; after most common prepositions, other than those taking the genitive, wo + preposition is used; if the preposition begins with a vowel, an 'r' is inserted (e.g. woraus):

das. wozu er berechtigt ist	*what he is entitled to*

Es ist das einzige, wofür es sich lohnt, Richter zu sein (V. Baum)	*It is the only thing for which it is worth while being a judge*
Er hat sein Examen bestanden, worüber ich mich sehr freue	*He has passed his examination about which I am very pleased*

183. wo + preposition (cf. note at end of 182) **is frequently used with ordinary substantival antecedents if they are things**, though rarely if they are plural; but prep. + rel. pron. is both better style and more commonly used: Der Füller, mit dem (womit) ich gewöhnlich schreibe, war ganz billig.

Note:

i Distinguish 'wovon' *about which, concerning which* and 'von wo' *from where, from which*.

ii da + prep. is used as an alternative to wo + prep. with ordinary substantival antecedents, but is not recommended for imitation. E.g.

... Masken oder Faschingsnasen, dahinter sich der Genius verbirgt (E. Penzoldt)	*... masks or carnival noses, behind which genius hides*

184. If the antecedent is one of the personal pronouns ich, du, wir, ihr, Sie, the pers. pron. is generally repeated after the relative, but this rather stilted construction is avoided in conversation:

Du, der du so viel erlebt hast, wirst mich verstehen	*You, who have experienced so much, will understand me*
Sie, der Sie so viel erlebt haben, werden mich verstehen	
Doch nicht nur ich, der ich mich schließlich irren kann, ... (H. Broch)	*But not only I, who after all may be wrong, ...*

Note: This construction is not used where the pers. pron. antecedent is introduced by the verb 'sein' + 'es'; here the verb in the rel. clause goes into the 3rd person: ihr wart es also, die es getan haben; warst du es, der es getan hat?

185. wer and was may be used as compound relatives, combining antecedent and relative: *who* or *he who*; *what* or *that which*:

Wer viele Freunde hat, ist glücklich	*He who has many friends is happy*
Und was noch schlimmer ist, er realisiert es selber nicht	*And what is worse, he doesn't realize it himself*
Woran die Menge glaubt, ist leicht zu glauben (Goethe, quoted in Du. Gram. 6210)	*What the mob believes in is easy to believe in*

Note:

i The comprehensiveness of wer and was may be strengthened by the addition of auch, nur or immer:

Jeder Vater, jede Mutter und wer immer der wachsenden Generation gegenübersteht (*FAZ*)	*Every father, every mother and whoever has to deal with the younger generation*

ii Where the suppressed antecedent and the relative are in different cases, the former is generally represented by a demonstrative, in the case required, at the beginning of the main clause:

Wem du traust, der wird auch dir trauen	*He whom you trust will also trust you*
Wen die Götter lieben, der stirbt jung	*Whom the gods love, die young*

iii wer and was cannot be used as compound relatives where the antecedent is preceded by a preposition, even if antecedent and relative are in the same case:

Wir lachten über das, was er getan hat	*We laughed about what he had done*

iv Referring to specific persons, or to restricted groups, the demonstrative 'der' is used in the same way, i.e. for 'he who':

Der da sitzt, ist mein Onkel	*The man sitting there is my uncle*
Die da arbeiten, waren aber nicht eben heiter (*Zeit*)	*Those who work there were, however, not exactly cheerful*

186. Some other forms of the relative

weshalb	*for which reason*
der Grund, weshalb (or warum) . . .	*the reason why . . .*
die Art, wie . . .	*the way in which . . .*
die Stadt, wo er wohnt,	*the town where he lives*
die Stadt, wohin wir fahren,	*the town to which we are driving*
die Stadt, woher ich komme,	*the town from which I've come*
Er beantwortete all unsere Fragen, wobei er sich oft räusperte	*He answered all our questions, often clearing his throat*

Note: For the translation of 'when' introducing relative clauses (e.g. the day when . . .) see 534(f).

N.B. All the miscellaneous adjectives and pronouns treated in 187–239 always have a small letter with the following exceptions: Er hat ein gewisses Etwas an sich; ein gewisser Jemand; das Nichts *nothingness, void; a trifle*; viele Wenig machen ein Viel.

187. aller, alle, alles *all*; uninflected: all (also alle and alles)

(a) **The inflected aller is declined like dieser** (with the exception given in i N. 1 below).

i **used adjectivally**

aller Wein	*all wine*
Alles Zögern wäre verhängnisvoll	*Any hesitation would be fatal*
in aller Heimlichkeit	*in all secrecy*

Note:

1. The masc. and neut. gen. sing. are frequently allen; see 89 N.i:

trotz allen Spottes, den sie im Herzen . . . trug (H. Böll)	*in spite of all the feelings of derision that she harboured in her heart*
allen Ernstes	*in all seriousness* (set phrase)

2. The plur. alle is generally used to convey both 'all' and 'all the':

Alle Frauen sind neugierig	*All women are inquisitive*
Ich habe alle Fehler korrigiert	*I've corrected all the mistakes*

3. An attrib. or subst. adj. following the inflected aller has the weak endings (with occasional variations): aller gute Wein; alle Deutschen.

ii **used pronominally**

Alles ist bereit	*Everything is ready*
Alle waren anwesend	*Everyone was present*
Alles lachte	*Everyone laughed* (idiomatic)
Er ist die Hoffnung aller	*He is the hope of all*
Sind das alle?	*Is that the lot?*

Note: The gen. sing. alles is not used alone; the gen. of das (demonstrative) must be added:

Ich erinnere mich alles dessen, was er sagte[2]	*I remember everything that he said*

(b) **all (uninflected)** is used before the def. art. and before a demonstr. or possess. adj. or pron.; only in the fem. nom. and acc. and in the nom. and acc. plur. is the inflected alternative at all common (cf. Du. Gram. 2880):

all das schlechte Wetter; all das Schöne, was ich gesehen habe; nach all diesem Regen; mit all diesem; wir sehen uns kaum—ich mit all meiner Arbeit und sie mit all ihrer; all/alle unsre Freunde.

Note: Thorolf Hansen (*Deutschunterricht für Ausländer*, 13. Jahrgang 5/6,

---

[1] For a list of the words treated, with paragraph numbers, see CONTENTS.
[2] from Eggeling, op. cit., p. 24.

p. 139) suggests, with some corroborating quotations, that 'alle unsre Freunde' implies 'without exception' more strongly than 'all unsre Freunde'.

(c) alle (uninflected)

i It is very occasionally found as an alternative to the uninflected 'all'; cf. two fixed phrases:

Bei alledem bin ich hoffnungsvoll	*For all that, I'm hopeful*
trotz alledem	*despite all this*

ii Regionally and colloquially, it has the sense of 'finished, used up':

Der Wein ist alle	*The wine's finished*
Die Kataloge sind leider alle	*I'm afraid there are no more catalogues*
Meine Geduld ist alle[1]	*My patience is exhausted*
Es muß alle werden[2]	*It's got to be eaten up*

(d) alles (uninflected) (coll.) has two uses:

i See interrog. pron. 173(b)

Wer kommt denn alles?	*What people are coming?*

ii It may precede a plural complement of the verb sein with the sense of lauter (all, nothing but):

Es sind alles Lügen	*It's all lies*
Seine Freunde waren alles Geschäftsleute	*His friends were all business men*

(e) alls, generally spelt als, is used adverbially with the sense of 'continually' or 'occasionally'. It is regional and colloquial, but should be recognized:

Er hat als geflucht	*He kept on cursing*
Er kommt als (einmal) am Sonntag	*He sometimes comes on a Sunday*
Sie tut als weinen	*She keeps crying*

(f) Some order points

i alle follows a personal pronoun:

Ich habe mit ihnen allen gesprochen	*I have spoken to all of them*
wenn sie ihn alle gern haben	*if they all like him*
cf. sing.: Ich habe es alles getan	*I have done it all*

ii The demonstr. pronouns das, dies(es) and diese (plur.) are preceded by the uninflected all (the commonest usage), but may be preceded or followed by inflected alles etc.:

all das/alles das/das alles	*all that*
Mit all diesem werde ich nicht fertig	*I can't cope with all this*
Aus diesem allen[3] sieht man, daß ...	*From all this one can see that ...*

Both forms precede the gen. dessen

Ich war mir all/alles dessen unbewußt	*I was unconscious of all that*

alles is less emphatic if separated from the demonstrative by the verb:

Dies muß alles getan werden	*This must all be done*
Dies alles muß getan werden	*All this must be done*

---

[1] from Collinson op. cit., p. 60.
[2] from Corbett op. cit. 49(h)(v).
[3] the weak form allen is here more usual.

iii A declined 'all' may follow its noun in the fem. and neut. nom. and
  acc. and in the nom., acc. and dat. plur.

Note: 1. Where it limits the subject, 'all' follows the verb.
  2. This usage is colloquial except in the nom. and acc. plur.

Das Brot ist alles trocken; ich habe die Hoffnung alle aufgegeben; die Kinder
spielten alle im Garten; ich habe mit den Kindern allen gesprochen.

188. The rendering of all by 'ganz'

(a) all + the/demonstr./possess. (+ adj.) + sing. noun may usually be rendered by ganz *whole*. It has a more unifying effect than 'all' and is,
  in general, the preferred usage. (Clearly, all the English equivalents
  that follow could alternatively be expressed with 'whole' or 'the whole
  of'.)

Die ganze Butter ist schlecht	*All the butter is bad*
diese ganze Unsicherheit	*all this uncertainty*
Er hat sein ganzes Geld (or: all sein Geld) verloren	*He has lost all his money*
mit seiner ganzen jugendlichen Energie	*with all his youthful energy*

With a plural noun, this use of 'ganz' is purely colloquial, e.g.

Die ganzen Straßen waren voll Menschen	*All the streets were full of people*

(b) 'ganz' is essential before collective nouns such as the following: das
  ganze Regiment *all the regiment*, die ganze Familie, in der ganzen
  Schule.

(c) 'ganz' is essential in time phrases of the type 'all the morning', 'all
  day' (see 315); cf. der ganze Januar war kalt *all January it was cold*.

(d) Before the names of continents, countries and towns, 'all' is rendered
  by 'ganz'; see 116(c).

189. 'all' with the relative pronoun

Sometimes a free rendering is necessary; the relevance of 187(f)iii will be
noticed; otherwise the following examples must speak for themselves.

REL. PRON. IN NOM. SING.

Der Wein, der ohne Ausnahme (without exception) gut ist, . . .	*the wine, which is all good,* . . .
Die Butter, die alle schlecht ist,	*The butter, that is all bad*

REL. PRON. IN ACC. SING.

Der Park, den Sie jetzt ganz (completely) gesehen haben,	*The park, all of which you've now seen*
Das Brot, das er alles gegessen hat,	*The bread, all of which he's eaten*

REL. PRON. IN GEN. SING.

Mein Freund, dessen ganzes Geld gut angelegt ist,	*My friend, all of whose money is well invested*
Diese Stadt, deren Kirchen ich alle kenne,	*This town, all of whose churches I know*
Das Schloß, in allen dessen Zimmern ich gewesen bin (or: in dem ich in allen Zimmern gewesen bin),	*The palace, in all of whose rooms I have been*

REL. PRON. IN DAT. SING.

Der Garten, in dem überall Unkraut wächst,	*The garden, in all parts of which weeds are growing*
Seine Arbeit, mit der ich ohne Ausnahme zufrieden bin,	*His work, with all of which I'm satisfied*

REL. PRON. IN THE FOUR CASES OF THE PLURAL

Die Bücher, die alle interessant sind,	*The books, which are all interesting*
Die Bücher, die ich alle gelesen habe,	*The books, all of which I've read*
Die Kinder, deren Eltern ich alle kenne,	*The children, all of whose parents I know*
Die Kinder, mit denen ich allen gesprochen habe,	*The children, with all of whom I've spoken*

190. ander *other*

(a) **ander is declined like an ordinary adjective or subst. adj.:**

der andere Student	*the other student*
der andere	*the other one*
irgendein anderer	*some (or any) other one*
kein anderer (als Müller)	*none other, no one else (but Müller)*
die drei anderen, die anderen drei	*the three others, the other three*
alle anderen	*all the others*
Er war anderer Meinung (als ich)	*He was of a different opinion (from me)*
etwas (or was) anderes	*something different, something else*
irgend etwas anderes	*something (or anything) else*
ganz was anderes	*something quite different, quite another matter*
alles andere	*everything else*

Note:

i Regionally and colloquially ander is frequently used without an ending in the neut. acc. after ein, kein or a possess. adj., e.g. Wir haben ein ander Haus gekauft; wir haben unser ander Haus verkauft.

ii we others = wir anderen; you others = ihr anderen. ('Sie anderen' is not used.)

(b) **The inflection of an attrib. adj. following ander**

i if ander is preceded by an article, a demonstr. or a possess. adj., ander and the other adjective have the same orthodox ending: der andere deutsche Student.

Note: After a possessive, and especially after unser and ihr, the second adjective is sometimes given a weak ending in conversation, e.g. unser anderer neue Sekretär (not to be imitated).

ii ander + adj. + noun: the predominant literary practice is to give the adjective the strong endings, i.e. the same endings as ander (cf. Hansen, pp. 129–37 of loc. cit. in 187(b)N.), except in the masc. and neut. dat. sing., where the weak ending preponderates (Du. Gram. 2110).

anderes dummes Gerede	*other stupid talk*
mit anderer moderner Musik	*with other modern music*
anderer italienischer Maler	*of other Italian painters*

cf. ander + subst. adj. or participle:

die Erfahrungen anderer Reisender	*the experiences of other travellers*

While the above would not sound stilted in conversation, there is a collo-quial tendency to give the second adjective weak endings, except in the nom. and acc. plur., e.g. anderes dumme Gerede, mit anderer modernen Musik, anderer italienischen Maler.

(c) **Orthography**: wherever ander has an ending, one of the e's is fre-quently dropped, especially in spoken German, though it is not wrong, or even particularly unusual, to retain them both.

With -e and -er, only the e of the stem can be dropped.
With -en, it is commoner to drop the e of the ending.
With -em, it is much commoner to drop the e of the ending.
With -es, it is much commoner to drop the e of the stem, in contrast with the special (adverbial) form anders, treated in 191.

Therefore:
der andre Student, ein andrer, die andern (or andren) Studenten, mit etwas anderm, ein andres Buch.

191. The invariable anders *else, different, differently*

It is an (adverbial) genitive (see Eggeling, op. cit., pp. 32 and 205: jemand, niemand: 2). It is used in three ways:

(a) meaning 'else' after jemand, niemand and wer.

Note:
i Here it is sometimes written and pronounced 'anderes'.
ii It is not used with the genitive.
iii In the dative, the forms 'jemand anderm' and 'niemand anderm' are not uncommon, especially where there is no preposition to indicate the case, as in: Dieser Schirm gehört jemand anderm (or anders) (coll.: Dies ist jemand anders sein Schirm: see end of 61)
iv Other South German variants cause no difficulty of comprehension.

EXAMPLES:

(irgend) jemand anders; mit jemand anders; niemand anders (als) *no one else (but)*; wer anders kann es getan haben? (commoner: wer kann es sonst getan haben? cf. 194).
die Ansichten von jemand anders (or: eines anderen) *someone else's views*

(b) meaning 'else' in conjunction with wo, wohin, woher, nirgendwo:

woanders, anderswo	*somewhere else*
Wo anders könnte es sein?	*Where else could it be?*
irgendwo anders	*somewhere/anywhere else*
Ich gehe irgendwo anders hin	*I'm going somewhere else*
Ich gehe woandershin	
Ich gehe anderswohin	
Er kommt anderswoher, nicht aus Hamburg	*He comes from somewhere else, not from Hamburg*
nirgendwo anders	*nowhere else*
Ich gehe nirgendwo anders hin	*I'm not going anywhere else*

(c) it is used independently, meaning 'different' or 'differently'.

Er ist ganz anders (als sein Bruder)	*He is quite different (from his brother)*
Es ist etwas anders[1]	*It's a bit different*
Es ist nicht viel anders	*It's not very different*
Wie anders das klingt!	*How different that sounds!*
Er hat es anders getan	*He did it differently*

Note:

i wenn anders *provided that* is archaic.

ii else, otherwise, if not=sonst (see 194(f)), e.g. sonst muß ich es selber tun; the use of anders in this sense is rare.

192. Some miscellaneous instances of the use of 'ander' and the rendering of 'other'

alles andere als	*anything but*
Er hat uns ganz andere Dinge erzählt	*He told us far worse/stranger things*
cf. e.g. ganz andere Szenen	*cf. far worse scenes*
ganz andere Schnitzer	* far worse howlers*
Es geht nicht anders	*It's got to be done, there's no other way*
Es war nicht anders zu erwarten	*One could expect nothing else*
Eins kommt zum andern	*It's not just one thing*
Ein Wort gab das andere	*One word led to another*
Er sagte kein Wort mehr	*He didn't say another word*
jeder außer dir	*anyone other than yourself*
Diese Männer sind Verbrecher wie andere auch	*These men are criminals like any others*

193. other, different, various, varied; distinguish the following:

Dies ist ein anderes Buch	*This is another (a different) book*
Er trank noch eine Tasse Kaffee	*He drank another cup of coffee*
Gibt es noch weitere Fragen?	*Are there any other questions?*
Er ist anders als sein Bruder	*He is different from his brother*
(less common: Er ist verschieden von seinem Bruder)	
Die zwei Brüder sind sehr verschieden	*The two brothers are very different*
Er reagierte anders	*He reacted differently*
Die zwei Brüder reagierten verschieden	*The two brothers reacted differently*
Der Lehrer gebrauchte verschiedene Methoden	*The teacher used various methods*
Die zwei Lehrer gebrauchten verschiedenartige Methoden	*The two teachers used different methods*
Wir besuchten die verschiedenen Museen	*We visited the different (various) museums*
ein abwechslungsreiches Programm	*a varied programme*

194. 'sonst' is a common variant for 'anders' in the sense of 'else' and for some other uses of 'ander'; this and the other uses of 'sonst' may conveniently be treated here.

(a) with etwas, alles, nichts, jemand and niemand, either word can be used, except where 'else' has a strong sense of 'different', when only 'ander(e)s' is used, as in the last two examples:

Kannst du etwas anderes/sonst etwas vorschlagen?	*Can you suggest anything else?*

---

[1] contrast: Es ist etwas and(e)res *It's something else.*

War noch jemand anders/sonst
(noch) jemand da?

Was anyone else there?

Niemand anders/Niemand sonst hat
mir geholfen (or: Sonst hat mir
niemand geholfen)[1]

No one else helped me

Mir hat er etwas anderes gesagt

He told me something else

Das ist Professor Neumann
und niemand anders

*That's Professor Neumann
and no one else*

(b) with 'wer?' either word can be used to denote 'what other person(s)',
but only 'sonst' to denote 'what further person(s)':

Wer anders kann es getan haben?/
Wer kann es sonst getan haben?
(commoner)

Who else can have done it?

Wer kommt sonst noch?

Who else is coming?

Mit wem hast du sonst (noch)
gesprochen?

With whom else did you speak?

(c) with 'was?', only 'sonst' is used:

Was soll ich denn sonst tun?

What else am I to do?

Was hat er sonst (noch) gesagt?

What else did he say?

(d) in conjunction with wo, wohin, woher, nirgendwo, either word can be
used; compare 191(b) with the following:

sonstwo, sonst irgendwo, irgendwo
sonst

somewhere else, anywhere else, elsewhere

Wo könnte es sonst sein?

Where else could it be?

wo auch (immer) sonst noch

wherever else

Ich muß noch sonstwohin

I still have to go somewhere else

Ich gehe sonst nirgendwo hin

I'm not going anywhere else

(e) in conjunction with a noun, either word can be used, meaning 'any
other':

Brauchst du noch (irgend)ein anderes
Buch/sonst noch (irgend)ein Buch?

Do you need any other book?

Wenn noch andere Probleme/sonst
noch Probleme auftauchen, . . .

If any other problems arise, . . .

(f) Some further uses of 'sonst':

sonst irgendwann

at some (or any) other time

und sonst noch allerhand

and all kinds of other things

Gibt es sonst noch Neues?

Is there any other news?

Sonst geht alles gut

Otherwise all is well

Wir müssen uns eilen, sonst verpassen
wir den Zug

*We must hurry up, otherwise we shall miss
the train*

länger als sonst

longer than usual

Er ist sonst viel lebhafter

He's usually much more lively

(g) **'ansonsten'** is an archaic variant of 'sonst', in the sense of
otherwise, else, in other respects, and is a current journalistic
'Modewort'.

Ansonsten aber war das Gemini-
Experiment ein voller Erfolg (*Die
Zeit* on American astronauts)

*But in other respects the gemini experiment
was a complete success*

[1] 'sonst' never immediately precedes 'niemand' or 'nichts' at the beginning of a sentence.

195. beide *both, two.*

(a) beide is frequently the equivalent of two, but only when it is preceded by the def. art., a demonstr. or possess. adj. or a personal pronoun: die beiden Brüder.

(b) Used after the def. art., a demonstr. or a possess. adj., beide has the weak endings: diese beiden (Männer), meiner beiden Brüder.

Otherwise, it is declined like dieser (apart from the exceptions noted in (c) below): beide Schwestern; sie sind beide krank; die Bewohner beider Stadtteile.

An attrib. or subst. adj. following beide has weak endings: beide neuen Lehrer; die Beschwerden (*complaints*) beider Angestellten.

(c) After a personal pron., beide has the weak endings:

i generally after the nominative ihr:

Ihr beiden/beide müßt mitkommen	*You two must come too*

ii always when placed between the nominatives wir, ihr and a noun:

wir beiden (alten) Freunde	*we two (old) friends*
wir beiden Heimatlosen	*we two homeless ones*

Otherwise, following a personal pron., it has strong endings:

wir beide	*we two*
für euch beide alten Freunde	*for you two old friends*
Ich habe sie beide gesehen	*I saw them both*

196. The use of the neut. sing. beides *both, either*

(a) Referring to persons, it is used colloquially as the subject of sind or waren + plural noun:

Ich habe mit den Brüdern Schmidt zu Mittag gegessen; beides (better: beide) sind Vegetarier	*I had lunch with the Schmidt brothers— they're both vegetarians*

(b) Referring to two different things, it may be more widely used; as subject it is followed by a singular verb, except before sind or waren + plural noun:

Das Hotel und die Landschaft:	*The hotel and the scenery:*
beides enttäuscht mich	*they both disappoint me*
beides ist wunderbar	*they are both wonderful*
beides sind Enttäuschungen	*they are both disappointments*

(c) Referring to two different small specific things, beides is only used as object, or as subject of sind or waren + plural noun:

Sie hatte einen Ring und eine Uhr und hat beides verloren	*She had a ring and a watch and she's lost them both*
Ihr Ring und ihre Uhr, beides waren (or: es waren beides) Wertgegenstände	*Her ring and her watch, both were valuables*

BUT:

Ihre zwei Ringe, sie hat beide verloren	*Her two rings—she's lost them both*
Der Ring und die Uhr, beide gefielen ihr	*The ring and the watch—she liked them both*

(d) Further examples of beides:

Ich will beides tun	*I'm going to do both things*
Beides ist möglich	*Either is possible*

(e) The neut. dat. beidem is only used referring to verbal nouns:

Kochen und Putzen, ich kann mit beidem nicht fertig werden	*Cooking and cleaning—I can't cope with either*
Der Ort und das Hotel, ich bin mit beiden zufrieden	BUT: *The place and the hotel—I'm satisfied with both*

197. Miscellaneous instances of the use of 'beide' and the rendering of 'both'

Wir waren alle beide enttäuscht[1]	*We were both of us disappointed*
Ich will alles beide(s) tun[1]	*I'm going to do both things*
Einer von beiden könnte uns helfen	*One/Either of the two could help us*
An beiden Enden des Ganges hängt ein Bild	*There's a picture at either end of the corridor*
in beiden Fällen	*in either case*
Keiner von beiden ist gekommen	*Neither of them has come*
Sowohl seine Frau als (auch) seine Tochter sind krank[2]	*Both his wife and his daughter are ill*

198. dergleichen, desgleichen

(a) dergleichen *of such a kind, suchlike*: indeclinable adjective and pronoun, e.g. dergleichen Behauptungen *suchlike assertions*, nichts dergleichen *no such thing*, und dergleichen (mehr) (u. dgl. (m.)) *and so forth*.

(b) desgleichen:
i *similar, suchlike*: indecl. adj. (less serviceable than 'dergleichen').
ii *in like manner, likewise*: adverb.
Ould wurde abgelöst (*was relieved*), der schläfrige Matrose auf dem Achterdeck (*quarter-deck*) desgleichen (E. Schnabel).

199. ein, einer *a, one, someone*

(a) For the declension of **ein** (*a* or *one*) + adj. + noun, see 90.

(b) **Used after the def. art., a demonstr. or possess. adj.:**
i **ein** *one* is declined like an ordinary adjective, whether followed by a noun or used pronominally.
ii ein is stressed.
iii a following attrib. or subst. adj. has the same endings as ein.

Der eine deutsche Tourist beschwerte sich	*The one German tourist complained*
Das eine Gute ist, daß er Mut hat	*The one good thing is that he has courage*
das eine, das ich brauche	*the one thing that I need*
Die Mutter des einen ist französisch	*The mother of the one is French*
die einen . . ., die andern	*some . . ., others*
Mit dieser einen Hand konnte er Wunder tun	*With this one hand he could do wonders*
Ihr eines neues Kleid ist blau	*Her one new dress is blue*

---

[1] colloquial and emphatic.
[2] cf. 523 ff.

(c) **Used as a pronoun, with no preceding def. art., demonstr. or possess.,** ein is declined like dieser, i.e. like the indef. art. except for masc. nom. einer and neut. nom. and acc. eines, usually pronounced and written 'eins'.

Einer (commoner: Irgendeiner) muß es getan haben	*Someone must have done it*
Ist einer (commoner: irgendeiner) bereit, mir zu helfen?	*Is anyone ready to help me?*

einer der Männer; einer von uns; einer, der ihn kannte, hat ihn mir beschrieben; ein Fenster war offen, und eins war zu; eins von Karls Büchern; ich sprach mit einer der Damen; ich besorge das alles in einem.

Note:

i The gen. 'eines' is literary and is little used except before a gen. plur.:

Dies war der Eindruck eines Menschen, der ihn kannte/eines seiner Freunde	*This was the impression of one who knew him/of one of his friends*

ii The neut. 'eins' may be used where an alternative male or female reference is required:

Die beiden alten Geschwister lebten zusammen; eins half dem andern	*The old brother and sister lived together; one helped the other*

200. Some idiomatic uses of 'einer' and 'eins' and renderings of 'one'

Das ist einer!	*He's quite a lad*
Du bist mir einer!	*You're a nice one!*
Er ist belesen wie selten einer (from Du. Stil.)	*He's uncommonly well read*
Eins wollt' ich noch sagen	*There's one more thing I wanted to say*
Trinken wir noch eins!	*Let's have another one (i.e. glass)*
einen heben	*to drink (lit. raise) a glass of beer, etc.*
Ich hab' ihm eins/eine [Ohrfeige] gegeben	*I gave him one (a blow/a box on the ears)*
Es ist mir alles eins	*It's all the same to me*
Es läuft auf eins hinaus	*It comes to one and the same thing*
Er redet in einem fort	*He talks without stopping*
ein gewisser Pinneberg	*one Pinneberg*
Ich bin keiner, der sich leicht beklagt	*I'm not one to complain easily*
Sie waren alle miteinander zufrieden	*One and all were satisfied*
Das Kind ist ihr ein und alles	*The child is her one and all*
Er ist mein einziger Freund	*He's my one (i.e. only) friend*

201. Note:

i For further information on the numeral eins, see 241.
ii For man *one, you, they, people* (cf. Fr. on), see 216.

202. (a) **ein und derselbe** *one and the same*
     (b) **ein oder der andere** *one or another*

In both, 'ein' is generally uninflected:

An ein und demselben Tag machten drei Firmen Pleite	*On one and the same day three firms went bankrupt*

Ein (or: Einer) oder der andere machte   *One or another made a short remark*
eine kurze Bemerkung
Ich kaufte noch ein oder das andere   *I bought one or two things more*

203. ein bißchen (dialectally ein bissel, ein bisserl) *a little*; generally uninflected, a following adjective having the strong endings: Ich hatte noch ein bißchen deutsches Geld, mit ein bißchen Geld, BUT: die Wirkung eines bißchen gesunden Humors (commoner: von).

Note:

i The 'ein' may be replaced by das, a demonstr. or possess. adj., which are duly declined: mit ihrem bißchen Talent.

ii its common adverbial use: *a bit, somewhat, rather*: ein (klein) bißchen schneller, ein bißchen spät, ich will ein bißchen lesen.

204. ein paar *a few* (often pronounced 'n paar)[1]

(a) It is indeclinable; a following adjective, whether attributive or substantival, has strong endings: ein paar hundert Pfund, mit ein paar Freunden, ein paar gute Bücher, ein paar Vorübergehende *a few passers-by*.
There is a tendency to avoid using it in the gen.: mit der Hilfe von ein paar alten Freunden.

(b) If 'paar' is preceded not by 'ein', but by the def. art., a demonstr. or possess. adj., these are declined and the gen. is freely used:

Was soll ich mit den paar Mark   *What am I to do with these few marks?*
anfangen?
der Wert meiner paar Möbel   *the value of my few bits of furniture*

(c) the translation of 'few' and 'a few':

Er hat ein paar/einige Freunde   *He has a few friends*
Er hat wenige Freunde   *He has few friends*
Ich habe ganz viele Bücher   *I've got a good few books*
alle paar Stunden   *every few hours*

205. einige

(a) **In the singular (einiger, einige, einiges)**:

i it means *some, a certain amount (of)*.

ii it is declined like dieser, except in the masc. and neut. gen., which are einigen.

iii a following attrib. or subst. adj. usually has the weak endings.

iv it is used as follows, 1–4 being common uses, 5–7 relatively restricted:

1. before Entfernung and Zeit, e.g. in einiger Entfernung (von), vor einiger Zeit.

2. before a neuter substantival adjective:

Er hat einiges Interessante erzählt   *He related a few interesting things*
Er hat einiges Nützliche getan   *He did some useful things*

3. as a neuter collective:

Ich habe noch einiges zu tun   *I've still got a certain amount to do*
einiges davon   *some of it*

---

[1] Collinson, op. cit., p. 61.

4. before a good many abstract nouns, e.g.

Seine Rede hat einigen Eindruck gemacht	*His speech made a certain amount of impression*
Er zeigte einige Energie	*He showed a certain amount of energy*
Hierin habe ich einige Erfahrung	*I have some experience of this*
mit einiger Sicherheit	*with some certainty*
mit einiger Ungeduld (V. Baum)	*with some impatience*
bei einigem guten Willen (Th. Mann, quoted in Du. Gram. 2120)	*with a certain amount of good will*

5. before a few collectives:

Er hatte einiges Gepäck bei sich	*He had a certain amount of luggage with him*
Ich hatte noch einiges Geld	*I still had a certain amount of money*

6. occasionally, before an infinitive used as a noun:

nach einigem mühsamen Graben	*after some hard digging*
nach einigem Überlegen	*after some reflection*

7. before some nouns with the prefix Ge-, formed from verbs and denoting a protracted activity:

Immerhin erregte es doch einiges Gemurmel (H. Fallada)	*Nevertheless it caused a certain amount of muttering*
cf. einiges Geschwätz/einiges Geflüster	*a certain amount of gossip/of whispering*

(b) **In the plural (einige):**

   i it means *some*, *a few* and is widely used, both pronominally and adjectivally.

   ii it is declined like dieser and a following attrib. or subst. adj. usually has the strong endings (cf. 113(b)).

Einige mußten stehen	*Some had to stand*
einige tausend Bücher	*a few thousand books*
einige fünfzig Bücher	*some fifty books or more*
Es ist das Streben einiger weniger, aber doch vorhandener Zeitgenossen, ihren Pkw zum 'Statussymbol' zu erheben (*Wochenpost*, Ostberlin)	*It is the aim of some few of our contemporaries, who nevertheless do exist, to make their car a status symbol*

206. etwas (indeclinable)

(a) **something, anything**

Etwas störte mich	*Something disturbed me*
Hat er etwas gesagt?	*Did he say anything?*

For etwas Neues *something new*, see 111: type (a).

(b) **some, any, a little**; a following attrib. adj. has the strong endings:

Ich brauche etwas (frisches) Fleisch	*I need some (fresh) meat*
Hast du etwas Butter?	*Have you any butter?*
etwas von seinem Geld	*some of his money*
etwas davon	*some of it*

(c) etwas is not used in the genitive; even when it is followed by an adjective, which would show the case, 'von' is more usual:

der Genuß von etwas frischem Obst	*the eating of some fresh fruit*

(d) **etwas and was**

i In conversation, etwas meaning *something, anything* is more often than not shortened to was:

Hat er was (Interessantes) gesagt?   *Did he say anything (interesting)?*

ii In the nom. was can be used only if preceded by 'so' or followed by a subst. adj.:

So was interessiert mich   *Anything like that interests me*
Was Erfrischendes (commoner: etwas   *Something refreshing would do us good*
Erfrischendes) würde uns gut tun

(e) For irgend etwas, irgendwas *something (or other)*, *anything (at all)*, see 207(c); for so etwas, so was *something like this*, see 304(d).

(f) not . . . anything = nichts; not . . . any = kein.
Ich habe heute nichts getan   *I haven't done anything today*
Ich brauche kein Fleisch   *I don't need any meat*

(g) etwas is much used adverbially meaning **somewhat, a bit**: Er ist etwas nervös; es geht ihm etwas besser; er zögerte etwas *he hesitated slightly*.

(h) etwas must not be confused with the adverb and particle etwa (see 295).

207. irgend: adverb, signifying or emphasizing indefiniteness

(a) **Used as an independent adverb,** it has the sense of irgendwie *somehow, anyhow, in any way*:[1]

Wenn es irgend geht, wäre ich froh   *If it's somehow possible, I should be glad*
wenn irgend möglich   *if at all possible*
Die Gelegenheit war so günstig wie nur   *The opportunity was as favourable as it*
irgend möglich (Ompteda)[2]   *could possibly have been*

(b) When **prefixed to the interrog. adverbs wann, wie, wo, wohin, woher,** it converts them into indef. adverbs:

irgendwann   *some time or other; any time*
irgendwie   *somehow; anyhow*
Du mußt es irgendwie machen   *You must do it somehow*
Du kannst es irgendwie machen   *You can do it any way you like*
irgendwo   *somewhere; anywhere*
Er geht heute nachmittag irgendwohin   *He's going somewhere or other this afternoon*
irgendwoher   *from somwhere; from anywhere*
N.B. Ich gehe nirgendwohin   *I'm not going anywhere*
(or nirgendswohin)

(c) **It increases the indefiniteness of jemand** *someone, anyone*, **etwas and was** *something, anything*; irgendeiner (see (f) below) and irgendwer *someone, anyone* are commoner than einer and wer used in this sense (see 199(c) and 173(d)):

Irgend jemand muß dich gesehen   *Someone (or other) must have seen you*
haben
Hier ist irgend jemands Schirm   *Here is someone or other's umbrella*

---

[1] noted by Stopp, op. cit., 62(c).
[2] example quoted by Eggeling, op. cit., p. 202.

Irgendwann wurden von irgendwem diese . . . Briefe aus dem Kasten genommen (H. Böll)	*At some time or other these letters were taken out of the letter-box by someone or other*
Versteht er irgend etwas/irgendwas vom Wein?	*Does he know anything (at all) about wine?*
irgend so etwas	*something/anything like this*

Note:

i For practical purposes:

jemand *someone*; irgend jemand *someone (or other)*, *anyone (at all)*

etwas *something*; irgend etwas (irgendwas) *something (or other)*, *anything (at all)*

ii an irgend etwas and irgendworan:

With a number of common prepositions, the second alternative is sometimes found and heard, but its use is very limited and it is not to be recommended:

Ich habe mich an irgend etwas (irgendworan) gestoßen	*I knocked against something or other*
Ist das zu irgend etwas (irgendwozu) zu gebrauchen?	*Can that be used for anything?*

(d) **irgendein** is an indefinite adjective meaning *some (or other)*, *any (whatsoever)*; it is declined like ein and a following adjective is declined as after ein (cf. 90); its plural is irgendwelche (see (e) below).

Er zeigte mir irgendein (neues) Buch	*He showed me some (new) book or other*
Machte er irgendeine Bemerkung?	*Did he make any remark?*
Irgendein anderer antwortete	*Someone else answered*

(e) **irgendwelcher -e -es** *some (or other)*, *any (whatsoever)* has the endings of dieser and a following attrib. or subst. adj. has the weak endings, with some fluctuation in the gen. plur. It is used in the following instances:

i as the plural of irgendein (cf. (d) above):

Er zeigte mir irgendwelche (neuen) Bücher	*He showed me some (new) books (or other)*
der Besuch irgendwelcher Verwandten	*the visit of some relatives*

ii instead of irgendein (sing.):

1. before collective nouns which are not used after the indef. art.:

irgendwelches magere Vieh	*some lean cattle (or other)*

2. before the names of substances and abstract nouns, unless they are individualized, when 'irgendein' is more usual:

Haben wir irgendwelchen Käse im Haus?	*Have we some cheese of any sort in the house?*
Er hat mir irgendeinen neuen Käse empfohlen	BUT: *He recommended some new cheese or other*
Wenn ich irgendwelche Angst hätte, . . .	*If I felt any fear, . . .*
ohne irgendwelche Schwierigkeit	*without any difficulty*
Es gab irgendeine unerwartete Schwierigkeit	BUT: *There was some unexpected difficulty or other*

'von' is preferred to the genitive:

die Folge von irgendwelchem unnötigen Zögern	*the consequence of any unnecessary hesitation*

3. colloquially, before the names of concrete objects, where irgendein is the correct German:

Er hat mir irgendwelche Broschüre gegeben	*He gave me some brochure or other*

(f) **irgendein may be used pronominally**: irgendeiner, -eine, -eines; plur.: irgendwelche; the gen. sing. is only used before a gen. plur., as in the last example:

Irgendeiner muß dich gesehen haben	*Someone (or other) must have seen you*
Ich habe mehrere Bücher über München; Sie können irgendeins/ irgendwelche haben	*I've got several books about Munich; you can have any one/any (ones) you like*
Nennen Sie mir den Titel irgendeines seiner Romane	*Give me the title of any (one) of his novels*

(g) **irgend so ein** (plur. irgend solche) *one/some of those, any/some such* (frequently pejorative):

Wer war es?—Es war irgend so ein Vertreter für Waschmittel (Du. Stil.)	*Who was it?—It was one of those men selling washing powders*
Er machte irgend solche komischen Bemerkungen	*He made some such strange remarks*

Pronominally (sing. only): irgend so einer *some fellow of that sort.*

(h) **Orthography**: irgend and the word with which it is used are written as one word (e.g. irgendwie, irgendein, irgendwelche) with four exceptions: 1. when irgend is used as an independent adverb (see (a) above) 2. irgend jemand 3. irgend etwas (BUT: irgendwas) 4. irgend so ein, irgend solche.

208. jeder *each, every;*[1] *everyone, everybody*

(a) Used adjectivally, it is declined like dieser; exc.: masc. and neut. gen. sing. are occasionally jeden (see 89 N.i). An attrib. adj. following jeder has the weak endings.

das Törchen jedes (kleinen) Gartens	*the gate of every (little) garden*
Funktionäre jeden Ranges (*Spiegel*, quoted in Du. Gram. 2955)	*civil servants of every grade*

(b) Used pronominally, it is declined like dieser, but is not used in the gen.; the masc. jeder and the neut. jedes may have common gender:

Jeder muß um ein Uhr bereit sein	*Everyone must be ready at one o'clock*
Seine Eltern waren sehr tüchtig, jedes auf seine Weise	*His parents were very able, each in their own way*

Note the appositional use:[2]

Meine Brüder schenkten mir jeder ein Buch	*My brothers each gave me a book*

(c) Used after the indef. art., mainly pronominally, jeder has the mixed declension. 'Ein jeder' is a slightly emphatic variant for jeder and

---

[1] see also 239(b).
[2] cf. Schulz-Griesbach, op. cit., D 848.

usefully supplies the missing gen. of the pronominal jeder (cf. (b) above):

Ein jeder wollte was sagen	*Everyone wanted to say something*
Die Wünsche eines jeden (or: jedes einzelnen) wurden berücksichtigt	*The wishes of every individual were taken into account*

(d) While correctly jeder can only be used in the sing., colloquially it is often used instead of 'alle' in phrases of this type: jede fünf Minuten, jede paar Jahre, jede zehn Schritte; also: in jeden Ferien[1] (*in*) *every holiday*

209. jedermann *everyone, everybody* takes a singular verb and inflects only in the gen. (jedermanns). It is less used than 'jeder'.

Jedermann/Jeder hatte die Nachricht gehört	*Everyone had heard the news*
Er zeigt jedermann/jedem seine neue Uhr	*He shows everyone his new watch*
Das ist nicht jedermanns Sache	*That's not everyone's line*

210. jedweder *each, every; everyone*: (a) it is declined and used like 'jeder' with two exceptions: 1. its gen. sing. before a masc. or neut. noun of Groups 1–6 can only be 'jedweden' 2. it is not used after the indef. art. (b) it is archaic, emphatic and confined to elevated style, e.g.

Nutznießer . . . jedweden Luxus (Th. Mann, quoted in Du. Gram. 2965)	*beneficiaries of every luxury*

211. jeglicher *each, every, any; everyone*: (a) it is declined and used like 'jeder', but its gen. sing. before a masc. or neut. noun of Groups 1–6 can only be 'jeglichen'. (b) it is obsolescent, rarely heard in modern conversation, but still used in literary language as an effective and emphatic variant:

. . . Verständlichkeitsstörungen, die jegliche Deutung nahezu jeglicher Szene zulassen (from a film review in the *Hbg. Abendblatt*)	*. . . lapses in intelligibility which allow any interpretation of almost every scene*

212. jemand *someone, somebody*; **niemand** *no one, nobody, not . . . anyone*

(a) Declension

N.	jemand	niemand
A.	jemand, jemanden	niemand, niemanden
G.	jemand(e)s	niemand(e)s
D.	jemand, jemandem	niemand, niemandem

In the acc. and dat., both forms are used in conversation, but the inflected form predominates in literary German.

Ich habe heute niemand (or niemanden) gesehen; ich habe jemand (or jemandem) das Paket gegeben.

Examples of genitive:

Ist das nicht jemandes Aktentasche? (Commoner: Hat nicht jemand diese Aktentasche liegenlassen?)

[1] mentioned by Stopp, op. cit., 83(b)(2)

Es scheint niemandes Sache zu sein, hierfür zu sorgen (Commoner: Es scheint niemanden anzugehen, hierfür zu sorgen.)

(b) jemand/niemand + adj.: the following is the commonest usage, both colloquial and literary; deviations will cause no difficulty of comprehension.

    N.A.   jemand/niemand Intelligentes
    G.   (avoid)
    D.   jemand/niemand Intelligentem

Das ist der Brief von jemand Intelligentem	*That's the letter of someone intelligent*

Note: someone/anyone/no one else: here 'anders' is rather more common than 'anderem' in the dat.: mit jemand/niemand anders; see 191(a) and 194(a).

(c) Miscellaneous

so jemand	*someone like that*
Das tut/sagt/weiß kein Mensch	*Nobody does/says/knows that* (idiomatic)
niemand als mein Bruder	*no one but my brother*
Er ist eine Null	*He's a nobody* (*a mere cipher*)

(d) For irgend jemand *someone* (*or other*), *anyone* (*at all*), see 207(c).

213. kein, keiner *not a, no, not any; no one, none*

(a) Used adjectivally, kein is declined like ein in the sing. and like dieser in the plur.; a following attrib. or subst. adj. has the mixed declension:

Es war kein angenehmer Anblick	*It wasn't a pleasant sight*
Kein Erwachsener war zugegen	*No adult was present*
Kennst du keine Deutschen?	*Don't you know any Germans?*

(b) Used pronominally, it is declined like dieser, but 1. it is not used in the gen. and 2. in the neut. nom. and acc. 'keins' is commoner than 'keines' in conversation.

Keiner im Dorf wollte was sagen; keiner von uns (euch etc.); haben Sie ein Radio? Nein, wir haben keins; keins der neuen Häuser (or: von den neuen Häusern); keiner von beiden *neither of them.*

Note: The neut. keins (von beiden) is used to refer to a small group, or a pair, of different sexes, e.g. Ich fragte meine Geschwister/meine Eltern, aber keins (von beiden) hatte davon gehört.

214. kein and nicht

(a) kein is used even where the corresponding affirmative statement does not contain an indef. art.: Er hat (kein) Geld; er ist (kein) Arzt; er hat (keine) Arbeit gefunden;[1] wir hatten (keine) Schwierigkeiten;[2] haben wir keine frischen Brötchen?[3]

(b) Where an object is so closely connected with the verb that it is felt as the equivalent of a sep. prefix, nicht is used in the negative version:

---

[1] cf. Schulz-Griesbach, op. cit., J 261.
[2] cf. Schulz-Griesbach, op. cit., H 735.
[3] cf. N. A. Bulach: Zum Wesen und Gebrauch der Negation 'kein' (*Deutsch als Fremdsprache*, 6/1968).

Er spielt nicht Klavier; er läuft nicht Schi; er hat in Berlin nicht Wurzel gefaßt. Sometimes either nicht or kein may be used: Er spricht nicht/kein Deutsch; wir haben heute nicht/kein Tennis gespielt; er hat nicht/keinen Abschied von mir genommen. Sometimes only kein is idiomatic: Ich habe keine Lust, es zu tun; er hat sich keine Mühe gegeben.

(c) The idiomatic penchant for kein is illustrated by the following examples, in the first three of which nicht instead of kein would be perfectly correct:

Er ist noch keine zehn Jahre alt	*He's not yet ten*
Es ist noch keine acht Uhr	*It's not yet eight o'clock*
Er ist noch keine fünf Minuten hier	*He hasn't been here five minutes*
keine zwei Stunden vor meiner Abreise	*within two hours of my departure*
Er ist kein Kind mehr	*He's no longer a child*

(d) When the sentence opens with an emphatically placed complement or object and this is to be negatived, it may be done either by means of nicht or by means of keiner, placed later in the sentence; keiner is regional and colloquial (cf. Du. Gram. 2980):

Ein Diplomat ist er nicht	*He's no diplomat*
Ein Diplomat ist er keiner	
Geld habe ich nicht	*I haven't got any money*
Geld habe ich keins	

215. kein and nicht ein

(a) After wenn *if*, nicht ein is more usual than kein: Man hätte ihn kaum bemerkt, wenn ihm nicht ein Schnurrbart etwas Distinguiertes verliehen hätte.

(b) nicht ein is sometimes used before sondern: Dieses Buch ist nicht ein Roman, sondern eine Biographie.

(c) nicht ein may be used to render 'not one', ein being stressed:

Nicht *ein* Junge wußte die Antwort	*Not one boy knew the answer*
Einer kann das nicht zustandebringen	cf. *No one man can achieve that*

216. man *one, you, they, people etc.* (cf. French 'on')

(a) Forms N. man (derived from 'ein Mann')
A. einen (borrowed from 'einer')
G. (none)
D. einem (borrowed from 'einer')
REFLEXIVE: sich
POSSESSIVE: sein *one's* (not used in nom.)

(b) Examples   NOM.

Man sollte nichts riskieren	*One shouldn't risk anything*
Als man sich zum Abendcsscn setzte, fehlte der alte Herr	*When they (or we) sat down for supper, the old gentleman was missing*

ACC.

Man weiß nie, ob er einen erkannt hat	*You never know if he's recognized you*

DAT.

So leid es einem tut, man muß manchmal hart sein	*However much you regret it, you sometimes have to be hard*

REFLEXIVE

Man hat sich nach dir erkundigt	*People have been inquiring about you*

POSSESSIVE

Verwandte können lästig sein	*One's relatives can be a nuisance*
Die Ansichten, die man hat, sind selten originell	*One's opinions are rarely original*
Man sollte seinen Freunden helfen	*One should help one's friends*

(c) Note:

i Not infrequently, the object 'einen' is omitted:

durch einen ... Nebel, der [einen] nur ein paar Schritte weit sehen ließ (G. Gaiser)	*through a fog that only let one see a few steps ahead*

ii It is well to be aware of the North German colloquial adverb 'man' *only, just*; a sometimes untranslatable expletive, it is often close to 'einmal, mal':

Das ist man en bißchen wenig	*That's (only) rather little*
Geh du man vor!	*You just go ahead*
Der hat's man eilig	*He's in a hurry, isn't he?*

217. mancher; uninflected: manch

(a) **Meanings**

SING.: *many a (man, one)*; *quite a lot of things*

PLUR.: *some* (frequently: some as opposed to others)

many, quite a number of (slightly poetic and fewer than 'viele')

(b) **The inflected mancher -e -es**

i Used as a pronoun, it is declined like dieser, but is not used in the genitive:

Mancher hat es nicht geglaubt	*Many a man did not believe it*
Das ist schon manchem passiert	*That has happened to many a man*
Ich habe noch manches zu tun	*I still have quite a lot of things to do*
Manche (Leute) trinken Tee, manche (or andere) trinken Kaffee	*Some (people) drink tea, some (or others) drink coffee*
Manche meiner Bekannten (or: von meinen Bekannten)	*some of my acquaintances*

ii Used adjectivally, it is declined like dieser; one exception: masc. and neut. gen. sing. are frequently manchen (see 89 N.i). An attrib. or subst. adj. following mancher has the weak endings, though strong endings are also found and heard in the plural:

manches Reich	*many an empire*
die Geschichte manchen Reiches	*the history of many an empire*
manches Studenten (Group 7 Noun)	*of many a student*
An manchen Tagen bleibt er im Bett	*On some days he stays in bed*
die Schwierigkeiten manchen/manches jungen Lehrers	*the difficulties of many a young teacher*
Ich habe manche schönen/schöne Tage in Deutschland verlebt	*I have spent many happy days in Germany*
manche Arbeiter und Angestellte (*Die Welt*)	*some workers and employees*

iii mancher is frequently preceded by gar or so (cf. Du. Gram. 2990):

gar strengthens it quantitatively and is rather literary; so is expletive and normal:

Gar mancher erinnert sich daran	*Many a man (indeed) remembers it*
so mancher junge Lehrer	*many a young teacher*
so manches Mal	*many a time*

(c) **The uninflected manch** may be used before the following; in the case of iii, iv and v manch is archaic or poetic in flavour:

i einer (pronominal); not used in the gen.:

Manch einer (commoner: Mancher) hat es nicht geglaubt	*Many a man did not believe it*

ii ein (+adj.)+noun:

manch ein (erfahrener) Arzt (commoner: mancher (erfahrene) Arzt)	*many an (experienced) doctor*

iii adj.+noun; the adjective has strong endings:

manch reiches Land	*many a rich land*
manch reiche Länder	*many rich lands*

iv a subst. adj., which has the strong endings; not used in the gen. sing.:

Manch anderer hätte uns nicht geholfen	*Many another would not have helped us*
Er hat manch Gutes getan	*He has done many good things*

v certain neut. nouns in the nom. and acc. sing., e.g.:

manch Abenteuer (from Du. Gram. 2995), manch Fest, manch Mädchen

218. meinesgleichen *people like me, the likes of me, my equal(s)*: indeclinable pronoun, e.g.

Ich und meinesgleichen interessieren uns für so was nicht.

Mit mir und meinesgleichen spricht er nie.

cf. deinesgleichen, seinesgleichen, unseresgleichen, euresgleichen, ihresgleichen, Ihresgleichen.

219. nichts *nothing, not anything*[1] (coll. also nix; S. German: nit)

(a) It is invariable and may be used in the nom. and acc. and, after a preposition, in the dat.

Aus nichts wird nichts	*Nothing produces nothing* (proverb)
nichts als Schwierigkeiten	*nothing but difficulties*

(b) For nichts Neues *nothing new*, see 111; cf. nichts Besseres; ich kann mit nichts anderem schreiben.

220. niemand: see 212.

221. sämtlich *all (without exception), complete*

(a) Use and endings:

    i When not preceded by a def. art., demonstr. or possess. adj., it has the strong declension and a following adjective then commonly has the weak endings with some fluctuation in the gen. plur.

---

[1] For an account of the historical origins of nichts and of the true nature of a following subst. adj., see Eggeling, op. cit., nichts.

ii It is not much used in the singular.

iii The last example in (b) below illustrates its uninflected use.

(b) Examples:

Sämtliche neuen Häuser sind verkauft.	*All the new houses are sold*
Goethes sämtliche Werke	*Goethe's complete works*
Meine sämtlichen Verwandten haben mir geschrieben	*All my relatives (without exception) wrote to me*
sämtliche politische Propaganda	*all political propaganda*
Sie haben es sämtlich bestätigt	*They confirmed it, one and all*

222. solcher *such*; uninflected: solch

(a) The inflected solcher -e -es

i Except after jeder, mancher, ein and kein, solcher is declined like dieser (though the masc. and neut. gen. is frequently solchen: cf. 89 N.i) and a following attrib. or subst. adj. has the weak endings:

solches (gute) Wetter	*such (good) weather*
Ich habe solchen Durst	*I'm so thirsty*
Der Stoff als solcher gefällt mir	*I like the material as such*
Bist du mit deinen neuen Schuhen zufrieden? Ich habe auch solche	*Are you satisfied with your new shoes? I've got some like that too*

ii After jeder and mancher, solcher has weak endings, except that after manche (nom. and acc. plur.) the strong form solche is commoner; a following adjective has weak endings throughout:

jeder solche (kühne) Gedanke	*every such (bold) idea*
manche solche deutschen Bücher	*some such German books*

iii After ein and kein, solcher and a following adjective have the mixed endings:

ein solches dummes Spiel; mit keiner solchen (persönlichen) Freiheit; ein solcher ist für die Stellung nicht geeignet

(b) The uninflected solch

i A following attrib. adj. has mixed endings if the phrase contains ein or kein; otherwise strong endings.

ii It may be used in the following cases:

1. before the indef. art. (commoner: so ein): solch ein Wetter, solch ein großes Haus.

2. before an attrib. adj. (somewhat literary; commoner: so): solch gutes Wetter, ein solch großes Haus, mit solch unermüdlichem Eifer.

3. colloquially, before certain neut. nouns in the nom. and acc. sing.: Solch Wetter ist wirklich furchtbar; ein solch Gespräch; ein solch Gefühl.

223. 'so' is much used to render 'such', particularly in conversation

(cf. the commoner alternatives given in 222(b)ii). It may be used:

(a) before ein+noun or +subst. adj. and before einer (pronominal):

so ein Geschenk	*such a present*
in so einer Stadt	*in such a town*

so ein Armer	*such a poor man*
(Commonest plur.: solche armen Leute	*such poor people*)
so einer (or: ein solcher)	*such a man, a man like that*
(Commonest plur.: solche Männer	*such men*)

Note: 'so ein' is often pronounced 'so'n', e.g. in so'ner Stadt (cf. Collinson op. cit. p. 53).

(b) before adj.+noun, with or without ein, or before a subst. adj.:

ein so großes Haus	*such a big house*
so ein großes Haus	
so große Häuser	*such big houses*
bei so gutem Wetter	*in such good weather*
Er sagt immer so Komisches	*He always says such funny things*

Note: In the first example, the order 'so ein großes Haus' is more collo-quial than 'ein so großes Haus'; further, it may convey 'a big house like that', e.g.: So ein großes Haus macht viel Arbeit; cf. So ein kleines Kind (not: ein so kleines Kind) sagt die drolligsten Dinge.

(c) between kein and adj.+noun:

Es ist keine so wichtige Sache	*It's not such an important matter*

(d) so etwas, so was: *such a thing, something like that.*

224. Note:

i For such-and-such (a one), see 165 x.
ii such as=wie zum Beispiel; see also 142.
iii travelling as such (or in itself): das Reisen an (und für) sich.

225. unsereiner (fem. unsereine) *people like us, people of our social class,*[1] *the likes of us* is sing. only, with the endings of dieser, but is not used in the gen. The neut. nom. and acc. unsereins is used colloquially for either sex.

Unsereiner (Unsereins) kann das nicht wissen	*People like us can't know that*
Er würde unsereine (unsereins) nie heiraten	*He would never marry the likes of us*
Mit unsereinem spricht er nie	*He never speaks to people like us*

226. viel, viele *much, many*; **wenig, wenige** *little, few*

Used substantivally in the neut. sing. they have the following forms:

N.A.	viel or vieles	wenig or weniges
G.	(not used)	
D.	viel or vielem	wenig or wenigem

The uninflected forms are more general and collective in their connota-tion, the inflected forms more particular and distributive.

This distinction is succinctly made by Betteridge (op. cit.: viel) with the tag 'nicht vieles, sondern viel': non multa, sed multum. Further examples:

Er ist mit wenig zufrieden	*He is content with little*
Mit vielem bin ich nicht ein-verstanden	*There's much that I don't agree with*

[1] Eggeling's apposite rendering (op. cit., p. 126).

Used substantivally in the plur. they are declined like dieser: wenige dieser Bücher; die Hoffnungen vieler wurden enttäuscht.

227. viel (wenig) + noun: commonest usage:

SINGULAR

MASC. AND NEUT.	FEM.
N. viel, wenig	viel, wenig
A. viel, wenig	viel, wenig
(Exc. Vielen Dank!)	
G. vielen; commoner: von vielem	vieler
von wenig	weniger (or: von wenig)
D. i after a preposition:	
viel, wenig	viel, wenig
ii without a preposition:	
vielem, wenigem	vieler, (weniger) (if 'weniger' might mean 'less', it must be circumvented)

PLURAL

N.	viele (viel)	wenige, wenig
A.	viele (viel)	wenige, wenig
G.	vieler	weniger
D.	vielen (viel)	wenigen (wenig)

Note on the plural forms:
i The uninflected forms are more general and collective, stressing sheer quantity, the inflected forms more particular and distributive (cf. Du. Gram. 3030); this distinction is not, however, consistently observed.
ii In time phrases the inflected forms are used, e.g. Die Firma bestand nur wenige Jahre; vor vielen Jahren.

EXAMPLES:

NOM. SING.
Dazu ist viel Mut nötig — *Much courage is needed for that*

ACC. SING.
Ich trinke wenig Milch — *I drink little milk*

GEN. SING.
der Genuß vielen Obstes — *the eating of much fruit*
der Genuß von vielem Obst
das Ergebnis vielen Nachdenkens — *the result of much reflection*
die Wirkung von bloß wenig Wein — *the effect of only a little wine*
infolge vieler/weniger Opposition — *as a result of much/little opposition*

DAT. SING.
Er handelte mit viel Geschick — *He acted with much skill*
mit wenig Zucker — *with little sugar*
Er hat vielem Übel vorgebeugt — *He forestalled much evil*
Er begegnete vieler Opposition — *He met with much opposition*
Er widerspricht jetzt in geringem Maße der Kritik[1] — *He now rebuffs little criticism*

---

[1] 'weniger' could mean 'less' and is therefore circumvented.

Nom. Plur.
Viele Probleme wurden besprochen   *Many problems were discussed*
Acc. Plur.
Er hat viel (or viele) Freunde   *He has many friends*
Gen. Plur.
die Reden vieler Politiker   *the speeches of many politicians*
Dat. Plur.
mit vielen Ausnahmen   *with many exceptions*
mit ganz wenig Ausnahmen[1]   *with very few exceptions*

228. viel (wenig) + adj. + noun: commonest usage:

Singular

viel (wenig) uninflected; adj. has the strong endings (von + dat. is more
used than the gen.; see Variations below).

Examples:

Nom.
Viel indischer Tee wird in England   *Much Indian tea is drunk in England*
  getrunken
Acc.
Ich habe wenig moderne Kunst   *I have seen little modern art*
  gesehen
Gen.
der Genuß viel frischen Obstes   *the eating of much fresh fruit*
infolge viel unerwarteter Opposition   *as a result of much unexpected opposition*
Dat.
mit viel kaltem Wasser   *with a lot of cold water*
nach viel unnötigem Zögern   *after much unnecessary hesitation*
Ich mißtraue so viel abstrakter   *I distrust so much abstract theory*
  Theorie

Variations
In the gen. some Germans give viel (wenig) the strong endings and the
  adjective -en, but -er before fem. abstract nouns: die Wirkung vielen
  frischen Obstes, vieler guten Milch, vieler scharfer Kritik. **Far commoner than the gen. is von + dat.**: die Wirkung von viel frischem
  Obst, von viel scharfer Kritik.
In the dat., before abstract nouns, some Germans give viel (wenig) the
  strong endings and the adjective -en in the masc. and neut., -er in the
  fem.: nach vielem unnötigen Zögern; ich mißtraue so vieler abstrakter
  Theorie.

Plural

viele (wenige) and the adjective have the strong endings.

In the gen., some Germans give the adjective the weak ending -en;
  colloquially, von + dat. is again preferred. For example, see 113(b).

229. viele (wenige) + attrib. adj. + subst. adj. in the plur.: see 113(b),
  substituting viele (wenige) for mehrere.

[1] from Du. Gram. 3030.

230. Declension of viel (wenig) + neut. subst. adj. in the sing.:

N.A.   viel Gutes (vieles Gute), wenig Nützliches
G.   der Eindruck vieles Guten (commoner: von viel Gutem), von wenig
      Nützlichem
D.   außer viel Gutem (vielem Guten), wenig Nützlichem

231. viel and wenig may be used substantively or adjectivally after the def. art., a demonstrative or a possessive; they then have the ordinary adjective endings:

Ich staunte über das viele, was er erledigt hatte	*I was amazed at the large number of matters that he had seen to*
Ich staunte über das viele Geld, das er ausgab	*I was amazed at the large amount of money that he spent*
die wenigen, die ihn erkannten	*the few who recognized him*
Er war mit diesem wenigen zufrieden	*He was satisfied with this small amount*
Sie hat ihr weniges Geld verloren (Commoner: ihr bißchen Geld)	*She has lost her small amount of money*

232. ein wenig *a little* is invariable; it is not used before a genitive; a following attributive adjective has strong endings. E.g.

Ich habe mich ein wenig ausgeruht; die Sehnsucht ... nach ein wenig Freundschaft (Th. Mann); mit ein wenig weiblicher Eitelkeit; ich bin ein ganz klein wenig eifersüchtig *I'm a tiny bit jealous*

233. An ambiguity: Wir bekamen wenig gutes Fleisch

This sentence could mean one of two things:
i We got not very good meat ('wenig' being an adverb limiting 'gutes').
ii We got little meat that was good ('wenig' being an uninflected adjective).

One solution is to stress, underline or italicize 'wenig' to produce the first sense and 'gutes' to produce the second.
Alternatively, 'wenig' may be replaced by 'nicht sehr' to produce the first sense and by 'nicht viel' to produce the second.

In the plural, a clear distinction is made:

Wir bekamen wenig gute Brötchen	*We got not very good rolls*
Wir bekamen wenige gute Brötchen	*We got few good rolls*

Distinguish similarly 'viel' and 'viele' before a comparative adj.:

Später schrieb er	*Later he wrote*
viel bessere Bücher	*much better books*
viele bessere Bücher	*many better books*

For the ambiguity inherent in weniger *less*, see 234(d).

234. The comparative of viel and wenig: mehr: *(some) more*
weniger: *less, fewer*

(a) These are undeclined and a following adjective has strong endings:
Er hat weniger Geld als ich; er kam mit mehr nutzlosem Plunder (*rubbish*); er kaufte noch mehr deutsche Bücher; wir haben keine Butter mehr.

(b) 'von' is used in place of the genitive:

die Wirkung von mehr (starkem) Kaffee — *the effect of more (strong) coffee*

der Verlust von weniger Stunden — *the loss of fewer hours*

(c) weiter *further* is frequently used instead of mehr, where 'further' could be substituted for 'more' in English:

nach weiterem (unnötigem) Zögern — *after more (unnecessary) hesitation*

Er schickte mir die Titel weiterer deutscher Romane — *He sent me the titles of more German novels*

(d) An ambiguity: Sie trinken jetzt weniger guten Wein. This sentence could mean one of two things:

i They now drink inferior wine.

ii They now drink less wine of good quality.

To ensure the first sense, replace 'weniger' by 'nicht so'; to ensure the second sense, replace 'weniger' by 'nicht so viel'.

235. soviel, zuviel, wieviel (sowenig etc.): one word or two?

Note: I am here accepting the ruling given in *Duden: Rechtschreibung* and *Hauptschwierigkeiten* and using some of their examples.

(a) With 'so':

They are written as one word when they are conjunctions or adverbs and in certain set phrases:

soviel ich weiß; soviel (wie) du willst; sowenig du auch gelernt hast (*however little you've learnt*), du wirst die Antwort wissen.

ich bin sowenig schuldig wie du; ich kann es ebensowenig wie du (*I can do it just as little as you can.*)

soviel wie möglich; das ist soviel wie eine Absage (*that is the equivalent of a refusal*). N.B. soundso viel.

They are written as two words if 'so' is a straightforward adverb of degree:

Er muß immer so viel arbeiten — *He always has to work such a lot*

Du hast so wenig gelernt, daß . . . — *You've learnt so little that . . .*

Ich habe so viel (Geld) wie du — *I have as much (money) as you*

(b) With 'zu':

They are written as one word if the stress falls on viel or wenig and they are uninflected:

Er gab mir viel zuvìel; das ist zuvìel des Guten (*too much of a good thing*); Sie haben zuwènig Erfahrung.

They are written as two words:

i if they are inflected: Ich habe zu viele Eier gekauft.

ii if the stress falls on 'zu': Sie haben für diese Stellung zù wenig Erfahrung.

(c) With 'wie': wieviel: one word, unless inflected.
    wie wenig: always two words.

Wieviel Birnen haben wir dieses Jahr! Wie viele Pfirsiche hast du gekauft?

236. Renderings of miscellaneous phrases with little, few, less[1]

Ich habe mich nicht wenig geärgert	*I was not a little annoyed*
in nicht viel weniger als einem Jahr	*in little less than a year*
Er machte einige wenige (ironische) Bemerkungen	*He made some few (ironical) remarks*
Es ist geradezu skandalös	*It's nothing less than monstrous*

237. welcher -e -es used as an indefinite pronoun *some, any*

It has the following characteristics:

  i it refers back to a preceding noun, except occasionally in the plural when it may mean 'some people' (see the last example).
  ii in the singular it generally refers to a substance.
  iii it has the strong endings.
  iv it is not used in the genitive, nor after 'nicht'.
  v it is primarily colloquial, but is widely used by German authors and not merely in conversational contexts (cf. Eggeling, op. cit., pp. 383 f.).

Hast du (etwas) Käse?	*Have you got some cheese?*
—Ja, ich habe welchen (or etwas)	*—Yes, I've got some*
—Nein, ich habe keinen	*—No, I haven't got any*
Es gab ja nur wenig Tabak, aber das Mädchen beschaffte mir immer welchen (J. Federspiel)	*As you know, there wasn't much tobacco going, but the girl always got hold of some for me*
Ich brauche Marken—kannst du mir welche geben?	*I need some stamps—can you give me any (or some)?*
Von seinen Zeitgenossen waren kaum noch welche am Leben	*Of his contemporaries hardly any were still alive*
Es gibt welche, die sind froh, der Wirklichkeit ins Auge zu sehen (I. Wendt)	*There are some who are glad to look reality in the face*

238. wenig, wenige: see 226 ff.

239. The main equivalents of any (some), anyone, anything

(a) any (some): miscellaneous uses:

Hast du (etwas) Geld bei dir?	*Have you any/some money on you?*
Hast du (ein paar) Bananen gekauft?	*Did you buy any/some bananas?*
Nein, sie hatten keine	*No, they hadn't any*
Kannst du mir irgendein Buch hierüber leihen?	*Can you lend me any/some book about this?*
Ich brauche Marken—kannst du mir welche geben?[2]	*I need some stamps—can you give me any/some?*
Hast du noch mehr (noch ein bißchen, noch ein paar)?	*Have you any more/some more?*
Ich ging nicht mehr (more emphatic: nie wieder) hin	*I did not go there any more*
(noch) länger	*any longer*
Ist noch etwas übrig?	*Is there any/some left?*
Wenn ich (etwas) Geld hätte, . . .	*If I had any/some money, . . .*
Wenn du (irgendwelche) Schwierigkeiten hast, . . .	*If you have any difficulties, . . .*

[1] see also 128.
[2] see 237.

Wenn (irgend)einer/irgendwelche von
meinen Freunden es wüßte/
wüßten, . . .

If any of my friends knew, . . .

(b) When its basic meaning is every or all, any=jeder (or sometimes
'aller'):

Das weiß jeder Schuljunge	*Any schoolboy knows that*
Jeder Aufschub wäre verhängnisvoll	*Any delay would be fatal*
Er kann jeden Augenblick aufwachen	*He may wake up at any moment*
Er ist ohne jede (or alle) Erfahrung	*He is without any experience*
Es war ein Tag wie jeder andere	*It was a day like any other*

(c) anyone

Hast du irgend jemand gesehen?	*Did you see anyone?*
Jeder wird dir das gleiche sagen	*Anyone will tell you the same thing*

(d) anything

Hast du (irgend)was gekauft?	*Did you buy anything?*
Er ist für irgend etwas/für alles dankbar	*He's grateful for anything*
Er ist alles andere als faul	*He's anything but lazy*
Er tut alles eher als arbeiten	*He does anything rather than work*
Er hat nichts gesagt	*He didn't say anything*

VII NUMERALS[1]

A. CARDINALS

240. Cardinals (die Kardinalzahlen or Grundzahlen)

0 null	18 achtzehn	101 hunderteins	
1 eins	19 neunzehn	102 hundertzwei	
2 zwei	20 zwanzig	151 hunderteinundfünfzig	
3 drei	**21 einund-**	200 zweihundert	
4 vier	**zwanzig**	1000 tausend *a thousand*	
5 fünf	22 zweiund-	eintausend *one thousand*	
6 sechs	zwanzig	1001 tausendundeins	
7 sieben	**30 dreißig**	1099 tausendundneunundneunzig	
8 acht	40 vierzig	1100 tausendeinhundert	
9 neun	50 fünfzig[3]	2000 zweitausend	
10 zehn	**60 sechzig**	1,000,000 eine Million	
11 elf	**70 siebzig**	2,000,000 zwei Millionen	
12 zwölf	80 achtzig	5,200,789 fünf Millionen zweihundert-	
13 dreizehn	90 neunzig	tausendsiebenhundertneunundachtzig	
14 vierzehn	100 hundert		
15 fünfzehn[2]	*a hundred*	1,000,000,000 eine Milliarde	
16 sechzehn	einhundert	1,000,000,000,000	
17 siebzehn	*one hundred*	eine Billion	

241. eins (ein, einer) (see also 199 and 216)

(a) in counting and calculating: eins, cf. hunderteins, BUT: einundzwanzig, einunddreißig etc.

(b) used before a noun and not preceded by the def. art., a demonstr. or possess. adj.: ein, declined like the indef. art. To indicate that it means 'one' (and not 'a') it is vocally stressed and often italicized:

Er brachte nur *ein* Buch	*He brought only one book*
aus mehr als *einem* Grunde	*for more than one reason*

Note:

i In 'ein oder zwei' and 'ein bis zwei', ein is generally uninflected: Ich

---

[1] for punctuation see 745.
[2] illiterate pronunciation: fuffzehn.
[3] illiterate pronunciation: fuffzig.

pflückte ein oder zwei Rosen; ich sprach mit ein oder zwei anderen; in ein bis zwei Jahren.[1]

ii Before Uhr, ein is uninflected: kurz nach ein Uhr.

iii 101, 1001 etc. used before a noun: normal usage is an uninflected hunderteins, tausendundeins etc., e.g. ein Buch mit dreihunderteins Seiten. Exc. hundertundeine Mark; Tausendundeine Nacht *The Arabian Nights*

(c) used as a pronoun, ein is declined like dieser: einer der Männer, eines/ eins der Bilder.

242. zwei and drei

(a) These have the slightly literary genitive forms zweier and dreier; a following attrib. or subst. adj. usually has the strong endings. These forms are used only if the case is not indicated by a preceding def. art., demonstr. or possess. adj.; in conversation 'von' is more usual. E.g.

Mutter zweier Kinder (V. Baum); die Garantie zweier alter Herren (= Adenauer and de Gaulle) (*Zeit*); die Ansichten zweier Deutscher, zweier Experten/von zwei Deutschen, von zwei Experten, BUT: die Ansichten dieser zwei Expe∴en; während dreier Tage (normally: während drei Tagen).[2]

(b) In stating telephone numbers, in military parlance and often in other contexts, the old feminine form 'zwo' is used instead of 'zwei', to avoid phonetic confusion with 'drei'. This is frequently extended to the ordinal 'der zwote', although there can be no confusion of 'der zweite' and 'der dritte'.

243. The cardinals 2-6 and 8-12

(a) These can have -en in the dative plural (though not when used attributively):

nur einer von zweien (or zwei) ist als   *only one out of two can be called*
gesund zu bezeichnen (*Zeit*)   *physically fit*

The commonest uses of this form are in the phrase 'auf allen vieren' *on all fours* and in the formula 'zu zweien, zu dreien' etc. *in twos, in threes,* where, however, the alternative 'zu zweit, zu dritt, zu viert' is commoner. (This form in -t may be used up to 10.)

diesen Spaziergang zu zweien   *this walk together (à deux)*
(Th. Mann)
Wir waren zu dritt   *There were three of us*
Die Tänzer traten zu fünft auf   *The dancers came on to the stage in fives*

(b) 2-6 and 8-12 have a form in -e, in poetry, archaic style, popular speech and certain set phrases:

Bei Nacht im Dorf der Wächter rief: Elfe! (Mörike: *Elfenlied*); ich habe alle fünfe gesehen; ich muß um fünfe aufstehen; alle viere von sich strecken 1. *to stretch oneself out* 2. *to give up the ghost.*

244. Cardinals have a form in -er (indeclinable except for -n in the dat.

---

[1] The case of Jahren is determined by 'in'.
[2] während is also used with the dative.

plur. when used substantivally) **to denote value** (generally in Pfennig) **and decades**:

zwei zwanziger Marken, bitte	*two 20 pfennig stamps, please*
zwei Zwanziger, bitte	
Er gab mir eine Zehner (Marke)	*He gave me a 10 pfennig stamp*
Er gab mir einen Zehner	*He gave me a 10 pfennig piece*
Er gab mir einen Zehner (Schein)[1]	*He gave me a 10 mark note*
in den siebziger Jahren des	*in the seventies of the nineteenth century*
neunzehnten Jahrhunderts	
Er ist (hoch) in den Sechzigern	*He's in his (late) sixties*
ein Sechziger (or Sechzigjähriger)	*a sexagenarian*
ein Vierundsechziger	*a 1964 wine*
Er ist Anfang/Mitte/Ende (der)	BUT: *He's at the beginning/in the middle/*
Dreißig	*at the end of his thirties*

245. hundert, tausend and Dutzend

(a) Only hundert and tausend are used adjectivally (uninflected and written with a small letter):

hundert/zweihundert Häuser	*100/200 houses*
viele hundert Häuser	*many hundreds of houses*
mit mehreren hundert Häusern	*with several hundred houses*

(b) All three are used substantivally (always with a capital): das Hundert (-e), das Tausend (-e), das Dutzend (-e).

das zweite Dutzend	*the second dozen*
Hunderttausende von Häusern	*hundreds of thousands of houses*
Es geht in die Hunderte	*It runs into hundreds*
Die Menschen verhungerten zu	*People starved in hundreds and thousands*
Hunderten und Tausenden[2]	

Note:

i If they are in the gen. plur. and this is not shown by an accompanying word, they take the adjectival gen. plur. ending -er:

die Beschwerden Dutzender von	*The complaints of dozens of tourists*
Touristen	
Die Ersparnisse Tausender gingen	*The savings of thousands were lost*
verloren	
die Ersparnisse vieler Tausende	BUT: *the savings of many thousands*

ii Dutzend does not take the form of the plural in combinations such as drei Dutzend (Eier): see 56(a).

246. eine Million, eine Milliarde and eine Billion are only used substantivally and are always inflected in the plural: fünf Millionen Bücher; viele Millionen sind ihm dankbar.

247. Substantival numeral (+adj.) +noun (or subst. adj.)

There are three ways in which a following noun may be linked to a substantival numeral: (a) is the safest (b) is also common (c) is rather literary:

---

[1] Schein is omissible if it is clear from the context that a 10 mark note and not a 10 pfennig piece is meant.

[2] Duden's example: Gram. 3110.

(a) with 'von':

Dutzende von Anfragen	*dozens of inquiries*
Tausende von jungen Arbeitslosen	*thousands of young unemployed*
in Hunderten von deutschen Dörfern	*in hundreds of German villages*

(b) The following noun may be in apposition. (Here the substantival numeral is often written with a small letter.)

Hunderte neue Häuser	*hundreds of new houses*
Tausende junge Arbeitslose	*thousands of young unemployed*
Sie wurden von tausenden West-Berlinern freudig begrüßt (*FAZ*)	*They were cheered by thousands of West Berliners*

(c) If preceded by an attrib. adj., the following noun may be in the genitive:

ein Dutzend südamerikanischer Radioreporter (*Zeit*)	*a dozen South American radio-reporters*
Millionen grauer Stäubchen (H. Fallada)	*millions of tiny grey particles*

Note: Where Millionen is preceded by a cardinal and/or a def. art., demonstr. or possess., the first preceding word determines the inflection of a following attrib. or subst. adj.:

drei Millionen Weiße	*three million whites*
die drei Millionen Weißen	*the three million whites*
unsrer Millionen jungen Arbeiter	*of our millions of young workers*

248. Qualification of cardinals

E.g. Er besitzt über (*over*), rund, ungefähr (*approximately*), knapp (*barely*) 10 000 Briefmarken.

Note:

i an + acc. signifies 'getting on for, almost': Da standen an siebenhundert deutsche Kriegsgefangene (Th. Plievier).

ii an and um are frequently followed by die + cardinal, but a following attrib. or subst. adj. has the strong ending: Im Hotel waren zur Zeit um die vierzig deutsche Gäste.

iii (a) an, bis zu, gegen, über, um, unter and zwischen used adverbially before cardinals have no effect on the case of a following noun. (But see (b) below.)

Bis zu zehn Kinder können mitfahren	*Up to ten children can come with us*
Sie ist zwischen 30 und 40 Jahre alt	*She is between 30 and 40 years old*

(b) When they introduce an attributive phrase, an, bis zu, unter and zwischen take the dative; gegen, über and um take the accusative: Kinder unter sieben Jahren zahlen die Hälfte; Kinder über sechs Jahre zahlen voll, BUT: Kinder von über sechs Jahren (dat. after 'von').

B. ORDINALS

249. Ordinals (die Ordinalzahlen or Ordnungszahlen)

(a) Apart from the deviations given below, **the ordinals are formed by adding -te to the cardinals 2–19 and -ste from 20 upwards**

(This gives the ending required after der, die, das, the ordinals always
being inflected):
der zweite Tag, die zwanzigste Sitzung, das tausendste Flugzeug

(b) Deviations:

der erste *the first*   der siebte[1] *the seventh*
der dritte *the third*   der achte (one 't') *the eighth*

(c) In compound ordinals, only the last component has the ordinal suffix:
auf der, man muß es ausschreiben, dreihundertneununddreißigsten Sitzung [of a
Geneva conference] (*FAZ*); der hunderterste[2] Tag.

(d) Ordinals are always inflected and are declined like ordinary adjectives:

Das ist sein viertes Buch   *That is his fourth book*
eine Leistung ersten Ranges   *a first-rate achievement*

(e) **to be the first to**: the following quotation from *Die Zeit* (25.11.66)
illustrates the two possibilities:

Die Russen waren die ersten, die   *The Russians were the first to send an*
einen künstlichen Erdsatelliten um   *artificial satellite round the earth; they*
den Globus schickten; sie brachten   *were the first to put a man into space*
als erste einen Menschen in den
Weltraum
Ich war als erster an Ort und Stelle   *I was the first to be on the spot*
cf. Ich hatte ihn als einziger gesehen   *I was the only one to have seen him*

(f) Three idiomatic uses of ordinals:

mein x-ter (pronounce ikster)   *my nth/umpteenth attempt*
Versuch
Er war im siebten Himmel   *He was in the seventh heaven*
Er kam vom Hundertsten ins   *He kept digressing*
Tausendste

(g) **erstens** (*firstly*), zweitens, drittens, siebtens etc.; a regional alternative: zum ersten, zum zweiten etc. (See also 642(c)vi).

(h) die zweitbeste (*second best*) Arbeit, die drittgrößte Stadt.

C. FRACTIONS

250. Fractions (die Bruchzahlen)

(a) Except for half (see 251), **fractions are formed by replacing the
final -te of the ordinals by -tel** (= Teil *part*). They are neuter and
are declined like a Group 1 noun, except that they have no -n in the
dat. plur.

In general, decimals take the place of fractions and only a few of the latter,
with low numbers, are used. E.g.

ein Drittel ($\frac{1}{3}$), ein (und) zwei Drittel[3] ($1\frac{2}{3}$), dreiviertel[4] ($\frac{3}{4}$), dreieinviertel[4] ($3\frac{1}{4}$).

Zwei Drittel des Materials ist gut   *Two thirds of the stuff is good*
die Bezahlung eines Drittels des   *the payment of a third of the sum/of two*
Betrags/von zwei Drittel des Betrags   *thirds of the sum*

---

[1] commoner than the older form 'der siebente'.
[2] more usual than 'der hundertunderste'.
[3] after 'ein', 'und' is generally omitted.
[4] almost always written as one word.

(b) Examples of fractional compounds: eine Viertelstunde, ein Vierteljahr, ein Viertelpfund Leberwurst, ein Viertel(liter) Weißwein, Dreiviertelkilo Bohnen.

251. half: 1. halb (noun, adjective or adverb)
2. die Hälfte (noun)

(a) half (noun)

(Ein) Halb ist mehr als ein Drittel	*Half is more than a third*
Er gab mir nur die Hälfte (or: nur halb) (davon)	*He gave me only half (of it)*
halb so viel (wie)	*half as much (as)*
die eine (die größere) Hälfte	*the one (the bigger) half*

(b) half a and half the (this, my)
A serviceable working rule is to use 'halb' for 'half a' and 'die Hälfte' for 'half the (this, my, your etc.)', though for the latter 'halb' may also be possible:

Ich aß einen halben Apfel	*I ate half an apple*
ein halbes Dutzend	*half a dozen*
die Hälfte der Jungen	*half the boys*
Die Hälfte der Butter (or: die halbe Butter) ist schlecht	*Half the butter is bad*
Er aß die Hälfte des Kuchens (or: den halben Kuchen)	*He ate half the cake*
die Hälfte des/dieses Geldes	*half the/this money*
die Hälfte meines Geldes	*half my money*

(c) half (adverb)

halb angezogen	*half dressed*
Er weiß alles nur halb	*He only half knows things*

(d) Phrases and idioms[1]

zum halben Preis	*at half the price*
mit halber Geschwindigkeit	*at half speed*
nach der ersten Halbzeit, bei Halbzeit	*at half-time* (football)
Er ist mir auf halbem Wege entgegengekommen	*He met me half way* (lit. and fig.)
Das ist nichts Halbes und nichts Ganzes	*That's neither fish nor flesh*
Ich nehm' noch ein Halbes	*I'll have another small glass*
seine bessere Hälfte	*his better half* (his wife)
Die Besucher waren zur Hälfte Deutsche	*Half the visitors were Germans*

(e) For equivalents of the many idiomatic uses and compounds of 'half', a dictionary must be consulted. E.g.

Das ist lange nicht gut genug	*That's not good enough by half*
Ich hätte beinah Lust, schwimmen zu gehen	*I've half a mind to go swimming*

(f) $1\frac{1}{2}$, $2\frac{1}{2}$ etc.
$1\frac{1}{2}$: anderthalb, einundeinhalb, eineinhalb Stunden.[2]
$2\frac{1}{2}$: zwei(und)einhalb. $7\frac{1}{2}$: sieben(und)einhalb.

---

[1] I am particularly indebted to Du. Stil. for the examples in this section.
[2] anderthalb (i.e. das zweite (andre) nur halb) is more used than the other two, of which einundeinhalb is the commoner.

Note:
i In normal usage, these forms are not declined: Er ist vor zweiundeinhalb Stunden angekommen.
ii For comprehension purposes, the archaic forms dritt(e)halb ($2\frac{1}{2}$), viert(e)halb ($3\frac{1}{2}$) etc. may be mentioned.

D. EQUAL DISTRIBUTION (5 MARKS EACH Etc.)

252. Numerically equal distribution is expressed by 'je' (from MHG ie = always):

Ich gab den Jungen je 5 Mark	*I gave the boys 5 marks each*
A. und B. wurden zu je drei Jahren Haft verurteilt (*SZ*)	*A and B were sentenced to three years' imprisonment each*

Three less common uses of this 'je':

Je zwei von ihnen kamen herein (normal usage: Sie kamen zu zweit herein)	*They came in in twos*
nach je sechs Monaten (normal usage: alle sechs Monate)	*(after) every six months*
Je der (= Jeder) zehnte Baum war ein Kirschbaum	*Every tenth tree was a cherry-tree*

E. SINGLE, TWOFOLD

253. single, twofold etc.: einfach, zweifach etc.

eine einfache Karte	*a single ticket*
ein dreifacher Sieg	*a treble victory*
... stiegen die Grundstückspreise zunächst aufs Zehnfache (H. Böll)	*... the price of land in the first instance went up tenfold*

cf. vielfach or mehrfach *manifold, frequent(ly), repeated(ly)*, mannigfach[1] *manifold, varied.*

ein vielfacher Millionär	*a multi-millionaire*
Er wird vielfach kritisiert	*He is frequently criticized*
Die Preise sind aufs Mehrfache gestiegen	*Prices have multiplied several times*

Parallel to the above are the forms **zwiefältig, dreifältig** etc., vielfältig, mannigfaltig, e.g. ein dreifältiger Sieg, seine mannigfaltigen Gaben.

Note:
i double = doppelt.
ii zweifach has the literary variant zwiefach.
iii einfältig generally means simple-minded.
iv the Trinity = die Dreifaltigkeit (or die Dreieinigkeit, die Trinität).
v mehrfältig does not exist.
vi single, individual, separate = einzeln, e.g. Er betrachtete die einzelnen Fotos (or: jedes Foto einzeln).
vii Er hat keinen einzigen Freund *He hasn't a single friend.*

---

[1] less used than mannigfaltig.

F. ONCE, TWICE AND THE USES OF 'MAL'

254. Once, twice, three times etc.: einmal, zweimal, dreimal etc.

Ich habe es hundertmal bereut	*I've regretted it a hundred times*
anderthalbmal so groß (wie)	*one and a half times as big (as)*
Also, Herr Ober, zweimal Gulasch	*Well now, waiter, goulash for two*

See also 258: multiplication.

einmal, zweimal etc. form adjectives in -ig:

eine einmalige Gelegenheit	*a unique opportunity*
Kleists *Penthesilea* ist etwas Einmaliges	*Kleists* Penthesilea *is something unique*
nach dreimaligem Durchlesen seines Briefes	*after reading his letter through three times*
mehrmalig	*repeated, reiterated*

255. A selection of the uses of Mal *time, occasion*

In the sing. Mal is written as a separate word, with a capital: Ich habe ihn oft besucht; das eine Mal zeigte er mir seine Markensammlung. Das letzte Mal war das schönste; das erste Mal, daß ich ihn sah; dieses *eine* Mal *this once*; kein einziges Mal *not once*; ein ums andere Mal *every other time*; nächstes Mal.[1]

Exc. 1. where a combination of def. art. + adj. + mal, often with zu (or bei), is regarded simply as an adverb phrase: Als er das letztemal hier war; heute kam er zum drittenmal (hintereinander)/zum erstenmal (seit langem); das nächstemal, das übernächstemal, das vorletztemal, zum wievieltenmal? beim erstenmal.

Exc. 2. a few common adverbs and adverb phrases, e.g. diesmal, jedesmal, ein andermal. (For einmal, see 294(a)(b)).

In the plur. Mal is written as a separate word with a capital when it is inflected: Die letzten paar Male war er nicht zu Hause; beide Male; viele (hundert) Male.

BUT: hundertemal, ein (halbes) dutzendmal, ein paar dutzendmal, dutzendemal, ein paarmal; x-mal, zigmal *umpteen times*.

vielmals is much used in three contexts only:
Ich danke Ihnen vielmals/Danke vielmals! *Many thanks.*
Ich bitte vielmals um Entschuldigung. *Many apologies.*
Er läßt Sie vielmals grüßen. *He sends you his kind regards.*

G. TWO KINDS OF ETC.

256. two, three etc., many kinds of: zweierlei, dreierlei, vielerlei

Note:
i These forms consist of a gen. of the cardinal or indefinite + MHG lei(e) *kind, sort* (see also 95(b)).
ii They are used attributively and substantivally.
iii They are indeclinable and a following adjective has the strong endings.

---

[1] nächstes Mal cannot be used with a verb in the past; therefore: Das nächstemal war er nicht zu Hause.

Examples:

Ich ziehe zweierlei Bohnen	*I grow two kinds of beans*
Er hat hunderterlei Pläne	*He's got hundreds of different plans*
Ich habe ihm dreierlei vorgeschlagen	*I suggested three different things to him*

Uses of einerlei:

Die Schwestern trugen einerlei Kleider	*The sisters wore identical dresses*
Die Stühle sind alle einerlei	*The chairs are all the same*
Es ist mir ganz einerlei	*It's all the same to me*
Ich ziehe nur eine Art Bohnen	BUT: *I only grow one kind of beans*

H. MISCELLANEOUS NUMERICAL USAGES AND FORMULAE

257. Miscellaneous usages[1]

3 525 400 DM/Einwohner/Bücher	*3,525,400 marks/inhabitants/books*
71 83 22 (einundsiebzig dreiundachtzig zwoundzwanzig)	*718322 (telephone number)*
3 21 (drei einundzwanzig)	*321 (telephone number)*
einmal erster Bremen einfach	*first single Bremen*
zweimal zweiter Bremen Rückfahrkarte (or: hin und zurück)	*two second returns Bremen*
3,75 (dreikommasiebenfünf)	*3·75 (decimal)*
0,5 (nullkommafünf)	*0·5 (decimal)*
Das Zimmer ist 5,50 m (Meter) lang und 4,20 m breit	*The room is 5·5 metres long and 4·2 metres wide*
Das Zimmer ist 5,50 mal 4,20 (fünfkommafünfnull mal vierkommazweinull)	*The room is 5·5 by 4·2 metres*
10,75 DM (zehn Mark fünfundsiebzig)	*10 marks 75 pfennig*
ein Motor von 1700 cm³ (ein Motor von 1700 Kubikzentimeter)	*an engine of 1700 c.c.*
ein 60-PS-Motor (PS = Pferdestärke)	*a 60 b.h.p. engine*
Er hat einen Ford 1500	*He's got a Ford 1500*
Er hat einen fünfzehnhunderter	*He's got a 1500*
Er hat einen 3,2 l (Liter) BMW	*He's got a 3·2 litre BMW*
Das Thermometer steht auf null Grad (0°C)	*The thermometer is at zero (Celsius, i.e. centigrade)*
ein Winkel von neunzig Grad (90°)	*an angle of 90°*
ein rechter Winkel	*a right angle*
Die zwei Mauern stehen in einem Winkel von 70° zueinander	*The two walls form an angle of 70°*

Note: 7 is often written 7̸, to distinguish it from 1.

258. Some mathematical processes and equations

Note: In all the following except the last two, 'ist' may be used in place of 'gleich'; for multiplication 'macht' is also used.

addieren	*to add*
vier plus (or und) fünf gleich neun	$4+5=9$ (footnote[2])
abziehen or subtrahieren (von)	*to subtract (from)*

---

[1] See also 565(e).   [2] same symbols in German.

zwölf minus (or weniger) zwei gleich zehn	$12 - 2 = 10$ (footnote [1])
multiplizieren (mit)	*to multiply (by)*
sieben mal drei gleich einundzwanzig	$7 \times 3 = 21$ (footnote [2])
das Einmaleins	*multiplication table(s)*
dividieren (durch or mit)	*to divide (by)*
zwanzig (geteilt) durch fünf gleich vier	$20 \div 5 = 4$ (footnote [3])
vier hoch zwei (or: vier Quadrat) gleich sechzehn	$4^2 = 16$ (footnote [1])
zwei hoch minus fünf gleich eins durch zwei hoch fünf	$2^{-5} = \frac{1}{2^5}$ (footnote [1])
n-te Wurzel aus b gleich a	$\sqrt[n]{b} = a$ (footnote [1])
a verhält sich zu b, wie 9 zu 7	*a is to b as 9 is to 7*

259. Some contemporary mathematical terms

die Mengenlehre	*theory of sets*
x ist Element der Menge A	$x \in A$
die Untermenge or Teilmenge	*subset*
Vereinigung von zwei Mengen	*union of 2 sets*
Durchschnitt von zwei Mengen	*intersection of 2 sets*
die Allmenge	*the universal set*
gleichmächtige Mengen (mit derselben Kardinalzahl)	*equivalent sets (with the same number of elements)*
eineindeutige Entsprechung	*one-to-one correspondence*

Abbildung *mapping*	Drehung *rotation*
Kongruenz *isometry*	Verschiebung *translation*
Spiegelung *reflection*	Identität *identity*

fünf größer drei	$5 > 3$
a größer oder gleich b	$a \geqslant b$
a kleiner oder gleich b	$a \leqslant b$

260. A typical German address

> Herrn
> Dr. Friedrich Lehmann
>
> Lindenstraße 16
>
> 2800 Bremen 5

16 is the number of the house; where a house contains numbered flats or individual letter-boxes, write e.g. W18 (=Wohnung 18) after the house-number.

The sender's name and address should be written on the back of the envelope; cf. the provision made for this on postcards obtained at a German post-office.

---

[1] same symbols in German.
[2] The German alternative symbol is $7 \cdot 3$ (not: $7 \cdot 3$).
[3] German symbol: $20 : 5 = 4$.

If the above letter were for Dr. Lehmann's wife, it would be addressed e.g. :

Frau
Else Lehmann

if it were for both of them :

Herrn
Dr. Friedrich Lehmann und Frau

VIII ADVERBS

A. INTRODUCTORY

261. All adjectives and participles with suitable meanings can be used as adverbs; they are then, of course, uninflected. E.g.

Er hat die Sache überraschend schnell erledigt	*He has settled the matter surprisingly quickly*
ein Dokument . . . zeigt doch, daß er mäßigend und bremsend zu wirken versuchte (*Zeit*)	*one document nevertheless shows that he tried to exercise a moderating and retarding influence*

Note:
i Sometimes what appears to be adverb + adjective is really two adjectives, the first one being uninflected, e.g.

Nicht, was lebendig, kraftvoll sich verkündigt, Ist das gefährlich Furchtbare (Schiller)	*Not that which proclaims itself in vital power is that which is dangerous and terrible*

ii For the comparative and superlative of adverbs, see Chap. IV.

262. There are also a considerable number of words which are exclusively adverbs, some of them corresponding to an adverb phrase in English, e.g. außerdem *besides, in addition*, gleichsam *so to speak, as it were*, notfalls *in case of need*, oben *up above, upstairs*, (cf. 726).

B. SOME ADVERBS OF DEGREE

263. sehr

i *very*: sehr schwer; er weiß es sehr gut; das ist sehr nett von dir.
ii *very much, greatly*, limiting a verb or phrase and denoting degree: Das interessiert mich sehr; ich bewundere ihn sehr; er ist sehr dafür; das ist sehr nach meinem Geschmack.
iii *much* denoting degree after so, wie, zu: Nicht so sehr die Handlung (*plot*) wie der Stil hat mich gefesselt. Wie sehr ich es bedaure! Er hat es sich zu sehr zu Herzen genommen.

264. lange and längst, generally preceded by noch, are used interchangeably before a negative to denote a substantial difference in degree.[1]

Das ist noch lange nicht gut genug	*That's not nearly good enough*
Dieses Buch ist lange nicht so gut wie sein letztes	*This book is not nearly as good as his last one*
Das ist noch längst kein Grund	*That is far from being a reason*
Er hat's lange gut	N.B. Idiom: *He's extremely fortunate*

265. Miscellaneous idiomatic adverbs of degree

Er arbeitet recht gut	*He works very well*
Er ist noch arg jung für diese Stellung	*He's still awfully young for this post*
Er ist ausgesprochen begabt	*He's distinctly gifted*
Er ist durchaus zuverlässig	*He is thoroughly reliable*
Wenn ich gegen etwas bin, so tut er's erst recht	*If I'm against anything, he does it all the more*
Das hatte ich glatt vergessen (coll.)	*I had completely forgotten that*
Er ist richtig faul (coll.)	*He's downright lazy*
Sie hat tüchtig geweint (coll.)	*She had a good cry*

C. ADVERBS AND ADVERB PHRASES OF PLACE: SOME SPECIAL POINTS OF USAGE

266. Wo? Wohin? etc. In contrast with English usage, German consistently differentiates between rest and motion in the following cases:

Wo ist er? *Where is he?*	Er geht dahin *He is going there*
Wohin geht er? *Where is he going?*	Er ist hier *He is here*
Er ist da *He is there*	Er kommt hierher *He is coming here*
In den Ferien fahren wir dahin, wo ihr letztes Jahr wart[2]	*In the holidays we're going where you were last year*
Komm hierher, wo ich stehe[2]	*Come where I'm standing*
Er geht heute nachmittag irgendwohin (coll. wohin)	*He's going somewhere or other this afternoon*
Er geht überallhin	*He goes everywhere*

Note:

i As is apparent from the examples above and below (with a few idiomatic exceptions), 'hin' denotes motion away from the speaker or his original situation, whereas 'her' denotes motion towards the speaker or his present situation. (For 'the speaker' it may be necessary to substitute 'the person concerned'.)

ii Especially in conversation, the two elements of wohin and dahin are often separated, hin going to the end in the manner of a separable prefix:

Wo gehört dieses Buch hin?	*Where does this book belong?*
Da geh' ich nie hin	*I never go there*
ein kleines, gutes Restaurant . . ., wo keine Amerikaner hinkamen (V. Baum)	*a small, good restaurant, to which no Americans came*

---

[1] coll. (As adverbs of time, lange=*for a long time*, längst=*long since*; see 315 and 330).
[2] cf. Schulz-Griesbach, op. cit., J 170.

iii hierher is always treated as a sep. prefix, dahin only when it has a meaning other than 'to that place': Er ist heute hierhergekommen; wir sind gestern dahin gegangen; die Tage sind schnell dahingegangen (cf. 706).

iv dahin and hierher are often replaced by the prefixes hin and her:[1]

Ja, ich werde hingehen	*Yes, I shall go there*
Wenn er das nächstemal her-kommt, ...	*When he next comes here, . . .*

267. from where? whence? from there, thence

Von wo kommt er? Woher kommt er? Wo kommt er her?	*Where does he come from?*
Weißt du, wo er herkommt?	*Do you know where he comes from?*
Ja, er kommt von da	*Yes, he comes from there*
Ja, da kommt er her	*Yes, that's where he comes from*
Wo ist er her?—Er ist aus Berlin	*Where is he from?—He's from Berlin* (a Berliner)
Wo hast du das her?	*Where have you got that from?*
Wo soll ich das Geld hernehmen?	*From where shall I take the money?*

268. da and dort, dahin and dorthin etc.

(a) dort is more definite and incisive and is rather less used.
(b) dort only has local force; thus: Die letzte Hoffnung ist dahin (not dorthin) (Du. Stil.) *The last hope has vanished.*

269. hin and her are frequently used to strengthen or complete a preceding place phrase (cf. 594(b)N.iii):

Wir wanderten bis zu den Bergen (hin); der Hof ist zur Straße hin offen.
Die Stimmen kamen von oben her, von innen her, von überall(her); von rechts (her), von Süden (her); von weit her; ringsum(her) *all around*, rings um mich (her). Cf. Ich kenne ihn von früher (her).

270. hin und her to and fro, hierhin und dorthin hither and thither.

Note:

Ich habe hin und her überlegt	*I've considered the matter from every point of view*
Freund hin, Freund her, er hat mich beleidigt (Du. Stil.)	*Friend or no friend, he's offended me*

271. worein into which and darein into it, into them are virtually obsolete, apart from the use of darein (often drein) as a separable prefix (see 706) and in the compounds obendrein *in addition, into the bargain* and hinterdrein 1. *subsequently, later* (Hinterdrein habe ich es bereut) 2. (less common) *following after, bringing up the tail.*

Eggeling (op. cit.: wo(r)) gives an example in which worein does not sound antiquated:

Das sind Sachen, worein (or: in die) ich mich niemals mische	*Those are matters in which I never meddle*

---

[1] for the treatment of hin and her as sep. prefixes, see 695 ff.

272. at the top of, at the bottom of

oben auf dem Turm	*at the top of the tower*
oben im Haus	*at the top of the house*[1]
oben im Baum	*at the top of the tree*
oben auf dem Schrank	*on top of the cupboard*
Er lehnte den Arm oben auf die Mauer	*He leant his arm on top of the wall*
am oberen Ende der Treppe, oben	*at the top of the stairs*
zuoberst	*on top (of everything else)*
unten im Kasten	*at the bottom of the box*
unten am Bein	*at the bottom of my leg*
auf der nächsten Seite unten	*at the bottom of the next page*
zuunterst	*at the bottom, under everything else*
von oben bis unten	*from top to bottom*

For figurative uses, consult a dictionary, e.g.

aus voller Kehle	*at the top of one's voice*

273. (da) drüben – hier drüben   *over there – over here*

hüben und drüben, hüben wie drüben	*here and over there* (e.g. in Europe and America, in the Bundesrepublik and the DDR)

Note: Instead of by hier drüben, 'over here' is often rendered by hier followed by a specific indication of place: hier im Schatten *over here (in the shade)*, hier in England *over here (in England)*.

274. mitten

(a) mitten is an adverb meaning *in the middle* and is generally followed by a preposition. It is very freely used, as shown by the following examples:

Mitten im Garten ist ein Teich	*In the middle of the garden there is a pond*
Sie stellte die Vase mitten auf den Tisch	*She put the vase in the middle of the table*
mitten auf der Leiter	*halfway up the ladder*
mitten in der Nacht	*in the middle of the night*
mitten in der Aufregung	*in the midst of the excitement*
Er war mitten aus seinem Urlaub zu der Konferenz gekommen	*He had come to the conference in the middle of his leave*
Ich war . . . mitten unter den Leuten auf der Straße (C. Zuckmayer)	*I was in the midst of the people in the street*
Er bahnte sich mitten durch die Menge einen Weg	*He forced his way through the middle of the crowd*

(b) Many of the above examples could be rendered with **die Mitte**, e.g. in der Mitte des Gartens, auf die Mitte des Tisches, in der Mitte der Nacht.

'Mitte' is essential in the following: Er ging in der Mitte des Weges *He walked in the middle of the path*.

Note the set phrase: Wir freuen uns, dich in unserer Mitte zu sehen (Du. Stil.)

[1] cf. ein Zimmer hinten im Haus *a room at the back of the house*.

(c) mitten is also used:

i in conjunction with the sep. prefix entzwei:

Der Stock brach mitten entzwei	*The stick broke in two in the middle*

ii before adverbs of place formed with da(r)-:

mitten darin, mittendrin (coll.)	*in the middle of it, in the centre*
Er sortierte seine Papiere; mitten darunter/mittendrunter fand er eine Fotografie	*He sorted his papers; in the midst of them he found a photo*

D. ADVERBS IN -WEISE

275. Adverbs formed from noun + weise (= *way, manner*)

i beispielsweise	*by way of example*
beziehungsweise (bzw.)	*respectively, as the case may be*
dutzendweise	*by the dozen*
gruppenweise	*in groups*
pfundweise	*by the pound*
stellenweise	*in places*
ii ausnahmsweise	*by way of exception, exceptionally*
paarweise	*in pairs*
probeweise	*on approval, on probation*
ruckweise	*by jerks*
schrittweise	*step by step*
stückweise	*piece by piece, piecemeal*
stundenweise	*by the hour*
teilweise	*partly*
versuchsweise	*by way of experiment, tentatively*
zeitweise	*intermittently; temporarily*
zwangsweise	*compulsorily*

Originally and organically, both groups were exclusively adverbs:

Sein Sohn und seine Tochter sind 10 bzw. 14 Jahre alt (from Du. Haupt.)	*His son and daughter are 10 and 14 years old respectively*
Übergeben Sie den Brief dem Chef beziehungsweise seinem Stellvertreter	*Hand the letter to the manager or his deputy, as the case may be*
Sein neues Buch ist stellenweise ganz gut	*His new book is quite good in parts*
Er wird stundenweise bezahlt	*He is paid by the hour*

The words in group ii above have also come to be used as attrib. adjectives, and others may go the same way:

eine probeweise Anstellung	*a probationary appointment*
eine schrittweise . . . Verminderung der Streitkräfte in Europa (SZ)	*a gradual . . . reduction of armed forces in Europe*
die stundenweise Bezahlung	*payment by the hour*
ein teilweiser Erfolg	*a partial success*

276. Adverbs formed from adj. + weise (being a one-word adverbial gen.)

merkwürdigerweise	*strange to say*
vernünftigerweise	*sensibly enough*

(a) Instead of having the direct, qualifying function of an adverb, these adverbs convey the speaker's or writer's view of the occurrence in question.

Contrast:

i Er war merkwürdig müde — *He was strangely tired*
ii Er war merkwürdigerweise müde — *Strange to say, he was tired*

i Er hat vernünftig geantwortet — *He replied sensibly*
ii Vernünftigerweise hat er geantwortet — *Sensibly enough, he replied*

Similarly:

bedauerlicherweise	*regrettably enough*
begreiflicherweise	*understandably*
dummerweise	*foolishly enough*
erstaunlicherweise	*astonishingly enough*
glücklicherweise	*fortunately*
interessanterweise	*interestingly enough*
komischerweise	*funnily enough*
liebenswürdigerweise	*obligingly enough*
möglicherweise	*possibly, perhaps*
überflüssigerweise	*superfluously enough*
unglücklicherweise[1]	*unfortunately*

(b) The following, all much used, deviate from the typical connotation of these adverbs:

falscherweise	*wrongly*
Ich hatte falscherweise angenommen, daß . . .	*I had wrongly assumed that . . .*
natürlicherweise	*in the natural course of events*
normalerweise	*in the normal course of events*
notwendigerweise	*of necessity*
unnötigerweise	*unnecessarily*
unvermuteterweise	*unexpectedly*

E. GERN

277. gern (or gerne) *gladly, willingly* is used to form the commonest German equivalent of 'to like, to be fond of'.

etwas/jemanden gern haben — *to like something/someone*
etwas gern tun — *to like doing something*

E.g. Ich habe dieses Bild/seine Schwester gern; ich radle gern; ich gehe gern ins Kino; ich bin gern in London.

Regarding the form gerne: In MIIG -e was the regular ending of adverbs; in New High German this -e survives in a few alternative forms, cf. lang(e), fern(e), nah(e). As Duden rightly observes (Du. Haupt. Adverb 6), 'gerne' sounds warmer than 'gern'.

278. Synonyms of 'gern haben'

i **lieben** *to love* implies greater intensity and depth of feeling than gern haben.

[1] or leider.

ii **lieb-haben** *to be fond of, to love* is warmer and more intimate than gern haben; it is only applied to persons, particularly when speaking of the affection felt for parents, sons, daughters, brothers and sisters: Sie hat ihren jüngsten Sohn besonders lieb.

iii **gefallen + Dat.** *to please* and gern haben are often interchangeable, but while 'gefallen' is used to convey a first impression, 'gern haben' expresses an established and lasting fondness. E.g.

Ja, dieses Bild gefällt mir	*Yes, I like this picture*
Ich habe dieses Bild gern	*I'm fond of this picture*

iv **mögen** *to like* and gern haben are virtually synonymous; gern haben is the commoner of the two; mögen is mainly used negatively: Ich mag ihn nicht.

gern is frequently used in conjunction with mögen:

Ich mag ihn gern	*I like him*
Ich möchte gern mit ihm sprechen	*I should like to speak to him*

279. Miscellaneous points connected with 'gern'

(a) Of **intensifying words and phrases used with gern** (sehr, recht, so etc.) two may be illustrated:

Ich habe das Kindchen *zu* gern/*gar* zu gern (coll.)	*I just adore the little child*
Ich gehe für mein Leben gern in die Oper	*I adore going to the opera*

(b) For **to like food and drink**, etwas gern essen/trinken is more usual than etwas gern haben, e.g. Ich trinke Kaffee gern.

(c) The negative form **ungern** gives a sharper edge to an aversion than nicht gern; it may also express reluctance (see also 124):

Ich gehe ungern ins Kino	*I dislike going to the cinema*
Ich habe ihn ungern unterbrochen	*I was reluctant to interrupt him*

(d) **Colloquially gern haben is used for to like doing something** (though not in a brief remark e.g. I like cycling): it is used with 'es' to anticipate an infinitive phrase with 'zu' (cf. 512); the same construction may be used with a passive infin. (2nd example):

Ich habe es gern, nach dem Mittagessen einen Spaziergang zu machen (better: Ich mache gern nach dem Mittagessen einen Spaziergang).
Er hat es gern, gelobt zu werden (Commoner: Er liebt es, gelobt zu werden).[1]

(e) In complicated contexts **es gern haben, wenn** may be used, e.g.

Ich habe es gern, wenn er uns sonntags besucht	*I like to have him visiting us on Sundays*

Compare the idiomatic formula:

Ich würde es gern sehen, wenn du eine bessere Stellung bekämst	*I should very much like you to get a better job*

280. The comparative and superlative of gern

(a) The forms are lieber and am liebsten, the comparative and superlative of lieb.[2] They are used in the same way as gern. Thus:

---

[1] 'Er wird gern gelobt' would be slightly ambiguous; it could idiomatically mean: *People are fond of praising him.*
[2] cf. Es wäre mir lieb/lieber/am liebsten, wenn Sie nichts darüber sagten *I'd be glad/I'd prefer if you said nothing about it.*

Ich habe München gern; ich habe Hamburg lieber (als München); ich habe Frankfurt am liebsten.
Ich radle gern; ich reite lieber; ich schwimme am liebsten.

(b) Intensifications: viel, weit, bei weitem lieber; am allerliebsten.

(c) preference of one activity or course of action to another:

Ich habe Reiten lieber als Radeln	*I prefer riding to cycling*
Ich stehe lieber früh auf als hetzen zu müssen	*I prefer getting up early to having a rush*

With a change of subject, 'als daß' must be used:

Ich möchte es lieber selber tun, als daß er sich einmischt	*I would rather do it myself than that he should interfere*

(d) Both 'lieber' and 'am liebsten' may be used in place of 'gern' in the constructions discussed in 279(d) and (e).

(e) 'lieber' is frequently used to convey a wiser course of action, corresponding to English 'better'; 'besser' is also possible, but not in conjunction with 'wollen'. Thus:

Sie behalten das lieber (or: besser) für sich	*You had better keep that to yourself*
Ich will es lieber selber tun	*I had better do it myself*

(f) The use of lieber indicated in (e) above does not apply to am liebsten:

Sie behalten das am besten für sich	*You had best keep that to yourself*
Es wird am besten sein, ich tue es selber	*I had best do it myself*

281. Position of gern/lieber/am liebsten in the sentence

(a) With gern haben, gern generally stands at the end of the sentence, like a sep. prefix:

Ich habe meinen Onkel trotz all seinen Schwächen gern	*I like my uncle despite all his weaknesses*

The same applies to lieber and am liebsten

(b) Otherwise:

i gern normally has the position of an unemphatic adverbial limitation of manner (cf. 658):

Er hilft seinem Onkel samstags gern im Garten	*He likes helping his uncle in the garden on Saturdays*

If gern bears on some particular word or phrase, this is placed at the beginning of the sentence, but gern is not moved:

Seinem Onkel hilft er samstags gern im Garten	*It's his uncle he likes helping in the garden on Saturdays*

ii lieber, am liebsten normally precede the word or phrase on which they bear:

Ich möchte es meinem Vater am liebsten erst nächste Woche zeigen	*I'd rather not show it to my father till next week*

cf. the examples in 280(e).

(c) gern, lieber and am liebsten can themselves be emphasized by being placed at the beginning of the sentence, followed by inversion.

282. Some idiomatic uses of gern and lieber

Ich will dir gern helfen	*I'll gladly help you*
Das glaub' ich gern	*I'm quite ready to believe it*
Du kannst das gern tun	*You can certainly do that as far as I'm concerned*
Gern geschehen!	*Don't mention it*
Er ist überall gern gesehen	*He is welcome everywhere*
Diese Zigarre wird gern geraucht	*This cigar is very popular (commercialese)*
Er verdient gut und gern 2000 Mark im Monat	*He may very well earn 2000 marks a month*
Lieber aushalten als nachgeben!	*Better hold out than give in*
je länger, je lieber	*the longer, the better*
Ich ginge lieber nach Hause	*I'd rather go home*
Ich wüßte nicht, was ich lieber täte	*There's nothing I'd rather do*

IX PARTICLES[1]

283. Introductory

Colloquial German stands or falls by an ample scattering of denn, doch, ja, mal, schon, so etc., without which it sounds bleak and impersonal; their correct use is a considerable test for the foreigner.

For the sake of completeness, the purely adverbial use of the particles has been briefly included, e.g. eben *just* (*now*), einmal *once*, etwa *about*, *approximately*; *perhaps*, *by chance*, nämlich *namely*, nun *now*, nur *only*, schon *already*; this, too, frequently offers points of interest.

For a list of the particles treated, with paragraph numbers, see CONTENTS.

284. aber[2]

(a) **It gives emphasis**:
　i to an expression of satisfaction or admiration:

Der Film war aber gut	*The film really* was *good*

　ii to an expression of reproach:

Du kommst aber spät heute	*You are late today*

　iii to ja, nein, sicher and the like:

Hast du was dagegen?—Aber nein!	*Have you any objection?—Of course not*

(b) **aber auch** gives strong emphasis, often to a repeated word:

Er hat (alles,) aber auch alles vergessen	*He's forgotten absolutely everything*

(c) **oder aber** *or on the other hand*:

Seine Befürwortung könnte der Sache helfen oder aber schaden	*His support might help the cause or on the other hand it might harm it*

(d) **aber can mean 'again'** (cf. abermals *once more*) (elev.):

tausend und aber tausend	*thousands and thousands*

(e) **Its substantival use may here be noted**:

Die Sache hat *ein* Aber	*There's one difficulty* (or *objection*)

---

[1] I am here occasionally indebted to articles by Gisela Schröder and Siegfried Colditz in *Deutsch als Fremdsprache* (1/1965 and 1/1966 respectively) and to W. E. Collinson: 'Some German Particles and their English Equivalents' in *German Studies presented to H. G. Fiedler* (Oxford, Clarendon Press, 1938).

[2] For the use of aber as an orthodox conjunction 'but' and as 'however', see 517 ff.

285. allerdings, freilich, zwar

Note: 'freilich' never means 'freely', which is primarily 'frei' (e.g. Du kannst ganz frei entscheiden), with many alternatives according to the context.

(a) **Their commonest meaning is concessive: admittedly, to be sure, certainly, indeed, it is true**

i Where they have the force of the conjunction 'although', either allerdings or freilich is used:

Ich will mein Bestes tun, allerdings /freilich kann ich nichts garantieren	*I'll do my best, though certainly I can't guarantee anything*

ii Otherwise all three may be used, but, whereas 'zwar' must be balanced by 'aber', 'doch' or 'jedoch', 'allerdings' and 'freilich' need not be:

Es ist zwar/allerdings/freilich ein gutes Buch, aber seine anderen gefallen mir besser	*It is certainly a good book, but I prefer his other ones*
Es ist allerdings/freilich ein gutes Buch	*It is certainly a good book*

(b) **allerdings and freilich are used to express agreement or to give an affirmative reply**; both may contain a hint of indignation:

Er hat sich wirklich angestrengt.— Allerdings!	*He really exerted himself.—Indeed he did*
Kannst du es auch alles besorgen? —(Ja,) freilich!	*Can you see to it all?—Certainly I can* (or: *Obviously I can*)

(c) **Less commonly, allerdings and freilich may serve to correct a previous negative statement:**[1]

Die Lage ist nicht ernst.—Freilich ist sie ernst	*The situation isn't serious.—Of course it's serious*

(d) **und zwar** introduces a phrase giving greater precision to what precedes: and moreover, and what is more, and in fact, namely:

Ich habe ihn für heute abend eingeladen und zwar für 7 Uhr	*I've invited him for this evening, (namely) for 7 o'clock*
Mein Freund ist Schauspieler, und zwar ein ganz bekannter	*My friend is an actor and in fact quite a well-known one*

286. auch

(a) **also, too, and, duly, what's more**

Mein Bruder ist auch krank	*My brother is also ill*
Ich habe ihn gestern gesehen.—Ich auch	*I saw him yesterday.—So did I*
Er bat mich, den Brief zu beantworten, was ich (dann) auch tat	*He asked me to answer the letter, which I duly did*
Ich habe ihn eingeladen, und er kommt auch	*I've invited him and what's more he's coming*

(b) **even**

Auch[2] die besten Schüler machen Fehler	*Even the best pupils make mistakes*

---

[1] cf. Eggeling, op. cit.: allerdings 1(a) and freilich 1.   [2] or sogar or selbst.

Auch nicht sein bester Freund kann ihn beeinflussen[1]	*Not even his best friend can influence him*
Er ist auch noch stolz darauf	*He's even proud of it*
und wenn auch	*even so, no matter*

(c) **auch nur** *even* (= *as few as, as little as*)[2]

wenn ich auch nur zwei Freunde hätte	*if I had even two friends*
ohne auch nur zu fragen[3]	*without as much as asking*
Ich war außerstande, die Szene auch nur annähernd zu schildern	*I was incapable of giving even an approximate description of the scene*

(d) **oder auch** *or else; or even*

Du kannst Birnen kaufen oder auch Pflaumen	*You can buy some pears or else some plums*

(e) **nor, neither, either** (with negative) (cf. 527)

Ich wußte nichts davon.—Ich auch nicht	*I knew nothing about it.—Nor (did) I/ Neither did I*
Das wird ihm auch nichts helfen (from Du. Stil.)	*That won't help him either*

(f) **confirmatory**

Er scheint intelligent zu sein.—Das ist er auch	*He seems to be intelligent.—So he is*

(g) **correcting a false impression**

Das hättest du nicht tun sollen.— Ich hab' es auch gar nicht getan	*You shouldn't have done that.—But I never did it*
Er ist aber nicht sehr intelligent.— Das hab' ich auch gar nicht gesagt	*But he's not very intelligent.—Well, I never said he was*

(h) **reinforcing a request or admonition**

Kauf mir eine Zeitung und vergiß es auch nicht![4]	*Buy me a paper and be sure you don't forget*
Hörst du auch zu?	*Are you sure you're listening?*

(i) **giving emphasis to a comment on the remark of another speaker**

Was *hast* du auch für seltsame Ideen!	*What strange ideas you have, upon my word!*
Das will ich (aber) auch tun	*I'll certainly do that*
Wer *gibt* auch so ein Versprechen?	*What fool would make such a promise?*

cf. in a question:

Bist du auch glücklich?	*And are you really happy?*

(j) **compliant**

Du bist anscheinend dagegen; wir können es auch lassen	*You seem to be against it; if you prefer, we'll leave it*

(k) **explanatory**

Er hat die Stellung bekommen; sein Vater hat auch viel Einfluß	*He's got the job, but then his father has a lot of influence*
Ich konnte es nicht tun; was hätten die andern auch gedacht?	*I couldn't do it, for what would the others have thought?*

[1] or: Nicht einmal sein bester Freund . . ..
[2] cf. Kolisko and Yuill: *Practice in German Prose*, p. 89.
[3] from Betteridge, op. cit.
[4] from Muret-Sanders, op. cit.: auch.

Wie trocken ist der Rasen!—Es hat auch nur wenig geregnet[1]	How dry the lawn is!—Don't forget, we haven't had much rain

(l) concessive[2]

Wer es auch sein mag, ich kann nichts für ihn tun	Whoever it may be, I can do nothing for him

287. dabei

(a) proximity and inclusion

die Dabeistehenden	the bystanders
Waren Sie auch dabei?	Were you there too? (Were you at the meeting, in the army etc., too?)
Er war nur halb dabei	He was only half taking part/attending
Einige haben Ferngläser dabei (*Zeit*)	Some have brought binoculars

(b) at the same time, yet

Sie erzählte mir davon und strickte dabei	She told me about it and knitted as she did so
Er ist gescheit und dabei fleißig	He is clever and industrious besides
Er suchte nach dem Brief, und dabei hatte er ihn in der Hand	He looked for the letter, yet he had it in his hand
Er lebt sehr einfach, dabei ist er ganz wohlhabend	He lives very simply, yet he's quite well off

(c) idiomatic (basically often 'in the matter')

Das Merkwürdige dabei ist . . .	The strange thing about it is . . .
Was ist denn da dabei?	Whatever is there to object to? What does it matter?
Es ist nichts dabei	There's no objection, it's quite all right
Ich finde nichts dabei	I see no objection
Es kam nichts dabei heraus	It led to nothing
Da kann man nichts bei machen (H. Fallada) (dabei divided)	One can do nothing in such a matter (coll.)
Er denkt sich nichts dabei	He thinks nothing of it (i.e. sees no harm in it)
Wir wollen es dabei lassen	We'll leave it at that
Es bleibt dabei	We are not changing our decision

288. dazu (see also 511 i)

(a) purpose (stress as indicated)

Dàzu braucht man ein scharfes Messer	For this you need a sharp knife
Dàzu ist er nicht intelligent genug	He's not intelligent enough for that
Ich hatte keine Gelegenheit/keinen Grund dazù	I had no opportunity/no reason to do it
Ich bin nicht dàzù da, um deine Arbeit zu tun	I'm not there in order to do your work
Ich kann nichts dàzù tun	I can't do anything about it

(b) addition (stress on 'zu') (cf. 706)

Es wäre das eine Ungerechtigkeit und ein Fehler dazu (*FAZ*)	This would be an injustice and in addition a mistake
Dazu kommt noch das Porto	To this must be added the postage
Er schenkte mir ein Hemd und einen Schlips dazu	He gave me a shirt and a tie to go with it

---

[1] from Muret-Sanders, op. cit.: auch.   [2] see 471–4.

289. denn

(a) **conjunction 'for'**: see 521

(b) **used for 'than'**: see 131(d)

(c) **Inserted in a question,** 'denn' implies a lively interest or impatience on the part of the questioner, or makes the question less abrupt:[1]

Wie geht es dir denn?	*Tell me, how are you?*
Was ist denn los?	*Whatever's the matter?*
Wer redet denn von nachgeben?	*Come now, who is talking of giving in?*
Der Bus hält ja. Sind wir denn schon da?[2]	*Why, the bus is stopping. Have we arrived?*
Wieso denn?	*How so?*

It may also convey doubt or perplexity:[3]

Ist das denn so wichtig?	*Is that really so important?*
Was soll ich denn machen?	*Whatever am I to do?*

(d) **denn noch** is used when trying to recall a fact:[4]

Wie *heißt* er denn noch?	*What is his name now?*

(e) **denn auch** indicates the result of a previous fact:

Es war schwül im Zimmer; er nickte denn auch bald ein	*It was sultry in the room and so he soon dozed off*

(f) Often preceded by 'so', denn is used **in an exclamation expressing surprise** at some piece of news:

So hat er denn die Stellung erhalten!	*So he has got the job!*

(g) **denn doch** (unstressed) expresses indignation or protest:

Das ist denn doch unerhört!	*But that really is scandalous!*
Das ist denn doch zuviel verlangt!	*I must say, that's asking too much*

(h) **es sei denn, (daß)** is a common conjunctional phrase meaning *unless*, mainly used in Open Conditions (cf. 462):

Ich komme also gegen ein Uhr, es sei denn, daß ich aufgehalten werde (or: es sei denn, ich werde aufgehalten)	*So I'll come about one o'clock unless I'm delayed*
Das kann dir niemand sagen, es sei denn ein Fachmann	*No one can tell you that except, perhaps, an expert*

The idea of 'unless' can be conveyed by 'denn' alone (archaic and literary) or by 'denn' coupled with the imperfective subjunctive of 'müssen' (rather literary):

'Ich lasse dich nicht fort', rief sie, 'du sagst mir denn, was du im Sinn hast.' (F. Wiechert)[5]	*'I shan't let you go', she cried, 'unless you tell me what you have in mind'.*
Er kommt noch, er müßte denn krank sein[6]	*He is sure to come unless he is ill*

(i) **geschweige denn** *not to mention, let alone, much less* (The phrase stands

---

[1] Eggeling's admirable formulation, op. cit.: denn (adverb).
[2] Es geht weiter (B.B.C.), p. 95.
[3] cf. Schröder loc. cit. (see p. 145, footnote 1).
[4] cf. Collinson, loc. cit., p. 119.
[5] quoted by Eggeling, op. cit.: denn (adverb).
[6] from Betteridge, op. cit.: müssen.

for 'ich geschweige' *I am silent about, I do not mention*.)[1] Occasionally the 'denn' is omitted.

Er wollte mir kein Geld leihen, geschweige denn schenken	*He wouldn't lend me any money, let alone give it me*
Ich glaube nicht, daß er sich für Tennis interessiert, geschweige denn, daß er selber spielt	*I don't think he's interested in tennis, much less that he plays himself*
Er kann kein Französisch, geschweige denn Deutsch	*He doesn't know French, not to mention German*

(j) **In North Germany, 'denn' is often used colloquially for 'dann'**; this should not be imitated (cf. Du. Gram. 3630):

Na, denn geht es eben nicht	*Well, then it just can't be done*

290. doch

(a) **yet, but, nevertheless**

Ich sehe ihn oft, doch kennen wir uns kaum	*I often see him, yet we hardly know each other*

Note: 'doch wir kennen uns kaum' would be possible, if slightly less usual; after 'und doch' only the inverted order is possible.

(b) Vocally stressed, it has the sense of **after all, all the same, despite everything**:

Ich hab' ihm abgeraten, aber er hat es (nun) *doch* getan	*I advised him against it, but he has done it all the same*
Zwingen kann ich ihn ja *doch* nicht	*Why* (ja), *in any case I can't compel him*
Also *doch!*[2]	*What did I tell you?/There you are!*
Lieber nicht drüber nachdenken. Oder *doch?* (Arno Schmidt)	*Better not think about it. Or should one after all?*
lieber *doch* nicht	*better not after all*

(c) **intensifying an imperative**, often with a pleading or impatient note;[3] 'doch mal' often conveys encouragement, as in the last example:[4]

Lassen Sie mich doch mal das Foto sehen!	*Do let me have a look at the photo*
Reg dich doch nicht so auf!	*For heaven's sake, don't get so excited*
Gehen Sie doch mal nach Italien!	*Why don't you go to Italy?*

(d) **turning a statement into a question that hopes for, or expects, a favourable or corroborative reply**; often the equivalent of 'nicht wahr':

Du kannst mir doch helfen?	*Surely you can help me?* *You can help me, can't you?*
Er kommt doch heute? Er kommt heute, nicht wahr?	*He is coming today, isn't he?*

With a negative, the remark may convey incredulity or surprise:

Du glaubst doch nicht, daß ich es getan habe?	*Surely you don't think that I did it?*

---

[1] cf. Eggeling, op. cit.: denn: adverb.
[2] from Betteridge, op. cit.: doch.
[3] Eggeling amusingly illustrates its nuances: op. cit.: doch (adverb) 2(b).
[4] cf. Collinson, loc. cit., p. 112.

(e) **In the following reactions to a statement or question of another speaker**:

i contradicting another speaker's negative statement:

Er hat nie etwas für uns getan.—   *He's never done anything for us.—Yes he*
Doch, er hat mir einmal 100 Mark   *has: he once lent me 100 marks*
geliehen

ii expressing agreement with an affirmative statement:

Er ist eigentlich ganz intelligent.—   *He's really quite intelligent.—Indeed he is*
Doch, (doch)

iii lending emphasis to a statement by protesting against an imaginary remark to the contrary:

Und die Anzeigen, doch, das   *And the announcements* (on the radio),
interessiert mich immer (I. Seidel)   *oh yes, that always interests me*

iv giving an affirmative reply to a question expecting a negative one (cf. Fr. 'si'):

Bist du nicht zufrieden?—Doch!   *Aren't you satisfied?—Yes, I am*

v used alone, or mildly emphasizing e.g. ich glaube, ich denke, ich dächte, in an affirmative reply:

Kommt er bald?—Doch!   *Is he coming soon?—Oh, yes*
Haben Sie eine [Antwort]?—Ich   *Have you got an answer?—Yes, I think I*
dächte doch (Th. Mann)   *have*

vi strengthening 'nein' or 'nicht' in a negative reply:

Mutti, kann ich ein Stück   *Mummy, can I have a piece of chocolate?*
Schokolade haben?—Nein doch, du   *—Certainly not, you've had enough to eat*
hast jetzt genug gegessen   *now*

(f) **intensifying an exclamatory remark**:

Wie *haben* wir doch gelacht!   *How we did laugh!*
Wie *winzig* doch alles von hier oben   *But how tiny everything looks from up*
aussieht!   *here!*

(g) **in exclamations expressing a wish** (cf. 476(b)):

Wenn er doch jetzt käme!   *If only he would come now!*

(h) **straining one's powers of memory or comprehension**:

Wie *hieß* er doch (or noch)?   *What was his name?*
Was *hat* er doch gesagt?   *What was it he said?*
Wie *konnte* er doch so was tun?   *However could he do such a thing?*

(i) **oder doch** *or at least, or at any rate*:

Es geht ihm wieder gut, oder doch   *He's well again, or at any rate much*
viel besser   *better*

See also 298: a common analogous use of ja and doch

291. eben

N.B. Used adverbially, eben never means 'even', which is sogar or selbst; as an adjective, it means 'even, level'.

(a) **When accented, it is the equivalent of just (just now) in two different senses:**

i **temporal,** referring to past, present or future:

Er ist eben[1] (erst) angekommen	*He has (only) just arrived*
Wovon sprachen wir eben?	*What were we talking about just now?*
Das wollte ich eben sagen	*I was just going to say that*
Eben geht mir ein Licht auf	*It's just dawning on me*
Ich komme eben	*I'm coming in a moment*

ii **denoting 'by a narrow margin'** (often followed by 'noch'):

Mit 500 Mark im Monat komme ich eben (noch) aus	*I can just manage on 500 marks a month*

(b) **When unaccented:**

i **it means 'just, exactly, precisely':**[2]

Eben dieses Haus hatte mir zugesagt	*It was just this house that attracted me*
Das wäre mir eben[3] recht	*That would be just what I should like*
Eben dàran hatte ich nicht gedacht	*That's the one thing I hadn't thought of*
Die Lage ist nicht eben ernst	*The situation is not exactly serious*

Compare the colloquial rejoinders:

Er müßte eine andere Stelle suchen.— (Ja) eben![3]	*He ought to look for another job.— Exactly*
Der Chef war eigentlich ganz verständnisvoll.—Na eben![3]	*The director was really quite understanding.—Of course he was (That's just what I said he'd be)*

Compare with the last example the reminding function of 'eben' in a context such as this: enumerating the main nationalities to visit Baden-Baden, the speaker might conclude: 'und dann eben Amerikaner' *and then, as I said before, Americans.*

Compare the compounds of 'eben' (in all of which it is accented) e.g. ebensoviel, ebensosehr *just as much,* ebenderselbe *the very same.*

ii **it suggests an explanation:**

Ich kann ihn nicht überreden; er ist eben hartnäckig	*I can't persuade him; the thing is that (or: you see,) he's obstinate*
Peter hat das Examen *doch* bestanden.—Er hat eben Glück gehabt	*Peter has passed the exam after all.— It's just that he was lucky*

iii **it expresses the resigned acceptance of a situation or the necessity for such an attitude:**

Aber so ist es eben!	*But there, that's how it is*
Nun ja, alles ist eben anders	*Ah well, everything's different and it can't be helped*
Karl hat angerufen, er hätte den Zug verpaßt; wir essen eben eine halbe Stunde später	*Karl has rung up to say he's missed the train; we'll just have to have dinner half an hour later*
Gut, dann eben nicht	*Well, then we won't (petulantly)*
Ich tue es, so gut ich eben kann	*I'll do it as well as I can in the circumstances*

---

[1] or, more emphatic: soeben.
[2] cf. 298(a), 2nd pair of examples.
[3] accented.

Note: The widely used South German dialectal **halt** could be substituted for eben in any of the examples in (b)ii and iii.

292. eher

(a) **sooner, earlier** (comparative of 'bald')[1]

Ich konnte nicht eher kommen	*I couldn't come any sooner*
je eher, desto besser	*the sooner, the better*

(b) **rather** (= more, to a greater extent)

Er sah eher wie ein Geschäftsmann als wie ein Schriftsteller aus	*He looked more like a businessman than like an author*
Das Gerücht seines Mißgeschicks hatte sie eher gereizt als abgeschreckt (A. Seghers)	*The rumour of his misfortune had attracted rather than deterred them*
Das ist eher möglich	*That is more likely*
Das geht schon eher	*That's rather more feasible*

eher must here be distinguished from **vielmehr,** which is strongly corrective; contrast i and ii:

i Es ist eine Ehre eher als eine Schande	*It's an honour rather than a disgrace*
ii Es ist keine Schande, (sondern) vielmehr eine Ehre	*It's no disgrace; rather it's an honour*
Ich achte ihn, vielmehr ich bewundere ihn[2]	*I respect, nay I admire him*

(c) **rather** (= in preference to)

Ich tue alles andere eher als nachgeben	*I'll do anything rather than give in*
Eher als daß ich ihn belästige, will ich es selber tun	*Rather than trouble him I'll do it myself*

(d) **if anything** (one thing rather than the opposite)

Es geht ihm eher besser	*He's if anything better*
Ich hatte eher bedauert, daß das Hotel so leer war	*I had been sorry rather than glad that the hotel was so empty*

(e) **um so eher** *all the more probably* (or *all the sooner*)

Er wird um so eher kommen, als er weiß, daß du da bist	*He's the more likely to come as he knows that you're here*

(f) **am ehesten**

i In the temporal sense (*soonest*), this is not much used: Wer ist am ehesten angekommen? (normal usage: zuerst.) Rather commoner is the form **ehestens** *at the earliest*: Er kann ehestens morgen früh hier sein (normal usage: frühstens) (Du. Stil.)

ii By a figurative extension of 'soonest', it may mean *with greatest probability, most readily, most easily*:

Du wirst es am ehesten in der Mansarde finden	*You're most likely to find it in the attic*
Man könnte ihn am ehesten mit Gottfried Keller vergleichen	*One could most nearly compare him to Gottfried Keller*

---

[1] Colloquially one may occasionally hear 'bälder'.
[2] Normal order is more incisive than inversion after vielmehr.

293. eigentlich: see 307.

294. einmal, mal

(a) **once (as opposed to twice etc.**) is 'einmal', with the first syllable stressed:

Ich habe ihn nur einmal getroffen	*I've met him only once*

Compare some idiomatic uses:

Dieses Paket ist noch einmal¹ so schwer wie das da	*This parcel is as heavy again as that one*
einmal (or erstens) . . ., sodann . . .²	*in the first place . . ., in the second place*
Ich kann nicht alles auf einmal tun	*I can't do everything at once*
Alle antworteten auf einmal	*Everyone answered at the same time*
Auf einmal erschien er	*All at once he appeared*

Note: In all the following uses either 'einmal' or the colloquial 'mal' can be used. The form selected in the examples is, on balance, the more convincing in the particular case. Only in the last example of (b) the alternative could not be used.

(b) **once, some time, one day, for once in a way**

Es war einmal eine alte Hexe	*Once upon a time there was an old witch*
Ich hab' ihn mal besucht	*I once visited him*
Ich werd' ihn mal besuchen	*I'll visit him one day*
irgend einmal	*some time or other*
Er wird es (noch) einmal bereuen (Du. Stil.)	*He'll regret it yet*
Da ich einmal im Zuge war, erzählte ich weiter	*Having once got going, I went on with my story*
Hier konnte er sich einmal richtig satt essen	*Here for once he was really able to eat his fill*
mal zur Abwechslung	*for once in a way*
Na ja, so *mal*	*Well, for once in a way*

(c) **With an imperative or its equivalent, it corresponds to 'just':**

Komm (eben) mal her!	*Just come here*
Denken Sie mal, er hat hundert Pfund gewonnen!	*Just think, he's won £100*
Überleg dir's mal!	*Just think about it*
Moment mal!	*Just [wait] a minute*
Das muß man sich mal vorstellen	*I ask you, just picture that*

With suitable intonation, it may express protest or indignation:

Erlauben Sie mal!/Hören Sie mal! So was hab' ich nie gesagt	*Pardon me/Look here, I never said that*

Sometimes, while it is essential in German, it is better left untranslated:

Laß mal sehen!	*Let's have a look*
Sieh mal, ich habe es mir *so* gedacht	*Look, this is what I thought (we'd do)*
Sag mal, *wo* wohnst du jetzt?	*(Just) tell me, where do you live now?*

(d) **After 'wollen', it frequently corresponds to 'just':**

Ich will (doch) mal sehen, wer es ist	*I'll just (or: I'll go and) have a look who it is*

---

¹ or, colloquially, noch mal.
² from Eggeling, op. cit.: einmal 1.

| Ich will ihn (schnell) mal anrufen | *I'll just give him a ring* |
| Jetzt will ich dir mal was sagen | *Now I'll (just) tell you something* |

(e) **noch einmal** (also 'nochmals') **and wieder**: noch einmal *once again*, *once more* is limited to the repetition of a clearly defined action; wieder *again* is more general:

Er öffnete noch einmal die Tür und rief 'Auf Wiedersehen!'	*He opened the door once more and called 'Good-bye'*
Im folgenden Jahr war er wieder krank[1]	*In the following year he was ill again*
Nach zwei Jahren kam er wieder nach Hause	*After two years he came home again*

(f) **nicht einmal (nicht mal)** *not even*

| Nicht einmal der Bürgermeister war dagegen | *Not even the mayor was against it* |

(g) **nun einmal** expresses resigned acceptance of a fact:

Es ist nun einmal so	*There you are, that's how things are (implying: and there's nothing to be done about it)*
Er will nun mal nicht—da ist nichts zu machen	*He just doesn't want to—there's nothing to be done about it*
Er braucht nun einmal viel Schlaf	*He happens to need a lot of sleep*
So was verkauft sich nun einmal	*Surprisingly or not, that kind of thing sells*

(h) **Examples of further idiomatic uses and nuances of 'mal'**

Du sollst mal sehen, wie das Geld geflitzt kommt (H. Fallada)	*You'll be surprised how the money comes pouring in*
Sie haben ja erst mal die Arbeitslosenunterstützung (H. Fallada)	*To start with, of course (ja), you'll have the unemployment benefit*
Da du (schon) einmal hier bist, könnten wir die Sache besprechen	*Seeing that you are here, we could discuss the matter*
Mal sehen	*We'll see*
Das sollte mal einer tun!	*Do that and see what happens!*
Gestern hab' ich mir's mal angesehen ('mal' is purely expletive)	*I had a look at it yesterday*

295. etwa

(a) about, approximately: Es kostet etwa dreißig Mark.

(b) perhaps, by chance (in a question or condition): Ist er etwa verreist? *Can he be away?* Wenn er etwa verreist ist, . . .

(c) After nicht, etwa often implies that a certain conclusion has been, or might be, drawn:[2]

| Sie wollen doch nicht etwa nach London ziehen? | *You don't mean to say that you intend moving to London?* |
| Sie müssen nicht etwa denken, daß ich ihn verteidigen will | *Now don't go and think that I'm trying to defend him* |

296. freilich: see 285.

---

[1] noch einmal would give an almost impatient emphasis.
[2] well analysed by Eggeling, op. cit., p.140.

297. ja.

Note: ja is moderately accented as used in (a), (b) and some items of (g); heavily accented in (f); otherwise unaccented.

(a) **yes.** The following example illustrates the effect of some idiomatic additions:

Bist du zufrieden?	—Ach ja! *Oh yes, I think so*
—Ja, ja! *Oh yes*	(also: *Yes, of course (I remember)*)
—Jawohl[1] *Yes/Yes, indeed*	—Nun ja! *Yes, I suppose so*
—Ja, freilich! *Certainly/Of course*	—Na ja! *Yes, I suppose so*

N.B.: As S. Colditz points out (loc. cit. p. 145, footnote 1), Ja, ja! may convey nostalgia:

Ja, ja! Das waren schöne Zeiten   *Yes, those were happy days*

(b) Placed before the second and more intense of two analogous words, it corresponds to English **nay** or **indeed**:

Es war ein Erfolg, ja ein Triumph	*It was a success, indeed a triumph*
Es war ein unerwarteter, ja ein sensationeller Erfolg	*It was an unexpected, indeed a sensational success*

(c) **It underlines the inevitable consequence of a fact stated by another speaker:**

Ich habe den Brief gelesen.—So? Dann weißt du ja alles	*I've read the letter.—Have you? Then, of course, you know everything*

(d) **of course, certainly, to be sure, indeed, before 'aber' or in a conditional clause:**

Ich will ihm ja helfen, aber leicht wird es nicht sein	*Certainly I'll help him, but it won't be easy*
Wenn er ja kommt, kann er das Paket mitbringen	*If, of course, he's coming, he can bring the parcel with him*

(e) **It conveys a wide range of feelings,** according to the context and intonation (see also 298):

Surprise:

Da ist ja Onkel Fritz!	*Why, there's Uncle Fritz!*
Er hat ja ein neues Auto!	*Why, he's got a new car!*

Indignation:

Das ist ja unerhört!	*That really is a scandal*

Agreement (concessive):

Es ist ja wahr	*It's true, to be sure*

Satisfaction:

Da kommt ja der Arzt	*Good—here comes the doctor*

(f) A stressed 'ja' emphasizes the importance of an action, or of avoiding it, and appears most frequently **in conjunction with an imperative** (**Be sure to . . .**):

Bleibe *ja* hier!	*Be sure to stay here*
Tu das *ja* nicht!	*Be sure not to do that*
Er soll *ja* nichts sagen	*On no account must he say anything*
Ich tat mein Bestes, damit er *ja* zufrieden wäre	*I did my best to ensure his being satisfied*

---

[1] regulation affirmative reply in the Bundeswehr; coll. pron. jawoll.

(g) Miscellaneous

Ja, wissen Sie, so was ist nie leicht	*Well, you know, that kind of thing is never easy*
Ja, was will er denn?	*Well, and what does he want?*
Ja und?	*1 And what then? 2 Well then?*
Ja (often stressed and prolonged), wenn das der Fall ist	*Well, of course, if that's the case*
Ja so, das ist etwas anderes[1]	*Ah, that's another matter*
Ja, was ich sagen wollte[2]	*Oh, by the way I was going to tell you*
Du hattest ja herrliches Flugwetter	*You had grand weather for flying, didn't you?*
ja sagen	*to give one's consent*
Er antwortete mit einem eindeutigen Ja	*He replied with an unequivocal affirmative*

298. A common analogous use of 'ja' and 'doch'

They are both used to enlist the understanding of the person addressed or of the reader, often protesting at the simplicity of a question (3rd pair of examples) or recalling a circumstance which justifies a preceding statement (4th pair of examples). The difference between 'ja' and 'doch' lies in the fact that 'doch' often conveys a stronger note of protest[3] or impatience. The main English equivalents are: *why, surely, don't you see, after all, you know, of course.*

(a) parallel examples:

Du könntest dir ja Karls Rad leihen	*You could borrow Karl's bike, couldn't you?*
Du könntest dir doch Karls Rad leihen	*Surely you could borrow Karl's bike?*
Das ist es ja eben	*Why, that's just the point* (or: *the difficulty*)
Das ist es doch eben	*Don't you see, that's just the point*
Warum gehst du nie ins Kino? —Du weißt ja, daß ich Filme nicht leiden kann	*Why do you never go to the cinema?* —*Why, you know that I can't stand films*
—Du weißt doch, daß ich Filme nicht leiden kann	—*You know very well that I can't stand films*
Er kann unmöglich kommen; er ist ja krank er ist doch krank	*He can't possibly come; he's ill, you know don't you see, he's ill*
Ich habe ihn ja/doch noch gestern gesehen!	*You know, I saw him only yesterday*

(b) further examples of 'ja':

Es ist nicht meine Schuld, wenn du dich langweilst; du hättest ja zu Hause bleiben können	*It's not my fault if you're bored; after all, you could have stayed at home*
Niemand drängte ihn, es eilte ja auch nicht (H. E. Nossack)	*No one pressed him, nor, after all, was there any hurry*

---

[1] from Eggeling op. cit.: ja 2(b).
[2] from Betteridge op. cit.
[3] cf. *Es geht weiter* (B.B.C.), p. 15.

(c) further examples of 'doch':

Das hätte ich doch nie gedacht	*You know, I should never have thought that*
Sie wissen doch, was ich meine?	*You know what I mean, don't you?*
Der Clown fiel wieder hin; die Kinder lachten; es war doch unendlich komisch, wie er immer hinfiel	*The clown fell down again; the children laughed; it was, after all, extraordinarily funny, the way he always fell down*

(d) example of **ja doch**:

Ich zählte die Kratzer an der Wand; ich mußte mich ja doch mit etwas beschäftigen	*I counted the scratches on the wall; after all, I had to occupy myself with something*

(e) a slightly literary usage, peculiar to 'doch'; here the 'doch' sentence has the inverted word-order, without being a question:

Natürlich leihe ich ihm das Geld; ist er doch mein Freund	*Of course I'll lend him the money; after all, he's my friend*

Analogous to this, is the use of 'doch' to express surprise and indignation:

Ist doch der Junge wieder am Zucker gewesen! (from Erben, op cit., 81)	*I'm blowed if that boy hasn't been at the sugar again!*

Plötzlich guckte ich aus dem Fenster, schleppten doch zwei Polizisten meinen Wagen ab—er war ja nicht abgeschlossen und außerdem falsch geparkt (*Zeit*)

299. nämlich

(a) **namely**

diese zwei Städte, nämlich Hamburg und Bremen	*these two cities, namely Hamburg and Bremen*

(b) **explanatory: you know, you see, for . . .**

Du mußt etwas lauter sprechen, er ist nämlich taub	*You must speak a bit louder; he's deaf, you know*
Sonst hätte ich es nämlich selber getan	*Otherwise, you see, I would have done it myself*

300. noch[1]

(a) **temporal**

  i *still, yet*; often 'immer noch' or 'noch immer', where continuation is denoted; Er war (immer) noch krank.

  ii some idiomatic applications of this meaning:

Ich werde das Problem noch lösen	*I'll solve the problem yet*
Ich habe nur noch zwei Mark	*I've only got two marks left*
Mein alter Vater kann nur noch wenig tun	*My old father can do very little now*
Weißt du noch?	*D'you remember?*
Du hast seinen Brief gelesen und da fragst du noch?	*You've read his letter and yet you ask?*
Diese Aufgabe ist so schwer.—Nun, das ist noch die einfachste	*This problem is so hard.—Well, it's the simplest compared with the rest*

  iii **noch nicht** *not yet*, **noch nie** *never (yet), never before*

---

[1] see also 290(h), 472, 523 ff.

(b) **still, yet, more, further,** with a comparative and, analogously, in other combinations (cf. Fr. encore): noch schneller; noch drei Tage; ich nehme noch ein Bier (*another glass of beer*); was willst du denn noch? *what else do you want?* noch etwas.

301. nun

(a) **now (temporal)**: less incisive than 'jetzt':

Nun (or jetzt) wollen wir umkehren	*Now we'll turn back*
Geht es dir nun (or jetzt) besser?	*Are you better now?*
nun endlich	*now at last*
cf. Als es nun Winter wurde, . . .	*Now when it turned to winter, . . .*

(b) **well (often 'na')** and some further colloquial equivalents:

Nun?	*Well?*
Nun und?	*And then what?*
Na und?	1. *Well, what's the outcome?* 2. *So what?*
Nun ja (or: Na ja), klassisches Deutsch ist es gerade nicht (Th. Valentin)	*Well (to be sure), it's not exactly classical German*
Nun, meinetwegen	*All right then, as far as I'm concerned*
Nun/Na, wir werden ja sehen	*Well, we shall see*
Haben Sie nu was retten können?[1]	*Now were you able to save anything?*
weil ich die ja nun sehr gut kenne,[1] (nun is purely expletive)	*because, of course, I know her very well*

(c) **nun einmal**: see 294(g).

302. nur

(a) **only**

Man kann ihn nur bewundern	*One can only admire him*

(b) **It may have intensifying force:**

Das macht es nur noch schlimmer	*That makes it even worse*
Wie kann er so taktlos sein?	*However can he be so tactless?*
Was können wir nur tun, um ihm zu helfen?	*Whatever can we do to help him?*
so schnell wie nur möglich	*as quickly as ever you can*

(c) **Used with an imperative or an imperative equivalent it expresses an exhortation or a warning:**[2]

Sehen Sie nur, was Sie gemacht haben!	*Just look what you've done*
Denken Sie sich nur!	*Just imagine*
Geh nur!	*Go along*
Treten Sie nur ein!	*Come right in*
Er soll nur kommen	*By all means let him come*
Nur weiter!	*Carry on* (often implying: *It's all right so far*)
Nur her damit!	*Come on, hand it over*
Nur nicht ängstlich!	*Don't be afraid*
Nur Mut!	*Be brave*

---

[1] taken from an article by Ulrich Engel in *Forschungsberichte des Instituts für deutsche Sprache*, Jan. 1968, pp. 85 ff.; 'nu' for 'nun'.

[2] cf. Schulz-Griesbach, op. cit., H 623 and H 626, Betteridge, op. cit., Collinson, loc. cit., and Du. Stil.

Nimm dich nur in acht!	*You be careful!*
Geh *nur* nicht in diesen Laden!	*Whatever you do, don't go into this shop*
Nur nicht!	*For heaven's sake, don't!*

(d) **nur so**: see 304(l)

(e) For the use of nur **in concessive clauses**, see 471(c)iii, e.g.

Wo er sich nur zeigte, . . .	*Wherever he showed himself, . . .*

303. schon

(a) **already.** With this basic meaning it will often require a different
　　rendering in English or can barely be translated:

Er war schon angekommen	*He had already arrived*
schon am nächsten Tag	*the very next day*
Da bist du ja schon wieder!	*Why, there you are back again*
Sind Sie schon in Köln gewesen?	*Have you been to Cologne yet?*
Sind Sie schon einmal in Köln gewesen? (slight stress on 'schon')	*Have you been to Cologne before?*
Sind Sie (schon) einmal in Köln gewesen? (slight stress on 'Köln')	*Have you ever been to Cologne?*
Ich hab' ihn auch schon in der Bibliothek gesehen	*I've sometimes seen him in the library*
Nicht alles, was nicht demokratisch ist, ist auch schon faschistisch (W. Alff)	*Not everything that is not democratic is necessarily fascist*

(b) **even, no more than, (if) only**:

Schon dieses 'good morning' war unvorsichtig genug (A. Goes)	*Even this 'good morning' was imprudent enough*
Schon der Gedanke (allein) ist mir unsympathisch	*The mere thought is repugnant to me*
Wenn ich ihn schon sehe, ärgere ich mich	*I've only to see him and I feel annoyed*
schon ihrer Kinder wegen	*if only because of their children*
Das geht schon daher nicht, weil . . .	*That's impossible if only because . . .*

(c) **expressing confidence or reassurance**:

Er wird uns schon helfen	*He'll help us all right*
Es wird schon gehen	*Don't worry, we'll manage*
Sie verstehen schon, nicht wahr?[1]	*I'm sure you understand, don't you?*

(d) **It may have a concessive slant,** often accepting the view of another
　　speaker:

Das ist schon möglich	*That's quite possible*
Das stimmt schon, aber es könnte auch anders kommen	*I admit that that is so, but things might turn out differently*
Ja, ich glaube schon, aber . . .	*Yes, I think so, but . . .*
Es ist schon besser du gehst (H. Böll)	*I think it would be better if you went*

(e) **giving persuasive force to what is usually a rhetorical ques-
　　tion: but then, after all**:

Wer kann schon dem Angebot widerstehen, für die Hälfte des normalen Preises bis Ostafrika und Bangkok zu fliegen? (*Zeit*)	*After all, who can resist the offer of a flight to East Africa and Bangkok for half the normal fare?*

[1] *Es geht weiter* (B.B.C.) p. 18.

Was sagt die Regierung zu Ungarn? —Nichts. Was sollen sie schon sagen? (M. Horbach)	*What does the government say to events in Hungary?—Nothing, but then what are they to say?*

(f) giving a note of preference or encouragement to an imperative or its equivalent:

Ein Achtel. Nein, bring schon ein Viertel. Wenn wir doch einmal so üppig sind (H. Fallada)	*An eighth of a pound. No, you'd better bring a quarter, as we're being so extravagant*
'Nun machen Sie schon, daß Sie weiterkommen!' sagte er zu seinem Fahrer (Th. Plievier)	*'Come on, now, let's get a move on', he said to his driver*

(g) Used in an Open Condition and sometimes strengthened by 'einmal', it has the force of überhaupt *at all*:

Wenn ich ihm schon (einmal) schreiben muß, so mach' ich es lieber heute	*If I've got to write to him at all, I'd rather do it today*

(h) Some fixed phrases

Schon gut!	*1. All right. Very well 2. That will do (You've said enough)*
und wenn schon!	*even so; what about it?*
Wenn schon, denn schon	*What is worth doing at all is worth doing well*
Das will schon etwas sagen (or bedeuten or heißen)	*That is saying a good deal*
schon gar nicht	*less than ever, even less*

304. so

(a) so (to such a degree)

Er ist so alt, daß er alles vergißt	*He is so old that he forgets everything*
soundso oft	*ever so often*

(b) as . . . as

Er ist so alt wie ich	*He is as old as I am*

(c) so (ein): such (a); a/that kind of; one of those etc.

so ein großes Haus	*such a big house*[1]
So ist das Leben	*Such is life*
Ich habe so ein Gefühl[2]	*I have a kind of feeling*
Er trug so eine Baskenmütze	*He was wearing one of those berets*
Sometimes pejorative:	
Das ist auch so eine Firma	*That's another of those shady firms*
So ein Wetter!	*What weather!*
Das sind so Fragen (idiomatic)	*Those are difficult questions*
Das sind so Sachen (idiomatic)	*Those are strange things*

(d) so etwas, so was[3]

Haben Sie so etwas/so was?	*Have you got something like this (or: that)?*
irgend so etwas	*anything like this*

---

[1] see also 223.
[2] cf. Collinson, op. cit., p. 53; 'Gefühl' is stressed.
[3] cf. so jemand *someone like that*.

So etwas Dummes hab' ich noch nie gelesen	*I've never read anything so stupid*
So was von Frechheit hab' ich noch nie erlebt (from Du. Stil.)	*I've never met with such impertinence*
Er ist so etwas wie ein Dichter	*He's something of a poet*
Er hat so ein gewisses Etwas	*There's something about him*

With omission of 'etwas':

Jedenfalls hatte das Mädchen eine Stelle in einem Kino. An der Kasse oder so [etwas] (J. Federspiel) (*in the box-office or something like that*).

(e) **thus, like this, like that, in this way, in such a way; as things are, as it is** ('so' is stressed in all but the 4th and 5th examples):

Du mußt es *so* tun	*You must do it like this*
Er handelte *so*, daß wir alle erstaunt waren	*He acted in such a way that we were all surprised*
So oder *so*, die Frage muß erledigt werden	*One way or another, the question has got to be settled*
Es kann Ihnen auch so gehen	*The same thing may happen to you*
Sieh mich nicht so an!	*Don't look at me like that*
So wirst du nie damit fertig	*Like this you'll never get it done*
So brauchte er es nicht zu erwähnen	*In this way he didn't have to mention it*
Auch *so* können wir nur eben auskommen	*Even as it is we can only just make both ends meet*
Ich bin *so* schon müde	*I'm tired anyhow/as it is*

(f) **'just' and other renderings underlining the casualness of the remark, the ordinariness of the action or situation referred to:**

Ich will dir keine Vorwürfe machen, ich meinte nur so . . .,(from Du. Stil.)	*I'm not trying to reproach you; I just thought . . .*
Die Schiffe beobachten, die da so vorbeikommen (W. Kempowski)	*To watch the ships that just happen to pass*
Was halten Sie eigentlich so von Picasso? (Th. Valentin)	*What do you think offhand of Picasso?*
Können Sie uns nicht 'nen Tip geben? So als Klassenlehrer (Th. Valentin)	*Can't you give us a hint? You know, as our form master*
Wie kommst du darauf?—Nur so (F. Dürrenmatt)	*What makes you ask?—Oh, nothing special*
Was machen Sie denn so abends?	*What do you generally do in the evening?*
was Manager so verdienen (*Zeit*)	*the kind of salaries that managers (usually) get*
Der Posten: 'Ja, um sechs ist hier Essensausgabe, dann ist Schluß. Nur noch so Streifenzug.' (A. Goes)	*The sentry: 'Yes, at six there's supper; that's the last thing. Only the usual patrolling.'*
Das weiß niemand so recht zu sagen	*No one can really say* (expletive)

(g) **about** (giving vagueness to numerals)

'Seit wann sitzt ihr hier?'. . . 'So seit neun.' (Th. Valentin)	*Since when have you been sitting here?—Since about nine*

(h) **so, thus**

Und damit, so möchte man meinen, war es eigentlich erledigt	*And with that, so one would think, the matter was really settled*

(i) **so, therefore**

Es war schon elf Uhr, so mußten wir uns eilen	*It was already eleven o'clock, so we had to hurry*

(j) **if, when** (archaic and literary)

so Gott will	*if it please God*
und auch dann nur, so es ganz still ist, dann hört man es [das Meer] singen und brausen (H. Broch)	*and moreover only then, when it's quite still, can one hear the sea singing and roaring*

(k) **used as a relative pronoun** (archaic, biblical and poetic):
Die Wanduhr pickt, im Zimmer singet leise
Waldvöglein noch, so du im Herbst gefangen (*which you caught*)
(Eichendorff: *Das Alter*)

(l) **nur so** has intensifying force, generally corresponding to the idiomatic 'fairly'. (The context will distinguish this sense of 'nur so' from that of 'nur so' as it figures in several examples of (f) above.)

Der Wagen sauste nur so dahin (from Du. Stil.)	*The car fairly whizzed along*
Es strömt nur so	*It's simply pelting down*
Er hat ihn heruntergemacht, daß es nur so eine Art hatte	*He told him off with a vengeance* (idiom)

(m) **Further colloquial and idiomatic uses** (see also 639, 641)

So?	*Really? Is that so?*
So! (often clipped short)	*Well, that's that*
soso	*so so, tolerably well*
So, du hast es vergessen	*I see; you've forgotten*
Wie geht's Ihnen heute?—So ziemlich	*How are you today?—Not too bad*
Das ist so recht nach meinem Geschmack (suggested by Du. Stil.)	*That's exactly according to my taste*
Er hat nicht so ganz unrecht	*He's not so far wrong*
Er tut nur so	*He's only pretending*
Er schlägt sich so durch	*He just manages to make a living*
. . ., so Brandt, . . .	*. . ., so says/according to Brandt, . . .*

(n) For the use of 'so':
to introduce subordinate clauses: see 467(c), 471, 542(f), 545–6 (e.g. so daß er alles wußte; so schnell er auch lief, . . .)
to follow subordinate clauses: see 462(c), 470(c), 473(c)N., 542(d) (f), 544(a) (e.g. Wenn ich ihm heute schreibe, so bekommt er den Brief morgen.) (Analogous to this: 464(a).)

305. **überhaupt** (accented on the last syllable)

(a) Only dialectally 'überhaupt' sometimes means 'above all, especially'; this use is best ignored; above all = vor allem, vor allen Dingen.

(b) **The basic meaning of überhaupt is 'considered as a whole, in a general way'**; this generalizing function requires the presence, or implication, of a particular case, a point well made by Eggeling (op. cit.: überhaupt).
The main English equivalents are: in general, altogether, at all; in certain types of question: really, in fact; a few of the following illustrations require other renderings.

(c) used affirmatively:

Er liebte die italienische Sprache, die Sprachen überhaupt (A. Goes)	He loved the Italian language and languages in general
Er ist flüchtig, faul und uninteressiert; überhaupt ist er ein schlechter Schüler	He is careless, lazy and uninterested; altogether, he's a bad pupil
Seinen Mut müßte man haben, dachte ich. Oder überhaupt Mut. (M. Walser)	One ought to have his courage, I thought. Any sort of courage
Ich komme morgen auf diesen Punkt zurück; überhaupt habe ich noch einiges zu erklären	I'll come back to this point tomorrow; for that matter, I've still got a number of things to explain
Wir müssen uns eilen, damit wir ihn überhaupt noch sehen.	We must hurry up in order to see him at all
Und überhaupt! (coll.)	and really, you know! (or: if you think about it)

(d) in conditional clauses:

Wenn ich überhaupt komme, wird es nicht für lange sein	If I come at all, it won't be for long

(e) in questions:

Er singt nicht besonders gut.—Kann er überhaupt singen?	He doesn't sing particularly well.—Can he sing at all?
Wie konntest du überhaupt so was tun?	How could you do such a thing at all? (i.e. under any circumstances)
Hier ist der Brief nicht; wo kann er überhaupt sein?	The letter isn't here; wherever can it be?
Was will er überhaupt?	What does he really want? (or, with aggressive intonation: What the dickens does he want?)
Weißt du überhaupt, was dieses Wort bedeutet?	Do you in fact know what this word means?

(f) used with a negative:

Du hättest es überhaupt nicht tun sollen, und besonders jetzt nicht	You shouldn't have done it at all, and particularly not now
Er ist überhaupt kein Dichter	He isn't a poet at all
Ich kann dir nicht sagen, ob er in die Schweiz will; ich weiß überhaupt nichts von seinen Plänen	I can't tell you if he intends going to Switzerland; indeed I know nothing whatever of his plans[1]

306. weiter

(a) **main meanings: further** (Er ging weiter als ich; weiter hinten), **else** (Wer war weiter da? weiter niemand, weiter nichts), **continuation** (Wir spielten weiter; immer weiter *on and on*).

(b) **coupled with a negative: not particularly, no particular:**

Es sah weiter nicht schlimm aus (Th. Plievier)	Things didn't look particularly bad
Es machte weiter keinen Eindruck auf ihn	It made no particular impression on him
Das hat weiter nichts zu sagen	That has no particular significance

---

[1] Without the preceding sentence, 'nothing whatever' would be 'gar nichts', merely an emphatic negative. Cf. Eggeling, op. cit.: überhaupt: 2.

307. (a) **'wirklich' must be distinguished from 'eigentlich'**

wirklich can always, and eigentlich can generally, be rendered by 'really',
   yet the two German adverbs are never interchangeable:
wirklich means: in truth, positively, I assure you;
eigentlich means: at bottom, in actual fact, actually, in reality, generally
   implying 'contrary to appearances, expectations or later developments';
   colloquially it may mean no more than 'tell me'.
Some pairs of examples may illustrate this difference:

Er ist wirklich sehr fleißig	*He really is* (I can assure you) *very hard-working*
Er scheint manchmal faul zu sein, aber er ist eigentlich sehr fleißig	*He sometimes appears to be lazy, but he's really* (in actual fact) *very hard-working*
Das geht wirklich nicht	*That really* (positively) *can't be done*
Eigentlich geht das nicht, aber . . .	*Really* (strictly speaking) *that can't be done, but . . .*
Es ist wirklich schade, daß er nicht hier ist	*It really is a pity that he isn't here*
Es ist eigentlich schade, daß er nicht hier ist	*Come to think of it, it's a pity that he isn't here*
Ist er wirklich krank?	*Is he really ill?*
Ist er eigentlich krank?	*Tell me, is he ill?*

N.B. Wirklich? So? Tatsächlich? Wahrhaftig? *Really?*

(b) **As adjectives, the two words have the same basic difference**

Es war ein wirklicher Triumph	*It was a real* (positive) *triumph*
im wirklichen Leben	*in real life*
Was ist die eigentliche Ursache?	*What is the real* (fundamental) *cause?*

(c) **Some further examples of eigentlich**

Was willst du eigentlich?	*What exactly do you want?*
Eigentlich könntest du mir helfen	*Really* (in actual fact) *you could help me*
Wir wollten eigentlich nach München (from Du. Stil.)	*We really* (originally) *intended going to Munich*
Wo ist eigentlich der Büchsenöffner?	*Tell me, where is the tin-opener?*

308. wohl

(a) **As an adjective** (never used attributively) it means well (in health);
   also: happy, at ease:

Er ist wieder wohl	*He's well again*
Mir ist heute nicht sehr wohl	*I'm not very well today*
Wohler habe ich mich nie gefühlt	*I've never felt better*
In Italien fühl' ich mich am wohlsten	*I am happiest* (or: *It suits me best*) *in Italy*
Ich fühle mich immer sehr wohl bei Ihnen	*I always feel very much at my ease when staying with you*

(b) **As an adverb, it does *not* mean 'well, excellently'**; thus: Er
singt gut (not: wohl); exceptions are some idiomatic phrases (cf. v

below) and some compounds (e.g. wohlschmeckend *tasty*). **The following are its main uses as adverb and particle:**

i Stressed, **it may mean 'well' in the sense of 'fully, full well, carefully':**

Er weiß sehr wohl, daß er unrecht getan hat	*He knows very well that he has done wrong*
Du hättest wohl kommen können[1]	*You might very well have come*
und er war so geartet, daß er solche Erfahrungen wohl vermerkte (Th. Mann)	*and he was so constituted that he took careful note of such experiences*

ii **wohl aber** (with stress on wohl): **but certainly, but (on the other hand):**

Herr Gérade, der mitnichten ein Tor, wohl aber ein Träumer war (A. Kolb)	*Herr Gérade, who was by no means a fool, but certainly a dreamer*
Ich habe ihn nie gesprochen, wohl aber oft gesehen	*I've never spoken to him, but (on the other hand) I've often seen him*

iii Unstressed, and sometimes preceded by 'ja', it expresses uncertainty or probability: **I suppose, probably etc.:**

Er ist noch nicht hier; er hat wohl den Zug verpaßt	*He's not here yet; I suppose he's missed the train*
heute nicht, wohl aber morgen	*not today, but probably tomorrow*
Das weißt du ja wohl	*No doubt you know that*
Ob er wohl alles verstanden hat?	*Do you think/I wonder if he's understood everything?*
Würden Sie wohl so liebenswürdig sein und den Brief mitnehmen?[2]	*I wonder if you'd be so good as to take the letter with you?*

By an extension of the meaning 'probably', **wohl auch** may mean 'sometimes': Er besuchte uns oft und brachte wohl auch ein kleines Geschenk mit.

iv Moderately stressed, it may have concessive force: **admittedly, indeed, certainly** (cf. 285):

Er ist wohl mein Freund, aber ich kann ihm nicht helfen	*He is indeed my friend, but I can't help him*
Er besuchte uns wohl manchmal	*Certainly he occasionally visited us*
Das ist wohl möglich	*That may be so (I admit)*

v **Some idiomatic phrases**, with 'wohl' stressed where indicated:

Das kann man wohl sagen	*You're right there*
Ich möchte wohl wissen, warum . . .	*I'd really like to know why . . .*
Kinder, wollt ihr wohl endlich still sein!	*Children, now at last will you be quiet!*
Siehst du nun wohl, daß ich recht habe? (from Du. Stil.)	*Now do you at last see that I'm right?*
Wohl bekomm's!	*I trust it may do you good* (or, ironically: *Much good may it do you!*)
Leb *wohl!*	*Farewell, good-bye*
Schlaf *wohl!*	*Sleep well*
wohl oder *übel*	*willy-nilly, come what may*

[1] with unstressed 'wohl': You could probably have come (cf. iii)).
[2] from Collinson, loc. cit., p. 116.

309. zwar: see 285.

310. Some examples of multiple particles

Ich will eben mal nachgucken	*I'll just go and have a look*
Du wirst doch wohl nicht meinen, daß ich es war?	*Surely you don't think it was me?*
Und das heißt ja schon eigentlich, daß dieser Jüngling ein Sinnierer war (H. von Doderer)	(a young man's hobby was bee-keeping): *and, you know, that in itself really means that this young man was a dreamer*
Das hatte ich während meiner literarischen Laufbahn ja nun doch auch immerhin gelernt (Arno Schmidt)	*Now that, after all, was something I had learnt during my literary career*
Ja, aber ich bin doch nun mal mit Marek und Jan befreundet und nicht mit einem Österreicher (Th. Valentin)	*Yes, but don't you see I happen to be friends with Marek and Jan and not with an Austrian*
Es ist doch nun mal so	*After all, that's how it is*
So schlecht wie ihr Ruf ist die Stadt nun auch wieder nicht	*On the other hand the town is not as bad as its reputation*

X TIME PHRASES

A. TIMES OF THE CLOCK

311. Wieviel Uhr ist es?

	What time is it?
Wie spät ist es?	*What time is it?*
Es ist ein Uhr/eins	*It's one o'clock/one*
Wieviel Uhr haben Sie?	*What time do you make it?*
(Es ist) drei Uhr	*I make it three o'clock*
Es ist zehn (Minuten) vor eins	*It's ten (minutes) to one*
Es ist zehn (Minuten) nach eins	*It's ten (minutes) past one*
Es ist Viertel nach (elf)	*It's quarter past (eleven)*
Es ist Viertel (auf) zwölf[1]	
Es ist fünfundzwanzig nach (elf)	*It's twenty-five past (eleven)*
Es ist fünf vor halb (zwölf)	
Es ist halb zwölf	*It's half past eleven*
Es ist zwanzig vor zwölf	*It's twenty to twelve*
(Es ist fünf Minuten vor dreiviertel zwölf)	
Es ist Viertel vor zwölf	*It's quarter to twelve*
Es ist dreiviertel (auf) zwölf[1]	
Um wieviel Uhr kommt er?[2]	*What time is he coming?*
Er kommt um halb sechs	*He's coming at half past five*
um drei Uhr nachts	*at 3 a.m.*
um neun Uhr vormittags (vorm.)	*at 9 a.m.*
um zwölf Uhr mittags	*at twelve o'clock noon*
um sechs Uhr nachmittags (nachm.)	*at 6 p.m.*
um sieben Uhr abends	*at 7 p.m.*
um Mitternacht	*at midnight*
Es ist Punkt/genau/gerade[3] neun Uhr	*It's exactly nine o'clock*
Es ist gerade[3] halb	*It's just half past*
Schlag neun (Uhr)	*on the stroke of nine*
Es ist ungefähr/gegen neun Uhr	*It's about nine o'clock*
Es ist neun Uhr vorbei	*It's past nine o'clock*
Er kommt ungefähr um neun Uhr (not: um ungefähr)	*He's coming about nine o'clock*
Er kommt gegen neun Uhr (see Note i below)	

[1] This alternative is often used in Central and South Germany; the auf (upon, i.e. towards) explains its logic but is normally omitted.

[2] The 'Um' is often omitted in rapid speech. (This does not apply to the examples that follow.)

[3] pron. grade.

Er will um neun Uhr herum da sein   *He intends being here round about nine*
(coll.)   *o'clock*

Note:
i **'gegen' before a time of the clock** (e.g. Er kam gegen zwei Uhr an)
signifies for some Germans 'towards, getting on for', for others
'about, approximately'. To convey the first sense without ambiguity,
the sentence would run: Er kam kurz vor zwei Uhr an; for the second
sense: Er kam ungefähr um zwei Uhr an.

ii **Some further less common variants**
Es ist vier ein Viertel   *It's quarter past four*
Es ist viereinhalb   *It's half past four*
Es ist vier dreiviertel   *It's quarter to five*
Es ist sechzehn ein Viertel/ein halb/   *It's 16.15/16.30/16.45*
dreiviertel

312. The 24-hour clock

(a) This is exclusively used in time-tables, television and radio programmes,
in all official announcements of theatrical performances, meetings,
hours of business etc. and on printed invitations.
In conversation and letters German practice varies a good deal. Most
Germans use it in connection with the times of a journey; beyond
that, and where there is no ambiguity, the tendency is to use the 12-
hour clock; it would be slightly unusual to say: Die Tante hat uns
für fünfzehn Uhr dreißig zum Kaffee eingeladen.

(b) In time-table parlance, 'Uhr' is omissible in spoken German only in
giving the full hours 1–12:
Mein Zug fährt um neun   *My train goes at 9.00*
Mein Zug fährt (um) neun Uhr   *My train goes at 9.15*
fünfzehn
Wir kommen (um) siebzehn Uhr in   *We arrive in Hamburg at 17.00*
Hamburg an

(c) In connection with '13–23 Uhr' and with 'null Uhr', only time-table
parlance is used, e.g. Die Vorstellung beginnt um neunzehn Uhr
dreißig (19.30 Uhr) (not: um halb zwanzig Uhr); similarly: um
neunzehn Uhr fünfundvierzig (not: um Viertel vor zwanzig Uhr).
One possible exception is given in 311 N.ii.

(d) **vierundzwanzig Uhr or null Uhr?**
A performance is scheduled to finish 'gegen 24.00 Uhr', but a train
leaves at 0.23 (null Uhr dreiundzwanzig).

B. DATES

313. (a) **Der wievielte ist heute?**   *What's the date today?*

Den wievielten haben wir heute?   *What's the date today?*
Welches Datum ist heute?
Heute/Es ist der erste März   *It's the first of March*
Wir haben den ersten März
Es ist der Zwanzigste   *It's the 20th.*

Am wievielten kommt er zurück?	*What's the date of his return?*
Er kommt am zehnten Juni (am 10. Juni) zurück	*He's returning on the tenth of June*
Er kommt am Zehnten zurück	*He's returning on the tenth*
Er kommt am zehnten sechsten zurück	*He's returning on the tenth of the sixth*
am ersten Oktober nächsten Jahres (commoner: nächstes Jahr)	*on the first of October (of) next year*

(b) **Where the day of the week precedes the date**, there are three alternatives; the third is the most formal:

Er kommt	*He's returning*
Montag, den zehnten Juni,	*on Monday, the tenth of June*
am Montag, den zehnten Juni,	
am Montag, dem zehnten Juni,	
zurück	
Die Premiere findet Freitag, den 3. Januar (1971), statt	*The first night is on Friday, 3 January (1971)*

(c) **At the head of a letter**:

Köln, 20.10. (or x.) 69 or Köln, (den/d.) 20. Oktober 1969; spoken:
Köln, den zwanzigsten Oktober neunzehnhundertneunundsechzig

C. LAST NIGHT ETC.

314.
gestern abend	*last night* (before bedtime)
heute nacht	*last night, in the night*
heute morgen, heute vormittag	*this morning*
heute früh	*(early) this morning*
heute nachmittag, heute mittag	*this afternoon*
heute abend	*this evening, tonight* (before bedtime)
heute nacht	*tonight* (after bedtime)
morgen früh	*tomorrow morning*
morgen ganz früh	*early tomorrow morning*
morgen in aller Frühe	

D. DURATION

315. Duration: adverbial accusative (+**lang**). Wherever, in the following examples, 'lang' is bracketed, it is an optional addition which has no effect on the meaning and is purely a matter of personal choice:

Ich war einen Monat (lang) in Berlin	*I was in Berlin for a month*
drei Monate (lang) '	*for three months*
viele Jahre (lang)	*for many years*
monatelang	*for months*
ganze Stunden lang	*for hours on end*
eine Weile	*for a while*
eine Zeitlang	*for a time*
einige Zeit (lang)	*for some time*
lang(e)[1], eine lange Zeit	*for a long time*
wie lang(e)?[1]	*how long?*
kurz, eine kurze Zeit (lang)	*for a short time*

[1] The e of lange (see 277) is frequently dropped (cf. Du. Gram. 4445).

Ich bin jede Woche einen Tag (zwei Tage) in Frankfurt	*I'm in Frankfurt one day (two days) every week*
den ganzen Morgen (lang)	*all the morning*
den ganzen Tag (lang)	*all day*
den ganzen Winter (lang)	*all the winter*
die ganze Zeit (lang)	*all the time, all this time*
die ganze letzte Zeit	*throughout these last few weeks (or months)*
sein ganzes Leben (lang)	*all his life*

E. DEFINITE TIME (e.g. next week)

316. Definite time: adverbial accusative. This applies to time units, parts of the day, days of the week, months, preceded by **this, next, last, every**; often a prepositional phrase is a common alternative:

Wir werden dieses Jahr (in diesem Jahr) nicht verreisen	*We are not going away **this** year*
Er kommt nächste Woche	*He's coming **next** week*
Er kommt nächsten/kommenden/ am nächsten Dienstag	*He's coming next Tuesday*
Den nächsten Morgen (am nächsten Morgen) starb er	*The next morning he died*
Das nächste/im folgenden Jahr war er wieder krank	*The next/the following year he was ill again*
Kommende Woche (in der kommenden Woche) will ich ihn besuchen	*In the coming week I'm going to visit him*
Er kommt nächsten Mai (commoner: im Mai)	*He's coming next May*
Ich sah ihn (am) letzten/(am) vorigen/am vergangenen Freitag	*I saw him **last** Friday*
Wir waren die letzten drei Jahre in der Schweiz	*The last three years we've been to Switzerland*
Er kam jeden Tag	*He came **every** day*
Er kam alle zwei Tage	*He came every other day*
Er kam alle drei Wochen	*He came every three weeks*
alle paar Jahre	*every few years*
jede halbe Stunde	*every half hour*

Note:

i In the case of **'the' and 'that'**, a prepositional phrase is normal usage:

Am Tag nach seinem Tode starb auch seine Frau	*The day after his death, his wife died too*
An diesem Morgen war er schlechtgelaunt	*That morning he was in a bad mood*
Wir waren in jenem Jahr in Italien gewesen	*We had been in Italy that year*

ii A common rendering of **'the next'** or 'the following' is **'ander'**, but its use is confined to: am andern Tag, Morgen, Nachmittag, Abend and (less common) in der andern Nacht and it is not used of the future; thus: Am nächsten/folgenden Morgen werden wir weiterfahren.

iii **this morning**, this evening etc. = heute morgen, heute abend (see 314).

F. INDEFINITE AND HABITUAL TIME

317. Indefinite and habitual time: adverbial genitive

eines Tages	*one day*
eines schönen Tages	*one fine day* (lit. and idiomatic)
eines schönen Sommers (M. Frisch)	*one fine summer*
eines Sonntags	*one Sunday*
eines Morgens	*one morning*
eines Sonntagmorgens	*one Sunday morning*
eines nebligen Morgens (A. Kolb)	*one misty morning*
eines Nachts (by analogy, although fem.)	*one night*
donnerstags	*on Thursdays*
wochentags, werktags	*on weekdays*
morgens (rather less common: des Morgens), vormittags	*in the mornings*
nachts; tags	*at night; by day*
donnerstagabends	*on Thursday evenings*

Note:

i morgens, abends etc. are also frequently used with reference to one occasion, e.g. Nachmittags machten wir einen Spaziergang *In the afternoon we went for a walk*. The same applies to frühmorgens *early in the morning* and spätabends (or abends spät).

ii Ich habe ihn letzte Woche (einmal) gesehen   *I saw him one day last week*

iii In einer Woche (in einem Monat, in einem Jahr) war er schwer krank   *One week (one month, one year) he was seriously ill*

G. AGO, BEFORE, AFTER

318. ago: main construction: vor + dative.

vor einem Jahr, vor zwei Jahren, vor Jahren *years ago*, vor langer Zeit, vor einiger Zeit, vor kurzem (less common: vor kurzer Zeit), unlängst *not long ago*.

gestern vor acht Tagen	*a week ago yesterday*
Wie lange ist es her?	*How long ago is it?*
Es ist schon lange her	*It's a long time ago*
Es ist schon einen Monat her	*It's a month ago*

319. before: main construction: accusative + vorher.

Ich war ein Jahr vorher dagewesen	*I had been there a year before*
zwei Jahre vorher	*two years before*
am Tag (or: den Tag) vorher, am vorhergehenden Tag, tags zuvor	*(on) the day before*

cf. lange vorher, einige Zeit vorher, kurz vorher

Distinguish 'vorher' and 'vorhin'

vorher *previously, beforehand* can refer to past or future:

Ich hatte ihn vorher gesprochen	*I had spoken to him previously* (or: *before that*)
Ich muß ihn vorher sprechen	*I must speak to him beforehand*

vorhin *a short time ago, just now* refers to the past only:

Ich habe vorhin mit ihm gesprochen   *I spoke to him just now*

320. after, later

Einen Monat nach seiner Verhaftung wurde er freigelassen	*A month after his arrest he was released*
Ich habe ihn einen Monat danach/ später gesehen	*I saw him a month after*
lange danach, lange nachher, nach langer Zeit, lange Zeit danach	*a long time after*
einige Zeit danach nach einiger Zeit	*some time after*
kurz danach, kurz nachher, nach kurzer Zeit	*a short time after*
nach einer Weile	*after a while*
nach Wochen, Jahren etc.	*weeks, years etc. later*
tags darauf	*the day after*

H. ERST

321. erst: i. *at first, first of all* (cf. zuerst)
ii *only, not until, (so far) not more than:*

Er kommt erst am Montag	*He is only coming on Monday*
	He is not coming till Monday
Es ist erst acht Uhr	*It's only eight o'clock*
erst heute	*not till today*
Ich kam erst letzten Sommer nach Heidelberg	*I never got to Heidelberg till last summer*
Er ist erst sieben Jahre alt	*He is only seven years old*
Ich habe erst zwei deutsche Romane gelesen	*I have only read two German novels so far*
Es hatte eben erst zu schneien aufgehört (E. Jünger)	*It had only just stopped snowing*
Wäre er doch erst zu Hause! (H. Fallada)	*If only he were home!*
Wenn er erst zu Hause ist, . . .	*Once he is home, . . .*
Dieser Garten ist ganz schön, aber du solltest erst mal unsern sehen!	*This garden is quite nice, but wait till you see ours*
erst wenn (erst als)	*only when, not until*

I. GUIDE TO THE USE OF PREPOSITIONS BEFORE NOUNS DENOTING TIME

322. an + dat.: before days and parts of the day: am Montag, an einem Wochentag, am ersten Mai, an besonderen Tagen (BUT: in diesen kritischen Tagen); am Tag *in the daytime, by day*, am Abend, am Montagabend; **Exc.** in der Nacht.

Idiomatic variants: Er kommt Montag (Montagabend) zurück; bei Tag, tags; bei Nacht, nachts; abends etc. (see 317 N.i).

323. in + dat.

(a) before Augenblick, Minute, Woche, Monat, Jahr, Jahrhundert,

Zeitalter *period, age,* Epoche, the months and the seasons (see also 326):

im Augenblick	*at the moment*
im letzten Augenblick	*at the last moment*
in letzter Minute	
in der Woche vor Weihnachten	*in the week before Christmas*
in den letzten paar Jahren	*in the last few years*
im Jahre neunzehnhundertfünfzig (or merely: neunzehnhundert-fünfzig)[1]	*in 1950*
im Januar	*in January*
im Sommer	*in summer*
im Sommer 1963	*in the summer of 1963*
in dieser Jahreszeit	*in this season*
zu dieser Jahreszeit	BUT: *at this time of the year*

Idiomatic variants: Er kam Juli/Sommer 1963 zurück.

(b) to denote a period within or after which something is done or occurs:

Ich habe die Arbeit in zwei Stunden gemacht	*I did the work in two hours*
Er kommt in einer halben Stunde	*He's coming in half an hour*
heute in acht Tagen	*in a week's time, a week today*
heute über acht Tage	

Note:

Man kann dies an einem Morgen/ an (or: in) einem Tag/in zwei Tagen schaffen	*One can get this done in one morning/ in one day/in two days*

324. um: 'at' before times of the clock: um zehn Uhr.

325. zu: usually before Weihnachten, Neujahr, Ostern, Pfingsten: zu Weihnachten (S. Germ. also 'an') *at/for Christmas*

Idiomatic variant:

Er kommt Weihnachten (Ostern, Pfingsten)	*He's coming at Christmas (Easter, Whitsun)*

N.B. an Silvester *on New Year's Eve,* BUT: Wir fahren zu Silvester (*for New Year's Eve*) nach Mannheim.

326. zu or in + dat. before 'Zeit'?

(a) 'zu' is used in contexts denoting one or more specific points or limited periods of time:

zur Zeit (or: dèrzeit)	*at present, at the moment, at the time*
zur Zeit der letzten Wahlen	*at the time of the last election*
zur Zeit Shakespeares	*in Shakespeare's day*
Zu *einer* Zeit (or: Elnmal) hatte ich gehofft, Arzt zu werden	*At one time I had hoped to become a doctor*
zu *der* Zeit, zu dieser Zeit ('damals' is rather less precise)	*at that time*

---

[1] But: im Jahre tausendsechsundsechzig *in 1066.*
Duden condemns 'in 1950', which is sometimes found, as an Anglicism (Du. Haupt.p. 47).

zu der Zeit, als du hier warst	*at the time when you were here*
zu einer anderen Zeit	*at some other time*
zu jeder Zeit (jederzeit)	*at all times, at any time*
zu keiner Zeit (nie, niemals)	*at no time*
zu gewissen Zeiten	*at (certain) times*
zur gewohnten Zeit	*at the usual time*
gerade noch zur rechten Zeit	*in the nick of time*
zu gleicher Zeit (zugleich, gleichzeitig)	*at the same time, simultaneously*
Zu meiner Zeit war alles anders	*In my time (in my day) everything was different*
Ich habe in meinem Leben viele Veränderungen mitgemacht	BUT: *I've seen many changes in my time (in my day)* (cf. (b) i below)

(b) in + dat. is used:

i to denote a period within or after which something is done or occurs:

| In all der Zeit (in der ganzen Zeit) haben wir ihn nicht gesehen | *In all that time we didn't see him* |
| In kurzer Zeit war er wieder da | *In a short time he was back again* |

ii in phrases which are felt to denote duration and not merely a point or limited period of time:

In unserer Zeit tut man das nicht mehr	*In our times that is no longer done*
in einer Zeit, in der die Städte wachsen	*at a time when towns are growing*
in einer solchen Zeit wie heute	*at a time like the present*
in früheren Zeiten	*in days past*
in künftigen Zeiten	*in days to come*
in der ersten Zeit	*at first (in the first few weeks or months)*

327. Phrases with 'Stunde'

zur Stunde (elev.)	*at the present moment; so far; now, at once*
zu dieser Stunde	*at this hour*
zu jeder Stunde	*at any time*
zur selben Stunde	*at the same hour*
zu später Stunde (elev.)	*at a late hour*
in ruhigen Stunden	*in peaceful hours*
in elfter (or zwölfter) Stunde	*at the eleventh hour*

328. The translation of 'for'

(a) for a period of time lying completely in the past or the future:

| Wir waren drei Wochen (lang) in Deutschland | *We were in Germany for three weeks* |
| Wir werden drei Wochen (lang) in Deutschland sein | *We shall be in Germany for three weeks* |

Note: 'für' is also used in this type of context, e.g. Sie ging zurück ins Schlafzimmer . . . und . . . saß für zehn Minuten ganz reglos auf ihrem Bett (V. Baum). Wir waren für drei Wochen in Italien.

(b) for a period of time beginning in the past and still continuing in the present or at a more recent point in the past:

Er ist seit drei Wochen hier (or: Er ist jetzt schon drei Wochen (lang) hier)[1]	*He has been here for three weeks*
Er war schon seit drei Wochen krank, als ich ankam[1]	*He had been ill for three weeks when I arrived*

(c) for a period of time beginning in the present (or at some indicated point of time) and extending thence into the future:

Ich gehe für drei Wochen nach Deutschland (or, somewhat stilted: auf drei Wochen (acc.))	*I'm going to Germany for three weeks*
Am nächsten Tag fuhren wir für einen Monat in den Schwarzwald	*The next day we went to the Black Forest for a month's stay*

Colloquial variant:

Ich gehe eine halbe Stunde (lang) ins Café	*I'm going to the café for half an hour*

329. No preposition before Anfang, Mitte and Ende in a number of time phrases. (The examples apply to all three words):

Anfang Januar (Februar etc.)	*at the beginning of January (February etc.)*
Mitte des/dieses Monats	*in the middle of the/this month*
Ende nächster Woche	*at the end of next week*
Ende letzten Jahres	*at the end of last year*
Anfang 1960	*at the beginning of 1960*
Anfang der zwanziger Jahre	*at the beginning of the 1920s*
Er ist Mitte (der) Dreißig	*He is in his middle thirties* (between 30 and 40 years of age)

With Anfang and Ende only:

Anfang des Winters	*at the beginning of the winter*
Ende der Ferien	*at the end of the holidays*

Note:

i The above usage is essential in the types: Anfang Januar, Anfang 1960, er ist Mitte Dreißig; in the others, am Anfang, in der Mitte, am Ende are possible, but less idiomatic.

ii Note the absence of an article in analogous phrases with prepositions, e.g. seit Ende Januar, bis Mitte des Monats, vor Anfang 1960, seit Anfang des Winters.

J. FURTHER SELECTED TIME PHRASES AND TIME WORDS

330. Selected time phrases and time words not covered in 311–29, arranged in alphabetical order of the English equivalents.

Note:

For the use of Mal ('time', as in 'three times, next time') see 254 f.

For noch *still*, noch nicht *not yet* etc., see 300(a).

For 'in the twenties' etc., see 244.

---

[1] Regarding the tenses used, see 554.

For the difference between e.g. 'my three weeks' holiday' and 'our three-weekly conference', see 720, -lich, N.3.

(ungefähr) um diese Zeit	*about this time*
A.D. (=Anno Domini) (little used)	A.D.
n. Chr. (=nach Christus)	
n. Chr. G. (=nach Christi Geburt)	(Christi=gen. of Christus)
Er ist im richtigen Alter	*He's the right age* (see also 'at')
Jahrgang 1950	*of the 1950 age-group;* also used to denote the vintage of a wine
die ganze Zeit	*all along*
(noch) länger	*any longer*
Ich konnte keine Zeitung mehr bekommen	*I couldn't get a paper any more*
	around: see *round about*
zu jeder Tageszeit	*at any hour*
bei Tagesanbruch	*at daybreak*
bei Einbruch der Nacht	*at nightfall*
bei Sonnenaufgang	*at sunrise*
im Alter von 15 (Jahren)	*at the age of 15*
mit 15 (Jahren)	
in aller Herrgottsfrühe	*at the crack of dawn*
seinerzeit	*at the time,* e.g.
Ich habe sie seinerzeit besucht	*I visited them at the time*
gleich am Anfang	*at the very beginning*
zu diesem Zeitpunkt	*at this point of time*
zu dieser (or: um diese) Tageszeit	*at this time of day*
um diese Zeit	*at this time of day/of night*
v. Chr. (=vor Christus)	B.C.
v. Chr. G. (=vor Christi Geburt)	
Ich bin bis Montag zurück	*I'll be back by Monday*
rückwirkend vom 1. März	*back-dated to 1st. March*
bis dahin	*by that time,* cf.
Bis dahin bin ich längst zurück	*I'll be back well before that*
bis zum dritten Januar	*by the third of January*
morgen um diese Zeit	*(by) this time tomorrow*
bis wann?	*by when?*
bis in unsere Tage	*down to our own day*
bis auf den heutigen Tag	*down to the present day*
den Tag über, tagsüber	*during the day*
Hast du ihn je gesehen?	*Have you ever seen him?*
Es ist der beste Film, den ich je gesehen habe	*It's the best film I've ever seen*
bis tief in die Nacht hinein	*far into the night*
zu guter Letzt	*finally, to finish up, to cap everything*
Ich habe ihn ewig nicht gesehen	*I haven't seen him for ages*
für alle Zeiten	*for all time*
Wenn Sie länger da sind, ... (cf. 129)	*If you are there for any length of time, ...*
auf ewig	*for ever*
ganze drei Wochen	*for a full three weeks*
Ich habe ihn seit langem/lange/seit Jahr und Tag (idiomatic) nicht gesehen	*I haven't seen him for a long time*
für immer, auf immer	*for good*
auf Monate hinaus	*for months to come*
seit einiger Zeit	*for some time past*

augenblicklich	*for the moment*
bis auf weiteres, vorderhand	*for the present*
einstweilen, vorderhand, vorerst	*for the time being, meanwhile*
vorläufig	*for the time being, provisionally*
von Anfang bis Ende	*from beginning to end*
von Kindesbeinen an	*from early childhood*
von morgens bis abends	*from morning till evening*
von neun Uhr an	*from nine o'clock onwards*
von heute auf morgen	*from one day to the next, overnight*
von Anfang an	*from the beginning, from the start*
von vornherein	*from the first, from the outset*
von da an	*from then onward*
von der Zeit an ('der' is stressed)	
seit Menschengedenken	*from time immemorial*
seit undenklicher Zeit	
von jeher	*from time immemorial, always*
von Jugend auf	*from his (my etc.) youth upwards*
Er war eine gute Stunde bei mir	*He was with me a good hour*
vor einer guten Woche	*a good week ago (see also quite)*
stundenlang	*hour after hour, for hours*
Er wohnt stundenweit (drei Stunden weit) von hier	*He lives hours (three hours) from here*
Wie lange sind Sie noch da?	*How much longer will you be here?*
im voraus	*in advance, beforehand*
in alter Zeit, anno dazumal (coll.)	*in days of yore*
in künftigen Zeiten	*in days to come*
zur rechten Zeit	*in due course*
Schließlich kam auch Herr G.	*In due course Herr G. also arrived (coll. use)*
rechtzeitig	*in good time*
in seinem Alter	*in his old age*
auf seine alten Tage	
im Handumdrehen	*in no time*
im Lauf der Zeit, mit der Zeit	*in the course of time*
im Lauf von vier Jahren	*in the course of four years*
in absehbarer Zeit	*in the foreseeable future*
auf die Dauer	*in the long run*
inzwischen, mittlerweile, indessen, währenddessen, solange	*in the meantime, meanwhile:* = *during this period of time*
inzwischen, mittlerweile	= *since then*
in der Nacht von Sonntag auf Montag	*in the night from Sunday to Monday*
rechtzeitig, beizeiten	*in (good) time*
vor alten Zeiten	*in times of old, in days gone by*
auf unabsehbare Zeit	*indefinitely*
Ich kam noch eben zurecht	*I was just in time*
Es ist gleich halb fünf	*It's just on half past four*
zu allerletzt	*last of all*
der vorletzte Tag	*the last day but one*
der zweitletzte Tag	
der drittletzte Tag	*the last day but two*
längst	*long since (long ago, for a long time)*
Ich weiß es schon längst	*e.g. I have known it for a long time*
Es ist noch lange hin	*It's a long time to come*
mittelalterlich	**medieval**
in mittlerem Alter	**middle-aged**
die meiste Zeit	*most of the time*
den größten Teil der Zeit	

dann, sodann	*next, then*
nicht mehr	*no longer*
nicht mehr lange	*not much longer*
bald . . ., bald . . .	*now . . ., now . . .*
ab und zu	*on and off*
an diesem Datum	*on that date*
auf die Minute	*on the dot*
einmal (zweimal etc.)	*once (twice etc.) a week*
in der Woche pro Woche	
die Woche wöchentlich	
jede Woche	
dieser Tage	*one of these days, shortly; recently*
	(see 331)
übers (or: am) Wochenende	*over the weekend*
über Nacht	*overnight, during the night*
am vorhergehenden Dienstag	*(on) the previous Tuesday*
Er war gut zwei Stunden bei mir	*He was with me quite two hours*
vor gut drei Wochen	*quite three weeks ago*
	recent, recently: see 331
bis in den Herbst hinein	*right into autumn*
um Weihnachten herum	*round about Christmas*
um/ungefähr 1930	*round about 1930*
nach wie vor	*the same as before, the same as ever*
von alters her	*since ancient times*
seitdem, seit damals	*since that time, since then*
seit Mittwoch voriger Woche	*since Wednesday of last week*
früher oder später	*sooner or later*
über kurz oder lang	
vom ersten Oktober an	*starting on October the first*
heutzutage	*these days*
gestern um diese Zeit	*this time yesterday*
heuer	*(in) this year (Austrian dialect)*
sein ganzes Leben hindurch	*throughout his life*
zeit seines Lebens	
den ganzen Winter hindurch	*throughout the winter*
den ganzen Winter über	
verschieben auf + acc.	*to postpone till*
bis spät in die Nacht	*till late at night*
bis dann, bis dahin	*till then*
Ist es Zeit?	*Is it time?*
Ist es schon soweit? (idiomatic)	
anfangs	*to begin with, at first*
zuerst, zunächst	*to begin with, first of all*
bis auf den heutigen Tag	*to this day*
die heutige Sitzung	*today's meeting*
die Sitzung heute	
bis zu eineinviertel Stunden	*up to an hour and a quarter*
gleich am nächsten Tag	*the very next day*
Woche um Woche	*week after week*
übernächste Woche	*the week after next*
vorletzte Woche	*the week before last*
am Freitag vorletzter Woche	*on Friday of the week before last*
nach Feierabend	*when the day's work is done*
heute über ein Jahr	*a year today, a year hence*
heute übers Jahr	
die Stunde Null	*zero-hour*

331. recently

kürzlich, vor kurzem, unlängst	1. *a short time ago, a short time previously*
neulich	2. *the other day*
neulich morgens	*the other morning*
dieser Tage,[1] in diesen Tagen	3. *the other day, on one of the last few days*
letzthin, in letzter Zeit, seit kurzem, (neuerdings)	4. *latterly, during the last few weeks or months*, e.g.
Ich habe ihn letzthin nicht gesehen	*I haven't seen him recently*
bis vor kurzem	*until recently*
Ich habe ihn noch später gesehen als du	*I have seen him* **more recently** *than you*
Karl hat ihn zuletzt gesehen	*Karl has seen him* **most recently**

recent: There is no satisfactory German adjective; 'kürzlich' is an adverb and is unconvincing as an adjective, while 'neuerlich' also means 'renewed, fresh' (cf. Eggeling op. cit., p. 284):

beim kürzlichen Staatsbesuch von Bundespräsident Lübke (*SZ*)	*during the recent state-visit of Federal President Lübke*
die neuerliche Verletzung des vereinbarten Viermächtestatus (*FAZ*)	*the recent* (or *renewed?*) *violation of the agreed four-power status* [of Berlin]

One is therefore driven to circumlocutions and substitutions such as the following:

bei der kürzlich stattgefundenen Konferenz	*at the recent conference*
bei unserer Begegnung (von) neulich	*at our recent meeting*
als er vor kurzem krank war	*during his recent illness*
die jüngsten Zwischenfälle auf Zypern (*Zeit*)	*the (most) recent incidents in Cyprus*
eine neuere Verordnung	*a* **more recent** *regulation*
eine erst kürzlich eingeführte Neuerung	*a more recent innovation*
bei unserer letzten Begegnung	*at our* **most recent** *meeting*
die neuesten Verordnungen	*the most recent regulations*
sein neuestes/jüngstes/letztes Buch	*his most recent book*

332. der Termin *date, fixed day; appointment; court summons*

Er zahlte zu dem vereinbarten Termin	*He paid on the day agreed upon*
den Termin ein-halten/ versäumen	*to keep to/miss the date*
der (äußerste) Termin	*the deadline*
die Ferientermine	*the dates of the holidays*
Nennen Sie mir bitte einen Termin!	*When could I have an appointment?*
der Terminkalender	*engagement-diary*

---

[1] 'dieser Tage' may also mean 'on one of these coming days, shortly'.

XI VERBS

A. CONJUGATION

333. Conjugation of verbs: introductory

German verbs are of two main types, weak and strong.

Weak verbs form their imperfect by adding -te to the stem and their past
participle by prefixing ge- and adding -t to the stem; the stem is obtained by cutting off the -en (or -n)[1] of the infinitive. E.g.

> holen *to fetch* – holte – geholt

Strong verbs change the vowel of their stem in the imperfect; in the past
participle the vowel of the stem may again change or it may be the
same as that of the infinitive or of the imperfect. In the 1st and 3rd pers.
sing. of the imperfect, strong verbs have no ending; in the past participle
they prefix ge- and add -en to the stem. E.g.

> singen *to sing* – sang – gesungen
> tragen *to carry* – trug – getragen
> schreiben *to write* – schrieb – geschrieben

(For verbs with no ge- in the past part., see 343).

Most strong verbs with the stem-vowels e, a, au and o have a vowel
change or modification in the 2nd and 3rd pers. sing. of the present
indicative, where e becomes ie or i, while a, au and o modify (see 341).

There follow below:

i the full conjugation of haben *to have*, sein *to be* and werden *to become*. In
their simple tenses, these are not typical of either a weak or a strong
verb; as auxiliaries they help to form the compound tenses of all
other German verbs.

ii the full conjugation of a typical weak and of a typical strong verb
(holen and tragen respectively) in the active voice.

iii the full conjugation of the passive of loben.

iv variations in verb forms.

Note on the paradigms that follow:

1. The polite form of the 2nd pers., sing. or plur., is, except in the imperative, not given separately. It is the same as the 3rd pers. plur., except

---

[1] -n where the infinitive ends in -eln or -ern: see 340(g).

that Sie *you* has a capital letter: sie haben = *they have*; Sie haben = *you have*.[1]

2. In the compound tenses, the past part. and infin. go to the end of the sentence, except in a subordinate clause (see 649).
Perfect: Ich habe das Buch geholt
Pluperfect: Ich hatte das Buch geholt
Future: Ich werde das Buch holen
Future Perfect: Ich werde das Buch geholt haben

In the following paradigms, dots are inserted in the fut. perf. and condit. perf. to divide off the part that goes to the end (i.e. the perfect infinitive). The same device has been used in all tenses of the passive paradigm.

3. The compound tenses of 'haben' typify the compound tenses of all verbs conjugated with haben.

4. The compound tenses of 'sein' typify the compound tenses of all verbs conjugated with sein.

334. haben *to have*

Indicative	Subjunctive
PRESENT	
ich habe	ich habe
du hast	du habest
er hat	er habe
wir haben	wir haben
ihr habt	ihr habet
sie haben	sie haben
IMPERFECT	
ich hatte	ich hätte
du hattest	du hättest
er hatte	er hätte
wir hatten	wir hätten
ihr hattet	ihr hättet
sie hatten	sie hätten
PERFECT	
ich habe gehabt	ich habe gehabt
du hast gehabt etc.	du habest gehabt etc.
PLUPERFECT	
ich hatte gehabt	ich hätte gehabt
du hattest gehabt etc.	du hättest gehabt etc.
FUTURE	
ich werde haben	ich werde haben
du wirst haben	du werdest haben
er wird haben	er werde haben
wir werden haben	wir werden haben
ihr werdet haben	ihr werdet haben
sie werden haben	sie werden haben
FUTURE PERFECT	
ich werde . . . gehabt haben	ich werde . . . gehabt haben
du wirst . . . gehabt haben etc.	du werdest . . . gehabt haben etc.

[1] For the use of the familiar, as opposed to the polite 2nd pers., see 140.

Conditional	Conditional Perfect
ich würde haben	ich würde . . . gehabt haben
du würdest haben	du würdest . . . gehabt haben
er würde haben	er würde . . . gehabt haben
wir würden haben	wir würden . . . gehabt haben
ihr würdet haben	ihr würdet . . . gehabt haben
sie würden haben	sie würden . . . gehabt haben

Imperative	Infinitives	Participles
2nd sing. hab(e)!	PRES. haben	PRES. habend
2nd plur. habt!	PERF. gehabt haben	PAST gehabt
2nd polite haben Sie!		

335. sein *to be*

Indicative	Subjunctive
	PRESENT
ich bin	ich sei
du bist	du sei(e)st
er ist	er sei
wir sind	wir seien
ihr seid	ihr seiet
sie sind	sie seien

	IMPERFECT
ich war	ich wäre
du warst	du wär(e)st
er war	er wäre
wir waren	wir wären
ihr wart	ihr wär(e)t
sie waren	sie wären

	PERFECT
ich bin gewesen	ich sei gewesen
du bist gewesen etc.	du sei(e)st gewesen etc.

	PLUPERFECT
ich war gewesen	ich wäre gewesen
du warst gewesen etc.	du wär(e)st gewesen etc.

	FUTURE
ich werde sein	ich werde sein
du wirst sein etc.	du werdest sein etc.

	FUTURE PERFECT
ich werde . . . gewesen sein	ich werde . . . gewesen sein
du wirst . . . gewesen sein etc.	du werdest . . . gewesen sein etc.

Conditional	Conditional Perfect
ich würde sein	ich würde . . . gewesen sein
du würdest sein etc.	du würdest . . . gewesen sein etc.

Imperative	Infinitives	Participles
2nd sing. sei!	PRES. sein	PRES. (seiend)[1]
2nd plur. seid!	PERF. gewesen sein	PAST gewesen
2nd polite seien Sie!		

[1] barely used.

eg.- I hope that I become

336. werden *to become*

Indicative

Subjunctive

PRESENT

ich werde	*I become*
du wirst	*you become*
er wird	
wir werden	
ihr werdet	
sie werden	

that I become

that you become

ich werde
du werdest
er werde
wir werden
ihr werdet
sie werden

IMPERFECT

ich wurde[1]
du wurdest
er wurde
wir wurden
ihr wurdet
sie wurden

ich würde
du würdest
er würde
wir würden
ihr würdet
sie würden

For compound tenses (ich bin geworden, ich sei geworden etc.) see 335.

Imperative		Infinitives		Participles	
2nd sing.	werde!	PRES.	werden	PRES.	werdend
2nd plur.	werdet!	PERF.	geworden sein	PAST	geworden
2nd polite	werden Sie!				

337. Weak Verb: holen *to fetch*

Indicative

Subjunctive

PRESENT

ich hole
du holst
er holt
wir holen
ihr holt
sie holen

ich hole
du holest
er hole
wir holen
ihr holet
sie holen

IMPERFECT

ich holte
du holtest
er holte
wir holten
ihr holtet
sie holten

ich holte
du holtest
er holte
wir holten
ihr holtet
sie holten

For compound tenses (ich habe geholt, ich hatte geholt etc.) see 334.

Imperative		Infinitives		Participles	
2nd sing.	hol(e)!	PRES.	holen	PRES.	holend
2nd plur.	holt!	PERF.	geholt haben	PAST	geholt
2nd polite	holen Sie!				

[1] The singular forms ich ward, du wardst, er ward are archaic and poetic.

338. Strong Verb: tragen *to carry*

Indicative	Subjunctive
PRESENT	

Indicative	Subjunctive
ich trage	ich trage
du trägst	du tragest
er trägt	er trage
wir tragen	wir tragen
ihr tragt	ihr traget
sie tragen	sie tragen

IMPERFECT

Indicative	Subjunctive
ich trug	ich trüge
du trugst	du trüg(e)st
er trug	er trüge
wir trugen	wir trügen
ihr trugt	ihr trüg(e)t
sie trugen	sie trügen

For compound tenses (ich habe getragen, ich hatte getragen etc.) see 334.

Imperative		Infinitives		Participles	
2nd sing.	trag(e)!	PRES.	tragen	PRES.	tragend
2nd plur.	tragt!	PERF.	getragen haben	PAST	getragen
2nd polite	tragen Sie!				

339. Passive of loben *to praise* (Weak)

Indicative	Subjunctive
PRESENT	

Indicative	Subjunctive
ich werde . . . gelobt	ich werde . . . gelobt
du wirst . . . gelobt	du werdest . . . gelobt
er wird . . . gelobt	er werde . . . gelobt
wir werden . . . gelobt	wir werden . . . gelobt
ihr werdet . . . gelobt	ihr werdet . . . gelobt
sie werden . . . gelobt	sie werden . . . gelobt

IMPERFECT

Indicative	Subjunctive
ich wurde . . . gelobt	ich würde . . . gelobt
du wurdest . . . gelobt etc.	du würdest . . . gelobt etc.

PERFECT

Indicative	Subjunctive
ich bin . . . gelobt worden	ich sei . . . gelobt worden
du bist . . . gelobt worden etc.	du sei(e)st . . . gelobt worden etc.

PLUPERFECT

Indicative	Subjunctive
ich war . . . gelobt worden	ich wäre . . . gelobt worden
du warst . . . gelobt worden etc.	du wär(e)st . . . gelobt worden etc.

FUTURE

Indicative	Subjunctive
ich werde . . . gelobt werden	ich werde . . . gelobt werden
du wirst . . . gelobt werden etc.	du werdest . . . gelobt werden etc.

FUTURE PERFECT

Indicative	Subjunctive
ich werde . . . gelobt worden sein	ich werde . . . gelobt worden sein
du wirst . . . gelobt worden sein etc.	du werdest . . . gelobt worden sein etc.

etc.

Conditional	Conditional Perfect
ich würde . . . gelobt werden	ich würde . . . gelobt worden sein
du würdest . . . gelobt werden etc.	du würdest . . . gelobt worden sein etc.

Imperative		Infinitives	
2nd sing.	sei (werde) gelobt!	PRES.	gelobt werden
2nd plur.	seid (werdet) gelobt!	PERF.	gelobt worden sein
2nd polite	seien Sie (werden Sie) gelobt!		

Participles: PRES. gelobt werdend   PAST (gelobt worden)

Note:

i The future perf. passive is virtually never used; see 362.

ii The imperative passive with 'werden' is rare; thus, from the end of a letter: Seien Sie herzlich von uns beiden gegrüßt.

iii The passive present participle is very rarely used.

iv The passive past part.: except when forming part of an active compound tense, the active past part. of all transitive verbs is passive in meaning, e.g. mein verlorener Schirm *my lost umbrella*; cf. 435 ff.

B. VARIATIONS IN VERB FORMS

340. Miscellaneous variations

(a) **1st sing. pres. indic.**: the ending -e normally drops away in spoken German (and often, for rhythmic reasons, in literary German), e.g. Ich kauf' noch was; ich les' ganz gern. (But see (f) and (g) below).

(b) **1st sing. imperf. indic. of weak verbs**: the -e of the -te ending often drops away in spoken German (and, for rhythmic reasons, in literary German), especially before a vowel, e.g. Ich sucht' ihn überall, BUT: ich suchte meinen Bruder.

(c) **When the stem ends in a vowel or in h**, the -e of the -en ending generally drops away in spoken German (and often, for rhythmic reasons, in literary German) in the following forms:

Pres. Infin.: schaun, sehn.

1st and 3rd plur. Pres. Indic. and Subj.: wir/sie schaun, sehn; e.g. (Pres. Subj.): Gehn wir jetzt in den Garten!

Polite form of Imperative: schaun Sie! sehn Sie!

With strong verbs only:

1st and 3rd plur. Imperf. Indic. and Subj.: wir/sie sahn, sähn.

Past Part.: gesehn.

N.B. Pres. Indic. and Imperative of 'tun':

ich tu(e), du tust, er tut, wir tun, ihr tut, sie tun.

tu(e)! tut! tun Sie!

(d) **When the stem ends in a sibilant**:

i In the 2nd sing. pres. indic. the s of the ending drops away: lesen: du liest; schließen: du schließt; heizen: du heizt. Exc.: when the sibilant is sch: waschen: du wäschst.

ii In the 2nd sing. imperf. indic. of strong verbs the s of the ending is retained and an e is inserted: lesen: du lasest; schließen: du schlossest; waschen: du wuschest. (colloquially also: du last, du schloßt, du wuschst).

(e) When the stem ends in d or t:

i The stem of a weak verb ending in d or t is always followed by an e, e.g.

Pres. Indic.: du redest, er redet, ihr redet.
Imperfect: ich antwortete, du antwortetest etc.
Past Part.: geredet, geantwortet.
Imperative plur.: redet! antwortet!

Note: The ending e of the 1st sing. pres. indic. and of the imperative sing. is frequently dropped in spoken German, e.g. Ich antwort' nicht; antwort doch! See also ii N. below.

ii The stem of a strong verb ending in d or t adds -est (instead of -st) in the 2nd sing. pres. indic. (but not in the imperfect) and -et (instead of -t) in 3rd sing. pres. indic. and 2nd plur. pres. indic., imperf. indic. and imperative. (For strong verbs with a vowel change in pres. indic., see 341(c)).

e.g. du findest, du bittest (BUT: du fandst, du batst)
  er findet, ihr findet, ihr fandet, findet!

Note: In rapid speech frequently no e is inserted in the 2nd sing. pres. indic. (whether weak or strong) e.g. Du redst zu viel; findst du es komisch?

(f) The stem of a weak verb ending in -m or -n preceded by a consonant is followed by an e if without it the word would be awkward or impossible to pronounce, e.g. atmen *to breathe*, segnen *to bless*. In this case, moreover, the e is never dropped in the 1st sing. pres. indic. or in the imperative sing. (There are no strong verbs in this category).

Pres. Indic.: ich atme, du atmest, er atmet, ihr atmet.
Imperf.: ich atmete, du atmetest etc.
Past Part.: geatmet.
Imperative: atme! atmet! atmen Sie!

Contrast e.g., filmen *to film*, lernen *to learn*: no necessity to insert an e.

(g) Weak verbs with infinitives in -eln and -ern: the stem is obtained by cutting off the -n, giving principal parts e.g. segeln, segelte, gesegelt; rudern, ruderte, gerudert.

Pres. Indic.:

ich seg(e)le	wir segeln	ich rud(e)re
du segelst	ihr segelt	du ruderst
er segelt	sie segeln	er rudert etc.

Imperative:
  seg(e)le! segelt! segeln Sie!   rud(e)re! rudert! rudern Sie!

Note:
i The bracketed e of the 1st sing. pres. indic. and of the imperative sing. is generally omitted with verbs in -eln, but is often retained with those in -ern.

ii The pres. subj. is identical with the pres. indic., except for the 3rd sing.: er seg(e)le, er rud(e)re.

(h) **In shops, restaurants and hotels**, the 3rd person is often used as a polite form of address, e.g. Was wünscht der Herr? Wollen die Herrschaften zu Mittag essen?

341. Vowel changes and modification in Pres. Indic. of Strong Verbs

(a) Rule: In the 2nd and 3rd sing. of the pres. indic. of strong verbs, the following changes occur:

long e	becomes	ie: lesen:	ich lese	du liest	er liest
short e	,,	i: helfen:	ich helfe	du hilfst	er hilft
a	,,	ä: fangen:	ich fange	du fängst	er fängt
au	,,	äu: laufen:	ich laufe	du läufst	er läuft
o	,,	ö: stoßen:	ich stoße	du stößt	er stößt

N.B. e is long before a single consonant or before h + consonant.
e is short before two or more consonants, other than h + consonant.

(b) Exceptions:
i The following strong verbs, with the above stem-vowels, have no vowel change in the pres. indic.:

bewegen *to induce*[1]	heben *to lift*	schaffen *to create*
erschallen *to resound*	kommen *to come*	scheren *to shear*
gehen *to go*	melken *to milk*	stehen *to stand*
genesen *to recover*	saugen *to suck*	weben *to weave*[2]
hauen *to hew, cut*		

ii geben and nehmen change long e to i: du gibst, er gibt; du nimmst, er nimmt.

iii erlöschen *to go out* (of light or fire): du erlischst, er erlischt.

(c) Strong verbs with a vowel change or modification in 2nd and 3rd sing. pres. indic. and whose stem ends in a t, add -st in 2nd sing. and nothing in 3rd sing.:

schelten *to scold*: ich schelte, du schiltst, er schilt.
cf. fechten *to fight*, flechten *to twine, plait*, gelten *to be valid, carry weight, be considered (as)*
N.B. du fichtst, flichtst are often pronounced du fichst, flichst.

raten *to advise; to guess*: ich rate, du rätst, er rät.
cf. braten *to roast, fry*, halten *to hold*; *to stop*

The following (with stems in -t and -d) show individual variations of the above rule:

bersten	*to burst*	ich berste	du birst	er birst
treten	*to step, go*	ich trete	du trittst	er tritt
werden	*to become*	ich werde	du wirst	er wird
laden	*to load; to summon*	ich lade	du lädst	er lädt

---

[1] strong with this meaning; see principal parts in 351.
[2] generally weak in current usage.

342. The forms of the Imperative

(a) The orthodox forms of the imperative may be summed up thus:

2nd sing. (du)	hole!	lies!	sprich!
2nd plur. (ihr)	holt!	lest!	sprecht!
polite (sing. or plur.)	holen Sie!	lesen Sie!	sprechen Sie!

Three further imperatives may be added:

sein:	sich setzen (Refl.):	auf-stehen (sep. prefix):
sei!	setze dich!	stehe . . . auf!
seid!	setzt euch!	steht . . . auf!
seien Sie!	setzen Sie sich!	stehen Sie . . . auf!

Regarding the use of the exclamation mark after imperatives, see 744(d)ii.

(b) 2nd sing.: add e to the stem.
Note:
i Strong verbs that change e to ie or i in the 2nd and 3rd sing. of the pres. indic. (cf. 341(a)(b)) have the same vowel change in the imperative sing. and do not add an e; the same applies to erlöschen: erlisch. (In regional colloquial German this vowel change is (incorrectly) frequently not made in the imperative sing. (cf. Du. Gram. 1025), e.g. Nehm doch meinen Schirm! Vergeß es *ja* nicht!)
ii sehen has siehe in certain exclamations (e.g. Siehe da! *behold*) and in giving references in books: s. S. 90 = siehe Seite 90!
iii nehmen and treten have nimm! and tritt!
iv werden has werde! wissen has wisse!
v Strong verbs that modify the stem vowels a, au, o in the pres. indic. (cf. 341(a)) do not modify in the imperative: fange, laufe, stoße!
vi The e ending is generally dropped in spoken German (and sometimes, for rhythmic reasons, in literary German): Komm in den Garten! Stör mich nicht! Setz dich! Schlaf gut! It is never dropped in verbs such as atmen and segnen and rarely in verbs with infinitives in -eln and -ern. (See 340(f)(g)).
vii Occasionally a stressed 'du' is used after the imperative sing. for the sake of emphasis, e.g. Bestell *du* inzwischen das Frühstück (I. Wendt) *Meanwhile, you order breakfast.*

(c) 2nd plur.: as in the pres. indic., omitting ihr.
Note:
i In verse this imperative sometimes ends in -et, where it is not phonetically necessary: Nun danket alle Gott (Martin Rinkart).
ii Occasionally a stressed ihr is used after this imperative for the sake of emphasis: Kinder, wir kommen gleich; geht ihr schon vor!

(d) Polite form: as in the pres. indic., but verb and pronoun are reversed.

343. Verbs with no ge- in the Past Part. (These are verbs that are not stressed on the first syllable, except for type iii below and verbs of types iv and v when used with a separable prefix):

i verbs with inseparable prefixes (cf. 368)
e.g. besuchen: besucht; erfinden: erfunden.

ii verbs with variable prefixes, when the prefix is inseparable
e.g. second pair of examples in 371.

iii verbs with double prefixes (cf. 370)
e.g. ànvertrauen *to entrust*: ànvertraut.

iv foreign verbs in -ieren (cf. 675(c))
e.g. arrangieren: arrangiert; àufforcieren: àufforciert.

v a few others:

aùs-posaunen *to trumpet forth*	rumòren *to rummage noisily*
miaùen *to mew*	schmaròtzen bei *to sponge on*
offenbàren *to reveal*	trompèten *to blow (on the trumpet)*,
prophezèien *to prophesy*	*to trumpet forth*

e.g. Er hat sein eignes Lob ausposaunt — *He blew his own trumpet*

Note:

1. werden has no ge- in the past part. when used as an auxiliary to form the passive (cf. 339); thus: Er ist gelobt worden, BUT: Er ist Schauspieler geworden.

2. For the use of the infinitive form as past part., see 389(c)ii, 420.

344. The auxiliary of the perfect and particularly of the pluperfect tense is sometimes elegantly omitted in a subordinate clause, mainly in literary German:

Nachdem er dem Minister alles gesagt [hatte], stand er auf	*After he had told the minister everything, he stood up*
. . . daß die Gruppe den Verband, gegen den sie angesetzt worden [war], nicht entdeckt hatte (G. Gaiser)	*. . . that the wing had not found the formation, against which it had been brought into action*

Note:

(a) This omission should not be made where the past part. is identical with the 3rd sing. pres. indic. and a temporal ambiguity might result:

Da er nichts entdeckt hat; geht er nach Hause	*As he has discovered nothing, he's going home*

(b) A comparable omission is that of 'sein' as a copulative verb in a subordinate clause (elev.) (cf. Du. Haupt: Hilfsverb):

Ich weiß, wie schwer die Aufgabe (ist) — *I know how hard (is) the task*

345. The forms of the Subjunctive (cf. paradigms in 334ff.)

(a) Rules:
    i The subjunctive is always regular. (No vowel changes in pres. subj.).
    ii 2nd sing. always ends in -est.
       2nd plur. always ends in -et.
    iii 3rd sing. is always the same as 1st sing.
    iv imperf. subj. weak: same as imperf. indic.[1]
       imperf. subj. strong: start it by adding -e to imperf. indic. and modifying if possible.

(b) Exceptions to (a)ii:
    i sein: du sei(e)st, du wär(e)st, ihr wär(e)t. The bracketed e is generally omitted in spoken German.

---

[1] In South German, brauchen frequently has imperf. subj. bräuchte.

ii Weak verbs in -eln and -ern: see 340(g)N.ii.

iii In the imperf. subj. of strong verbs, the e of the 2nd sing. and 2nd plur. endings (-est and -et) is generally omitted in spoken German provided that modification distinguishes subjunctive from indicative: du trüg(e)st, ihr trüg(e)t, BUT: du schriebest, ihr schriebet.

If the stem ends in a sibilant, the 2nd sing. *must* end in -est: du schlössest, ihr schlösset (schlößt); du läsest, ihr läset ('ihr läst' would be too similar to pres. indic. 'ihr lest').

If the stem ends in d or t, the 2nd plur. *must* end in -et: du fänd(e)st, ihr fändet.

(c) The following strong verbs have an irregular imperf. subj.:[1]

INFIN.	IMPERF. INDIC.	IMPERF. SUBJ.
beginnen	begann	begönne
gewinnen	gewann	gewönne
helfen	half	hülfe
schelten	schalt	schölte
schwimmen	schwamm	schwömme
schwören	schwor	schwüre
spinnen	spann	spönne
stehen	stand	stünde
sterben	starb	stürbe
verderben	verdarb	verdürbe
werben	warb	würbe
werfen	warf	würfe

Most of these irregular imperfect subjunctives sound stilted and are generally avoided in conversation, e.g.

Wenn das Konzert früher beginnen sollte, . . . (not: begönne)
Wenn er mich schelten sollte/würde, . . . (not: schölte)

346. The 9 mixed verbs

In the imperf. and past part. these verbs have (a) the weak endings -te and -t (b) a vowel change and, in the case of 'bringen' and 'denken', a consonant change. The form of their imperf. subj. must also be noticed:

INFIN.	3rd sing. PRES. INDIC.	IMPERF. INDIC	IMPERF. SUBJ.	PAST PARTICIPLE
brennen	brennt	brannte	brennte	gebrannt
bringen	bringt	brachte	brächte	gebracht
denken	denkt	dachte	dächte	gedacht
kennen	kennt	kannte	kennte	gekannt
nennen	nennt	nannte	nennte	genannt
rennen	rennt	rannte	rennte	gerannt
senden	sendet	sandte sendete	sendete	gesandt gesendet
wenden	wendet	wandte wendete	wendete	gewandt gewendet
wissen	weiß	wußte	wüßte	gewußt

Note:

i For their meanings and for the use of the alternative forms of senden and wenden, see 351.

[1] With a few others, an irregular form is less common than the regular.

ii Pres. indic. of wissen: ich weiß, du weißt, er weiß, wir wissen, ihr wißt, sie wissen; imperative sing.: wisse!

347. The 6 modal verbs: dürfen, können, mögen, müssen, sollen, wollen. For the forms of these verbs see 389; they are also included in 351.

C. THE AUXILIARIES HABEN AND SEIN[1]

348. The following verbs are conjugated with 'haben':

(a) **all transitive verbs**: Ich habe ihn gesehen; ich habe mein neues Auto gefahren.

EXCEPTIONS:
i a few compounds of gehen, e.g.

Er ist die Strecke abgegangen	*He paced the distance*
Er ist die Arbeit mit dem Schüler durchgegangen[2]	*He went through the work with the pupil*
Er ist die Wette eingegangen[3]	*He made the bet*

ii Gefahr laufen *to run a risk*: Er ist Gefahr gelaufen, sein ganzes Vermögen zu verlieren.

iii los-werden *to get rid of someone or something*: Ich bin ihn endlich losgeworden.

(b) **all reflexive verbs**:

Ich habe mich erholt	*I have recovered*
Ich hatte mich aus dem Zimmer gestohlen	*I had stolen out of the room*
Ich habe mich müde gelaufen	*I have run* (or: *walked*) *till I'm tired out*
Ich hatte mir alles nur eingebildet	*I had only imagined everything*

EXCEPTIONS:
i Du bist dir gleichgeblieben　　　*You haven't changed*

ii Where the reflexive pron. is used reciprocally (=each other) with a verb conjugated with 'sein', the auxiliary remains 'sein':

Sie sind sich ausgewichen	*They evaded each other*
Wir sind uns in der Stadt begegnet	*We met in town*

(c) **impersonal verbs and expressions**:
Es hat geregnet; es hat geklopft; es hat mir vor ihm gegraut *I shuddered to look at him.*

EXCEPTIONS:
i gelingen, mißlingen, glücken, mißglücken.
ii impersonal expressions based on verbs normally conjugated with 'sein', e.g. Es ist mir kalt geworden *I began to feel cold.* Wie ist es Ihnen in Berlin gegangen? *How did you fare in Berlin?*

(d) **intransitive verbs other than those mentioned in 349**, e.g.
Ich habe gearbeitet; ich habe gepfiffen; ich habe gut geschlafen.

---

[1] see also 351 N.iii.
[2] cf. Du. Haupt. durchgehen.
[3] Among other objects of 'eingehen' are: ein Bündnis *an alliance*, eine Ehe *a marriage*, ein Risiko *a risk*, einen Vergleich *a compromise*, Verpflichtungen *obligations*.

Note: liegen, sitzen and stehen are conjugated with 'sein' in South German, but the North German 'ich habe gelegen, gesessen, gestanden' is normal usage.

349. Four groups of intransitive verbs are conjugated with 'sein':

(a) **verbs denoting change of place,** e.g.

an-kommen *to arrive,* aufstehen *to get up,* entkommen *to escape,* erscheinen *to appear,* fahren, fallen, fliegen, gehen, klettern, kommen, paddeln *to canoe,* radeln, reiten, rudern, Schi fahren or Schi laufen, schwimmen, segeln, stürzen *to rush; to fall, plunge,* tanzen, treten *to step, tread, go,* verschwinden.

Note: Some such verbs of motion are sometimes conjugated with 'haben' if the activity as such is referred to, without mention of direction or destination:

Ich habe als junger Mensch viel getanzt	*I did a lot of dancing when I was young*
Sie ist aus dem Zimmer getanzt	BUT: *She danced out of the room*
Ich habe den ganzen Morgen gesegelt	*I've been sailing the whole morning*
Ich bin nach der Insel gesegelt	BUT: *I sailed to the island*

This practice is on the decline and, of the verbs in the above list, it is normal only with paddeln, rudern, segeln and tanzen. Thus current usage favours:

Ich bin den ganzen Morgen geklettert, geritten, geschwommen.
Ich bin in der Schweiz Schi gelaufen.
Er ist gut gesprungen.
Ich bin auch im Krieg etwas geflogen (V. Baum).

(b) **verbs denoting change of state,** e.g.

altern *to age*	platzen *to burst*
auf-wachen *to wake up*	reifen *to ripen, mature*
ein-schlafen *to go to sleep*	schmelzen *to melt* (intr.)
entstehen *to come into being, begin, arise*	verbluten *to bleed to death*
erblassen *to turn pale*	vergehen *to pass* (of time)
erklingen *to ring out, resound*	verhallen *to die away* (of sound)
erschrecken (str.) *to get a fright*	wachsen *to grow* (intr.)
ertrinken *to drown* (intr.)	welken *to fade*
heilen *to heal* (intr.)	

Er ist schon eingeschlafen; die Glocken sind erklungen; der Junge war gewachsen.

(c) **5 verbs denoting 'to happen':** geschehen, passieren (coll.), vor-gehen, vor-kommen, zu-stoßen + Dat. *to happen to someone* (only of misfortune). E.g. Was ist (ihm) denn passiert? (stattfinden *to take place* is conjugated with haben).

(d) **8 others**

begegnen *to meet* (by chance)	glücken *to succeed*
bleiben *to remain*	mißglücken *to fail*
fehl-schlagen *to fail, come to nothing*	mißlingen *to fail*
gelingen *to succeed*	sein *to be*

Er ist zu Hause geblieben; es ist mir gelungen, ihn zu überzeugen; der Plan ist mißglückt.

350. Selected instances of the use of 'haben' and 'sein' with the same verb

i bekommen

Ich habe einen Brief bekommen	*I have received a letter*
Das Essen ist mir gut bekommen	*The dinner agreed with me*

ii fahren

Ich habe meinen neuen Wagen gefahren	*I drove my new car*
Ich bin nach Stuttgart gefahren	*I drove to Stuttgart*
Ich bin zu schnell gefahren	*I drove too quickly*
Ich bin diese Strecke öfters gefahren	*I have often driven along this stretch of road*

('diese Strecke' is an adverbial extension, not the object, of 'fahren'. Cf. Er war einen Baum hinaufgeklettert.)

iii folgen

Er hat mir gefolgt	*He obeyed me*
Er ist mir gefolgt	*He followed me*

iv frieren

Es hat heute nacht gefroren	*There was a frost last night*
Ich habe (or: Es hat mich) bei dem eisigen Wetter gefroren	*I felt frozen in the icy weather*
Das Wasser ist gefroren	*The water has frozen*
Der See ist gefroren (or: zugefroren)	*The lake has frozen*

v gären

Der Wein hat gegoren	*The wine has been fermenting* (process)
Der Wein ist gegoren (or: ausgegoren)	*The wine has fermented* (completed process, resultant state)

vi **treten** *to kick, tread, step, come etc.* It is conjugated **with 'haben'**:
1. when transitive: Er hat mich mit dem Fuß getreten *He kicked me*; sie hat das Spinnrad getreten.
2. when intransitive, but denoting sheer activity, e.g. *to pedal* (cycle): Ich habe sehr schnell getreten.

It is conjugated **with 'sein'** when it denotes change of place: Er ist ins Zimmer getreten.

A further distinction:
Er hat/ist mir auf den Fuß getreten: 'hat' denotes deliberately; 'ist' denotes by mistake.

Note: The following are conjugated with 'haben':
zu-nehmen *to increase* (intr.), *to put on weight*
ab-nehmen *to decrease* (intr.), *to lose weight*
kochen *to boil, come to the boil*.

D. PRINCIPAL PARTS OF STRONG, MIXED AND IRREGULAR VERBS

351. Note on, and list of, principal parts

i A very few verbs, rarely used in current German, are not included in the list that follows.

ii Alternative forms are avoided as far as possible in favour of the one
   most commonly used in current German.
iii 'ist' before the past part. indicates that the verb is conjugated with
   'sein'; all others are conjugated with 'haben'; where a verb is conjugated with either auxiliary, according to sense, this is shown.
iv Two past participles are given for the 6 modal verbs (see 389(c)ii and
   (d) and 392) and for heißen, helfen, lassen, sehen (see 420 f.).

INFINITIVE	3rd SING. PRES. INDIC.	2nd SING. IMPERATIVE	IMPERF. INDIC.	IMPERF. SUBJ.	PAST PART.	MEANING
backen	backt	back(e)!	backte	backte	gebacken	*to bake*
bedürfen	bedarf		bedurfte	bedürfte	bedurft	*to need*
befehlen	befiehlt	befiehl!	befahl	befähle	befohlen	*to command*
beginnen	beginnt	beginn(e)!	begann	begönne	begonnen	*to begin*
beißen	beißt	beiß(e)!	biß	bisse	gebissen	*to bite*
bergen	birgt	birg!	barg	bärge	geborgen	*to salvage, bring to safety*
bersten	birst	birst!	barst	bärste	ist geborsten	*to burst* (intr.)
betrügen	betrügt	betrüg(e)!	betrog	betröge	betrogen	*to deceive*
bewegen	bewegt	beweg(e)!	bewog	bewöge	bewogen	*to induce s.o. to do s.th.*[1]
biegen	biegt	bieg(e)!	bog	böge	hat gebogen	*to bend*
					ist gebogen	*to turn* (um die Ecke)
bieten	bietet	biet(e)!	bot	böte	geboten	*to offer*[2]
binden	bindet	bind(e)!	band	bände	gebunden	*to bind, tie*
bitten (um)	bittet	bitt(e)!	bat	bäte	gebeten	*to ask (for), request*
blasen	bläst	blas(e)!	blies	bliese	geblasen	*to blow*
bleiben	bleibt	bleib(e)!	blieb	bliebe	ist geblieben	*to remain*
braten	brät	brat(e)!	briet	briete	gebraten	*to roast, fry*
brechen	bricht	brich!	brach	bräche	hat gebrochen	*to break* (tr.)
					ist gebrochen	*to break* (intr.)
brennen	brennt	brenn(e)!	brannte	brennte	gebrannt	*to burn*
bringen	bringt	bring(e)!	brachte	brächte	gebracht	*to bring*
denken	denkt	denk(e)!	dachte	dächte	gedacht	*to think*
dreschen	drischt	drisch!	drosch	drösche	gedroschen	*to thresh*
dringen	dringt	dring(e)!	drang	dränge	ist gedrungen	*to penetrate, force one's way*[3]
dünken	mich (or mir) deucht		deuchte	deuchte	gedeucht	*to think o.s., to seem*[4]
dürfen	darf		durfte	dürfte	gedurft, dürfen	*to be allowed to*
empfangen	empfängt	empfang(e)!	empfing	empfinge	empfangen	*to receive* (letters, presents, guests)
empfehlen	empfiehlt	empfiehl!	empfahl	empfähle	empfohlen	*to recommend*
empfinden	empfindet	empfind(e)!	empfand	empfände	empfunden	*to feel*
erkiesen	erkiest	erkies(e)	erkor	erköre	erkoren	*to choose* (obs. and elev.)
erlöschen	erlischt	erlisch!	erlosch	erlösche	ist erloschen	*to go out* (of light, fire)[5]

INFINITIVE	3rd SING. PRES. INDIC.	2nd SING. IMPERATIVE	IMPERF. INDIC.	IMPERF. SUBJ.	PAST PART.	MEANING
erschallen	erschallt	erschall(e)!	erscholl	erschölle	ist erschollen	*to resound*[6]
erschrecken	erschrickt	erschrick!	erschrak	erschräke	ist erschrocken	*to be startled*[7]
erwägen	erwägt	erwäg(e)!	erwog	erwöge	erwogen	*to weigh up, consider*
essen	ißt	iß!	aß	äße	gegessen	*to eat*
fahren	fährt	fahr(e)!	fuhr	führe	hat gefahren	*to drive* (tr.)[8]
					ist gefahren	*to drive, travel* (intr.)[8]
fallen	fällt	fall(e)!	fiel	fiele	ist gefallen	*to fall*
fangen	fängt	fang(e)!	fing	finge	gefangen	*to catch*
fechten	ficht	ficht!	focht	föchte	gefochten	*to fight, fence*
finden	findet	find(e)!	fand	fände	gefunden	*to find*
flechten	flicht	flicht!	flocht	flöchte	geflochten	*to twine, plait*
fliegen	fliegt	flieg(e)!	flog	flöge	hat geflogen	*to fly* (tr.), *to pilot* (a plane)
					ist geflogen	*to fly* (intr.)
fliehen	flieht	flieh(e)!	floh	flöhe	hat geflohen	*to flee* (tr.)[9]
					ist geflohen	*to flee* (intr.)
fließen	fließt	fließ(e)!	floß	flösse	ist geflossen	*to flow*
fressen	frißt	friß!	fraß	fräße	gefressen	*to eat* (of animals)
frieren	friert	frier(e)!	fror	fröre	hat gefroren	*to freeze, be cold*[10]
					ist gefroren	*to freeze* (over)[10]
gären	gärt	gär(e)!	gor	göre	gegoren	*to ferment* (of wine)[11]

[1] meaning to move (physically) and to stir (emotionally), bewegen is weak.
[2] generally: an-bieten, BUT e.g. Er bot einen traurigen Anblick.
[3] (h) in a few specialized senses, e.g. Er hat darauf gedrungen *He insisted on it.*
[4] e.g. Er dünkt sich sehr wichtig; die Sache dünkt mir schwierig. Mainly archaic or facetious; commoner wk.
[5] löschen *to extinguish* is weak.
[6] also weak. Commonest current usage for (er-) (ver-) schallen: schallen *to resound*: weak; erschallen *to resound* erschallt, erschallte, ist erschollen; verschallen *to die away* (of sound): weak (ist verschallt). BUT: Er ist verschollen *He's never been heard of again* (fixed phrase).
[7] meaning to frighten, erschrecken is weak.
[8] see 350 ii.   [9] e.g. Ich habe seine Gegenwart geflohen; der Schlaf hat mich geflohen (Du. Stil.).
[10] see 350 iv.   [11] see 350 v; used fig, gären is weak, e.g. Es gärte in den Köpfen *There was a ferment in men's minds.*

Infinitive	3rd Sing. Pres. Indic.	2nd Sing. Imperative	Imperf. Indic.	Imperf. Subj.	Past Part.	Meaning
gebären	gebärt	gebär(e)!	gebar	gebäre	geboren	*to give birth to*
geben	gibt	gib!	gab	gäbe	gegeben	*to give*
gedeihen	gedeiht	gedeih(e)!	gedieh	gediehe	ist gediehen	*to thrive*
gehen	geht	geh(e)!	ging	ginge	ist gegangen	*to go*
gelingen	gelingt	geling(e)!	gelang	gelänge	ist gelungen	*to succeed* (mainly impers.)
gelten	gilt	gilt!	galt!	gälte	gegolten	*to be valid, carry weight, be considered (as)*
genesen	genest	genese!	genas	genäse	ist genesen	*to recover* (from illness)
genießen	genießt	genieß(e)!	genoß	genösse	genossen	*to enjoy*
geraten	gerät	gerat(e)!	geriet	geriete	ist geraten	*to turn out (well), to get (into some state)*[1]
geschehen	geschieht		geschah	geschähe	ist geschehen	*to happen*
gewinnen	gewinnt	gewinn(e)!	gewann	gewönne	gewonnen	*to win*
gießen	gießt	gieß(e)!	goß	gösse	gegossen	*to pour*
gleichen	gleicht	gleich(e)!	glich	gliche	geglichen	*to equal, resemble*
gleiten	gleitet	gleit(e)!	glitt	glitte	ist geglitten	*to glide, slide*
glimmen	glimmt	glimm(e)!	glomm	glömme	geglommen	*to glimmer*[2]
graben	gräbt	grab(e)!	grub	grübe	gegraben	*to dig*
greifen	greift	greif(e)!	griff	griffe	gegriffen	*to grip, seize*[3]
haben	hat	hab(e)!	hatte	hätte	gehabt	*to have*
halten	hält	halt(e)!	hielt	hielte	gehalten	*to hold; to stop* (intr.)
hängen	hängt	häng(e)!	hing	hinge	gehangen	*to hang* (intr.)[4]
hauen	haut	hau(e)!	hieb	hiebe	gehauen	*to hew, cut*[5]
heben	hebt	heb(e)!	hob	höbe	gehoben	*to lift*
heißen	heißt	heiß(e)!	hieß	hieße	geheißen, heißen	*to be called; to mean; to bid*
helfen	hilft	hilf!	half	hülfe	geholfen, helfen	*to help*
kennen	kennt	kenn(e)!	kannte	kennte	gekannt	*to know, to be acquainted with* (person, place, film etc.)
klimmen	klimmt	klimm(e)!	klomm	klömme	ist geklommen	*to climb*[6]
klingen	klingt	kling(e)!	klang	klänge	geklungen	*to sound*

Infinitive	3rd sing. Pres. Indic.	2nd sing. Imperative	Imperf. Indic.	Imperf. Subj.	Past Part.	Meaning
kneifen	kneift	kneif(e)!	kniff	kniffe	gekniffen	to pinch
kommen	kommt	komm(e)!	kam	käme	ist gekommen	to come
können	kann		konnte	könnte	gekonnt, können	to be able to, can
kriechen	kriecht	kriech(e)!	kroch	kröche	ist gekrochen	to creep, crawl[7]
laden	lädt	lad(e)!	lud	lüde	geladen	to load; to invite[8]
lassen	läßt	lass(e)!	ließ	ließe	gelassen, lassen	to leave (alone); to let, cause to, allow
laufen	läuft	lauf(e)!	lief	liefe	hat gelaufen	to run, (walk) (tr. and refl.)[9]
					ist gelaufen	to run (walk) (intr.)
leiden	leidet	leid(e)!	litt	litte	gelitten	to suffer
leihen	leiht	leih(e)!	lieh	liehe	geliehen	to lend
lesen	liest	lies!	las	läse	gelesen	to read
liegen	liegt	lieg(e)!	lag	läge	gelegen	to lie
lügen	lügt	lüg(e)!	log	löge	gelogen	to (tell a) lie
mahlen	mahlt	mahl(e)!	mahlte	mahlte	gemahlen	to grind
meiden	meidet	meid(e)!	mied	miede	gemieden	to avoid[10]
melken	melkt	melk(e)!	molk	mölke	gemolken	to milk[11]
messen	mißt	miß!	maß	mäße	gemessen	to measure
mißlingen	mißlingt		mißlang	mißlänge	ist mißlungen	to fail (mainly impers.)
mögen	mag		mochte	möchte	gemocht, mögen	to like (to)
müssen	muß		mußte	müßte	gemußt, müssen	to have to, must

[1] e.g. Er ist in Gefahr (Schulden, Schwierigkeiten, Wut) geraten.
[2] also weak, especially in the imperf.
[3] e.g. Die Räder griffen nicht. Transitively, 'ergreifen' is more serviceable.
[4] archaic and dialectal: hangen, hangt, hing, gehangen, to hang (tr.) = hängen (wk.).
[5] The imperf. is generally weak and must be weak for hauen to thrash and sich hauen to fight.
[6] sometimes weak; elev.; commoner is the trans. verb erklimmen to climb, scale.
[7] kriechen vor + dat. to cringe before someone (h).
[8] in the sense of 'invite, summon', 3rd sing. pres. indic. is also ladet (archaic and regional); ein-laden is the normal verb 'to invite'.
[9] e.g. Er hat einen Weg für mich gelaufen He did an errand for me. See also 348(a) Exc. ii and (b).
[10] commoner: vermeiden.
[11] There is a weak alternative, and 'melkte' is commoner than 'molk'.

INFINITIVE	3RD SING. PRES. INDIC.	2ND SING. IMPERATIVE	IMPERF. INDIC.	IMPERF. SUBJ.	PAST PART.	MEANING
nehmen	nimmt	nimm!	nahm	nähme	genommen	to take
nennen	nennt	nenn(e)!	nannte	nennte	genannt	to name, call
pfeifen	pfeift	pfeif(e)!	pfiff	pfiffe	gepfiffen	to whistle
preisen	preist	preis(e)!	pries	priese	gepriesen	to praise
quellen	quillt	quill!	quoll	quölle	ist gequollen	to gush, well up
raten	rät	rat(e)!	riet	riete	geraten	to advise; to guess
reiben	reibt	reib(e)!	rieb	riebe	gerieben	to rub
reißen	reißt	reiß(e)!	riß	risse	hat gerissen	to tear (tr.)
					ist gerissen	to tear (intr.)
reiten	reitet	reit(e)!	ritt	ritte	hat geritten	to ride (a horse) (tr.)
					ist geritten	to ride (on a horse) (intr.)
rennen	rennt	renn(e)!	rannte	rennte	hat gerannt	to run, thrust (tr.)[1]
					ist gerannt	to run, race (intr.)
riechen	riecht	riech(e)!	roch	röche	gerochen	to smell
ringen	ringt	ring(e)!	rang	ränge	gerungen	to wrestle, struggle
rinnen	rinnt	rinn(e)!	rann	ränne	ist geronnen	to flow, trickle
rufen	ruft	ruf(e)!	rief	riefe	gerufen	to call
salzen	salzt	salz(e)!	salzte	salzte	gesalzen	to salt
saufen	säuft	sauf(e)!	soff	söffe	gesoffen	to drink (of animals), to booze
saugen	saugt	saug(e)!	sog	söge	gesogen	to suck[2]
schaffen	schafft	schaff(e)!	schuf	schüfe	geschaffen	to create[3]
schallen: see erschallen						
scheiden	scheidet	scheid(e)!	schied	schiede	hat geschieden	to separate (tr.)
					ist geschieden	to part (from), depart (intr.)
scheinen	scheint	schein(e)!	schien	schiene	geschienen	to shine; to seem
schelten	schilt	schilt!	schalt	schölte	gescholten	to scold
scheren	schert	scher(e)!	schor	schöre	geschoren	to shear[4]
schieben	schiebt	schieb(e)!	schob	schöbe	geschoben	to shove, push
schießen	schießt	schieß(e)!	schoß	schösse	hat geschossen	to shoot
					ist geschossen	to shoot, rush[5]
schinden	schindet	schind(e)!	schund	schünde	geschunden	to flay; to ill-treat, overwork[6]

Infinitive	3rd. sing Pres. Indic.	2nd sing. Imperative	Imperf. Indic.	Imperf. Subj.	Past Part.	Meaning
schlafen	schläft	schlaf(e)!	schlief	schliefe	geschlafen	to sleep
schlagen	schlägt	schlag(e)!	schlug	schlüge	geschlagen	to hit, beat
schleichen	schleicht	schleich(e)!	schlich	schliche	ist geschlichen	to creep
schleifen	schleift	schleif(e)!	schliff	schliffe	geschliffen	to grind, sharpen[7]
schließen	schließt	schließ(e)!	schloß	schlösse	geschlossen	to close
schlingen	schlingt	schling(e)!	schlang	schlänge	geschlungen	to wind, twine
schmeißen	schmeißt	schmeiß(e)!	schmiß	schmisse	geschmissen	to fling, chuck
schmelzen	schmilzt	schmilz!	schmolz	schmölze	hat geschmolzen	to melt (tr.)
					ist geschmolzen	to melt (intr.)
schneiden	schneidet	schneid(e)!	schnitt	schnitte	geschnitten	to cut
schreiben	schreibt	schreib(e)!	schrieb	schriebe	geschrieben	to write
schreien	schreit	schrei(e)!	schrie	schriee	geschrie(e)n	to shout, scream
schreiten	schreitet	schreit(e)!	schritt	schritte	ist geschritten	to stride
schweigen	schweigt	schweig(e)!	schwieg	schwiege	geschwiegen	to be silent
schwellen	schwillt	schwill!	schwoll	schwölle	ist geschwollen	to swell (intr.)[8]
schwimmen	schwimmt	schwimm(e)!	schwamm	schwömme	ist geschwommen	to swim
schwinden	schwindet	schwind(e)!	schwand	schwände	ist geschwunden	to contract, disappear[9]
schwingen	schwingt	schwing(e)!	schwang	schwänge	geschwungen	to swing, brandish
schwören	schwört	schwör(e)!	schwor	schwüre	geschworen	to swear, vow[10]
sehen	sieht	sieh(e)!	sah	sähe	gesehen, sehen	to see
sein	ist	sei!	war	wäre	ist gewesen	to be

[1] e.g. Er hat ihm den Degen durch den Leib gerannt; er hat ihn zu Boden gerannt *he ran him down.*

[2] commoner weak.

[3] schaffen *to work, to be busy; to convey* is weak.

[4] scheren *to concern* and sich scheren (um) *to clear off, depart; to bother about* are weak, e.g. Was scherte das den Beamten? *What did that matter to the official?*

[5] e.g. Das Blut ist ihm ins Gesicht geschossen; er ist aus dem Zimmer geschossen.

[6] The imperfect is rarely used.

[7] schleifen *to drag; to raze to the ground* is weak.

[8] schwellen (tr.) is weak e.g. Der Wind schwellte die Segel.

[9] e.g. Holz schwindet beim Trocknen (Du. Stil.). For 'to disappear' verschwinden is commoner.

[10] regionally also weak: imperf. indic. also schwur (obsolescent).

INFINITIVE	3RD SING. PRES. INDIC.	2ND SING. IMPERATIVE	IMPERF. INDIC.	IMPERF. SUBJ.	PAST PART.	MEANING
senden	sendet	send(e)!	sandte / sendete	sendete	gesandt / gesendet	to send[1]
sieden	siedet	sied(e)!	sott	sötte	gesotten	to boil (tr.)[2]
singen	singt	sing(e)!	sang	sänge	gesungen	to sing
sinken	sinkt	sink(e)!	sank	sänke	ist gesunken	to sink (intr.)[3]
sinnen	sinnt	sinn(e)!	sann	sänne	gesonnen	to meditate[4]
sitzen	sitzt	sitz(e)!	saß	säße	gesessen	to sit
sollen	soll		sollte	sollte	gesollt, sollen	am to
spalten	spaltet	spalt(e)!	spaltete	spaltete	hat gespalten / ist gespalten	to split, cleave (tr.)[5] / to split, divide (intr.)
speien	speit	spei(e)!	spie	spiee	gespie(e)n	to spit, spew[6]
spinnen	spinnt	spinn(e)!	spann	spönne	gesponnen	to spin
sprechen	spricht	sprich!	sprach	spräche	gesprochen	to speak
sprießen	sprießt	sprieß(e)!	sproß	sprösse	ist gesprossen	to sprout
springen	springt	spring(e)!	sprang	spränge	ist gesprungen	to jump
stechen	sticht	stich!	stach	stäche	gestochen	to prick, sting
stecken	steckt	steck(e)!	steckte / stak	steckte / stäke	gesteckt	to be (fixed) in a place[7]
stehen	steht	steh(e)!	stand	stände (stünde)	gestanden	to stand
stehlen	stiehlt	stiehl!	stahl	stähle	gestohlen	to steal[8]
steigen	steigt	steig(e)!	stieg	stiege	ist gestiegen	to climb (intr.), rise[9]
sterben	stirbt	stirb!	starb	stürbe	ist gestorben	to die
stieben	stiebt	stieb(e)!	stob	stöbe	ist gestoben	to fly up (like dust)[10]
stinken	stinkt	stink(e)!	stank	stänke	gestunken	to stink
stoßen	stößt	stoß(e)!	stieß	stieße	hat gestoßen / ist gestoßen (auf)	to knock, thrust / to encounter, come across[11]
streichen	streicht	streich(e)!	strich	striche	hat gestrichen / ist gestrichen	to run one's hand over; to spread (butter, bread)[12] / to roam, pass over[13]
(sich) streiten	streitet	streit(e)!	stritt	stritte	gestritten	to quarrel, contend

INFINITIVE	3rd SING. PRES. INDIC.	2nd SING. IMPERATIVE	IMPERF. INDIC.	IMPERF. SUBJ.	PAST PART.	MEANING
tragen	trägt	trag(e)!	trug	trüge	getragen	to carry; to wear
treffen	trifft	triff!	traf	träfe	getroffen	to meet; to hit (e.g. a target)
treiben	treibt	treib(e)!	trieb	triebe	hat getrieben	to drive (e.g. cattle); to pursue (an activity)
					ist getrieben	to drift (intr.)
treten	tritt	tritt!	trat	träte	hat getreten	e.g. to kick[14]
					ist getreten	to tread, step, come etc.[14]
trinken	trinkt	trink(e)!	trank	tränke	getrunken	to drink
tun	tut	tu(e)!	tat	täte	getan	to do
verderben	verdirbt	verdirb!	verdarb	verdürbe	hat verdorben	to spoil, ruin (tr.)[15]
					ist verdorben	to spoil, go bad (intr.)
verdrießen	verdrießt	verdrieß(e)!	verdroß	verdrösse	verdrossen	to vex
vergessen	vergißt	vergiß!	vergaß	vergäße	vergessen	to forget
verlieren	verliert	verlier(e)!	verlor	verlöre	verloren	to lose
verschallen: see 'erschallen'						

[1] The forms 'sandte, gesandt' are commoner, but 'sendete, gesendet' *must* be used in the sense of to broadcast by radio, e.g. Das heutige Konzert wird gesendet. 'schicken' is the commoner word for 'to send'.

[2] also weak; only weak when intr.; 'kochen' is commoner for both uses.

[3] There is one transitive use: Man *hat* im Bergwerk einen neuen Schacht gesunken *A new shaft has been sunk in the mine.* To sink (a ship) = versenken (wk.).

[4] elev.; nach-sinnen (über), also rather literary, is commoner.

[5] past part. also gespaltet, e.g. Die Partei hatte sich in zwei Teile gespaltet.

[6] The normal word is spucken (wk.).

[7] stak is literary; stecken *to put* is exclusively weak.

[8] to steal, creep=sich stehlen.

[9] to climb, ascend (tr.) = besteigen.

[10] e.g. Die Funken sind zum Himmel gestoben (Du. Haupt.)

[11] e.g. Wir sind auf den Feind/auf Schwierigkeiten gestoßen; also with 'sein' in the sense of 'to join up with': Unser Regiment ist zur Hauptarmee gestoßen.

[12] also: *to cross out, cancel, paint*; for constructions and further meanings, see dictionary.

[13] e.g. Die Vögel sind über das Land gestrichen.

[14] see 350 vi.

[15] verderbt (adj.) *corrupt, depraved.* To spoil, pamper=verwöhnen (wk.).

Infinitive	3rd sing. Pres. Indic.	2nd sing. Imperative	Imperf. Indic.	Imperf. Subj.	Past Part.	Meaning
verzeihen	verzeiht	verzeih(e)!	verzieh	verziehe	verziehen	to pardon
wachsen	wächst	wachs(e)!	wuchs	wüchse	ist gewachsen	to grow (intr.)[1]
wägen	wägt	wäg(e)!	wog	wöge	gewogen	to weigh (one's words)[2]
waschen	wäscht	wasch(e)!	wusch	wüsche	gewaschen	to wash (tr.)
weben	webt	web(e)!	wob	wöbe	gewoben	to weave[3]
weichen	weicht	weich(e)!	wich	wiche	ist gewichen	to yield, give way
weisen	weist	weis(e)!	wies	wiese	gewiesen	to point, show[4]
wenden	wendet	wend(e)!	{wandte / wendete}	wendete	{gewandt / gewendet}	to turn[5]
werben	wirbt	wirb!	warb[6]	würbe	geworben	to recruit; für: to canvass for; um: to woo
werden	wird	werde!	wurde[6]	würde	ist geworden	to become
werfen	wirft	wirf!	warf	würfe	geworfen	to throw
wiegen	wiegt	wieg(e)!	wog	wöge	gewogen	to weigh[7]
winden	windet	wind(e)!	wand	wände	gewunden	to wind, twist
wissen	weiß	wisse!	wußte	wüßte	gewußt	to know (facts, e.g. date, rule, name, answer, the way, that ...)
wollen	will	wolle!	wollte	wollte	gewollt, wollen	to want (to)
ziehen	zieht	zieh(e)!	zog	zöge	hat gezogen / ist gezogen	to pull / to go, pass; to move[8]
zwingen	zwingt	zwing(e)!	zwang	zwänge	gezwungen	to force

[1] wachsen to smear with wax is weak; to grow (tr.) = an-bauen (e.g. Kartoffeln), züchten (e.g. Rosen).
[2] sometimes weak; for 'to weigh up, consider', use 'erwägen', exc. Erst wägen, dann wagen Look before you leap.
[3] generally weak in current usage.
[4] for further meanings and constructions, see dictionary.
[5] The forms 'wandte, gewandt' are commoner, also with prefixes. Main exceptions: 1. Er wendete den Anzug, das Auto, den Braten, das Heu 2. Der Bus, das Schiff hat gewendet 3. Das Glück, die Lage, das Wetter, der Wind hat sich gewendet 4. entwenden to purloin, verwenden to use.
[6] The sing. forms ich ward, du wardst, er ward are archaic and poetic.
[7] wiegen (wk.) = to rock (e.g. a baby).
[8] e.g. Die Truppen zogen durch die Stadt; er ist nach Berlin gezogen.

E. THE USE OF THE TENSES

352. Scheme of the German tenses and their English equivalents
(This is modified and completed in the paragraphs that follow. It will be noted that there is no continuous form in German).

Active

PRESENT
ich schreibe

I write
I am writing

IMPERFECT
ich schrieb

I wrote
I was writing

PERFECT
ich habe geschrieben

I wrote
I have written
I have been writing

PLUPERFECT
ich hatte geschrieben

I had written
I had been writing

FUTURE
ich werde schreiben

I shall write
I shall be writing

FUTURE PERFECT
ich werde geschrieben haben

I shall have written
I shall have been writing

CONDITIONAL
ich würde schreiben

I would write
I would be writing

CONDITIONAL PERFECT
ich würde geschrieben haben

I would have written
I would have been writing

Passive

PRESENT
ich werde gestört

I am disturbed
I am being disturbed

IMPERFECT
ich wurde gestört

I was disturbed
I was being disturbed

PERFECT
ich bin gestört worden

I was disturbed
I have been disturbed

PLUPERFECT
ich war gestört worden

I had been disturbed

FUTURE
ich werde gestört werden

I shall be disturbed

(FUTURE PERFECT
ich werde gestört worden sein

I shall have been disturbed)

CONDITIONAL
ich würde gestört werden

I would be disturbed

CONDITIONAL PERFECT
ich würde gestört worden sein   *I would have been disturbed*

353. The rendering of the English continuous form

(a) Frequently, no special device is required:

Was hast du heute morgen getan?   *What have you been doing this morning?*
Ich habe Briefe geschrieben   *I've been writing letters*
Ich werde heute fortwährend gestört   *I'm constantly being disturbed today*

(b) If it is desired to emphasize the continuous nature of an activity, various means are available:

i the insertion of gerade or eben *just*:

Ich schreibe eben Briefe   *I'm writing letters*

ii (gerade or eben) dabei sein zu + infin.:

Ich bin gerade dabei, ein bißchen   *I'm tidying up a bit*
aufzuräumen

iii beim (or am) + infinitive used as a noun; when the verb has an object, this construction is only occasionally possible, and never when it has an adverbial qualification:

Als ihr Mann zurückkam, war sie   *When her husband returned, she was*
beim/am Kochen (Briefeschreiben)   *cooking (writing letters)*
Es ist immer noch am Regnen[1]   *It's still raining*

iv begriffen sein in + dat.:

Ich war gerade im Anziehen   *I was just dressing when he rang up*
begriffen, als er anrief

v Other insertions will suggest themselves to fit the context, e.g.

Ich habe ihn letzthin (*recently*)   *I've been meeting him twice a week*
zweimal in der Woche getroffen

354. Four special uses of the Present

(a) In describing a state or activity beginning in the past and still continuing (e.g. Ich warte seit zwanzig Minuten *I've been waiting for twenty minutes*; ich kenne ihn schon lange); see 532(b), 554.

(b) The historic present, sometimes sustained over many pages, is commoner in German than in English:

Mit zuckenden Nerven marschieren sie näher, noch immer versuchen sie sich gegenseitig zu täuschen, so sehr sie alle schon die Wahrheit wissen: daß die Norweger, daß Amundsen ihnen zuvorgekommen ist. Bald zerbricht der letzte Zweifel ... (Stefan Zweig: *Der Kampf um den Südpol* in *Sternstunden der Menschheit*)

Compare its effective colloquial use: Ich ging gestern ins Café—auf einmal, da seh' ich meinen Vetter.

(c) As in English, the present is the accepted tense for summaries of plays or stories and for 'history notes'.

(d) The use of 'ich komme' for English 'I have come' in sentences such as the following deserves mention:[2]

Ich komme die Miete zu bezahlen   *I've come to pay the rent*

---

[1] beim is not used with Regnen, Schneien, Frieren etc.
[2] cf. Collinson, op. cit., p. 80.

355. Present and Future[1]

(a) The future tense is relatively little used in German; where a time phrase or the context shows that the future is referred to, the present tense is preferred; the future is, as it were, experienced as if it were the present:

Ich gehe nächstes Jahr nach Amerika	*I'm going to America next year*
Morgen um diese Zeit bin ich in Wien	*This time tomorrow I shall be in Vienna*
Ich bin gleich fertig	*I'll be ready in a moment*
Er findet uns nie	*He will never find us*
Ich weiß, was wir machen	*I know what we'll do*
Also, du holst mich um 7 Uhr ab	*Well then, you'll call for me at 7 o'clock*
(Es) wird gemacht	*It shall be done*

(b) Where the present is thus used in a sub. clause + a main clause or in a series of sentences, the effect can be particularly vivid:

Wenn Sie herauskommen (*when you come out of prison*), nimmt kein Hund ein Stück Brot von Ihnen, Ihre Kinder kennen Sie nicht mehr. Sie sind dann eine alte Frau (W. Schreyer).

(c) The future tense may be used to underline the contrast between present and future:

Nächstes Jahr wird alles besser sein	*Next year everything will be better*

(d) The future tense may be used to express the speaker's intention:[2]

Ich werde es ihm morgen bestimmt sagen	*I'll tell him tomorrow without fail*

(e) A series of future tenses has emphatic or prophetic force:

Ich werde nicht mehr wie ein Irrer durch die Welt laufen. Ich werde nicht mehr eifersüchtig sein (Ch. Wolf).

(f) For the use of the future tense to express probability and as an imperative equivalent, see 358 and 459(b) respectively.

356. Two special uses of the Imperfect

(a) In describing a state or activity beginning in the past and still continuing at a more recent point in the past (e.g. Ich wartete schon seit zwei Stunden *I had been waiting for two hours*); see 532(c) and 554 N.iv.

(b) It is occasionally used in the course of a narrative in the past to point into the future; the conditional is the more usual tense:

Die Felsennase raste auf mich zu. Sekunden noch, dann überrollte und begrub uns die Lawine (K. Mundstock)[3]	*The sharp crag was rushing towards me. A few more seconds and the avalanche would roll over us and bury us*

357. Imperfect and Perfect

(a) Apart from sentences with 'since' or its equivalent (see 354(a)), the

---

[1] This paragraph owes much to an article 'Präsens oder Futur' (*Deutsch als Fremdsprache* 2/1967) by W. A. Sherebkow, including the examples in (b) and (e).

[2] cf. Schulz-Griesbach, op. cit., B 564.

[3] from Pawel Petkov: Futurische Verhältnisse im präteritalen Zeitplan (*Deutsch als Fremdsprache* 3/1969).

English forms 'I have done, I have been doing, he has done, he has been doing etc.' are rendered by the German perfect.

But the simplest past form (he did, he wrote etc.) may be either imperfect or perfect, depending on the context and the distinctive character of the two tenses.

(b) **The imperfect is used to record events or scenes belonging definitively to the past and without reference to the present; it is the staple narrative tense of German fiction.** E.g.

Es klingelte. Sie öffnete ihm die Tür. Er stand da, der Knecht Persenning, und starrte sie an. Seine Kopfschmerzen schwanden augenblicklich. Sie nickte mit dem Kopf, trat zur Seite und sagte dann: 'Bitte sehr, mein Herr.' (W. Altendorf)

(c) **The perfect looks back from the present into the past** or, to put it differently, **it links up the past with the present.** From this stem its two main uses:

i **It is used to record past events whose influence extends into the present**:

Er [Lessing] hat der deutschen Dichtung nicht nur ihre ersten unsterblichen Dramen, sondern auch der deutschen Prosa Klarheit und Beweglichkeit, Stil geschenkt. (H. Röhl: *Wörterbuch zur deutschen Literatur*, 1931)

ii **It is the predominant past tense of German conversation and, to a lesser extent, of German letter-writing.** (It particularly preponderates in South Germany):

Mutter, es hat geklopft	*Mother, there was a knock at the door*
Ich habe neulich Ihren Bruder gesehen	*I saw your brother the other day*[1]
Wo haben Sie ihn gesehen?	*Where did you see him?*
Lieber Karl!	*Dear Karl,*
Wir sind gestern nachmittag hier angekommen und Peter hat sofort gebadet	*We arrived here yesterday afternoon and Peter immediately went for a bathe*

(d) This fundamental difference between the imperfect and the perfect is stated in different terms by H. T. Betteridge in two articles on 'The Preterite (= Imperfect) and the Perfect in Modern German',[2] in which he stresses 'the essentially subjective notion underlying the perfect tense', while 'The preterite is the more "objective" tense'.

To quote one of H. T. Betteridge's illustrations, it is the subjective element which explains the use of the perfect in the following: 'Für dasselbe haben meine Väter den Kopf auf den Henkerblock legen müssen' (G. von le Fort).

(e) The perfect may be used to record a habitual or repeated action in the past as well as a state or condition, though for the latter the imperfect is commoner and safer:

Wenn das Wetter schön war, habe ich früher nach dem Mittagessen einen Spaziergang gemacht	*When the weather was fine, I used to go for a walk after lunch*

---

[1] Significantly, a German speaking imperfect English will say: I have seen your brother the other day.

[2] *Modern Languages*, December 1958 and March 1959.

| Ich habe ihn früher gekannt | *I used to know him* |
| Das Haus hat schrecklich ausgesehen | *The house looked awful* |

(f) In North Germany, even in conversation, the imperfect is by no means unidiomatic, while its greater brevity is a merit. In practice, **German conversation (and letter-writing) is often an unthinking mixture of the two tenses, in which an instinctive sense of rhythm plays its part**: Als ich nach Hause kam, hab' ich zu Abend gegessen und hab' noch ein paar Briefe geschrieben; dann ging ich früh zu Bett, aber ich konnte nicht schlafen.

(g) In certain domains the imperfect is used where one would expect the perfect:

| Sie sahen soeben . . . | *You have just seen . . . (on TV)* |
| Wilson selbst übernahm die Gesamtverantwortung für das Wirtschaftsministerium (from 'Informationen', a summary of the past week's news in *Die Zeit*) | *Wilson himself has assumed overall responsibility for the Department of Economic Affairs* |

In headlines it has the obvious merit of brevity:

| Zug raste in Arbeitskolonne: 5 Tote (*Bild-Zeitung*) | *Train hurtles into gang of workmen—5 dead* |

358. **A special use of the Future and Future Perfect**: to express a supposition or probability:

| Er ist nicht gekommen; er wird wieder zu viel zu tun haben | *He hasn't come; presumably he's again got too much to do* |
| Er wird den Zug verpaßt haben | *He's probably missed the train* |

359. **Apart from the use indicated in 358, the future perfect is relatively rare**; in conversation it is frequently rendered by the perfect:

| Bis morgen um diese Zeit habe ich alles geregelt | *By this time tomorrow I shall have settled everything* |

Compare the use of the perfect in both languages in e.g.

| Wenn ich von ihm gehört habe, werde ich dir schreiben | *When I've heard from him, I'll write to you* |

360. For the use of **the conditional and conditional perfect**, see 462 f., 466, 473, 479 ff.

For the use of **the subjunctive tenses**, see 460 ff.

F. THE USE OF THE PASSIVE[1]

361. **Paragraphs 354(a) and (b), 355(a) and 356(a) apply equally to the passive voice**

Present (or imperf.) tense in a sentence with 'seit':

| Diese Sache wird schon seit Wochen erörtert | *This matter has been under discussion for weeks* |

[1] see also 381, 419, 432, 496.

Present tense with future meaning:

Ich werde nächsten Montag benachrichtigt	*I shall be informed next Monday*

The conversational preference for the perfect (357(c)ii) applies less to the passive, where the shorter imperfect (Ich wurde gestern von meinem Neffen besucht) is preferred.

362. The cumbersome **Future Perfect Passive** exists in theory, but is virtually never used, e.g.

Bis sieben Uhr wird man mich von dem Ergebnis benachrichtigen	*By seven o'clock I shall have been informed of the result*

363. The equally cumbersome **Conditional Perfect Passive** is used rather more, in conjunction with conditional clauses, though the alternative tense, the Pluperfect Subjunctive, will generally be preferred (see 462):

Ich wäre gestört worden *I would have been disturbed*, instead of: Ich würde gestört worden sein.

In a subordinate clause, these forms would run: obwohl ich gestört worden wäre, and: obwohl ich gestört worden sein würde.

364. While the passive is used less in German than in English, sentences like the following, which could obviously be turned into the active, are completely convincing in their passive form:

Dieses Haus wurde von Studenten gebaut	*This house was built by students*
Das Hotel ist anscheinend seit Jahren nicht angestrichen worden	*The hotel can't have been painted for years*

A preference for the active form, with or without 'man', is perhaps strongest in the future:

Natürlich wird man ihn kritisieren	*Of course he will be criticized*
Sogar seine Freunde werden ihn kritisieren	*He will be criticized even by his friends*

365. Constructions where the passive is used in English but cannot be used in German:

Ein Vorbeigehender sah ihn in das Haus einbrechen	*He was seen breaking into the house by a passer-by*
Man hörte ihn singen	*He was heard singing*
Man fand ihn auf dem Fußboden liegen	*He was found lying on the floor*
Er ist bekanntlich unzuverlässig	*He is known to be unreliable*
Man glaubt, er ist verreist	*He is thought to have gone away*
	It is thought that he has gone away

366. Some substitutes for the passive:

(a) man (one, someone, cf. Fr. 'on')+active:

Man hatte ihn davor gewarnt	*He had been warned about it*
Das macht man nicht	*It isn't done*

(b) verloren-gehen *to be lost, to get lost*:
Der Schlüssel ist verlorengegangen   *The key has been lost*

(c) Verbs used reflexively with an inanimate subject:
Das lernt sich rasch   *That is quickly learnt*
Das erklärt sich leicht   *That is easily explained*
Der Schlüssel hat sich gefunden   *The key has been found*
Mein Verdacht hat sich bestätigt   *My suspicion has been confirmed*

(d) bekommen or kriegen (coll.) + past part. is the German equivalent of
  an analogous English alternative for a direct passive:
Ich bekomme/kriege das Geld   *I have the money paid out to me*
  regelmäßig ausgezahlt   *regularly*
Wir haben viel gezeigt bekommen   *We had a lot shown to us, we were*
                                             shown a lot

(e) A noun with a verbal content introduced by a suitable verb:[1]
seine Vollendung finden (for 'vollendet werden') *to be completed.*
eine große Vereinfachung erfahren *to be greatly simplified* (for 'sehr vereinfacht
  werden')
eine Veränderung erleiden   *to be changed*
zur Erörterung gelangen   *to be discussed*

For some comments on Nominalstil (i.e. a current preference for nouns
  as opposed to verbs and clauses), of which these phrases are examples,
  see Du. Haupt., pp. 456 f. and Moeller, op. cit., pp. 53 ff., 65 ff. and
  115 ff.; see also 404 in this book.

367. 'Das Zustandspassiv'

(a) A distinction must be made between the true passive, with its stress
  on the action, and the resultant state, expressed by 'sein' (not
  'werden'); the past part. is here a complement:
Der Tisch wird gedeckt   *The table is being laid*
Der Tisch ist gedeckt   *The table is laid*
Die Stadt wurde allmählich von   *The town was gradually surrounded by*
  Truppen umringt   *troops*
Die Stadt war von Truppen umringt   *The town was surrounded with troops*
Dieser Bericht ist von einem   *This report is written by a friend of*
  Freund von mir geschrieben   *mine*
Früher waren die zwei Teiche   *Formerly the two ponds had been*
  verbunden gewesen   *connected*

(b) Sometimes the right choice is less clear:
Die zwei Dörfer werden (coll. sind)   *The two villages are separated by a wood*
  durch einen Wald getrennt
Dort werden Mechaniker gebraucht   *Mechanics are required there*
  (J. Ziem)
Ich war die ganze Zeit versucht,   *The whole time I was tempted to help him*
  ihm zu helfen
Das will überlegt sein   *That needs thinking about*
Der Schreiber war bald festgestellt   *The writer was soon identified*
  (A. Goes) (more incisive than
  imperf. or pluperf. passive)

---

[1] The first three examples are taken from an article by Herbert Kolb in *Sprache im tech-
nischen Zeitalter*, 19/1966.

(c) **was born**: a serviceable rule is to use 'ist geboren' of the living and 'wurde (or: war) geboren' of the dead:

Wann sind Sie geboren? *When were you born?*
Ich bin 1940 geboren *I was born in 1940*
Goethe wurde/war 1749 geboren *Goethe was born in 1749*

G. VERBS WITH PREFIXES:
INSEPARABLE, SEPARABLE, DOUBLE, VARIABLE

368. The 8 Inseparable Prefixes:

be- emp- ent- er- ge- miß-[1] ver- zer-

Characteristics:
(a) In contrast with the separable prefixes, none of these exists as an independent word.
(b) They are never separated from the stem of the verb.
(c) They never carry the stress.
(d) A verb with an insep. prefix has no ge- in the past part.: besuchen: besucht.

EXAMPLES:
beeinflussen *to influence*, entkommen *to escape*, erröten *to blush*, geleiten *to escort*, zerreißen *to tear to pieces*

The force of the insep. prefixes is treated in 677 ff.

369. Separable Prefixes:

All prefixes other than the 8 insep. prefixes are, or—in the case of the 9 variable prefixes—may be, separable.

Characteristics:

(a) In contrast with the insep. prefixes, these are words with a meaning, the majority being independent parts of speech as well as prefixes, e.g. prepositions (aus-gehen *to go out*), adverbs (dazwischen-treten *to intervene*), nouns (teil-nehmen *to take part*), adjectives (frei-lassen *to release*), infinitives (spazieren-gehen *to go for a walk*).
Only a few are meaningless except as prefixes: danieder-, ein-, einher-, hernieder-, herzu-, hintan-, hinzu-, inne-, umhin-.
For the 3 types of sep. prefix and for the individual prefixes, see 692 ff.

(b) A sep. prefix always carries the main stress. Nouns formed from these verbs are likewise accented on the prefix: der Àbflug, die Voraùssage.

(c) Position of a sep. prefix, illustrated by 'aus-gehen':
i It stands at the end of the sentence in the imperative, and in the present and imperfect tenses except in a subordinate clause; here the verb itself comes last, forming one word with the prefix:[2] Gehen Sie früh aus! Er geht (ging) früh aus. Obwohl er früh ausgeht (ausging), . . .

---

[1] miß- does not entirely qualify as an insep. prefix; it is fully treated in 691.
[2] Exc. Indirect Statements and other noun clauses without 'daß'; here normal order is used: Er sagte (ich glaubte), er gehe früh aus (cf. 484(b)).

ii It precedes the ge- of the past part., which is written as one word:
Er ist früh ausgegangen.

iii Where the infinitive is used with 'zu', the latter comes between the
sep. prefix and the simple verb, the whole being written as one
word: um auszugehen.

iv Present part.: ausgehend.

370. Double Prefixes:

When a sep. prefix is attached to a verb with an insep. prefix, the verb is
treated as separable, except that there is no ge- in the past part. Thus
the principal parts of an-vertrauen *to entrust* are:
anvertrauen – vertraut an – vertraute an – anvertraut

Infin. with 'zu': um es mir anzuvertrauen.

Pres. tense in sub. clause: wenn er es mir anvertraut, . . .

Imperative: Vertraue es mir an!

Further common examples:
an-erkennen *to acknowledge*
aus-verkaufen *to sell out* (one's stock)
bei-behalten *to keep on, retain* (e.g. a high standard of living, an old custom)
vor-enthalten *to withhold*

Note:
i In modern German some verbs with double prefixes are sometimes
treated as inseparable verbs (though not in the infinitive) with the
effect of a certain incisiveness. This occurs particularly: 1. when the
insep. prefix is er- or ent- 2. in written rather than spoken German
3. in Swiss and Austrian authors. (cf. Du. Haupt. Verb 2d).
e.g. Das anerkannte Tuzzi voll und ganz (R. Musil, quoted by Duden)
Er vorenthält ihnen den Lohn, BUT: statt ihnen den Lohn vorzuenthalten.

ii The opposite combination, i.e. an insep. prefix attached to a verb with a
sep. prefix, does not occur. What at first sight appear to be instances
of it in reality consist of an insep. prefix attached to a compound
noun or adjective to form an inseparable verb; such verbs are always
weak. E.g.
beauftragen *to commission, instruct* formed from 'der Auftrag'
benachteiligen *to treat disadvantageously* formed from 'nachteilig'
veranlassen *to occasion, cause* formed from 'der Anlaß'

iii Regarding 'wieder' when prefixed to a verb with a sep. prefix, see
689(b)ii.

371. The 9 Variable Prefixes:

über	durch	voll	hinter
unter	um	wider	miß
		wieder	

Characteristics:

(a) These are sometimes sep., sometimes insep., and are correspondingly
stressed or unstressed.

(b) über, unter, durch, voll, wider and hinter show the following tendencies:
   i When the prefix is separable:
1. verb and prefix each retain their original meaning.
2. where the simple verb is intransitive, the compound verb is intransitive.
   ii When the prefix is inseparable:
1. a derived or figurative meaning arises from the combination of verb and
prefix.
2. even where the simple verb is intransitive, the compound verb is
transitive.

These tendencies may be illustrated by some instances where a prefix
is used both separably and inseparably with the same simple verb:

Das Obergeschoß steht etwas über	*The upper storey overhangs a bit*
Er übersteht alle Schwierigkeiten	*He surmounts all difficulties*
Ich hatte ihm eine Decke übergelegt	*I had put a rug over him*
Ich hatte mir die Sache überlegt	*I had considered the matter*
Ich fand ein Loch im Zaun und schaute durch	*I found a hole in the fence and looked through*
Ich schaute die Papiere durch	*I glanced through the papers*
Ich durchschaute ihn/seine Absichten	*I saw through him/his intentions*

The force of the variable prefixes is treated in 683 ff.

H. IMPERSONAL VERBS AND EXPRESSIONS

372. Introductory

(a) Impersonal verbs and expressions are of two kinds:
   i **genuinely impersonal verbs and expressions** in which the 'es'
cannot be equated with, or replaced by, a specific noun, a phrase
or a clause, e.g. Es regnet; es fehlt mir an Geld; es ist mir warm; es
graut mir vor Schlangen; es wurde mir schlecht; wie geht es
Ihnen?
   ii **pseudo-impersonal expressions**, in which the 'es' anticipates, or
stands for, the real subject. Thus the sentences 'Es freut mich sehr,
Sie wiederzusehen' and 'Es freut mich sehr, daß Sie wieder
gekommen sind' could be recast in more emphatic form to read:
'Sie wiederzusehen freut mich sehr' and 'Daß Sie wieder ge-
kommen sind, freut mich sehr'. Compare the following:
A.: Kurt hat das Examen bestanden.
B.: So? Es freut mich sehr, in which 'es' stands for 'daß er das
Examen bestanden hat', and could be replaced by 'sein Erfolg'.
The 'es' may similarly be regarded as introductory when the expres-
sion is followed by a 'wenn' clause: Es würde mich freuen, wenn
Sie morgen kämen.
In what follows, debatable cases have been classified as genuinely
impersonal verbs.

(b) The main practical difficulty in connection with impersonal expressions of both the types mentioned in (a) above is that of the retention

or omission of 'es' in a main clause beginning with something other than the 'es' and in a subordinate clause.

373. Impersonal verbs and expressions which never drop the 'es'

(a) weather phrases, e.g. es ist warm (kalt, kühl etc.) *it is warm (cold, cool etc.)*: warm ist es heute; heute ist es warm; da es warm ist, . . . es wird warm *it is getting warm,* es ist Winter, es wird Winter *winter is coming on,* es dämmert 1. *it is dawning, growing light* 2. *it is growing dusk,* es donnert, es friert, es gießt *it is pouring,* es schneit.

(b) onomatopoeic verbs used impersonally, e.g. es klingelt *there's a ring,* es klopft *there's a knock,* es knallt *there's a report, a shot,* es läutet 1. *there's a ring* 2. *the bells are pealing.*

(c) fire and draught: Es brennt! es brennt in der Stadt; es zieht.

(d) miscellaneous:

es fehlt mir an + dat.	*I lack*
es fehlt mir an Geld[1]	*I'm short of money*
es fragt sich, ob	*the question is whether*
es fügte sich, daß	*it so happened that*
es gefällt mir in Heidelberg/bei ihm	*I like it (I like being) in Heidelberg/at his place*
es geschieht Ihnen recht	*it serves you right*
Jetzt gilt es zu handeln	*Now the thing is to act*
es handelt sich um + acc.	*it is a question of* (Fr.: il s'agit de)
es hängt davon ab, ob	*it depends on whether*
es heißt (daß) (see N.i below)	*it is said (that)*
es kommt darauf an,[2] (ob)	*it depends (on whether)*
es kommt auf seine Reaktion an	*it depends on his reaction*
es kommt zu + dat.	*'it comes to', there occurs,* e.g.
Am Abend kam es zu neuen Zusammenstößen	*In the evening there were fresh clashes*
es liegt an + dat.	*it is due to*
woran liegt es, daß . . .?	*why is it that . . .?*
es macht (or: tut) nichts	*it doesn't matter*
es steht Ihnen frei, zu gehen oder zu bleiben	*you are free to go or stay*
es verhält sich	*it is (the case),* e.g.
Ähnlich verhält es sich im Baugewerbe	*Things are similar in the building-trade*

Note:

i es heißt (daß) *it is said (that)*
    e.g. Es heißt, er wäre angekommen. Er ist nach Wien geflogen, heißt es.

cf. In der Erklärung heißt es, die Bundesregierung werde . . . (*FAZ*)	*In the declaration it says that the Federal Government will . . .*
'Schade!' hieß es überall	*'A pity,' people were saying everywhere*

Two idiomatic uses:

Wie heißt es doch im 'Faust'?	*What's that bit in 'Faust'?*
Hier heißt es handeln	*Now the thing is to act*

[1] Compare: es fehlt mir das (nötige) Geld, um diese Reise zu machen *I haven't the (necessary) money to go on this journey*; contrast: es fehlt mir Geld *some of my money is missing.*
[2] Many idiomatic uses include: es kommt darauf an zu handeln *the thing is to act*; auf ein paar Mark (mehr oder weniger) kommt es mir nicht an *I don't mind a few marks more or less.*

ii In literary German, a wide range of verbs are used impersonally, generally conveying the feeling of an impersonal force at work (cf. 143(f)):

Anna stand am Fenster und schaute hinaus. Es wirbelte, wogte, es schlug den Schnee gegen das Glas, als wollte er alles zuschütten (G. Kölwel)	*Anna stood at the window and gazed out. There was a whirling and surging. The snow was beaten against the glass, as if it would block up everything*

374. Pseudo-impersonal expressions which never drop the 'es'

Es ist mir unangenehm, das zu tun/daß er kommt	*It's disagreeable for me to do that/ that he's coming*

Mir ist es unangenehm/Unangenehm ist es mir, ... Natürlich ist es mir unangenehm, ... Obwohl es mir unangenehm ist, ...

es ärgert mich	*it annoys me*
es fällt mir leicht/schwer	*it is easy/difficult for me*
es fehlt nur noch, daß er auch krank ist[1]	*if he's ill too, it's the last straw*
es gelingt (glückt) mir	*I succeed*
es hat keinen Sinn/Zweck, das zu tun	*there is no point in doing that*
es ist (nicht) der Mühe wert	*it's (not) worth while*
est ist mir eine Freude	*it's a pleasure for me*
es ist ein Glück	*it's fortunate*
es ist eine Schande	*it's a disgrace* (or *shameful*)
es ist (mir) gleich,[2] ob er kommt oder nicht[3]	*it's all the same (to me) whether he comes or not*
es ist leicht/schwer[3]	*it's easy/difficult*
es ist möglich[3]	*it's possible*
es ist nötig	*it's necessary*
es ist (mir) peinlich	*it's embarrassing (for me)*
es ist mir recht	*I agree to it, I'm agreeable*
es ist schade	*it's a pity*
es ist (mir) wichtig[3]	*it's important for me*
es ist zu bedauern, zu befürchten, zu hoffen (etc.), daß[4]	*it is to be regretted, to be feared, to be hoped that*
es kann passieren, daß[3]	*it may happen that*
es läßt sich nicht bestreiten, daß[4]	*it cannot be denied that* (or: *the fact remains that*)
es liegt mir fern, Schwierigkeiten zu machen	*the last thing I want to do is to make difficulties*
es liegt nahe, daraus zu schließen, daß	*the obvious thing is to conclude that*
es lohnt sich (nicht)	*it's (not) worth while*
es macht mir Freude, das zu tun	*it gives me pleasure to do that*
es macht nichts aus	*it doesn't matter*
es macht mir Spaß	*it amuses me* (or: *I enjoy*)
es mißlingt (mißglückt) mir	*I fail*
es spricht sich herum, daß	*the word is going round that*
es stellt sich heraus, daß[3]	*it turns out that*
es versteht sich von selbst, daß	*it goes without saying that*
es ziemt sich nicht	*it's not fitting*

[1] The 'es' may be omitted with inversion. [2] for variants of 'gleich', see 117: gleich. [3] The 'es' is sometimes omitted with inversion. [4] The 'es' may be omitted except in normal order.

375. With the following impersonal and pseudo-impersonal expressions, if, in a main clause, the personal pronoun (other than 'sie' or 'Sie') is placed first, the 'es' is often omitted; in most cases, its retention, especially in the form 's, is colloquially more usual, while its omission is more literary and sometimes old-fashioned; with a noun, the 'es' is usually retained.

Es ist mir warm Mir ist/ist's warm	*I am feeling warm*
Es ist meinem Vater warm Meinem Vater ist es/ist's warm	*My father is feeling warm*
Mich hat('s) gewundert/Meinen Bruder hat es/hat's gewundert, daß sie nichts gesagt hat	*I was surprised/My brother was surprised that she didn't say anything*

impersonal:

es graut mir vor + dat.	*I have a horror of* (e.g. snakes)
es ist mir, als ob	*I feel as if, it seems to me that*
es ist mir kalt, es friert mich	*I am feeling cold*[1]
es kommt mir vor, als ob	*it seems to me as if*
es schaudert mir[2] bei dem Gedanken/ wenn ich daran denke	*I shudder at the thought/ when I think of it*
es scheint mir, daß/als ob	*it seems to me that/as if*
es wird mir warm/kalt	*I am getting warm/cold*

pseudo-impersonal:

es enttäuscht mich, daß	*I am disappointed that*
es erstaunt mich, daß	*I am astonished that*
es fällt mir auf, daß	*it strikes me as strange that*
es freut mich, daß/zu + infin.	*I am glad that/to*
es interessiert mich, daß/zu + inf.	*I am interested that/to*
es ist mir lieb, daß	*I am glad* (lit.: *it is agreeable to me*) *that*
es tut/es ist mir leid, daß	*I am sorry that*

Note:

i With some of the above expressions the 'es' is not infrequently omitted in cases other than that mentioned in the rubric.

E.g. Wenn (es) dir zu warm ist, ziehe die Jacke aus.

Natürlich graut (es) mir vor Schlangen.

Obwohl (es) mich interessieren würde, ihn zu sehen, . . .

BUT: Obwohl es mich enttäuschen würde, ihn nicht zu sehen.

Some 'Sprachgefühl' is here desirable.

ii es hungert mich (mich hungert) and es dürstet mich (mich dürstet) belong here, but are obsolete, poetic and biblical; modern usage: ich bin hungrig/durstig or ich habe Hunger/Durst.

376. The following impersonal expressions usually drop the 'es', except: i in normal order.

       ii when applied to a noun in a direct question.

       iii when applied to a proper name.

---

[1] also: ich friere.

[2] slightly less common: es schaudert mich.

Es ist mir (nicht) wohl[1]	*I am (not) well*
Gestern war meinem Bruder nicht wohl	*Yesterday my brother wasn't well*
Gestern war es Karl nicht wohl	*Yesterday Karl wasn't well*
weil meinem Bruder nicht wohl ist	*because my brother isn't well*
War dir nicht wohl?	*Weren't you well?*
War es deinem Bruder nicht wohl?	*Wasn't your brother well?*
es ist mir besser	*I'm feeling better*
es ist (or wird) mir schlecht	*I feel sick*
es ist (or wird) mir übel	*I don't feel well*
es ist mir gut zumute[2]	*I'm in good spirits*
es träumt mir von + dat./daß[3]	*I dream about/that*

377. In the following expressions the 'es' is omitted except in normal order:

Es steht in der Zeitung, daß . . .	*It says in the paper that . . .*
Gestern stand in der Zeitung, daß . . .	*Yesterday it said in the paper that . . .*
Obwohl in der Zeitung steht, daß . . .	*Although it says in the paper that . . .*
es fällt mir ein, daß	*it occurs to me that*
es liegt mir viel/wenig/nichts daran (dies zu tun)	*I attach great/little/no importance to it (to doing this)*
es ist mir viel/wenig/nichts daran gelegen (dies zu tun)	

378. Impersonal expressions with 'gehen'; 'es' is always retained:

es geht	1. *it can be done*
	2. *so so; pretty well*
es geht nicht	*it can't be done*
es wird schon gehen	*it will be all right*
es wäre auch ohne ihn gegangen	*we could have managed without him*
so geht es im Leben	*such is life*
aber wie es so geht	*but as is so often the case*
Wie geht es Ihnen?[4]	*How are you?*
Es geht mir gut, danke[4]	*I'm all right, thank you*
Jetzt geht es wieder	*I'm better again now*
wie wird mir's gehen?	*how shall I fare?*
es ist mir geradeso gegangen	*the same thing happened in my case*
wenn es nach mir ginge	*if I had my way*
es geht um Leben und Tod	*it's a matter of life and death*
es geht um seine ganze Zukunft	*his whole future is at stake*
Mit dem Zug geht's freilich schneller	*Certainly it's quicker by train*
Wo geht's nach Osnabrück?	*Which is the way to Osnabrück?*
Heute geht's nach Freiburg	*Today I'm (we're) going to Freiburg*

---

[1] used more negatively than affirmatively; cf. the more colloquial: es ist mir nicht gut.
[2] 'gut' can be replaced by e.g. schlecht, sonderbar, traurig.
[3] elev.; normal usage: ich träumte von/daß.
[4] more colloquial: Wie geht's? Gut, danke.

Note: Other verbs with numerous impersonal uses are an-kommen, gelten, kommen, stehen; with few exceptions, the 'es' is always retained.

379. In spoken German, the 'es' of a number of the impersonal expressions listed in the preceding paragraphs is often omitted or slurred in normal order. Such are:

Es ist warm (kalt) heute, es geschieht dir recht, es macht (tut) nichts, es kommt darauf an, es hängt davon ab, es scheint mir, daß . . ., es kommt mir vor, als ob . . ., es freut mich, daß . . ., es ist mir lieb, es tut mir leid, es ist mir leid, es geht nicht, es geht mir gut (schlecht); and all those in 374 beginning with 'es ist'. E.g.

Is' warm heute	*It's warm today*
'Scheint so', sagt Pinneberg. 'Fragt sich nur wie lange.' (H. Fallada)	*'It seems so', says Pinneberg. 'The question is only for how long'*
Freut mich sehr	*I'm very glad*

380. A reflexive impersonal construction, generalizing an activity; the 'es' always remains. E.g.

Es schreibt sich so leicht mit dieser Feder	*It's so easy writing with this pen*
Im eignen Bett schläft es sich noch einmal so gut	*One sleeps twice as well in one's own bed*

381. The Impersonal Passive

This is a much used construction, denoting a general activity not attributed to a particular agent. The 'es' drops out except in normal order:

Es wurde im Nebenzimmer geredet	*There was talking in the next room*

Wurde im Nebenzimmer geredet? Hin und wieder wurde im Nebenzimmer geredet. Da im Nebenzimmer geredet wurde, . . .

Vor Hunden wird gewarnt	*Beware of dogs*
Bei Müllers ist eingebrochen worden	*The Müllers have had burglars*
Von einem Nachfolger wird nicht gesprochen	*There is no talk of a successor*
Hier wird gelegen, gestöhnt, geliebt, gestorben (A. Goes)	*Here men lie, moan, love, die* (from a description of a military hospital)

See also 459(e) and 496(b)iii.

I. THERE IS

382. There are two specific German equivalents of 'there is' (for other renderings see 387).

(a) es gibt + accusative

The origin and explanation of this phrase, 'it gives', is: Nature (or Providence) gives (provides, produces). This is a clue to the uses of 'es gibt', e.g. Es hat letztes Jahr eine gute Ernte gegeben *There was a good harvest last year*. The 'es' is thus a real subject, which is retained whatever the word order, e.g. Letztes Jahr hat es eine gute Ernte gegeben.

(b) **es ist, es sind + nominative**

Here the 'es' is merely an introductory subject, which drops away in inversion or a subordinate clause, when it is no longer separated, by the verb, from the real subject; the number of the latter determines that of the verb (ist or sind). E.g. Es ist eine Maus in der Küche; oft ist eine Maus in der Küche; wenn eine Maus in der Küche ist, . . .; es sind zwei Hunde im Garten.

383. es gibt is used:

(a) **to denote existence as such, without reference to a particular place:**

Wenn es uns nicht gegeben hätte, wäre er verloren gewesen	*But for us* (lit. *if we had not existed*), *he would have been lost*
Es gibt verschiedene Gründe dafür	*There are various reasons for it*
Urlaub gibt es jetzt sowieso nicht (G. Gaiser)	*In any case there is no leave at present*
Gleichmaß und Ruhe hat es da nur selten gegeben (*Zeit*: from a review of Zuckmayer's autobiography)	*There was rarely proportion and tranquillity in his life*

Typical of this use are broad, general statements:

Es gibt Tage, wo alles schiefgeht	*There are days when everything goes wrong*
So etwas gibt es nicht	*There's no such thing*
Es hat immer Kriege gegeben (Th. Valentin)	*There have always been wars*
O ja, Unglückliche gibt es in allen Häusern, in jedem Stand! (M. Walser)	*Oh yes, there are unhappy individuals in every kind of home, in every walk of life*

Occasional fluctuations are found, e.g. Es gab/es war/wir hatten keine Zeit, das zu tun. Warum sollte ein Unterschied sein, zwischen einem weißen und einem schwarzen Mann? (I. Wendt) (Also possible: Warum sollte es einen Unterschied geben, . . .)

(b) **to denote existence in a large area**, e.g. a town, a country (but see 384(b)):

Es gibt drei alte Kirchen in unserer Stadt	*There are three old churches in our town*
Es gibt in München so viel zu sehen	*There is so much to see in Munich*
Es gab Holme in dem Fjord (G. Gaiser)	*There were islets in the fjord*
Es dürfte in der Bundesrepublik wenige geben, die so gut wie er informiert sind (*Zeit*)	*There are probably few persons in the Federal Republic who are as well informed as he is*

(c) **in recording the consequences of some event:**

Wenn du das tust, gibt's ein Unglück (Du. Stil.)	*If you do that, there'll be a calamity*
Bei den Unruhen soll es bisher vier Tote gegeben haben (*FAZ*)	*So far there are said to have been four killed in the course of the disturbances*
Er mußte auswärts ein Konzert dirigieren . . . So gab es eine kleine Pause in ihrem gemeinsamen Glück (H. H. Jahnn)	*He had to conduct a concert away from home . . . Thus there was a break in their joint happiness*

384. es ist is used:

(a) **to denote permanent or temporary presence in a definite and limited place** (e.g. a house, a room):

Es war eine kleine Gastwirtschaft im Keller (V. Baum). Schade, daß hier im Haushalt keine Nähmaschine ist (H. Fallada). Es ist irgend jemand an der Tür.

Note:

i When 'es ist' is used in this context and in that described in 384(b), the sentence must contain a word or phrase denoting place; if there is none, supply da, darin etc.:

Auf dem Kaminsims ist eine Uhr; es sind auch zwei Vasen da (or: da sind auch zwei Vasen)	*On the mantelpiece there is a clock; there are also two vases*
Es ist ein Brief für Sie da	*There's a letter for you*

ii Occasionally 'es gibt' is used in this context, particularly if it is desired to underline the distinctive character of the thing concerned. (With 'es gibt' the stress is on the thing, not on the place.)

In dieser Diele gab es gegenüber der Tür einen offenen Kamin (I. Wendt)	*In this lounge there was a fireplace opposite the door*

(b) **to denote temporary presence in a large area:**

Es waren noch viele Menschen auf den Straßen	*There were still a lot of people in the streets*
Es sind heute viele Auswärtige in der Stadt	*There are many strangers in town today*
Es waren Wolken am Himmel	*There were clouds in the sky*
Es war ein Frühlingsgefühl in der Luft	*There was a feeling of spring in the air*

N.B. See Note i in (a) above.

(c) **in recording events** (though here practice varies a good deal):

Letzte Woche war in Hamburg ein Streik. Gestern war das zweite Sinfoniekonzert. Im Fernsehn war eine Diskussion darüber (Th. Valentin). [es] war ein Gehen und Schieben hinter der Reling hin (G. Gaiser) *There was much moving about and pushing behind the ship's rail.* In Mainz war ein Aufenthalt (or: gab es einen Aufenthalt) von fünf Minuten.

When 'es gibt' is used in this context, it is especially in connection with events of a striking or exceptional character and with future events:

Es gab in der Fabrik eine Explosion	*There was an explosion in the factory*
Eine Verhandlung wie diese hat es in der Geschichte der deutschen Luftfahrt noch nie gegeben (*Zeit*)	*In the history of German aviation there has never been an investigation such as this one*
Es wird nächste Woche in Hamburg einen Streik geben	*Next week there will be a strike in Hamburg*

(d) **in speaking of weather conditions** (though 'es gibt' is also sometimes used, especially referring to the future):

Es war in diesem Winter wenig Schnee (Es hat . . . wenig Schnee gegeben)	*There was not much snow this winter*
Am nächsten Morgen war dichter Nebel	*Next morning there was a thick fog*

Es ist zuviel Strömung (S. Lenz)	*There's too much current*
Es wird ein Gewitter geben	*There's going to be a thunderstorm*

385. Some idiomatic uses of 'es gibt'

Was gibt's?	1. *What's the news?*
	2. *What's the matter?*
Was gibt's heute (zu Mittag)?	*What is there for lunch today?*
Gestern gab es Kalbsbraten	*Yesterday there was roast veal*
Was gibt es heute abend im Theater?[1]	*What's on at the theatre tonight?*
Es gibt nichts zu lachen	*There's nothing to laugh at*
Es gibt noch viel zu tun	*There's still a lot to do*
Nein, das gibt's nicht	*No, you're/we're not doing that*
Gleich gibt's was[1]	1. *In a minute you'll get a box on the ears*
	2. *There'll be a thunderstorm in a minute*
	3. *Lunch will soon be ready*

386. Two special uses of 'es ist'

i Once upon a time there was . . . Es war einmal . . .
ii in describing a picture:

Im Hintergrund ist ein Wald	*In the background there is a forest*

387. Other renderings of 'there is' (important)

Where 'there is' is normal in English, German frequently uses neither 'es ist' nor 'es gibt', but some other, generally more definite, verb. E.g.

In der Diele steht ein Flügel	*There's a grand piano in the lounge*
Auf dem Tisch lagen Äpfel	*There were some apples on the table*
Es lagen Wolken um den Gipfel	*There were clouds round the summit*
Vor mir war der Hafen: zuerst sah ich die Dampfer, sodann . . .	*Before me was the harbour: first, there were the steamers, then . . .*
Es herrschte tiefe Stille	*There was deep silence*
An unseren Schulen herrschte Disziplin (Th. Valentin)	*In our schools there was discipline*
Letzte Woche wurde in Hamburg gestreikt	*Last week there was a strike in Hamburg*
Im Gebüsch knisterte es	*There was a crackling sound in the undergrowth*
Es ist eingebrochen worden	*There's been a burglary*
Es kamen letztes Jahr viele Ausländer nach England	*There were a lot of foreigners in England last year*
Es besteht kein Zweifel, daß . . .	*There is no doubt that . . .*

See also 143(e) and 373 N.ii.

J. THE MODAL VERBS

388. können[2] *to be able to, can*   müssen *to have to, must*
dürfen *to be allowed to, may*   sollen *am to*
mögen *to like, to like to*   wollen *to want, to want to, to be willing to*

---

[1] from Wahrig, op. cit.
[2] 'können' has been placed first as being the commonest of the six and therefore the most suitable as a model in the paragraphs that follow.

These 6 verbs are generally known as the Modal Verbs or Modal Auxiliaries because they are mainly used in conjunction with other verbs whose significance they *modify*. As may be seen from the above table, the modals respectively express ability, permission, inclination, necessity, obligation and volition to perform the action of the verb dependent on them (cf. Stopp, op. cit., 63).

389. The forms of the Modal Verbs

(a) The singular of the present indicative is irregular, being an extinct strong imperfect:

> können: ich kann, du kannst, er kann, wir können, ihr könnt, sie können
> dürfen: ich darf, du darfst, er darf, wir dürfen etc.
> mögen: ich mag, du magst, er mag, wir mögen etc.
> müssen: ich muß, du mußt, er muß, wir müssen etc.
> sollen: ich soll, du sollst, er soll, wir sollen etc.
> wollen: ich will, du willst, er will, wir wollen etc.

(b) The present subjunctive is regular:

> ich könne ich dürfe, du dürfest etc.
> du könnest ich möge, du mögest etc.
> er könne ich müsse, du müssest etc.
> wir können ich solle, du sollest etc.
> ihr könnet ich wolle, du wollest etc.
> sie können

(c) i The imperf. indic. and past part. are weak, but where the infinitive is modified this modification is dropped; mögen also has a consonant change.

ii The modals have two past participles; the second is identical with the infinitive and is used when, as is preponderantly the case, there is an infinitive dependent on the modal, e.g.: Er hat das Buch gewollt, BUT: Er hat das Buch lesen wollen.

(d) The principal parts are therefore as follows:

INFIN.	PRES. INDIC.	IMPERFECT.	PAST PARTICIPLE
können	kann	konnte	gekonnt, können
dürfen	darf	durfte	gedurft, dürfen
mögen	mag	mochte	gemocht, mögen
müssen	muß	mußte	gemußt, müssen
sollen	soll	sollte	gesollt, sollen
wollen	will	wollte	gewollt, wollen

(e) The imperf. subj. is the same as the imperf. indic., but where the infin. is modified, the modification is here restored:

> ich könnte, dürfte, möchte, müßte, sollte, wollte

(f) The -e of the 1st and 3rd sing. imperf. indic. and subj. is often dropped in conversation, especially before a vowel, e.g. Er konnt' uns nicht finden; er möcht' mitgehen.

(g) Owing to their meanings, the modals are not found in the imperative, apart from some curios of 'wollen' not worth quoting.

390. Infinitives dependent on the modals are used without 'zu': Er will sein Haus verkaufen; er kann nichts als arbeiten.

391. Straightforward examples of the modals in their four commonest tenses

(a) **Present Indicative**:

Darf ich heute Tennis spielen?	*May I play tennis today?*
Ich soll ihm das Buch morgen zurückgeben	*I'm to return the book to him tomorrow*

(b) **Imperfect Indicative**:

Ich konnte gestern nicht kommen	*I couldn't come yesterday*
	I wasn't able to come yesterday
Ich mochte ihm nichts davon sagen	*I didn't like to tell him about it*
Ich mußte fleißig arbeiten	*I had to work hard*

(c) **Imperfect Subjunctive**:

Ich könnte morgen kommen	*I could come tomorrow*
	I would be able to come tomorrow
Ich dürfte morgen kommen	*I would be allowed to come tomorrow*
Ich möchte das Buch (gern) lesen	*I should like to read the book*
Wenn er darauf bestehen würde, müßte ich das Buch lesen	*If he insisted on it, I should have to read the book*
Ich sollte das Buch lesen	*I ought to read the book*
Ich wollte dir gern helfen	*I would be very willing to help you*

(d) **Pluperfect Subjunctive**:

Ich hätte das Buch lesen können	*I could have read the book*
Ich hätte das Buch lesen dürfen	*I would have been allowed to read the book*
Ich hätte das Buch lesen mögen[1]	*I would have liked to read the book*
Ich hätte das Buch lesen müssen	*I would have had to read the book*
	I ought to have read the book[2]
Ich hätte das Buch lesen sollen	*I ought to have read the book[2]*
(Ich hätte das Buch lesen wollen[3]	*I would have liked to read the book*)

392. (a) **A special order rule**: when a modal is used concurrently 1. in a compound tense 2. in a subordinate clause 3. with a dependent infinitive, then the auxiliary of the compound tense precedes the dependent infinitive, instead of coming at the end.

(b) Examples:

Da er heute hat schwimmen dürfen, muß es ihm besser gehen	*As he has been allowed to swim today, he must be better*
Es war klar, daß er sich würde anstrengen müssen	*It was clear that he would have to exert himself*
Das Buch, das ich hätte kaufen sollen, kostet 30 Mark	*The book that I should have bought costs 30 marks*
daß die letzte Filmaufnahme ... hat verschoben werden müssen (I. Wendt)	*that the final shooting of the film has had to be postponed*

(c) Where another word or phrase forms a unit with the dependent infinitive, the auxiliary generally precedes the complete unit:

---

[1] commoner: Ich hätte das Buch gern gelesen.
[2] 'sollen' expresses a stronger sense of duty than 'müssen'.
[3] 'wollen' is rarely used in this tense.

Obwohl er hat Fußball spielen dürfen, . . .	*Although he has been allowed to play football,* . . .
Obwohl er hat nach Hause gehen müssen, . . .	*Although he has had to go home,* . . .
Obwohl er sich hätte geschmeichelt fühlen sollen, . . .	*Although he ought to have felt flattered,* . . .

(d) In conversation, and even in letters, most Germans avoid the above construction by using a simple tense; thus the first two examples in (b) would normally become: Da er heute schwimmen durfte and Es war klar, daß er sich anstrengen müßte (imperf. subj.).

(e) A modal may have a second modal dependent on it, the second modal itself having a dependent infinitive:

Er müßte einen raschen Erfolg erzielen können	*He ought to be able to achieve a rapid success*

Where this occurs in a subordinate clause, there is an occasional tendency to place the first modal, though it is not in a compound tense, in front of the dependent infinitives. Of the following examples 1. is correct, while 2. illustrates the tendency just noted:

1 Sein Lehrer behauptete, daß er es eigentlich übersetzen können müßte	*His teacher maintained that really he should be able to translate it*
2. Das war ein merkwürdiges Liebespaar, das da sich abmühte, damit eines das andere sollte behalten können (G. Gaiser)	*It was a strange pair of lovers who toiled and laboured in order that the one should be able to keep the other*

393. The ellipsis of verbs of motion (gehen, fahren and others) **after the modals is very common**; the idea of movement is wholly conveyed by the adverb or adverb phrase indicating the destination.

(a) With mögen, this ellipsis occurs only after the imperf. subj.:

Ich möchte jetzt nach Hause	*I'd like to go home now*

With the other five, it occurs mainly after the present and imperfect (indic. or subj.):

Wo wollen Sie morgen hin?	*Where are you going tomorrow?*
Ich will nach Frankfurt	*I'm going to Frankfurt*
Ich sollte zu meinem Onkel	*I was to go to my uncle's I ought to go to my uncle's*
Ich könnte heute abend ins Theater	*I could go to the theatre this evening*

With können and müssen, and occasionally with dürfen, also after the pluperf. subj.:

Er hätte gestern ins Kino gedurft[1]	*He would have been allowed to go to the cinema yesterday*

With müssen occasionally also after the perf. and pluperf. indic.:

Er hat ins Geschäft gemußt[1]	*He's had to go to the office*

(b) This usage is preponderantly, but not exclusively, colloquial (as in the examples in (a) above). According to the context, the omitted verb

---

[1] In the perf. and pluperf. there is not pure ellipsis, in that, with the omission of gehen, the past part. is changed from können, dürfen, müssen to gekonnt, gedurft, gemußt (cf. 389 (c) ii).

may be fliegen, klettern, kommen, rudern, schwimmen, springen, ziehen or some other verb of motion:

Er wollte über die Mauer [klettern]	*He wanted to climb over the wall*
Die Strömung war so stark, daß er nicht bis ans Ufer [schwimmen] konnte	*The current was so strong, that he couldn't swim as far as the bank*
Er mußte in den Krieg [ziehen] (H. Böll)	*He had to go to the war*

(c) The modals may be similarly used (i.e. without 'gehen' or some analogous verb) with a large number of separable prefixes signifying motion, e.g.

Ich will ihm nach	*I'll go after him*
Er kletterte über die Mauer, aber er konnte nicht zurück	*He climbed over the wall, but he couldn't get back*
Ich möchte jetzt fort	*I'd like to leave now*
Ich hätte eigentlich hingemußt	*I really ought to have gone there*
Mich wundert, daß er um diese Zeit noch hinausdarf (Th. Valentin)	*I'm surprised that he's allowed out at this time of night*

The verbs in these sentences may be regarded as 'jemandem nach-wollen' *to want to go after someone,* 'zurück-können' *to be able to go back* etc.

The tense-restrictions given in 393(a) again apply, except that 'können' and 'müssen' can here often be used in the future:

Ich glaub', ich werd' vorbeikönnen	*I think I'll be able to get past*
Wir werden bald zurückmüssen	*We shall have to go back soon*

The main prefixes in question are:

dahin	heraus	herunter	hinaus	nach
durch	herein	hierher	hinein	vorbei
fort	herüber	hin	hinüber	weg
herauf	herum	hinauf	hinunter	weiter
				zurück

394. Other ellipses with the modals

(a) As in English (though sometimes 'es' is added):

Ich wollte Tennis spielen, aber ich konnte/durfte nicht	*I wanted to play tennis, but I couldn't/ wasn't allowed to*
Soll ich?	*Shall I?*
Ich versuchte, ihn zu überzeugen, aber ich konnte (es) nicht (habe es nicht gekonnt)	*I tried to convince him, but I couldn't*
Mußt du diesen Brief lesen?	*Must you read this letter?*
—Natürlich muß ich ('s)	*—Of course I must*

(b) Idiomatic ellipsis of 'tun': Das kann ich nicht; das darfst/sollst du nicht; was soll ich damit? *What am I to do with it?*

(c) Idiomatic ellipsis of other verbs:

Ich kann nichts dafür [machen]	*I can't help it*
Ich kann nicht mehr [weitermachen]	*I'm tired out*
Was soll dieser Brief eigentlich [bedeuten]?	*What is really the point of this letter?*

395. The following paragraphs deal with the various uses of the individual modals; in each case, section (a) covers the basic meaning of the verb, of which further examples are to be found in 391: Straightforward examples of the modals in their four commonest tenses.

396. können

(a) to be able to, to know how to, to be in a position to (cf. 391):
Kann er Auto fahren?   *Can he drive a car?*

(b) elliptical use with the above meanings (cf. 394(b)(c)):

Was andere können, kann ich auch	*What others can do, I can do too*
Ich kann nicht anders	*I cannot act otherwise*
Oh ja, er kann etwas	*Oh yes, he's quite able*

(c) to know things learnt,[1] e.g. languages, other school subjects, homework (Aufgaben, Vokabeln, ein Gedicht), one's craft (sein Handwerk), a skill. This is really an elliptical use, as indicated in the first example:

Er kann Französisch [sprechen]	*He knows French*
Er kann gut Physik (commoner: Er ist gut in Physik)	*He's good at physics*
Er wird nie eine richtige Stellung bekommen, weil er nichts kann	*He'll never get a proper job because he's not trained for anything*

(d) used colloquially for 'dürfen':

Kann ich herein?	*May I come in?*
Du kannst den Bleistift behalten	*You can keep the pencil*

(e) it denotes possibility:

Das kann sein	*That may be*
Ich kann mich irren	*I may be mistaken*
Er kann krank sein	*He may be ill*
Er kann krank gewesen sein	*He may have been ill*
Er könnte krank sein	*He might be ill*
Er könnte krank gewesen sein	*He might have been ill*

Note: To express a negative possibility, often some further word must be inserted in addition to 'nicht', or 'vielleicht' must be used, as the mere insertion of 'nicht' may exclude the possibility: Er kann nicht krank gewesen sein *He can't/couldn't have been ill.* Thus:

Er *kann* auch *nicht* krank gewesen sein	*He may (on the other hand) not have been ill*
Er ist vielleicht gar nicht krank gewesen	*He may/might not have been ill at all*

(f) miscellaneous:

Ich konnte nicht anders, ich mußte lachen	*I couldn't help laughing* 1. normal usage
Ich mußte einfach lachen	
Ich konnte nicht umhin zu lachen	2. old-fashioned
Ich lief, was ich nur konnte	*I ran for all I was worth*
So etwas kann mich ärgern[2]	*That kind of thing always annoys me*
Ich bezweifle nicht sein Können	*I'm not questioning his ability*

---

[1] cf. S. Latzel: 'wissen, kennen und können' in *Deutschunterricht für Ausländer*, Heft 3/4, 12. Jahrgang (1962), pp. 81–6 and Heft 1/2, 13. Jahrgang (1963), pp. 52–3.
[2] from Wahrig, op. cit.

397. dürfen

(a) to be allowed to, may: see 391.

(b) polite turns of phrase, based on the above meaning:

Hierher, wenn ich bitten darf	*This way, if you please*
Verkäufer: Was darf es sein, bitte?	*Shop-assistant: What can I get you?*
Dürfte ich Sie um das Salz bitten?	*Might I ask you for the salt?*
Ich darf Ihnen mitteilen, daß . . .	*May I inform you that . . .* (commercial)

(c) used with a negative, it denotes 'must not, may not':

Das darfst du nicht (tun)	*You mustn't do that*
Aber ich darf mich nicht loben	*But I mustn't praise myself*
(E. Langgässer)	

Note: Logically, 'du mußt das nicht tun' means 'you are not obliged to do that', but it is quite commonly used in the sense of 'you musn't do that'; the situation and vocal inflexion will show which is meant; in the first sense 'mußt' will have a more drawn out emphasis.

(d) instead of 'sollen', in negative sentences:

Er hätte so etwas nicht tun dürfen	*He shouldn't have done that kind of thing*
Er durfte so etwas nicht tun	—a more incisive version

(e) instead of 'können':

Das darf als Vorzug betrachtet werden	*That can be regarded as an advantage*
Von der Mannschaft durfte er [Blücher] das Unmögliche verlangen, wenn sein 'Vorwärts' aus seinen Augen blitzte (Treitschke)	*He could demand the impossible of his troops, when 'Advance!' flashed from his eyes*

(f) it denotes probability; 'dürfte' implies greater probability than 'könnte', but is at the same time more tentative and polite (cf. Collinson, op. cit., pp. 87 f.):

Er dürfte krank gewesen sein	*He might well have been ill*
Wenn dies der Fall ist, dann dürfte dieser Anzug auch für Mondfahrer unbrauchbar sein (*Zeit*)	*If that is the case, then this space-suit would probably be of no use to lunar astronauts either*

398. mögen

(a) to like, to like to (cf. 391):

Mögen sie sich auch? (Du. Stil.)	*And are they fond of each other?*
Ich mag nicht	*I don't like to*
Ich möchte nicht, daß er heute kommt	*I would not like him to come today*

(b) instead of 'können':

Wer mag das (nur) sein?	*Who can that be?*
Wie mag das gekommen sein?	*How can that have come about?*
und da mit diesem [Toten] schon jemand sich abgab, mochte das genügen (G. Gaiser)	*and as someone was already seeing to this dead man, there was no need to do anything* (lit. *that could suffice*)

(c) it is used to express a wish or command: see 476(a): e.g. Möge er glücklich sein! *May he be happy!* In an **indirect command**, 'Ich sagte ihm, er möchte kommen' (*I told him to come*) is less peremptory than 'Ich sagte ihm, er sollte (or müßte) kommen'. 'Ich sagte ihm, daß er kommen sollte (müßte)' is possible, but not 'daß er kommen möchte'. Cf. Ich hoffte, er möchte kommen (only without 'daß').

(d) it is used in concessive clauses: see 471, 472, 474.

(e) it denotes possibility or probability:

Das mag sein	*That may be*
Er mag krank sein	*He may be ill*
Er mag sein Bestes getan haben, aber er hat nicht viel erreicht	*He may have done his best, but he hasn't achieved much*
Das Kind mochte vier Jahre alt sein	*The child was perhaps four years old*
ein korrektes, sehr britisches Englisch, das sie in irgendeinem Pensionat gelernt haben mochte (V. Baum)	*a correct, very British English, that she had probably learnt in some boarding-school*

(f) 'möchte' often conveys a hesitant or polite doubt:

Sie möchten zu rasch gehandelt haben	*Maybe you acted too quickly*
Man möchte meinen, daß . . .	*One would almost think that . . .*

399. müssen[1]

(a) to have to, must: compulsion, necessity, inevitability (cf. 391):

Wenn Sie studieren wollen, müssen Sie das Abitur gemacht haben	*If you want to go to a university you must have passed the Abitur (school leaving examination)*
Muß das sein?	*Is that really necessary?*
Es mußte so kommen	*It had to come like this*
Er hat es gut gemacht, das muß man sagen	*He certainly did it well* (idiomatic)
Das muß man gesehen haben	*It's worth seeing* (idiomatic)

Note: For the rendering of 'must not', see 397(c).

(b) instead of 'sollen', in the imperf. (or pluperf.) subj., if there is little or no emphasis on duty:

Deutschlands Kohle ist teurer, als sie sein müßte (*Zeit*)	*Germany's coal is dearer than it should be*
Sie ist hübsch, nur müßte sie schlanker sein (Du. Stil.: nur)	*She's pretty, only she ought to be slimmer*
Wo ist der Brief?—Er müßte (not 'sollte') in dieser Schublade sein	*Where's the letter?—It should be in this drawer*
Jeder müßte einmal auf einem Bauernhof gearbeitet haben	*Everyone ought to have worked on a farm some time*

(c) it denotes logical deduction:

Er spielt heute Tennis, also muß es ihm besser gehen	*He's playing tennis today, so he must be better*

Note:
i logical deduction in the context of a narrative in the past; note the tense:

Draußen stieg . . . jemand, der den gleichen Gang haben mußte wie Fräulein Gröschel, die Hintertreppe . . . hinauf (E. Fried)	*Outside, someone who must have had the same gait as Fräulein Gröschel was coming up the back stairs*

[1] Regarding the uses of müssen, sollen and wollen, I am indebted to an article by Gerhard Kaufmann in *Deutschunterricht für Ausländer* (1962 Heft 5/6 and 1963 Heft 1/2; also 1965 Heft 1/2); some of the examples are his.

ii müssen may question a logical deduction:

Er war nicht im Büro, aber deshalb muß er nicht krank sein (Commoner: aber deshalb braucht er nicht krank zu sein)	*He wasn't at the office, but that doesn't mean that he's ill*

iii a negative logical deduction is denoted by können + negative:

Er spielt heute Tennis, also kann er nicht krank sein	*He's playing tennis today, so he can't be ill*

400. sollen[1]

(a) am to, ought to, should: it conveys a moral obligation or an action that is fitting or advisable or that has been decided on beforehand (cf. 391):

Du sollst Vater und Mutter ehren	*Thou shalt honour thy father and thy mother*
Man soll (or sollte) immer geduldig sein	*One should always be patient*
Ich soll nicht so viel rauchen	*I'm not supposed to smoke so much*
Wir sollten uns gestern treffen	*We were to have met yesterday*
Du solltest doch deinem Freund helfen?	*Surely you were to have helped your friend?*
Du hattest doch deinem Freund helfen sollen?	
Wie weit sollen (or wollen) wir gehen?	*How far shall we go?*
Was soll ich in Hamburg (tun)?	*What am I to do in Hamburg?*
Warum sollte ich denn nicht ins Theater gehen?	*Why shouldn't I go to the theatre?*
Ich weiß nicht, was ich tun soll	*I don't know what to do*
Ich wußte nicht, an wen ich mich wenden sollte	*I didn't know whom to apply to*

Note on the last 2 examples: Attention is drawn to the clauses with sollen which render English infinitives. 'Ich weiß nicht, was zu tun' is not German. 'Ich weiß nicht was tun' is possible, but only with 'tun' or with 'anfangen' used colloquially for 'to do', e.g. Diese zwei Zimmer sind übriggeblieben, und kein Mensch hat gewußt, was damit anfangen (H. Fallada).

(b) it may express intention:

Eine zweite Fabrik soll bald gebaut werden	*A second factory is soon to be built*
Soll das ein Kompliment sein?	*Is that supposed to be a compliment?*
Was soll das (heißen)?	*What's the meaning of this?* (generally indignantly)
Es sollte eine Überraschung sein	*It was meant to be a surprise*

Note the ironical application of this use, conveying indignation:

Und in diesem Gebäude soll sich einer zurechtfinden!	*And you're supposed to find your way about this building!*

(c) it may express a promise or warning:

Ja, du sollst mitgehen	*Yes, you shall go too*
Es soll nicht wieder vorkommen	*It shan't happen again*
Du sollst das noch bereuen	*You'll live to regret this*

[1] see 399: footnote to 'müssen'.

(d) it may express what was, or was not, destined to happen:

Er sollte früh sterben	*He was (destined) to die young*
Er sollte niemals nach Deutschland zurückkehren	*He was never to return to Germany*
Es hat so sein sollen	*It was meant to be*

(e) it may express a rumour or report:

Er soll steinreich sein	*He is said to be enormously rich*
Bei den Unruhen soll es bisher vier Tote gegeben haben (*FAZ*)	*So far four are reported killed in the course of the disturbances*
Das soll *er* gewesen sein?	*Do you mean to say it was him?*
Der Geschäftsführer sollte schon nach Hause gegangen sein	*The manager was said to have gone home already*

(f) it may be used instead of 'können' in certain questions:

Wie sollte (konnte) ich das wissen?	*How could I have known that?*
Sollte (könnte) es doch ein Mißverständnis gewesen sein?	*Could it have been a misunderstanding after all?*
Warum sollte (könnte) er nicht einmal in London gewesen sein?	*Why shouldn't he have been to London some time?*

(g) it may be used in conditional clauses: see 462(e)(f).

E.g. Sollte es regnen, so komme ich nicht.

cf. the use of sollte, with the sense of 'would, should', in the two following idiomatic expressions:

Man sollte meinen, er würde es gern tun	*One would think he'd be glad to do it*
Es sollte (or: Es würde) mich wundern, wenn . . .	*I should be surprised if . . .*

(h) it is used to express a command or wish:

Du *sollst* das tun[1]	*You're to do that*
Du sollst *fleißig* sein[1]	*I want you to work hard*
Er soll sich in acht nehmen	*Let him beware!*
Sie sollen sofort kommen	*Let them come at once*
	They/you are to come at once
Nein, soll[2] Groenewold mit ihnen über diesen Film sprechen—du nicht (Th. Valentin)	*No, let Groenewold talk with them about this film (if he wants to)—not you*

Note: It may voice a command which ironically conveys a threat or a challenge:

Der soll noch mal kommen und Geld pumpen wollen![3]	*Let him come again to borrow some money!*

The imperf. and pluperf. subj. may be used with similar effect:

Das sollte er mal mit unserem Chef versuchen![3]	*He should try that on with our boss*
So hätte der früher mal mit mir reden sollen![3]	*If he had spoken to me like that in the past!*

Compare the phrase:

Das sollte mir mal passieren!	*If I were to do that, there'd be a fine row!*

---

[1] from Collinson, op. cit., p. 90; Collinson points out the effect of stress and tone on the meaning of sollen, the first remark expecting absolute obedience.

[2] in place of the optative subjunctive 'möge'; not to be imitated.

[3] G. Kaufmann's example (see 399: footnote to müssen)

(i) it is used in **indirect commands**:

Ich sagte ihm, er solle (or: sollte) es tun	*I told him to do it*
Ich will, daß er es tut	BUT: *I want him to do it*
Ich wollte, daß er es tat	*I wanted him to do it*

401. wollen[1]

(a) to want, to want to, to wish (to) (cf. 391):

Ich will meine Ruh'	*I want peace and quiet*
Ich will nur dein Bestes	*I only want what is best for you*
Ich will ihm nichts (Böses)	*I wish him no harm*
Was wollen Sie von mir?	*What do you want of me?*
Nun denn, mach, was du willst (Du. Stil.)	*Well then, do what you like* (implying: I don't care)
Der Arzt will, daß ich mir mehr Bewegung mache	*The doctor wants me to take more exercise*
Ich wollte (imperf. subj.), ich wäre zu Hause	*I wish I were at home*
Ich wollt', ich könnt' es	*I wish I could do it*

(b) to be willing to (cf. 391(c)):

Willst du mir helfen?	*Will you help me?*
—Ja, ich will dir helfen	*—Yes, I'll help you*
Er will es nicht zugeben	*He won't admit it*
Ich bat ihn es zu tun, aber er wollte nicht	*I asked him to do it, but he wouldn't*
Ich wäre Ihnen sehr dankbar, wenn Sie es tun wollten (= imperf. subj.)	*I'd be very grateful to you if you'd do it*

Note: In sentences such as the first two in (b), the ordinary future tense (Wirst du mir helfen? Ja, ich werde dir helfen) would sound cold and impersonal. Contrast: Wirst du bald bereit sein? *Will you soon be ready?*

(c) it may express intention:

Wir wollen uns bald einen neuen Fernseher anschaffen	*We intend getting a new TV soon*
Wie wollen Sie ihm das klarmachen?	*How do you intend explaining that to him?*
Ich will ihn jetzt anrufen	*I'm going to phone him up now*
Ich wollte Sie darüber fragen	*I was going to ask you about it*
Was wollen Sie damit sagen?	*What do you mean by that (remark)?*
Sie wollen doch nicht behaupten, daß ich es getan habe?	*Surely you're not trying to say that I did it?*
Wollen (or: Sollen) wir uns den Dom ansehen?	*Shall we have a look at the cathedral?*

Note: In the last example 'wollen' implies that the speaker is in favour; 'sollen' leaves the decision entirely to the other.

(d) to claim, maintain, pretend:

Er will eine Mosquito abgeschossen haben (G. Gaiser)	*He claims to have shot down a Mosquito (plane)*
Er wollte mich nicht erkennen	*He pretended not to recognize me*
Zur gleichen Zeit, da ich das Judenauto gesehen haben wollte, . . . (F. Fühmann)	*At the same time at which I said I had seen the car with the Jews, . . .*
cf. Keiner will es getan haben	*No one admits having done it*

[1] See 399: footnote to müssen.

(e) with inanimate subjects:
  i basic meaning generally 'to need, demand':

Tomaten wollen viel Sonne	*Tomatoes need a lot of sun*
Eine solche Arbeit will Zeit haben	*A piece of work of that sort demands time*
Solche Dolmetscherarbeit will gelernt sein, das darf man mir glauben (M. Walser)	*This kind of interpreter's work needs learning, believe me*

  ii with nicht: basic meaning 'to refuse to':

Der Koffer wollte nicht zugehen	*The suit-case refused to close*
Meine Beine wollen nicht mehr	*My legs won't carry me any further*
Das will mir nicht in den Kopf	*I can't grasp that*

(f) with impersonal subject:

Es will mir scheinen, daß er zuviel unternimmt	*I have the impression that he undertakes too much*
Es scheint regnen zu wollen	*It looks as if it were going to rain*

(g) as a substitute for the imperative: see 459(a).

(h) miscellaneous idiomatic uses:

Na, dann wollen wir mal (anfangen) (Du. Stil.)	*Well then, let's start*
Er will eben (or gerade) fort	*He's just going*
Er wollte eben (or gerade) fort, als ich ankam	*He was about to leave when I arrived*
Er hat allerhand versprochen, aber das will nicht viel sagen	*He has promised all sorts of things, but that doesn't mean much*
Das will ich gern glauben	*I quite believe it*
Ich will nur hoffen, daß er . . .	*I do hope he . . .*
Ich will nichts gehört/gesehen/ gemerkt haben	*I shall do as if I hadn't heard/seen/ noticed anything*
Also, ich will nichts gesagt haben	*Well then, act as if I hadn't said anything*
Da ist nichts/nicht viel zu wollen	*There's nothing/not much one can do about it*
Mit ihm ist nichts zu wollen	*There's nothing to be done with him*
Dagegen ist nichts zu wollen	*You can't prevent that*
eine gewollte Beleidigung[1]	*a deliberate insult*
Der Schluß des Romans ist zu gewollt[2]	*The end of the novel is forced*

402. Miscellaneous points relative to the modals

(a) Where possibility or logical deduction is to be expressed and können, dürfen, mögen and müssen might equally well have their literal meaning, adverbs such as 'vielleicht', 'wahrscheinlich' or 'sicher' should be used instead. (The context and vocal inflection make these ambiguities relatively rare). E.g.

Er wird mir vielleicht helfen   *He might help me*
  ('Er könnte' would mean: He could . . .)
Er ist heute sicher in Frankfurt   *He must be in Frankfurt today*
  ('Er muß' might mean: He has to be . . .)

(b) Distinguish:

Er muß es getan haben	*He must have done it*
Er hat es tun müssen	*He has had to do it*

[1] from Schulz-Griesbach, op. cit., B 833.
[2] from E. Agricola, op. cit., p. 751.

Er kann es getan haben	*He may have done it*
Er hat es tun können	*He has been able to do it*
Er könnte es getan haben	*He might have done it*
Er hätte es tun können, (wenn er gewollt hätte)	*He could have done it (if he had wanted to)*
Ich hätte ihn gern einmal gesehen	*I should have liked to see him some time*
Ich möchte die Sache vor meiner Abreise erledigt haben	*I should like to have settled the matter before my departure*
Er hätte heute ankommen müssen (or sollen)	*He should have arrived today* (implying: but he hasn't)
Er müßte schon längst angekommen sein	*He should have arrived long ago* (implying: and he probably has)

(c) **etwas zu tun haben** *to have to do something* is sometimes the equivalent of 'etwas tun sollen' (Type i below), sometimes of 'etwas tun müssen' (Type ii). Though not uncommon, it is used less than 'sollen' or 'müssen'.

Type i (=sollen) (See also 459(c))

Eva Dumont überlegte, was sie zu tun habe (G. Gaiser)	*Eva Dumont considered what she ought to do*

Type (ii) (=müssen)

Ein Schuß, zwei Schüsse? Die Verhandlung wird es zu klären haben (*Spiegel*)	*One shot or two shots? The question will have to be cleared up at the trial*

Note: The above use of 'etwas zu tun haben' should be distinguished from its use in sentences such as the following, in which the infinitive phrase qualifies the object and the element of necessity or obligation is far weaker:

Er hat ein Haus zu verkaufen	*He has a house to sell*
Ich habe mehrere Briefe zu schreiben	*I have several letters to write*

See also 434(a)ii.

K. THE USES OF THE INFINITIVE WITHOUT 'ZU'

403. Survey of uses of the infinitive without 'zu':[1]
1. as a verbal noun 404
2. as the nominative complement of heißen 405
3. as the objectival complement of nennen and heißen 406
4. in elliptical exclamations 407
5. in place of an imperative 408
6. after the 6 modal verbs 409
7. after 11 other verbs (e.g. sehen, lassen, lehren) 410–21
8. in certain applications of bleiben, gehen, haben, legen, schicken, tun 422

404. The infinitive without 'zu' is used as a verbal noun, always neuter, often corresponding to an English form in -ing (see also 713):

Das Bekleben der Wände ist verboten (Erben, op. cit., 88)	*Stick no bills*

---

[1] for punctuation, see 743 (f) iii.

Ich hörte das laute Bellen eines Hundes	*I heard the loud barking of a dog*
Der Fuß tut mir beim Gehen weh	*My foot hurts me when walking*
Der Wagen kam ins Gleiten	*The car got into a skid*

Dann kam das Schiff, und ich beobachtete, wie so viele Male schon, das vorsichtige Längsfahren, Stoppen, Zurückweichen in dem Sprudeln und Rauschen und Räderklatschen (*the slapping sound of the paddle-wheels*), das Taueschleudern und Festbinden (Emil Strauß).

The extensive and often elaborate use of the infinitive as a noun is undoubtedly one of the hallmarks of modern German style. Two examples may illustrate the arresting possibilities (and temptations) of this usage:

| Jede Nacht bedeutete für ihn ein Nichts, ein Grab, ein Ausgelöscht-werden (R. Musil) | *Every night meant for him a void, a grave, extinction* |
| In der Bundesrepublik beginnt sich diese Basis humanen Miteinander-lebens, Untereinanderaussprechens und Miteinanderwirkens aufzulösen (quoted in *FAZ*) | *In the Federal Republic this foundation of humane living together, freely exchanging ideas and co-operating, is beginning to dissolve* |

405. It is used as the nominative complement of 'heißen' *to mean, to be (the equivalent of)*:

| Das heißt lügen | *That amounts to lying* |
| Das hieße wieder von vorne anfangen | *That would mean starting again from the beginning* |

406. It is used as the objectival complement of 'nennen' and 'heißen' *to call*. (In current usage nennen is by far the commoner.):

| Das nennst du höflich sein! | *You call that being polite!* |

407. In elliptical exclamations the infin. is generally used without 'zu', e.g. Einen Menschen danach bewerten, wieviel Hosen er verkaufen kann! (H. Fallada).

408. It is used in place of an imperative (cf. 459(g)):

| Nicht rauchen! Bitte anschnallen! | *No smoking. Please fasten seat-belts* |

This 'imperative infinitive' is sometimes effectively used in the course of a narrative to render a thought-stream, as in the second sentence of the following:

Es hatte ihm wohlgetan, bei der Rückkehr den exotischen Wagen umstanden zu sehen von Passanten, die sich über das kleinstädtische Nummernschild (*the provincial number-plate*) wunderten. Dann in aller Ruhe einsteigen, anlassen, über die Schulter blicken (*Then get in quite calmly, start the engine, glance over your shoulder*) (U. Johnson).

409. It is used after the 6 modal verbs: see 388 and 390.

410. The infinitive without 'zu' is used, with varying consistency (treated in the subsequent paragraphs), **after the following 11 verbs:**

5 verbs of perception:
sehen *to see*
hören *to hear*
fühlen *to feel*
spüren *to feel, perceive*
finden *to find*

3 causative verbs:
heißen *to bid*
lassen *to let* (causative and permissive)
machen *to make*

3 others:
helfen *to help*
lehren *to teach*
lernen *to learn*

Ich sah ihn ins Zimmer kommen	*I saw him come into the room*
Ich hörte das Kind weinen	*I heard the child crying*
Ich ließ ihn das Geld behalten	*I let him keep the money*
Er lehrt mich schwimmen	*He is teaching me to swim*

411. After sehen and hören, and even more after **fühlen and spüren**, a 'wie' or 'daß' clause is the commoner construction in colloquial German, especially if the sentence is of any length or complexity:

Ich sah, wie sich der Polizist nach dem alten Mann umsah	*I saw the policeman looking out for the old man*
Ich fühlte mein Herz klopfen	*I felt my heart beating*
Ich fühlte, wie er zitterte	*I felt him trembling*
Ich spürte seinen Einfluß wachsen	*I sensed how his influence was growing*
Ich spürte, wie er mir die Hand auf die Schulter legte	*I felt him lay his hand on my shoulder*

412. After finden the infin. construction is used for finding someone or something standing or lying somewhere:

Ich fand ihn am Fenster stehen	*I found him standing by the window*
Ich fand die Bücher auf dem Tisch liegen	*I found the books lying on the table*

In other contexts, either the pres. part. or some different construction is used:

Ich fand ihn in seinem Sessel (sitzend)	*I found him sitting in his armchair*
Ich fand ihn schlafend	*I found him sleeping*
Ich fand ihn lesend (commoner: beim Lesen)	*I found him reading*
Ich fand ihn bei einer Tasse Kaffee	*I found him having coffee*
Ich fand ihn dabei (or: damit beschäftigt), seine Papiere zu sortieren	*I found him sorting his papers*

413. heißen is used almost exclusively with a plain infinitive:

Er hieß mich über meine Zukunft entscheiden	*He bade me decide about my future*

Note: heißen, in the sense of 'to bid, order,' is little used in everyday German, where it sounds stilted and literary. Thus normal usage for the above sentence would be: Er sagte mir, ich müßte über meine Zukunft entscheiden.

414. lassen may mean 1. to let, allow 2. to cause to, make; it is generally clear from the context which of the two meanings applies; it is used exclusively with a plain infinitive.

1. to let, allow:

Er ließ mich das Buch behalten	*He let me keep the book*

2. to cause to, make:

Er ließ die Mannschaft halten	*He stopped his men*
Die Nachricht ließ ihn erblassen	*The news made him turn pale*

415. machen *to make, cause to* is used far less than lassen, being relatively rare apart from the idiomatic expression 'Er machte von sich reden' *He caused a stir.*

Er machte mich lachen (commoner: Er brachte mich zum Lachen). Du mußt Kurt glauben machen, daß ich bei dir bin (V. Baum).

416. After helfen, lehren and lernen, practice varies a good deal, but the following rule is the most serviceable: a mere infinitive, with no object, adverb etc., is used without 'zu'; where there is an object or adverbial limitation, 'zu' is used:

und jetzt hilf mir anpacken (E. M. Remarque)	*and now give me a hand*
Er . . . half Carla, die Weinflaschen zu öffnen (M. Horbach)	*He helped Carla open the wine-bottles*
Sie lehrte mich kochen	*She taught me to cook*
Sie lehrte mich, Suppe zu kochen	*She taught me to prepare soup*
Ich habe schwimmen gelernt	*I've learnt to swim*
Ich habe ja nie richtig kochen gelernt (H. Fallada)	*You know, I've never properly learnt to cook*
Ich habe schneller zu schwimmen gelernt	*I've learnt to swim more quickly*

Note: After lehren and lernen, a 'wie' clause is common usage:

Ich habe gelernt, wie man eine durchgebrannte Sicherung repariert	*I've learnt to repair a fuse*

417. After 'merken' and 'bemerken' *to notice* **and 'erblicken'** *to catch sight of, behold,* the infinitive is so rare that its use is best ruled out; it is never used after 'beobachten' or 'zusehen' *to watch.* After all these verbs, relative, 'daß' and 'wie' clauses are the accepted constructions:

Ich erblickte einen Bettler, der auf mich zukam	*I caught sight of a beggar coming towards me*
Ich merkte, daß er hinkte	*I noticed his limping*
Knudsen sah ihr zu, wie sie sich wieder auf die Bank setzte (A. Andersch)	*Knudsen watched her sitting down on the seat again*

418. After 'brauchen' *to need to do something* normal usage is zu + infin., but a plain infinitive is sometimes used colloquially; brauchen is used almost exclusively interrogatively or in conjunction with a negative word, with 'nur' or with 'bloß' *merely:*

Warum brauchst du in die Stadt zu gehen?	*Why need you go into town?*

Ich brauche nicht hinzugehen (or: hingehen)	*I needn't go there*
Du brauchst bloß anzurufen (or: anrufen), und ich komme	*You need only phone up and I'll come*
Er muß fleißiger arbeiten	BUT: *He needs to work harder*

Used in a compound tense or in a subordinate clause, brauchen always encloses the dependent infinitive: Du wirst dieses Fensterchen niemals aufzumachen brauchen; obwohl ich es nur dem Chef zu erwähnen brauche, . . .

Like the modals, it may be used elliptically:

Ich brauch' heute nicht mehr ins Büro	*I needn't go to the office again today*

See also 420 f.

419. After sehen, hören, heißen *to bid* **and lassen, the active infin. may have a passive meaning**; with lassen this is common; with the other three it is unusual:

Er läßt sich (dat.) ein Haus bauen	*He is having a house built*
Er ließ sich sehen	*He showed himself*
Er sah die Kisten auf den Laster laden (commoner: wie die Kisten auf den Laster geladen wurden)	*He saw the packing-cases being loaded onto the lorry*

The origin and explanation of these active infinitives with passive meanings is doubtless the omission of the accusative of an active accusative and infinitive construction.[1] Thus the above examples are contractions of: Er läßt einen Architekten für ihn ein Haus bauen; er ließ die Leute ihn sehen; er sah Männer die Kisten auf den Laster laden. This explanation is reinforced by the fact that the accusative is frequently omitted before a straightforward active infinitive: Auf der Straße sah ich [Leute] tanzen; in der Küche hörte ich [jemand] lachen. The following quotation, where 'tollen' can only have active force, is particularly revealing: Ich hörte drin tollen und Türen aufreißen (Max Mell) *Inside I heard people romping about and flinging doors open.*

Despite this explanation, the infinitive in sentences such as our three original examples is undoubtedly regarded as having passive force. This is shown by expanding the first example to 'Er läßt sich von dieser Firma ein Haus bauen', where there can no longer be any question of an omitted accusative.

Finally it should be mentioned that on no account can an orthodox passive infinitive be used after the four verbs in question. Thus 'I heard him being called' is 'Ich hörte, wie man ihn rief'; theoretically it could be 'Ich hörte ihn rufen', but this is obviously ambiguous; it could *not* be: Ich hörte ihn gerufen werden.

Further examples of lassen + active infin. with passive meaning:

Er ließ sich um 7 Uhr wecken	*He had himself wakened at 7 o'clock*
Laß dich nicht beschwindeln!	*Don't let yourself be cheated*
Er ließ seine Überraschung nicht merken	*He concealed his surprise*

---

[1] cf. Eggeling, op. cit., accusative and infinitive.

Ich hätte mir doch ein Zimmer nach vorne 'raus geben lassen sollen (A. Andersch)	*I ought after all to have asked for a front room*
Das läßt sich leicht ändern	*That can easily be changed*

420. Six of the 11 verbs used with a plain infinitive (cf. 410) **and one other have a second past participle, identical with the infinitive,** which is used, with varying consistency, when they have a dependent infinitive preceding the past participle (cf. the Modal Verbs, 389(c)(ii), e.g. Er hat das Buch lesen wollen).

These verbs are: sehen   heißen   and brauchen *to need,*
                 hören   lassen   though generally used
                 fühlen   helfen   with zu + infin. (cf. 418)

With **sehen and hören**, the infinitive form of the past part. predominates: Ich habe ihn hereinkommen sehen/hören. In modern conversation the 1st past part. (Ich habe ihn hereinkommen gesehen) sounds slovenly, though Eggeling (op. cit., p. 10) quotes numerous instances of its use by authors from Storm to Werfel, both colloquial and narrative. A more usual colloquial alternative would be: Ich habe gesehen, wie er hereinkam.

With **fühlen**, a 'wie' clause is commoner: Ich habe gefühlt, wie das Fieber kam, rather than: Ich habe das Fieber kommen fühlen.

heißen (little used in conversation, cf. 413): with a plain dependent infin., the 2nd past part. is used:
Er hat's mich tun heißen   *He bade me do it*
But with a more elaborate dependent infinitive phrase, 'geheißen' followed by zu + infin. is preferred:
Er hatte seine Truppen geheißen, die Burg bis zum letzten Mann zu verteidigen.

With **lassen**, the infin. form predominates and *must* be used when it means 'to cause to' (3rd example):

Ich hatte den Brief fallen lassen	*I had dropped the letter*
Ich habe meine Aktentasche irgendwo liegenlassen (more usual than 'liegengelassen')	*I've left my brief-case somewhere*
Ich habe ihn zu mir kommen lassen	*I sent for him*

With **helfen**, the 2nd past part. is mainly literary (Er hat das Vaterland verteidigen helfen) while colloquial usage is 'geholfen' followed by zu + infin.: Sie hat mir geholfen, die Küche zu reinigen

With **brauchen**, the infin. form predominates:
Du hättest nicht zu kommen brauchen   *You needn't have come*
(occasionally: gebraucht)

Note: There are two cases in which the 1st past part. of the above seven verbs (i.e. gesehen, gehört etc.) *must* be used:
(a) in the passive:
Der Plan wurde fallengelassen   *The plan was dropped*

Except with fallen-lassen (see 710) and liegen-lassen, such passives are rare. Thus: 'He was seen to enter' is 'Man sah ihn hereinkommen' (not: Er wurde hereinkommen gesehen) (cf. 365).

(b) in the perfect infin. (rarely used with a dependent infinitive) (cf. 433):

Ich glaubte ihn hereinkommen gesehen zu haben	*I thought to have seen him enter*

Normal usage: Ich glaubte, ich hätte ihn hereinkommen sehen, or, more coll., Ich glaubte, ich hätte gesehen, wie er hereinkam.

421. When the 2nd past part. of the 7 verbs treated in 420 is used in a subordinate clause, the auxiliary precedes the dependent infinitive instead of coming at the end. (Cf. the modals: Da er heute hat schwimmen dürfen, muß es ihm besser gehen (392)).

Da ich ihn habe spielen sehen, weiß ich, daß es ihm besser geht	*As I have seen him playing, I know that he's better*
obwohl du nicht hättest (zu) kommen brauchen	*although you needn't have come*
Ich hob den Brief auf, den er hatte fallen lassen	*I picked up the letter which he had dropped*

The man in the street will avoid this construction, saying e.g. (for the 1st example above) Ich sah ihn spielen, also weiß ich, daß es ihm besser geht.

The order of the future and conditional of these 7 verbs, used in a subordinate clause and with a dependent infinitive, is not affected, in contrast with the modals, e.g.

Ich wußte nicht, ob ich ihn kommen sehen würde	*I didn't know if I would see him come*
Ich wußte nicht, ob ich es würde tun können (normal usage: ob ich es tun könnte)	BUT: *I did not know if I should be able to do it*
	For good measure:
Ich wußte nicht, ob ich ihn würde kommen sehen können (normal usage: ob ich ihn kommen sehen könnte)	*I did not know if I should be able to see him come*

422. The infin. without 'zu' is used in certain applications of (a) bleiben (b) gehen (c) haben (d) legen (e) schicken (f) tun

(a) **bleiben** *to remain* is used with a number of plain infinitives denoting postures or situations (stehen bleiben, sitzen bleiben) with both literal and derived connotations: see 710; also: bestehen-bleiben *to continue*, e.g. of an old custom, and wohnen bleiben: Er will in Hamburg wohnen bleiben.

(b) After **gehen** it is used to denote purpose 'where the emphasis lies not so much on 'gehen' as on the idea expressed in the infinitive':[1]

Ich gehe heute (im Fluß) schwimmen	*I'm going swimming (in the river) today*
Ich gehe bald schlafen	*I'm soon going to bed*
Er ist einen neuen Anzug kaufen gegangen	*He's gone to buy a new suit*
Er ist in die Stadt gegangen, um einen neuen Anzug zu kaufen	BUT: *He's gone to town to buy a new suit*

[1] Eggeling, op. cit., p.159.

Note:

i Though it occurs less frequently, 'kommen' can be used like 'gehen' above, especially in the 2nd person: Kommst du heute schwimmen? Komm doch mit mir einkaufen!

ii Colloquially, the past tenses of 'sein' are used with a plain infinitive to convey 'I went swimming' etc.:

Ich war heute morgen schwimmen	*I went swimming this morning*
Ich bin einkaufen gewesen	*I went/I've been shopping*

iii In spazieren-gehen (spazieren-fahren etc.) the infin. spazieren is treated as a separable prefix (cf. 709).

(c) **haben** + plain infin.:

i to have something in a certain position somewhere, e.g.:

Ich hatte ein paar Bücher auf dem Tisch liegen; ich habe drei Sack Kartoffeln im Keller stehen. Cf. fig.:

Wir haben eine Anfrage/mehrere Aufträge vorliegen	*We have an inquiry/several orders*

Applied to persons, this usage is virtually limited to 'wohnen', e.g. Wir haben eine alte Tante in Hamburg wohnen.

ii Du hast gut reden/lachen   *It's easy enough (it's all very well) for you to talk/laugh*

(d) (**sich**) **schlafen legen**: Die Mutter legte das Kind schlafen (*put the child to bed*); ich legte mich schlafen (*I went to bed*)

(e) After **schicken** the plain infin. of a certain number of verbs may be used to denote purpose, e.g. Sie schickte das Kind schlafen (commoner: zu Bett); ich habe ihn einkaufen geschickt (BUT: Ich habe ihn geschickt, um eine Zeitung zu kaufen); meine Mutter schickt mich immer Blumen pflücken.

(f) **tun** + plain infin.:

i a very colloquial, pleonastic use (bad German):

Ich tu jetzt ins Kino gehen	*I'm going to the cinema now*
Gern tät' ich ins Kino gehen	*I'd like to go to the cinema*
Tust du mich auch verstehen?	*Are you sure you understand me?*

This use of 'tun' is, however, an accepted means of starting the sentence with an emphasized infinitive:

Bewundern tu ich ihn nicht, aber er imponiert mir doch	*I don't admire him, but he impresses me all the same*
Aber schmerzen tat es darum nicht weniger (G. Reuter)	*But it was no less painful on that account*

ii nichts tun als:

Er tut nichts als arbeiten   *He does nothing but work*

L. THE USES OF THE INFINITIVE WITH 'ZU'

423. In all cases other than those treated in 404–22, the infinitive is used with 'zu'; most of these offer no difficulty; for punctuation see 743(f).

424. It is the commonest usage where the infin. is the subject of a verb or the complement of 'sein', except in proverbs or comparable formulations:

Meiner Großmutter zu helfen macht mir immer Spaß	*I always enjoy helping my grandmother*
So etwas zu erlauben ist unerhört	*To allow that kind of thing is preposterous*
Sein Ziel ist, einen Roman zu schreiben	*His aim is to write a novel*
	BUT:
Irren, ist menschlich	*To err is human*
Früh aufstehen ist etwas Schreckliches	*Getting up early is horrible*

'zu' is essential
    i where the infin. is the real subject after an introductory 'es':

Es wird schwer sein, ihn zu überzeugen	*It will be difficult to convince him*

    ii where the infin. has a relative pronoun as its object:

Wir erörterten die Frage, die zu erledigen so wünschenswert wäre	*We discussed the question to settle which would be so desirable*

425. After all verbs other than the 6 modals and those treated in 410 ff.: Er begann zu singen; er verdient, belohnt zu werden.

426. After impersonal and pseudo-impersonal expressions: Es ist mir viel daran gelegen, dies zu tun; es ist unmöglich, alles zu wissen.

427. To complete the sense of adjectives and adjectival participles: Diese Frage ist schwer zu entscheiden; ich war erstaunt, ihn zu Hause zu finden, BUT:

Er war der erste (der letzte, der einzige, der beste Redner), der kam	*He was the first (the last, the only one, the best speaker) to come*

428. In comparative phrases: after als *than* practice varies, zu + infin. being commoner; after so *as*: zu + infin. E.g. Schwimmen ist besser als im Garten (zu) arbeiten; du kannst nichts Besseres tun, als zu Hause (zu) bleiben; ich bin nicht so dumm, das zu glauben (Du. Stil.).

429. To limit nouns:

Gibt es eine Möglichkeit, ihm zu helfen?	*Is there a possibility of helping him?*

430. After prepositional constructions with verbs, adjectives and nouns, provided there is no change of subject, e.g. Ich freue mich darauf, ihn wiederzusehen: see 504.

431. After 'um'; and after 'ohne' and '(an)statt', provided there is no change of subject:

Ich konnte nichts tun, (um) ihn zu beruhigen	*I could do nothing to reassure him*
Er verließ das Haus, ohne gesehen zu werden	*He left the house without being seen*

Er verließ das Haus, ohne daß ich ihn sah	BUT: *He left the house without my seeing him*
statt sich aufzuregen	*instead of getting excited*

Note:

i The 'um' of 'um . . . zu + infin.' *in order to* is sometimes omitted (cf. the first example above); it is safer to include it.

ii For 'in order that, so that' see 467.

iii Note the two following formulae, which do not express purpose:

Er ist zu alt, um das zu tun	*He is too old to do that*
Er ist alt genug, (um) das zu wissen	*He is old enough to know that*

With a change of subject, 'um . . . zu' becomes 'als daß' (cf. 469(a)) and 'daß' respectively, e.g. Er ist alt genug, daß man sich auf ihn verlassen kann.

iv Provided there is no glaring ambiguity, um . . . zu + infin. may be used without any implication of purpose as an effective substitute for a second main clause; it tends to suggest the idea of 'destined to' (cf. Du. Gram. 6080 and English usage):

Mit achtzehn Jahren verließ er Deutschland, um niemals wiederzukehren (= und sollte niemals wiederkehren)	*At eighteen he left Germany never to return*

432. Used after sein *to be*, zu + active infin. has a passive meaning, e.g. Er war nirgends zu sehen *He was nowhere to be seen*. This construction is the equivalent either of können + passive infin., as in the foregoing example, or of müssen or sollen + passive infin.

= können + passive infin.:

Dieses Buch ist nicht zu haben	*This book is unobtainable*
Ist der Direktor heute zu sprechen?	*Can I see the manager today?*
An Schachspielen war nicht zu denken (V. Baum)	*There could be no question of playing chess*

= müssen + passive infin.:

Das ist unbedingt zu vermeiden	*That must be avoided at all costs*
Es ist zu befürchten, daß . . .	*It is to be feared that . . .*

= sollen + passive infin.:

Dieses Haus ist zu verkaufen	*This house is for sale*

The attributive counterpart of this construction is present-participial in form; it is limited to transitive verbs taking an object in the accusative:

eine nicht zu vermeidende Schwierigkeit	*an unavoidable difficulty*
Er sprach mit einer nur zu bewundernden Sachlichkeit	*He spoke with an objectivity which was only to be admired*
Dies ist ein Versprechen, dem zu mißtrauen ist (commoner: dem man mißtrauen muß)	BUT: *This is a promise to be mistrusted*

433. After verbs indicating 'certain mental processes or actions associated with these',[1] an infinitive (most frequently a perfect

[1] Stopp, op. cit., 107(e)2.

infinitive) **with 'zu' is often used**, though a clause is commoner. The subject of the infinitive phrase must be the same as that of the introductory verb:

Er behauptete (erinnerte sich, glaubte, meinte, war überzeugt, gab zu), mich gesehen zu haben	*He maintained (remembered, thought, was convinced, admitted) that he had seen me*

N.B. Commoner e.g. Er glaubte, er hätte mich gesehen.

Further examples:

Sie . . . glaubte zu lesen, zu häkeln, tat aber nichts als warten (V. Baum)	*She thought she was reading, crocheting, but she was doing nothing but wait*
A. behauptet von B. bedroht worden zu sein (*Hbg. Abendblatt*)	*A asserts that he was threatened by B*

Note: The above must not be confused with an English accusative and infinitive construction, which requires a clause in German, e.g. I believed him to be ill = Ich glaubte, er sei krank (cf. 484(a)).

434. Three remaining uses of zu + infin. may be grouped together:

(a) **after 'haben':**

i 'etwas zu tun haben' as the equivalent of 'etwas tun sollen or müssen': see 402(c).

ii other uses after haben cause no difficulty, e.g.

Ich habe viel zu tun	*I have a lot to do*
Ich habe an seinem Vorschlag nichts auszusetzen	*I have no fault to find with his suggestion*
Sie haben hier nichts zu suchen	*You have no business here* (idiomatic)

(b) **after 'kommen', denoting chance or result:**

Wir kamen auf Rußland zu sprechen	*We got on to the subject of Russia*
Wir arrangierten es so, daß wir nebeneinander zu sitzen kamen	*We arranged things so that we came to sit next to each other*

(c) **after 'wissen',** *to know how to, to be able to:*

Er weiß mit den Leuten umzugehen	*He knows how to deal with people*
Er wußte alles schnell zu finden	*He was able to find everything quickly*

Note: The English infinitives in 'He told me what to do', 'I didn't know when to come' etc. require clauses in German; see 400 (a): last two examples and Note.

M. PARTICIPLES

435. The adjectival and substantival use of participles is treated in detail in 97 f. and 106 ff.; **their adverbial use** is illustrated in 261.

EXAMPLES: ein lachendes Kind; mein verlorener Schirm; er war sehr aufgeregt; ein Angestellter; die Sterbenden; sie kocht überraschend gut.

It will become clear in the course of the following pages that participles are less widely used in German than in English.

436. The attributive participial phrase

(a) A distinctively German feature is that an attributive participle may be preceded by an object and/or by qualifying adverbs and adverb phrases. Where there are several items, they are arranged according to the guide-lines given in 652 ff.

Ihr gegenwärtig in München Chemie studierender Sohn hat sie kürzlich besucht	*Their son, at present studying chemistry in Munich, recently visited them*
Ich habe dieses von meinem Vetter warm empfohlene Buch sehr genossen	*I very much enjoyed this book which was strongly recommended by my cousin*
Wegen Überproduktion entlassene Arbeiter demonstrierten im Fabrikhof	*Workers who had been dismissed on account of overproduction demonstrated in the factory yard*

(b) This construction is not common in conversation, where the first two of the above examples would probably run:

Ihr Sohn, der gegenwärtig in München Chemie studiert, hat sie kürzlich besucht.
Mein Vetter hat mir dieses Buch warm empfohlen, und ich habe es sehr genossen.

But a letter recently received from Germany contained a typical example: Wir waren erlebnisreiche, im ganzen von gutem Wetter begünstigte drei Wochen unterwegs.

(c) The attributive participial phrase is much used, and abused, in literary and journalistic German. One example of each must suffice:

Meta Nackedey, ein ewig errötendes, jeden Augenblick in Scham vergehendes Geschöpf von einigen dreißig Jahren (Th. Mann)	*Meta Nackedey, some thirty years old, a perpetually blushing creature, who every moment almost died of bashfulness*
Zwar gilt der in den vergangenen vier Jahren auf der Basis einer deutsch-amerikanischen Regierungs-vereinbarung für bislang 552 Millionen Mark entwickelte Panzer als Spitzenmodell seiner Klasse (*Spiegel*)	*Admittedly the tank which has been developed during the past four years, so far at a cost of 552 million marks, on the basis of an agreement between the German and American governments is regarded as the outstanding one of its class*

(d) The same type of attributive phrase may be found with an adjective instead of a participle, e.g. Er hielt eine von rhetorischen Effekten völlig freie Rede.

437. Other types of participial phrase and the position of the participle

In the attributive participial phrase dealt with in 436 the participle must come last.
Other types of participial phrase are:
(a) absolute participial expressions.
(b) phrases with adjectival or adverbial force following the noun to which the participle refers.
(c) phrases with adverbial force standing at the beginning of the sentence.
Discounting rare literary effects, the position of the participle is as follows: in type (a) it comes last.

in types (b) and (c) the present part. comes last, while the past part. may come first or last, as determined by emphasis or rhythm; where the participial phrase is long and intricate, the past part. comes first.

EXAMPLES:

Type (a)

Ihre Zustimmung vorausgesetzt, möchte ich ...	*Assuming your consent, I should like to ...*
Die Geschäfte beendet und signiert, kam Isaak Landauer[1] ... (L. Feuchtwanger)	*The transactions completed and signed, Isaak Landauer came ...*

Type (b)

das Gehege, ... zusammengebrochen, niedergelegt durch das Gewicht der auf ihm Lastenden (H. Mann)	*the enclosure, collapsed, flattened by the weight of those who pressed upon it*
Zwar hatte dieses Mal der Dolch, durch ein seidenes Unterkleid abgelenkt, das Opfer nicht sogleich tödlich getroffen (P. Heyse)	*This time, indeed, deflected by a silken undergarment, the thrust of the dagger had not been immediately fatal*

Type (c)

Ein altes Lied summend, wanderte er durch den Garten	*Humming an old song, he strolled through the garden*
Geblendet von dem Glanz einer Krone, bemerkte Wallenstein den Abgrund nicht, der zu seinen Füßen sich öffnete (Schiller)	*Dazzled by the glitter of a crown, Wallenstein did not see the abyss that yawned at his feet*
Von der Wucht seiner Rede hingerissen, brachen die Zuhörer immer wieder in Beifall aus	*Carried away by the force of his speech, the audience continually broke out into applause*

438. Absolute participial expressions

(a) A German passive past participle may form an absolute participial expression: see 437: Examples: Type (a).

(b) Those with an active past participle or a present participle in English are rendered in German by a subordinate clause, a main clause or a prepositional phrase:

Als der Vorsitzende angekommen war, (or: Nach Ankunft des Vorsitzenden) begann die Konferenz	*The chairman having arrived, the conference began*
Da der Fluß rasch stieg, wurden Notmaßnahmen getroffen (or: Der Fluß stieg rasch, und Notmaßnahmen wurden getroffen)	*The river rising rapidly, emergency measures were taken*
Er saß in seinem Sessel mit den Füßen auf einem Schemel	*He sat in his armchair, his feet resting on a footstool*

439. An English participial phrase which constitutes a separate statement and is thus the equivalent of a main clause is rendered as such in German, especially where the two actions are consecutive, as in the first of the following examples:

Er öffnete die Schublade und nahm das Testament heraus	*Opening the drawer, he took out the will*

[1] quoted by R. Kurth in *Muttersprache*, 1958, pp. 122 ff.

Er saß an seinem Pult und schrieb einen Brief (literary alternative: einen Brief schreibend)	*He sat at his desk writing a letter*

440. An English participial phrase conveying manner may be rendered in two ways: (a) by a German participial phrase (rather literary) (b) by an 'indem' clause (normal usage):

Nach jedem Satz pausierend, erzählte er seine Geschichte Er erzählte seine Geschichte, indem er nach jedem Satz eine Pause machte	*Pausing after every sentence, he told his story*

441. English participial phrases which are the equivalent of temporal, causal or concessive clauses are mostly rendered by these in German:

Nachdem ich die Briefe beantwortet hatte, ging ich spazieren	*Having answered the letters, I went for a walk*
Da ich wußte, daß er verreist war, habe ich ihn nicht angerufen	*Knowing that he was away, I didn't ring him up*
Obwohl ich wußte, daß er absagen würde, habe ich ihn trotzdem eingeladen	*Knowing that he would refuse, I nevertheless invited him*

In two cases a participial phrase may, however, be used:
 i where a past part. has a passive meaning, being that of a transitive verb:

Vor Einbrechern gewarnt, brachte er das Geld auf die Bank	*Warned against burglars, he took the money to the bank*

 ii where a past part. has an active meaning, being that of an intransitive verb conjugated with 'sein' and signifying a completed action:

Zu Hause angelangt, ging ich bald zu Bett	*Having reached home, I soon went to bed*

cf. An einer schmerzhaften Krankheit jung gestorben, hatte er doch ein halbes Dutzend Bücher geschrieben.

442. The English elliptical construction: While waiting for you, ... Though admiring his achievements, ... etc. is restricted in German to obwohl (obgleich etc.) followed by a passive past participle; otherwise a clause must be used:

Obwohl von seinen Kollegen geachtet, war er nicht sehr beliebt	*Though respected by his colleagues, he was not very popular*
BUT: Als ob er vor Einbrechern gewarnt war, brachte er das Geld auf die Bank	*As if warned against burglars, he took the money to the bank*

443. wie + passive past participle is used in a number of contracted and parenthetical phrases:[1]

Also, wie ausgemacht: wir treffen uns um acht Uhr	*Well then, as arranged, we'll meet at eight o'clock*
wie gesagt	*as I said*

[1] cf. Eggeling, op. cit.: wie 2 (c).

| wie erwartet | *as expected* |
| wie vorausgesehen | *as foreseen* |

Cf. the set phrase:

| Er blieb wie angewurzelt stehen | *He stopped as if rooted to the ground* |

444. For the past part. as an imperative equivalent, see 459(f).

445. The past part. of a verb conjugated with 'sein' may be used with 'kommen' to describe the manner of coming, corresponding to a pres. part. in English:

Er kam ins Zimmer gelaufen	*He came running into the room*
Er kam herbeigeeilt	*He came hurrying along*
Ein Dachziegel kam auf den Bürgersteig heruntergefallen	*A tile came crashing onto the pavement*

446. Certain participles are used as prepositions or conjunctions or to form prepositional or conjunctional phrases, e.g. entsprechend *in accordance with*, vorausgesetzt, daß *assuming that, provided that*. These are not listed here, but are included with the appropriate prepositions and conjunctions.

ausgenommen *excepting* and **eingeschlossen** *including*, though prepositional in force, are better dealt with here. (Both words are somewhat stilted, normal usage being außer + dat. and auch respectively.)
The commonest usage is for the noun or pronoun to follow ausgenommen and to precede eingeschlossen, its case being determined by the main verb of the sentence; eingeschlossen is often strengthened with 'mit':
Alle waren da, ausgenommen mein Bruder.
Ich traue allen, ausgenommen dem neuen Sekretär.
Alle waren da, er mit eingeschlossen.
Er hat alle eingeladen, meinen Bruder eingeschlossen.
Versicherung eingeschlossen *including insurance.*

Note:

i Where the noun on which the exception depends is dat. after a preposition, ausgenommen is followed by the acc.: Ich hatte keine Zeit, mit den anderen zu sprechen, ausgenommen meinen Vetter.

ii eingeschlossen is not preceded by a dative: Ich traue allen, den neuen Sekretär mit eingeschlossen.

447. Some idiomatic uses of the past participle

ein (aus)gedienter Soldat	*one who has completed military service*
ein gelernter Glaser	*a trained* (or *skilled*) *glazier*
Das Bild ist sehr geschmeichelt	*The picture is very flattering*
Er sah seinen Verdacht bestätigt	*He saw his suspicions confirmed*
offen gesagt	*to be frank*
strenggenommen	*strictly speaking*
Verstanden?	*Understand?*

448. The German renderings of English participles in the following cases are dealt with in the paragraphs indicated:

1. the English continuous form: I am writing etc.: 353.
2. a participle as the objective complement of to see, to hear, to feel, to find, e.g. I saw him coming: 410–12.

3. He is having a house built: 419.
4. certain uses of the participles with to remain (he remained seated) and to have (I had a few books lying on the table): 422(a) and (c).
5. for the German construction 'eine nicht zu vermeidende Schwierigkeit' *an unavoidable difficulty*, see 432.

See also 455: Miscellaneous illustrations of the rendering of the verb form in -ing.

N. THE TRANSLATION OF THE ENGLISH GERUND

449. **The English gerund** (the verb form in -ing used as a noun) has no fixed equivalent in German and **is rendered in a variety of ways. One of these is to use an ordinary German noun** if a suitable one suggests itself, e.g. Der Anstrich des Hauses geht gut voran *The painting of the house is going ahead well*. This method is possible in any of the contexts treated in the following paragraphs; it will not be mentioned again as such, but is illustrated in some of the examples.

450. **The English gerund may frequently be rendered by a German infinitive used as a noun** (always neut.) (cf. 404) **or simply by the infinitive, generally with 'zu':**

(a) as subject:

Ihn zu überzeugen wird nicht leicht sein	*Convincing him won't be easy*

(b) as object:

Ich hörte das laute Bellen eines Hundes	*I heard the loud barking of a dog*
Er begann zu lachen	*He began laughing*

(c) as complement:

Sein Hobby ist Briefmarkensammeln	*His hobby is stamp-collecting*
Das nennst du höflich sein[1]	*You call that being polite*

(d) in prepositional phrases limiting a noun or completing the sense of an adjective:

Ich habe keine Zeit zum Üben	*I have no time for practising*
Ich habe keine Zeit, im Garten zu arbeiten	*I have no time for working in the garden*
die Freuden des Schilaufens	*the pleasures of skiing*
die Wichtigkeit einer baldigen Entscheidung	*the importance of deciding soon*
Er ist nicht fähig, so etwas zu tun (or: Er ist einer solchen Tat nicht fähig)	*He is not capable of doing that kind of thing*

451. **'without' and 'instead of'** + gerund: see 431

452. **by or through** + gerund, **expressing means**: use a clause introduced by 'indem' or 'dadurch, daß'; 'indem' should only be used

[1] no 'zu'; see 406.

when the action of the 'indem' clause is simultaneous with that of the main clause:

Er rettete sich, indem er aus dem Fenster sprang	*He saved himself by jumping out of the window*
Er erreichte sein Ziel dadurch, daß wir ihm geholfen haben	*He attained his goal through our having helped him*

Note: Where there is a strong causal element, 'dadurch, weil' is also used (cf. Du. Haupt.: daß 3):

Seine Lage wird dadurch schwierig, weil sògar seine Freunde nicht mehr an ihn glauben	*His position is becoming difficult through even his friends' no longer believing in him*

453. Prepositions such as after, before, since, in spite of, followed by a gerund, are rendered by adverb clauses:

Trotzdem er mir geholfen hatte (or: Trotz seiner Hilfe), kam ich spät	*In spite of his having helped me, I was late*

454. For a gerund or a gerundial phrase following the preposition of a verbal, substantival or adjectival construction (e.g. I rely on finding him at home; his indignation at our not having told him) see 504 ff.

455. Miscellaneous illustrations of the rendering of the verb form in -ing. Since the use of participles is more restricted in German than in English and since German has no fixed equivalent of the English gerund, language sense is often required to produce an organic German equivalent of the English verb form in -ing. This may be illustrated by a number of examples:[1]

Es muß jedenfalls ein schreckliches Leben sein, dauernd erst um sieben Uhr abends nach Hause zu kommen	*It must be a dreadful existence anyhow, not getting home till seven in the evening*
Wenn er nur als ein unbestimmtes, graugrünes Gebilde erscheint, dessen Baumgruppen sich bloß als blasse Schatten zeigen, ...	*If it [Brensham Hill] appears only as a vague grey-green shape with the clumps of trees showing only as faint shadows ... (J. Moore)*
Er verbringt seine Zeit mit Lesen	*He spends his time reading*
Er verbringt seine Zeit damit, daß er über der Vergangenheit brütet	*He spends his time brooding about the past*
Er ging in Gedanken versunken dahin, während die Kinder weiter voran waren	*He walked along brooding, the children being farther ahead*
Wenn man seine Nervosität berücksichtigt, sprach er recht gut	*Allowing for his nervousness, he spoke very well*

[1] The first two are taken from A and S Level proses set by the Oxford and Cambridge Schools Examination Board in 1962 and 1963.

So weilten sie, bis die Stunde, wo man sich für die Nacht trennt, längst vorbei war	*Thus they lingered on till the hour of separating for the night was long past* (Ch. Dickens)
Haben Sie etwas dagegen, daß mein Bruder es erfährt?	*Have you any objection to my brother hearing about it?*
Ich schreibe sein Verbrechen der Tatsache zu, daß er als Kind nie geliebt worden ist	*I ascribe his crime to his never having been loved as a child*

See also 497 and 502.

O. THE IMPERATIVE AND ITS EQUIVALENTS[1]

456. Straightforward examples of the imperative: Hans, sei nicht so dumm! Kinder, bringt ein paar Stühle in den Garten! Kommen Sie bald wieder! Bitte, setzen Sie sich!

Note the following difference between English and German usage:

Seien Sie so gut und schließen Sie die Tür!	*Be so good as to shut the door*

457. (a) **Occasionally a stressed 'du' and 'ihr' are used after the familiar forms for the sake of emphasis**; see 342(b)vii and (c)ii.

(b) For **the intensification of the imperative by a particle,** see 286(h), 290(c), 294(c), 297(f), 302(c), 303(f).

458. The function of the imperative proper is a direct command in the 2nd person; **for the rendering of a wish or exhortation in all persons and of a command in the 3rd pers., see 476.**

459. Imperative equivalents (cf. Du. Gram. 1040, 1045)

(a) Modal verbs: müssen, sollen (400(h)), dürfen (397(c)) and one use of wollen: Willst du gleich still sein! *Will you be quiet now!*

(b) 2nd sing. or plur. of pres. or future indic.: either a question or a statement, to which the intonation gives their imperative force:

Hörst du jetzt zu?	*Are you going to listen now?*
Wirst du jetzt zuhören?	
Ihr hört jetzt zu!	*You're going to listen now*
Ihr werdet jetzt zuhören!	
'Du hebst das [ein Bonbon] auf bis nach dem Abendessen', erklärte das Fräulein (V. Baum)	'*You're keeping that [a sweet] till after supper*', *declared the governess*

(c) haben zu+infin.:

Du hast dir jetzt die Hände zu waschen	*You're to wash your hands now* (a sharp injunction)

(d) a 'daß' clause, generally containing a stressed 'ja':

Daß du *ja* zum Mittagessen pünktlich bist!	*Be sure you're punctual for lunch*

[1] For the forms of the imperative, see 342.

(e) the impersonal passive (cf. 381):

Jetzt wird gearbeitet!	*You're going to work now*
Jetzt wird nicht gelacht!	*No laughing now!*

(f) a past participle:[1]

Stillgestanden!	*Attention!* (military command)

(g) an infinitive:[2]

Antreten! Wegtreten!	*Fall in! Dismiss!*
Einsteigen und Türen schließen!	*Take your seats! Close the doors!*
4 Eiweiß zu sehr steifem Schnee schlagen	*Beat 4 whites of egg stiffly*

(h) a noun, an adjective, an adverb, a phrase, all used elliptically: Achtung! *Look out!* Ruhig! *Be quiet!* Vorwärts! *Forward!* Tür zu! *Shut the door!*

Es erscholl das Einsatzkommando 'Knüppel frei! Räumen!' (*Spiegel*)	*The order to act rang out: Truncheons ready! Clear the street!*

P. THE SUBJUNCTIVE AND ITS USES

460. Survey of the uses of the subjunctive[3]

1. Introductory 461
2. Conditional Clauses 462–5
3. 'as if' clauses 466
4. Final Clauses 467
5. Other clauses with a final element 468
6. Negative contexts 469
7. Concessive Clauses 470–74
8. The Subjunctive of Modest Assertion 475
9. The Optative Subjunctive 476
10. Indirect Speech 477–85

461. Introductory

(a) The fundamental difference between the indicative and subjunctive moods is that the indicative expresses fact, certainty and agreement, while the subjunctive expresses the hypothetical, the unreal, supposition, doubt and disagreement. The imperf. subj. is not a past tense.

(b) In spoken German there is a strong tendency to replace the subjunctive by the indicative, a tendency which is strongest among, but not confined to, the less educated.

(c) In subordinate clauses, the imperf. subj. is more used by North Germans, the pres. subj. by South Germans, especially in the Alemannic area: Baden-Württemberg, Switzerland and parts of Bavaria and Austria (cf. Du. Gram. 6750). In general, the imperf. subj. is gaining ground at the expense of the pres. subj., which, in conversation, is felt to be stilted and affected. (Perhaps for that very reason the pres. subj. continues to flourish in journalistic and literary German:

---

[1] Duden's explanation (Gram. 1045): the command is regarded as fulfilled.
[2] used elliptically, 'Sie sollen', or something similar, being omitted.
[3] For the forms of the Subjunctive, see 334 ff., 340(c)(g), **345 f.**, 389(b)(e)(f).

Du. Gram. 6750). More specifically, the 2nd sing. and 2nd plur. of the pres. subj. (e.g. du kommest, ihr kommet) are the forms that sound most affected and are most regularly avoided. The singular of the pres. subj. of 'sein' is freely used, 'er sei' perhaps more frequently than any other pres. subj. form in the language.

(d) Per contra, many imperfect subjunctives with the root vowels ä, ü and particularly ö (e.g. er läse, er grübe, er löge, from lesen, graben and lügen) sound stilted and are likewise avoided; these include all the irregular imperfect subjunctives given in 345(c).

(e) The method of avoiding the forms of the subjunctive that sound stilted (e.g. by an interchange of present and imperfect subjunctive or by the use of the conditional or a modal verb) varies according to the grammatical context and is treated under the separate uses of the subjunctive.

(f) A glance at the conjugational paradigms in 334 ff. and 389 will show that, except for 'sein' and the modal verbs, the 1st sing., 1st plur. and 3rd plur. of the pres. indic. and the pres. subj. are identical; that the imperf. subj. of all weak verbs is the same as the imperf. indic.; and that strong verbs with a vowel that cannot modify have identical forms in the 1st and 3rd plur. of the imperf. indic. and subj. The extent to which, and the methods by which, German usage takes account of this factor is referred to under the separate uses of the subjunctive. It may be said that the identity of subjunctive and indicative is felt to matter less in the imperfect than in the present.

462. Conditional Clauses

(a) **Basic types**

i **Open Condition (no *would* or *would have*)**: indic. in both parts.
Wenn ich ihm heute schreibe, bekommt er den Brief morgen
If I write to him today, he'll get the letter tomorrow

ii **Improbable Condition (*would*)**
    'wenn' clause: imperf. subj.
    main clause: imperf. subj. or condit.
Wenn ich ihm heute schriebe,
    ⎰bekäme er den Brief morgen
    ⎱würde er den Brief morgen bekommen
If I wrote to him today, he would get the letter tomorrow

iii **Rejected Condition (*would have*)**
    'wenn' clause: pluperf. subj.
    main clause: pluperf. subj. or condit. perf.
Wenn ich ihm heute geschrieben hätte,
    ⎰hätte er den Brief morgen bekommen
    ⎱würde er den Brief morgen bekommen haben
If I had written to him today, he would have got the letter tomorrow

Note:
i In the main clause of type ii, the conditional is commoner in conversation than the imperf. subj.

ii **A warning**: 'would' expressing habit or meaning 'was willing to' is not rendered by 'würde'.

After lunch he would go for a walk:
> Nach dem Mittagessen pflegte er einen Spaziergang zu machen (slightly stilted)/machte er immer (or: gewöhnlich) einen Spaziergang (normal usage).

I asked several of my friends but none would go with me:
> Ich forderte mehrere meiner Freunde auf, aber keiner wollte mitgehen.

(b) **An Open Condition, with the indic. in both parts, may occur in the past:**

Wenn man Schwierigkeiten hatte, konnte man sich an den Werkmeister wenden	*If one was in difficulties, one could apply to the foreman*

(c) Where, as in all the examples in (a) above, the condit. cl. precedes the main cl., the latter often begins with 'so' or 'dann' (Engl. then) (See also 463(a)N.i):

Wenn ich ihm heute schreibe, so (or: dann) bekommt er den Brief morgen.

(d) It is not unusual to use normal order in the main clause following a conditional clause, the effect being to give additional emphasis to the main clause:

Wenn ich es nicht mit eignen Augen gesehen hätte, ich hätte es nie geglaubt	*If I hadn't seen it with my own eyes, I should never have believed it*

(e) **Stilted, awkward or ambiguous forms of the imperf. subj.** (cf. 461(d)(e)(f)) **may be avoided** by using either the conditional or 'sollte' or 'wollte'. The conditional should preferably not be used in both the condit. clause and the main clause.

Wenn du schneller arbeiten würdest (better: wolltest) (in place of 'arbeitetest'), könntest du mehr verdienen.
Wenn das Konzert früher beginnen sollte (in place of 'begönne'), . . .
Wenn er mich fragte (or: fragen sollte), würde ich ihm alles sagen.[1]
Wie wäre es, wenn wir ihm helfen wollten? (in place of 'hülfen').

Colloquially, the imperf. indic. is sometimes used:

Wenn er die Notleine zog (in place of 'zöge'), würde der Zug sofort stehenbleiben (E. Kästner)	*If he pulled the communication cord, the train would stop at once*

Finally, the imperf. subj. of 'tun' is sometimes enlisted (bad German):
> Wenn ich ihm schreiben täte, würde er den Brief morgen bekommen.

(f) In addition to the function noted in (e), 'sollte' may be used to increase the improbability, the remoteness, of an Improbable Condition:

Wenn ich einmal in diese Lage kommen sollte,[2] . . .	*If ever I were to find myself in that situation, . . .*

---

[1] If the weak imperf. subj. were used in both parts (Wenn er mich fragte, sagte ich ihm alles), this would be more likely to mean: When he asked me, I used to tell him everything.
[2] from Erben, op. cit., 68.

463. Alternatives for 'wenn'

(a) In place of 'wenn' with the verb at the end, inversion of verb and subject, without 'wenn', may be used.

Note:

i Following a conditional clause of this type, the main clause usually begins with 'dann' or 'so', 'so' being a shade literary.

ii Used in Open or Improbable Conditions (types i and ii in 462(a)), the inversion construction is slightly more literary (cf. Du. Gram. 6375).

iii In contrast with English, there is in German no restriction on this usage, except that it is uncommon where the condit. clause follows the main clause.

Thus the examples in 462(a) could run:
Schreibe ich ihm heute, dann bekommt er den Brief morgen.
Schriebe ich ihm heute, . . . Hätte ich ihm heute geschrieben, . . .
and, from 462(e): Sollte er mich fragen, so würde ich ihm alles sagen.

(b) The following words and phrases are used with the same tenses as 'wenn'; in practice, they mainly introduce Open Conditions (462(a): type i) (for punctuation see 743 (e) ii):

vorausgesetzt, daß	*assuming that, provided that*
angenommen, (daß)	
falls; sofern; im Falle, daß	*in case*
für den Fall, daß	
unter der Bedingung, daß	*on condition that*
unter der Voraussetzung, daß	*on the assumption that*
sofern; wofern (relatively rare)	*provided that*
gesetzt, (daß)	*supposing that*
gesetzt den Fall, daß	

Note:

i angenommen, (daß) and gesetzt, (daß): without 'daß' these are followed by normal order; with 'daß' the verb goes to the end: Angenommen, er hat dein Telegramm erhalten/Angenommen, daß er dein Telegramm erhalten hat, wird er bald hier sein.

ii für den Fall, daß is used in a context with an element of purpose, such as: Er gab mir seine Telefonnummer für den Fall, daß ich ihn erreichen wollte.

iii for 'even if', see 473.

464. Conditional Clause equivalents

(a) An imperative, or a sentence with 'sollen . . . nur' or 'brauchen . . . nur', may be the equivalent of a conditional clause if followed by so (or dann) + a second sentence:[1]

Gib mir das Geld, so kann ich die Plätze besorgen	*Give me the money, then I can get the seats*
Er soll nur anrufen/Er braucht nur anzurufen, so sage ich ihm Bescheid	*Let him ring up/He need only ring up and I'll give him the information*

[1] cf. Schulz-Griesbach, op. cit., G 418.

(b) A noun clause or a relative clause may be the equivalent of a conditional clause; thence the tenses in the following:

Wer (or: Jemand, der) diese Entwicklung vorausgesehen hätte, hätte viel Geld verdienen können	*Anyone foreseeing this development could have made a lot of money*

(c) An adverb or a prepositional phrase may take the place of a conditional clause; thence the tenses in the following simple sentences:

Sonst würde ich es nicht tun	*Otherwise I would not do it*
Unter anderen Umständen wäre ich erfolgreicher gewesen (from Du. Gram. 6465)	*Under other circumstances I should have been more successful*

(d) A conditional clause may be implied; thence the tenses in the following simple sentences:

Lieber bliebe ich zu Hause [wenn ich die Wahl hätte]	*I would rather stay at home [if I had the choice]*
Ich hätte dasselbe getan [wenn ich an deiner Stelle gewesen wäre]	*I would have done the same thing [if I had been in your place]*

465. unless

i wenn . . . nicht: tenses as for 'wenn'.
ii außer wenn;[1] ausgenommen, wenn[1] *except if*: used mainly in Open Conditions (462(a): type (i)).
iii es sei denn, daß:[1] used mainly in Open Conditions; see 289(h).
iv denn (with imperf. subj. of 'müssen'): archaic and literary; see 289(h).

Wenn er nicht bald kommt, wird es zu spät sein	*Unless he comes soon, it will be too late*
Er kommt immer pünktlich nach Hause, außer wenn Sitzung ist	*He always comes home punctually except if there's a meeting*

Note: The 'nicht' of 'wenn . . . nicht' must follow a pronoun object, generally follows def. art., demonstrative or possessive+noun, must precede words like jemand, etwas, alles, einiges, and generally precedes other types of object:

Wenn du ihn nicht fragst, . . .
Wenn du meinem Bruder nicht hilfst, . . .
Wenn du ihr nicht alles sagst, . . .
Wenn er nicht (deutsche) Zeitungen liest, . . .

466. 'as if' clauses (Comparative-cum-Conditional): als ob, als wenn

(a) **Basic types** (Both alternatives, als ob and als+inversion, are widely used; the latter is slightly more literary.)

i **Appearances are accepted as probably true**

Er sicht (sah) aus, {als ob er krank sei / als sei er krank}   pres. subj.
He looks (looked) as if he were ill

{als ob er krank gewesen sei / als sei er krank gewesen}   perf. subj.
as if he had been ill

---

[1] for punctuation see 743(e).

$\begin{cases} \text{als ob er zuverlässig sein werde} \\ \text{als werde er zuverlässig sein} \end{cases}$ fut. subj.
as if he would be reliable

Note: Colloquial usage prefers the conditional (sein würde) to the future subj.

ii Appearances are regarded as misleading

Er tut (tat), $\begin{cases} \text{als ob er krank wäre} \\ \text{als wäre er krank} \end{cases}$ imperf. subj.
He acts (acted) as if he were ill

$\begin{cases} \text{als ob er krank gewesen wäre} \\ \text{als wäre er krank gewesen} \end{cases}$ pluperf. subj.
as if he had been ill

$\begin{cases} \text{als ob er in zwei Jahren ein reicher Mann sein würde} \\ \text{als würde er in zwei Jahren ein reicher Mann sein} \end{cases}$ condi-   tional
as if he would be a rich man in two years' time

or appearances are regarded as purely imaginary

Er arbeitete mit der Zahnbürste, als wenn viel davon abhinge (V. Baum)	*He plied his toothbrush, as if much depended on it*
Das wird ganz laut und ist fast fort, als hätte es der Wind geschluckt (H. Fallada)	*It [the distant roar of a big city] grows quite loud and almost vanishes, as if the wind had swallowed it*

Note: In the English of all the examples, 'as though' would, of course, be an alternative for 'as if'.

(b) The distinction between these two basic types, made in Du. Gram. 6705, is borne out by the preponderant practice of a considerable range of authors and by the reaction of Germans tested on the above examples.

Nevertheless, this distinction is one of which the average German, and many German authors, are not consciously aware and it is frequently infringed. Moreover it is often overridden by the instinctive aversion for subjunctive forms that sound affected or awkward (cf. 461(c) and (d)); these may be avoided by using the 'wrong' tense, by a modal or by some other means, e.g. instead of: Er tat, als ob er hervorragend schwömme, say: als ob er hervorragend schwimme/schwimmen könnte, or: als ob er ein hervorragender Schwimmer wäre.

(c) Colloquially, 'als ob' is frequently used with the indic.
Note:
i this is common when the main verb is in the present, relatively rare when it is in the past.
ii als + inversion cannot be used with the indic.

E.g. Er sieht aus, als ob er krank ist; er tut, als ob er oft an seine Eltern schreibt; mir war, als ob er mich nicht verstand.

(d) To introduce an illustrative parallel, 'as if' may be rendered by 'wie wenn': Das wäre, wie wenn (or: als wenn) ein Kommunist zum Katholizismus bekehrt würde.

(e) **'als wenn'** can also mean **'than if, than when'**; the context will make this clear:

Man kann ihn nicht besser ärgern, als wenn man ihm fortwährend Rat gibt	*One cannot annoy him more effectively than if one constantly gives him advice*

467. Final Clauses

(a) **In spoken German,** they generally have the indicative and often use können:[1]

Ich helfe ihm, damit[2] er rechtzeitig abfährt/abfahren kann	*I'm helping him so that he leaves on time*
Ich half ihm, damit er rechtzeitig abfahren konnte/damit alles gut ging	*I helped him so that he should leave on time/so that everything should be all right*

(b) **In literary German,** the pres. or imperf. subj. is often used,[1] especially when the main verb is in a past tense, as in the first example, but also when it is in the present, as in the second:

Er half ihnen, damit sie rechtzeitig abführen.

Und damit diese Autorität intakt bleibe, wird ihm [dem Bundespräsidenten] angeraten, sich möglichst wenig in aktuelle Streitfragen einzumischen (*to interfere as little as possible in current controversies*) (*Zeit*)

(c) **Alternatives for damit** *in order that, so that*

  i (so) daß: Arbeite fleißig, (so) daß du das Examen bestehst.

  ii auf daß is a specifically literary alternative. Thus, in a passage too long to quote, Thomas Mann tells of the building of the pyramids in long years of agonizing forced labour 'auf daß Gottkönig Chufu tief innen darunter ruhe'.

  iii When the subject of the main clause is also that of the final clause, it is neater and more usual to use um zu + infin.:

Ich gehe nach Hause, um ihm zu helfen	*I'm going home so that I may help him*

(d) **lest** = damit . . . nicht or daß . . . nicht.

Ich helfe ihm, damit er nicht zu spät abfährt	*I am helping him lest he should leave too late*

Note: I fear lest . . . = Ich fürchte, daß . . .

468. The imperf. or pluperf. subjunctive may be used in a relative clause or in a temporal clause introduced by 'bis', 'ehe' or 'bevor', which has a final sense:

Er suchte . . . nach jemandem, der ihn anspräche (G. Gaiser)	*He was looking for someone who might address him*
Sie beschlossen zu warten, bis er käme (or: kam, or: kommen würde)	*They decided to wait for him to come*
Er weigerte sich, den Vertrag zu unterzeichnen, bevor wir ihm weitere Zugeständnisse gemacht hätten (or: machten)	*He refused to sign the agreement before we had made further concessions*

---

[1] cf. Collinson, op. cit., p. 133.
[2] accented on the second syllable.

469. Use of the subjunctive in negative contexts

(a) Because of their negative character, their concern with what did *not* happen or was *not* the case, **nicht daß, ohne daß, (an)statt daß and zu (alt), als daß are frequently followed by the imperf. or pluperf. subj.** The effect is less brusque than that of a straightforward indicative tense, which is always a possible alternative (cf. Du. Gram. 6485, 6680):

Nicht, daß er faul wäre (or: ist), aber er kommt in seinem Beruf nicht vorwärts	*Not that he's lazy, but he's not getting on in his profession*
nicht daß ich wüßte (set phrase; indic. not possible)	*not that I know*
und er [Zuckmayer] hat, ohne daß es ihm geglückt wäre, immer wieder . . . versucht, seine Herkunft vom wohlanständigen Bürgertum abzustreifen (*Zeit*)	*and, without succeeding, he tried again and again to divest himself of his respectable middle-class origin*
Statt daß er mir geholfen hätte (statt daß er mir half, statt mir zu helfen), las er die Zeitung	*Instead of helping me, he read the paper*
Er ist zu vernünftig, als daß ich dies von ihm erwartet hätte	*He is too sensible for me to have expected this of him*

(b) Similarly, the imperf. or pluperf. subj. may on occasion be used **in other subordinate clauses** where the main clause or the subordinate clause or both are negative. Again, the indic. is perfectly possible, but more brusque (cf. Du. Gram. 6485, 6690, 6720):

Dies bedeutet keineswegs, daß ich mit allem zufrieden wäre (or: bin)	*This by no means signifies that I'm satisfied with everything*
Nicht eine einzige Großstadt, keine Mittel- oder Kleinstadt, kein Dorf, die nicht ihr Gesicht in zwei Jahrzehnten gründlich . . . gewandelt hätten[1]	*Not a single large, medium-sized or small town, not a village, that has not radically changed its appearance in the course of two decades*

(c) Similarly, the pluperf. subj. is often used **in sentences containing 'fast' or 'beinah'** (with their negative implications), with or without nicht:[2]

Ich wäre fast nicht gekommen	*I almost didn't come*
Wir hätten das Spiel beinah gewonnen	*We almost won the game*

470. Concessive Clauses beginning with although or its equivalent

(a) The relevant conjunctions are:
  i obgleich *although*; its variants: obwohl, obschon; and the rarer obzwar and wiewohl.
  ii trotzdem (stressed on 'dem') *despite the fact that.*
  iii ungeachtet (daß) *notwithstanding that.*
  iv zugegeben, daß *granted that.*
  Of these, obwohl is the commonest in current usage.

(b) The mood is normally the indicative.

---

[1] from an article on 'Das Bergische Land', south of the Ruhr, in *Die Zeit* (11.11.1966).
[2] cf. Schulz-Griesbach, op. cit., B 739.

(c) Where the concessive clause precedes the main clause, the contrast between them may be emphasized by the use of so ... doch,[1] or occasionally of normal order, in the main clause:

Obwohl sie sehr bescheiden leben, so scheinen sie doch ganz glücklich zu sein	*Although they live very modestly, they seem to be quite happy*
Obwohl er mein Vetter ist, ich kann nichts für ihn tun	*Although he's my cousin, I can do nothing for him*

471. Concessive Clauses beginning with whoever, however, whenever etc.

(a) Here there is an immense range and complexity of variations and no attempt will be made to include them all.

(b) **The following four types represent normal usage and cover most requirements**; they start respectively with 1. an indefinite pronoun 2. an indefinite adverb 3. however + adjective 4. however + adverb.

Wer er auch ist/sein mag, ich kann nichts für ihn tun	1. *Whoever he may be, I can do nothing for him*
Wann er auch ankommt/ ankommen mag, ich will ihn sofort sprechen	2. *Whenever he may arrive, I want to speak to him at once*
Wie (or: So) teuer das Bild auch ist/sein mag, ich will es doch kaufen	3. *However expensive the picture may be, I'll buy it all the same*
Wie (or: So) schnell er auch lief/ laufen mochte, der Polizist holte ihn ein	4. *However quickly he ran, the policeman caught him up*

(c) **Comments on the above types**

   i Following these concessive clauses, the main clause has normal order; this emphasizes the contrast between the two clauses, the magnitude of the concession: e.g. sentence 2 conveys: No matter at what hour he may arrive, I want to speak to him at once. Occasionally, where this element of contrast is weaker, the main clause may have inversion, e.g. Wo er sich auch zeigte, wurde er mit Beifall begrüßt *Wherever he showed himself, he was cheered.*

   ii If these clauses are in the present, the verb may be either indicative or subjunctive. Normal usage is the indicative (as above); the subjunctive may make the concession a shade more sweeping and is stylistically more *recherché*, e.g. Wer er auch sei/sein möge, ich kann nichts für ihn tun. In the past (illustrated in type 4), the verb can only be in the indicative.

   iii Alternatives for 'auch' (though 'auch' is commonest and safest): nur, auch nur, immer, auch immer, nur immer; 'immer' generally

cf. Collinson, op. cit., p. 131.

comes immediately after the pronoun or adverb and is not used in types 3 and 4:

Sie verstehen sich ohne Worte, was immer sich begibt (*whatever occurs*) (W. Dieß).
Wo immer er sich zeigte/Wo er sich auch nur (auch immer) zeigte, wurde er mit Beifall begrüßt.

iv In types 3 and 4, 'wie' is slightly commoner than 'so', but for 'however much', expressing degree, 'sosehr' is commoner than 'wie sehr'; these, like 'sowenig', may be used alone or followed by 'auch':

Sosehr ich es (auch) bedauere, ich kann unmöglich mitgehen	*However much I regret it, I can't possibly go with you*
Sowenig er mir gefällt, ich muß ihn doch bewundern	*Little as I like him, I can't help admiring him*

(d) **'whatever' used as an indefinite adjective** is rendered by 'was für (ein)' or 'welcher':

Was für Schwierigkeiten du auch hast, es ist der Mühe wert	*Whatever difficulties you may have, it's worth the bother*
... diese Vorgänge, von welcher Seite man sie auch betrachtet (*SZ*)	*these events, from whatever side one considers them*

Note: 'welcher' may be used elliptically:

aus welchem Land auch immer	*from whatever country*
mit welchen Mitteln auch immer (*SZ*)	*with whatever resources*

472. 'noch so' is the equivalent of '(n)ever so' with concessive force:[1]

Er mag noch so gescheit sein, (er) paßt aber für diese Stellung nicht	*He may be ever so intelligent, but he's not suitable for this post*
Nein, er war kein guter Ehemann, so dachte Xanthippe, mochte er ein noch so großer Philosoph sein (S. Andres)	*No, he was not a good husband, thought Xanthippe, though he might be never so great a philosopher*

According to the context, 'noch so' may require other English renderings:

jede noch so nebensächliche Bemerkung	*every remark, however trivial,*
Es mögen sich (auch) noch so viele Leute beschweren, es wird nichts geschehen	*No matter how many people complain, nothing will happen*

473. Concessive Clauses of the Conditional type: even if, even though:

German renderings are of four kinds, (a) being the commonest; the same tenses are used as in conditional clauses (see 462(a)).

(a) selbst wenn, auch wenn, sogar wenn; a following main clause generally has inversion:

Selbst wenn ich ihm heute schriebe, würde er den Brief morgen nicht bekommen.

(b) wenn ... auch; also, relatively rare: ob ... auch, wenngleich (divisible), wennschon (divisible); in a following main clause, normal order is more emphatic and more usual:

Wenn ich ihm auch heute geschrieben hätte, er hätte den Brief morgen (doch) nicht bekommen.

Note:

i The 'auch' of 'wenn ... auch' must follow a pronoun object, generally

[1] contrast its colloquial use: He was ever so nice: Er war wirklich furchtbar nett.

follows def. art., demonstrative or possessive + noun, but must precede all other types of object:

Wenn du ihr auch alles gesagt hättest, . . .
Wenn du das/dieses/dein Haus auch verkauft hättest, . . .
Wenn du auch kein Buch von ihm gelesen hast, . . .
Wenn er auch (deutsche) Bücher liest, . . .

ii 'wenn auch', 'wenngleich' and 'wennschon' may be used elliptically:
Das Buch ist, wenn auch nicht hervorragend, (so) doch interessant.
Er hatte viel zu berichten, wennschon nichts sehr Wichtiges.

(c) Inversion with auch or with gleich, the latter being old-fashioned; in a following main clause, normal order is more emphatic and more usual:

Ist er auch (or gleich) ein alter Freund, ich kann ihm nicht helfen. Hätte ich ihm auch heute geschrieben, er hätte den Brief morgen nicht bekommen.

Note: After any of the 'even if' clauses mentioned in (a) (b) and (c), a following main clause frequently begins with so (+ inversion) and/or contains doch *nevertheless*:

Wenn ich ihm auch heute geschrieben hätte, so hätte er den Brief morgen doch nicht bekommen.[1]

(d) An 'even if' clause which is closely linked to a preceding noun or pronoun may be rendered by 'und' + conditional clause:

Keiner von den Arbeitern, und wenn man ihm die dreifache Bezahlung verspricht, wird diese Aufgabe übernehmen	*Not one of the workers, even if he is promised treble pay, will take on this job*
Gervaise, und wäre sie eine Göttin, ist eine klägliche Partie (A. Kolb)	*Gervaise, even if she were a goddess, is a poor match*

474. Miscellaneous types of clause with concessive force

Ich mag tun, was ich will, es hilft doch nichts	*Whatever I do, it doesn't help*
koste es, was es wolle	*whatever the cost*
Gleichviel, wer es getan hat, er soll bestraft werden	*No matter who has done it, he shall be punished*
(Einerlei) ob er Erfahrung hat oder nicht, ich werde ihn anstellen	*Whether he has experience or not, I shall engage him*
Ich habe ihn eingeladen; nicht, daß ich seine Gesellschaft besonders schätze[2]	*I have invited him, not that I particularly value his company*
wie dem auch sei (set phrase)	*be that as it may*
das mochte sein, wie es wollte,	*however that might be,*
wie auch immer (*Zeit*) (elliptical)	*however that may be*

475. The Subjunctive of Modest Assertion, a hallowed and admirable phrase, which, in conjunction with the following examples, requires no explanation. Its main tense is the imperfect, though it may occur in the pluperfect. In every case a blunt indicative would be possible, e.g. (first example) Ich weiß, was zu tun ist.

---

[1] cf. Schulz-Griesbach, op. cit., G 553.   [2] for nicht daß, see also 469(a).

Ich wüßte wohl, was zu tun wäre (Du. Gram. 6470)	*I think I know what ought to be done*
Eine Frage hätte ich *doch* noch (Th. Valentin)	*There's one more thing I* would *like to ask*
Da wäre er nun aufgewacht (F. Dürrenmatt)	*He seems to have woken up*[1]

This subjunctive is frequently used in registering the completion of a task or the reaching of one's destination:

Diese Sache hätten wir also geregelt	*That would appear to be completed*
Da wären wir also endlich	*So here we are at last*

A question may likewise be made less blunt by the use of the subjunctive:

Wäre das alles?	*Will that be all?*
Wären Sie also jetzt zufrieden?	*Well, are you satisfied now?*

476. The Optative Subjunctive is used to express a wish, exhortation or command in a main clause (as in (a) below) or in a conditional clause, the main clause being suppressed (as in (b) below).

(a) Present Subjunctive
1st pers. sing. (relatively rare)

Möge ich's nicht bereuen!	*May I not regret it!*

(Somewhat stilted; normal usage: Hoffentlich werd' ich's nicht bereuen).

Sage ich's lieber ganz offen	*I'd better say so quite frankly*

2nd pers. sing. and plur.: A direct command in the 2nd person being the function of the imperative, the optative subjunctive is limited to the expression of a wish or exhortation by means of 'mögen':

Mögest (or: Möchtest) du immer so denken!	*May you always think thus!*

(Somewhat stilted; normal usage: Hoffentlich wirst du immer so denken.)

3rd pers. sing.
i it is used in a number of set phrases expressing a wish:

Gott segne dich!	*God bless you!*
Gott behüte dich!	*May God protect you!*
Gott behüte![2]	*God forbid! Certainly not!*
Gott (dat.) sei Dank!	*Thank heavens!*
Es lebe die Freiheit!	*Long live freedom!*
Er lebe hoch! (or: Er soll leben!)	*Long may he live! Here's to his health!*

ii the pres. subj. of 'mögen' may be used to express a wish:
Möge er glücklich sein! Möge es ihm gelingen! (Somewhat stilted; normal usage: Hoffentlich wird er glücklich sein. Hoffentlich gelingt es ihm.)

iii with 'man' as subject, it is fairly common as the equivalent of an imperative addressed to whom it may concern:

Im Notfall wende man sich an den Hausmeister!	*In case of need apply to the caretaker*
Man bedenke, was die Folgen sein könnten	*Consider what the consequences might be*

---

[1] thus translated by L. Forster in his edition of Dürrenmatt: Der Verdacht (Harrap).
[2] short for: Gott behüte mich davor!

iv it may express an exhortation or command, but only in literary
    language:

Bezähme jeder die gerechte Wut	*Let each man curb his righteous anger and*
Und spare für das Ganze seine Rache	*save his vengeance for the common*
(Schiller: *Wilhelm Tell*)	*cause*
Er komme sofort!	*Let him come at once*
Er möge sofort kommen!	—less peremptory
Er soll sofort kommen	—normal usage

1st pers. plur.

Na also, gehen wir ganz langsam.	*Well then, let's walk quite slowly. Take*
Faß mich unter (H. Fallada)	*my arm*
Seien wir dankbar, daß nichts passiert ist!	*Let's be thankful that nothing happened*
Gehen wir in den Garten!	*Let's go into the garden*
Also, spielen wir jetzt Karten!	*Well, let's play cards now*

Note:
i Laß uns/Laßt uns + infin. is here frequently used instead of the pres. subj.,
    but would not be idiomatic in the last example above. 'Laßt uns' may
    be used in talking to someone one addresses as 'Sie', e.g. Laßt uns in
    den Garten gehen!
ii Let's see the letter (coll.) = Laß mich mal den Brief sehen!

3rd pers. plur.
A wish may be expressed by means of 'mögen'; a command is expressed
by means of 'sollen':

Mögen sie es nicht bereuen!	*May they not regret it!*

(Normal usage: Hoffentlich werden sie es nicht bereuen.)

Sie sollen sofort kommen!	*Let them come at once*

(b) **Imperfect Subjunctive, Pluperfect Subjunctive and Conditional**: to express a wish (If only . . .)
Note:
i Instead of 'wenn' with the verb at the end, inversion of verb and subject
    may be used with the pluperf. subj. and, in the case of strong verbs,
    but less commonly, with the imperf. subj.
ii The inclusion of doch, nur, bloß, doch nur or doch bloß is virtually
    essential to convey that it is a wish.

Wenn er doch nur käme!	*If only he would come!*
(Käme er doch nur!)	
Wenn er bloß besser arbeitete!	*If only he worked better!*
Hätte mein Vater doch dieses Haus nie gekauft!	*If only my father had never bought this house!*
Wenn er Ihnen das Geld doch bloß geben würde!	*If only he would give you the money!*

Q. INDIRECT SPEECH

477. Survey of the treatment of Indirect Speech

6. Notes on 479–83: 484, e.g. 484(b): the use of 'daß', 484(d): subordinate clauses in reported speech
7. Deviations from the rules given in 479–83: 485

478. Introductory

German practice varies immensely in the handling of indirect speech. It has been thought best to start by giving and illustrating a set of definite rules (for Indirect Statement, Indirect Question and Noun Clauses depending on verbs other than those of saying and asking) which represent preponderant usage and which will rarely produce impossible German. Thereafter deviations from those rules will be considered. The user is recommended to read 484(b) (on the use of 'daß') before proceeding.

479. Indirect Statement

The main verb will here be 'sagen' or one of its equivalents, e.g. antworten *to answer*, behaupten *to maintain*, erklären *to declare; to explain*, erwähnen *to mention*, erzählen *to relate*, leugnen *to deny*, meinen *to say*,[1] versichern *to assure*, zugeben *to admit*.

Rules

(a) If sagen, or its equivalent, is present, future or imperative, it is generally followed by the indicative: Er sagt, er ist krank. Er wird sagen, daß er nichts davon weiß. Sagen Sie ihm, er soll sofort kommen!

(b) If sagen is past, it is normally followed by the subjunctive or conditional, with the following scheme of tenses:

TENSE OF ORIGINAL DIRECT STATEMENT	TENSE OF INDIRECT STATEMENT	
	CONVERSATIONAL	LITERARY
Present	Imperf. Subj.	Pres. Subj.
Past {Imperfect, Perfect, Pluperfect}	Pluperf. Subj.	Perf. Subj.
Future	Conditional (but Fut. Subj. in 3rd sing.)[2]	Fut. Subj.

EXAMPLES

'Ich schreibe einen Brief'	Er sagte, er schriebe (schreibe) einen Brief
'Ich schrieb einen Brief' 'Ich habe einen Brief geschrieben' 'Ich hatte einen Brief geschrieben'	Er sagte, er hätte (habe) einen Brief geschrieben
'Ich werde einen Brief schreiben'	Er sagte, er werde einen Brief schreiben

---

[1] The basic meaning of meinen, 'to be of the opinion', is frequently extended to 'to express an opinion' or 'to say', e.g. 'Das geht aber nicht', meinte sie.

[2] This applies to Indirect Statement only; not to Indir. Questions (481) or after indefinite verbs (482).

(c) The above scheme of tenses is modified by the principle that distinctive subjunctive forms should be used whenever possible. Therefore:

CONVERSATIONAL TENSES: Weak Verbs: as their imperf. subj. is the same as their imperf. indic., use the pres. subj., where it is different from the pres. indic.: Er sagte, Hans spiele Tennis (not: spielte)

LITERARY TENSES: where these have the same form as the indicative, use the corresponding conversational tense:
Er sagte, sie sängen alte Volkslieder (not: singen)
Er sagte, sie hätten nichts vergessen (not: haben)
Sie sagten, sie würden nie heimkehren (not: werden)

In the case of the pres. subj. this rule should be followed even where the imperf. subj. is likewise identical with the indicative. Thus:
'Wir arbeiten fleißig'   Sie sagten, sie arbeiteten fleißig
                                (not: arbeiten)

480. When sagen (or its equivalent), fragen (cf. 481), hören etc. (cf. 482) are in the perfect, they are often followed by the indicative

(a) This will generally be the case when the perfect refers to the recent past and thus approximates to the present:
Was hat er gesagt? Er hat gesagt, daß er krank ist/Er hat erwähnt, daß er dich gesehen hat. Er hat eben gefragt, ob wir zufrieden sind. Ich habe gerade gehört, daß er angekommen ist.

(b) Where the occasion of 'Er hat gesagt', 'Er hat gefragt' etc. lies further back, the subjunctive is more usual, especially where the matter referred to in the statement or question may have changed in the meantime (2nd and 3rd examples):
Letzte Woche hat er mir gesagt, er hätte sein Haus verkauft (or: daß er sein Haus verkauft hat) (cf. 484(b)).
Letzte Woche hat er mir gesagt, er wäre krank.
Er ist letzte Woche hier gewesen und hat gefragt, ob du zu Hause wärst.

481. Indirect Question

(a) If 'fragen' is present, future or imperative, it is normally followed by the indicative: Er fragt, ob Sie zu Hause sind. Frage ihn, wer ihm geholfen hat.

(b) If 'fragen' is past, it is normally followed by the subjunctive or conditional, with the same scheme of tenses as in 479 (see also 480):
'Ist Herr A. zu Hause?'—Er fragte, ob Sie zu Hause wären (seien).
'Was hast du verloren?'—Ich fragte ihn, was er verloren hätte (habe).
'Wann werden Sie Ihren Bruder sehen?'—Er fragte mich, wann ich meinen Bruder sehen würde.

482. Noun Clauses depending on indefinite verbs. Such are:

ahnen *to have a presentiment, to suspect*
annehmen *to assume*
denken *to think*

sich einbilden *to imagine* (generally erroneously)
erwarten* *to expect*

fühlen *to feel*
fürchten* *to fear*
glauben *to believe, think*
hoffen* *to hope*
hören *to hear*
meinen *to be of the opinion*
schreiben *to write*

träumen *to dream*
vermuten *to presume*
voraussetzen *to presuppose*
sich vorstellen *to imagine* (deliberately)
wünschen* *to wish*
zweifeln* *to doubt*

(a) If these verbs are present, future or imperative, the indicative is normally used in the noun clause: Er schreibt, daß er krank ist. Er wird glauben, daß ich krank bin.

(b) If these verbs are past, the subjunctive or conditional is normally used in the noun clause, with the same scheme of tenses as in 479 (see also 480):

Er glaubte, ich wäre (sei) krank   *He thought I was ill*
                              (Original thought: A. is ill)
Ich hörte, er hätte (habe) die Schlange   *I heard he killed the snake*
  getötet

Note: After the five verbs marked with an asterisk, only the Conversational Tense will always be correct, e.g.

Ich fürchtete, er würde zu spät   *I feared he would come too late*
  kommen

483. Noun Clauses depending on verbs denoting certainty. Such are:

bedauern *to regret*[1]
beweisen *to prove*
entdecken *to discover*
erfahren *to hear, learn* (as a fact)
sich erinnern *to remember*
es tut mir leid *I am sorry*[1]
feststellen *to ascertain, establish*

gewiß sein *to be certain*
herausfinden *to find out*
merken *to notice*
sehen *to see*
sicher sein *to be sure*
überzeugen *to convince*
wissen *to know*

After these verbs, the indicative is normally used in the noun clause:

Ich wußte, daß er es getan hat *I knew that he had done it*; ich weiß nicht, ob er krank ist; ich wußte nicht, daß er krank war; wenn ich nur wüßte, wo er geblieben ist! Ich entdeckte, daß er Frankfurt verlassen hatte; es tat ihm leid, daß er dich nicht gesehen hat.

Note:

i Where the context requires the conditional, the imperf. subj. is a common alternative (as in conditional clauses): Ich wußte nicht, ob er kommen würde/käme; cf. ich wollte wissen, wann er nach Hause käme (*when he was coming* (=*would come*) *home*).

ii Other deviations from wissen + indic. are not infrequent and are generally to be explained by sometimes subtle contextual factors. A straightforward instance may be cited:

Ich wußte nicht, ob er krank wäre/sei   *I didn't know if he were ill*
(introductory verb in the past + complete uncertainty)

iii Note the elliptical use of ob:

[Ich möchte wissen] Ob er mich   *Can he have misunderstood me after all?*
doch mißverstanden hat?

[1] denotes certainty in the sense that one regrets something that one regards as a fact.

484. Notes on 479–83

(a) **After many of the verbs listed in 482 and 483, an accusative and infinitive construction is frequently used in English**, e.g. I believed (presumed, expected, knew, discovered) him to be ill. **This is impossible in German**, where a clause must be used: Ich glaubte, er sei krank; ich wußte, daß er krank war. Compare:

Dies ist ein Buch, von dem ich weiß,   *This is a book that I know to be reliable*
daß es zuverlässig ist

(b) **The use of 'daß'**

  i In indirect statements and after the indefinite verbs,[1] the use of 'daß' is optional, except that it *must* be used after the indefinite verbs when they are negative and is more usual after 'sagen' or its equivalent when negative. Apart from this exception, the form without 'daß' is preferred before a subjunctive, especially in conversation.

Er sagte, er wäre krank/daß er krank wäre.
Er glaubte, ich wäre krank/daß ich krank wäre.
Er sagte nicht, daß er krank wäre.
Er glaubte nicht, daß ich krank wäre.

  ii Before an indicative practice varies, but it is in general commoner (and safer) to use 'daß', which, in the absence of a subjunctive, makes it clearer that here is a subordinate clause. After bedauern, beweisen, sich erinnern, es tut mir leid, feststellen, herausfinden and überzeugen, 'daß' is essential.

Ich wußte, daß er krank war (or: er war krank)
Ich habe herausgefunden, daß er jetzt in Berlin lebt.

  iii From ii it follows that not infrequently daß + indic. is an alternative to the subjunctive without 'daß': Er hat mir gesagt, er hätte sein Haus verkauft/daß er sein Haus verkauft hat.

(c) **The subjunctive may be required in a noun clause depending on a noun** (usually with 'daß' or some other introductory word) e.g. das Gerücht, daß . . ., meine Frage, ob . . .

(d) In reported speech in the subjunctive, all **subordinate clauses** that were part of the original direct statement or question go into the subjunctive, e.g.

Er sagte, er werde das Buch kaufen,   *He said he would buy the book, as his*
da sein Onkel, dessen Urteil er hoch   *uncle, whose judgement he greatly*
achte, es ihm empfohlen hätte   *respected, had recommended it to him*

But the reporter may independently add some information in a subordinate clause and this will go into the indicative:

Er sagte, er bewerbe sich um diese   *He said he was applying for this job, for*
Stelle, für die er gar nicht geeignet   *which he is not at all suitable*
ist

(e) **After 'hoffen' and 'wünschen', modals are sometimes used**:

Er hoffte, daß ich seinem Sohn helfen   *He hoped that I might help his son*
möge

Er wünschte, ich sollte ihm alles   *He wanted me to explain everything to him*
erklären

---

[1] zweifeln *to doubt*, used affirmatively, is followed by ob *whether*.

(f) **The subjunctive can neatly show that a statement is a reported one without the insertion or repetition of a verb of saying:**

Bei seiner Vernehmung berief sich H. auf Notwehr. Er sei mit S. in Streit geraten und habe sich von diesem bedroht gefühlt (*SZ*)

In the course of his cross-examination H. pleaded self-defence. He said he had become involved in a quarrel with S. and had felt himself to be threatened by him

Papa möchte auch gern selbst lenken, Mama will es aber nicht, weil es die Nerven angreife (R. Huch)

Daddy would also like to drive, but Mummy doesn't want him to, because, she says, it's a strain on the nerves

(g) In **hybrids of direct and indirect speech** such as the following, the subjunctive is used:

Der Laden, sagte er, sei erst seit kurzem eröffnet, mache aber schon ganz gute Geschäfte

The shop, he said, has only been going for a short time, but is already doing quite good business

(h) According to German grammarians,[1] the domain of the present subjunctive is reported speech, while the domain of the imperfect subjunctive is the hypothetical (Wenn ich ihm heute schriebe, . . .), the imagined (Ich träumte, ich wäre zu Hause), the erroneous (Ich dachte, der Zug führe eine Stunde später). While Erben and Duden are able to muster plentiful illustrations supporting this differentiation, they admit, and show, that it is by no means consistently adhered to. According to Duden the imperf. subj. may be used in indirect speech to imply a greater degree of scepticism towards the statement reported than would the pres. subj. (Gram. 6440 and 6668).

To the present writer all this seems too doctrinaire to be advocated as a basic guide-line. The following figures for the use of tenses in indirect speech resulted from an examination of Ricarda Huch's *Der letzte Sommer, eine Erzählung in Briefen* (1910), the correspondents being cultured people; cases where the choice was determined by the desirability of using a distinctive subjunctive form were ignored:

Literary Tenses (Pres., Perf., Fut. Subj.): 75
Conversational Tenses (Imperf., Pluperf. Subj., Condit.): 301

It is significant 1. that the most sustained use of the literary tenses occurs in an account of a serious political discussion (in the letter dated 28. Mai) and 2. that the imperf. subj. of weak verbs is frequently used even where the pres. subj. would supply a distinctive subjunctive form.

485. Deviations from the rules for the use of the Subjunctive in Indirect Speech given in 479–83

Introductory

As indicated in 478, the above rules for the use of the subjunctive in indirect speech and in other noun clauses are subject to variations and these must now be considered in some detail.

Basic to these deviations are the general considerations regarding the functions and use of indicative and subjunctive stated in 461(a)(b), which the user should re-read at this point. It should, however, be

---

[1] e.g. J. Erben: Zur Frage des Konjunktivs (*Zeitschrift für deutsche Sprache*, Band 22, Heft 3), with confirmatory references to W. Flämig, O. Behaghel and others; also Duden: Grammatik 6580 ff.

added that the subjunctive is the normal medium of reported speech and does not necessarily imply disbelief in, or disagreement with, the statement reported.

(a) Examples of the conversational tendency to replace the subjunctive by the indicative:

Er sagte, er schwimmt gern	*He said he likes swimming*
Ich sah nach, ob mein Vater noch schlief	*I had a good look whether my father was still asleep*
Er glaubte, ich war krank	*He thought I was ill*

We may repeat the well-tailored sentence given in 484(d) to illustrate the use of the subjunctive in the subordinate clauses of reported speech, followed by what it would probably become in workaday conversation:

Er sagte, er werde das Buch kaufen, da sein Onkel, dessen Urteil er hoch achte, es ihm empfohlen hätte.

Er sagte, er werde das Buch kaufen; sein Onkel hat es ihm nämlich empfohlen und anscheinend gibt er viel auf sein Urteil.

(b) Choice of indicative explained by its fundamental function:

Ich sagte ihm, von wo wir gekommen sind	*I told him where we've come from*

('where we've come from' represents a definite fact.)

Ich habe schon gehört, daß er angekommen ist	*I've already heard that he's arrived*

(the speaker has accepted his arrival as a fact.)

Ich fühlte, daß ich ihn beleidigt hatte	*I felt [pretty sure] that I had offended him*
Er ahnte nicht, was sich indessen ereignet hatte	*He did not suspect what had meanwhile occurred*

(the speaker is thinking of what actually did take place.)

(c) When the main verb is pres. tense but 3rd person, a subjunctive often follows, especially without 'daß'

i Miscellaneous instances:

Er sagt, er müsse (muß) nach Hause (BUT: Er sagt, daß er nach Hause muß)	*He says he's got to go home*
Man sagt, er sei gestorben (strong element of uncertainty)	*They say he's died*
Er glaubt, ich wär' (bin) krank	*He thinks I'm ill*
Er meint, es sei besser mit dem Auto zu fahren	*He thinks it's better to go by car*

('meinen' strongly indicates a personal opinion.)

Er schreibt, er sei krank	*He writes that he's ill*

(the sense of 'er schreibt' is past, not present.)

ii Where, in a narrative, sagen is used in a vivid historic present, which is thus the equivalent of 'sagte':

Und er sagt zu ihr, daß es besser sei, man verschwinde, ehe der Kerl zurück-komme (W. Heinrich).

iii In newspaper reporting; here the subjunctive (always the literary tenses) is used whatever the tense of the introductory verb:

Die Opposition behauptet, diese Politik sei verkehrt. Man müsse die Frage ganz anders anpacken.

(d) **Further illustrations of the use of indicative and subjunctive**:

Du sagst, du bist müde	*You say you're tired*
Sagst du, du wärst müde?	*Do you say you're tired?*

Er fragte mich, ob ich krank bin   *He asked me if I were ill*
  (Indic.: 1. indic. tends to replace subj. 2. the answer is known.)
Ich fragte ihn, ob er krank sei   *I asked him if he were ill*
  (Subj.: the answer is not known.)

Ich möchte wissen, ob er kommt	*I wonder if he's coming*
Ich fragte mich, ob er käme	*I wondered if he were coming*

Der Angeklagte konnte beweisen, daß er unschuldig war	*The accused was able to prove that he was innocent*
Der Angeklagte versuchte zu beweisen, daß er unschuldig sei	*The accused tried to prove that he was innocent*

Er erzählte mir, was er in Wiesbaden   *He told me what he did in Wiesbaden*
getan hat
  (Indic.: the emphasis is on what he actually did.)

Glauben Sie, ich hätte nichts davon   *Do you think I knew nothing about it?*
gewußt? (from Du. Gram.)
  (Subj., implying: but I did.)

i A. gab zu, daß Peter intelligent ist
ii A. gab zu, daß Peter intelligent wäre (sei)
  For the first reporter of A's admission, Peter's being intelligent is an
  accepted fact; the second reporter is subconsciously giving greater
  weight to the fact that he is reporting what A admitted.

R. VERBS FOLLOWED BY THE DATIVE

486. Introductory

As the name indicates, the dative case is the case of the recipient. As such,
it is occupied preponderantly by persons rather than things, persons to
whom something is given (shown, told, allowed etc.) or to whom
something pleasant or unpleasant, beneficial or injurious, is done. The
old concepts 'Dative of Advantage' and 'Dative of Disadvantage' are
helpful for getting the feel of the dative and its use; in some instances
the more neutral 'Dative of the Person Concerned' is more apt. In
many instances, the indirect (dative) object depends on the presence of a
direct (accusative) object; the latter may be a noun or pronoun, an infinitive-phrase or a subordinate clause (cf. examples in 488).

Note: The following are not included here:
i Verbs concerned with parts of the body and articles of clothing, where
  a pronoun in the dative is generally used instead of a possess. adj.:
  see 82(b)–(f).
ii Impersonal verbs and expressions taking the dative: see 372 ff.

487. Verbs of the basic type: to give something to someone, e.g. Er gab dem Lehrer den Bleistift.

Here may be included: an-bieten *to offer*, beweisen *to prove*, bringen *to bring*, empfehlen *to recommend*, leihen *to lend*, opfern *to sacrifice*, reichen *to hand, pass*, schenken *to present*, schicken *to send*, schulden *to owe*, vererben *to bequeath*, verkaufen *to sell*, zeigen *to show*, zu-flüstern *to whisper*, zu-teilen *to allot*.

jemandem ein Rätsel, eine Hausarbeit auf-geben	*to set s.o. a riddle, homework*
jemandem Mut, Vertrauen ein-flößen	*to inspire s.o. with e.g. courage, confidence*
jemandem etwas verschaffen	*to procure s.th. for s.o.*
and many analogous instances	

Note:

i beweisen:

Er bewies mir, daß . . .	*He proved to me that . . .*
Nichts konnte ihm bewiesen werden	*Nothing could be proved against him*

ii **bringen**: used in the sense of to take, it is followed by 'zu', e.g. Er hat seinen Sohn zum Arzt gebracht.

iii **schicken**: also used with an+acc., the effect being less personal, e.g. Schicken Sie ein Telegramm an den Minister (cf. Erben, op. cit., 122).

iv **vererben**: also used with an+acc., which gives greater emphasis to the legatee.

v **verkaufen**: also used with an+acc., which gives greater emphasis to the purchaser, e.g. Er hat sein Haus an einen Fabrikanten verkauft.

488. The personal object of verbs meaning to say, to tell, to answer, to advise, to command, to allow, to forbid, to obey, to forgive is in the dative; here, as generally in 487, there is frequently an indirect and a direct object, the latter being another noun or pronoun, an infinitive-phrase or a clause, e.g.

Der Arzt hat meinem Bruder Ruhe angeraten.
Das kann ich ihm nicht verzeihen.
Er riet mir, mein Haus zu verkaufen.
Er versicherte mir, daß er alles erledigt hätte.

Note:

i Most of these verbs may also be used only with a direct object, e.g. Wer hat das befohlen? Die Polizei hat die Versammlung erlaubt (more official: genehmigt)/verboten.

ii **antworten**: Er hat mir geantwortet; er hat auf meinen Brief/auf meine Frage geantwortet (or: Er hat meinen Brief/meine Frage beantwortet.)

iii Before the beginning of a quotation, 'sagen zu' is more usual: Dann sagte er zu mir: 'Du bist schuld daran.'

489. Examples of the dative of advantage (cf. 486 and 83)

jemandem seine Arbeit, ein Paket ab-nehmen	*to relieve s.o. of their work, of a parcel*
jemandem zur Verfügung stehen	*to be at s.o.'s disposal*
Das werde ich dir nie vergessen	*I shall never forget that you did that for me*

jemandem etwas vor-machen[1]	*to demonstrate s.th. to s.o.*
jemandem zugute kommen (s)	*to stand s.o. in good stead*
Seine lange Erfahrung kommt ihm nun zugute (Du. Stil.)	*His long experience now stands him in good stead*

490. Examples of the dative of disadvantage (cf. 486 and 83)

jemandem etwas auf-drängen	*to force s.th. on s.o.*
jemandem etwas rauben	*to rob s.o. of s.th.*
jemandem etwas verheimlichen (or verschweigen)	*to keep s.o. in ignorance of s.th.*
jemandem etwas zu-muten	*to demand or expect s.th. of s.o.*
Das kann man ihm nicht zumuten	*One cannot expect that of him*
jemandem zur Last fallen (s)	*to be a burden or charge on s.o.*

491. Examples of the dative of the person concerned (cf. 486)

jemandem etwas an-hören[2]	*to tell s.th. by s.o.'s speech*
Man kann ihm den Franzosen anhören	*You can tell by his accent that he's French*
jemandem etwas verdanken	*to be indebted to s.o. for s.th.*
jemandem etwas zu-schreiben	*to ascribe s.th. to s.o.*
jemandem etwas zu-trauen	*to credit s.o. with s.th.*
Ich hätte ihm mehr Vernunft zugetraut	*I should have credited him with more sense*

492. to escape (from): ent-+various verbs of motion+dat. (All are conjugated with sein.) E.g.

Der Name ist mir entfallen	*The name has escaped my memory*
Er ist der Gefahr/der Strafe entgangen	*He escaped the danger/the punishment*
Es ist mir nicht entgangen, daß . . . (Du. Stil.)	*It did not escape my notice that . . .*
Er ist den Wärtern entschlüpft	*He escaped from the warders*

Note:

i to escape from prison: aus dem Gefängnis aus-brechen, entfliehen, entwischen.

ii to escape from a cage: aus einem Käfig aus-brechen (for large, fierce animals), entwischen (for any animals).

iii For 'to escape' without either a noun in the dat. or a prepositional phr., entkommen and entweichen are most used, e.g. Die Polizei war sofort zur Stelle, aber die Diebe entkamen.

493. The following verbs, outside the preceding groups, also take the dative:

jemandem ab-sagen	*to refuse s.o.'s invitation*
jemandem ab-schreiben	1. *to refuse s.o.'s invitation*
	2. *to put s.o. off, to ask them not to come*
ähneln	*to resemble*
auf-fallen (s)	*to strike, astonish*
Sein merkwürdiges Benehmen ist mir aufgefallen	*I was struck by his strange behaviour*

---

[1] cf. 693, vor-: 2nd example

[2] cf. start of 515.

aus-weichen (s)	*to evade*
jemandem/einer Sache aus dem Wege gehen (s)	
begegnen (s)	*to meet* (by chance)[1]
bei-stehen	*to stand by, help*
bei-stimmen	*to agree with* (e.g. a suggestion)
bekommen (s)	*to agree with one* (of food)
danken	*to thank*
dienen	***to serve*** (e.g. one's master, the state, the truth)
Sie servierte das Mittagessen	BUT: *She served the lunch*
Sie bediehte die Gäste (mit Bier)	*She served the customers (with beer)*
drohen	*to threaten*
ein-fallen (s)	*to occur to* (one's mind), e.g.
Plötzlich fiel mir der Name ein	*Suddenly I remembered the name*
entgegen-gehen (s)	*to go to meet; to face* (e.g. difficulties)
entsagen	*to renounce*
entsprechen	*to correspond to*
fehlen	***to be lacking, missing***
Ihm fehlt der nötige Mut	*He lacks the necessary courage*
Er fehlt mir sehr	*I miss him a lot*
Was fehlt dir?	*What's wrong with you?*
Mir fehlt nichts	*There's nothing wrong with me*
folgen (s)	*to follow*[2]
frönen	*to be a slave to* (e.g. fashion, a vice), *to be addicted to*
gefallen	*to please* (see 278 iii)
gegenüber-stehen	*to stand opposite, face*
gehören	***to belong to*** (possession)
Diese Uhr gehört mir	*This watch belongs to me*
Er gehört zu unserm Klub	BUT: *He belongs to our club*
Er gehört unserm Klub an	
Dieses Feld gehört zu unserm Garten	*This field belongs to our garden*
genügen	*to suffice*
geraten (s)	*to succeed*, e.g.
Der Kuchen ist ihr gut geraten	*Her cake turned out well*
glauben	***to believe*** (a person)
Ich glaube ihm	*I believe him*
Das glaube ich ihm nicht	*I don't believe him (I don't believe that statement of his)*
Ich glaube diese Nachricht nicht	BUT: *I don't believe this news*
Ich glaube an ihn	*I believe (have faith) in him*
Er glaubt an Gespenster, an den Kommunismus, an sein Glück	*He believes in ghosts, in Communism, in his luck*
gleichen	*to be equal to; to resemble*
gleich-sehen	*to resemble*
jemandem etwas gönnen	*not to begrudge s.o. s.th.*, e.g.
Ich gönne ihm seinen langen Urlaub	*I'm pleased for him that he's got a long holiday*

---

[1] treffen (h) + Acc. = to meet by chance or by arrangement.
[2] to follow, succeed = folgen (s) auf + acc., e.g. Auf die Egmont-Ouvertüre folgte die siebte Sinfonie.

gratulieren	*to congratulate*
helfen	*to help*
imponieren	*to impress*
kondolieren	*to express one's sympathy with*
jemandem kündigen	*to give s.o. notice*
mißtrauen	*to distrust*
munden	*to taste good*, e.g.
Die Suppe hat mir gemundet	*I enjoyed the soup*
nach-jagen (s)[1]	*to pursue s.o.* (also fig. e.g. wealth, success)
nahe-gehen (s)	*to grieve, affect*, e.g.
Sein Tod ist mir (sehr) nahegegangen	*I felt his death keenly*
sich nahen, sich nähern	*to approach*
nutzen, nützen	*to benefit, be of use to*, e.g.
Das nützt mir nichts	*That's of no use to me*
passen	*to suit; to fit*
schaden	*to harm*
schmecken	*to taste good*: see 'munden'
schmeicheln	*to flatter*
schreiben[2]	*to write to*
sein	*to belong to* (regionally coll.) e.g.
Ist dieser Schirm dir?	*Is this umbrella yours?*
Was ist dir?	*What's the matter with you?*
Ihm ist etwas	*There's something the matter with him*
trauen	*to trust*
trotzen	*to defy*
voran-gehen (s)	*to go ahead of*
vor-beugen	*to forestall* (e.g. difficulties)
(sich) weh tun	*to hurt* (*o.s.*), e.g.
Du hast deinem Bruder weh getan	*You've hurt your brother*
Sein Bein tut ihm weh	*His leg hurts him*
Ich habe mir weh getan	*I've hurt myself*
sich widersetzen	*to oppose* (e.g. an order)
widersprechen	*to contradict*
widerstehen	*to resist*
winken	*to beckon, wave to*
jemandem zu-jubeln	*to cheer s.o.*
zu-reden[3]	*to urge, encourage s.o.* (*to do s.th.*)
zuvor-kommen (s)	*to anticipate, forestall*

494. Reflexive Verbs with the reflexive pronoun in the dative

(a) A large number of verbs and expressions in the preceding paragraphs may also be used reflexively, e.g.

Ich erlaubte mir, ihm zu widersprechen	*I allowed myself to contradict him*
Ich muß mir Arbeit verschaffen	*I must find work*
Ich habe mir zuviel zugemutet	*I've taken on too much*

---

[1] see also 693, nach-.

[2] Ich habe meinem Bruder (einen Brief) geschrieben; rather less personal: Ich habe (einen Brief) an den Betriebsleiter geschrieben (cf. Erben, op. cit., 122).

[3] see also 693: zu-.

(b) The following is a selection of commonly used refl. verbs (with refl. pronoun in dat.) which are not merely reflexive adaptations of verbs already given; the first four are exclusively reflexive:

sich etwas an-eignen	*to appropriate, acquire s.th.*
Er hat sich meinen Schirm angeeignet	*He's appropriated my umbrella*
sich ein-bilden	*to imagine* (generally erroneously)
sich gleich-bleiben (s)	*to remain unchanged*
sich etwas verbitten	*to refuse to tolerate s.th.*
Solche Bemerkungen verbitte ich mir	*I won't tolerate such remarks*
sich vor-nehmen, etwas zu tun	*to make up one's mind to do s.th.*
sich vor-stellen	*to imagine, visualize*

See also 679(a).

495. Accusative or Dative?

(a) **Ich klopfte ihm/ihn auf die Schulter**
Either is possible and Duden's distinction (Du. Haupt. p. 600) seems sound: ihm (which is commoner) gives greater emphasis to 'on the shoulder'; ihn gives greater emphasis to 'him'. Cf. Der Hund biß ihm/ihn ins Bein. Er schoß mir/mich ins Bein.

(b) **to imitate**
nach-ahmen in current usage takes the accusative not only meaning 'to mimic s.o.', but also meaning 'to follow s.o.'s example', e.g. Er versucht, seinen Bruder nachzuahmen.
nach-machen + acc. = to imitate, mimic, e.g. Er machte den Lehrer nach. It can, however, be used with a direct and an indirect object, e.g. Mein Söhnchen macht mir alles nach. Das soll mir einer nachmachen! *I defy anyone to do the same.*

(c) **Verbs with a double accusative**
i A double accusative is the normal construction with kosten and lehren, e.g.
Die Reise hat mich 900 Mark gekostet; es kostet meinen Vater viel Zeit; er lehrt mich Deutsch.

ii A dative of the person is, however, also to be found and heard, in the case of 'kosten' especially in figurative contexts, e.g.
Das kann ihm/ihn den Hals kosten; es hat ihm/ihn das Leben gekostet; es kostete ihm/ihn große Überwindung (*a great effort*)

iii A double accusative also occurs with fragen, e.g.
Er fragte mich etwas; er fragte mich allerlei Schwieriges.

496. The dative object of the active voice cannot be the subject of the passive; it is thus impossible to say: Er wurde von seinen Freunden geholfen.

(a) There are two exceptions:
i 'folgen' and particularly the participial phrase 'gefolgt von': Zwei Männer trugen die Bahre, gefolgt von Lene (G. Hauptmann).
ii the phrase 'Ich fühlte mich geschmeichelt' *I felt flattered.*

(b) In English, this prohibition generally does not apply (e.g. He had been promised a new bike); moreover, what is in German a dative object is often a direct object in English (e.g. His friends helped him). The resultant English passive sentences may be rendered in German in one of three ways:

i With verbs taking a direct and an indirect object, the direct object of the active version can be made the subject of the passive:

Ein neues Fahrrad war ihm von seinen   *He had been promised a new bike by his*
Eltern versprochen worden   *parents*
(or, with introductory es: Es war
ihm von seinen Eltern ein neues Fahrrad versprochen
worden)

ii The sentence can be turned into the active, with or without 'man':

Seine Freunde halfen ihm   *He was helped by his friends*
Man half ihm   *He was helped*

iii Most verbs taking the dative that are conjugated with 'haben' can be used impersonally in the passive (cf. 381)

Es wurde ihm (von seinen Freunden)   *He was helped* (*by his friends*)
geholfen (or: Ihm wurde (von seinen
Freunden) geholfen)
Es ist mir empfohlen worden,   *I have been recommended to visit Baden-*
Baden-Baden zu besuchen[1]   *Baden*
Es wird ihm nie widersprochen   *He is never contradicted*

The following verbs + dat., conjugated with 'sein', may be found in the impersonal passive, generally without the 'es': ausweichen, nachgehen, nachjagen, nachlaufen, nachsetzen, e.g.

Dem Feind wurde geschickt   *The enemy was skilfully evaded*
ausgewichen
Dem Problem ist nachgegangen   *The problem has been investigated*
worden

N.B. Reflexive Verbs cannot be used in the passive.

497. When the dative object is, in English, a gerundial phrase, in German a suitable noun must be supplied, followed by a 'daß' clause or an infin. phr. in apposition; often a free translation is a less cumbersome alternative or, as in the last two examples, the only satisfactory solution:

zu-schreiben *to ascribe*: see 455, last example.
vor-beugen *to forestall, guard against*
  I guarded against his finding out
  Ich beugte der Möglichkeit vor (or: Ich verhütete), daß er es herausfinden könnte.
sich widersetzen *to oppose*
  I opposed his being entrusted with the task
  Ich widersetzte mich dem Versuch, ihm diese Aufgabe anzuvertrauen.
  Ich war dagegen, daß man ihm diese Aufgabe anvertraute.
That is equal to ruining his life
  Das heißt sein Leben ruinieren.

---

[1] Strictly speaking, the 'es' is here not impersonal, but an introductory subject, the infinitive phrase being the real subject.

He escaped being interrogated
Er entging einem Verhör.
Er konnte es vermeiden, verhört zu werden.

S. VERBS FOLLOWED BY THE GENITIVE

498. Introductory

A verb used with the genitive tends to sound stilted, and alternative constructions or verbs are normally preferred in spoken German. (This applies least to reflexive verbs.) In literary and official German these verbs are by no means eschewed; it will be noted that a number of them are of a judicial character (cf. Du. Gram. 5320).

The following lists are confined to verbs which are still used in current German; wherever an alternative construction exists, it is given.

499. Non-reflexive Verbs used with the genitive

jemanden (wegen) eines Verbrechens an-klagen	*to accuse s.o. of a crime*
Er wurde wegen Diebstahl(s) angeklagt	*He was accused of theft*
bedürfen (conjug. like dürfen)	*to need, require*[1]
jemanden seines Geldes berauben jemandem sein Geld rauben	*to rob s.o. of their money*
jemanden eines Verbrechens beschuldigen or bezichtigen	*to accuse s.o. of a crime* (two official verbs)
entbehren	*to lack* (elev.)
Es entbehrte . . . der Folgerichtigkeit (H. Risse)	*It lacked consistency*[2]
gedenken	*to remember, recall* e.g.
Wir haben deiner gedacht	*We gave you a thought*
jemanden eines Verbrechens überführen	*to convict s.o. of a crime*
jemanden einer Sache versichern	*to assure s.o. of s.th.*
Ich versichere Sie meines Interesses	*I assure you of my interest*
jemanden einer Sache würdigen	*to deem s.o. worthy of s.th.* e.g.
Er würdigte mich seiner Freundschaft (from Betteridge op. cit.)	*He honoured me with his friendship*

500. Reflexive Verbs used with the genitive

sich jemandes/einer Sache an-nehmen	*to show interest in, assist, befriend s.o.; to take an interest in, look after a matter*
sich einer Sache bedienen[3]	*to use, make use of s.th.*
sich jemandes /einer Sache bemächtigen	*to gain possession of s.o. or s.th.*
sich einer Sache enthalten	*to abstain, refrain from s.th.* (e.g. laughter, criticism)

---

[1] normal conversational equivalents: ʼɔrauchen or nötig haben + Acc.
[2] BUT: Ich kann das Buch gegenwärtig nicht entbehren *I can't do without the book at present*; ich entbehre ihn sehr *I miss him very much*.
[3] commoner: benutzen + acc.

sich jemandes/einer Sache (less common: an jemanden etc.) entsinnen	to recollect s.o. or s.th.
sich jemandes erbarmen	to take pity, have mercy on s.o.
sich jemandes/einer Sache (or: an jemanden etc.) erinnern[1]	to remember s.o. or s.th.
sich einer Sache erwehren	to refrain from (e.g. laughter), to resist (e.g. an urge)
sich einer Sache rühmen	to boast of, pride o.s. on s.th.
sich jemandes (für jemanden)/ (wegen) einer Sache schämen	to be ashamed of s.o. or s.th.
sich einer Sache vergewissern (less common : über eine Sache)	to make sure of s.th. (e.g. the time of departure)
sich jemandes versichern	to make sure of, gain control of s.o.
sich einer Sache versichern	to make sure of, secure s.th. (e.g. s.o.'s consent)

501. Idiomatic uses of certain verbs with the genitive

sich bester Gesundheit erfreuen	to enjoy the best of health
sich eines guten Rufes erfreuen	to enjoy a good reputation
der Ruhe pflegen	to take a rest
Es spottet jeder Beschreibung	It beggars description
ehe ich mich dessen (or: mich's) versah	before I was aware of it, all of a sudden
seines Amtes walten	to discharge the duties of one's office; sometimes facetious, e.g.
Also, walte deines Amtes!	Now then, do your job
sich seines Lebens (or: seiner Haut) wehren	to fight for one's life
Er würdigte mich keines Blickes	He didn't deign to look at me

502. How to deal with verbs followed by the genitive when the 'genitive object' is, in English, a gerundial phrase or a noun clause. The following are the main relevant verbs:

(a) After an-klagen, beschuldigen, sich entsinnen, sich erinnern, sich rühmen, sich schämen, überführen, use zu + infin. or a 'daß' clause:

Er wurde beschuldigt, das Geld gestohlen zu haben	He was accused of stealing the money
Ich schämte mich, daß mein Bruder es getan hatte	I was ashamed at my brother's having done it

(b) sich enthalten: use sich davon zurückhalten + zu + infin.:

Ich hielt mich davon zurück, mich in seine Angelegenheiten einzumischen	I abstained from interfering in his affairs

(c) würdigen: use the corresponding noun:

Man würdigte ihn einer öffentlichen Ehrung	He was deemed worthy of being publicly honoured

(d) With the phrase 'sich (dat.) einer Sache bewußt sein', use dessen + 'daß' clause:

Ich bin mir dessen bewußt, daß ...	I am conscious (of the fact) that ...

[1] 'eine Sache erinnern' is regional; 'sich (dat.) eine Sache erinnern' is obsolete.

T. VERBS, ADJECTIVES AND NOUNS WITH PREPOSITIONAL CONSTRUCTIONS[1]

503. Examples

Ich verlasse mich auf deine Hilfe	*I am relying on your help*
Ich bin von diesem Geld abhängig	*I am dependent on this money*
Seine Empörung über den Zeitungsartikel war begreiflich	*His indignation at the newspaper article was understandable*

504. Where verbs with prepositional constructions are directed not at a noun or pronoun, but at something happening or being done (frequently a gerund in English), normal usage is to prefix da (or dar, before a vowel) to the preposition, followed by an infinitive phrase, with 'zu', where the subject of the infinitive is the same as the subject of the introductory verb and by a 'daß' clause where the subject changes.

The same applies, mutatis mutandis, in the case of adjectives and nouns with prepositional constructions.

Ich verlasse mich darauf, ihn zu Hause zu finden	*I rely on finding him at home*
Ich verlasse mich darauf, daß er alles arrangiert	*I rely on his arranging everything*
Ich bin davon abhängig, dieses Geld zu bekommen	*I am dependent on receiving this money*
Ich bin davon abhängig, daß mir mein Bruder hilft	*I am dependent on my brother helping me*
Seine Empörung darüber, niemand zu Hause zu finden, war begreiflich	*His indignation at finding no one at home was understandable*
Seine Empörung darüber, daß wir ihm nichts davon gesagt hatten, war begreiflich	*His indignation at our not having told him anything about it was understandable*

Note:

i It would not be wrong to have a 'daß' clause in the first, third and fifth of the above examples, e.g. Ich verlasse mich darauf, daß ich ihn zu Hause finde.

ii An infinitive phrase may also be used where its subject is the same as the object of the introductory verb:

Er hinderte mich daran, den Brief zu schreiben	*He hindered me from writing the letter*
Ich werde meinen Freund davor warnen, es zu tun	*I shall warn my friend against doing it*

iii da + prep. is enclosed in a compound tense, a subordinate clause or an infinitive phrase:

Ich hatte mich darauf verlassen, daß er kommen würde.
Obwohl ich mich darauf verlasse, ihn zu Hause zu finden, . . .
Anstatt mich darauf zu verlassen, daß er es tun wird, . . .

---

[1] This section owes much to Gunnar Bech, op. cit. Regarding the position of the prepositional phrase, see 653 N.ii and 658(c).

505. Deviations from the rule and examples given in 504

i with a large number of verbs, adjectives and nouns the inclusion of da + prep. is optional.
ii with a small number da + prep. is omitted.

Examples of i

Ich ärgerte mich (darüber), daß er so wenig getan hatte	*I was annoyed that he had done so little*
Ich bin (davon) überzeugt, daß er sein Bestes tut	*I'm convinced that he's doing his best*
Er hat eine Abneigung (dagegen), Einkäufe zu machen	*He has an aversion to doing shopping*

(See 509, List A).

Note: The inclusion or omission of da + prep. is purely a matter of personal choice; its inclusion tends to produce a more intensive effect, while its omission is a shade more colloquial.

Examples of ii

Ich hoffe auf seine Unterstützung; ich hoffe, ihn heute zu sprechen; ich hoffe, daß du kommen wirst.
Ich war überrascht über seinen Sinn für Humor; ich war überrascht, ihn zu sehen; ich war überrascht, daß er da war.
meine Bitte um Geld; meine Bitte, ihn zu sprechen, wurde mir gewährt.
(See 510, List B).

506. Where the preposition is 'wegen', a 'weil' clause is used, sometimes heralded by 'deswegen':

Er machte mir Vorwürfe (*reproached me*) wegen meiner Faulheit.
Er machte mir (deswegen) Vorwürfe, weil ich alles vergessen hatte.

Where 'für' is an alternative to 'wegen', 'dafür, daß' is preferable:

Ich lobte ihn wegen seines Fleißes/für seinen Fleiß.
Ich lobte ihn dafür, daß er alles erledigt hatte.

507. After some verbs, adjectives and nouns, the clause is introduced not by daß, but by some interrogative word, e.g. ob *whether*, wie, wann, wer, was. This arises naturally from the sense, e.g.

Ich dachte darüber nach, ob ich es unternehmen könnte/wie ich ihm helfen könnte/was er wohl dazu sagen würde.

508. The lists that follow cannot aim at completeness, but at the inclusion of most relevant words in common use. Verbs predominate as it is with them that prepositional constructions are most frequently used. After most verbs, adjectives and nouns not included in Lists A and B, the inclusion of da + prep. is essential.

509. List A: i Verbs ii Adjectives and Participles iii Nouns after which the inclusion of da + prep. is optional

i ab-halten (davon) zu *to deter*, jemandem ab-raten (davon) zu *to advise against*, acht-geben (darauf) zu/daß *to take care*, sich amüsieren (darüber) zu/daß/wie *to be amused*, sich ärgern (darüber) zu/daß *to be annoyed*, auf-fordern (dazu) zu *to invite s.o.* (e.g. to accompany one), auf-passen (darauf), daß *to take care,* autorisieren (dazu) zu *to authorize s.o. to do s.th.*

sich beklagen (darüber), daß *to make a complaint about,* benutzen/gebrauchen (dazu) (um) zu *to use in order to,* betteln (darum) zu/daß *to beg* (e.g. to be allowed to do s.th. or that s.o. should help one), (dazu) da-sein, um . . . zu *to be there in order to,* sich einigen (darüber), daß *to reach agreement,* ein-laden (dazu) zu *to invite,* es ekelt mich (davor) zu *it fills me with abhorrence,* sich entscheiden (dafür) zu *to decide to,* sich entschließen (dazu) zu *to make up one's mind,* erinnern (daran) zu/daß *to remind,* sich erinnern (daran), daß *to remember that,* BUT: sich erinnern daran zu ('daran' is essential) *to remember to*

sich freuen (darüber) zu/daß *to be glad,* sich fürchten (davor) zu *to be afraid,* sich (dazu) herab-lassen zu *to condescend,* hindern (daran) zu *to hinder, prevent,* sich hüten (davor) zu *to take care not to,* jammern (darüber), daß *to lament that,* klagen (darüber), daß *to complain*

sich schämen (darüber) zu/daß *to be ashamed,* sich scheuen (davor) zu *to shrink from* (doing s.th. unpleasant), sich sehnen (danach) zu *to long to,* sich sträuben (dagegen) zu/dagegen, daß *to oppose, boggle at,* sich streiten (darüber), wer, wieviel etc. *to quarrel about who, how much etc.,* mit jemandem (darin) überein-stimmen, daß *to agree with s.o. that,* überzeugen (davon), daß *to convince,* urteilen (darüber), ob, wie gut etc. *to judge whether, how good etc.,* sich wundern (darüber) zu/daß *to be surprised*

ii ärgerlich (darüber) zu/daß *annoyed,* empört (darüber) zu/daß *indignant,* entsetzt (darüber) zu/daß *shocked,* enttäuscht (darüber) zu/daß[1] *disappointed,* entzückt (darüber) zu/daß[1] *delighted,* erfreut (darüber) zu/daß *pleased,* erstaunt (darüber) zu/daß[1] *astonished,* froh (darüber) zu/daß[1] *glad,* (dazu, dafür) geeignet sein zu *to be fitted to,* (darauf) gespannt sein zu *to be (expectantly) eager to,* (darauf) gespannt sein, ob *to wonder whether,* stolz (darauf) zu/daß *proud,* traurig (darüber) zu/daß[1] *sad,* überzeugt (davon), daß *convinced,* unentschieden (darüber), ob, wer, wann etc. *undecided,* vorbereitet (darauf) zu/daß *prepared*

iii ein Abkommen (darüber) zu/daß *an (official) agreement,* eine Abneigung (dagegen) zu *aversion,* Angst haben (davor) zu/daß *to be afraid,* Aussicht haben (darauf) zu *to have prospects of,* eine Beschwerde (darüber), daß *complaint,* die Empörung (darüber), daß *indignation,* das Erstaunen (darüber) zu/daß *astonishment,* die Freude (darüber) zu/daß *joy, pleasure,* aus Furcht (davor), daß *for fear that,* der Gedanke (daran) zu/daß *thought,* der Grund (dafür), daß *reason,* die Sehnsucht (danach) zu *longing,* sich Sorgen machen (darum), daß, ob etc. *to worry,* die Überraschung (darüber) zu/daß *surprise,* das Verlangen (danach) zu *desire, craving,* im Zweifel sein (darüber), ob *to be in doubt*

510. List B: i Verbs ii Adjectives and Participles iii Nouns after which da + prep. is omitted

i an-klagen wegen (Er wurde angeklagt, das Geld gestohlen zu haben) jemanden um etwas bemühen (Dürfte ich Sie bemühen, ihm dies zu geben?)
bitten um (Ich bat ihn, mir zu helfen)
erzählen von/über (Er erzählte uns, daß . . .)
hoffen auf (Ich hoffe, es zu tun; ich hoffe, daß . . .)

ii begeistert von *in raptures about* (Er war begeistert, sie zu sehen)

---

[1] generally without darüber in both constructions.

begierig nach (Ich bin begierig, ihn zu sehen; ich bin begierig (zu erfahren),
 ob ... *anxious to hear*)
bereit zu (Ich bin bereit, es zu tun)
böse über (Ich war böse, daß er nicht gekommen war)
enttäuscht über/von (Ich war enttäuscht, ihn nicht zu sehen/daß er nicht
 da war)
neugierig auf *curious as to, anxious to know* (Ich bin neugierig, ob er kommen
 wird; ich bin neugierig (zu hören), was er dazu sagt)
überrascht über (Ich war überrascht, ihn zu sehen/daß ...)

iii Angst haben um *to be anxious about* (Ich hatte Angst, daß er sich erkälten
 könnte *I was afraid lest ...*)
die Anklage wegen (die Anklage, Geld gestohlen zu haben)
der Anlaß, die Veranlassung zu *occasion, cause for* (Ich habe keine Veranlassung, ihm Geld zu geben)
die Bitte um (Er ignorierte meine Bitte, pünktlich zu sein)
die Furcht vor (seine Furcht, beschwindelt zu werden)
eine Gelegenheit zu *an opportunity for* (Ich hatte keine Gelegenheit, mit ihm
 zu sprechen)
die Hoffnung auf (meine Hoffnung, ihn zu sehen/daß er kommen würde)
eine Neigung zum Pessimismus *inclination, proneness to* (seine Neigung,
 alles zu kritisieren)
das Recht auf (das Recht zu streiken)

511. Some special cases

i the idiomatic use of 'dazu' with the following verbs:[1]
Er hat mich dazu gebracht *induced me*, (dazu) erzogen *brought me up*, dazu
getrieben *driven me*, (dazu) überredet *persuaded me*, dazu verführt *en-
ticed me*, dazu verleitet *led me astray*, (dazu) gezwungen *forced me*
es zu tun.

Er ist (dazu) geboren, Künstler zu sein	*He is born to be an artist*
Wie kommt er nur dazu, so was zu tun?	*However did he come to do such a thing?*
Ich bin dazu verurteilt, seine Launen hinzunehmen	*I am condemned to put up with his whims*

ii streben nach *to strive after*

Er strebte (danach), anerkannt zu werden	*He strove to win recognition* (recognition = a desired goal)
Er strebte, seinen Mitmenschen zu helfen	*He strove to help his fellow-men* (continuous endeavour)

iii träumen von *to dream of*

Er träumte davon, einmal Italien zu sehen	*He dreamt of seeing Italy some day* (= hoped to)
Er träumte, daß man ihm gekündigt hätte	*He dreamt that he had been given notice* (= an actual dream)

iv warnen vor + dat. *to warn about or against*

Er warnte mich davor, allein in die Stadt zu gehen	*He warned me against going into the town alone*

[1] cf. Gunnar Bech, op. cit., 289, and 613(f) in this book.

Er warnte mich, nicht allein in die Stadt zu gehen	*He warned me not to go into the town alone*
Er warnte mich (davor), daß der Chef es übelnehmen könnte	*He warned me that the director might take it badly*

N.B. similarly after 'seine Warnung'.

v zweifeln an + dat. *to doubt*

Ich zweifle (nicht) an seiner Ehrlichkeit	*I doubt (do not doubt) his honesty*
Ich zweifle nicht (daran), daß er kommen wird	*I don't doubt that he will come*
Ich zweifle, ob er kommen wird	BUT: *I doubt if he will come*

U. THE USE OF THE ANTICIPATORY 'ES'[1]

512. The use of 'es' to anticipate zu + infin. or a 'daß' clause

(a) The following are typical examples of verbs having zu + infin. or a 'daß' clause as their object:

Er begann zu singen; er versprach zu kommen; er erlaubte mir, nach Hause zu gehen.

Ich wußte, daß er krank war; er versprach, daß ich alles sehen sollte; er wollte, daß mein Bruder kommen sollte.

(b) After some such verbs, the infinitive phrase or the 'daß' clause is regularly or usually anticipated by an accusative 'es', to which the infinitive phrase or the 'daß' clause is in apposition:

Ich konnte es kaum ertragen, ihn so leiden zu sehen	*I could hardly endure to see him suffer so*
Evelyn hatte es abgelehnt zu essen (V. Baum)	*Evelyn had declined to have lunch*
Ich konnte es nicht ertragen, daß er so litt	*I could not endure that he should suffer so*
Ich habe es erlebt, daß Riemann die beste Rede gehalten hat	*I've known Riemann to give the best speech*

(c) After others, the anticipatory 'es' is optional:

Er hat (es) unternommen, einen neuen Plan zu entwerfen	*He has undertaken to draw up a new plan*
Er will (es) verhindern, daß die Kundgebung stattfindet	*He wants to prevent the demonstration from taking place*

(d) There is no 'es':

   i if, for the sake of emphasis, the infinitive phrase or the 'daß' clause is placed at the beginning of the sentence, but 'das', in apposition to the inf. phr. or the 'daß' clause, is possible: Ihn so leiden zu sehen, (das) konnte ich kaum ertragen.

   ii if the infin. phrase is enclosed in a main sentence or in a subordinate clause: Ich habe ihn zu warnen unternommen; ich fragte ihn, ob er zu singen abgelehnt hätte.

513. Notes on the lists that follow:

   i They cannot aim at completeness, but at including a high proportion of relevant verbs in common use.

[1] This section owes much to Gunnar Bech, op. cit.

ii Verbs of which the English equivalent has 'it' corresponding to the German 'es' are not included, e.g.

es jemandem ermöglichen zu	*to make it possible for s.o. to do s.th.*
es für ratsam halten zu	*to consider it advisable to*
es zustande/zuwege bringen, daß	*to bring it about that*

iii With a few verbs 'wie' is substituted for 'daß', as required by the sense, e.g. erklären *to explain.*

514. List A: Verbs after which the anticipatory 'es' is essential or usual

es ab-lehnen zu	*to decline to do s.th.*
es jemandem hoch an-rechnen, daß	*to think highly of s.o. for doing s.th.*, e.g.
Ich rechne es ihm hoch an, daß er dieses Opfer gebracht hat	*I think highly of him for making this sacrifice*
es aus-halten zu/daß	*to endure doing s.th./that . . .*
es über sich bringen zu	*to bring o.s. to do s.th.*
es durch-setzen zu/daß	*to succeed (in the face of opposition) in doing s.th. or in arranging that*
es eilig haben zu	*to be in a hurry to do s.th.*
es erleben, daß	*to have known s.th. to happen, to live to see s.th. happen*
es erreichen zu/daß	*to manage to do s.th.*
es jemandem ersparen zu	*to save s.o.'s having to do s.th.*
es ertragen zu/daß	*to endure doing s.th./that . . .*
es fertig-bringen zu	*to manage to do s.th.*
es genießen zu	*to enjoy doing s.th.*
es lassen zu	*to refrain from doing s.th.*, e.g.
Ich konnte es nicht lassen, dies zu tun	*I couldn't refrain from doing this*
es leicht haben, zu	*to be easy for s.o. to do s.th.*, e.g.
Ich hatte es leicht, ihn zu überzeugen	*It was easy for me to convince him*
es leid sein zu	*to be tired of doing s.th.*
es sich leisten können zu	*to be able to afford to do s.th.*
es lieben zu	*to love doing s.th.*
es jemandem nach-tragen, daß	*to bear s.o. a grudge for having done s.th.*
es (nicht) nötig haben zu	*(not) to need to do s.th.*
es satt haben zu	*to be sick of doing s.th.*
es unterlassen zu	*to omit doing s.th.*
es jemandem nicht verdenken, wenn	*not to blame s.o. for doing s.th.* e.g.
Man kann es ihm nicht verdenken, wenn er protestiert	*He can't be blamed for protesting*
es verlernen zu	*to forget how to do s.th.*
es verschmähen zu	*to disdain to do s.th.*
es verstehen zu	*to know how to do s.th.*
Ich habe es ihm zugute gehalten, daß er alles offen zugab	*I took into favourable consideration the fact that he frankly admitted everything*
es jemandem zu-muten zu	*to expect s.o. to do s.th.*, e.g.
Man kann es diesem alten Mann nicht zumuten, Überstunden zu machen.	*One cannot expect this old man to work overtime*

515. List B: Verbs after which the anticipatory 'es' is optional

(es) sich ab-gewöhnen zu	*to break o.s. of doing s.th.*
(es) sich an-gewöhnen zu	*to become accustomed to doing s.th.*
(es) jemandem an-hören, daß	*to tell by s.o.'s speech that*, e.g.

Man kann (es) ihm anhören, daß er Franzose ist	*You can tell by his accent that he's French*
(es) jemandem an-merken, daß	*to notice that* (e.g. s.o. is tired)
(es) jemandem an-sehen, daß	*to tell from s.o.'s appearance that* (e.g. they have been ill)
(es) auf-geben zu	*to give up doing s.th.*
(es) auf-schieben zu	*to put off doing s.th.*
(es) begreifen, daß/warum	*to grasp (comprehend) that/why*
(es) bereuen zu/daß	*to repent, regret having done s.th./that . . .*
(es) erfassen, daß	*to grasp (comprehend) that . . .*
(es) gewohnt sein zu/daß	*to be used to doing s.th/that . . .*
(es) jemandem gönnen, daß	*to be glad for s.o. that, e.g.*
Ich gönne (es) ihm, daß er wieder ausgehen kann	*I'm glad for him that he can go out again*
(es) lernen zu/wie	*to learn (how) to do s.th., e.g.*
Ich habe (es) gelernt, ihn taktvoll zu behandeln	*I've learnt to treat him tactfully*
(es) leugnen, daß	*to deny that . . .*
(es) unternehmen zu	*to undertake to do s.th.*
(es) jemandem verbieten zu	*to forbid s.o. to do s.th.*
(es) jemandem vergeben, daß	*to forgive s.o. for doing s.th.*
(es) jemandem verheimlichen, daß	*to conceal from s.o. that . . .*
(es) verhindern, daß	*to prevent s.th. happening*
(es) vermeiden zu/daß	*to avoid doing s.th. or s.th. happening*
(es) vermögen zu	*to be able to do s.th.*
(es) versäumen zu	*to omit or miss doing s.th.*
(es) jemandem verschweigen, daß	*not to tell s.o. that . . .*
(es) jemandem verzeihen, daß	*to pardon s.o. for doing s.th.*
(es) vor-ziehen zu	*to prefer to do s.th.*
(es) wagen zu	*to dare or venture to do s.th.*
(es) jemandem zu-trauen zu	*to believe s.o. capable of doing s.th.*

XII CONJUNCTIONS

A. INTRODUCTORY NOTE

516. Note: Some textbooks include in their chapter on Conjunctions a class known as **Adverbial Conjunctions**, e.g. jedoch *however, nevertheless*, dagegen *on the other hand*, deshalb *therefore*, sonst *else*. When they stand at the beginning of a sentence, these are normally followed by inversion. In this book they are regarded as adverbs. Where they require comment or illustration, they are dealt with elsewhere; the Index should be consulted.

B. THE SIX SIMPLE CO-ORDINATING CONJUNCTIONS

517. The simple co-ordinating conjunctions are:

und[1] *and*	aber *but*	sondern *but* (*on the contrary*)
oder[1,2] *or*	allein *but*	denn *for* (*because*)

Where they introduce a clause, they take normal order unless they are followed by something other than the subject (cf. 642(d)).

518. 'aber' may also stand inside a sentence with the sense of 'however':

Alle verloren den Kopf; er aber blieb
ganz ruhig
Everyone lost their head, but he (or: *he, however,*) *remained quite calm*

Where two verbs have the same subject, 'aber' is frequently used in this way, being placed after the second verb:

Er runzelte die Stirn, sagte aber
nichts (more idiomatic than: aber
sagte nichts)[3]
He frowned but said nothing

N.B. For 'aber' as a particle, see 284.

519. aber and sondern[4]

sondern is only used after a negative and then only when a wrong idea is

---

[1] for punctuation, see 743(a).
[3] cf. Erben, op. cit., 186.

[2] for agreement rules, see 524(c).
[4] for punctuation, see 743(b).

replaced by a correct one;[1] in other words, nicht . . ., sondern . . . presents two ideas which are incompatible:

Er ist nicht reich, sondern arm	*He is not rich, but poor*
Wir gingen nicht ins Kino, sondern arbeiteten im Garten	*We didn't go to the cinema, but worked in the garden*

aber, too, may be used after a negative, but nicht . . ., aber . . . presents two ideas which are compatible, which may co-exist (cf. 657(d)iiN):

Er ist nicht reich, aber ehrlich	*He is not rich but honest*
Wir gingen nicht ins Kino, aber wir wollten doch nicht zu Hause bleiben	*We didn't go to the cinema, but yet we didn't want to stay at home*

Note: 'nicht nur' is always followed by 'sondern auch' (see 523 ff.).

520. allein is rather literary; its characteristic use is to introduce, or explain, the non-fulfilment of a hope or expectation;[2] it is lightly stressed, in contrast with allein *alone, only*. For punctuation, see 743(b).

Ich hatte gehofft, ihn nach der Sitzung zu sprechen, allein er war nicht zugegen	*I had hoped to speak to him after the meeting, but he was not present*

521. denn,[3] as a co-ordinating conjunction, is the exact equivalent of English 'for'. Thus a 'denn' clause can never precede the clause with which it is co-ordinate, nor can it be used alone: Er kann nicht kommen, denn er hat Grippe. Warum ist er nicht gekommen? Weil er Grippe hat.

522. und and sondern are sometimes omitted between two sentences, as a stylistic device, e.g. Julika holt Aschenbecher in der Art einer Gastgeberin, [und] bittet mit Geste, Platz zu nehmen (M. Frisch).

C. CO-ORDINATING CONJUNCTIONAL PHRASES[4]

523. Co-ordinating conjunctional phrases

sowohl . . . als (auch) sowohl . . . wie (auch) sowie (auch)	*as well as, both . . . and*
nicht nur . . ., sondern auch	*not only . . ., but also*
entweder . . . oder	*either . . . or*
weder . . . noch	*neither . . . nor*
sei es, daß/weil . . ., sei es, daß/weil[5]	*whether . . . or whether*

[1] cf. W. J. Hearn and G. Seidmann, *Graded German Composition* (Macmillan, 1966) 97, Note 3.
[2] cf. Du. Synonymwörterbuch: aber etc.
[3] for denn as a particle see 289.
[4] for punctuation see 743(b)(c) (d) Exc..
[5] somewhat literary.

(gleichviel,) ob . . . oder (ob)   *whether . . . or (whether)*
teils . . ., teils   *partly . . ., partly*

524. Agreement of verb with singular and plural subjects

(a) After sowohl . . . als (auch), sowohl . . . wie (auch) and sowie (auch),
the verb is generally plural, even when they connect two singular
subjects:
Sowohl mein Bruder als auch meine Schwester sind dagegen; A. sowie (auch)
B. sind dagegen

(b) After weder . . . noch and teils . . ., teils the verb is generally singular
if both subjects are singular, otherwise plural:
Weder mein Bruder noch meine Schwester ist dagegen; weder meine Brüder noch
meine Schwester sind dagegen

(c) Where nicht nur . . ., sondern auch, entweder . . . oder or oder alone
connect two singular subjects, the verb is singular: Entweder Hans
oder Karl wird mir helfen; where they connect one singular and one
plural subject, the verb agrees with the nearer subject: Entweder
Hans oder seine Brüder werden mir helfen; where both subjects are
plural, the verb is, of course, plural. (In the case of (entweder . . .)
oder there is no deviation from this practice.)

525. Agreement of verb where the subjects differ in person

The following examples should cover most contingencies:
Sowohl mein Bruder wie auch ich sind dagegen.
Nicht nur meine Brüder, sondern auch ich bin dagegen.
Entweder du hast recht oder ich.
Weder mein Bruder noch ich sind dagegen.
Ob du es tust oder ich, ist einerlei.

526. Word order in two sentences joined by the co-ordinating conjunctional phrases

(a) sowie (auch): normal order in main clause, verb to end in the 'sowie'
clause:
Ich bewundere ihn, sowie ich ihn   *I admire as well as fear him*
auch fürchte

(b) nicht nur . . ., sondern auch: inversion in the first, normal order in the
second:
Ich bleibe zu Hause: nicht nur regnet   *I'm staying at home: not only is it rain-*
es, sondern ich habe auch viel zu   *ing, but also I've got a lot to do*
tun

(c) entweder . . . oder: inversion in the first, normal order in the second:
Entweder leihst du mir das Geld,   *Either you lend me the money or I shall*
oder ich gebe den Plan auf   *give up the plan*

Note: Normal order is possible in the first, giving the whole a more
menacing note.

(d) weder . . . noch: inversion in both:

Weder habe ich seinen Brief bekommen, noch habe ich sonst von ihm gehört	*Neither did I receive his letter, nor did I hear from him in any other way*

(e) (gleichviel) ob . . . oder (ob): verb to the end in both; a following main clause has normal order:

Ob er nun krank ist oder nicht kommen will, er hat jedenfalls abgesagt	*Whether he's ill or doesn't want to come, in any case he's refused the invitation*

(f) teils . . ., teils: inversion in both.

527. nor (without a preceding neither) may generally be rendered by 'noch'; 'auch nicht' or 'auch kein' are common alternatives:

Ich kenne nicht ihn noch seinen Bruder (or: Ich kenne ihn nicht und auch seinen Bruder nicht)	*I don't know him nor (or) his brother*[1]
Sie ist nicht sehr hübsch, noch hat sie Geld (or: und hat auch kein Geld)	*She's not very pretty nor has she any money*

Only 'auch nicht' is possible in the following:

Ich mag ihn nicht sehr.—Ich auch nicht	*I don't like him much.—Nor I (either)*

N.B.

Ich sagte, ich hätte es nicht getan, und das stimmte auch	*I said I hadn't done it, nor had I*

D. SUBORDINATING CONJUNCTIONS

528. Introductory notes on the subordinating conjunctions

i Survey of types
1. Conjunctions of Time 529–35
2. Conjunctions of Place 536 f.
3. Conjunctions of Manner and Degree 538–42
4. Causal Conjunctions 543 f.
5. Consecutive Conjunctions 545 f.
6. Final Conjunctions 467
7. Conditional Conjunctions 462–5
8. Concessive Conjunctions 470–74

Within each type, the conjunctions are arranged in the alphabetical order of the English equivalents, except for types 2 and 8.

ii All these introduce subordinate clauses, with the verb at the end.

iii Unless indicated, they are normally followed by the indicative. The main exception occurs when they form part of reported speech: see 484(d).

iv For ob *whether* and daß *that* introducing noun clauses, see the section on Indirect Speech, especially 481 and 484(a)–(c).

[1] while 'or' would here be more usual in English, 'oder' could not be used in German.

E. CONJUNCTIONS OF TIME

529. Conjunctions of time

nachdem *after*
wie, indem, als *as (while, when)*
solang(e) *as long as*
sooft *as often as, whenever*
sobald, sowie *as soon as*
bevor, ehe *before*
kaum (daß) *hardly . . . when,*
  no sooner . . . than

seitdem, seit *since*
bis *till, until; by the time*
wann, als, wenn, *when*
da, wo
während *while*
(indes, indessen) *while*

530. Notes on conjunctions of time

(a) as (while, when)

i 'wie' is commonly used in this sense, but is mildly colloquial.

ii 'indem' can only be used, and 'wie' should only be used, when the action of the time clause is simultaneous with that of the main clause: Indem/Wie ich mir die Sache überlegte, kamen mir mancherlei Zweifel.

(b) as long as

i stylistically, 'solange' is preferable to 'solange als' or 'solange wie'.

ii 'solang(e)' may have a purely temporal sense (1st example) or a temporal-cum-conditional sense (2nd example), but not a purely conditional sense (3rd example):

Solange ich zu Hause war, hat niemand angerufen	*As long as I was at home, no one rang up*
Solange er sein Bestes tut, bin ich zufrieden	*As long as he does his best, I shall be satisfied*
Wenn er nur heute pünktlich kommt, wird alles klappen	*As long as he's punctual today, everything will be all right*

iii see 532(d)

(c) as often as, whenever

Sooft er kam, brachte er uns Geschenke	*Whenever he came, he brought us presents*

This purely temporal sense of 'whenever' must be distinguished from its concessive use, treated in 471, e.g. Whenever he may arrive, I want to speak to him at once.

(d) as soon as

i stylistically, 'sobald' is preferable to 'sobald als' or 'sobald wie'.
ii 'sowie' is common in conversation.

(e) before and till (see also 468)

When the main clause is negative, a pleonastic 'nicht' is frequently inserted in the subordinate clause:

Ehe (or Bis) du das nicht getan hast, brauchst du nicht nach Hause zu kommen	*You needn't come home before (or until) you've done that*

531. hardly . . . when, no sooner . . . than

(a) the conjunctional phrase 'kaum daß':

Kaum daß wir das Wirtshaus erreicht hatten, begann es zu regnen (or: als es zu regnen begann)	*No sooner had we reached the inn than it began to rain*

(b) Commoner than (a) are the following alternative versions in which kaum is an adverb:

Kaum hatten wir das Wirtshaus erreicht, (so) begann es zu regnen.
Wir hatten das Wirtshaus kaum erreicht, als (*when*) es zu regnen begann.

(c) With any of these constructions, the swift sequence of events may be emphasized by inserting 'auch schon': Wir hatten das Wirtshaus kaum erreicht, als es auch schon zu regnen begann.[1]

(d) 'kaum daß' (in (a) above) must be distinguished from the restrictive phrase 'kaum, daß' (cf. Du. Haupt. p. 337):

Ich kann dir kein Geld leihen; kaum, daß ich für mich selber genug habe (commoner: ich habe kaum für mich selber genug)	*I can't lend you any money—I've hardly got enough for myself*

532. since

(a) 'seitdem' is used rather more than 'seit'.

(b) When the since clause refers to a state or activity beginning in the past and still continuing, the present tense is used in German. The same applies to the main clause with the following qualifications:

i When a series of actions or states is referred to, the perfect is used (3rd example) unless it is desired to indicate a continuing habit (4th example).

ii When the main clause is negative, the perfect is used (5th example) except in cases of clear continuity (6th example).

1. Seitdem ich die Tabletten (nicht mehr) nehme, fühle ich mich wohler	*Since I've (no longer) been taking the tablets, I've been feeling better*
2. Seitdem er sein Haus verkauft hat,[2] wohnt er in einem Hotel	*Since he sold his house, he's been living in a hotel*
3. Seitdem ich ihn kenne, ist er mehrmals krank gewesen	*Since I've known him, he has been ill several times*
4. Seitdem ich ihn kenne, besuche ich ihn jeden Sonntag	*Since I've known him, I've been visiting him every Sunday*
5. Seitdem ich ihn kenne, haben wir uns nie gestritten	*Since I've known him, we have never quarrelled*
6. Seitdem ich im Dorf wohne, bin ich nie einsam	*Since I've been living in the village, I'm never lonely*

(c) When the since clause refers to a state or activity which, beginning in the past, still continued at a more recent point in the past, the imperfect tense is used in German, with the same qualifications as in (b) above, substituting the pluperf. for the perf.:

Seitdem ich ihn kannte, besuchte ich ihn jeden Sonntag	*Since I had known him, I had been visiting him every Sunday*

[1] cf. Schulz-Griesbach, op. cit., G 351 ff.
[2] The sale of his house was a self-contained action, completed in the past; therefore not present tense.

Seitdem ich ihn kannte, hatten wir uns nie gestritten	*Since I had known him, we had never quarrelled*
Seitdem ich im Dorf wohnte, war ich nie einsam	*Since I had been living in the village, I was never lonely* (neg., but a continuous state)

(d): (b) and (c) apply equally to solange *as long as*, which could be substituted for seitdem in all the above examples except 2. and 3. in (b). In Example 1. in (b), solange could be used, but with a different sense: As long as I take . . .

(e) **ever since**: the German rendering depends on the context:

Von der Zeit an, wo er das Vermögen seines Onkels erbte, . . .	*Ever since he inherited his uncle's fortune,* . . .
Solang ich ihn kenne, . . .	*Ever since I've known him,* . . .
Soweit ich zurückdenken kann, . . .	*Ever since I can remember,* . . .

533. till, until

(a) See 530(e).

(b) **not until**:
    i 'erst als' or 'erst wenn' *only when* (cf. 321).
    ii less common: nicht eher . . . als bis ('not sooner . . . than till').

Erst als mein Bruder zurück war, ging ich aus	*Not until my brother was back did I go out*
Ich werde erst ausgehen, wenn mein Bruder zurück ist	*I shan't go out till my brother is back*
Ich werde nicht eher ausgehen, als bis mein Bruder zurück ist	

(c) 'bis' may also render **by the time**, as in: Bis du zurückkommst, habe ich alles erledigt. Cf. the use of the preposition: Ich bin bis Montag zurück.

534. when

(a) **wann**, used as an interrog. adv. to introduce direct questions, is used conjunctionally in noun clauses, i.e. in reported speech and the like:
Wann kommt er nach Hause? Ich fragte ihn, wann er nach Hause käme. Ich weiß nicht, wann ich nach Hause komme.

(b) **als** introduces adverb clauses referring to a single occurrence or state in the past:
Als ich ihn sah, bekam ich einen Schreck. Als ich jung war, las ich seine Bücher gern.

Note: als is used with the present tense in two cases:
    i the historic present: Gerard wird heftiger, als er sein [Grouchys] Zögern sieht (St. Zweig: *Die Weltminute von Waterloo* in *Sternstunden der Menschheit*) ('wie', cf. 530(a), is also frequently used thus).
    ii in summaries of plays or stories: Als Othello die Wahrheit erfährt, nimmt er sich das Leben.

(c) **wenn** introduces adverb clauses in the present[1] or future or referring to a repeated occurrence in the past:

Wenn er kommt, werde ich ihm alles sagen. Wenn ich zum Zahnarzt mußte, weinte ich immer.

Note the following case:

Ich wollte zu Hause sein, wenn Karl ankam	*I wanted to be at home when Karl arrived*

(wenn is used because, as viewed by the speaker, Karl's arrival lay in the future)

(d) **da** is an archaic alternative for 'als' in its main use: Die Sonne schien an einem wolkenlosen Himmel, da er seinen Heimatort verließ (F. Dürrenmatt). See also 534(f).

(e) Following an 'als' clause, the main clause often begins with 'da' *then*; following a 'wenn' clause, it often begins with 'da' or 'dann':[2]

Als ich in Hamburg ausstieg, da sah ich ihn sofort.
Wenn du mit der Arbeit fertig bist, dann wollen wir alles besprechen.

(f) 'when' introducing relative clauses

i Stylistically, the best rendering is prep. + rel. pron.:

Ich werde den Tag, an dem er ankam, nie vergessen	*I shall never forget the day when he arrived*
in einer Zeit, in der die Jugend immer unabhängiger wird	*at a time when youth is becoming ever more independent*
Es war eine Gelegenheit, bei der Sie ihn hätten sprechen können	*It was an occasion when you could have spoken to him*

ii Other common renderings are wo, da, als and wenn:

Es vergeht kaum ein Tag, wo er mich nicht anruft	*Hardly a day passes when he doesn't give me a ring*
Ach, wo sind die Zeiten, da Pinneberg sich für einen guten Verkäufer hielt? (H. Fallada)	*Oh, where are the times when Pinneberg considered himself a good salesman?*
aber in dem Augenblick, als der Hund aufsprang, schrie er: . . . (Th. Valentin)	*but at the moment when the dog jumped up he shouted*
an seinem nächsten Geburtstag, wenn er volljährig wird (from Erben, op. cit., 257)	*on his next birthday when he comes of age*

In place of prep. + rel. pron. in i above, 'wo' could be used in any of the examples, 'als' in the first, 'da' in the second.

N.B. Es war das erste Mal, daß   *It was the first time that I had seen*
ich ihn gesehen hatte   *him*

iii Where the relative 'when' is not restrictive but continuative, it is generally rendered in German by a second main clause:

Es war jetzt drei Uhr. Zu dieser Zeit ging er immer spazieren	*It was now three o'clock, when he always went for a walk*
Letztes Jahr ist er nach München gezogen und seitdem habe ich ihn nicht gesehen	*Last year he moved to Munich since when I haven't seen him*

[1] with the two exceptions noted in 534(b)N.
[2] cf. Schulz-Griesbach, op. cit., G 057 and G 538.

(g) **when clauses with concessive force**

Wie konntest du das tun, obwohl du wußtest (or: wo du doch wußtest), daß es unrecht war?   *How could you do that, when you knew it was wrong?*

(h) **than when**: see 131(d)i

535. while

(a) 'während' is the normal equivalent, 'indessen' and 'indes' being archaic ('indessen', less commonly 'indes', is quite a usual equivalent of 1. meanwhile 2. nevertheless).

Du kannst mich füttern, indes ich die Ente rupfe (E. Langgässer)   *You can feed me while I'm plucking the duck*

(b) All three conjunctions, as well as 'wogegen', may also denote contrast (while, whereas), 'während' again being the normal choice:

Ich lese gern Romane, während mein Bruder sich mehr für Politik interessiert.

F. CONJUNCTIONS OF PLACE

536. Conjunctions of place

wo *where*
wohin *whither, where to, to which*
woher *whence, from where, from which*

worin *wherein, in which, in what*[1]
worauf *(whereon), on which, on what*[1]
etc.

537. Notes on conjunctions of place

(a) **wo, wohin and woher** may introduce relative and noun clauses:

Der Ort, wohin wir jetzt fahren, ...   *The place to which we are now driving ...*

Er wohnt (dort), wo wir früher wohnten   *He lives where we used to live*

Ich fragte ihn, woher er käme   *I asked him where he came from*

Note:
i For the meanings of wo other than 'where' see (b) below.
ii For the use of wohin and woher, see also 266–7.

(b) **Further uses of 'wo'**
i as a rendering of 'when': see 534(f)(g).

ii as a colloquial rendering of 'seeing that' (causal); generally **wo doch**: Wir können morgen später aufstehen, wo es doch Sonntag ist.

iii **wo nicht** is a colloquial alternative for 'wenn nicht' *if not*: Wo du es nicht brauchst, kannst du es mir geben (bad German). Es wird schwierig sein, wo nicht unmöglich.

iv **wo möglich** *if possible* (coll.); **womöglich** *possibly, perhaps*.

v as a colloquial alternative for 'irgendwo' *somewhere*:
Die hab' ich doch schon wo gesehen   *Surely I've seen her somewhere*
(I. Wendt)

[1] see 171, 183.

vi as a dialectal and illiterate substitute for the rel. pron.:

diese Bilder, wo Sie hier sehen   *these pictures that you see here*
(heard on a conducted tour)

vii in the exclamations I wo! Ach wo (denn)! *Nonsense! Whatever makes you think that?*

G. CONJUNCTIONS OF MANNER AND DEGREE

538. Conjunctions of manner and degree

je nachdem (ob) *according as, according to whether etc.*
abgesehen davon, daß *apart from the fact that*[1]
wie, so wie, gleichwie *as, like*
soviel, soweit *as far as*
als ob, als wenn *as if, as though*[2]
indem; dadurch, daß *by* +gerund, expressing means[3]
außer daß; ausgenommen, daß *except that*[1]
inwiefern, (in)wieweit *how far, to what extent*
in dem (im) Maße, wie (or: in dem) (*in proportion*) *as* . . ., *so*
(in)sofern als, (in)soweit als *inasmuch as, in so far as*
(an)statt daß *instead of* +gerund[4]
(genauso) wie . . ., so *just as*
nur daß *only that*
als *than*
je . . ., um so; je . . ., desto; je . . ., je *the more* . . ., *the more*[5]
so . . ., so; so sehr . . ., so sehr *to the same extent that; as* . . ., *so*
zu (alt), als daß *too (old) for*[6]
ohne daß *without* +gerund[4]
indem: participial phrase conveying manner[7]

539. according as, according to whether etc.

(a) Je nachdem du dich anstrengst,   *According as you exert yourself, you will*
    bringst du mehr oder weniger   *get more work done or less*
    fertig

(b) Commoner than 'je nachdem' alone (as in (a) above) is 'je nachdem' followed by 'ob' *whether* or by an interrogative pronoun (wer, was), adjective (welcher) or adverb (wie, wann, wo, warum). E.g.

Je nachdem ob es ihm besser geht   *According to whether he is better, he is*
oder nicht, wird er morgen   *going away tomorrow*
verreisen

Je nachdem wen du sprichst, kannst   *According to whom you see, you can*
du mehr oder weniger Auskunft   *obtain more or less information*
erhalten

Je nachdem wie mir sein Gemälde   *According to how I like his painting, I*
gefällt, werde ich es kaufen oder   *shall buy it or not buy it*
nicht

---

[1] for punctuation see 743(e).
[2] see 466.   [3] see 452.   [4] see 431, 469(a).
[5] see 134.   [6] see 469(a).   [7] see 440.

(c) 'je nachdem' is sometimes used without a clause, the latter being implied by the context:

Kommst du morgen mit?—Je   *Are you coming with us tomorrow?—It*
nachdem [e.g. wie ich mich   *depends*
fühle]

540. as, like (see also 130 and 142)

(a) 'wie' clause truncated:

Er kämpfte wie ein Löwe (=wie ein   *He fought like a lion (=as a lion*
Löwe kämpft)   *fights)*
Wie gesagt, ich kann mit diesem Buch *As I said, I can't get on with this book*
nicht fertig werden

Note: In the first of the above examples 'so wie' or 'gleichwie' could be used; both are rather more emphatic than 'wie'; 'gleichwie' is also rather literary.

(b) 'wie' clause complete:

Faul, wie er ist, wird er es nie zu   *Lazy as he is, he'll never get on in the*
etwas bringen   *world*
Wie ich erwartet hatte, kam er spät   *As I had expected, he was late*
Wie Sie sehen, die Lage ist kritisch *As you see, the situation is critical*
(or: ist die Lage kritisch)

Note: After 'Wie Sie sehen', the main clause may have either normal order or inversion, the former being more emphatic.

541. as far as

(a) 'soviel' is used before 'wissen' and 'sich erinnern':

Soviel er wußte, ging es ihr besser   *As far as he knew, she was better*
soviel (or: soweit) ich mich erinnere *as far as I remember*

(b) 'soweit' is used in most other contexts:

Soweit man sehen konnte, war nichts   *As far as one could see, there was*
als Wald und Wiesen   *nothing but forest and meadows*
soweit ich urteilen kann   *as far as I can judge*
soweit dies möglich war   *as far as this was possible*
soweit bisher bekannt   *as far as is known up to now*

N.B. was mich betrifft   *as far as I'm concerned*
                                      (See also 582(b), 586(d))

542. Examples of further conjunctions of manner and degree

(a) **how far, to what extent**

Ich weiß nicht, inwieweit Sie davon   *I don't know to what extent you have*
informiert sind   *been informed about this*

(b) **(in proportion) as . . ., so**

Aber in dem Maße, wie seine   *But (in proportion) as his health*
Gesundheit geschwächt ward,   *suffered, so his artistry was sharpened*
verschärfte sich seine
Künstlerschaft (Th. Mann)

(c) **inasmuch as, in so far as**

Er ist insofern ein angenehmer
Mensch, als er nie klagt

*He is an agreeable person inasmuch as he
never complains*

einer Partei . . ., die er selbst nur
insoweit schätzt, als sie seine
Politik unterstützt (*Christ und Welt*)

*of a party, which he himself values only in
so far as it supports his policy*

(d) **just as**

Genauso wie er selber kocht, so
stopft er auch seine Socken

*Just as he does his own cooking, he darns
his own socks*

(e) **than**

i 'als' clause truncated:

Er läuft schneller als ich [laufe]

He runs quicker than I

ii 'als' clause complete:

Er diktiert schneller, als ich
stenographieren kann

*He dictates faster than I can take down in
shorthand*

(f) **to the same extent that; as . . ., so**

So international der Sport ist, so
national begrenzt ist oft das
Interesse seines Publikums (*FAZ*)

*To the same extent that sport is inter-
national, the interest of its devotees is
often narrowly national*

So sehr sie ihn liebt, so sehr
haßt sie uns[1]

As she loves him, so she hates us

H. CAUSAL CONJUNCTIONS

543. Causal conjunctions

da *as, since*
weil *because*
zumal (da) *especially as*

nun (da) *now that, seeing that*
da nun mal (coll.) *seeing that*
wo doch (coll.) *seeing that*

544. Notes on causal conjunctions

(a) The lighter 'da' and the heavier 'weil' exactly correspond to 'as' or 'since' and 'because' respectively; so, too, a 'da' clause tends to precede, and a 'weil' clause to follow, the main clause.

After a preceding 'da' clause, the main clause sometimes opens with 'so': Da er nicht gekommen ist, (so) wird er wohl anrufen.

(b) The causal clause may be given prominence by inserting 'darum', 'deshalb' or 'deswegen' in the main clause before a following 'weil' clause:[2] Ich muß deshalb heute zu Hause bleiben, weil ich Besuch erwarte.

(c) **all the more because** = um so mehr, als (or da):

Ich freute mich über seinen Erfolg,
um so mehr, als/da er völlig
unerwartet kam

*I was glad about his success, all the more
because it was totally unexpected*

(d) For 'denn' *for, because*, see 521.

---

[1] taken from Muret-Sanders, op. cit.
[2] cf. Schulz-Griesbach, op. cit., G 531.

(e) Examples of the remaining causal conjunctions:

Er wird uns sicher helfen, zumal er dich so gern hat *He's sure to help us, especially as he's so fond of you*

Nun alles geschehen ist, bleibt nur zu wünschen, daß . . . (*FAZ*, quoted in Du. Gram. 3590) *Now that everything has been done, one can only wish that . . .*

Ich muß es tun, da ich es nun mal (or: wo ich es doch) versprochen habe *I've got to do it seeing that I've promised to*

I. CONSECUTIVE CONJUNCTIONS

545. Consecutive conjunctions

so daß *so that, such that*
so . . ., daß

derart . . ., daß *so . . . that*
dermaßen, daß *to such an extent that*

546. Notes on consecutive conjunctions

(a) Examples:
Das Wetter war schlecht, so daß wir wenig wandern konnten.
Das Wetter war so schlecht, daß wir wenig wandern konnten.
Er hat sich derart aufgeregt, daß wir den Plan fallenlassen mußten.

(b) Occasionally 'daß' alone is used for 'so that':
Kleines Volk setzte sich lustig in Trab, daß der Eisbrei umherspritzte (Th. Mann) *Youngsters trotted off gaily so that the slush splashed in all directions*

(c) As a stylistic variant, consequence may be conveyed by two main clauses: Wir konnten wenig wandern, so schlecht war das Wetter.

(d) For consecutive clauses of the type 'zu (alt), als daß' see 469(a).

XIII PREPOSITIONS

Note:

i With few exceptions, **time phrases with prepositions** are not included here; **see Chap. X.**

ii **An asterisk denotes that the preposition is further dealt with in 597 ff.: Main figurative uses of German prepositions.**

A. PREPOSITIONS TAKING THE DATIVE

547. Nine common prepositions taking the dative[1]

*aus *out of, from*
außer (a) *outside, out of*
  (b) *except, besides*
*bei (a) *near, by*
  (b) *at the house of, with*
*gegenüber (a) *opposite*
  (b) *compared with*

mit *with*
*nach (a) *after* (b) *to* (especially before place-names)
seit *since*
*von (a) *from* (b) *by* (with passive)
  (c) *of*
*zu *to*

548. *aus

(a) *out of*: Er kam aus dem Haus; ich sah aus dem Fenster; er trank aus einer Tasse; er ging mir aus dem Weg; aus der Mode kommen/sein.

(b) *from*: where 'from' basically means 'out of', aus is used in German: Er stammt aus (*comes from*) Hamburg; er ist gerade aus der Schule gekommen; ein Zitat aus 'Faust'; dieser Schrank ist aus dem achtzehnten Jahrhundert; aus dieser Richtung *from this direction*.

549. außer

(a) *outside, out of*: it is mainly used in a large number of fixed phrases, e.g.

Wir essen heute außer Hause	*We are eating out today*
Die Fabrik ist außer Betrieb	*The factory is not working*
außer Dienst (a. D.)	*retired (Retd.)*
außer der Zeit	*out of season; not at the official time*

[1] for 17 less common ones, see 557.

außer der Reihe	*out of turn*
außer Kontrolle geraten	*to get out of control* (e.g. car)
Aber dies war etwas, das ganz außer seiner Macht lag (R. Musil)	*But this was something that lay quite outside his power*

cf. außer Atem, außer Form, außer Gefahr, außer Hörweite *out of earshot,* außer Mode, außer Sicht, außer Übung, außer Zweifel *beyond doubt*

(b) *except, besides*: Niemand hat ihn gesehen außer dem Nachtwächter; außer dienstags.

Note: außer *except* is sometimes treated as a conjunction and is then followed by the same case as the word to which it refers back: Ich konnte nichts außer Lichter sehen.

550. *bei[1]

(a) *near, by*

Er stand (nahe) bei mir (or: in meiner Nähe)[2]	*He stood near me*

cf. bei dem Rathaus/in der Nähe vom Rathaus; er saß beim Feuer; Bad Homburg ist (nahe) bei Frankfurt

(b) *at the house of, with*

Er wohnt bei seinem Onkel	*He lives at his uncle's (with his uncle)*
Ich habe dieses Fleisch beim neuen Metzger gekauft	*I bought this meat at the new butcher's*
Ich habe ihn bei Müllers getroffen	*I met him at the Müllers'*
bei uns	*at our house*
bei uns in der Fabrik	*in our factory* (idiomatic)

Note: bei cannot be used with verbs of motion; it is thus not synonymous with French 'chez'. E.g.

Er geht zu seinem Onkel	*He is going to his uncle's*
Er kam dicht an mich heran (or: in meine Nähe)	*He came near me*
Er kam dem Tode nahe	*He came near to death*

(c) *nearer, nearest (to)*

Er stand näher am Fenster als ich	*He stood nearer the window than I*
Mainz ist näher bei Frankfurt als Mannheim	*Mainz is nearer to Frankfurt than is Mannheim*
Er stand dem Fenster am nächsten	*He stood nearest the window*

551. *gegenüber, in both the senses treated here, follows a pronoun, but may precede or follow a noun, the latter position being the commoner.

(a) *opposite*: Ich saß ihr gegenüber; wir wohnen dem Krankenhaus gegenüber/gegenüber dem Krankenhaus.

N.B. schräg gegenüber	*almost* (lit. obliquely) *opposite*
am gegenüberliegenden (or anderen) Ufer	*on the opposite bank*

(b) *compared with*: Seinem Bruder gegenüber ist er ein Faulenzer; gegenüber dem Vorjahr *compared with last year*

---

[1] see also 590(b)N.ii and (c)ii iii.
[2] cf. Er stand in der Nähe *He stood near*

552. mit covers all straightforward meanings of *with*, e.g. Er kam mit ihr; Frankfurter Würstchen mit Kartoffelsalat; ich spiele oft mit ihm Tennis; er schreibt mit einem Füller. See also 560(c) and 631.

N.B. mit der Arbeit anfangen/aufhören *to start/stop work*

553. *nach

(a) *after*: nach drei Wochen; nach dem Konzert; nach Tisch; bitte, nach Ihnen!

Ich las ein Buch nach dem andern   *I read book after book*
Nach dem Chef hat der Betriebs-   *After the boss, the manager has the*
   leiter am meisten zu sagen   *biggest say*

(b) *to*: see 593.

554. seit *since*: seit dem Krieg, seit drei Wochen *for the last three weeks*, seit einiger Zeit *for some time past*.

Note on tenses used with 'since' phrases

i When the 'since' phrase applies to a state or activity which, beginning in the past, still continues, the present tense is used in German:

Ich arbeite seit acht Uhr   *I've been working since eight o'clock*
Seit Oktober liegt sie im   *Since October she's been in hospital*
   Krankenhaus
Seit wann wohnen Sie hier?   *Since when have you been living here?*
Seit meiner frühsten Kindheit habe   *Since my earliest childhood I've had an*
   ich eine Abneigung gegen Katzen   *aversion to cats*[1]
Ich habe ihn seit dem Tod seines   BUT: *I have only seen him once since his*
   Vaters nur einmal gesehen   *father's death*

ii When a series of actions or states is referred to, the perfect is used, unless it is desired to indicate a continuing habit (3rd example):

Er ist seit Weihnachten mehrmals   *He has been ill several times since*
   krank gewesen   *Christmas*
Ich habe ihn seit Weihnachten jeden   *I have visited him every Sunday since*
   Sonntag besucht   *Christmas*
Seit Weihnachten besuche ich ihn   *Since Christmas I've taken to visiting him*
   jeden Sonntag   *every Sunday*

iii In negative statements, the perfect is used, except in cases of clear continuity, as in the 2nd example:

Ich habe ihn seit langem nicht gesehen   *I haven't seen him for a long time*
Seit Anfang des Jahres arbeitet er   *He has not been working since the*
   nicht mehr   *beginning of the year*

iv When the 'since' phrase, or its equivalent, applies to a state or activity which, beginning in the past, still continued at a more recent point in the past, the imperfect tense is used in German, with the same qualifications as above, substituting the pluperf. for the perf.:

Ich wartete schon seit zwei Stunden   *I had been waiting for two hours when at*
   (or: schon zwei Stunden), als er   *last he arrived*
   endlich ankam

----

[1] BUT (less usual): Seit meiner frühsten Kindheit habe ich immer eine Abneigung gegen Katzen gehabt. While the sentence still implies that the aversion continues, 'immer' gives greater weight to its existence throughout the past.

| Ich hatte ihm seit Jahren (or: jahrelang) zugeredet, sein Haus zu verkaufen | *For years I had been urging him* (i.e. on a series of occasions) *to sell his house* |
| Als ich ihn besuchte, arbeitete er schon zwei Jahre nicht mehr | *When I visited him, he hadn't been working for two years* |

555. *von

(a) *from*

von covers all straightforward uses of 'from' (but see 548(b)), e.g. Ich fuhr von Frankfurt nach München; ich habe einen Brief von mcinem Vetter bekommen; ich wohne zwanzig Minuten vom Bahnhof (entfernt); ich war vom ersten bis zum zehnten Oktober in Berlin; von außen *from outside*; von zu Hause weg *away from home*; von da an *from there/from then onwards*.

Note:

i To denote a point of vantage or departure, von is frequently strengthened by another preposition, mainly 'aus', used adverbially:
Von diesem Fenster (aus) hat man eine gute Aussicht auf den See; von heute an *from today*.
from a German letter: Sie sind . . . vom Libanon aus mit dem Schiff nach Zypern gefahren. Wir sind gespannt (*we're wondering*), wie es nun von dort aus weitergehen wird.

ii Idiomatic:

Er war von Haus aus Lehrer, ist aber jetzt Schauspieler	*He was originally a teacher, but he's now an actor*
von Grund aus falsch	*completely wrong*
von mir aus	*as far as I'm concerned, if you like*

(b) *by* (with passive) (See also 560(c)):
Dieses Haus wurde von Studenten gebaut; cf. eine Sinfonie von Mozart.

(c) *of*: **'von' is used instead of the genitive case in the following instances**:

i **partitively**:

Wir aßen von dem Kuchen	*We ate some of the cake*
einer/der intelligenteste/viele von meinen Freunden (or: meiner Freunde)	*one/the most intelligent/many of my friends*
viel von seinem Leben	*much of his life*
ein Teil von dem, was er sagte	*part of what he said*

Similarly: einer von ihnen, einer von denen *one of whom*, jeder von uns, etwas von ihrem Charme, nichts von der Wirkung *none of the effect*, welches von diesen Büchern?

ii **in phrases which in some way characterize a preceding noun**:

ein Mann von Geschmack	*a man of taste*
eine Frau von deutscher Abstammung	*a woman of German descent*
Er war von bezaubernder Höflichkeit	*He was enchantingly courteous*
ein kräftiger Kerl, ein Klotz von einem Türken (*Zeit*)	*a strong fellow, a great lout of a Turk*

... einen völlig neuen Typ von Viermächte-Konferenz (*Spiegel*)	*a completely new type of Four-Power Conference*
ein Junge von fünfzehn (Jahren)	*a boy of fifteen (years)*

iii **to denote possession, or to render an objective genitive**[1] (last two examples), **where the genitive case is not shown**:

der Geschmack von Schokolade	*the taste of chocolate*
die Redakteure von Berliner Zeitungen	*the editors of Berlin newspapers*
die Herstellung von Knöpfen	*the manufacture of buttons*

iv **when the person or thing following a Saxon genitive**[1] **is itself in the genitive** (especially common after proper names):

die Ziele von Bismarcks Politik[2]	*the objectives of Bismarck's policy*

v **before proper names**
1. before geographical names forming part of a title or ending in a sibilant and which are not used with the def. art.:

der König von Schweden; die Straßen von Paris BUT: die Königin der Niederlande; die Dörfer des Elsaß.

Note: Up to 1918, 'von' was accorded for use before a surname as a title of nobility, e.g. Generalfeldmarschall Paul von Hindenburg; cf. French 'de', e.g. Alfred de Vigny.

2. frequently before geographical names in preference to a possible genitive, especially in conversation: die Kirchen von Nürnberg, im Süden von England (rather than Nürnbergs, Englands).

3. frequently to render the gen. sing. of proper names ending in a sibilant, e.g. die Operetten von Johann Strauß: see 51(g).

vi **in conversation**
1. von is much used instead of the genitive because the latter is felt to be somewhat affected, e.g. ein Teil von dem Kuchen, die Kinder von meinem Bruder.
This is particularly so in the case of a gen. plur. without a def. art., possessive or demonstrative:

die Gehälter von einigen neuen Angestellten (rather than: einiger neuer Angestellter); die Bilder von anderen italienischen Malern.

2. von generally replaces the first of two successive genitives, especially if they are masc. and/or neut., here avoiding a succession of sibilants:

Er klopfte an die Tür von dem Schlafzimmer des Generals (not: des Schlafzimmers des Generals)
Das ist die Schwester (von) der Frau meines Freundes.

556. ***zu** *to*, e.g. Er ging zum Bahnhof, zur Bank, and always for going to a person: Er ging zu seinem Onkel. See 594.

---

[1] cf. 60.
[2] A common error is 'die Ziele Bismarcks Politik', in which only one of the two genitives (Bismarck's) is rendered.

557. Seventeen less common prepositions taking the dative

ab *(starting) from, as from*
abgesehen von *apart from*
binnen *within* (a period of time)
dank *thanks to*
entgegen *contrary to, against*
entsprechend *in accordance with*
fern *far from*
gemäß *in accordance with*
gleich *like*
mitsamt *together with*

nächst *next after; next to*
nebst *together with, in addition to*
samt *together with*
zufolge i *in accordance with* ii *as the result of*
zuliebe *to please (s.o.), for the sake of*
zunächst *next to, close to*
zuwider *contrary to, against*

(a) **ab** *(starting) from, as from* is commercialese and officialese, but is fairly widely used in a time sense, where it takes the accusative.

Examples: i Place: ab (unserer) Fabrik *ex works*; ab Jericho folgten wir einer langen Kolonne israelischer Touristenbusse (*Zeit*) ii Time: ab neun Uhr, ab heute, ab ersten Mai, ab nächste Woche.

Note: The 1st example is a fixed phrase; otherwise, the normal equivalents are 'von ... ab' for places (von Jericho ab) and 'von ... an' in a time sense (vom ersten Mai an).

(b) **abgesehen von** *apart from*
abgesehen von allem andern   *apart from everything else*

(c) **binnen** *within* (a period of time). With a singular noun it may also take the genitive. E.g. binnen sechs Tagen, binnen eines Monats, binnen kurzem *before long, shortly.*
Commoner equivalents: in+dat. or innerhalb+gen.

(d) **dank** *thanks to*
dank seinen Bemühungen   *thanks to his efforts*

It is also used with the genitive:
dank seiner Sprachkenntnisse   *thanks to his knowledge of languages*
  (A. Goes)

(e) **entgegen** *contrary to, against* may precede or follow its noun:
entgegen den Erfahrungen früherer   *contrary to the experience of former years*
Jahre (*FAZ*)
seiner Gewohnheit entgegen   *contrary to his habit*

(f) **entsprechend** *in accordance with* may precede or follow its noun; it is largely commercialese:
Ihren Anordnungen entsprechend   *in accordance with your instructions*

(g) **fern** *far from* is elevated style, normal usage being fern von or weit von; only these can be used with pronouns:
Wir wollen ein paar schöne Stunden fern (von) der Stadt verbringen; er wohnt fern/weit von uns.

(h) **gemäß** *in accordance with* may precede or, more frequently, follow its noun: seiner Gewohnheit gemäß, ihren Wünschen gemäß. –

(i) **gleich** like
Meine Frau grüßt Sie gleich mir   *My wife sends you her kindest regards as*
  herzlich   *I do*

(j) **mitsamt** and **samt** *together with* are somewhat stilted; they may be
used slightly ironically, as in the 2nd example:

Er hat sein Haus samt allen Habseligkeiten verloren	*He has lost his house together with all his possessions*
Das große Krögersche Haus stand mitsamt seiner würdigen Geschichte zum Verkaufe (Th. Mann.)	*The great Kröger house, together with its stately history, came up for sale*

Normal equivalents: mit or zusammen mit.

(k) **nächst** *next after*; *next to* (rare)

Nächst Gott verdanke ich vor allem dir meine Rettung (from Du. Stil.; normal usage: nach)	*After God, I owe my being saved above all to you*
nächst dem Schrank (normal usage: neben)	*next to the cupboard*

(l) **nebst** *together with, in addition to* is mainly formal or officialese; sometimes used facetiously.

Herr Direktor Karl Müller ist nebst Gemahlin und Kindern eingetroffen	*Herr Direktor Karl Müller has arrived together with his wife and children*
nebst den Reisespesen	*in addition to travelling expenses*

Normal equivalents: (zusammen) mit, außer.

(m) **samt** *together with*: see (j) above.

(n) **zufolge**: meaning *in accordance with*, it is generally used with a preceding dative, e.g. seinem Befehl zufolge (normal equivalent: gemäß;
see (h) above); meaning *as the result of*, it is used with a following
genitive (normal equivalent: infolge + gen.).

(o) **zuliebe** *to please (s.o.), for the sake of* is much used; it follows its noun
or pronoun: Ich habe es meiner Mutter zuliebe getan; dir zuliebe
gibt es Spargel (*asparagus*).

(p) **zunächst** *next to, close to* may precede or follow a noun but must
follow a pronoun:
Zunächst dem Fenster stand ein Tischchen; mir zunächst stand ein
Italiener.
Normal equivalents: neben, dicht bei or dicht an (all + dat.).

(q) **zuwider** *contrary to, against* follows its noun, e.g. seinem Befehl zuwider.
Normal equivalent: gegen.

B. PREPOSITIONS TAKING THE ACCUSATIVE

558. Six common prepositions taking the accusative[1]

bis (a) *till, until* (b) *as far as*
durch (a) *through* (direction)
   (b) *through, throughout*
   (c) *through, by, by means of*
für *for*

*gegen (a) *against* (b) *contrary to*
   (c) *compared with* (d) *in return
for* (e) *towards* (f) *about,
approximately*
ohne *without*
*um *round, around, round about*

[1] for 10 less common ones, see 565.

559. bis[1]

(a) *till, until*: bis nächsten Sommer, bis letzte Woche, bis Sonnenuntergang, bis heute abend, bis jetzt, bis Ende 1967.

(b) *as far as*

Ich fahre nur bis Frankfurt	*I am only going as far as Frankfurt*
Bis dahin gehe ich mit	*I'll go with you as far as there*
bis hierher und nicht weiter	*thus far and no further*

Note:

i **not until = erst**, e.g. Er kommt erst am Montag (see 321).

ii **Used before an article or a demonstr., possess. or interrog. adj., 'bis' is followed by another preposition which determines the case.**

(α) **When it means 'till'** (or 'to', 'up to' with the sense of 'till'), this preposition is 'zu': bis zum vierten Mai, bis zu einer Krise, bis zu diesem Augenblick, bis zu seinem Tode, bis zu welchem Tag?

EXCEPTIONS:

(a) 'bis zu' with no article etc.: bis zu Beginn des Weltkrieges; von Anfang bis (zu) Ende; Kinder bis zu zwölf Jahren; von Alexander bis zu Napoleon.

(b) 'bis' before a demonstrative: bis diesen Montag (Dienstag) etc.

(β) **When it means 'as far as'**, the second preposition is the appropriate equivalent of 'to' (see 589 ff.):

Wir gingen bis zum Wald, bis zu seinem Haus.

Er ging bis zur Tür/bis an die Tür.

bis an den Rhein, bis an die Grenze *as far as the frontier.*

... standen sie im Wasser bis an die Knöchel (*up to their ankles*) (H. Mann).

Before the name of a country or town, 'as far as' is 'bis' or 'bis nach'; 'bis' is commoner, 'bis nach' is more intensive; whichever is used, a phrase in apposition is in the dative (cf. Du. Gram. 3385):

Ich fahre bis (nach) Lübeck, der alten Hansastadt	*I'm going as far as Lübeck, the old Hanseatic city*
Alexander der Große drang bis nach Indien vor	*Alexander the Great advanced as far as India*

N.B. Der Feind drang bis auf zwei Kilometer von der Stadt vor.

The enemy advanced to within two kilometres of the town.

bis über die Ohren verschuldet	*up to one's ears in debt*
bis zu vierzig Mark pro Tag	*up to 40 marks a day*

iii **bis auf + acc.** may mean *down to* (*and including*) or *all but, except*:

Die Kabinen waren mit 447 Passagieren bis auf das letzte Klappbett belegt (*Zeit*)	*With 447 passengers, the cabins were full down to the last camp-bed*
Die Passagiere kamen alle um bis auf drei	*All but three of the passengers were killed*

Ambiguity can be avoided by using einschließlich + gen. and außer + dat. respectively.

---

[1] see also 248 N.iii and 330: 'by' and 'till'.

560. durch

(a) *through* (direction): Ich ging durch das Dorf; er atmet durch den Mund.

(b) *throughout*

durch viele Generationen hindurch	*throughout many generations*
die ganze Nacht (hindurch)	N.B. *throughout the night*
im ganzen Land	*throughout the country*

(c) **through, by,**[1] **by means of, with: durch, mit, von**

durch indicates the animate or inanimate agent or means through whom or which an action is performed:

Mein Onkel hatte mich durch seinen Sohn/durch ein Telegramm gewarnt	*My uncle had warned me through his son/ by a telegram*
Durch harte Arbeit hat er sein Ziel erreicht	*By hard work he attained his aim*

mit indicates the instrument used in performing an action:

Er hat ihn mit einem Messer getötet	*He killed him with a knife*

Compare: Er kam mit der Bahn, mit dem Schiff, mit dem Flugzeug, mit seinem Wagen, mit einem Taxi, mit dem Rad; cf. mit der Post, mit Luftpost.

Note: All these phrases except 'mit seinem Wagen' and 'mit dem Rad' could also be turned, colloquially and commercially, with 'per': per Bahn, per Schiff etc.

In passive sentences:

i **von** is used to indicate the author or doer of a deed:

Ich war von meinem Onkel durch seinen Sohn gewarnt worden	*I had been warned by my uncle through his son*
Er wurde von zwei Polizeibeamten verhaftet	*He was arrested by two police-officers*

ii the inanimate cause of an occurrence is normally indicated by **durch**:

Die Ernte wurde durch Hagel vernichtet	*The crop was destroyed by hail*
Ich wurde durch den starken Verkehr aufgehalten	*I was delayed by the heavy traffic*
Er wurde von einem Auto überfahren	BUT: *He was run over by a car*

(The accident was caused by car and driver)

Das Haus war von Bäumen umgeben (fixed usage)	N.B. *The house was surrounded with trees*

Where an action is conveyed, not by a passive verb, but by a noun with verbal force, the doer is indicated by 'durch':

die Annahme des Kaisertitels durch den König (Bismarck)	*the assumption of the imperial title by the King*
der Ersatz der Muskelkraft durch die Maschine	*the replacement of muscular strength by the machine*

561. für is the equivalent of *for* in a wide range of senses, e.g. Er hat viel für mich getan; das ist kein Buch für Kinder; es war sehr unangenehm

---

[1] see also 621.

für mich; genug für heute; für einen Ausländer spricht er recht gut Englisch; ein gutes Mittel für (or: gegen) Kopfweh; ich habe die Bücher für vierzig Mark bekommen/verkauft.
See also 117 N.ii and 175.

562. *gegen

(a) *against*
Er warf den Ball gegen die Mauer; er schwamm gegen den Strom (lit. and fig.); er verteidigte sich gegen seine Verleumder (*slanderers*); ich bin gegen diesen Plan; haben Sie etwas dagegen?

(b) *contrary to*
Ich handelte gegen seinen Befehl; das geschah gegen seinen Wunsch; gegen die Natur; gegen alle Erwartungen; gegen alle Vernunft *contrary to reason.*

(c) *compared with*

Gegen ihn bin ich nur ein Stümper	*Compared with him I'm a mere bungler*
gegen früher	*compared with formerly*

(d) *in return for*

Er gab mir das Geld gegen eine Quittung	*He gave me the money in return for a receipt*
Ich tauschte meinen Füller gegen seinen Kugelschreiber	*I exchanged my fountain-pen for his ball-point pen*

(e) *towards* (see also 311 N.i)

Wir fahren jetzt gegen Süden (elev.) (normal usage: nach Süden)	*We are now driving in a southerly direction*
Er kam gegen Abend an	*He arrived towards evening*
Es war schon gegen Ende März	*It was already near the end of March*

(f) *about, approximately* (see also 311 N.i)
Es waren gegen 400 Personen im Saal

563. ohne *without*[1]

The indef. art. is generally omitted after ohne, e.g. Er geht gern ohne Hut (from Du. Stil.); er kam ohne Bleistift in die Stunde; bitte, ein Frühstück ohne Ei; ein Zimmer ohne Tisch (BUT: Ohne ein Wort verließ er das Zimmer).

Where there is no ambiguity, the possess. adj. is sometimes omitted: Sie kam heute ohne Brille, ohne Fahrrad, ohne Kinder. See also 74(a).

One elliptical use may be noted, its meaning varying according to the context: Sein Vorschlag ist nicht so ohne *His suggestion is not at all bad/ not without its difficulties* (or *risks*)

564. *um[2] *round, around, round about* is frequently strengthened with one of the adverbs 'rings' and 'herum':

Rings um den Garten lief eine Mauer; wir standen rings um den Teich.
Um das Haus (herum) liegt ein Garten; um mich herum (or: her) war alles still; er kam um die Ecke (herum); er kommt gewöhnlich um diese Zeit (herum), um Ostern (herum); ich habe um hundert Mark herum.

---

[1] see also 632.
[2] see also 311, second group of examples.

Idiomatic use of 'um' in conjunction with 'bringen' and 'kommen':

jemanden um eine Sache bringen	*to deprive s.o. of s.th.*
Die Aufregung hat mich um den Schlaf gebracht	*The excitement deprived me of my sleep*
Sie haben ihn ums Leben gebracht	*They killed him*
Er hat sich ums Leben gebracht	*He has killed himself*
um eine Sache kommen	*to lose something*
Er ist um sein ganzes Geld gekommen	*He has lost all his money*
Er ist bei dem Unfall ums Leben gekommen	*He lost his life in the accident*

565. Ten less common prepositions taking the accusative

ab *(starting) from, as from*[1]	hindurch *throughout*[3]
betreffend *with regard to*	per *per, by* etc.
eingerechnet *including* (in the account)	pro *per* (meaning 'for each')
entlang *along, alongside*[2]	sonder *without*
gen *towards*	wider *against, contrary to*

(a) **betreffend** *with regard to* (commercialese) generally follows its noun:
Ihr Schreiben vom 1. Oktober betreffend, . . .

(b) **eingerechnet** *including* (in the account) (commercialese) follows its noun:

meine Unkosten eingerechnet	*including my expenses*

(c) **gen** *towards* is a contraction of 'gegen' and is only used in poetic style (e.g. Er wanderte gen Norden) and in a few set phrases (e.g. Schreit es nicht gen Himmel? *Isn't it revolting?*)

(d) **per** *per, by* etc. is mainly officialese and commercialese, e.g. viermal per Jahr, per Post, per Schiff, 500 DM per (or pro) Tonne. (See also 560(c)N.)

per Luftfracht	*by air* (for goods)
per Einschreiben	*by recorded delivery*[4]
per LKW (Lastkraftwagen)	*by road*
per Adresse (p.A.)	*care of* (c/o)
Die Waren sind per 1. Januar bestellt	*The goods are ordered for 1 January*
per Anhalter fahren	*to hitchhike*
per Autostopp reisen	

(e) **pro** *per* (meaning 'for each') is commercialese and colloquial, e.g. Die Pfirsiche kosten 30 Pf. pro Stück. Was ist der Preis pro Tag? Wir fuhren 100 Kilometer pro Stunde (or: die Stunde) (100 km/st). Fünf Prozent (5%)

Unsere Reisekosten betragen im Schnitt pro/je Vertreter pro/je Monat 920 DM	*Our travelling expenses average 920 marks per traveller per month*

(f) **sonder** *without*: archaic; limited to a few rare phrases, e.g. sonder Zweifel, sonder Zahl *countless*.

---

[1] see 557(a).   [2] see 618.   [3] see 560(b).
[4] by registered letter = als Wertbrief.

Commoner is the indeclinable adjective sondergleichen *unequalled, unparalleled*, which follows its noun, e.g. Es war ein Erfolg sondergleichen.

(g) **wider** *against, contrary to* is biblical, poetic and used in certain stock phrases:

Wer nicht mit mir ist, der ist wider mich	*He who is not with me, is against me*
wider Erwarten	*contrary to expectation*
wider Willen	*reluctantly*
Das geht mir wider den Strich	*That goes against the grain*

C. NINE PREPOSITIONS TAKING DATIVE OR ACCUSATIVE

566. Nine prepositions take:

the dative when they denote 1. rest 2. movement within a place or area;
the accusative when they denote movement towards or to a new position.

Grouped mnemonically they are:

in *in; into*
*an *at, on (up against)*;
to, on (to) (up against)
*auf *on; (down) on (to)*

*über *above, over, across*
*unter i *under, below, beneath*
ii *among*

*vor *before, in front of*
hinter *behind*

neben *beside, next to*
zwischen *between*

EXAMPLES:

in

Er wohnt in diesem Haus	*He lives in this house*
Wir gingen im Wald spazieren	*We went for a walk in the forest*
Ich ging ins Eßzimmer	*I went into the dining-room*

an

Das Bild hing an dieser Wand	*The picture hung on this wall*
Ich hängte das Bild an die Wand	*I hung the picture on the wall*

über

Ein Flugzeug kreiste über der Stadt	*A plane was circling over the town*
Ich ging über die Brücke	*I went across the bridge*

unter

Der Fluß floß träge unter der Brücke[1]	*The river flowed sluggishly under the bridge*
Ich fand das Rezept unter meinen Papieren	*I found the recipe among my papers*
Er tauchte den Kopf unters Wasser	*He dipped his head under the water*

---

[1] dative, as the prep. does not denote movement to a new position.

neben

Neben mir ging ein junger Kerl[1]	*A young fellow was walking beside me*
Sie stellte die eine Vase neben die andere	*She stood the one vase next to the other*

zwischen

Sein Laden ist zwischen dem Kino und der Post	*His shop is between the cinema and the post-office*
Der Junge ging zwischen seinen Eltern[1]	*The boy was walking along between his parents*
Der Junge drängte sich zwischen seine Eltern	*The boy pushed himself between his parents*

567. Note:

i 'an' and 'auf'

At an earlier stage of the language 'an' was used in the sense of 'down on' and this use has survived in the phrases 'am Boden, an der Erde' (beside: auf dem Boden, auf der Erde) meaning 'on the floor, on the ground'.

Note the following:

Am Flußufer lag Seetang	*Seaweed lay on the river bank*
Am Strande lagen Boote	*Boats lay on the beach*
am Berg	*on the mountain-side*
auf dem Berg	*on the mountain-top*
Ich drückte auf den Knopf	*I pressed the button*
Ich klopfte ihm auf die Schulter	*I patted him on the shoulder*
auf diesem Bild	*in this picture*

ii unter: *under* and *among*: where the meaning might be ambiguous, 'among' is best rendered by 'zwischen' or by a free translation, e.g.

Das Häuschen stand unter Bäumen	*The cottage stood under some trees*
Das Häuschen stand zwischen Bäumen (or: war von Bäumen umgeben)	*The cottage stood among trees*

iii For the use of in, an and auf in the translation of to, into, at and in, see 589 ff.

568. In temporal senses: dative or accusative?

(a) in, an and vor take the dat. (exc. 'in' meaning *into*): im Sommer, am Montag, vor dem Krieg, BUT: Er arbeitete bis tief in die Nacht hinein.

(b) auf takes the acc.:
Ich reise auf (or: für) vierzehn Tage nach Deutschland.

569. In verbal constructions: dative or accusative?

(a) *auf and *über take the acc., e.g. sich verlassen auf *to rely on*, sich freuen über *to be glad about*.
SIX EXCEPTIONS:

basieren auf + dat.	*to be based on*
beharren auf + dat.	*to insist on, persist in* (elev.)

---

[1] dative, as the prep. does not denote movement to a new position.

beruhen auf+dat.	to rest, be based on (e.g. a misunderstanding)
bestehen auf+dat. (occasionally+acc.)	to insist on
fußen auf+dat.	to be based on
brüten über +dat. (also +acc.)	to brood, meditate on

N.B. In a sentence such as 'Er ruhte auf der Couch', 'auf' is clearly not an essential part of the verbal construction.

(b) *vor takes the dat., e.g. sich fürchten vor *to be afraid of.*

(c) *an varies, e.g. erkennen an+dat. *to recognize by*; denken an+acc. *to think of.*

570. In other contexts: dative or accusative?

Elsewhere, if the concepts of rest and movement cannot be even figuratively applied:

(a) in, an, unter, vor, zwischen preponderantly take the dat.:[1]

im ganzen	on the whole
der Bedarf an Arbeitskräften	the demand for labour
unter dieser Bedingung	on this condition
vor allem	above all
Was ist der Unterschied zwischen diesen zwei Wörtern?	What is the difference between these two words?

(b) auf and über preponderantly take the acc.:[1]

auf diese Weise *in this way*	über alle Maßen *beyond measure*

571. Dative or Accusative? Some special cases

(a) **There are certain instances of an action being denoted either by means of a simple verb or, more explicitly, by a verb with a separable prefix.** Used in conjunction with the simple verb, these prepositions take the acc.; used in conjunction with the compound verb, they are used with the dat.; they are then felt to denote an action occurring in a place.

EXAMPLES:
(an-)binden *to tie, fasten*
   Das Pferd war an einen Baum gebunden (an einem Baum angebunden, festgebunden, festgemacht).
(auf-)hängen (wk.) *to hang (up)* (tr.)
   Er hängte das Bild an die Wand (an der Wand auf).
(auf-)schreiben *to write (down)*
   Ich schrieb seine Adresse in mein Notizbuch (in meinem Notizbuch auf).

(b) In the case of **the prefix hin-** *down*, there is much fluctuation of usage, but the dative is probably commoner: Er stellte die Lampe neben mir hin; er legte das Buch vor mir hin.

(c) **In conjunction with the prefix ein-, 'in' generally takes the accusative,** e.g.
Er stieg in den Zug ein; er wickelte/schlug das Buch in ein Stück Papier

[1] cf. Du. Gram. 3360 and in this book 597 ff.

ein; sie hüllte sich in eine Reisedecke ein *she wrapped herself up in a travelling rug*; ich trug seinen Namen in meine Liste ein; wir haben ihn in das Geheimnis eingeweiht *we have initiated him into the secret.* Cf. unser Einzug in unsre neue Wohnung *our move into our new flat.*

Note:

i 'in' here generally takes the acc. even when the sentence denotes not action but the resultant state, though in the latter case the dat. may also be found, as in the last two examples:

Sie war in eine Reisedecke eingehüllt	*She was wrapped up in a travelling-rug*
Ich bin in das Geheimnis eingeweiht	*I have been initiated into the secret*
Das Buch war in ein/einem Stück Papier eingewickelt	*The book was wrapped up in a piece of paper*
Ich fand seinen Namen in die/der Liste eingetragen	*I found his name entered in the list*[1]

ii (sich) ein-schließen in + acc. or dat.: Sie schloß sich in ihr/ihrem Zimmer ein *She locked herself up in her room.*

iii in einem Wirtshaus ein-kehren *to turn in at an inn*: this unexpected dative is a fixed usage.

iv The dative is used in conjunction with ein-treffen (as with all verbs meaning *to arrive*) and with sich ein-finden *to appear*, e.g. (journalese):

Am Bahnhof hatten sich eingefunden . . .	*The following were present at the station . . .*

v for ein-bringen and ein-führen, see 573.

572. Miscellaneous cases that may cause doubt or difficulty. (In a few instances, either case is possible without a substantial difference in meaning; only the commoner usage is given below.)

(a) The dative is used in conjunction with the following:

an-bringen *to fix*: An dieser Wand könnten wir ein Bücherbrett anbringen.
an-kommen, an-langen *to arrive*, e.g. in der Stadt (cf. zu Hause)
befestigen an *to fasten to*
drucken *to print*, e.g. auf schlechtem Papier gedruckt.
empor-ragen über *to tower above*
fest-halten an *to stick to* (e.g. one's opinions)
sich fest-halten an *to cling to, hold on to*
gipfeln in *to culminate in*
hervor-gucken/hervor-treten hinter *to peep out/step forth from behind*: Er trat hinter dem Baum hervor.
hervor-kriechen unter *to creep out from under*
landen e.g. am Ziel *at one's destination*; Menschen auf dem Mond (tr. and intr.)
notieren *to note down* e.g. auf einem Zettel *on a slip of paper*
die Richtung *direction*:
   Ich schlenderte in der Richtung der Stadt.
   Wir müssen in dieser Richtung weitergehen.

---

[1] cf. Eggeling, op. cit.: ein-

BUT: Wir müssen jetzt in diese Richtung gehen.
(N.B. Wir fuhren in Richtung Rom.)
der Unterschied zwischen *the difference between*
(sich) verbergen, (sich) verstecken *to hide*, e.g. hinter dem Schrank.
verschwinden *to disappear*: Er verschwand in dem Haus.
verstauen in *to stow away in*

(b) **The accusative is used in conjunction with the following:**

an-bauen an *to build on to*: Wir haben eine Garage an das Haus angebaut.
sich an-schließen an *to adjoin*: An unseren Garten schließt sich ein Wäldchen an.
beugen: gebeugt über *bent over*: Sie saß über ihre Arbeit gebeugt.
grenzen an *to border on*
hinaus-ragen über *to jut out over*
sich klammern an *to cling to, hold on to*
schauen, sehen *to look*: Er schaute/sah über die Mauer.
sich setzen: Ich setzte mich ans Fenster. Ich setzte mich nahe am Bahnhof in ein Kino (H. Böll).
der Sieg (*victory*) der Athener über die Perser.
(sich) stützen auf *to support* (*o.s.*) *on* e.g. den Tisch; cf. das Kinn in die Faust gestützt (M. Frisch).
verteilen unter or an *to distribute* (e.g. money) *among, to*
vertieft/versunken in *buried/engrossed in*: Er war in die Zeitung vertieft.
verwickelt in *involved in*: in eine Sache verwickelt sein.

573. Verbs with which dative and accusative are used in different contexts or with different meanings

auf-nehmen in + acc.
Er ist in den Chor/in das Krankenhaus aufgenommen worden
He has been admitted to the choir/to the hospital

auf-nehmen in + dat.[1]
Ich wurde in seiner Familie sehr freundlich aufgenommen
I was very amiably received in his family

ein-bringen in + acc.
Getreide in eine Scheune einbringen
to bring grain into a barn

ein-bringen in + dat.
ein Gesetz im Parlament einbringen
to introduce a law in parliament

ein-führen in + acc.
jemanden in eine Familie, in eine Gesellschaft einführen
Waren in ein Land einführen
1. *to introduce s.o. into a family, a society etc.*
2. *to import goods into a country*

einführen in + dat.
Er will dieses Buch/diese Sitte in unserer Schule einführen
in other figurative senses, e.g.
He intends to introduce this book/this custom in our school

[1] cf. Du. Haupt.

halten with dat.

Er hielt den Hut vor dem Gesicht	*He held his hat in front of his face* (emphasis on posture)

halten with acc.

Er hielt den Hut einen Augenblick vors Gesicht	*For a moment he held his hat in front of his face* (emphasis on gesture)

kleben an + dat.   *to stick to* (intr.)

Die Haare klebten an seiner Stirn	*His hair stuck to his forehead*
nie am Manuskript klebend (*Zeit*)	*never sticking to his manuscript*

etwas kleben an, auf + acc.   *to stick s.th. to, on* (tr.)

Ich klebte die Marke auf den Brief	*I stuck the stamp on the letter*

klopfen an, auf + acc.

Ich klopfte an die Tür/auf den Tisch	*I knocked at the door/on the table*

klopfen an + dat.

Es klopfte an der Tür	*There was a knock at the door*
ein Klopfen an der Tür	*a knock at the door*

cf. Der Regen prasselte (*pattered*) an die Fensterscheiben, BUT: das Prasseln des Regens an den Fensterscheiben.

lehnen an + dat.

Das Brett lehnte an der Mauer	*The board was leaning against the wall*

(sich) lehnen an + acc. (or gegen)

Er lehnte sein Rad an (or gegen) die Mauer	*He leant his bike against the wall*
Er lehnte sich an (or gegen) die Wand[1]	*He leant against the wall* (action)
Er stand (saß) an (or gegen) die Wand gelehnt	*He was leaning against the wall* (position)

(sich) an-lehnen an + acc.

Er lehnte das Bild an die Wand an	*He leant the picture against the wall*
Er lehnte sich an die Wand an	*He leant against the wall*

D. PREPOSITIONS TAKING THE GENITIVE

574. Thirteen common prepositions taking the genitive, grouped mnemonically:

während *during*	innerhalb *inside, within*
wegen *because of, an account of*	außerhalb *outside*
statt, anstatt *instead of*	oberhalb *above*
trotz *in spite of*	unterhalb *below*
diesseits *on this side of*	um . . . willen *for the sake of*
jenseits *on the other side of, beyond*	. . . halber *for the sake of,*
beiderseits *on both sides of*	*because of*

---

[1] cf. Er lehnte sich über die Brüstung der Brücke *He leant over the parapet of the bridge.*

575. Forty-seven less common prepositions taking the genitive

abseits *away from*
abzüglich *deducting, less*
angesichts *in view of, in the face of*
an Hand (anhand) *with the aid of*
anläßlich *on the occasion of*
an Stelle (anstelle) *in place of*
auf Grund (aufgrund) *on the strength of*
auf seiten *on the side of*
ausschließlich *exclusive of, excluding*
behufs *for the purpose of*
betreffs (betr.) *with regard to*
bezüglich (bez.) *with regard to*
eingangs *at the beginning of*
einschließlich *inclusive of, including*
exklusive (exkl.) *excluding*
gelegentlich *on the occasion of*
hinsichtlich *with regard to*
in betreff *with regard to*
infolge *in consequence of*
inklusive (inkl.) *including*
inmitten *in the midst of*
kraft *by virtue of, by dint of*
längs *along, alongside*
längsseits *alongside* (nautical)
laut *according to, in accordance with*
mangels *for want of*

mittels(t) *by means of*
namens *in the name of*
ob *on account of*
(in) punkto *with regard to*
rücksichtlich *with regard to*
seitens *on the part of, from*
unbeschadet 1. *without prejudice to* 2. *in spite of*
unerachtet *notwithstanding, in spite of*
unfern *not far from*
ungeachtet *notwithstanding, in spite of*
unweit *not far from*
vermittels(t) *by means of*
vermöge *by dint of*
von seiten *on the part of, from*
vorbehaltlich *subject to*
zeit seines Lebens *during his lifetime*
zufolge *as the result of*
zugunsten *for the benefit of, in favour of*
zuungunsten *to the detriment of, to the disadvantage of*
zuzüglich *in addition to, plus*
zwecks *for the purpose of*

576. (a) The following are also used with the dative; but see 578.

während	anläßlich	hinsichtlich	ob
wegen	ausschließlich	inklusive	unbeschadet
statt, anstatt	betreffs	längs	ungeachtet
trotz	bezüglich	laut	vermittels(t)
	einschließlich	mangels	vermöge
angesichts	exklusive	mittels(t)	zugunsten[1]
			zuungunsten[1]

(b) **The following are often used with von + dative.** (They are then technically adverbs.)

diesseits	außerhalb	abseits	infolge
jenseits	oberhalb	an Hand	unfern
beiderseits	unterhalb	an Stelle	unweit
innerhalb		auf Grund	

577. The prepositions listed in 576 are generally used with the dat. and with von + dat. respectively in the following three contexts:

(a) If they are followed by a plural noun, not preceded by an article or adjective with a distinctive gen. plur. ending:

während fünf Jahren   *during five years*

[1] used with preceding dative.

wegen ein paar Hindernissen	*because of a few obstacles*
ungeachtet allerhand Protesten	*notwithstanding various protests*
innerhalb von vier Jahren	*within four years*
anstelle von Briefen	*in place of letters*
infolge von allerhand Protesten	*as a consequence of various protests*

BUT:

wegen dieser Hindernisse	*because of these obstacles*
ungeachtet scharfer Proteste	*notwithstanding sharp protests*

(b) If the noun they govern is preceded by a noun in the genitive denoting possession (the Saxon genitive):

während Vaters (kurzem) Urlaub	*during father's short holiday*
hinsichtlich des Kanzlers (langem) Schweigen	*with regard to the Chancellor's (long) silence*
anstelle von Beethovens letztem Streichquartett	*in place of Beethoven's last string quartet*

(c) If they govern an adjective or participle used substantivally in the neut. sing. and not preceded by a qualifying word with a distinctive gen. sing. ending:

wegen verschiedenem	*because of various things*
Mangels etwas Neuem hat er nur das Alte wiederholt	*For want of something new, he only repeated the old stuff*
anstelle von jemand Intelligentem[1]	*in place of someone intelligent*

BUT:

trotz des Schönen in diesem Gedicht	*in spite of the beautiful things in this poem*
einschließlich alles Neuen	*including everything new*

578. Apart from the three cases treated in 577:

(a) **während, wegen, statt and trotz** are often used with the dative, either colloquially or for the sake of euphony, as in the fourth example: während dem Mittagessen; wegen dem schlechten Wetter; ach, wegen so 'nem Quatsch (H. Fallada); trotz dem Rollen des Zuges (Th. Mann).

(b) In the case of **längs, laut, ob, zugunsten and zuungunsten,** the dative is a recognized alternative (with the last two, a preceding dative): Wir wanderten längs dem Flusse (normal usage: am Fluß entlang); laut neuem Vertrag *in accordance with the new agreement.*

(c) **The remaining prepositions listed in 576(a)** are only used with the genitive.

(d) **The prepositions listed in 576(b)** are often used with von + dative, either colloquially or for the sake of euphony, as in the second example: oberhalb von der Straße; infolge von dem plötzlichen Tod des Pfarrers.

579. The genitives of the personal pronouns (meiner, deiner etc.) sound stilted and **are usually avoided in conversation,** e.g.:

wegen mir	*because of me*
Ich bin an seiner Stelle (or: für ihn) gekommen	*I have come instead of him*

---

[1] The genitive of 'jemand Intelligentes' is avoided (cf. 212(b)).

Note:

i It should be stated that not all Germans would eschew 'statt seiner' in the second example above.

ii See also 153(a).

580. The following of the 47 less common prepositions taking the genitive are stilted officialese and/or commercialese:

abzüglich	einschließlich	mangels	vermittels(t)
ausschließlich	exklusive	mittels(t)	vermöge
behufs	inklusive	rücksichtlich	vorbehaltlich
betreffs	kraft	unbeschadet	zuzüglich
bezüglich	laut	ungeachtet	zwecks

These are preferably replaced by simpler prepositions or by other constructions. The following illustrations of this are based on the examples given in 587, which should be referred to:

ausschließlich: ohne Heizungskosten.

mangels: da es keine anderen Verwertungsmöglichkeiten gab.

unbeschadet: ohne seine Ansprüche zu gefährden.

vorbehaltlich: vorausgesetzt, daß er zustimmt.

zuzüglich: wozu noch die Versandkosten kommen (or: plus Versandkosten).

zwecks: um die Lage gründlich zu erörtern.

581. The following prepositions, most of them listed in 580, are frequently used with an unqualified and uninflected noun, especially in commercial and official phrases:

ausschließlich	in betreff	mangels	wegen
behufs	infolge	mittels(t)	zuzüglich
einschließlich	inklusive	(in) punkto	zwecks
exklusive	laut	trotz	

die Kosten ausschließlich Porto	*the expenses excluding postage*
(in) betreff Marktsituation in Belgien	*regarding the state of the market in Belgium*
infolge Kurzschluß	*owing to a short circuit*
laut Faktura	*as per invoice*
trotz Schnee	*in spite of snow*
Wegen Umbau geschlossen!	*closed for alterations*
wegen Diebstahl(s)[1]	*because of theft*

Junge Dame ... möchte netten, gebildeten Herrn zwecks Heirat kennenlernen (from a personal column in the *FAZ*)

See also 51(c).

E. ILLUSTRATIONS AND PECULIARITIES OF INDIVIDUAL PREPOSITIONS TAKING THE GENITIVE:
582–7 (order as in 574 f.)

582. wegen *because of, on account of*

(a) While it normally precedes its noun, it also frequently follows it, particularly, though not exclusively, in elevated style:

---

[1] BUT: wegen fortgesetzten schweren Diebstahls (*SZ*).

wegen des Wetters	*because of the weather*
des Wetters wegen (*Zeit*)	
dieser schweren Opfer wegen	*because of these great sacrifices*

(b) **Used with personal pronouns, wegen has the following forms**: meinetwegen *for my sake*, deinetwegen, seinetwegen, ihretwegen, unsertwegen, euertwegen, ihretwegen, Ihretwegen; cf. the demonstrative and relative forms dessentwegen and derentwegen (see 165 N.iv, 176(a)N.ii).

Alongside these, there are the colloquial wegen mir (dir) etc. *because of me (you)* and the rare and regional wegen meiner (deiner) etc. (cf. Du. Gram. 3450).

Note the idiomatic meaning:

| Meinetwegen/unsertwegen kannst | *As far as I'm/we're concerned, you* |
| du ins Kino gehen | *can go to the cinema* |

(c) The formula '**von+noun in gen.+wegen**' is mainly used in a number of set phrases, e.g. von Amts wegen *ex officio*, von Berufs wegen *in virtue of/on account of one's profession*, von Rechts wegen *by rights*.

(d) **von wegen+dat.** (generally 'because of') is very colloquial:

| Jetzt hört mir nur auf von wegen | *For heaven's sake stop talking about* |
| Idealismus! (Th. Valentin) | *idealism* |

It is also used by itself to challenge the statement of another speaker:

| Also, du bezahlst heute abend alles.— | *Well now, you're paying for everything* |
| Von wegen! | *tonight.—That's what you think!* |

(e) Where 'for' means 'because of', it generally either is, or can be, rendered by 'wegen':

Er bat um Entschuldigung wegen	*He apologised for being late*
seiner Verspätung	
Ich lobte ihn wegen seines Fleißes	*I praised him for his industry*
(or: für seinen Fleiß)	

583. statt, anstatt *instead of*

| Statt eines Grammophons habe ich | *Instead of a gramophone I've bought* |
| mir ein Radio gekauft | *myself a radio* |

statt is frequently used not as a preposition, but as a conjunction, the equivalent of 'und nicht' (which may indeed be preferred); the case of the following noun or pronoun is then determined by the part it plays in the sentence.

This use may avoid ambiguity:

| Ich besuchte meinen Vetter anstatt | *I visited my cousin instead of (visiting) my* |
| (or: und nicht) meinen Bruder | *brother* |

or it may avoid using the genitive of the personal pronoun:

Sein Haus hat er mir anstatt ihm	*He bequeathed his house to me instead of*
(preferably: und nicht ihm)	*to him*
vermacht	

Further example:

Ich schreibe jetzt mit einer Füllfeder statt mit einem Kugelschreiber	*I now write with a fountain-pen instead of a ball-point pen*

See also 729(a) ii.

584. trotz *in spite of, notwithstanding*

trotz seines letzten Briefes	*in spite of his last letter*

trotz is much used with the dat., and not only colloquially. The dative is fixed in 'trotz allem' *despite everything* and 'trotz alledem' *for all that*; cf. the adverb and conjunction 'trotzdem' *nevertheless*; *in spite of the fact that, although.*

585.

diesseits des Waldes	*on this side of the forest*
jenseits der Grenze	*beyond the frontier*
beiderseits der Straße	*on both sides of the road*
innerhalb des Lagers	*inside the camp*
innerhalb dieser Grenzen	*within these limits*
innerhalb eines Monats	*within a month*
Ich war nicht mehr als eine Stunde/eine Meile von zu Hause, als das Unglück sich ereignete	BUT: *I was within an hour/a mile of home when the accident happened*
Er wohnt in Reichweite von London	N.B. *He lives within easy reach of London*
außerhalb der Arbeitszeit	*outside working hours*
Oberhalb der Straße war ein Felsenvorsprung	*Above the road there was a rocky ledge*
Der Loreleifelsen liegt oberhalb der Stadt St. Goar	*The Lorelei Rock lies above (upstream from) the town of St. Goar*

Note:

i Colloquially, 'hinter' is used more than 'jenseits': Das Dorf liegt hinter der Grenze, hinter dem Wald, hinter Hannover.

ii 'innerhalb' and 'außerhalb' only denote rest, or movement within or outside a place. BUT: We went inside/outside the hut = Wir gingen in die Hütte hinein/aus der Hütte hinaus.

iii All the prepositions dealt with in this paragraph may also be used adverbially.

586. for the sake of (see also 582(b))

(a) **um + gen. + willen** *for the sake of*

Ich tat es um meiner Mutter willen	*I did it for my mother's sake*
um Mutters willen (cf. 51(f))	*for mother's sake*
um ihrer Ruhe willen	*for the sake of her peace of mind*
um Himmels (or Gottes) willen	*for heaven's sake*
Um Gottes willen! Was ist denn das?	*Heavens! Whatever's that?*
um seiner selbst willen	*for his own sake*

(b) (**um**) **meinetwillen** *for my sake*; cf. (um) ihretwillen, (um) unsert-
willen etc., um wessentwillen? Demonstrative and relative: (um)
dessentwillen, (um) derentwillen.

(c) **gen.+halber** *because of, for the sake of*
der Umstände halber   *because of the circumstances*
der Wahrheit halber   *for the sake of the truth*
nur der Form halber   *only for the sake of form*
  Note the compounds formed with some feminine nouns:
    krankheitshalber *because of illness*
    sicherheitshalber *for safety's sake*
    vorsichtshalber *as a precaution, to be on the safe side*
  also: anstandshalber (from *der* Anstand) *for propriety's sake*

(d) **meinethalben** *for my sake*; cf. ihrethalben, unserthalben etc.; dessenthalben, derenthalben (demonstr. and rel.)
IDIOMATIC: Meinethalben/   *As far as I'm/we're concerned, he can*
Unserthalben kann er tun, was   *do what he likes*
er will

587. Illustrations of the 47 less common prepositions+gen.

Unser Haus liegt **abseits** der   *Our house is situated away from the main*
  Hauptstraße   *street*
abzüglich der Unkosten   *less charges*
angesichts der ernsten Lage   *in view of the serious situation*
angesichts des Zahlenverhältnisses   *in view of the numerical relationship of the*
  der Rassengruppen (*FAZ*)   *racial groups*
Ich will die Regel **an Hand** einiger   *I will explain the rule with the aid of a*
  Beispiele erklären   *few examples*
Anläßlich seines 70. Geburtstags   *On the occasion of his 70th birthday he*
  wurde er zum Ehrenbürger   *was made a freeman of the city*
  ernannt
anstelle einer Antwort   *in place of an answer*
auf Grund seiner juristischen   *on the strength of his legal training*
  Ausbildung (*FAZ*)
Er steht **auf seiten** der Regierung   *He is on the side of the government*
die Miete **ausschließlich** der   *the rent exclusive of the charge for heating*
  Heizungskosten (from Du. Haupt.)
behufs einer Verhandlung   *for the purpose of a discussion*
betreffs (**bezüglich**) Ihres   *with regard to your offer*
  Angebots

Note on 'with regard to': betreffs, bezüglich and in betreff are officialese; the commonest German equivalents are: in bezug auf+acc.,
hinsichtlich+gen. and, especially, the clause 'was—object—betrifft
(or: anbelangt)': Was seinen Bruder betrifft, bin ich nicht so sicher
With regard to his brother, I'm not so sure.

eingangs der Zielgeraden   *at the beginning of the straight* (racecourse)
einschließlich der Angehörigen   *including their dependants*
  (*SZ*, referring to immigrants)
exklusive: see 'ausschließlich'
gelegentlich seines Besuchs   *on the occasion of his visit*
hinsichtlich (or: in Hinsicht auf+acc.): see 'betreffs' and Note
in betreff: see 'betreffs' and Note

infolge der neuen Steuer   *in consequence of the new tax*
inklusive Bedienung/Heizung[1]   *including service/heating*

inmitten *in the midst of*: also used with the dative.
inmitten üppiger Blütenpracht   *in the midst of a riot of blossom*
  (*Hbg. Abendblatt*)

kraft seines Amtes   *in virtue of his office*
das Spiel, kraft der Intelligenz   *the game of exerting power*
  unauffällig Macht auszuüben   *unostentatiously by dint of intelligence*
  (Th. Valentin)

längs *along, alongside*: also used with the dative:
längs des Flusses/dem Flusse   *along the river bank*

längsseits des Schiffes   *alongside the ship*

laut *according to, in accordance with*: also used with the dative:
laut einer Rundfunkmeldung   *according to a wireless report*
laut dem Plan der O.E.C.D.   *in accordance with the plan of the*
  (*Spiegel*)   *O.E.C.D.*[2]

ich fand dieses Haus vor, das   *I found this house awaiting me, which,*
  mangels anderer Verwertungs-   *for want of other possible uses, had*
  möglichkeiten . . . zur Arztwohnung   *been earmarked as the doctor's house*
  bestimmt worden war (II. Broch)
mittels(t) eines gefälschten Passes   *by means of a forged passport*
namens[3] der Opposition   *in the name of the Opposition*

ob *on account of* (archaic, poetic or ironical): also found with the dat.
Lax, glücklich ob des Tumultes,   *Lax, glad of the commotion, goes on*
  schürt weiter (H. Broch)   *stirring it up*

Note: 'ob' here means 'über', in the sense of 'about, concerning'; its
main original meaning 'over, above' survives in Rothenburg ob der
Tauber (= Rothenburg on the River Tauber); cf. words like das
Obdach *shelter*, die Obhut *care, protection*. It has no connection with the
conjunction ob *if, whether*.

(in) punkto *with regard to* (from Latin); used colloquially:
(in) punkto seines Einwands   *with regard to his objection*
(in) punkto Geld (cf. 581)   *as regards the question of money*

rücksichtlich dieses Beschlusses (rare)   *with regard to this decision*
Die neuesten Vorschläge **seitens** der   *The latest proposals on the part of the*
  Russen müssen sorgfältig erwogen   *Russians must be carefully con-*
  werden[4]   *sidered*

unbeschadet 1. *without prejudice to* 2. *in spite of*: it may precede or, less commonly,
follow its noun.
unbeschadet seiner Ansprüche   *without prejudice to his claims*
Heute ist London das kulturelle   *Today London is the cultural centre of the*
  Zentrum der Welt, unbeschadet   *world despite the foreign trade deficit*
  des Außenhandelsdefizits und des   *and the ailing state of sterling*
  kränklichen Pfund Sterling
  (*Zeit*, 26.8.66)

[1] cf. 581.
[2] = Organization for European Co-operation and Development.
[3] In the sense of 'by the name of, named', namens is followed by the nom., e.g. ein Kollege namens Hessenberg.
[4] Used with personal pronouns, seitens has the forms meinerseits *for/on my part*, deinerseits etc. (unsererseits and euererseits are rare).

unerachtet: obsolescent: see 'ungeachtet'

unfern *not far from*: colloquially it is also used with the dat.

unfern des Bahnhofs	*not far from the station*

ungeachtet *notwithstanding, in spite of*: it may precede or, less commonly, follow its noun.

ungeachtet dieser Lage auf dem Arbeitsmarkt (*Die Welt*)	*notwithstanding this situation in the labour market*

unweit des Dorfes	*not far from the village*

vermittels, vermittelst: see 'mittels', which is commoner.

vermöge seines unermüdlichen Fleißes	*by dint of his indefatigable industry*

von seiten: see 'seitens'

vorbehaltlich seiner Zustimmung	*subject to his consent*
zeit seines Lebens (set phrase)	*during his lifetime*

zufolge: see 557(n)

zugunsten *for the benefit of, in favour of*: can also be used with a preceding dative and must be so used with a personal pronoun:

eine Sammlung . . . zugunsten der Niedersächsischen Staats- und Universitätsbibliothek (*Die Welt*)	*a collection for the benefit of the State and University Library of Lower Saxony*
Ich bin ihm zugunsten (von meinem Amt) zurückgetreten	*I have resigned (my office) in his favour*

zuungunsten *to the detriment of, to the disadvantage of*: can also be used with a preceding dative and must be so used with a personal pronoun.

zuungunsten des Angeklagten	*to the detriment of the defendant*

Das bestellte Gerät kostet 200 Mark **zuzüglich** der Versandkosten (from Du. Haupt.)	*The instrument ordered costs 200 marks plus forwarding costs*
Er besucht mich heute **zwecks** einer gründlichen Erörterung der Lage	*He is visiting me today for the purpose of a thorough discussion of the situation*

588. north of the town

After the points of the compass, the genitive may be used, though 'von' is commoner, especially with place-names; these are also found uninflected, without 'von':

nördlich (von) der Stadt	*to the north of the town*
östlich von Köln	*to the east of Cologne*
nordwestlich Saigon (*Zeit*)	*to the north-west of Saigon*

F. THE TRANSLATION OF 'INTO, TO' and 'IN, AT' IN LITERAL CONTEXTS

Note:
i In what follows, some alternatives have deliberately been omitted.
ii For the translation of **as far as**, see 559(b) and N.ii(β).

589. in + acc. is used for going into a place, and generally for 'to' implying 'into', and **in + dat.** for being in or at that same place:

Er ging ins Büro, ins Dorf, ins Kino, in die Kirche *to church*, in ein Museum, in ein (neues) Restaurant, in die Stadt *to (the) town*, ins Tal, ins Theater, in den Wald, in sein Zimmer, in den Zoo.
Correspondingly: Er ist im Büro, im Haus, in der Kirche *at church* etc.

Note:
i By extension of 'Er ging ins Kino' etc.: Er ging in einen Film, in ein Konzert, in die Oper, in ein Schauspiel.

ii 'zu' is used with the nouns listed above:
  (a) where 'to' specifically means 'as far as, up to' and not 'into': Ich ging zum neuen Kino und wartete auf ihn; dieser Pfad führt zum Wald; die Straßenbahn fährt zum Zoo (from Du. Haupt.)
  (b) where the sentence concerns the journey rather than the reaching of an objective: Wir machten einen Ausflug zum Dorf; ich war auf dem Weg zu einem einsamen Tal; er wanderte zum Wald.

iii With some nouns, 'zu' is also found with the same connotation as in + acc.; this applies to four of those listed above: Er ging zum Dorf, zur Kirche, zur Stadt, zum Zoo.

iv **He went to his room**: if he went upstairs to his room, 'Er ging auf sein Zimmer' and 'Er ist auf seinem Zimmer' are often used, especially in hotels.

590. auf + acc. is used for *to (into)* and **auf + dat.** for *in* or *at*:

(a) **in a number of fixed phrases**, e.g.
Er ging auf den (Bauern)hof,[1] auf seine Bude *to his (student's) digs*, aufs Feld, auf den Flur *into the entrance-hall, passage*, auf den Gang, auf sein Gut *to his estate*, auf den Hof *into the courtyard*, aufs Land *into the country* (as opp. to town), auf die Straße,[2] auf die Toilette, auf die Wiese;[3] er stieg auf die Kanzel (*pulpit*).
Correspondingly: Er arbeitet auf dem Feld; er stand auf dem Flur, auf der Kanzel; er wohnt auf seinen Gütern etc.

Note:
i When 'Feld' denotes 'field' in the military sense (battlefield, front), auf is not used: ins Feld (or: zu Feld) ziehen *to take the field*; im Felde stehen *to be at the front*.
ii With 'Hof', 'in' is used to denote an enclosed courtyard, surrounded by buildings, e.g. Die Kinder können nur in sonnenlosen Höfen spielen (from Du. Stil.)
iii Er wohnt auf dem Lande, BUT: Er ist wieder im Lande *He is back in this country*; im ganzen Lande.

(b) **with public buildings and places (obsolescent)**
Er ging auf den Bahnhof, auf den Markt.
Er ist auf dem Bahnhof, auf dem Markt.
This use of auf was formerly more widespread; current usage fluctuates

---

[1] or zum Bauernhof, but only: Er ist auf dem Bauernhof.
[2] see also 595.
[3] 'in' is also used.

a good deal, with a preference for 'zu' for *to*, 'an + dat' for *at* and
'in + dat.' for *in*. In all the following cases auf would be possible;
where it is used in the right-hand column, this signifies that auf is
essential in the case in question.

Er ging/fuhr	Ich sah ihn
zum Bahnhof	am (im) Bahnhof
zur Bank	in der Bank
zur Bibliothek	in der Bibliothek
zur Börse (*Stock Exchange*)	an der Börse
zum Markt	auf dem Markt
zur Post	auf der Post
zum Rathaus	im Rathaus

Note:

i **To denote actual entry, use in + acc.**: Als ich ihn sah, ging er gerade in
den Bahnhof, in die Post.

ii Note the following:

Er ging zur Bahn; ich sah ihn an der Bahn (colloquial alternative for
'Bahnhof').

Er ist Kassierer bei einer Bank.

Er ist auf dem Rathaus (BUT: in der Bibliothek) beschäftigt *He works at
the town-hall* (*in the library*).

Der Zug hält nicht auf allen Stationen.

iii With **die Burg** *castle, stronghold* and **das Schloß** *castle, palace*, 'to' is
denoted by auf + acc. if they are situated high up; otherwise by zu or
in.

iv For **Schule** and **Universität**, see 595.

(c) **with formal occasions, e.g. a dance, wedding, conference**

i To denote going to these occasions, auf + acc. is obsolescent, normal
colloquial usage being zu:

Er ging zu einem (auf einen) Empfang, Kongreß, Tanz; zu einer (auf
eine) Hochzeit, Konferenz, wichtige(n) Sitzung.

ii To denote presence or occurrences at these occasions, auf is more
widely used, e.g. (from *Die Zeit*): auf einem abendlichen Empfang,
auf Parties, auf einer Pressekonferenz; it may be an alternative to
'bei': sie haben sich auf/bei einer Hochzeit kennengelernt.

iii Note the following:

1. die Ausstellung *exhibition*
   Er ging zur (or: in die) Ausstellung.
   Ich sah ihn in (or: auf) der Ausstellung.
2. with das Fußballspiel, das Pferderennen, die Regatta, only 'zu'
   and 'bei' are used.
3. auf die Jagd gehen *to go hunting*; auf der Jagd sein.
4. Ich habe in (or: bei) dieser Sitzung mehrmals gesprochen.
5. die Stunde *lesson*
   Ich gehe jetzt zur (or: in die) Musikstunde.
   Der Lehrer hat in der Geschichtsstunde über Luther gesprochen.

591. an + acc. denotes *to*, *up to*, generally implying greater closeness of approach than the rather vaguer 'zu'; correspondingly, **an + dat.** denotes *at*, *by*, *near*, *on* (e.g. on the coast).

an + acc. is mainly used:

(a) **with limited and precise objectives**
Er ging an den Tisch, an die Tür, an die Tafel, ans Mikrofon, an seinen Platz.
Er kam an die Bushaltestelle, an die Straßenkreuzung; an die Stelle, wo der Mann ermordet wurde; an eine Brücke.
Er brachte mein Gepäck ans Auto.

Correspondingly an + dat.: Er stand am Tisch; er zeigte sich am Fenster; er saß an seinem Platz; wir warteten an der Haltestelle; an jedem Zeitungskiosk erhältlich; an der Ecke der Straße.

Where an + acc. is used, the sentence often indicates the purpose of the action:
Er eilte ans Fenster und sah hinaus; er ging an die Schublade und nahm etwas heraus; er ging an die Kasse, um zu zahlen.

Note:
i In all the above examples of an + acc., zu could also be used with the slight difference in connotation explained above.
ii The same difference between an and zu applies when they are used after bis *as far as*, e.g.

Ich begleitete ihn	*I accompanied him*
bis zur Fabrik	*as far as the factory*
bis an die Fabrik	*to the factory gates*
bis an den Wald	*to the edge of the forest*

(b) **with objectives which extend lengthwise**
Er ging an den Fluß, an den Rhein, ans Flußufer, an den Strand, an die See *to the seaside*, an den Zaun *to the fence*, an die Theke *to the bar (counter)*, bis an den Fuß des Berges.
Er trat an den Rand der Brücke.
Wir kamen an die Front (milit.), an die Grenze *to the frontier*.

Correspondingly an + dat.: Rüdesheim liegt am Rhein; das Dorf liegt an der Küste.
Er wohnt an der Riviera, an der See *by the seaside*, am See *by the lake*, am Waldrand, am Marktplatz.
Er stand am Fuß des Berges, des Bettes.

592. A special use of an + dat.: before academic and similar institutions at which someone is employed, e.g.

Er ist Professor an der Universität Göttingen.
Er lehrt an dieser Schule, an einem Gymnasium (*grammar school*).
Er ist Pfarrer an der Peterskirche.
Er ist Intendant (*director*) am Staatstheater (cf. Das Stück wurde an vielen Theatern/an vielen Bühnen aufgeführt).
Er ist am Städtischen Krankenhaus tätig.

Correspondingly an + acc.:

Er erhielt einen Ruf an die Universität Kiel *He was offered a chair at the University of Kiel.*

Er wurde an eine andere Schule versetzt (*transferred*).

Er kam als Regisseur (*producer*) an die Frankfurter Oper.

593. nach is used for 'to':

(a) **before the names of continents, countries and towns:**

Er reiste nach Amerika, nach Deutschland, nach München.[1]

Er schlenderte nach Bacharach hinunter *He strolled down into Bacharach.*

BUT: Ich bin in Deutschland gewesen *I've been to Germany.*

Note:

i Before the names of countries and regions used with the def. art. (see 84(a)(b) and 6(b)) in + acc. is generally used: Ich reise in den Jemen, in die Schweiz (also: nach der Schweiz), in die USA (also: nach der USA), in das Elsaß.

ii With other geographical place-names, various prepositions are used, e.g. Wir fuhren in die Alpen, in den Harz, nach dem/auf den Feldberg, nach dem/an den Bodensee, nach der/an die Riviera; nach Korsika (N.B. Wir waren im Sommer auf Korsika; auf dem Balkan).

(b) **before points of the compass not limited by an adjective:** Wir fuhren nach Süden, BUT: Wir fuhren in den sonnigen Süden.

(c) **before adverbs of place:** Sie müssen nach rechts gehen; er kam nach vorne; er ging nach oben.

Note:

iii In addition to the above fixed uses, there is a tendency to use 'nach' for 'to' in the sense of 'towards, in the direction of': Er bewegte sich langsam nach der Tür; ich sah nach der Tür; er richtete seine Schritte (*turned his steps*) nach der alten Brücke; als ich nach dem Dorf eilte, begegnete ich dem Pfarrer.

iv See also 594(d).

594. zu

(a) **It *must* be used for going to a person,** both in the sense of going up to someone and of going to their house or shop: Er ging zu seinem Onkel, zu Müllers, zum Frisör.

Correspondingly: Er stand/wohnte bei seinem Onkel.

(b) **It is the commonest preposition for going to a place or to an occasion**; as such, it has already figured frequently in 589, 590 and 591 as an alternative for in, auf and an. There follow some further examples of its use; the right-hand column gives the preposition required to denote presence in the place in question.

Er ging	Er ist
zum Denkmal	am (beim) Denkmal
zur Fabrik	in der Fabrik[2]

---

[1] cf. Er fuhr nach einer süddeutschen Stadt.

[2] BUT: Der Arbeiter ist noch auf der Fabrik (still at work, not home yet).

zum Hafen	im Hafen
zur Höhle	vor (bei, in) der Höhle
zur Straßenbahn *tram*	in der Straßenbahn
zur Treppe	auf der Treppe
Sie kehrte zu ihrer Arbeit zurück	Sie ist wieder bei der Arbeit
Der Rauch stieg zur Decke	An der Decke war Rauch
Er fuhr zur Insel	Er ist auf der Insel
⌐eine Expedition zum Mond	ihr Aufenthalt auf dem Mond

Note:

i Before 'Denkmal' and 'Treppe', an + acc. could be used to convey 'up to' with greater proximity.

ii **To denote actual entry**, use in + acc., e.g. Als ich ihn sah, ging er gerade in die Fabrik.

iii **The prefix hin- is often used in conjunction with the preposition 'zu'**; the effect is to strengthen the idea that the objective was, is or will be reached. E.g. Er ging zur Post/zum Fenster hin; dieser Pfad führt zum Wald hin; ich werde morgen zu ihm hingehen.

(c) **A special use of 'zu'**: it means in (or: at), linking a prominent building with the town in which it is situated or indicating a birthplace; the alternative is generally in + dat. (Occasionally zu is found before the name of a town, instead of in + dat., outside these contexts.)

der Dom zu Köln (generally: der Kölner Dom)	*Cologne Cathedral*
im Wehrmachtheim zu Proskurov (A. Goes)	*in the transit-camp at Proskurov*
J. S. Bach wurde zu Eisenach geboren	*J. S. Bach was born in Eisenach*

(d) **North Germans have a marked tendency to use nach instead of zu**, e.g. Er ging nach dem Bahnhof, nach dem Hafen, nach der Tür; er fuhr nach der Insel.[1]

595. Some special cases

Schule etc.[2]

Er geht noch nicht in die Schule (or: zur Schule)	*He doesn't go to* (attend) *school yet*
Er ging um halb acht in die Schule (or: zur Schule)	*He went to school at half past seven*
Er ist noch auf der Schule (or: in der Schule)	*He is still at school* (= still attends school)
Er ist noch in der Schule	*He is still at school* (= not home yet)
Sie schicken ihr Kind in die Schule (or: zur Schule)	*They are sending their child to school*
Er geht aufs Gymnasium/in ein Internat	*He goes to a grammar-school/a boarding-school*
Er studiert an einer Technischen Hochschule	*He's studying at a technical college*

[1] cf. M. Tamsen in *Deutschunterricht für Ausländer*, Jan./Febr. 1957, pp. 6 ff.: Die Präpositionen nach und zu bei Verben der Bewegung.

[2] see also 592.

Straße

(a) **Where Straße means an open road** without contiguous houses—or preponderantly this—**'auf' is used**: Das Unglück ereignete sich auf dieser Straße (cf. auf der B-6 (Bundesstraße 6), auf der A-1 (Autobahn 1)); ich ging auf der gleichen Straße zurück, auf der ich gekommen war (Du. Stil.); in einer Zeit, in der noch Raum genug war auf unseren Straßen (*Zeit*).

(b) **Where Straße means a street** between contiguous houses (or 'road' used in this sense), **'auf' is used in 3 phrases**:

  i auf der Straße *in the street*: Die Kinder spielen auf der Straße; ich begegnete ihm/hörte ein Geräusch auf der Straße; der Mann auf der Straße.

  ii auf die Straße *into the street*: Ich ging auf die Straße; die Studenten gingen auf die Straße *the students took to the streets* (to demonstrate).

  iii auf den Straßen *in the streets*; 'in' is also possible: Es waren große Menschenmengen auf/in den Straßen.

Otherwise 'in' is used: Das Unglück ereignete sich in dieser Straße, in der Goethestraße; er spielt/wohnt in unserer Straße; das Auto hielt in einer engen Straße; er kam in die Straße, wo er früher gewohnt hatte; in den Geschäftsstraßen hastete die Menge wie in London (*Zeit*).

Note: Der Gasthof liegt an der Göttinger Straße (open road).
Der Gasthof liegt in der Bahnhofstraße (city street).

Universität

Im Oktober geht er auf die Universität; er ist auf der Universität (or simply: Er studiert).

Er geht an die Universität H.; er studiert (Jura) an der Universität H.; er ist Professor an der Universität H.[1]; an unseren Universitäten.

Ich gehe heute nachmittag zur Universität.

Karl ist noch nicht zu Hause; er arbeitet noch in der Universität.

596. Miscellaneous cases

bei Hofe	*at court*
am Hof Ludwigs XIV.	*at the court of Louis XIV*
Der Hund legte sich/lag mir zu Füßen	*The dog lay down/lay **at my feet***
Ein Apfel fiel zur Erde/zu Boden	*An apple fell **to the ground***
Der Junge fiel auf den Boden/auf die Erde	*The boy fell on the ground*[2]
Der Junge sprang auf den Boden/ zur Erde	*The boy jumped to the ground*[2]
Wir gehen heute in die Heide	*We're going **on to the heath** today*
ein winziges Häuschen in der Heide (Arno Schmidt)	*a tiny cottage on the heath*
Es waren Wolken am Himmel	*There were clouds **in the sky***

---

[1] cf. 592.

[2] Here Erde may refer to the ground outside or the floor inside; Boden only to the latter.

Ich sah eine Lerche/ein Flugzeug in der Luft	*I saw a lark/an aeroplane in the sky*
Das Flugzeug stieg in die Luft	*The aeroplane rose into the sky*
im Himmel	***in heaven***
Der Hund sprang an ihm hoch	*The dog jumped **up at** him*
Er kam/trat zu mir	*He came **up to** me*
Er trat an mich heran	
mein Besuch bei meinem Onkel	*my **visit to** my uncle*
ein Besuch des Zoos (or: ein Zoobesuch)	*a visit to the zoo*
eine Besichtigung des Doms	*a visit to the cathedral*
Ein Besuch in München (or: der Besuch von München) ist sehr lohnend[1]	*A visit to Munich is well worthwhile*

G. MAIN FIGURATIVE USES OF GERMAN PREPOSITIONS

597. an + dat.

(a) **in respect of, in the way of**: the 'an' phrase generally depends on, and qualifies, a word which denotes or implies amount:

ein großer Aufwand an Energie	*a great expenditure of energy*
Der Bedarf an Arbeitskräften verringert sich	*The demand for labour is decreasing*
Es fehlt ihm an Takt	*He is lacking in tact*
Wir haben 2 Mill. DM an Aufträgen vorliegen	*We have 2 m. marks worth of orders on the books*
Er ist seinem Bruder an Urteils- kraft überlegen/gleich/unterlegen	*He is superior/equal/inferior to his brother in power of judgement*
Sein Brief läßt an Klarheit nichts zu wünschen übrig	*His letter leaves nothing to be desired in the way of clarity*
Ich wage nicht, hier darzustellen, was alles an Komplikationen hier eintreten könnte (SZ)	*I do not dare describe here all that might arise in the way of complications*

cf. brauchen an *to need in the way of*, knapp sein an *to be short of*, aus Mangel an *for lack of*, reich an, ein großer Unterschied an (e.g. Begabung), an Boden verlieren *to lose ground*, an Höhe verlieren, ein großer Vorrat an *a large stock of*, an Wichtigkeit zu-nehmen *to increase in importance*

(b) **in connection with, about, in**

Er hat etwas Eigenartiges an sich	*He has something peculiar about him*
was mir an ihm auffiel	*what struck me about him*
Was gefällt dir an ihm?	*What do you like about him?*
Das hasse ich an den Schulmeistern am meisten (Th. Valentin)	*That's what I hate most about schoolmasters*
Das Schönste an der Sache ist, daß . . .	*The best of it is that . . .*

cf. Was ist komisch an meinem Hut? Es ist nichts an dem Gerücht; es ist was dran *there's something (some truth) in it*.

---

[1] commoner: Es lohnt sich sehr, sich München anzuschauen.

(c) **with verbs and nouns denoting being interested, participating or taking pleasure in something**

Er hat Anteil am Geschäft, am Gewinn	*He has an interest in the business, participates in the earnings*
Ich nehme Anteil an seinem Wohl	*I take an interest in his welfare*
Er hat viel Freude an seinen Kindern	*His children give him a lot of pleasure*

cf. sich beteiligen an, teil-nehmen an, die Augen/sich weiden an *to feast one's gaze on/to delight in, gloat over.* See also 634.

(d) **with verbs denoting falling ill with, suffering or dying from an illness**: erkranken an, leiden an, sterben an (cf. sein Tod an einem Herzschlag); cf. zugrunde gehen an *to be ruined by* (e.g. alcohol):

Er leidet an Schwindelanfällen	*He suffers from attacks of dizziness*
Er leidet unter der Einsamkeit/ unter der Hitze	BUT: *He suffers from loneliness/ from the heat*

598. an + acc.

(a) **introduces the objective of certain mental processes**[1]

Du erinnerst mich an ihn	*You remind me of him*
Ich erinnere mich an ihn	*I remember him*
die Erinnerung an	*the memory of*
zum Andenken an	*in memory of*

cf. denken an, der Gedanke an, sich gewöhnen an, glauben an *to believe in* (e.g. ghosts, Communism), der Glaube an.

(b) **is used to complete the sense of a number of nouns often corresponding to verbs taking the dative**, e.g.

Die Anpassung an die neuen Verhältnisse ist nicht leicht (sich an-passen + dat.	*Adapting oneself to the new circumstances is not easy* *to adapt o.s. to)*
Er hat keinen Anschluß an Deutsche (sich jemandem an-schließen	*He has made no contact with Germans* *to join s.o.* e.g. for a walk)

cf. seine Antwort an mich, sein Befehl an die Truppen, sein Bericht an die Direktion, viele Grüße (*love*) an Onkel Fritz, die Kriegserklärung an Japan, der Verkauf des Hauses an seinen Vetter, sein Vermächtnis (*legacy*) an seinen Neffen, der Verrat von Geheimnissen an den Feind.

599. Summary of two uses of 'an' that recur in their various contexts in Section H below:

i **an + dat.** is used before the feature *by* which one recognizes someone or notices a state of affairs and before an example *by* which one shows something or the phenomena *in* which one studies something. E.g. Ich bemerkte an seinem Benehmen, daß . . .; man kann diesen Instinkt an Tieren studieren; Experimente an Tieren.

ii **an + acc.** is used before the person *to* whom one addresses (richten) a request, one's words etc.; to whom one appeals; directs, addresses or writes a letter; passes s.th. on (weitergeben); or turns for advice: Ich werde mich an ihn um Rat wenden.

[1] cf. Collinson, op. cit., p. 107.

600. auf + acc.

(a) is used to denote the objective of a large number of actions and mental attitudes[1]

Note:

i This use of auf is the figurative parallel of zielen auf *to aim at*, schießen auf, feuern auf.

ii Whereas 'um' in its analogous use (cf. 609(a)) almost exclusively introduces something that it is sought to gain or obtain, 'auf' is wider in its application.

an-wenden auf	*to apply to*
Man könnte dieses Wort kaum auf ihn anwenden	*One could hardly apply this word to him*
Ich bin gespannt auf seine Antwort	*I'm curious as to what his answer will be*
Wir tranken auf sein Wohl	*We drank to his health*
	to refer to:
Seine Bemerkung bezog sich auf dich	*His remark referred to you*
Er wies auf die Schwierigkeiten hin	*He referred (pointed) to the difficulties*
Er wies mich auf die Vorschriften hin	*He referred me to the regulations*[2]
Du kannst dich auf mich berufen	*You can refer to me* (as a reference or witness)

cf. after verbs and nouns:

achten, acht-geben auf *to pay heed to, to keep an eye on*, an-spielen auf *to allude to, hint at*, eine Anspielung auf, Anspruch erheben/haben auf *to lay/have a claim to*, jemanden auf etwas aufmerksam machen *to draw s.o.'s attention to s.th.*, auf-passen auf *to keep an eye on*, Aussicht haben auf *to have prospects of*, sich beschränken auf *to confine o.s. to, to be limited to*, sich besinnen auf *to try to remember*, dringen auf *to demand urgently* (e.g. an interview, new measures), ein-gehen auf *to go into a matter; to agree to a suggestion*, sich erstrecken auf *to extend to, include*. sich freuen auf *to look forward to*, hoffen auf, die Hoffnung auf, sich konzentrieren auf, lauern auf *to lie in wait for*, coll.: *to await s.o. impatiently*, reagieren auf, ein Recht haben auf, schimpfen auf *to swear at, grumble at*, sich stürzen auf *to rush at*, (sich) vorbereiten auf *to prepare for*,[3] warten auf.

after adjectives and participles:

eifersüchtig auf, aufs Schlimmste gefaßt *prepared for the worst*, neidisch auf, neugierig auf *curious about* (e.g. the result),[4] stolz auf, versessen (or erpicht) auf *bent on having, mad about* (e.g. money).

(b) to rely on, to be based on and similar verbs

sich verlassen auf *to rely on, count on*, cf. bauen auf, rechnen auf, zählen auf; spekulieren auf *to speculate, gamble on* (e.g. a quick success); vertrauen auf *to put one's trust in*.

sich gründen auf, sich stützen auf; basieren auf + dat., beruhen auf + dat. *to be based on*; cf. ich gründe meine Meinung auf diese Tatsache.

(c) denoting 'in response to, as the result of'; the relevant expressions are sometimes strengthened through the addition of 'hin':

Auf meine Bitte (hin) hat er die Sache für sich behalten	*At my request he kept the matter to himself*

---

[1] cf. Collinson, op. cit., p. 108.
[2] BUT: Er wies mich an seinen Kollegen *He referred me to his colleague.*
[3] BUT: (sich) bereit-machen für, (sich) fertig-machen für; see also 622 i.
[4] neugierig auf is only applied to something that lies in the future; otherwise a paraphrase is used e.g. Ich möchte mehr über seine Vergangenheit wissen.

Auf meinen Brief hin hat er sofort gehandelt	*As the result of my letter he immediately took action*

cf. auf Anfrage *on application*, auf Anraten meines Onkels *on my uncle's advice*; antworten/die Antwort auf einen Brief, eine Frage; auf seine Empfehlung (hin) *on the strength of his recommendation*, auf seine Initiative, auf seinen Rat (hin); auf Verabredung *by arrangement, by appointment*; auf meine Verantwortung (hin) *on my responsibility*, auf einen Verdacht hin *on the strength of a suspicion*, auf ein Wort von ihm, auf Wunsch *by request*, auf meinen Wunsch (hin) *at my wish*.

601. aus

(a) to denote origin, reason, motive: from, out of

Er tat es aus Dankbarkeit	*He did it out of gratitude*
Ich weiß es aus Erfahrung	*I know it from experience*
Ich frage nur aus Interesse	*I'm just asking from interest*

cf. aus Furcht vor seinem Vater, aus Gewohnheit *from habit*, aus diesem Grund, aus Langerweile *out of boredom*, aus Liebe zu seiner Mutter, aus Neid, aus reiner Neugierde *out of sheer curiosity*, aus Spaß *for fun*, aus Überzeugung *out of conviction*, aus freiem Willen *of one's own free will*.

(b) to denote 'made of'

Die Kaffeekanne war aus Silber (gemacht); sie trug ein Kleid aus blauer Seide (commoner: ein blaues Seidenkleid) BUT: Er hat ein Herz von Stein.

Compare:

Er hat viel aus dem Geschäft gemacht	*He has developed the business very successfully*
aus der Not eine Tugend machen	*to make a virtue of necessity*
bestehen aus	*to consist of*
zusammengesetzt aus	*composed of*

602. bei

(a) on the occasion of, in the course of, at

bei dieser Gelegenheit	*on this occasion*
bei Gelegenheit	*when an opportunity occurs*
Ich half ihr beim Abwasch	*I helped her with the washing up*
bei dem bloßen Gedanken	*at the very thought*
Er erblaßte bei der Nachricht	*He turned pale at the news*
Bei *dem* Radau kann ich nicht arbeiten	*I can't work with that row going on*
Acht Menschen kamen bei diesem . . . Verkehrsunfall ums Leben (*FAZ*)	*Eight people were killed in this road accident*
bei Vollbeschäftigung	*in the case of full employment*

cf. bei diesem Anblick, bei seiner Ankunft, bei der Arbeit sein, er hinderte mich bei der Arbeit, bei der Erwähnung des 'Faust', beim Essen, beim Fußball, bei einem Glas Wein *over a glass of wine*, bei Straßenkämpfen, bei Tageslicht, bei Tisch, bei seinem Tod, bei näherer Überlegung (or: bei Licht besehen) *on further consideration*, bei schönem Wetter, bei jeder Wiederholung *at every repetition*, bei Wind, bei Wind und Wetter *in all weathers*, bei diesen Worten, bei unserer letzten Zusammenkunft.

(b) in view of, with

Bei seinem unzuverlässigen Charakter muß man vorsichtig sein	*In view of his unreliable character you have to be careful*
bei den immer steigenden Preisen	*in view of the constantly rising prices*
Bei diesem Gehalt kann ich mir kein Auto leisten	*With this salary I can't afford a car*

(c) **despite**

Bei all seinen Verlusten bleibt er ein Optimist	*Despite all his losses he remains an optimist*

cf. bei allen Vorteilen *for all the advantages*, bei alledem *for all that*, beim besten Willen *with the best will in the world.*

(d) **Various applications derived from its literal sense 'at the house of, with'** (see 550(b))

Bei ihm kann man nie sicher sein	*With him you can never be certain*
bei Hunden	*in the case of dogs*
Das hat ihm bei den Amerikanern sehr geschadet	*That did him a lot of harm in the eyes of the Americans*
beliebt bei	*popular with*
sich bei jemandem entschuldigen/ beklagen	*to apologize/to complain to s.o.*
sich bei jemandem erkundigen	*to inquire of s.o.*
Ich dachte bei mir	*I thought to myself*

cf. Er hat großen Einfluß bei dem Premierminister; wir haben Mathematik bei Dr. Schulze; dieses Wort kommt bei Goethe oft vor (*often occurs in Goethe*); bei uns tut man das nicht; er arbeitet bei dieser Firma; er hat bei der Infanterie/bei der Luftwaffe gedient.

(e) **4 common but somewhat unexpected uses**

Er war bei guter/schlechter Laune	*He was in a good/bad mood*
Er nennt mich beim Vornamen	*He calls me by my Christian name*
Er nahm mich beim Wort	*He took me at my word*
Er nahm mich bei der Hand	*He took me by the hand*

603. **gegen, gegenüber and zu are all used to denote conduct towards, a mental attitude towards, or relations with, someone or something** (cf. Fr. envers). Often two or all of them may be used in the same context, though each has its distinctive features.

(a) **zu**

i **It mainly, but not exclusively, denotes friendly attitudes and is mostly used with adjectives:**

Er war sehr freundlich zu mir	*He was very kind to me*

cf. frech zu *impudent to*, gerecht zu/gegen *just towards*, grausam zu/gegen *cruel to*, gut zu *good, kind to*, hart zu/mit/gegen *hard towards*, (un)höflich zu (*im*)*polite to*, nett zu *nice to*, respektvoll zu *respectful to*, unfreundlich zu *unkind to*.
BUT: seine Frechheit, Gerechtigkeit, Grausamkeit, Härte, (Un)höflichkeit gegen mich; sein Respekt vor mir.

ii It is used with a certain number of nouns, e.g.

Wir haben freundliche Beziehungen zu Müllers	*We are on friendly terms with the Müllers*
die Einstellung Rulls zur Schule (Th. Valentin)	*Rull's attitude to school*
aus Freundschaft zu ihm	*out of friendship for him*
seine Liebe zu seiner Mutter/zur Musik	*his love for his mother/of music*
seine Neigung zu dem Mädchen	*his liking for the girl*
Stellung zu etwas nehmen	*to define one's attitude to s.th.*
das Verhältnis des Einzelnen zum Staat	*the relation of the individual to the state*

iii It is rarely used with adverbs; thus: Er benahm sich sehr höflich gegen mich.

(b) **gegen mainly,** but not exclusively, **denotes hostile attitudes**:
Er war mißtrauisch gegen mich   *He was distrustful towards me*

cf. with adjectives and participles:
abgehärtet gegen *hardened to,* abweisend gegen *unfriendly towards,* argwöhnisch gegen *suspicious of,* empfindlich gegen *sensitive to,* gesichert gegen *secure against,* gleichgültig gegen *indifferent to,* rücksichtslos, rücksichtsvoll gegen *(in)considerate towards,* taub gegen alle Warnungen *deaf to all warnings,* treulos gegen *disloyal to.*

with nouns:
die Abneigung gegen *aversion for,* der Haß gegen/auf + acc. *hatred of,* das Mißtrauen gegen *distrust of,* seine Pflicht gegen seine Eltern *his duty to his parents,* sein Verhalten gegen seinen Chef *his attitude to his employer.*

See also (a) above: i and iii.

(c) **gegenüber**
i It follows a pronoun; it may precede, but generally follows, a noun.

ii **It can generally be used as an alternative to 'zu' and 'gegen';** in the examples in (a) and (b) above, gegenüber could *not* be used in the following: gut zu, nett zu, Beziehungen zu, seine Liebe zu, seine Neigung zu, das Verhältnis zu, abgehärtet gegen, empfindlich gegen.

iii It is frequently the preferred preposition, e.g.: Er handelte durchaus gerecht mir gegenüber (gegen mich); seine Güte mir gegenüber (zu mir) war rührend *(touching).*

iv **It is flexibly used to denote 'towards, in relation to' in a variety of other and less straightforward contexts,** e.g.

die Politik der USA gegenüber Rußland	*the policy of the USA towards Russia*
Erhards Hilflosigkeit gegenüber Positionskämpfen und taktischen Finten (*Zeit*)	*Erhard's helplessness in the face of jockeying for position and tactical feints*
Doch auch Herr Lautenschlag verfügte über allerlei Schachzüge den Seinen gegenüber (A. Kolb)	*But, like a chess-player, Herr Lautenschlag too had at his disposal various moves in his dealings with his family*
Er konnte seiner Frau gegenüber ein Gefühl von unbezahlten Schulden nicht loswerden (V. Baum)	*He could not get rid of a feeling of unpaid debt towards his wife*

(d) **3 common adjectives have 'mit':** böse mit *angry with,* sanft mit *gentle with,* streng mit *strict with.*

604. nach

(a) **denotes the object of a desire, striving and numerous purposeful actions**

Er sehnt sich nach Ruhe	*He is longing for peace*
Er forscht nach der Wahrheit	*He is seeking after the truth*
Die Kinder schrien nach Brot	*The children cried for bread*

Ich telefonierte nach dem Arzt/nach einem Taxi	*I phoned for the doctor/for a taxi*
Ich sah mich nach ihm um	*I looked out for him*
die Forderung nach einer Lohnerhöhung	*the demand for a wage-increase*

cf. after verbs:

angeln nach *to fish for*, aus-schauen nach, dürsten nach *to thirst for*, crave for (e.g. fame) (intr. and impers.; elev.), nach Komplimenten fischen, graben nach, greifen/langen nach *to reach for*, jagen nach *to pursue* (e.g. fame, pleasure), schicken nach *to send for*, schlagen nach *to hit out at*, schmachten nach *to thirst for*, *pine for* (lit. and fig.; elev.), streben nach, suchen nach, tasten nach *to grope for*, verlangen nach *to crave for*; *to ask to see* (e.g. a doctor).

after adjectives:

begierig nach *eager, impatient, ambitious for*, gierig nach *greedy for*.

after nouns:

das Heimweh nach der Schweiz, die Jagd nach Glück, die Nachfrage nach diesen Waren *the demand for these goods*, die Sehnsucht nach, auf der Suche nach, die Sucht nach Genuß *the mania for pleasure*, das Verlangen nach *the craving for*, der Wunsch nach.

(b) according to, in accordance with

Note: In this sense, 'nach' sometimes precedes and sometimes follows its noun; an asterisk after the phrase indicates that both positions are possible; it always precedes a proper name or a personal pronoun, but is rarely used with the latter.

nach diesem Gesetz (more official: diesem Gesetz gemäß)	*according to this law*
nach dem Testament ihres Vaters	*under her father's will*
nach Art der Betrunkenen (H. Böll)	*after the manner of drunkards*
nach der Häufigkeit seiner Besuche zu urteilen	*to judge by the frequency of his visits*
Das ist ein Mann so recht nach meinem Herzen	*He's a man just after my own heart*
Ich kenne ihn nur dem Namen nach	*I only know him by name*
Es sieht nach (or wie) Regen aus	*It **looks like** rain*
Es sieht nach reiner Verschwendung aus	*It looks like sheer wastefulness*
Er trinkt zuviel.—Er sieht auch danach aus	*He drinks too much.—He looks like it too*
Er sah wie ein Landstreicher aus	BUT: *He looked like a tramp*

cf. with 'nach' preceding its noun:

nach allem, was ich höre; Namen nach dem Alphabet ordnen;* nach Ansicht meines Bruders *according to my brother*;[1] nach Ansicht Lessings/nach Lessing; nach diesem Bericht;* nach Geschmack *according to taste*; nach meinem Geschmack; nach Herzenslust *to one's heart's content*; nach der Karte essen *to eat à la carte*; nach (besten) Kräften *to the best of one's ability*; nach deutschen Maßstäben *by German standards*; nach dieser Methode; nach der Natur malen *to paint from nature*; nach der Regel;* riechen nach *to smell of*; schmecken nach *to taste of*; nach dem Sommerfahrplan; nach meiner Überzeugung* *I am convinced that . . .*; nach meiner Uhr ist es halb zwei; nach Wunsch *as desired*.

---

[1] In conversation, a paraphrase is more usual: Mein Bruder meint/ist der Ansicht/ behauptet, daß man diesem Mann nicht trauen kann.

cf. with 'nach' following its noun:

allem Anschein nach *to all appearances,* meiner Ansicht nach,* seinem Aussehen nach *to judge by his appearance,* meiner Meinung nach,* der Reihe nach *in turn,* aller Wahrscheinlichkeit nach, seinem Wesen nach *by its very nature.*

N.B. je nach *according to, depending on*

Je nach dem Preis kannst du ein oder zwei Pfund kaufen	*According to the price you can buy one or two pounds*
je nachdem	*all according, it depends*

605. über + acc: about, concerning. E.g.

sich ärgern über	*to be annoyed about*
Er hat mich über seine Pläne beruhigt	*He has reassured me about his plans*
Ich war über seinen Vorschlag empört	*I was indignant at his suggestion*
ein Aufsatz über 'Faust'	*an essay on 'Faust'*

cf. after verbs:

sich amüsieren über, sich beklagen/sich beschweren über *to make a complaint about,* erröten über *to blush at,* sich freuen über, klagen über *to complain of* or *about, to grumble about,* sich lustig machen über *to make fun of,* nach-denken über, sich wundern über *to be surprised at,* **and many others.**

after adjectives:

bekümmert über *worried about,* entsetzt über *shocked at,* enttäuscht über/von *disappointed at,* entzückt über/von *delighted about,* froh über, unentschieden über **and many others.**

after nouns:

die Ansicht über, ein Buch über Schmetterlinge, die Freude über, die Klage über *the complaint* or *lament about,* in Verzweiflung über *in despair about,*[1] im Zweifel sein über[2] **and many others.**

606. about, concerning: some common instances in which prepositions other than 'über' are used:

die wachsenden Zweifel an seiner Fähigkeit (*Zeit*)	*The growing doubts about his capability*
neugierig auf + acc.	*curious about* (see 600(a))
sich irren in + dat.	*to be mistaken about s.th., in one's judgement of s.o.*
begeistert von	*in raptures about*
Das kann ich nicht von ihm glauben	*I can't believe that of him*
Was halten Sie von ihm?	*What do you think of him?*
Es ist von einer Gehaltserhöhung die Rede	*There's talk of a pay-increase*
schwärmen von	*to rave, go into raptures about*
träumen von	*to dream about*
nervös wegen	*nervous about*

See 609(b) for the use of 'um' to denote 'about, concerning'.

---

[1] BUT: verzweifeln an + dat. *to despair of.*
[2] But see 606.

607. **about, concerning: verbs with alternative prepositions**

(a) **denken, hören, lesen, sagen, schreiben, sprechen** and **wissen** may be used with über or von: 'über' generally implies length and thoroughness, 'von' brevity and cursoriness:

Wie denken Sie darüber?	*What is your view of the matter?*
Was denken Sie von ihm?	*What do you think of him?*
Wir haben darüber gesprochen	*We talked about it*
Er hat davon gesprochen	*He mentioned it*
Er weiß viel über Flugzeuge	*He knows a lot about aeroplanes*
Ich wußte schon von seinem Tod	*I already knew of his death*

Note:
i lesen über may mean to give a course of lectures on:
Professor Schulze liest über Schillers Dramen.
ii sagen zu: to say to, to give as one's opinion about:

Was sagt die Regierung zu Ungarn?	*What does the government say to (events in)*
(M. Horbach)	*Hungary?*

iii for wissen um, see 609(b).
iv **erzählen** *to relate* is used with von or über, with no difference in meaning: Er hat viel von seinen Ferien/über seine Ferien erzählt.

(b) **sich erkundigen** and **fragen** may be used with i nach ii über.
i

Ich erkundigte mich nach ihm	*I inquired after his health*
Ich fragte nach ihm	1. *I asked about his health*
	2. *I asked to see him*
Ich erkundigte mich/fragte nach seinem Namen, nach dem kürzesten Weg	*I inquired after/asked for his name, the shortest way*

ii

Ich erkundigte mich über den neuen Film	*I inquired about the new film*
Ich fragte ihn über seine Arbeit	*I asked him about his work*

Note: fragen is also used with 'um':

Ich fragte ihn um Rat	*I asked him for advice*

(c) **reden** über:

Die Leute reden bereits über ihn	*People are beginning to talk (disparagingly) about him*
Darüber läßt sich reden	*That's a sensible idea (worth discussing)*

reden von:

Er redete von seinen Erlebnissen, von seiner Familie	*He spoke of his experiences, his family*
Reden wir von etwas anderem!	*Let us talk about something else*
(viel) von sich reden machen	*to cause a (great) stir*
nicht zu reden davon, daß . . .	*not to mention the fact that . . .*

(d) **schimpfen** über + acc.   *to grumble about*
    schimpfen auf + acc.   *to swear at*

(e) **sich streiten, sich zanken** *to* quarrel um/über: see 609(a).

(f) **sich täuschen** über + acc.   *to be mistaken about* (e.g. the probable difficulties)

sich täuschen in + dat.   *to be mistaken in* (e.g. one's expectations of s.o.)

608. über + acc.: other figurative uses

(a) it may denote superiority or control over

Kaiser Karl V. herrschte über viele Länder   *The Emperor Charles V ruled over many lands*

Er war nicht mehr Herr über seine Gefühle/über sich selbst[1]   *He was no longer master of his feelings/of himself*

cf. es über sich bringen, etwas zu tun *to bring o.s. to do s.th.*, über jeden Verdacht erhaben *above suspicion*, siegen über, der Sieg über, verfügen über *to have at one's disposal.*

Compare über + dat.: Im Geschäft habe ich nur den Chef über mir; er steht über der Sache *he has complete command of* (i.e. conversance with) *the matter.*

(b) it may denote 'over, (going) beyond'

Er lebt über seine Verhältnisse   *He lives beyond his means*

Ich bin über die Neugierde hinaus   *I am past curiosity*

Es geht nichts über ein Glas Rheinwein[2]   *There's nothing like a glass of hock*

cf. über alle Maßen *beyond measure*; er liebt die Ruhe über alles; über Erwarten *beyond expectation*; das geht über meine Kräfte, über meinen Verstand *that is beyond me*; über die Stränge schlagen *to kick over the traces.*

N.B. For über before a cardinal (e.g. über hundert Bücher), see 248 N.iii.

609. um

(a) it introduces the objective of some action (see 600(a)N.ii)

der Kampf ums Dasein   *the struggle for existence*

Er tat es nur um das Geld   *He only did it for the money*

Sie stritten sich (zankten sich) um das Geld   *They quarrelled over the money* (i.e. as to who should have it)

Sie stritten sich über den Preis   BUT: *They quarrelled about the price*

um Geld schreiben   *to write for money* (asking for it)

für Geld schreiben   BUT: *to write for money* (to earn it)

Wir liefen um die Wette   *We raced each other* (lit.: we ran for a wager)

Sie logen um die Wette   cf. *They vied with each other in telling lies*

Er wandte sich an mich um Rat   *He turned to me for advice*

cf. jemanden um etwas bemühen *to trouble s.o. for s.th.*, sich um eine Stelle bemühen (or bewerben) *to apply for a post*, zu Gott um etwas beten, betteln um, bitten um, die Bitte um, um etwas flehen, *to plead, beg for s.th.* kämpfen um *to fight for* (a strategic position, victory), konkurrieren um *to compete for*, losen um *to draw lots for*, um Hilfe schreien, um Geld spielen, streiken um *to strike for* (e.g. a wage increase), werben um *to woo.*

---

[1] more literary: Herr seiner Gefühle/seiner selbst.
[2] from Betteridge, op. cit., über.

(b) **it denotes 'about, concerning, regarding' in a limited number of cases**, e.g.

Ich beneide ihn um seine Schlagfertigkeit	*I envy him his quickness of repartee*
es handelt sich um	*it is a question of* (Fr.: il s'agit de)
Es ist schade um den Verlust	*It's a pity about the loss*
Es steht schlecht um meinen Bruder	*My brother is in a bad way*
Ich war um eine Entschuldigung verlegen (from Du. Stil.)	*I was at a loss for an excuse*

cf. die Angst ums Leben *fear for one's life*; sich ängstigen um *to be anxious about*; sich Sorgen machen um *to worry about*; die Sorge um ihren Sohn; trauern um *to mourn for*.

It frequently has a literary flavour:

der heilige Schmerz . . . um die Gegenwart des Vaterlandes (Treitschke on H. von Kleist)	*the sacred sorrow for the present state of his fatherland*
Es war etwas Besonderes um diese Landerziehungsheime (K. Mann)	*There was something special about these boarding-schools*
Ich wußte nicht um seinen Tod (normal usage: von seinem Tod)[1]	*I didn't know of his death*

(c) **it denotes degree of difference**

Er ist (um) einen Kopf größer als ich	*He is a head taller than I am*
Ich werde meinen Aufenthalt um zwei Tage verlängern	*I shall extend my stay by two days*
Er hat sich um zwei Mark verrechnet	*He was two marks out in his calculation (or accounts)*
um die Hälfte mehr	*half as much again*
Die Mehrheit der CDU hatte um 15 Sitze abgenommen	*The CDU (Party's) majority had decreased by 15 seats*
eine Erweiterung der EWG um England und andere EFTA-Länder (SZ)	*an expansion of the EEC by the inclusion of England and other EFTA countries*

610. unter + dat.

(a) **it is used to introduce the accompanying circumstances of an action or occurrence:**

unter diesen Umständen[2]	*under these circumstances*
unter dieser Bedingung	*on this condition*
unter diesem Vorwand	*on this pretext*
unter Tränen	*amid tears*
und unter wachsendem Hallo wurde auch dies bestätigt (Th. Mann)	*and amid the growing uproar this too was confirmed*

(b) **it is used in a number of straightforward figurative contexts** (English: *under, beneath, below*):

Ich habe zehn Arbeiter unter mir; ich kann es nicht unter 60 Mark verkaufen; es geschah unter meinen Augen; unter dem Schutz der Dunkelheit; unter Zwang handeln *to act under compulsion*; unter den Waffen *under arms*; dieser Film ist unter aller Kritik (sl. unter aller Kanone).

---

[1] Möller (op. cit., p. 88) calls 'um' a 'Modepräposition', especially when used with 'wissen'.

[2] cf. unter allen Umständen *in any case, without question*; unter Umständen *under certain circumstances, if need be, possibly.*

(c) **it denotes 'by' in the phrases:**

Was verstehst du unter einer Präposition/ unter 'Idealismus'?	*What do you understand (mean) by a preposition/ by 'idealism'?*
Er ist unter diesem Namen bekannt	*He is known by this name*

611. von

(a) **of, on the part of**

Es war sehr liebenswürdig/nett/ vernünftig von Ihnen	*It was very kind/nice/sensible of you*
Es war dumm von mir	*It was silly of me*
Es ist nicht recht von ihm	*It's not right of him*

(b) **about, concerning**: see 606, 607(a)(c).

(c) **it is used figuratively in a wide range of contexts,** most of which are included in Section H below; its appropriateness is in most cases not difficult to feel, e.g.

Das kommt vom vielen Trinken	*That comes of drinking so much*
Er tat es von selbst	*He did it of his own accord*
Er lebt von seinen Aktien	*He lives on his investments*

612. vor + dat.

(a) **it denotes the emotional or physical cause of some state or action**

Ich war außer mir vor Entzücken	*I was beside myself with delight*
Mir war vor Kälte elend	*I was miserable with cold*
fallend und sterbend . . . im Wüstenbrand vor übernatürlicher Anstrengung (Th. Mann)	*falling and dying in the burning heat of the desert from superhuman exertion*

cf. Ich konnte vor Aufregung nicht einschlafen; ich schwitzte vor Hitze; ich brüllte vor Lachen; er gähnte vor Müdigkeit; er war gelb vor Neid (*green with envy*); er stöhnte vor Schmerz; er strahlte vor Zufriedenheit *he beamed with satisfaction.*

N.B. Er starb vor Hunger; ich starb fast vor Langerweile BUT: Er starb an einer Lungenentzündung (*pneumonia*), an Altersschwäche.

(b) **it introduces a source of danger or aversion, which is feared, loathed or guarded against**

Ich fürchtete mich (hatte Angst) vor dem Hund	*I was afraid of the dog*
Ich erschrak vor dem Hund	*I was scared by the dog*
Ich erschrak über sein schlechtes Aussehen (Du. Stil.)	BUT: *I got a fright at his unhealthy appearance*
Alles war in heiligem Respekt vor ihm	*Everyone was in unholy awe of him*
Es ekelt mich vor ihm	*He fills me with abhorrence*
Er warnte mich vor dem Hund	*He warned me about the dog*
Gott bewahre mich vor meinen Freunden!	*Heaven protect me from my friends!*
Er drückt sich immer vor dem Abwasch	*He always gets out of washing up*

cf. after verbs:
sich in acht nehmen (sich hüten, auf der Hut sein) vor *to be on one's guard against, to beware of*; fliehen vor; sich vor jemandem schämen *to feel ashamed in s.o.'s*

presence; sich scheuen vor *to shrink from* (e.g. a formidable task, a lie), (sich) schützen vor; (sich) verbergen/verstecken vor *to hide from*

after nouns and adjectives:
der Abscheu/der Ekel vor *abhorrence of*; die Angst/Furcht vor; auf der Flucht vor *fleeing from*; der Schutz vor; sicher vor *safe from*; eine Warnung vor.

Note: **to rescue from**: Er rettete mich aus dem brennenden Haus; er befreite mich von den Banditen; er rettete mich vor dem Tod.

613. zu

(a) it denotes purpose

Wozu gebrauchst du dieses Messer?	*What do you use this knife for?*
Ich gebrauche es zum Kartoffel-schälen	*I use it for peeling potatoes*
Mach dich zum Ausgehen fertig!	*Get ready for going out*
Er ist zum Nachprüfen des Fernsehers da	*He's come to check the television*
Ich sage dir dies zu deiner Beruhigung	*I'm telling you this to reassure you*
Ich tue es zu deinem Besten	*I'm doing it for your own good*
Hier gibt es Möglichkeiten zum Schilaufen	*There are possibilities for skiing here*
der Mut zu einer Entscheidung	*the courage for a decision*

cf. Ich habe ihn zum Abendessen (BUT: ins Theater) eingeladen; zur Ansicht *on approval*; Stoff zu einem neuen Anzug; zum Besten der Armen *for the benefit of the poor*; zur Erholung verreisen *to go away to recuperate*.
Er war zum Wissenschaftler geboren (*born to be*); er hat mir zum Geburtstag diese Uhr geschenkt; er ist (nicht) zum Lehrer geeignet ((*not*) *fitted to be*); wir hatten keine Gelegenheit zu einem Gespräch; er paßt nicht zum Pfarrer *he is not made to be a parson*; ein Plan zur Lösung dieser Probleme; dieses Wasser ist nicht zum Trinken; ich hänge das Tuch hierhin zum Trocknen; ein Verein zur Verbreitung der Bibel *a society for the propagation of the Bible*; zu diesem Zweck; ein Mittel zum Zweck *a means to an end*; wozu machst du das?

Note:

dienen zu = to serve a purpose

Wozu dient dieser Apparat?	*What is this appliance used for?*
Er dient zur Entsaftung von Obst und Gemüse	*It is used as a liquidizer for fruit and vegetables*
Er dient dazu, Obst und Gemüse zu entsaften	*It is used to liquidize fruit and vegetables*

dienen als = to serve as, in the capacity of

Ich diene ihm als Sekretär	*I serve him as secretary*
Das frühere Schloß dient jetzt als Museum (Du. Stil.)	*The former palace now serves as a museum*
Dieser Satz könnte als Beispiel dienen	*This sentence might serve as an example*

Sometimes either can be used: Dieses Erlebnis diente mir zur/als Warnung.

(b) it denotes 'by way of, for, as'

Er murmelte etwas zur Antwort	*He muttered something by way of a reply*
Seine Rede hatte eine politische Krise zur Folge	*His speech resulted in a political crisis*
Er tat es mir zu Gefallen	*He did it to oblige me* (lit. *as a favour*)

| Du solltest dir deinen Bruder zum Muster nehmen | *You should take your brother as a model* |

cf. zur Abwechslung *for a change*; zum Andenken an + acc. *in memory of*; zum Beispiel; zum (or als) Dank für; ihm zu Ehren *in his honour*; er hat eine Deutsche zur Frau; zum (or als) Lohn für *as a reward for*; zum Scherz *by way of a joke*; zur Strafe; zum Überfluß *needlessly*; zum Vergnügen *for pleasure*.

(c) it denotes result or effect

| Zu meinem Erstaunen hat er das Examen bestanden | *To my astonishment he has passed the examination* |
| Diese Maßnahmen werden zum Vorteil/zum Schaden der Stadt sein | *These measures will be to the advantage/ to the detriment of the town* |

cf. zu meinem Ärger, zu meiner Befriedigung *to my satisfaction*, zu meiner Beruhigung *to my relief*, zu meiner großen Freude; es ist zum Lachen *it's laughable*; es ist zum Verrücktwerden *it's enough to drive you mad*.

(d) Sie wählten ihn zum Präsidenten *They elected him president*: 'zu' is similarly used with the following analogous verbs: befördern *to promote*, bestimmen *to destine to be*, degradieren *to demote*, ernennen *to appoint*, krönen *to crown* (s.o. king), machen *to make*, weihen *to ordain*.

Er wurde zum Major befördert	*He was promoted major*
Ich habe ihn mir zum Feind gemacht	*I've made an enemy of him*
Ich mache es mir zur Regel, dies zu tun	*I make it a rule to do this*

With nouns: seine Beförderung, Ernennung, Wahl zum Direktor.

See also 636(b).

(e) it denotes conduct towards, a mental attitude towards, or relations with: see 603.

(f) Apart from the specific cases dealt with above, 'zu' is used in a variety of abstract or figurative contexts, where English has 'to' or 'into':

Ich kam zu dem Schluß, daß . . .	*I came to the conclusion that . . .*
zur Sache kommen	*to come to the point*
Er trieb mich zur Verzweiflung	*He drove me to despair*
Er zwang mich zu einer Entscheidung	*He forced me into a decision*
Ich kam nicht zum Briefeschreiben	*I didn't get round to letter-writing*
Er ist zum katholischen Glauben übergegangen	*He has gone over to the Catholic faith*
der Schlüssel zur Wahrheit	*the key to the truth*
Er wurde zu allerlei Dummheiten verleitet	*He was misled into various foolish acts*
Er überredete mich zu einem Glas Wein	*He talked me into having a glass of wine*

H. THE RENDERING OF ENGLISH PREPOSITIONS IN FURTHER CONTEXTS

614. Turning English idiomatic phrases

Not infrequently, one realizes instinctively that a particular English phrase, involving a preposition, is highly unlikely to have an analogous

German equivalent; in such cases the basic meaning of the English idiom must be determined and a straightforward but convincing German rendering of it must be aimed at. E.g.

Lesen Sie es, wenn Sie einmal Zeit haben (or: gelegentlich)	*Read it at your leisure*
Ich wußte wirklich nicht (or: Ich war ratlos), wie ich ihm helfen könnte	*I was at a loss to know how I could help him*
Wir haben zusammen nur einen Schirm	*We've only got one umbrella between us*
Wenn ich mich nur ausruhen könnte!	*Oh, for a rest!*
Du kannst es mir glauben	*You can take it from me*
Das ist gerade was für mich	*That is just in my line*
Er lebt von meinem Geld	*He lives on me*
Es ist nun einmal mein sehnlichster Wunsch, Italien zu sehen	*I've set my heart on seeing Italy*

615. Note on the lists that follow

In a great many cases the German is far closer to the English than in the instances dealt with in 614. Phrases were selected for inclusion by a combination of three criteria: 1. that they seem essential or useful to know; 2. that the German preposition either differs from the English one or, in some cases, rather surprisingly tallies with it; 3. that they are not, at least in some cases, easily accessible in a dictionary.

The more advanced student may like to use the lists to test his knowledge and 'Sprachgefühl'.

The lists are in general arranged in alphabetical order of the English.

616. about

	What about it?
Wie wär's damit?	1. = *Shall we do it?*
Na und?	2. = *So what?*
Wie wär's mit noch einem Stück Kuchen?	*What about another piece of cake?*
Wie ist es mit dir?	*What about you?*
Was ist da zu machen?	*What can you do about it?*
Wir müssen (da) irgendwas machen	*We must do something about it*
Da ist nichts zu machen	*There's nothing you can do about it*
Er wanderte durch die Straßen	*He walked about the streets*
Er ging im Garten umher (or herum)	*He walked about the garden*

Note on 'herum' and 'umher' (cf. the last example):
The distinction between herum (circling round: Er lief um den Baum herum) and umher (criss-crossing) is no longer adhered to in current and particularly not in colloquial German, herum being frequently used for umher. Moreover, in a context such as the following, only herum is used: Er kramte in der Schublade herum *He rummaged about in the drawer* (cf. Du. Haupt: herum/umher).

617. against

Er hat mir davon abgeraten	*He advised me against it*
gegen meine bessere Einsicht	*against my better judgement*
Ich bin an das Pult angestoßen	*I knocked against the desk*
Ich habe mit dem Knie an das Pult gestoßen	*I knocked my knee against the desk*
Ich bin in der Klemme	*I'm up against it*

618. along (here treated both as adverb and as preposition)

Ich ging langsam dahin	*I was walking slowly along*
Als er so dahinging, . . .	*As he walked along (cf. 304(f))*
Er schritt einher	*He strode along (implying stateliness)[1]*
Er ging vor/neben/hinter mir her	*He was walking along in front of/beside/ behind me*
Ich ging den Weg entlang	*I walked along the path*
Ich ging am Fluß (less common: den Fluß) entlang	*I walked along the river*
Am Fluß entlang wuchsen Weiden	*Willows grew along the river*
entlang der Grenze	*along the frontier*
Packe dich! Mach dich fort!	*Get along with you! (lit.)*
Unsinn! Sei nicht so blöde!	*Get along with you! (fig.)*
Er kommt gut vorwärts	*He is getting along well*
Er macht gute Fortschritte	

See also 699, 700(b)(d), 706: daher.

619. among

in den Bergen	*among the hills*
unter anderem	*among other things*
unter manchem anderen	*among many other things*
Wir waren unter uns	*We were among ourselves*
Ich rechne/zähle ihn zu meinen Freunden	*I count him among my friends*
Er trat aus der Schar seiner Kollegen heraus	*He stepped forward from among his colleagues*

620. at   i with verbs

von vorn an-fangen	*to begin at the beginning*
Er warf mir einen wütenden Blick zu	*He cast a furious glance at me*
Ich schätze sein Einkommen auf 3000 DM[2] (acc.)	*I estimate his income at 3,000 marks (a month)*
hinter die Wahrheit kommen	*to get at the truth*
Was wollen Sie damit sagen?	*What are you getting at?*
Worauf wollen Sie (mit Ihren Bemerkungen) hinaus?	
Machst du dich über mich lustig?	*Are you getting at me?*
Gilt diese Bemerkung mir?	
Ich sah auf die Uhr	*I looked at my watch*
Er sah nach mir herüber	*He looked across at me*
Er nörgelt an mir herum	*He nags at me*
hinter den Büchern sitzen	*to sit at one's books*
Er warf einen Stein nach mir	*He threw a stone at me*
Er versuchte sich im Malen	*He tried his hand at painting*

[1] cf. Betteridge, op. cit., einher.   [2] often pronounced 'D-Mark'.

Er versuchte sich daran, Gedichte zu schreiben	*He tried his hand at writing verse*
an einer Sache arbeiten	*to work at something*

ii with adjectives

Er ist gut in Physik	*He is good at physics* (at school)
Er schreinert gut	*He is good at carpentry*
Stück Draht, ganz einfach. Ich bin gut mit Schlössern (E. M. Remarque) (coll.)	*Bit of wire—quite simple. I'm good at locks*

iii phrases

bei einem flüchtigen Blick	*at a casual glance*
in 200 Meter Höhe	*at a height of 200 metres*
mit 70 Stundenkilometer Geschwindigkeit	*at a speed of 70 kilometres an hour*
um jeden Preis	*at any price*
im Grunde (genommen), eigentlich	*at bottom, fundamentally, actually*
im Grunde meines (seines) Herzens, eigentlich	*at heart*
ein Paar Handschuhe zu 20 Mark	*a pair of gloves at 20 marks*
auf meine Kosten	*at my expense* (lit. and fig.)
auf eigne Kosten	*at my (his, our, etc.) own expense*
Das Hotel war gut und noch dazu billig	*The hotel was good and cheap at that*
auf Kosten + gen.	*at the expense of*
die Männer an der Spitze	*the men at the top* (of an organization)
zu diesem Preis	*at this price*
Auf diese Art werden wir nichts erreichen	*At this rate (in this way) we shall achieve nothing*
Er ist eifrig dran	*He is hard at it*
um keinen Preis	*not at any price*
Er lief hinauf und nahm dabei zwei Stufen auf einmal	*He ran upstairs two at a time*

621. by

i with verbs

Der Antrag wurde mit 90 gegen 31 Stimmen bei 17 Enthaltungen angenommen	*The motion was approved by 90 votes to 31 with 17 abstentions*
Wir fuhren diese Straße	*We came by this road*
zum Fenster hinaus-klettern	*to climb out by the window*
Ich kenne ihn nur vom Ansehen	*I only know him by sight*
jemanden an der Hand führen	*to lead s.o. by the hand*
Er faßte mich am Arm	*He seized me by the arm*
etwas an einem Beispiel zeigen	*to show s.th. by an example*
Er schwört auf diese Tabletten	*He swears by these tablets*
Ich konnte an seinem Gesichtsausdruck erkennen, was er sich dachte	*I could tell by his expression what he was thinking*

ii phrases

bei Tageslicht	*by daylight*
beim Feuerschein	*by fire-light*
Er ist von Natur (aus) schüchtern (Du. Stil.)	*By nature he is shy*
auf dem nächsten Wege	*by the nearest way*
Wir fahren über Stuttgart	*We are going by way of (via) Stuttgart*

622. for

	i with verbs
bewundern wegen	*to admire for*
Nach Baden-Baden umsteigen!	*Change for Baden-Baden*
ein Examen machen	*to go in for an examination*
Sein Hobby ist Fotografieren	*He goes in for photography*
Ich habe sie für[1] Dienstagabend (für[1] halb acht) eingeladen	*I have invited them for Tuesday evening (for half past seven)*
Er ist nach Hamburg abgereist	*He has left for Hamburg*
jemanden/sich auf etwas Unangenehmes ein-lassen	*to let s.o./o.s. in for s.th. unpleasant*
Er ging auf die Tür zu	*He made for the door*
Ich habe ihn auf deinen Besuch vorbereitet	*I've prepared him for your visit (= warned him about it)*
Ich habe alles für deinen Besuch vorbereitet	*I've prepared everything for your visit*
Um drei Uhr	*At three o'clock*
gingen wir ins Dorf/machten wir uns auf den Weg zum Dorf	*we set out for the village (on foot)*
fuhren wir ins Dorf	*(by car)*
gingen/fuhren wir nach Hause[2]	*we set out for home*
Man sieht das Fernsehen als etwas Selbstverständliches an	*One takes television for granted*
Ich setze voraus, daß . . .	*I take it for granted that . . .*
Ich nahm ihn mit zu einem Spaziergang	*I took him for a walk*
Ich führte das Kind/den Hund spazieren	*I took the child/the dog for a walk*
Das Mehl wird auf seine Reinheit (hin) geprüft	*The flour is tested for purity[3]*

ii with adjectives

Wir waren für den Angriff bereit/ zum Angriff bereit	*We were ready for the attack (to meet it/ to make it)*
bekannt wegen (or für)[4]	*well known for*

iii with nouns

ein Hilferuf	*a cry for help*
seine Abreise nach Hamburg	*his departure for Hamburg*
Es besteht kein Grund zur Beunruhigung	*There are no grounds for alarm*
der Grund für (or + gen.)	*the reason for*

iv phrases

für alle Fälle	*for all eventualities*
meinetwegen	*for all I care*
Es ist sehr gut möglich, daß er krank ist	*For all I know, he's ill*
Ich riskiere einmal, an ihn zu schreiben (or: Was auch dabei herauskommt, ich will einmal an ihn schreiben)	*For better or for worse, I'm going to write to him*
Er ist zunächst einmal zu alt	*For one thing, he's too old*
ich für meinen Teil (or: was mich betrifft)	*I for my part*
ich zum Beispiel	*I for one*

[1] less usual: auf.
[2] a rather literary alternative: traten wir den Heimweg/die Rückfahrt an.
[3] cf. Ich habe den Brief auf Fehler (hin) durchgesehen.
[4] Only für is idiomatic when a 'daß' clause follows: Er ist dafür bekannt, daß er immer auf sich warten läßt *He is well known for being late.*

Er ist hinter dem Geld her
Er ist auf Geld aus
Es hat etwas für sich

He is out for money

There is something to be said for it

623. from

Ich habe ihn davon abgebracht,
dies zu tun
Die Wäsche hing an der Leine
Ich habe die Bücher bei Rothmann
bestellt
Er hinderte mich daran, den Brief
zu schreiben
Er hat verhindert, daß ich den Brief
schrieb
Ich war verhindert, in die Kirche zu
gehen
etwas aus der Nähe/aus der Ferne
sehen

i with verbs

I dissuaded him from doing this

The washing hung from the line
*I have ordered the books from
Rothmanns*
*He prevented (i.e. hindered) me from
writing the letter*
*He prevented (i.e. stopped, barred) me
from writing the letter*
I was prevented from going to church

to see s.th. from close up/from far away

ii with adjectives and nouns

Ich bin müde von der vielen Arbeit
Ich habe keine Geheimnisse vor dir

I'm tired from so much work
I have no secrets from you

iii phrases

von Kopf bis Fuß
Er liest alles, von der Philosophie bis
zum Krimi
Bonn ist 35 Kilometer von Köln
entfernt (coll.: Von Bonn nach
Köln sind's 35 Kilometer)

from head to foot
*He reads everything, from philosophy to
thrillers*
Bonn is 35 kilometres from Cologne

624. in, into

vor Gericht erscheinen
zusammen-stoßen (s) mit
sich stoßen an + dat.
Er änderte etwas an dem Bild, an
seinem Plan
sich jemandem an-vertrauen
Sein Leben gliedert sich in drei
Abschnitte
zum Film gehen
Eins hatten wir alle gemeinsam
Diesen Zug haben wir mit den
Amerikanern gemein
zu jemandem/zu einer Sache
Vertrauen haben
An ihm hast du einen treuen Freund
einer Sache nach-gehen (s)
Er läßt sich nicht davon abbringen,
es zu tun
einen Schnitzer machen
einen Satelliten in eine Umlaufbahn
bringen
Wir fuhren gegen einen Baum
Ich bin ihm gestern zufällig begegnet
Wie sagt man das auf deutsch?
Er sagte es in gebrochenem Deutsch

i with verbs

to appear in court
to bump into (s.o.)
to bump into (s.th.)
*He changed s.th. in the picture, in his
plan*
to confide in s.o.
His life falls into three parts

to go into films
One thing we all had in common
*This trait we have in common with the
Americans*
to have confidence in s.o./in s.th.

In him you have a faithful friend
to look into a matter
He persists in doing it

to put one's foot in it
to put a satellite into orbit

We ran into a tree
I ran into him yesterday
How do you say that in German?
He said it in broken German

Wie sagt man das in Ihrer Sprache?	*How do you say that in your language?*
Ich sah es im Geiste vor mir	*I saw it in my mind's eye*
Ich konnte mir sein Erstaunen vorstellen	*In my mind's eye I could see his astonishment*
mit fester Stimme sprechen	*to speak in a firm voice*
Er hat dem Kuchen tüchtig zugesprochen/Er hat tüchtig zugelangt	*He tucked into the cake*
Er wurde am Bein verwundet	*He was wounded in the leg*

ii phrases

nach allen Seiten	*in all directions*
am hellen Tage	*in broad daylight*
in guten Verhältnissen sein	*to be in good circumstances*
(sehr) gefragt sein (sometimes: werden)	*to be in (great) demand*
in meiner Angst, in meiner Verlegenheit etc. (wandte ich mich an ihn)	*in my anxiety, in my dilemma etc. (I turned to him)*
Seine Bemerkung war sehr am Platz/sehr angebracht	*His remark was very much in place*
In der Praxis ist es nicht ganz so	*In practice it's not quite like that*
für jemanden voreingenommen sein	*to be prejudiced in s.o.'s favour*
die betreffende Zeitung	*the newspaper in question*
klein von Gestalt	*small in stature*
in diesem Fall/wenn das der Fall ist	*in that event*
Er war im Begriff, es zu tun	*He was in the act of doing it*
auf dem Gebiet der Politik	*in the domain of politics*
Schlagzeilen machen	*to be in the headlines*
(tief) in den roten Zahlen stecken	*to be in the red*
nichts auf der Welt	*nothing in the world*
an Ihrer Stelle würde ich . . .	*in your place I should . . .*

625. of   i with verbs

Note: Numerous verbs with 'of' will be found in 499 f. among verbs followed by the genitive.

Er wurde freigesprochen	*He was acquitted of the crime*
jemandem gegenüber mit etwas prahlen/protzen[1]	*to boast to s.o. of s.th.*
Er ist von deutschen Eltern (geboren)	*He was born of German parents*
Er stammt aus einer alten Bremer Familie	*He comes of an old Bremen family*
Das kommt davon	*That's what comes of it*
Es ist nichts daraus geworden	*Nothing has come of it*
Ich werd' aus seinem Brief nicht klug	*I can make nothing of his letter*
Was meinst du zu seinem Brief?	*What do you make of his letter?*
etwas in Besitz nehmen	*to take possession of s.th.*
Wie finden Sie dieses Buch?	*What do you think of this book?*
Was halten Sie von diesem Buch?	
—Ich finde es sehr langweilig	*—I think it very boring*
—Ich halte nicht viel davon	*—I don't think much of it*

---

[1] also = to show off, cf. an-geben mit: Er gibt mit seinem Mercedes an *He boasts of/shows off with his Mercedes.*

Ich traue ihm nicht/Ich habe ihn in Verdacht

Ich habe diesen Prozeß satt
Ich bin diesen Prozeß leid
Dieser Prozeß steht mir bis oben hin (sl.)
Ich habe es satt, von ihm belästigt zu werden
Das gilt nicht von ihm

ii with adjectives

I'm suspicious of him

I'm tired/sick of this lawsuit

I'm tired of his pestering me

That is not true of him

iii with nouns

die Kritik an der Regierung
der erste Blick auf Heidelberg
der Einfall in Polen (acc.)
der Mord an + dat. (or: die Ermordung + gen.)
die Beschäftigung mit einem Steckenpferd
ein Sinn für Naturschönheit
mein Anteil an dem Geld

criticism of the government
the first glimpse of Heidelberg
the invasion of Poland
the murder of

the pursuit of a hobby

a sense of natural beauty
my share of the money

iv phrases

Er war mir weit voraus
gar nicht zu reden von
ein eignes Haus
von selbst, aus eignem Antrieb
die Schlacht bei Leipzig

He was far ahead of me (lit. and fig.)
not to speak of
a house of one's own
of one's own accord
the Battle of Leipzig (see also 64(a))

626. on, upon

Wir haben uns über den Preis/auf den Preis von 1000 Mark geeinigt
Ich habe mich für diesen Hut entschieden
zur Bühne/zum Theater gehen
Ich hatte den Hund an der Leine
Ich habe kein Geld bei mir
auf einen Gedanken kommen
Er lebt von seinen Aktien
Er schaute eben bei seinem Freund herein
Mein Fenster geht auf den Garten (hinaus)
operieren + acc.
Er nahm den Hund an die Leine
eine neue Stellung an-treten
sein Geld für etwas verschwenden
seine Zeit mit etwas verschwenden
seine Zeit an jemanden verschwenden
Er trägt einen Ring (am Finger)

i with verbs

We've agreed on the price/on the price of 1000 marks
I've decided on this hat

to go on the stage (become an actor)
I had the dog on the lead
I have no money on me
to hit upon an idea
He lives on his investments
He looked in on his friend

My window looks out on to the garden

to operate on s.o.
He put the dog on the lead
to start on a new job
to waste one's money on s.th.
to waste one's time on s.th.
to waste one's time on s.o.
He wears a ring

ii phrases

Er ist darauf versessen/erpicht, es zu tun
ein Wagen nach dem andern
Er schwärmt für moderne Kunst

He is bent on doing it

car upon car
He's mad on modern art

Die Ausstellung war von großem/ kleinem Umfang	*The exhibition was on a large/small scale*
Dies wird per Saldo die beste Lösung sein	*On balance this will be the best solution*
an Bord (des Dampfers)	*on board (the steamer) (with 'to be' and 'to go')*
Er ist auf/an Deck	*He is on deck*
Er ging auf Deck spazieren	*He went for a walk on deck*
Ich ging an Deck	*I went on deck*
Ich habe heute abend Dienst	*I'm on duty this evening*
aus zuverlässiger Quelle	*on good authority*
Der Direktor ist in Urlaub gefahren	*The manager has gone on holiday*
Der Direktor ist im Urlaub	*The manager is on holiday*
am Horizont	*on the horizon*
Der Soldat kommt/ist auf Urlaub	*The soldier is coming/is on leave*
im Fernsehen	*on television*
im Erdgeschoß, im Parterre, zu ebener Erde	*on the ground floor*
im zweiten Stock	*on the second floor*
auf gut Glück, aufs Geratewohl	*on the off-chance*
obwohl es unwahrscheinlich ist, daß er zu Hause ist	*on the off-chance of his being at home*
Ich wollte es gerade tun	*I was on the point of doing it*
Ich war drauf und dran, es zu tun	
im stillen	*on the quiet*
auf der Stelle	*on the spot, immediately*
Die Feuerwehr war bald zur Stelle	BUT: *The fire-brigade was soon on the spot*
unterwegs	*on the way*
auf dem Weg zum Bahnhof[1]	*on the way to the station*
auf meinem Weg ins Dorf	*on my way to the village*
im Rundfunk, im Radio	*on the wireless*
Reihe auf Reihe	*row upon row*
auf/zu beiden Seiten	*on both sides, on either **side***
Ich legte meine Papiere beiseite	*I put my papers on one side (aside)*
Er trat zur Seite	*He stepped on one side (aside)*
Er stand auf einer Seite des Präsidenten	*He stood on one side of the President*
Ich nahm ihn beiseite/auf die Seite	*I took him on one side*
Er war immer auf unserer Seite	*He was always on our side*
Er ist eher ruhig	*He's on the quiet side*
Ich muß mich gut (or: auf guten Fuß) mit ihm stellen	*I must get on the right side of him*
Ich muß ihn richtig anpacken	*—the same, meaning to cajole on some particular occasion*
Ich darf mir sein Wohlwollen nicht verscherzen	*I must keep on the right side of him*
auf dieser Seite (des Hauses)	*on this side (of the house)*

627. out of

34 von hundert Patienten	*34 out of 100 patients*
Ich fühle mich ausgeschlossen (or: nicht zugehörig)	*I feel out of it*
Ich habe zehn Mark zu wenig	*I'm ten marks out of pocket*

---

[1] commoner than: unterwegs zum Bahnhof.

Mir fehlen zehn Mark
Ich habe zehn Mark dabei verloren
Er kommt nie aus sich heraus
   See also 549(a)

I'm ten marks out of pocket

He never comes out of his shell

628. over

Mein Plan hat gewisse Vorteile vor
   Ihrem
über der Arbeit ein-schlafen
Was er sagt, ist uns zu hoch

My plan has certain advantages over yours

to fall asleep over one's work
He talks over our heads

629. to   i with verbs

eine Frage/eine Bitte/seine Worte an
   jemanden richten
sich an die Vorschriften halten
Der Film hält sich eng an den Roman
sich mit jemandem versöhnen
sich mit etwas ab-finden
Wieviel macht das?
Die Sache kommt zur Krise
Er wurde zu fünf Jahren Gefängnis
   verurteilt
bei-tragen zu
für eine Zeitung schreiben
jemandem Gerechtigkeit widerfahren
   lassen
Um ihm gerecht zu werden, muß
   man zugeben, daß . . .
Er hat sich den Kalbsbraten
   schmecken lassen (or, slightly
   precious: Er hat dem K. tüchtig
   zugesprochen)
zu Ende gehen
Ich habe ohne Schwierigkeiten zu ihm
   gefunden
Diese Tradition geht auf Bismarck
   zurück
Seine neue Stellung ist ihm zu Kopfe
   gestiegen
Der Preis ist von 10 auf 12 Mark
   gestiegen

Ich hörte meinem Onkel/der Rede/
   der Musik zu
Ich höre gern klassische Musik/Mozart/
   Radio
Er wollte auf meinen Rat nicht hören
Vernunft an-nehmen[1]

Er murmelte etwas vor sich (acc.) hin
reduzieren auf + acc.
sich an die Arbeit machen
sich dran machen

to address a question/a request/one's words
to s.o.
to adhere to the regulations
The film adheres closely to the novel
to become reconciled to s.o.
to become reconciled to s.th.
What does it come to (cost)?
The matter has come to a head
He was sentenced to five years'
imprisonment
to contribute to
to contribute to a paper
to do (mete out) justice to s.o.

BUT: *To do him justice, one must admit*
that . . .
He did full justice to the roast veal

to draw to a close
I found my way to him without any
difficulty
This tradition goes back to Bismarck

His new post has gone to his head

The price has gone up from 10 to 12
marks

*I **listened to** my uncle/the speech/the*
music
I like listening to classical music/Mozart/
the radio
He wouldn't listen to my advice
to listen to reason

He muttered s.th. to himself
to reduce to
to set to work

---

[1] from Betteridge, op. cit.

zu jemandem sprechen — *to speak* (*talk*) *to s.o.* (without the idea of a conversation)[1]

Der Lehrer sprach zu der Klasse über dieses Thema (Du. Stil.) — *The teacher spoke to the form about this subject*

jemanden sprechen — *to speak to, to see s.o.* (generally on an official matter)

mit jemandem sprechen — *to speak* (*talk*) *to* or *with s.o.* (*to converse with*)

jemandem/seinen Grundsätzen treu bleiben — *to stick to s.o./to one's principles*

bei der Sache/bei der Wahrheit bleiben — *to stick to the point/to the truth*

Ich bleibe bei meinen Pferdebüchern (Th. Mann) — *I'll stick to my books about horses*

Er schlug ihn zu Boden — *He struck him to the ground*

sich jemandem zu-wenden — *to turn to* (*towards*) *s.o.*

sich an jemanden wenden — *to turn* (*apply*) *to s.o.*

Er wandte sich an mich um Rat — *He turned to me for advice*

(streng) nach Vorschrift arbeiten — *to work to rule*

ii with adjectives and participles

Diesen Charakterzug haben alle Engländer gemeinsam — *This trait is common to all Englishmen*

Dieses Unternehmen liegt ihm am Herzen — *This enterprise is dear to him*

Er hängt an seiner Mutter — *He is devoted to his mother*

angepaßt (with preceding dat.) — *geared* (*adapted*) *to*

Er neigt zu(m) Rheumatismus, zur Verschwendung — *He is prone to rheumatism, to extravagance*

bis auf die Haut durchnäßt — *soaked to the skin*

Er ist empfänglich für Schmeichelei/ für weibliche Schönheit — *He is susceptible to flattery/to female beauty*

iii with nouns

der Zugang zu — *access to*

ein Beitrag zu dem Fonds/zum menschlichen Wissen — *a contribution to the fund/to human knowledge*

am Eingang zum Bahnhof — *at the entrance to the station*

die Reaktion der Regierung auf diese Ereignisse — *the reaction of the government to these events*

Die Neuromantik war eine Reaktion gegen den Naturalismus — *Neo-Romanticism was a reaction to Naturalism*

Sie waren damit gemeint — *It was a reference to you*

iv phrases

Sie saßen sich gegenüber (or: Aug' in Auge) — *They sat face to face*

Der Saal war zum Bersten voll — *The hall was full to overflowing*

bis ans Ende der Welt — *to the ends of the earth*

Diese Entwicklung ist günstig — *This development is to the good*

rechts vom Haus — *to the right of the house*

in gleichem Maße — *to the same extent*

bis zu welchem Grade? — *to what extent?*

[1] cf. Corbett, op. cit., p. 215.

800 bis 900 Mark	*800 to 900 marks*
Wir haben zwei zu eins (2:1) über Österreich gesiegt	*We had a 2 to 1 win over Austria*

630. towards

Er kam auf mich zu	*He came towards me*
Er schaute nach mir herüber	*He gazed over towards me*
Ich sah nach der Tür	*I looked towards the door*
sich um-drehen nach	*to turn round towards* (or *after*)

631. with

i with verbs

Ich kaufe nicht bei diesem Bäcker ein	*I don't **deal with** this baker*
Er weiß mit den Leuten umzugehen	*He knows how to deal with people*
Ich werde die Sache erledigen	*I'll deal with the matter*
Dieses Buch handelt von der Französischen Revolution (or: behandelt die Fr.R.)	*This book deals with the French Revolution*
Er hat an allem etwas auszusetzen	*He finds fault with everything*
Glück haben; Schwein haben (sl.)	*to get away with it*
Er ist mit einem Armbruch davongekommen	*He got off with a fractured arm*
Er hat eine gewisse Art	*He has a way with him*
Schritt halten mit	*to keep up with* (lit. and fig.)
Mit meinem Rheumatismus muß ich mich abfinden	*I've got to live with my rheumatism*
sich behelfen mit	*to make do with*
sich trennen von	*to part with*
Leg dieses Buch zu den andern	*Put this book with the others*
Mit dem Lärm mußt du dich abfinden	*You'll have to put up with the noise*
Ich kann ihn nicht mehr aushalten	*I can't put up with him any longer*
Er ist bei einem Freund zu Besuch	*He's staying with a friend*
wimmeln von	*to swarm with*
Ich nehme Zucker zum Tee	*I take sugar with my tea*

ii with adjectives and participles

Ich bin vom Tennisspielen müde	*I'm exhausted with playing tennis*
Ich stehe vor einer schwierigen Entscheidung	*I'm faced with a difficult decision*
Ich habe das Tennisspielen satt	*I'm fed up with playing tennis*
Er ist sehr von ihr eingenommen	*He is very much taken with her*

iii phrases

Es geht mir genauso	*It's the same with me*
mit jemandem in Verbindung stehen	*to be in touch with s.o.*

632. without

entbehren + acc.	*to do without*
fertig werden ohne (coll.)	
Ich mußte auf das Mittagessen verzichten	*I had to go without lunch*
Ich mußte ohne Mittagessen gehen (coll.)	

I. SELECTED WORDS USED WITH PREPOSITIONS

633. to be accustomed (used) to[1]

Distinguish:

i eine Sache/jemanden gewohnt sein
> to be used to s.th. or s.o. through long habit or experience:

Ich bin diesen Kaffee/diesen Lehrer gewohnt.
Ich bin eine solche Behandlung nicht gewohnt.
Ich bin gewohnt, nach dem Mittagessen spazierenzugehen.

ii an eine Sache/an jemanden gewöhnt sein
> to be (to have become) accustomed to s.th. or s.o. through conscious habituation:

Ich bin jetzt an diesen Kaffee/an diesen Lehrer gewöhnt.
Ich bin jetzt daran gewöhnt, weniger zu rauchen.

634. to be interested in etc.

'für' is used where interest denotes intellectual curiosity: Er interessiert sich für Musik; er hat/zeigt lebhaftes Interesse für Musik.

'an + dat.' is used where interest denotes concern for personal advantage: Er versucht, mich an seinem Geschäft zu interessieren (as a potential partner). Hätten Sie Interesse (daran), dies zu kaufen? Ich hätte vielleicht Interesse an diesem Haus (as a potential buyer). Ich habe kein Interesse an diesem Angebot. Er ist an diesem Unternehmen beteiligt *He has a (financial) interest in this enterprise.*

635. to see to, look after

nach jemandem sehen	*to see to, attend to s.o.*
sich um eine Sache bekümmern	*to see to, attend to a matter* (often intermittently)
sorgen für (or: versorgen)	*to see to* (e.g. the household), *to look after* (e.g. children, old people)
Ich werde dafür sorgen, daß er kommt	*I'll see (to it) that he comes*
besorgen	1. *to see to* (e.g. the household, a task)
	2. *to procure s.th. for s.o.*
	3. *to buy* (coll.)
Ich habe alles besorgt	*I've seen to* (or *bought*) *everything*
erledigen	*to see to, deal with* (e.g. one's correspondence), *to settle* (a question)

636. 'werden' and 'werden zu'

(a) **werden + nom.** is used:

i before the names of professions and other types: Er wird Lehrer; er ist Katholik/Kommunist geworden; was will er werden?

---

[1] based on Du Haupt.: gewohnt/gewöhnt.

ii in two phrases: Sie wird Mutter *She is having a child*; sie wurden Freunde.

(b) **werden zu + dat.** denotes 'to change, turn, develop into':

Die Felder waren zu Seen geworden	*The fields had turned into lakes*
Es wurde zur Mode	*It became a fashion*
Das ist mir zur Gewohnheit geworden	*That's become a habit of mine*
Dieser Prozeß wurde zu einer Qual für ihn (V. Baum)	*This case became a torment for him*
Er wurde zum Verbrecher	*He became a criminal*

J. MISCELLANEOUS NOTES ON THE USE OF PREPOSITIONS

637. Miscellaneous points

i **Where two prepositions taking different cases are joined by 'und' or 'oder'**, the commonest usage is to put the noun or pronoun into the case required by the nearer preposition:
Kommen Sie nur, mit oder ohne Kinder! Menschen strömten in und aus dem Bahnhof.

ii **With co-ordinating conjunctional phrases, the preposition is generally repeated**:
Dieser Brief ist entweder für dich oder für deinen Vater

iii **As in English, a preposition may precede a prepositional phrase:**

außer am Donnerstag	*except on Thursday*
Diese Unterlagen sind für unter die Schüsseln	*These mats are for under the dishes*

iv **Where the force of a preposition is strengthened by a separable prefix**, it is important to remember that the preposition is the essential word:

Er kam in das Zimmer (herein)	*He came into the room*
Er ging über die Straße (hinüber)	*He crossed the road*
Er kam um die Ecke (herum)	*He came round the corner*

K. CONTRACTION OF PREPOSITION + DEFINITE ARTICLE

638. The following contractions of prep. + def. art. are usual unless the article is emphasized:

with 'den': hintern, übern, untern.
with 'das': ans, aufs, durchs, fürs, hinters, ins, übers, ums, unters, vors.
with 'dem': am, außerm, beim, hinterm, im, überm, unterm, vom, vorm, zum.
with 'der' (fem. dat.): zur.

Note:
i In some figurative and idiomatic uses of 'zu', 'zum' and 'zur' may be contractions of 'zu einem' and 'zu einer':
Er ist zum Lehrer geeignet; ich nehme mir ihn zum Muster; zur Abwechslung; zum Beispiel; zur Strafe; er wurde zum Verbrecher.

ii In time phrases and in most other prepositional formulae only the contracted form is used, e.g.

am Dienstag, am 10. Mai, im Frühling, zur Zeit.

Er läuft am schnellsten; ich nahm ihn beim Wort; sie war beim Kochen; im Freien; ins Freie; im Vertrauen; ein Jahrmarkt war im Gang *a fair was in progress*; zum Frühstück.

iii Where the noun is particularized, the uncontracted form is more usual:

an dem Nachmittag, an dem Sie anriefen	*on the afternoon when you rang up*
Er geht zu der Schule, wo sein Vater früher war	*He goes to the school where his father used to be*

iv Outside set phrases 1. the uncontracted form is more literary 2. the rhythm of the sentence will often determine the choice, e.g. Die Truppen marschierten durch das Tor. Dann ging ich durchs Tor.

In examining the first 200 pages of E. M. Remarque's novel *Drei Kameraden* and of Thomas Mann's *Doktor Faustus*, Witold Manczak found that before commonly used nouns the contracted form was by far the more frequently used; in Remarque the contracted form occurred in 83% of such cases, in Thomas Mann in 67%.[1]

v Where the article is strongly emphasized and is used as a demonstrative, the uncontracted form is essential:

Gerade an *dem* Nachmittag kann ich nicht kommen	*That's the one afternoon when I can't come*
Bei *dem* Radau kann ich nicht arbeiten	*I can't work with this row going on*

vi **Further contractions of prep.+def. art.** are purely colloquial (cf. Du. Gram. 1580), but many of them are very common in rapid speech:

an'n	for	an den	für'n	for	für den
auf'n	,,	auf den	gegen's	,,	gegen das
auf'm	,,	auf dem	in'n	,,	in den
aus'm	,,	aus dem	nach'm	,,	nach dem
bei'n	,,	bei den	vor'n	,,	vor den
durch'n	,,	durch den	zu'n	,,	zu den (dat. plur.)

Ich hab' das Buch auf'n Tisch gelegt. Nach'm Essen geh' ich in'n Garten.

vii **The indef. art. is similarly frequently slurred after prepositions in rapid speech**, e.g. Was hast du da für'n Bleistift? Wir kamen an'n Tor. Wir gingen zu'nem Fest.

---

[1] *Muttersprache* 1966: 5/6, pp. 144–8.

XIV INTERJECTIONS AND EXCLAMATIONS

639. A selection of interjections and exclamations expressing specific feelings and reactions

Au! Aua! Autsch! — *Ow! Ouch!* (pain)

Hu! — 1. coldness 2. horror

Pfui! Pfui Teufel! — *Ugh!* (nausea, disgust)

Sch! Pss! Pst! — *Hush!*

Bràvo! — *Bravo! Well done!*

Verflucht (noch mal)! — *Confound it!*

Verflixt! Zum Kuckuck!

Denk mal an! Ach! Ach was! — *Fancy! Would you believe it!*

Ach nein! Na, so was! Aber so was! — *Well I never!*

So? (drawn out, rising intonation) — *Really?*

Donnerwetter! — *By Jove!*

Sieh mal an! — *Well I never* (surprise + pleasure)

Ach, du lieber Himmel! — *Heavens above!* (dismay)

Oh, du liebe Zeit!

(O) Jemine![1] Herr Jemine! Oje! — *Good gracious!*

Wie lästig! — *What a nuisance!*

(Es ist) *zu* dumm! — *It really is a nuisance*

Na ja! — *Ah well* (resignation)

Unsinn! Blödsinn! Quatsch! — *Nonsense! Rubbish!*

Ach was! (gruff intonation) — (see also 537(b)vii)

Aber natürlich! (Na,) freilich! — *Rather! I should think so!*

Gehst du gern auf Reisen? — *Do you like travelling?*

—(Na,) und ob![2] — *—Rather!*

640. Notes on occasional exclamations

(a) hailing, greeting and leave-taking

Hallo! He! Heda! *Hi!* Hör mal! Du! *I say!* Guten Tag! *Good day + Good afternoon* ('Guten' is frequently omitted or slurred: Tag! Morgen! N'Abend! Gun'—amd (*Zeit*))

(Auf) Wiedersehen! (Auf) Wiederschauen! On the phone: (Auf) Wiederhören!

---

[1] a distortion of Latin Jesu domine! (Du. Rechtschreibung).

[2] = Und du fragst, ob ich das gern tue! i.e. no need to ask.

(b) **at meals**

Nehmen Sie noch etwas?	*Will you have some more?*
—Ja, danke!	—*Thank you* (helping oneself)
—Ja, bitte! Bitte!	—*Thank you* (when being helped)
—Nein, danke! Danke! Danke, nein!	—*No thank you*

(c) **seasonable greetings**: Frohe Weihnachten und ein glückliches Neues Jahr! Prost Neujahr! Fröhliche Ostern/Pfingsten!

(d) **miscellaneous good wishes** (in which German is very prolific)

Herzlichste Glückwünsche zum Geburtstag!	*Best wishes for your birthday* (*Many happy returns*)
Zum Wohl! Zum Wohlsein! Prost! Prosit!	*Your good health! Cheers!* (raising one's glass)
(Gesegnete) Mahlzeit!	*I hope you enjoy/have enjoyed your meal*
Angenehme Ruh'!	*I hope you sleep well*
Gute Besserung!	*I hope you'll soon be better*
Viel Vergnügen!	*Have a good time*
Schönen Sonntag!	*Have a nice Sunday*
Meinen herzlichsten Glückwunsch!	*Congratulations!*
(Ich) gratuliere!	

641. Miscellaneous interjections and exclamations (arranged in alphabetical order of the English) (see also 297(a))

Schön! Is' gut (coll.)	*All right. Right you are*
Na gut!	*All right then* (*if that's what you think*)
Lassen Sie nur!	*Don't bother*
Bitte sehr! Gern geschehen!	*Don't mention it*
Gott behüte/bewahre! (I) bewahre!	*Heaven forbid! Certainly not! Nothing of the kind*
Hast *du* 'ne Ahnung!	*If you knew!*
Laß mich in Ruh!	*Leave me alone*
Achtung!	*Look out!*
Klar!	*Obviously, of course*
(Also) los!	*Off we go* (or: *Fire away*)
Ach *so*! Ahà!	*Oh, I see*
Basta![1] Und damit basta!	*Settled. Finished*
(O) Verzeihung!	*Sorry. I beg your pardon*
Es war beim Zahnarzt gar nicht so schlimm.—Na also!	*It wasn't so bad at the dentist's.—There you are.* (*What did I tell you?*)
Na also!	*What more do you want?* (as a rejoinder)
Tja! (from 'ja')	*Yes* (implying: *But what can one do about it?*)

---

[1] Italian: it is enough

XV WORD ORDER

A. THE THREE ORDER-TYPES OF GERMAN SENTENCES AND CLAUSES

I Normal Order

642. Normal order = subject + verb + (if any) complement, objects, adverbial limitations. It is used in the following cases:

(a) **in a main clause beginning with the subject:**
Mein Vater liest die Zeitung im Eßzimmer. Wer arbeitet im Garten?

(b) **in a series of main clauses, each beginning with the subject, expressed or understood:**
Mein Vater liest die Zeitung, meine Mutter strickt, (und) mein Bruder schreibt einen Brief. Er kam ins Zimmer, machte das Licht an und nahm ein Buch aus dem Schrank.

(c) **in a main clause beginning with one of the following** (These are followed by a comma or exclamation mark, are regarded as standing outside the sentence and therefore do not cause inversion; contrast 643(b)):

i interjections and exclamations:
Ach, es regnet schon wieder! Um Gottes willen! Ich hab' den Schlüssel vergessen. Auf Wiedersehen! Ich muß jetzt gehen.

ii ja and nein: Ja, du hast recht.

iii the name or other designation of the person addressed:
Karl, ich habe dein Buch gefunden. Lieber Freund, ich kann nichts dafür.

iv a number of parenthetical words and phrases:

also *well now, well then*	siehst du *d'you see*
das heißt (d.h.) *that is (i.e.)*	so *well now, well then*
im Gegenteil *on the contrary*	um es anders auszudrücken *to put it*
kurz, kurzum, kurz gesagt, kurz und	*differently*
gut *in short*	unter uns (gesagt) *between ourselves*
mit andern Worten *in other words*	weiß Gott *Heaven knows*
mit einem Wort *in a word*	wie gesagt *as I said*
nun, na *well*	wissen Sie *d'you know*

Also, wir wollen jetzt zu Mittag essen. Kurz und gut, die Lage ist kritisch. Wissen Sie, ich habe ihn noch nie getroffen.

v. a 'was' clause, limiting the main clause as a whole, but placed parenthetically in front of it:

Was so wichtig ist, das Buch verkauft sich gut	*What is so important, the book is selling well*

vi A few introductory words and phrases may be followed either by a comma and normal order, or by inversion without a comma; inversion is more usual; normal order gives greater edge to the statement. (Ultimately, the ear must help to decide whether an introductory word or phrase belongs here or to (c)iv above.) E.g.

allerdings *admittedly, to be sure*	jedoch *however*
erstens *firstly*	natürlich *of course*
(zweitens etc.) (*secondly etc.*)	offen gesagt *to be frank*
freilich *admittedly, to be sure*	übrigens *incidentally*
immerhin *nevertheless, for all that*	zum Beispiel *for example*

Er ist unzuverlässig; zum Beispiel kommt er immer spät zum Beispiel, er kommt immer spät	*He's unreliable; for example, he's always late*

Note:

1. When they take normal order, erstens, zweitens etc. are usually followed by a colon.

2. No comma after jedoch with either order.

3. doch *yet, nevertheless* may be followed by normal order (without a comma) or by inversion; see 290(a).

(d) **after one of the 6 simple co-ordinating conjunctions: und, oder, aber, allein, sondern, denn** (see 517). E.g. Er kann nicht kommen, denn er hat Grippe. But if the conjunction is followed by something other than the subject, this causes inversion of verb and subject: Er kann nicht kommen, denn seit gestern hat er Grippe.

(e) **in indirect statements and other noun clauses, if 'daß' is not used**; see 484(b). E.g. Er sagte, er sei krank. Ich glaubte, ich hätte ihn schon einmal gesehen.

(f) See 645(e) and (f)ii.

(g) For word order in two sentences joined by the co-ordinating conjunctional phrases (e.g. nicht nur . . ., sondern auch . . .) see 526.

II Inversion

643. Inversion of verb and subject is used in the following cases (see also 646):

(a) **in direct questions**, unless the subject is an interrog. pron. (wer, was) or begins with an interrog. adj. (welcher, was für ein), as in the last two examples:

Arbeitet er im Garten? Wann kommt er gewöhnlich nach Hause? BUT: Wer arbeitet im Garten? Was für ein Kleid steht ihr am besten?

Note: Colloquially, a plain sentence in normal order may be given an interrogative twist by suitable emphasis and intonation, e.g. Du glaubst es nicht? (cf. Erben op. cit., 272 N.3).

(b) **in a main clause beginning with something other than the subject or preceded by a sub. cl.** A wide range of items may in German stand at the beginning of the sentence, causing inversion:

1. an adverb: Gestern war ich im Theater.
2. a prep. phr.: Im Garten war er nicht zu finden.
3. the object: Seinen Bruder sehe ich selten.
4, 5. the complement: Ein guter Kerl ist er trotz alledem. Merkwürdig ist (es) nur, daß er es nie erwähnt hat.
6. a phrase referring to the subject: Optimistisch wie immer, kaufte er ein paar hundert Aktien.
7. an infin.: Anzeigen wird sie ihn (H. Fallada) *Report him to the police, that's what she'll do.*
8. an infin. phr.: Ihm Geld zu leihen, habe ich nie versprochen.
9, 10. past part. of a compound tense:
   Gesehen hab' ich ihn noch nie, nur von ihm gehört.
   Zurückgeblieben war überall ein zäher Schlick aus Schlamm und ausgelaufenem Heizöl (*a thick slime composed of mud and escaped fuel oil*) (*Zeit*, 18.11.1966: Florence after the floods).
11. part of an idiomatic phrase: Sehr leid hat es mir getan, daß . . .
12. an adv. cl.: Als er mich rief, übte ich Klavier.
13. an objectival noun cl.: Nur, daß er sich selbst nicht sehen konnte, bedauerte er (G. Hauptmann).

Note: A preceding sub. cl. may be the subject of the main verb, in which case the sentence, regarded as a whole, has normal order:

Daß er das Examen nicht bestanden hat, erstaunt mich nicht	*That he hasn't passed the exam doesn't surprise me*

644. Inversion has several functions (The numbers below refer to the examples in 643(b)):

It may be a completely normal and neutral way of beginning a sentence, as in 1 and 12.

It may give emphasis to the part of the sentence placed at the beginning (its commonest function), as in 5, 6, 7, 8, 9, 10, 11 and 13. (In English this emphasis will generally be achieved merely vocally.)

It may give emphasis to another part of the sentence, as in 4: trotz alledem.

It may be determined by contextual factors:
   i by what precedes, including the remark of another speaker (as in the 4th example below):
Wir suchten im Garten, aber im Garten . . . (see 2)
Ich sehe *ihn* oft; seinen Bruder sehe ich selten. (see 3)
Reinhard hatte hier . . . ein Haus aus Rasenstücken (*pieces of turf*) aufgeführt; darin wollten sie die Sommerabende wohnen (Th. Storm).[1]
Ich war drei Wochen auf Sylt.—Darum siehst du auch so gut aus.

   ii by what is to follow:
Das Geld gab er seinem Bruder, der dann die Rechnung bezahlte.

[1] quoted in an article on Word Order by N. P. Fomina in *Deutsch als Fremdsprache*, 6/1968.

645. Special points relevant to inversion

(a) **If something other than the subject stands at the beginning of two or more main clauses**, normal usage is to have inversion only in the first clause (examples 1 and 2), unless the sense makes it essential (examples 3 and 4), or the speaker or writer desires (5), to emphasize the applicability of the opening word or phrase to all the main clauses:

1. Zu Hause schrieb Mutter Briefe, und Vater arbeitete im Garten.
2. Am Abend blieb ich zu Hause, (ich) spielte Klavier und ging früh zu Bett.
3. In diesem Hause bin ich aufgewachsen, haben wir die Kriegsjahre durchgemacht und ist meine Mutter gestorben.
4. Innerhalb von drei Tagen wurde sein Bruder überfahren und starb sein Onkel an einem Schlaganfall.
5. Bereitwillig . . . interpretierte er . . . die einzelnen Stellen seines Films, gab er Auskunft . . . und wich er allen Fragen aus (*Hbg. Abendblatt*).

(b) **When something other than the subject stands at the beginning of the second of two main clauses joined by und, oder, aber or sondern**, the second clause must have its own subject-word, to show the inversion. (Failure to observe this rule is a common error, due, no doubt, to its irrelevance in English.)

Ich schrieb ein paar Briefe, und dann ging ich zu Bett	*I wrote a few letters and then went to bed*

(c) **Mainly colloquially, the foregoing word that causes the inversion is sometimes omitted**, as in the following:

Du solltest früh zu Bett gehen	*You ought to go to bed early*
—[Das] Tu ich auch	*—But I do*
—[Das] Werd' ich auch	*—Yes, I shall*
[Da] Sagt mein Verteidiger: 'Kommen wir zur Sache!' (M. Frisch)	*Says my counsel: 'Let's come to the point'*

This frequently occurs in exclamations:

Ach, [wie] bin ich ungeschickt! (H. Fallada)	*Oh, how clumsy I am!*
[So] Hatte ich also doch recht!	*So I was right after all*
[Was] Ist *das* [für] ein Vergnügen![1]	*What a pleasure it is!* (e.g. to see you again)

(d) **A sentence does not normally start with two consecutive items other than the subject**, e.g. adverb, adverb phrase, adverb clause; the first item is immediately followed by the inversion of verb and subject:

Dann stand er plötzlich auf	*Then suddenly he got up*

Grubačić (op. cit. pp. 55 ff.) adduces numerous examples of exceptions to this, e.g. und gleich darauf, mit erregten Schwüngen, kam ein Reiher (*heron*) geflogen (H. Carossa). Recognized exceptions are: 1. two closely connected items (Um halb drei, kurz nach dem Mittagessen, hatte er einen Schlaganfall) and 2. the desire to produce exceptional emphasis (Dann, ganz plötzlich, stand er auf).

---

[1] 'was für ein' is divisible: cf. 175(e).

(e) **When words or phrases such as auch, nur, sogar** *even,* **wenigstens, allein** *only,* **nicht allein** *not only,* **nicht einmal** *not even* **stand at the beginning of the sentence and limit the subject, normal order is used:**

Auch der Bürgermeister war dagegen	*The Mayor too was against it*
Nicht einmal der Lehrer wußte die Antwort	*Not even the teacher knew the answer*

(f) **No inversion in the following cases:**
   i after one of the six simple co-ordinating conjunctions: see 642(d).
   ii after some types of concessive clause: see 470–74, especially 471(c)i.
   iii sce 642(c), e.g. Ja,/Kurz und gut, die Lage ist kritisch.

646. Other instances of inversion

(a) with a verb of saying or asking placed after or within a quotation:
   'Mein Bruder', sagte er, 'kann Ihnen helfen.'
   cf. Eine schöne Entschuldigung! dachte ich bei mir.

(b) the polite form of the imperative: Kommen Sie in den Garten!

(c) many forms of the optative subjunctive (see 476), e.g. Mögest du immer so denken! Hoffen wir das Beste! Hätte mein Vater doch dieses Haus nie gekauft!

(d) see also 298(e), 642(g), 647 N.vi 2.

III Verb to the end of Subordinate Clauses

647. The finite verb goes to the end in all subordinate clauses, apart from the exceptions listed in Note vi below.

Ich weiß, daß er krank ist (noun cl.)
Der Junge, der krank ist, ist mein Freund (rel. cl.)
Er bleibt zu Hause, weil er krank ist (adv. cl.)

Note:

   i Two subordinate clauses joined by und, oder, aber or sondern: verb to the end in both:

Obwohl er fast nie ausgeht, sondern die ganze Zeit arbeitet, scheint es ihm gut zu bekommen	*Although he hardly ever goes out but works all the time, it seems to agree with him*

   If the two clauses have compound tenses with the same auxiliary, the latter appears only once, at the end of the second clause:

Nachdem ich Tee getrunken und eine Weile gelesen hatte, machte ich einen Spaziergang	*After I had had tea and read for a while, I went for a walk*

   If the second clause has its own subject, it is more usual to repeat the conjunction:

Wenn deine Familie dagegen ist oder wenn du keine Zeit hast, dann wollen wir den Plan fallenlassen	*If your family is against it or you have no time, we'll drop the plan*

ii One subordinate clause enclosed in another:[1] **verb to the end in both clauses.** (This is, of course, to be expected, but is often a source of error.)

Ich weiß, daß mein Vetter, der nach Kanada ausgewandert ist, viel Geld verdient	*I know that my cousin, who has emigrated to Canada, is making a lot of money*

iii The introductory conjunction of a subordinate clause is normally followed by the subject. (But see 655(b), 656(b) and 664 (c).)

Da ich morgen zu Hause sein werde, ...	*As tomorrow I shall be at home, ...*

The same applies to a relative pronoun which is not itself the subject:

Der Minister, den Sie so oft kritisiert haben, ...	*The minister, whom so often you have criticized, ...*

If the conjunction is followed by an adverb or adverb phrase, this does not cause inversion; the verb still goes to the end:

Wir hoffen, daß nächstes Jahr wieder viele Ausländer nach England kommen.

iv In exclamations, the finite verb usually goes to the end, though inversion is also common:

Wie *kalt* es heute ist!	*How cold it is today!*
Was für *komische* Bemerkungen er immer macht!	*What funny remarks he's always making!*
Wie der Chef darüber *geschimpft* hat!	*How the boss swore about it!*
Wie (coll.: Was) *hat* der Chef darüber geschimpft!	
Was *haben* wir dieses Jahr für Birnen!	*What lovely* (or: *awful*) *pears we've got this year!*

Inversion *must* be used when the exclamation is in the form of a rhetorical question (Wie konntest du nur so etwas tun!) and in the elliptical type: Ach, [wie] bin ich ungeschickt! (see 645(c)).

v See 642(g).

vi Exceptions (i.e. subordinate clauses with the verb not at the end):
1. indirect statements etc. without 'daß': normal order is used (see 642(e)).
2. alternative versions of conditional, 'as if' and 'even if' clauses (see 463, 466(a), 473(c)), e.g. Schreibe ich ihm heute, dann bekommt er den Brief morgen.
3. see 649 N.ii.
4. see 666 ff.: The Freer Word Order.

vii For **the use of the comma with subordinate clauses,** see 743(d).

B. POSITION OF SEPARABLE PREFIXES

648. For **the position of separable prefixes** see 369(c), and 666 ff.: The Freer Word Order.

---

[1] A noun clause is never enclosed in another subordinate clause: see 651(e).

One point may be added: a separable prefix may enclose or exclude a short infinitive phrase, but does not enclose a longer one:
Er fing an zu singen or Er fing zu singen an. Er fing an, mit Gefühl ein altes Volkslied zu singen.

C. POSITION OF PARTICIPLES AND INFINITIVES

649. The past participles and infinitives of compound tenses go to the end, except in subordinate clauses, where the auxiliary, being the finite verb, comes last. (See also 666 ff.: The Freer Word Order.)

Ich bin heute morgen in der Stadt gewesen	*I've been in town this morning*
Obwohl ich heute morgen in der Stadt gewesen bin, . . .	*Although I've been in town this morning, . . .*
Vielleicht wird er uns das Geld leihen	*Perhaps he will lend us the money*
Da er uns das Geld leihen wird, . . .	*As he will lend us the money, . . .*

Note:
i Where a sentence ends with both an infinitive and a past participle or with two infinitives, the item on which the other depends comes last:

Er hat mich schwimmen gelehrt	*He has taught me to swim*
Ich werde es ihm sagen müssen	*I shall have to tell him*

This obviously does not apply where a phrase with zu+infin. is not enclosed by the compound tense on which it depends (cf. 650(d) ii)·

Ich habe meinem Sohn versprochen, mich darüber zu erkundigen	*I've promised my son to inquire about it*

ii There is one case in which the auxiliary does not go to the end of a subordinate clause, e.g.
Da er heute hat schwimmen dürfen, muß es ihm besser gehen (see 392).
Ich hob den Brief auf, den er hatte fallen lassen (see 421).

N.B. For the position of the participle in participial phrases, see 437.

650. The position of dependent infinitives and infinitive phrases[1]

(a) **An infinitive always stands at the end of its own phrase:**

Um den Vertrag zu unterzeichnen, mußte er nach Neuyork fliegen	*In order to sign the contract he had to fly to New York*
Seine Aufgabe, den Etat ins Gleichgewicht zu bringen, ist keine leichte	*His task of balancing the budget is not an easy one*

(b) **Where it depends on a verb in a simple tense and not in a subordinate clause, the infinitive goes to the end of the sentence:**
Ich muß das Buch so bald wie möglich finden.
Gestern versuchte ich, ihm bei seiner Arbeit zu helfen.

[1] See also 666 ff.: The Freer Word Order.

(c) **A verb that takes a plain infinitive without 'zu'** encloses the dependent infinitive phrase in the following cases:[1]
i where the verb is used in a compound tense:

Natürlich wirst du Tennis spielen dürfen	*Of course you'll be allowed to play tennis*
Ich hatte ihn gegen elf Uhr ins Haus kommen sehen	*I had seen him come into the house about eleven o'clock*

ii where the verb is used as a dependent infinitive:

Er schien die Sache nicht erwähnen zu wollen	*He seemed not to want to mention the matter*

iii where the verb is used in a subordinate clause:

Da er plötzlich nach Frankfurt fliegen mußte, ...	*As he suddenly had to fly to Frankfurt, ...*

(d) **A verb that takes zu + infinitive**
i when the verb is in a simple tense in a subordinate clause, it generally encloses the dependent infinitive phrase, provided it is not too long:
Ich weiß, daß mein Bruder sein Geschäft zu verkaufen versucht.

Note: Where an infinitive has a relative pronoun as its object, it is generally enclosed in the rel. cl.: das Spiel, das wir kaum zu gewinnen hofften (or gehofft hatten); das Liebesversprechen, das zurückzunehmen er sich nicht traute (U. Johnson).

ii when the verb is used 1. in a compound tense or 2. as a dependent infinitive, whether in a main clause or in a subordinate clause, it generally excludes the dependent infinitive phrase:

1. Er hat versucht, sein Geschäft zu verkaufen	*He has tried to sell his business*
Ich weiß, daß er versucht hat, sein Geschäft zu verkaufen	*I know that he has tried to sell his business*
2. Er muß versuchen, sein Geschäft zu verkaufen	*He must try to sell his business*

Note:
1. A pseudo-impersonal expression (cf. 372(a)ii, 374, 375) used in a compound tense never encloses a dependent infinitive phrase:
Es wäre nötig gewesen, das zu tun; es wird mir gelingen, ihn zu finden; es hat mir leid getan, das zu hören.

2. An infinitive phrase with a clause dependent on it is never enclosed:

Ich habe versucht zu erfahren, was geschehen ist	*I have tried to learn what happened*

(e) **um ... zu + infin., ohne ... zu + infin. and (an)statt ... zu + infin. are not usually enclosed in a sentence or clause:**
Er hat große Opfer gebracht, um dir zu helfen. Da ich Zeitung gelesen habe, anstatt zu arbeiten, ...

(f) See 648.

---

[1] The same applies to brauchen *to need*, even when used with zu + inf. (cf. 418).

D. FURTHER CASES OF ENCLOSING AND EXCLUDING PHRASES AND CLAUSES

651. The following further cases of enclosing and excluding should be noted:

(a) **Comparative phrases**
i The second element in a comparison ('than' or 'as') is not usually enclosed in a sentence or clause:

Gestern haben wir einen besseren Wein getrunken als diesen	*Yesterday we drank a better wine than this one*
Ich wußte, daß er ebenso ärgerlich war wie ich	*I knew that he was just as annoyed as I*

ii Comparative phrases beginning with 'wie', meaning 'like' or 'as': brief ones are enclosed, especially in sentences or clauses of any length:

da ... die Orangen und Zitronen von den Kindern wie Schneebälle über die Gartenmauern geworfen wurden (S. Andres).[1]

Otherwise, practice varies:

ein Mann, der aussah wie ein Italiener (or: der wie ein Italiener aussah); er hat mit mir gesprochen wie mit einem alten Freund.

(b) **A phrase beginning with 'als' meaning 'in the capacity of, by way of, as being'** is generally enclosed unless it is of some length:
Er hatte die Sache als Franzose beurteilt.

(c) **sondern and oder + object or phrase** may be enclosed or excluded, the latter being commoner; **oder nicht** is always excluded:
Ich habe nicht die 'Frankfurter Allgemeine' bekommen, sondern die 'Süddeutsche Zeitung'.
Da wir uns nicht in Köln, sondern in Hamburg treffen, ...
Die Proben (*rehearsals*) fanden durchweg nachts statt oder an späten Nachmittagen (C. Zuckmayer).
Ich weiß nicht, ob es wichtig ist oder nicht.

(d) **außer *except* + noun or pronoun** is generally excluded:
Ich habe alles gefunden außer dem Wörterbuch.

(e) **A noun clause** is never enclosed in:
a main cl.: Ich hatte vergessen, daß er hier wohnt.
Er gab zu, daß er sich irrte.
a sub. cl.: Da ich wußte, daß er hier wohnt, ...
um/ohne/anstatt ... zu + infin.
Er hat angerufen, um mir zu sagen, wo er wohnt.

The same applies to the introductory word of a truncated noun clause, e.g. Er ist heute nach Hamburg gefahren; er hat mir nicht gesagt, warum [er nach Hamburg gefahren ist].

Exc. A noun cl. in apposition, e.g. Ich konnte den Gedanken, daß wir ihn hintergangen hatten (*that we had deceived him*), nicht loswerden.

---

[1] from Grubačić, op. cit., p. 78.

(f) **A relative clause** is frequently excluded if its antecedent comes near the end of its sentence or clause, e.g.

Und wie dürfte man eine Zeitung verbieten, die sich wiederholt so nachhaltig (*effectively*) für die Wahl der staatstragenden Partei (*the party in office*) eingesetzt hat? (*Spiegel*)

(Exclusions with early antecedents are also found, cf. Grubačić, op. cit., pp. 67 ff.)

(g) **Adverb clauses** may be enclosed if not too long, e.g.

... in dem ... Sälchen, welches, sobald man die Fenster schloß, seinen Eigengeruch verströmte (*exuded its distinctive odour*) (E. Langgässer)

(h) See 504 N.iii.

E. THE POSITION AND ORDER OF COMPLEMENTS, OBJECTS AND ADVERBS

652. The position of complements, objects and adverbs: three introductory points:

(a) The items following the finite verb are normally arranged in order of increasing importance, passing from the known to the unknown, with the end of the sentence, as the climax, carrying the greatest emphasis.[1] Two instances of this pattern, which will be frequently referred to, may be given here:

i The complement, something essential, as its name implies, goes to the end: Er war zehn Jahre in Berlin Zeitungskorrespondent.

ii Pronouns, since they refer to persons or things already named, occupy an unemphatic position,[2] preceding adverbs, noun objects and even noun subjects:

Er hatte es mir sofort gegeben.
Er hat es seinem Vater gezeigt.
Gestern hat ihn mein Bruder gesehen.

(b) In the paragraphs that follow, frequent reference is made to changing the position of some element in the sentence in order to give it emphasis. It should be noted that in the spoken language emphasis through word order is strengthened, or rendered superfluous, by vocal stress, e.g. Ich habe den Pfirsich *ihr* versprochen, or: Ich habe *ihr* den Pfirsich versprochen.

(c) Wherever there is a reference to one of the above items (complements, objects and adverbs) coming at the end of the sentence, this implies 'or immediately before a closing past participle, infinitive, separable prefix or finite verb (in a subordinate clause)'.

653. The complement generally comes at the end of the sentence:

Er ist trotz all seiner Eigentümlichkeiten ein guter Kerl	*He's a good chap despite all his peculiarities*

---

[1] cf. Schulz-Griesbach, op. cit., H 702 f. and Du. Gram. 7065; but also see 666 ff. below: The Freer Word Order.
[2] cf. Du. Gram. 7065.

Er hat mich gestern abend im Beisein meiner Eltern einen Faulenzer genannt	*Yesterday evening he called me an idler in the presence of my parents*

Note: Two points relevant to this order rule:
i The majority of adjectives used with the dative normally follow the dative noun or pronoun dependent on them; for exceptions see 117 N.i; all adjectives used with the genitive except bar (see 118) follow the dependent noun.

Seine Entscheidung ist seinen Freunden unbegreiflich	*His decision is incomprehensible to his friends*
Er ist einer solchen Tat nicht fähig	*He is not capable of such a deed*

ii The majority of adjectives and adjectival participles used with prepositions can precede or follow the prepositional phrase, generally with no effect on the sense, e.g.:

Er war begeistert von dem Film/Er war von dem Film begeistert.
Er ist gegen Kälte empfindlich/Er ist empfindlich gegen Kälte.

The following usually precede the prepositional phrase: abweisend gegen *unfriendly towards*, ärgerlich über, gleichgültig gegen *indifferent towards*, stolz auf.

The following usually follow the prepositional phrase: argwöhnisch gegen *suspicious of*, beliebt bei, erpicht auf *eager for*, mad on, geeignet für, gefaßt auf, überlegen an *superior in*, überzeugt von, unterlegen an *inferior in*, versessen auf *bent on, mad about*, vorbereitet auf.

Where the preposition is 'gegenüber', the adjective follows the phrase: Er war mir gegenüber sehr höflich.

'voll von' and 'voll mit' always precede the prepositional phrase: Der Korb war voll mit Birnen.

654. The direct object (acc.) and the indirect object (dat.)

Note: The following rules apply to all verbs used with an accusative object and a dative object in German; in some of the examples it will be found that the English equivalent is differently compounded. See also 655(d).

(a) **something to someone** (the commonest type)
i Normal usage: the indirect object precedes the direct object unless the direct object is a personal pronoun:

Er gab seinem Vater den Brief	*He gave the letter to his father*
Er gab ihm den Brief	*He gave him the letter*
Er gab ihn seinem Vater	*He gave it to his father*
Er gab ihn ihm	*He gave it to him*
Ich habe meinem Freund das Haus abgekauft	*I have bought the house from my friend*
Ich habe es ihm abgekauft	*I have bought it from him*
Ich kann seinen Eltern ihre Enttäuschung nachfühlen	*I can feel for his parents in their disappointment*

ii Variants:
  1. If the indirect object is to be emphasized, it can follow the direct object even if this is a noun:

Er hat sein ganzes Vermögen seinem Neffen vermacht	*He left his whole fortune to his nephew*

Ich habe diesen Pfirsich ihr versprochen	*I have promised this peach to* her

2. Colloquially, the dir. obj. 'es' may follow the pronominal indir. objects 'mir' and 'dir' in the truncated form 's:

Er hat mir's/dir's gezeigt	*He showed it to me/to you*

(b) someone to something

Here the dir. obj. precedes the indir. (except when the dir. obj. is a noun and the indir. obj. is a pronoun, which is in practice rare):

Sie überantworteten den Verbrecher der Justiz	*They delivered up the criminal to justice*

(c) someone to someone

If both are nouns, either order is possible, the more emphasized item coming last:

Er stellte seinen Neffen dem Pfarrer vor	*He introduced his nephew to* the parson
Er stellte dem Pfarrer seinen Neffen vor	*He introduced* his nephew (not his son) *to the parson*

If one of the two is a pronoun, it comes first:

Er stellte ihn dem Pfarrer vor	*He introduced him to the parson*
Er stellte ihm seinen Neffen vor	*He introduced his nephew to him*

If both are pronouns, the dir. obj. precedes the indir., unless the dir. obj. is to be emphasized (3rd example):

Er stellte ihn ihr vor	*He introduced him to her*
'Damit ich dich mir vorstellen kann— später—, wenn du fort bist' (V. Baum)	*'So that I can picture you (to myself)— later on—when you've gone'*
Ich nahm mir *ihn* zum Muster	*I took* him *as a model*

(d) something to something

If both are nouns, the one that carries the natural emphasis comes last:

Er hat dem Experiment viel Zeit gewidmet	*He devoted much time to the experiment*
Er hat sein Glück seiner Karriere geopfert	*He has sacrificed his happiness to his career*
Er hat seiner Karriere sein ganzes Glück geopfert	BUT: *He has sacrificed his whole happiness to his career*

If one of the two is a pronoun, it comes first; if both are pronouns, the dir. obj. precedes the indirect.

655. Position of the object when it is a personal pronoun

(a) In normal order it usually follows the finite verb:

Mein Bruder hat ihn gestern in der Stadt gesehen	*My brother saw him in town yesterday*
Er hat mir oft davon erzählt	*He often told me about it*

(b) With inversion and in a subordinate clause, it usually precedes a noun subject (including jeder, jedermann, jemand, niemand), **but must follow a pronoun subject:**

Gestern hat ihn mein Bruder in der Stadt gesehen	*Yesterday my brother saw him in town*
Gestern hat er ihn in der Stadt gesehen	*Yesterday he saw him in town*

Da ihn jemand in der Stadt gesehen hatte, . . .	*As someone had seen him in town,* . . .
Er fragte, ob mir der Wein geschmeckt hätte	*He asked if I had enjoyed the wine*

Note: While the above is normal usage, it is neither wrong nor uncommon for a pronoun object to follow a noun subject with inversion or in a subordinate clause: Gestern hat mein Bruder ihn in der Stadt gesehen. Da mein Bruder ihn in der Stadt gesehen hatte, . . . This order is usual if the pronoun object is 'sie' and the noun subject is fem., neut., or plur., as there could otherwise be uncertainty as to which is the subject and which is the object:

Gestern hat meine Mutter sie in der Stadt gesehen	*Yesterday my mother saw her in town*
Da das Mädchen sie in der Stadt gesehen hatte, . . .	*As the girl had seen her in town,* . . .
Da meine Brüder sie in der Stadt gesehen hatten, . . .	*As my brothers had seen them in town,* . . .

(c) **If the subject is etwas, nichts or a neuter collective such as alles, mehreres, viel, vieles**, with inversion and in a subordinate clause the pronoun object almost always precedes the subject, especially when the verb is in a simple tense. In the first three examples, the reverse order would be impossible:

Eben ist mir etwas eingefallen	*Something has just occurred to me*
Gewöhnlich stört mich nichts bei der Arbeit	*Usually nothing disturbs me at my work*
Er wußte, daß ihm nicht viel fehlte	*He knew that there wasn't much wrong with him*
Obwohl mich mehreres ohne Grund beunruhigt hatte, . . .	*Although several things had worried me for no reason,* . . .

(d) **With verbs taking a direct and an indirect object the following is the commonest usage:**

with inversion

dir. obj.: a pronoun; indir. obj.: a noun

Dann hat mein Bruder ihn (sie, es) meinem Vater gegeben	*Then my brother gave it to my father*

indir. obj.: a pronoun; dir. obj.: a noun

Dann hat ihm (mir, uns etc.) mein Bruder den Brief gegeben	*Then my brother gave him (me, us etc.) the letter*

both objects pronouns: both pronouns follow the noun subject:

Dann hat mein Bruder ihn (sie, es) mir (dir, uns etc.) gegeben	*Then my brother gave it to me (you, us etc.)*

Exc. i in a simple tense:

Schließlich gab sie mir mein Bruder	*Finally my brother gave them to me*

    ii for phonetic reasons, 'ihn' is usually separated from 'ihm' or 'ihnen':

Dann hat ihn mein Bruder ihm/ihnen gegeben	*Then my brother gave it (masc.) to him/ to them*

in a subordinate clause: the pronoun object or objects generally follow the noun subject, though in a simple tense an indirect pronoun object tends to precede it (4th example):

Nachdem mein Bruder ihn [den Brief] meinem Vater gegeben hatte, . . .
Nachdem mein Bruder ihm den Brief gegeben hatte, . . .
Nachdem mein Bruder ihn ihm gegeben hatte, . . .
Als ihm mein Bruder den Brief gab, . . .

656. Position of the reflexive pronoun

(a) In normal order it follows the finite verb:

Der Deutsche beschwerte sich mit Recht über das Essen	*The German rightly complained about the food*

(b) With inversion and in a subordinate clause it usually precedes a noun subject, but must follow a pronoun subject:

Gestern beschwerte sich der Deutsche über das Essen. Gestern beschwerte er sich über das Essen.
Obwohl sich der Deutsche über das Essen beschwert hatte, . . . (less usual: Obwohl der Deutsche sich . . . beschwert hatte).
Obwohl er sich über das Essen beschwert hatte, . . .

Note: Where the refl. pron. follows the subject, it should follow it immediately, as in the above examples and e.g. Mein Vetter, der sich erst vor kurzem von einer schweren Krankheit erholt hatte, . . .

(c) If the subject is einer, etwas, jeder, jedermann, jemand, nichts, niemand or a neuter collective such as alles, mehreres, vieles, with inversion and in a subordinate clause the reflexive pronoun almost always precedes the subject, especially when the verb is in a simple tense. In the first two examples the reverse order would be impossible:

Plötzlich bewegte sich etwas	*Suddenly something moved*
In seiner Lebensweise ändert sich nichts	*Nothing changes in his mode of life*
Oder vielleicht hatte sich einer geduckt (F. Fühmann)	*or perhaps one of them had ducked down*
Da sich alles verbessert, . . .	*As everything is improving, . . .*
Nachdem sich jemand beschwert hatte, . . .	*After someone had complained, . . .*

(d) Note the order in the following sentences (reflexive verb + dative pronoun object):

Inversion:

Jetzt näherte sich mir das Auto/ etwas/jemand	*Now the car/something/someone was approaching me*

Inzwischen hatte sich das Auto/etwas/jemand mir genähert.

Subordinate clause:

Ich beobachtete, wie sich das Auto mir näherte.
Ich merkte, daß sich das Auto mir genähert hatte.
Ich merkte, daß sich jemand mir näherte.
BUT: Ich merkte, daß sich mir etwas näherte.

(e) In an infinitive phrase, the reflex. pron. comes first:

Ich habe vor, mich bei dem Ober über das Essen zu beschweren	*I intend complaining to the head waiter about the food*

Ich versuche, mir deine Lage   *I am trying to imagine your situation*
vorzustellen

657. nicht/nie and the object

(a) **Where it is merely the action denoted by the verb that is
negatived, 'nicht' follows the object or objects:**
Er erwähnte seinen Zweck nicht   *He did not mention his purpose*
Er hat mir das Buch nicht gegeben   *He didn't give me the book*
Verkaufe die Bücher nicht!   *Don't sell the books*

(b) **Where two persons or things are explicitly contrasted** (not A
but B), **'nicht' precedes the first of these**; if indirect objects are
contrasted, they generally follow the direct object, as in the second
example:
Er hat mir nicht das *Buch* gegeben,   *He did not give me the book but the*
sondern die *Zeitschrift*   *periodical*
Er hat das Buch nicht *mir* gegeben,   *He did not give the book to me but to my*
sondern meinem *Bruder*   *brother*

Alternatively, the element negatived may be placed at the beginning
of the sentence, with 'nicht' preceding it (rhetorical) or coming
later:
Nicht das *Buch* hat er mir gegeben, sondern die *Zeitschrift*.
Mir hat er das Buch *nicht* gegeben, sondern meinem *Bruder*

Where the contrast is implicit, the element negatived is generally placed
at the beginning of the sentence:
Mir hat er das Buch *nicht* gegeben [sondern wahrscheinlich jemand anderem].

(c) **'not a' is rendered by 'kein'**, though 'nicht ein' is sometimes used
before 'sondern':
Ich besitze keinen Atlas   *I don't possess an atlas*
Er hat nicht einen Roman   *He has not written a novel but a biography*
geschrieben, sondern eine
Biographie

(d) **nie *never* and the object**
i Where it negatives the action denoted by the verb, 'nie' follows a
pronoun object, but may precede or follow a noun object, the
former position being slightly more emphatic:
Ich habe ihn nie getroffen. Ich habe nie seinen Bruder getroffen, or: ich habe
seinen Bruder nie getroffen.

ii The contrasting of two persons or things through 'nie' is illustrated
by the following examples:
Er hat mir nie *Geld* geschenkt,   *He has never given me money but books*
sondern *Bücher*
Geld hat er mir nie geschenkt, sondern
Bücher
Mir hat er nie Geld geschenkt, aber   *He has never given money to me but to my*
meinem *Bruder*   *brother*

Note: Regarding the use of 'sondern' and 'aber' in the above examples,
see 519. The last example implies 'aber meinem Bruder hat er oft Geld
geschenkt'; his stinginess towards one brother does not exclude
generosity towards the other.

iii If 'nie' itself is to be emphasized, it is placed at the beginning of the sentence.

(e) **Where 'nicht' is used not in its negative sense, but in seeking confirmation or to make a question sound more polite and tentative:**[1]
it precedes a noun object:

Hast du nicht die Königin gesehen?   *Didn't you see the Queen?*

it may precede or follow a noun subject:[2]

War nicht dein Vater eigentlich   *Wasn't your father really a bit*
etwas enttäuscht? (or: War dein   *disappointed?*
Vater nicht . . .)

it follows a pronoun subject or object:

Sah er nicht ein bißchen blaß aus?   *Didn't he look a bit pale?*

'not a' is here better rendered by 'nicht ein' than by 'kein':

Könnte ich nicht ein Zimmer für   *Couldn't I have a room to myself?*
mich haben?

(f) for **'nicht' and the object in 'unless' clauses** (wenn . . . nicht), see 465 N.

658. The order of adverbs and adverbial phrases

(a) The traditional rule is that adverbial items are arranged in the order: time, reason, manner, place, as in the sentences:
1. Sie sind gestern wegen des schlechten Wetters zu Hause geblieben.
2. Er ist am 1. Mai hoffnungsvoll nach Bonn gefahren.

But what of the following perfectly normal sentences?
3. Der junge Tenor hat in Berlin gut gesungen.
   (place before manner)
4. Ich arbeite im Büro bis um 18 Uhr.
   (place before time)

(b) To understand the apparent discrepancy between the two pairs of sentences it is essential to distinguish between two functionally different types of adverb and adverb phrase, which we may call adverbial complements and adverbial limitations respectively.[3]
Adverbial complements are adverbs and adverb phrases which are essential to complete the sense of the verb, with which they form a unit. They therefore come last in the sentence or immediately before a closing past participle, infinitive, separable prefix or finite verb (in a subordinate clause) and are always stressed.
Adverbial limitations, on the other hand, while they may be important to convey precisely what the speaker or writer has to say, do not have that same close link with the verb, that same essential character.

---

[1] cf. Collinson, op. cit., pp. 114 f.
[2] cf. Erben, op. cit., 162.
[3] I owe this important distinction, usefully high-lighted by Colin H. Good in *Deutschunterricht für Ausländer* 6/1967, pp. 161 ff., to Schulz-Griesbach, op. cit., H415, K050 and p. 409, and to Du. Gram. 5255 ff. and 5650. 'Adverbial complements' corresponds to Schulz-Griesbach's 'Prädikatsergänzungen' and Duden's 'Umstandsergänzungen'; adverbial limitations' to the former's 'freie Angaben' and the latter's 'freie Umstandsangaben'.

In the first two of our initial examples, 'Sie sind . . . geblieben' and 'Er ist . . . gefahren' are meaningless without 'zu Hause' and 'nach Bonn'; the verbs have meaning only when we know where they stayed and whither he journeyed. (It would, of course, be possible for the context to have made clear that Bonn was his objective, in which case 'Er ist am 1. Mai hoffnungsvoll gefahren' would mean 'On 1 May he hopefully set out'.)

But the 3rd and 4th of the initial examples convey something even without any of the adverbs and adverb phrases: Der junge Tenor hat gesungen. Ich arbeite. Two adverbial limitations give precision to each statement. In the third, the important thing is to know how the young tenor acquitted himself and so, without acquiring exceptional emphasis, 'gut' comes last. In the fourth, the person addressed probably already knows that the speaker works in an office, so that 'im Büro' is unimportant, almost superfluous; what the speaker wishes to impart is the length of his working day and so 'bis um 18 Uhr' comes last.

As indicated, the order in the 3rd and 4th examples is determined by the context. This is frequently the case, as for instance in the following quotation from Storm's *Immensee*, where 'hier' is brought closer to 'Wiese': und dann liefen beide Kinder . . . hinaus auf die Wiese . . . Reinhard hatte hier mit Elisabeths Hilfe ein Haus aus Rasenstücken aufgeführt.

(c) **Further examples of adverbial complements:**
Causal: Der Brand entstand neulich in der Fabrik durch Unvorsichtigkeit.[1]
Temporal: Die Konferenz dauerte leider ganze fünf Stunden.
Set Phrase: So etwas würde in England nicht in Frage kommen.
Verbal Construction: Ich werde mich in Frankreich auf deine Sprachkenntnisse verlassen. Ich habe ihn gestern im Büro an sein Versprechen erinnert.

N.B. In practice, 'time, reason, manner, place' remains a serviceable guide, especially for adverbial limitations and as regards the end-position of place. But, as has now been shown, it is not 'a rule', deviations from which are 'exceptions'.

(d) Of **two or more time adverbs or phrases**, the more general precedes the more specific, unless the former is to be emphasized: Ich reise jedes Jahr im Juli in die Schweiz. Er kommt morgen um sieben Uhr an.

(e) For **the position of gern, lieber, am liebsten**, see 281.

659. The position of 'nicht' among adverbs

Its neutral position, where it applies to the statement as a whole, is before an adverb of manner or, failing this, of place:

Ich bin gestern nicht mit meinem Bruder in die Stadt gegangen.

[1] from Schulz-Griesbach, op. cit., H 729.

Other possible positions:

i If 'gestern' is to be negatived, 'nicht' will immediately precede it.

ii If 'mit meinem Bruder' is to be negatived, there are three possibilities:
1. commonest: 'nicht mit meinem Bruder' can be placed before 'gestern'.
2. rhetorical: 'nicht mit meinem Bruder' can be placed at the beginning of the sentence, followed by inversion.
3. 'mit meinem Bruder' can be placed at the beginning, 'nicht' being left where it is and stressed.

iii If 'in die Stadt' is to be negatived, it should be placed at the beginning, with 'nicht' (stressed) either remaining where it is or placed before 'gegangen'.

If, however, the sentence were followed by 'sondern ins Gebirge', it would run: Ich bin gestern mit meinem Bruder nicht in die Stadt gegangen, sondern ins Gebirge.

Note: 'nicht' never precedes the adverbs hoffentlich, glücklicherweise, unglücklicherweise and leider.

660. The position of 'nie' among adverbs

i Its neutral position is the same as that of nicht (see 659), e.g.

Ich bin diesen Sommer wegen des Wetters nie mit meinem Bruder ins Gebirge gegangen	*I've never been into the mountains with my brother this summer because of the weather*

ii If 'nie' is to be emphasized, it is placed at the beginning of the sentence.

iii If some other element in the sentence is to be particularly negatived, it should be placed at the beginning and stressed, 'nie' being left where it is and also stressed, e.g.

Ins Gebirge bin ich diesen Sommer *nie* mit meinem Bruder gegangen.

661. Emphasizing particular adverbs or adverb phrases: where something other than the natural emphasis is desired, this may be achieved in two ways:

1. By placing the adverb to be emphasized at the beginning of the sentence, followed by inversion (cf. 643(b)):

Hoffnungsvoll ist er am ersten Mai nach Bonn gefahren.

In Berlin hat der junge Tenor gut gesungen, aber nicht in Hamburg.

Durch Unvorsichtigkeit entstand der Brand neulich in der Fabrik.

2. By a change in the natural word order:

Er ist hoffnungsvoll am ersten Mai nach Bonn gefahren.

Der junge Tenor hat gut in Berlin gesungen, aber nicht in Hamburg.

Er hatte oft über seine Zukunft konzentriert nachgedacht.

662. In normal order, an adverb, adverbial phrase or adverb clause cannot in general come between subject and verb

Er kommt oft	*He often comes*

EXCEPTIONS:

i aber, jedoch, indessen (all in the sense of 'however') and dagegen *on*

the other hand, used unstressed to emphasize the subject: Die Kinder
aber gingen zu Bett.

ii occasionally, an adverb clause that is closely bound up with the subject.
(This should not be lightly imitated.)

Mein Freund, obwohl er nicht faul   *My friend, though he isn't lazy, never*
  ist, arbeitet nie abends   *works in the evenings*

663. The order of objects and adverbs

(a) **Pronoun objects normally precede all adverbs and adverb
phrases**: Ich habe ihn gestern im Theater gesehen. Er hatte es mir
heimlich gegeben.

Pronouns other than 'es' can be emphasized by placing them at the
beginning of the sentence, followed by inversion; 'es' must be
changed to 'das' if used thus.

(b) **Adverbs and noun objects**

i Where the adverb or adverb phrase is an adverbial complement, it
comes last (cf. 658(b)):

Er hat die Maschine in Gang   *He got the machine going*
  gebracht

Er lernt viele Gedichte auswendig   *He learns many poems by heart*

ii Where the object is analogous to an adverbial complement, being
essential to complete the sense of the verb, it comes last:

Ich spiele oft mit meinem Vetter im Club Tennis.
Er hat gestern in Berlin eine Rede gehalten
um im nächsten Dorf Hilfe zu suchen.

Such objects may be felt as the equivalent of a separable prefix.
They are always stressed and are not difficult to determine.
Further instances are:

Deutsch sprechen, Wurzel fassen *to take root*, (keine) Zeit haben, Briefe
schreiben, den Führerschein machen *to pass one's driving test*, die Macht
ergreifen *to seize power*, die Stirn runzeln *to frown*, jemandem einen Stoß
geben *to give s.o. a push*

iii Apart from the cases dealt with in i and ii, the item which has the
natural emphasis follows the other:

Er fand unerwartet in einer der   *Unexpectedly he found a will in one of*
  Schubladen ein Testament   *the drawers*

Er hat schnell ein Pfund Äpfel   *He quickly bought a pound of apples*
  gekauft

Er fand das Testament unerwartet   *He found the will unexpectedly in one*
  in einer der Schubladen   *of the drawers*

Er hat den Film warm empfohlen   *He warmly recommended the film*

iv A time adverb precedes a noun object without causing the latter to
be emphasized:

Ich habe gestern die ganze Sache   *I settled the whole matter yesterday*
  erledigt

Where the noun object is to be emphasized it is placed at the start.

F. THE POSTPONED SUBJECT

664. The subject, other than a personal pronoun, is sometimes postponed with inversion and in subordinate clauses

(a) Where there is inversion of verb and subject, the latter may be emphasized by being given the end position:
Nun begrüßte den Dirigenten (*conductor*) und den Virtuosen lautes Händeklatschen (G. Kapp).
Zwei Tage, darauf wurde gegen die Streikenden Militär eingesetzt (B. Brecht).[1]

Sometimes the postponement of the subject gives an easier rhythm to the sentence: Gestern hat mich den ganzen Tag niemand gestört.

In the following sentence from a letter from a German teacher 'die Klassenhefte' is slightly emphasized and is brought immediately before its relative clause:
Außerdem stapeln sich (*are piling up*) einmal wieder die Klassenhefte, die alle noch korrigiert werden müssen.

(b) In the case of verbs denoting to happen, this postponement of the subject is almost the norm; the colourlessness of the verb gives the subject an added importance:[2]
Gestern ereignete sich um 5.30 Uhr am Stadtrand ein Verkehrsunfall.

(c) Though less frequently,[3] the subject is sometimes similarly postponed in a subordinate clause for reasons of rhythm and/or emphasis:
Wir hoffen, daß nächstes Jahr wieder viele Ausländer nach England kommen.
Er erwähnte, daß morgen zugunsten der Armen in der Stadthalle ein Konzert stattfindet.

G. THE ORDER AND POSITION OF ADJECTIVES

665. The following points should be noted regarding the order and position of adjectives:

(a) Several adjectives are normally arranged in the same order as in English:
eine arme, heimatlose alte Frau   *a poor homeless old woman*
ein großes, braunes Paket   *a large brown parcel*

(b) Attributive adjectives normally precede their noun, but if there is more than one they may follow it, as in English, with a somewhat literary effect; see 86, second example.

(c) Adjectives are sometimes separated from their noun, the effect being to emphasize both the noun and the adjective; this construction, which

---

[1] from Grubačić, op. cit., p. 59.
[2] This is well noted by Schulz-Griesbach (op. cit. H 475), two of whose examples I have used in (b) and (c).
[3] Grubačić, op. cit., p. 61, came upon 274 instances of the postponed subject after inversion and 24 in subordinate clauses.

is not particularly to be recommended, is commonest with adjectives indicating number or quantity:

Menschen sind um diese Zeit wenige unterwegs (G. Gaiser)	There are few people about at this time
Fehler habe ich in seiner Arbeit mehrere/keine gefunden	I found several/no mistakes in his work
Beweise hat er äußerst triftige vorgebracht (from Du. Gram.)	The evidence that he produced was extremely cogent
cf. Er hat Geld/Bücher die Menge (coll.)	He's got lots of money/books

(d) See also 173(c) and 653 N. i and ii.

H. THE FREER WORD ORDER

666. The phrase 'the freer word order' is from *Modern German Usage* (1937) by W. Witte, who there notes and illustrates (pp. 12 ff.) the declining authority, in modern German prose, of the rule by which the past participles of compound tenses, infinitives and separable prefixes stand at the end of the sentence and subordinate clauses end with the verb. The same phenomenon is the subject of E. Grubačić's 'Untersuchungen' (see Bibliography) and, concerning separable prefixes only, of an article by Rainer Rath: Trennbare Verben und Ausklammerung (*Wirkendes Wort*, 1/1965).

667. We may first illustrate each of the **four types of freer word order** named above:

Part of sentence placed after a past participle
1. Vieles hatte Glum schon gesehen auf seinem Weg von seiner Heimat bis über den Rhein hinweg (H. Böll).
2. B. hätte das [=his taxi-driver's interest] merken können an den gelegentlichen Rückblicken und dem Arm, der entspannt auf der freien Vorderlehne lag (U. Johnson).

Part of sentence placed after an infinitive
3. Seitdem Rodrigue seine Chronik begonnen hatte, freute er sich darauf, sie zu beschließen mit der Darstellung der Regierung dieses seines lieben Schülers und Beichtkindes (*confessant*) (L. Feuchtwanger).[1]

Part of sentence placed after a separable prefix
4. Die Kunst des herrschenden Geschmacks im vergangenen Jahrhundert ist zwar verschwunden, ihr Einfluß dauert jedoch fort in der Gefühlsstruktur (*the emotional make-up*) des Publikums, der großen und der kleinen Diktatoren, der demokratischen Politiker und Regierungsleute.[2]
5. 'Du hebst das [ein Bonbon] auf bis nach dem Abendessen', erklärte das Fräulein. (V. Baum). '*You will keep that (sweet) till after supper*', *declared the governess.*

[1] from Grubačić, op. cit., p. 15.
[2] from Rath, loc. cit., p. 223.

Part of sentence placed outside a subordinate clause

6. ... und ihm bewies, daß Ulla doch recht zu haben <u>schien</u> mit ihrem Pessimismus (I. Wendt).

668. It will be noted that in all the above examples what is excluded from the framework of the sentence is one or more **prepositional phrases**, and these **constitute by far the commonest type of 'Ausklammerung' or exclusion.**

In the first four examples the exclusion is explained by the length of what is excluded: in 1, three interdependent phrases; in 2, two linked prepositional phrases, the second extended by a relative clause; in 3 and 4, a single prepositional phrase elaborated by genitives, which, in the case of 4, would threaten to split the seams of the sentence if the light-weight prefix 'fort' were placed last.[1]

If in these four examples the function of the exclusion is to give the sentence a more relaxed rhythm and to ease comprehension, in 5 the effect is to give emphasis to the part excluded (bis nach dem Abendessen), in 6 to emphasize what precedes the exclusion (recht zu haben schien).

669. Two sentences from letters received from Germany may serve to show that **'Ausklammerung' is not a purely literary phenomenon**: 1. Am 28.10.68 ist X. gestorben an einem Schlaganfall. 2. Ich freue mich, daß alles gut klappte auf Deiner Reise (*that your journey went off all right*).

670. Some statistics and conclusions

In the 52 works by 26 authors which he examined, Grubačić noted 1587 instances of exclusion, of which 1401 were prepositional phrases, while Rath found exclusions after a quarter of 552 sentences with separable prefixes—the longer the sentences, the more frequent were the exclusions.

In an examination of 25 consecutive pages by each of seven modern writers, the author came upon 54 instances of freer word order; of these 25 occurred in narrative and description, 29 in dialogue and thought-stream; over half the exclusions were from subordinate clauses; in 14 cases the placing was due to the length of the prepositional phrase excluded or to the fact that there were two phrases.

Both Grubačić and Rath conclude that exclusions can no longer be regarded as exceptions, but rather as an alternative type of syntactical structure.

Grubačić sees a tendency for the emphatic position in the German sentence to move, with the help of exclusions, from the end to the middle, giving 'die neue Satzmelodie' a relaxed and natural quality: 'Man schreibt gesprochenes Deutsch.' This he illustrates from Thomas Mann, who, instead of writing 'Raoul Überbein war in der Residenz nicht beliebt', wrote: 'Raoul Überbein war nicht beliebt in der Residenz.'

---

[1] cf. Rath, loc. cit., pp. 222f.

To put the matter in perspective: the frequent occurrence of the freer word order means that a number of 'rules' given earlier, while they retain their general validity, are by no means absolute. The paragraphs to which this modification specifically applies are 369(c) (on the position of separable prefixes), 647 (on the position of the finite verb in subordinate clauses), 649 f. (on the position of participles and infinitives) and 652.

XVI AGREEMENT

A. AGREEMENT IN NUMBER AND PERSON

671. (a) Where the complement precedes and the subject follows the verb, the verb still agrees in number with the subject:

Mein Lieblingsobst sind Kirschen   *My favourite fruit is cherries*

(b) When das, dies, es (as a demonstrative) and welches (as an interrog. pron.) are used with the verb sein, the latter agrees with the real subject: Das sind meine Brüder. Sind es deine Bücher? Welches sind deine Bücher?

(c) After a subject consisting of different grammatical persons, the verb form is determined as in English:

Du und ich (= wir) gehen heute aus   *You and I (= we) are going out today*
Du und deine Brüder (= ihr) habt   *You and your brothers (= you) have*
mich enttäuscht   *disappointed me*

(d) For the agreement of the verb, in number and person, after sowohl . . . als auch, nicht nur . . . , sondern auch, entweder . . . oder, weder . . noch, ob . . . oder (ob) etc., see 524 f.

(e) Where the finite verb precedes two or more singular subjects, it is often used in the singular, e.g. Links war der Fluß, die Brücke und die Burg.

(f) Where the writer feels two singular subjects as forming a unity, the verb may be in the singular:

Diese Haltung und Miene war ihm   *This posture and look were peculiar to him*
eigentümlich (Th. Mann)

(g) When a singular word of quantity, e.g. eine Anzahl, ein Dutzend, die Hälfte, ein Haufen, eine Herde, eine Menge, ein Paar *a pair*, eine Schar, is followed by a plural noun, German usage prefers a singular verb, though a plural verb is sometimes found:

Eine Gruppe von Studenten sprach aufgeregt; die Hälfte der Äpfel war schlecht; eine Schar Kinder kam um die Ecke; es war/waren eine Menge Leute da.

Note: In contrast with occasional English practice, die Familie, die

Polizei, die Regierung and similar collectives always take a singular verb:

Seine Familie weiß davon   *His family knows/know about it*

B. AGREEMENT IN GENDER[1]

672. (a) **Doktor and Professor used of women**

Sie ist Doktor der Philosophie; Frau (Professor) Doktor Meyer.
BUT: Sie ist Doktòrin (=Ärztin); sie ist Professòrin (or Professor) (an der Universität Köln).

(b) **Neuter diminutives referring to persons**

i das Fräulein *young lady*, das Mädchen, das Töchterchen, das Söhnchen etc. are often referred to as 'sie' (possess. 'ihr') and 'er', especially when 1. das Mädchen is not a little girl 2. the personal pron. is some way from the neut. diminutive 3. a fresh speaker replies to a question.
E.g. Das junge Mädchen da ist gestern abend angekommen; sie ist sehr liebenswürdig.
BUT: Dann wurde das kleine Mädchen geboren und füllte die stillen Wände mit seinem Geschrei (P. Ernst).
Was tut Ihr Söhnchen?—Er (or Es) spielt im Garten.

Note:
1. The relative pron. referring to these words must be 'das' or 'welches'.
2. 'das Kind' is referred to as 'es'.

ii Fräulein Müller (=Miss Müller) is treated as feminine except when preceded by an article and at the beginning of a letter. Thus: Fräulein Müller, die schon fort ist, hat ihren Schirm vergessen. Das junge Fräulein Müller, das schon fort ist, hat seinen Schirm vergessen. Liebes Fräulein Müller! (BUT: Grüßen Sie Ihre Fräulein Schwester!)

Note: Many unmarried women, especially professional women no longer young, officially call themselves 'Frau' and not 'Fräulein'.

iii **Proper names:** Before those in -el, def. art. and adj. are masc. or fem.: Lieber Hansel! die fleißige Liesel; before other endings they are neut.; Liebes Peterle! das fleißige Mariechen (cf. Du. Gram. 6945).
All are referred to as 'er' and 'sie' (with fem. possessive 'ihr'), except where the name has been preceded by 'das' (cf. 84(e)iii): Mariechen konnte nicht schlafen; sie dachte an ihre kranke Mutter, BUT: Das Mariechen konnte nicht schlafen; es dachte an seine kranke Mutter.

[1] see also 141.

C. MISCELLANEOUS AGREEMENT POINTS

673. Zwanzig Mark ist zu viel

Zwei Kilo Fleisch werden nicht
genug sein

vier und fünf ist neun

Alle drehten den Kopf

Wir nahmen den Hut ab

Viele haben ihr Leben dabei
verloren

das Haus und der Garten

mein Onkel und meine Tante

Lieber Herr Müller! Liebe Frau
Müller!

Warst du es, der es getan hat?
(see 184 N.)

Twenty marks is too much

*Two kilograms of meat won't be
enough*

four and five are nine

They all turned their heads

We took off our hats

Many lost their lives through it

the house and garden

my uncle and aunt

Dear Mr. and Mrs. Müller (letter)

Was it you who did it?

XVII WORD FORMATION[1]

A. INTRODUCTORY:
FOUR METHODS OF WORD FORMATION

674. German words are formed from simple root-words in four different ways:

(a) by means of Ablaut (vowel changes)[2] or Umlaut (modification): werfen–warf–geworfen *to throw*: der Wurf *the throw*.
scharf: schärfen *to sharpen*.

(b) by means of prefixes: siegen, besiegen; der Busch, das Gebüsch.

(c) by means of suffixes (sometimes with Umlaut): bunt, die Buntheit; der Tod, tödlich.

(d) by forming compound words, with or without a linking letter or syllable: der Bauernhof, hellblau.

Note:
i The word **productive** is used to indicate that new words are still being produced by the type of word-formation in question.

ii Considerations of space have necessitated restricting examples in most parts of this chapter to a bare minimum.

B. THE FORMATION OF VERBS OTHERWISE THAN BY A PREFIX

675. The most fruitful type of verb-formation is by means of a prefix (treated in 676–712); **three other types may be usefully mentioned:**

(a) **Factitive or causative verbs**
i The main type is a weak verb formed from the imperfect of an intr. strong verb by means of Umlaut, with ä often appearing as e: ertrinken *to drown* (intr.), ertrank: ertränken *to drown* (tr.); springen *to jump*, sprang: sprengen *to blow up, burst open*.

---

[1] At various points of this chapter I am indebted to articles by Wolfgang Fleischer in *Deutsch als Fremdsprache* 3, 4/1965 and 1/1967 and to his *Wortbildung der deutschen Gegenwartssprache* (see Bibliography), from which some of my examples are taken; a few others come from Wahrig, op. cit.

[2] More precisely, Ablaut is a vowel change, showing certain regularities, in the root syllable (Stammsilbe) of etymologically related words (Du. Gram. p. 759).

ii Deviations from the main type include fallen *to fall*, fiel: fällen *to fell*; hängen *to hang*, hing: hängen (wk.) *to hang up*.

(b) **A number of verbs in -eln**, with Umlaut, denote a weakened form of an action: husten, hüsteln; lachen, lächeln; others are mildly pejorative (productive): frömmeln *to affect piety*.

(c) **Foreign verbs naturalized with the suffix -ieren** (productive)
i These exist in vast quantities; stylistically, their excessive use is to be frowned upon. E.g. arrangieren, eskalieren, produzieren, trainieren.
ii Many verbs with the suffix -isieren are factitives, e.g. amerikanisieren, motorisieren, standardisieren.
iii Verbs in -ifizieren include exemplifizieren, identifizieren, klassifizieren.
iv A few verbs with German stems are also formed with -ieren, e.g. buchstabieren *to spell*, halbieren *to halve*, stolzieren *to strut*.
v A warning: some verbs in -ieren do not, or do not only, mean what they might appear to mean, e.g. absolvieren, sich blamieren, kombinieren, kontrollieren, phantasieren, raffinieren, referieren (über), reflektieren auf, sich rentieren, sich revanchieren, spendieren, taxieren. E.g.
kontrollieren 1. *to check, inspect* (e.g. brakes, passport) 2. *to control*
raffiniert 1. *refined* (e.g. sugar, oil) 2. *exaggerated* (luxury)
3. *sly, subtle* (e.g. swindler, question)

C. VERBS FORMED BY MEANS OF AN INSEPARABLE PREFIX[1]

676. Verbs are formed from nouns, adjectives and verbs by means of an insep. prefix; some knowledge of the main effects and functions of these prefixes is particularly useful for comprehension.

677. be-

Note: with few exceptions, verbs with be- are transitive.
(a) it makes intransitive verbs transitive: steigen *to go up, rise*: besteigen *to climb* (a mountain).
(b) it directs an action to a different object (productive): eine Mahlzeit kochen: eine Wandergruppe bekochen (*to feed*).
(c) it forms verbs from nouns, generally denoting 'to furnish with' (productive): der Reifen *tyre*: ein Auto bereifen.
(d) it forms mainly factitive verbs from adjectives: befreien.

678. ent-

(a) it denotes origin or beginning: entstehen (s) *to come into being, begin, arise* (of e.g. a law, a political party, a dispute), entwerfen *to draw up* (a plan), *to draft* (a letter).
(b) it forms opposites: entehren *to dishonour*, (sich) entspannen *to relax*.
(c) it denotes 'to deprive of' or 'to free from' (productive): enteisen *to de-ice* (a plane), enterben *to disinherit*.

[1] For the general characteristics of insep. prefixes, see 368.

(d) it denotes removal and separation: entgleisen (s) *to leave the rails,* jemandem etwas entreißen *to snatch s.th. away from s.o.*

(e) it gives the meaning 'to escape' to various verbs of motion: see 492.

Note: Through assimilation, ent- appears as **emp-** in empfangen *to receive,* empfehlen *to recommend,* empfinden *to feel.*

679. er-

(a) it denotes achievement (einen Erfolg, eine Wirkung erzielen) and, as a distinctive and productive application of this, it denotes 'to acquire s.th. by means of the action expressed by the simple verb': Er hat sich (dat.) eine bessere Stellung erarbeitet/erschlichen *He has obtained a better job by hard work/surreptitiously.*

(b) it denotes the beginning of an action or state: erklingen *to ring out;* und plötzlich erstrahlt ihr Gesicht (H. Fallada) *and suddenly she looks radiant.*

(c) it forms verbs from adjectives 1. denoting getting into the state described by the adjective: erröten *to blush* 2. factitive verbs: erfrischen *to refresh,* erleichtern *to make easier* (from compar.).

(d) it is prefixed to a number of verbs when they are used in a figurative or derived sense: Er öffnete das Fenster. Er eröffnete die Sitzung, die neue Bibliothek, ein Konto.

N.B. schließen *to close:* erschließen *to open up* (e.g. a new region).

680. miß-: see 691.

681. ver- (productive)

(a) it forms transitive verbs:

i with the explicit or implicit sense of 'away': verbrauchen *to use up,* consume, die Zeit verträumen.

ii with a broadly negative or unfavourable sense: destruction (vernichten), spoiling (der Ausflug war verregnet), error (verkennen *to fail to recognize, misjudge*). Cf. the opposites achten: verachten; lernen: verlernen *to unlearn, forget.*

(b) it forms intr. verbs with the sense of 'away', deterioration, out of existence (all (s)): verhallen *to die away* (of sound), verhungern *to starve to death.*

(c) it forms refl. verbs meaning to make a mistake in doing s.th.: sich verfahren *to take the wrong road,* sich versprechen *to make a slip of the tongue.*

(d) it makes a number of intr. verbs tr.: verfolgen *to pursue.*

(e) it forms verbs from nouns: verchromen *to plate with chromium,* verkörpern *to embody;* also some factitives e.g. ein Buch verfilmen.

(f) from adjectives it forms 1. factitives: vereinfachen *to simplify,* verbessern *to improve* 2. verbs denoting getting into the corresponding state: verstummen (s) *to become silent,* verwildern (s) *to become a wilderness/ depraved.*

682. zer- denotes apart, to pieces; mainly prefixed to verbs (productive): ein Problem zerreden *to discuss a problem ad nauseam,* zerreißen (h & s) *to tear* (*to pieces*) (tr. and intr.).

D. VERBS FORMED, MAINLY FROM VERBS, BY MEANS OF A VARIABLE PREFIX[1]

683. über

(a) Sep.

   i across: Wir setzten über *We ferried across.*[2]

   ii over: Er legte mir eine Decke über *He put a rug over me.*

(b) Insep.

   i over: überreden *to persuade* ('to talk over'), überschwemmen *to inundate* (also fig.), übersehen *to survey; to overlook.*

   ii over-, implying excess: übermüden *to overtire.*

(c) Sep. and Insep. with the same simple verb, e.g.

über-ragen *to project* (intr.); überragen *to tower above, surpass* (tr.)

über-setzen (h & s) *to ferry across* (tr. and intr.)

übersetzen *to translate.*

684. unter[3]

(a) Sep.: under: unter-bringen *to house, find a place for,* unter-gehen (s) *to go down* (sun, ship), *to go under* (drowning).

(b) Insep.

   i under (including insufficiency): unterdrücken *to suppress,* unterschätzen *to underrate,* unterschreiben *to sign* (a letter).

   ii corresponds to Latin 'inter' (between): unterbrechen *to interrupt,* unterscheiden *to distinguish.*

685. durch

(a) Sep.: through: durch-arbeiten *to work through* (1. a book 2. without a break), durch-fallen (s) 1. *to fall through* 2. *to fail* (e.g. in an exam), durch-lassen *to let through* (s.o. or water).

(b) Insep.: through: durchnässen *to soak,* durchsuchen *to search* (e.g. luggage).

(c) Sep. and Insep. with the same simple verb, e.g.

durch-reisen (s) (intr.) *to travel through* (*a country*) (generally = without a stay): Ich bin (durch Frankreich) durchgereist.

durchreisen (tr.) *to travel all over a country*: Letztes Jahr habe ich Frankreich durchreist.

Note: With a number of verbs denoting change of place, durch may be sep. or insep. with only a slight difference in sense: the sep. form, with the stress on 'durch', generally conveys the completed action; the insep. form, with the stress on the verb, emphasizes the action as such or in progress:

Er eilte durch die Vorhalle durch   *He hurried through the vestibule*

---

[1] For the general characteristics of variable prefixes, see 371.

[2] With some verbs denoting change of place, where the prefix über is possible, hinüber (or: herüber) is more usual, e.g. Wir fuhren hinüber *We crossed over* (*the river*); see also 704.

[3] see also 704.

Er durcheilte die Vorhalle   *He hurried through the vestibule*
cf. durch-schleichen, durch-schreiten, durch-ziehen *to pass through,
march through.*
durch-kommen can only be sep.
durchgehen (insep.) *to traverse* is very rare.

686. um[1]

(a) Sep.
  i turning: um-graben *to dig over* (e.g. a flower-bed), sich um-sehen *to
  look round, back, about one.*
  ii falling and upsetting: um-fallen (s) *to fall over*, um-kippen (h & s) *to
  tip over, overturn* (tr. and intr.).
  iii change: um-arbeiten *to recast* (e.g. a book), um-steigen (s) *to change
  (trains).*
(b) Insep.: surrounding: umarmen *to embrace*, umgeben *to surround.*
(c) Sep. and Insep. with the same simple verb, e.g.
um-ziehen 1. (s) *to move (to another house)* 2. (h) ein Kind um-ziehen *to
change a child's clothes*; sich um-ziehen *to change (one's clothes).*
umziehen *to surround, encircle* (elev.); sich umziehen *to cloud over*: Der
Himmel umzieht sich.

687. voll

(a) Sep.: full: voll-gießen, voll-stopfen (mit) *to cram (with)*
(b) Insep.: completion, carrying out: vollbringen *to accomplish* (e.g. a deed,
a task), vollenden 1. *to complete*[2] 2. *to die* (elev.).

688. wider

Note: 'wider' and 'wieder' were originally the same word (OHG widar,
MHG wider), not separating till the 17th century. Accordingly, as a
prefix, wider may mean:
i against, e.g. widerstehen+dat. *to resist.*
ii back, e.g. wider-hallen *to echo, resound* (intr.) (cf. wieder in wieder-
kommen).

(a) Sep.: Two verbs only: wider-hallen and (sich) wider-spiegeln; both
are occasionally used inseparably in the pres. and imperf.
(b) Insep.: widerlegen *to refute*, widersprechen+dat. *to contradict.*

689. wieder

Sep.: always, except in wiederholen *to repeat.*
(a) back: wieder-bekommen *to recover, get back*, wieder-kehren (s) 1. *to
come back* 2. *to recur.*
(b) again
  i Here wieder should be treated as a prefix provided that a new, distinctive meaning arises from its combination with the verb. (The

---

[1] see also 704.
[2] somewhat stilted; normal usage e.g. er erledigte seine Arbeit; er war mit seiner Arbeit
fertig; ich habe den Brief fertig.

English equivalent will generally begin with re-). Otherwise it is to be regarded as an adverb (Du. Haupt. p. 690). E.g.

Er hat sein Studium wieder-aufgenommen	*He has resumed his studies*
Er hat das Paket wieder auf-genommen	*He took up the parcel again*
Du sollst dies nicht wiedererzählen	*You're not to repeat this, you're not to pass this on*
Willst du den Witz, bitte, wieder erzählen?	*Will you please tell us the joke again?*

ii When prefixed to a verb which itself has a sep. prefix, wieder is written as a separate word in the imperative, and in a simple tense, exc. in a sub. cl.: Nimm deine Studien wieder auf! Er nimmt seine Studien wieder auf. Wenn er seine Studien wieder-aufnimmt, ...

iii Further examples: wieder-auf-leben (s) *to revive* (intr.) fig. (e.g. of trade), wieder-ein-führen *to re-introduce* (e.g. a custom), wieder-her-stellen *to restore* (a building, picture, law and order), *to cure* (s.o. ill), wieder-wählen *to re-elect*.

690. hinter

(a) Sep.: to the back or down, confined to a number of inorganic and unlovely regional colloquialisms, e.g. hinter-schlucken *to gulp down* (water), *to swallow* (a tablet).
(b) Insep.
i behind (after): hinterlegen *to deposit* (money as a security).
ii acting stealthily: Steuern hinterziehen *to evade full payment of taxes.*
(c) Sep. and Insep. with the same simple verb, e.g.
hinter-gehen (s) *to go to the back.*
hintergehen *to deceive.*

691. miß

Insep. (see N.i below)
(a) opposite: mißachten *to disdain, despise,* mißtrauen + dat. *to distrust.*
(b) badly or wrongly: mißdeuten *to misinterpret,* mißhandeln *to ill-treat,* mißverstehen *to misunderstand.*

Note:
i Correctly and normally, miß is insep., but in some verbs alternative variations occur, e.g. ohne ihn mißzuachten, ich hatte ihn mißgeach-tet/gemißachtet. These variations being less common than the norm, they may be ignored, exc. in the case of **mißverstehen**: 1. the stress is here always on miß 2. it is insep. except in the infin. used with 'zu': um ihn nicht mißzuverstehen; cf. in nicht mißzuverstehender Weise *in an unmistakable manner* (cf. 432).

ii The following are the only infinitives of verbs with miß which are commonly used as nouns:
das Mißglücken, Mißlingen, Mißraten *failure,* das Mißbehagen *uncomfortable feeling,* das Mißfallen *displeasure, dissatisfaction,* das Mißtrauen *distrust.*

E. VERBS FORMED, MAINLY FROM VERBS, BY MEANS OF A SEPARABLE PREFIX[1]

692. Separable prefixes may be divided into three types:
(a) simple, e.g. ab-, an-: 693–9.
(b) compound, e.g. herein-, voraus-: 700–706.
(c) special, e.g. teil-nehmen, offen-lassen, spazieren-gehen: 709–12.

693. The simple separable prefixes. Considerations of space preclude a semantic analysis of these prefixes, nor do the assimilation and comprehension of verbs formed with them offer particular difficulty; there follow two or three characteristic examples of each prefix, which include illustrations of the productive character of some of them.

ab-[2] (productive): ab-fliegen *to take off*, jemandem etwas ab-gaunern *to obtain s.th. from s.o. by fraudulent means* (der Gauner *swindler*), ab-reißen *to pull down* (a house), ab-lehnen *to reject*.

an-[2] (productive): an-probieren *to try on* (clothes), eine Stadt an-fliegen *to approach a town by plane* (or, of an airline, *to serve a town*), an-springen (s) *to start* (of an engine) (intr.).

auf-[2]: auf-bleiben *to stay up*, auf-räumen *to tidy up*, auf-setzen *to put on* (hat, water to boil), auf-schließen *to unlock*.

aus-[2] (productive): aus-arbeiten *to work out* (a plan), aus-fräsen *to mill out* (a hole), aus-schlafen *to have a good long sleep*.

bei-: bei-treten + dat. *to join* (e.g. a club), bei-tragen zu *to contribute to*, einen Streit bei-legen *to settle a disputo*.

da-: da-bleiben, da-sein, da-stehen; see 710, 712(e).

dar- means 'there' and so 'before s.o.'; one common product: dar-stellen 1. *to represent, portray* 2. *to perform* (a part) 3. *to constitute, be* (Die Sache stellt ein Problem dar).

ein-[2] replaces 'in' as a prefix (productive): ein-dosen *to tin* (fruit, etc.), ein-fahren (h) *to run in* (a new car); see also 571(c).

fehl- denotes error or failure: fehl-gehen (s) *to miss one's way*, fehl-greifen 1. *to miss one's hold* 2. *to make a blunder*.

fort- and **weg-** meaning 'away' are synonymous, though weg- is used more: weg-bleiben/fort-bleiben, weg-nehmen/fort-nehmen 1. *to take away* 2. *to take up* (space) etc. BUT: weg-sehen (not: fort-sehen) *to look away*.

fort- (but not weg-) also denotes continuation: fort-setzen (tr.).

her- and **hin-**: see 695–9.

inne- within; limited to 5 verbs, e.g. inne-haben *to occupy* (a position).

los-: los-gehen 1. *to come off* (e.g. a button) 2. *to go off* (e.g. a gun) 3. *to commence* (coll.), los-stürzen auf *to rush at*.

mit-, a flexible and pregnant prefix, denotes one of two things:
(a) with some specific person(s), determined by the context:
Gehst du mit? *Are you going with me/us/them etc.?*
Er brachte das Buch mit.

---

[1] For the general characteristics and handling of sep. prefixes, see 369.
[2] see also 704.

(b) more vaguely, 'with the rest', conveying joining in, co-operating or a joint experience: Du mußt mitsingen; unsre Arbeiter bestimmen über den Urlaub mit (*have a say in fixing holidays*); du hast diese Jahre nicht mitgemacht *you didn't go through those years*.

Note: 'mit' may also have independent adverbial force: together with others or with other things, also, partly: Er ist mit der Beste seiner Klasse (*one of the best*); er war mit verantwortlich (*partly responsible*).

nach-: nach-gehen+dat. *to follow* (s.o.), *to investigate* (a problem), *to pursue* (pleasure), nach-datieren *to post-date*, nach-geben *to give way*.

nieder-: nieder-brennen *to burn down*, nieder-lassen *to lower*.

ob-: sometimes insep.; elev. or facetious; 3 verbs: see dictionary.

vor-: vor-gehen *to go forward* or *ahead*; *to be fast* (clock), vor-spielen *to play a piece of music to s.o.*, viel vor-haben *to have a lot on* (engagements).

weg-: see fort-

zu-: zu-fahren+dat. or, more incisive, auf+acc. *to drive towards*, zu-drehen *to turn off* (tap), Geld zu-schießen *to give additional money*.

694. A number of sep. and variable prefixes are used elliptically, e.g.

Ich fühle mich etwas ab (coll.) [abgespannt]	*I feel a bit low*
Ich habe das Buch aus [ausgelesen]	*I've finished the book*

cf. Ist er schon auf? Die Tür war auf; das Licht war noch an; er ist schon fort; sie ist schon hinauf; zurück!

F. HIN- AND HER- AND THEIR COMPOUNDS[1]

695. The orthodox distinction between 'hin' and 'her' is that 'hin' denotes motion away from the speaker or his original situation, whereas 'her' denotes motion towards the speaker or his present situation (For 'the speaker' it may be necessary to substitute 'the person concerned'):

Heute ist die Wahlversammlung, und ich gehe hin	*Today is the election meeting and I'm going (there)*
Ich hielt ihm die Zeitung hin	*I held out the newspaper to him*
Ich hörte einen Ruf und sah hin	*I heard a shout and looked in the direction from which it came*
Komm mal her!	*Just come here*
Er hat mich mit dem Auto hergebracht	*He brought me here by car*
Halt den Teller her!	*Hold out your plate*
Setz dich her zu mir!	*Come and sit down next to me*

696. Where verbs formed with 'hin' or 'her' have a derived, abstract or figurative meaning, the basic directional force of 'hin' may still generally be felt, while the use of 'her' is generally purely idiomatic:

sein Leben für etwas hingeben	*to sacrifice one's life for s.th.*
Die Zeit ging rasch hin	*Time passed quickly*

[1] see also 266–70.

Sie fielen über ihn her	*They assailed him*
Ich will mich nicht dazu hergeben	*I won't lend myself (be a party) to that*
Es geht lustig her	*Things are going on merrily*

697. In nouns formed with 'hin' or 'her', their basic directional force generally holds:

die Hinreise, die Hinfahrt	*the outward journey*
auf der Herreise, Herfahrt	*on the journey here*
auf dem Hinweg[1]	*on the way there*

Purely idiomatic: der Hergang *course of events, occurrence*

698. A particular meaning of hin-: down, as in: Er legte das Buch hin; er legte sich hin; er fiel hin; setz dich hierhin! *Sit down here.*

699. A particular meaning of her-: along, i.e. movement along in relation to some other person or thing:

Er ging neben mir her	*He walked along beside me*
Ein ausländischer Wagen fuhr vor uns her	*A foreign car was going along in front of us*

cf. the compound prefixes: Er lief nebenher, hinterher; 'vorher' is not used thus.

700. Compound separable prefixes formed with hin- and her-

(a) **Six much used pairs**:

hinein, herein *in*	hinunter, herunter *down*
hinaus, heraus *out*	hinab, herab *down*
hinauf, herauf *up*	hinüber, herüber *over, across*

Note: hinunter, herunter and hinab, herab are synonymous; the former are commoner in conversation

Er kam (aus dem Haus) heraus	*He came out (of the house)*
Er starrte (in die Dunkelheit) hinaus	*He stared out (into the darkness)*
Darf ich Sie herüberbitten?	*May I ask you to come across?*

(b)
hinan *upward* (elev.)	hinzu *as an addition*
heran *along* (approaching), *up (to)*; *upward*	herzu *along* (approaching), *up* (rare)
Er trat an mich heran	*He came up to me*
Geh nicht zu nah heran!	*Don't go too near* (idiomatic)
Sie fügte etwas Zucker hinzu	*She added some sugar*

(c) **with 'hin' only**:

hindurch *through*	hinweg *away* (but often idiomatic)
Er drang (durch die Menschenmenge) hindurch	*He made his way through (the crowd)*
Die Rollbahn sauste unter uns hinweg	*The runway sped away beneath us*

[1] 'auf dem Herweg' is not used.

(d) **with 'her' only:**

herbei *along* (approaching), *up*
hernieder *down* (elev.; rare)

Polizisten kamen herbei
Er kam um die Ecke herum
Meine Bücher lagen auf dem Tisch
 herum
Plötzlich trat er (aus dem Gebüsch)
 hervor

herum[1] *round*; also static, as in
 3rd example
hervor *forth, out*
Some policemen came along
He came round the corner
My books lay around on the table

Suddenly he stepped forth (from the
 shrubbery)

701. to go/come up and to go/come down sometimes cause difficulty; the following plain examples may be helpful:

Er ging den Berg hinauf   *He went up the hill*
Er ging zum Gipfel hinauf *He went up to the summit*
Er kam die Treppe herunter *He came down the stairs*
Er ging ins Tal hinunter   *He went down into the valley*

Ich ging zu ihm   *I went up to him*
Ich trat an ihn heran
Mein Bruder kam heran (or: *My brother came up*
 herbei)

Note: In the 1st and 3rd examples, den Berg and die Treppe are adverbial accusatives, not direct objects, the perfect being 'Er ist den Berg hinaufgegangen' and 'Er ist die Treppe heruntergekommen'.

702. Colloquially these compound prefixes are often abbreviated, if the second element begins with a vowel

North German favours the abbreviation of her (e.g. 'reinkommen, 'raufkommen, 'runterkommen) and adheres to this, irrespective of direction, e.g. Gehen Sie 'rüber! Er nahm die Bücher 'rauf. Warten Sie, ich gehe gleich hier rein (H. Fallada).

South German favours the abbreviation of hin (e.g. 'neingehen, 'naufgehen, 'nuntergehen), but in general uses the correct abbreviation in respect of direction. E.g. Er ging 'naus, BUT: Er kam 'raus.[2]

An illustration from *Die Zeit*: Ob er nicht 'rausmöchte aus dem Loch, in eine anständige Wohnung? ... 'Hier kriegt mich keiner 'raus.'

703. Where the verb has a figurative meaning, the prefix is more frequently the form with her- than the form with hin- and the two forms are then rarely interchangeable. E.g.

with her-
herab-sehen auf + acc.   *to look down on, despise*
heraus-geben   *1. to edit, publish*
           2. to give money as change
Es stellte sich heraus, daß ... *It turned out that ...*
herunter-leiern   *to reel off* (e.g. a prayer)

with hin-
sich hinaus-ziehen   *to drag on* (e.g. of negotiations)

---

[1] see also 616: last example and Note.
[2] Du. Gram. 3240 and 3275.

with her- or hin-

die Preise herauf-/hinauf-setzen	*to put up prices*
Es kommt auf dasselbe heraus/hinaus	*It comes to the same thing*

704. An important distinction and warning

Although, as was shown in 703, verbs formed with the compound prefixes may have a figurative sense, they preponderantly have a literal and concrete meaning, denoting movement in the direction in question (cf. the examples in 700).

On the other hand, verbs formed with the simple prefixes ab-, an-, auf-, aus-, ein-, über-, um- and unter-, while they may have a literal and concrete meaning (cf. 693), often have a derived or figurative sense. (For the literal and derived meanings of the variable prefixes über, unter and um, see also 683, 684, 686.)

EXAMPLES

hincin-, herein-, ein-

Er ist hineingegangen	*He has gone in*
Die Zeitung ist eingegangen	*The paper has ceased publication*
herein-bringen	*to bring (carry) in*
ein-bringen	*to bring in* e.g. crops, money, a parliamentary bill

hinaus-, heraus-, aus-

Er stand auf und ging (aus dem Zimmer) hinaus	*He got up and went out (of the room)*
Ich gehe heute nachmittag aus	*I'm going out this afternoon*
Wer weiß, wie es ausgeht!	*Who knows how it will end*
Er kam heraus	*He came out*
Er kommt mit den andern Jungen gut aus	*He gets on well with the other boys*
Ich kann mit 20 Mark nicht auskommen	*I can't make do with 20 marks*
N.B. Er streckte die Hand aus	*He stretched out his hand*

hinüber-, über-

Ich ging zu ihm hinüber	*I went across to him*
Er ist zur SPD übergegangen	*He's gone over to the Social Democrats*

705. The 6 pairs of prefixes in 700(a) and also 'herum' may be compounded with 'da', 'dort' and 'hier', these carrying the stress. E.g.

Er ging dahinein	*He went in there*
Er kam hierheraus	*He came out of here*
Wir gehen jetzt dorthinauf	*We're going up there now*
Du kannst daherum gehen	*You can go round there*

G. OTHER COMPOUND SEPARABLE PREFIXES

706. Note: The following are used as prefixes with only one or two verbs and are not illustrated below: bevor, dahinter, daneben, danieder, darüber, darum, drauf, hintan, umhin, vorweg, zuvor.

dabei: presence, proximity: dabei-sein, dabei-stehen.

daheim: at home: daheim-bleiben.

daher: along (approaching): Er schlenderte daher.

dahin: away, past (and idiomatic): Eine Staffel Düsenjäger pfiff über Köln dahin (*Zeit*); die Zeit flog dahin.

daran, dran: 'to it': sich daran-machen *to set to work*

darein, drein: 'into it': sich darein-finden *to adapt o.s., resign o.s.*

davon: away: davon-brausen *to set off with a roar* (motor-bike).

dazu: addition (and idiomatic): Später kam er auch noch dazu.

dazwischen: 'in between': dazwischen-reden *to interrupt* (a conversation).

einher: along (implying stateliness):[1] Er schritt einher.

empor: upward (mainly elev.): sich empor-arbeiten, empor-blicken.

entgegen: 1. meeting: Er kam mir entgegen 2. opposition: in entgegengesetzter Richtung.

hierher: hither: see 266.

überein: agreement: Ich stimme mit ihm in dieser Sache überein.

umher: around, about:[2] umher-blicken, umher-wandern.

voran: ahead, forward: Er ist schon vorangegangen; die Arbeit geht gut voran.

voraus: in advance, ahead: voraus-bezahlen, voraus-sagen *to foretell*.

vorbei, vorüber: past, by; vorbei is commoner in conversation except in a time sense: Er ging (an unserem Haus) vorbei; der Winter ging vorüber.

vorher: before, in advance; commonest use: vorhergehend *preceding*.

vorüber: see vorbei.

zurecht: right, in order: zurecht-machen *to prepare*.

zurück: 1. back, backward, behind: zurück-gehen *to recede, go down* (e.g. of floods, earnings), zurück-lassen *to leave behind*. 2. back, returning: zurück-bekommen *to get back, recover*, zurück-gehen *to return*.

zusammen: together: zusammen-bringen, zusammen-rücken (h & s) *to move closer together* (in order to make room) (tr. and intr.). By a fig. extension of 'closer together': zusammen-fallen (s) *to collapse*, zusammen-fahren (s) *to start* (with surprise).

707. A certain number of **prepositional formations, analogous to some of the above compound separable prefixes,** are, in normal practice, not compounded with the verb (cf. Du. Gram. 5940), but their position in the sentence is that of a separable prefix, e.g.

außer acht lassen	*to leave out of account*
beiseite legen	*to lay aside*
instand setzen	*to repair, make ready*
zugrunde gehen	*to perish, be ruined*
zugrunde liegen (+dat.)	*to form the basis (of), to be at the bottom (of)*
zustande bringen	*to bring about, achieve*
jemandem zuteil werden	*to fall to s.o.'s share*

N.B. The corresponding adjectival participles, verbal nouns and derived nouns are, however, written as one word: die instandgesetzte Maschine, der zugrundeliegende Gedanke, das Zugrundegehen, die Instandsetzung.

---

[1] Betteridge, op. cit.
[2] see also 616: last example and Note.

708. Preposition+einander (*one another*) in relation to the verb[1]

(a) **prep.+einander is *not* joined to the verb:**
    i if the sentence expresses genuine reciprocity:

Wir haben aneinander gedacht	*We thought of each other*
Wir werden aufeinander warten	*We shall wait for each other*
Sie passen zueinander	*They suit each other*

ii if prep.+einander is the equivalent of an adverb:

Wir haben nacheinander mit ihm gesprochen	*We spoke to him in turn* (*successively*)

(b) **prep.+einander is joined to the verb**, like a separable prefix, if together they form a single concept:

Ich habe die Bücher aufeinandergelegt	*I have put the books on top of one another (stacked the books)*
aneinandergrenzende Grundstücke	*adjacent pieces of land*
Es hat sich gezeigt, daß die Meinungen hierüber auseinandergehen	*It has become evident that opinions differ about this*

This does not apply if the verb already has a prefix:

Sie haben aneinander vorbeigeredet	*They were at cross purposes*

II. SPECIAL SEPARABLE PREFIXES

709. The special separable prefixes are nouns, adjectives, participles, adverbs and infinitives which are used as separable prefixes (productive)

EXAMPLE: teil-nehmen an+dat. *to take part in*
    Er nimmt an dem Konzert teil.
    Da er an dem Konzert teilnimmt, . . .
    Er hat an dem Konzert teilgenommen.
    Er hat versprochen, an dem Konzert teilzunehmen.

FURTHER EXAMPLES:
Nouns: acht-geben (auf+acc.) *to pay heed (to)*, haus-halten *to keep house*, statt-finden[2] *to take place*
Adjectives: offen-lassen *to leave open*, sauber-halten *to keep clean*, eine Sache tot-schweigen *to hush a matter up*
Participles: gefangen-nehmen *to take prisoner*, verloren-gehen *to get lost, go astray* (of things)
Adverbs: blind-fliegen *to fly blind*, fest-halten *to hold fast*, schwarz-arbeiten[3] *to be a blackleg*
Infinitives:
kennen-lernen *to make the acquaintance of*
liegen-bleiben 1. *to stay in bed* 2. *to be left behind, to be forgotten* (of things) 3. *to remain unsold*
sitzen-lassen *to leave in the lurch, to jilt*
spazieren-gehen *to go for a walk*
    BUT N.B. (sich) schlafen legen (see 422(d))

---

[1] cf. Du. Haupt. pp. 718 f.
[2] for the noun die Statt, see 729(a)ii.
[3] BUT: schwarz färben *to dye black*.

14

710. **Limitation of the use of adjectives, adverbs and infinitives as separable prefixes:** some are treated as separable prefixes when their combination with the verb produces a new meaning, but not when both components retain their literal meaning.

EXAMPLES:

Adverbs/Adjectives

Du sollst dableiben	*You're to stay (on)*
Du sollst *da* bleiben	*You're to stay there* (where you are)
Wir können weiterspielen	*We can go on playing*
Er hat mir weitergeholfen	*He has helped me on*
Ich werde dir weiter helfen	*I shall continue to help you* (as in the past)
Er hat es mir leichtgemacht, die Stellung zu bekommen	*He made it easy for me to get the job*
N.B. Er hat es mir sehr leicht gemacht, . . . (adj. written separately when qualified)	*He made it very easy for me* . . .

Infinitives (the position of the infin. in the sentence is not affected)
fallen-lassen *to drop* (fig.), e.g. a plan, a member of a team, a remark, one's mask.
fallen lassen *to drop* (lit.), e.g. a book.

stehen-bleiben 1. *to stop, stand still* 2. *to stop* (of a clock) 3. idiomatic: Wo sind wir in der letzten Stunde stehengeblieben? *Where did we get to in the last lesson?*
stehen bleiben *to remain standing*

711. (a) **Verbs like the following are formed from compound nouns and are conjugated like simple weak verbs:**

frühstücken *to have breakfast*: um zu frühstücken, ich frühstücke, ich habe gefrühstückt.

làngweilen *to bore* (from die Làngweile *boredom*)

wètteifern (mit) *to compete, vie (with)* (from der Wètteifer *rivalry, competition*).

(b) A number of verbs, not formed from compound nouns, are nevertheless conjugated like simple weak verbs (cf. (a) above) E.g.

hàndhaben *to handle, manipulate*, lièbäugeln mit 1. *to give s.o. the glad eye* 2. *to toy with* (an idea), lièbkosen *to caress*, schlàfwandeln *to walk in one's sleep*.

712. **separable prefixes:** some are treated as separable prefixes when their

(a) **rad-fahren** *to cycle*: Ich fahre gern Rad; da ich gern radfahre, . . . Ich bin viel radgefahren. N.B. Auto fahren.

(b) **maschine-schreiben** *to type* is only used intransitively: Ich schreibe nicht Maschine; ich habe früher nicht maschinegeschrieben, BUT: Ich habe den Brief mit der Maschine geschrieben. One exception: the passive past part.: ein maschinegeschriebener Brief.

(c) **not-landen** *to make a forced landing*: wir sind notgelandet; um notzulanden; BUT: wir notlandeten.

---

[1] Du. Haupt. pp. 715 ff.

(d) **Some compounds exist only in the infinitive,** e.g. brustschwim-
men, kettenrauchen, kopfrechnen *to do mental arithmetic,* kugelstoßen
to put the weight, segelfliegen *to glide,* wettlaufen *to race;* **others, only
in the infin. and past part.,** e.g. seiltanzen *to walk the tightrope,*
uraufführen: Das Stück wurde in Frankfurt uraufgeführt *The play
was first performed in Frankfurt.*

(e) **Compounds of sein and werden** are written as one word only in
their non-finite forms:
Er ist dagewesen, BUT: wenn er da ist.
Es ist bald bekanntgeworden, BUT: wenn es bekannt wird.
um das Bild loszuwerden, BUT: wenn ich es los werde.

(f) **auf und ab, hin und her:** ich bin auf und ab gegangen; während die
Kinder hin und her liefen, BUT: mein langes Aufundabgehen.

(g) **Separable prefixes placed emphatically at the beginning of the
sentence** are written as a separate word:
Fest steht, daß . . .   *It is certain that . . .*
Hinzu kommt, daß . . .   *Add to this the fact that . . .*

(h) **Some cases where a separable prefix might be expected but
where it has not yet developed:**
auswendig lernen *to learn by heart,* jemandem Bescheid sagen *to inform s.o.,*
Bescheid wissen *to be informed, to know,* Klavier spielen, Posten stehen *to
be on guard duty,* sich satt essen *to eat one's fill,* Schach spielen, Schi
laufen, Schlitten fahren, Schlittschuh laufen.
BUT: das Auswendiglernen *learning by heart,* das Schilaufen *skiing* etc.

I. THE FORMATION OF NOUNS

713. All infinitives may be used as verbal nouns, always neut., often
corresponding to an English form in -ing (cf. 404): das Aufstehen
getting up, das Reiten *riding.*
In many cases, such nouns are felt as ordinary nouns, e.g. das Einkommen
income, das Essen *meal, lunch, food,* das Leben *life,* das Unternehmen
enterprise, venture; concern, business, das Versprechen *promise.* Though such
nouns may be used in the plur., there is a tendency, because of their
verbal origin, to avoid it or to use another noun, e.g. Wir verglichen
unser Einkommen *We compared our incomes;* verpfuschte Existenzen
wasted lives; all seine Versprechungen.

714. Some nouns (preponderantly masc.) **are formed from verb-stems
without a suffix:** der Lauf, der Stoß, der Rückfall *relapse,* das Lob;
also with Ablaut: der Schluß, der Stich *stab, sting,* der Ersatz (ersetzen)
substitute, replacement.

**715. Nouns are formed from verbs and/or adjectives and/or nouns
by means of a suffix**

(a)
-e: from verbs: die Grube *pit,* and adjectives (largely qualities): die
Größe.

-ei, -erei: from verbs (productive); often pejorative; -ei with verbs in -eln, -ern: die Prügelei *fight, scrap*; otherwise -erei: die Rekordhascherei *record hunting* (haschen *to snatch*); from nouns denoting professions: die Gärtnerei *gardening*; *nursery*.

-el: from verbs: der Hebel *lever*, der Stachel *thorn, prickle*.

-er (-ler, -ner) (productive): 1. professions and some other personal designations: der Bäcker, der Bühnenbildner *set designer*, der Witwer *widower*; -ler is sometimes pejorative: der Ausflügler *tripper*; name of a town + er forms the name of its inhabitants: der Frankfurter, mit den Kölnern (deviations include der Bremer, der Göttinger, der Hannoveräner, der Münchner) 2. instruments (see 2(c)) and some other inanimates: der Seufzer *sigh*.

-heit (-keit, -igkeit) (numerous and productive), mainly from adjectives: nouns denoting qualities and states: die Laxheit, die Gleichheit; -keit is used instead of -heit with adjectives in -bar, -ig, -lich, -sam (e.g. die Sparsamkeit) and with some in -el and -er (e.g. die Eitelkeit *vanity*, BUT: die Dunkelheit); -igkeit, originating in nouns such as Schwierigkeit, has become an independent ending, e.g. die Schwerelosigkeit *weightlessness*.

-ling (productive): personal designations; generally with Umlaut; often pejorative: der Flüchtling *fugitive, refugee*, der Schwächling.

-nis: largely from verbs 1. with prefixes 2. denoting the result of an action: die Ersparnis *saving*, das Vermächtnis *legacy*.

-schaft (productive): 1. collectives: die Gewerkschaft *trade union* 2. nouns denoting states: die Bereitschaft *readiness*, die Gefangenschaft.

-sel: from verbs: das Rätsel *puzzle* (raten *to guess*); sometimes acts as a diminutive (productive): das Einschiebsel *insertion*.

-tum (productive): mainly from nouns and denoting institutions and typical conduct or outlook: das Papsttum, das Gangstertum, das Deutschtum *German ethos*.

-ung: very common; productive, especially in denoting processes: die Frischhaltung *keeping fresh*, die Wasserung der Kapsel *splash-down*.

(b) **-chen and -lein form diminutives**, which are always neut.; both generally cause Umlaut. North Germans use -chen (productive); the South German -lein sounds stilted, and dialectal forms are preferred, e.g. das Häusle (in Baden), das Hunderl (in Bavaria), das Blättli (in Switzerland).

Note:

i Declension: Diminutives in -chen and -lein are Group 1 nouns (cf. 18). The dialectal forms (with local variations) are left uninflected, von + dat. replacing the gen. sing. E.g. (dat. plur.): Die Kinder spielten mit den Hundle/mit die [sic] Hunderl (also: mit den Hunderln)/mit den Blättli.

ii -chen is not used with nouns in -ch and generally not with nouns in -ng; here North German usually has a double diminutive: das Büchelchen, das Ringelchen.

iii The ending -e disappears before the diminutive endings: das Pflänzchen; likewise -en (das Kästchen), though it is sometimes changed to -el (das Wägelchen).

iv All the diminutive endings may also convey affection (Weibchen *wifie*, das Hundle), unless used ironically: Also, Freundchen . . ., ein nettes Sümmchen![1]

v The diminutive endings are virtually never used after the suffixes -ei, -erei, -heit, -in, -keit, -ling, -nis, -schaft, -ung; therefore: die kleine Lehrerin (not: das Lehrerinchen) (see (c) below).

(c) **-in forms nouns denoting the female of most persons and many animals**, often with Umlaut: die Ärztin, die Beamtin, die Hündin, die Landsmännin *fellow-countryman*. The following have no fem. form: der (Film)Star, der Gast, der Lehrling, der Liebling, der Minister, e.g. Sie ist der Liebling der Familie. For Doktor and Professor, see 672(a).

(d) 4 noun suffixes which are themselves nouns:[2] **-gut** (possession, goods) and **-werk** (work) form collectives: das Ideengut *stock of ideas*, das Steingut *stoneware*, das Balkenwerk *woodwork, beams*; **-wesen** (being, nature etc.) mainly denotes spheres of administration and of human activity (productive): das Schulwesen *educational system*, das Flugwesen *aviation*; **-zeug** (stuff, cloth etc.) forms collectives (das Schreibzeug) and instruments (das Werkzeug *tool*, das Fahrzeug *vehicle*).

716. **Nouns are formed from verbs and/or nouns by means of a prefix.** (These prefixes always carry the main stress, exc. Erz- as in 2nd example, Ge- and Miß-)

(a)
Erz-: der Erzbischof *archbishop*; der Erzgauner *thorough scoundrel*.
Ge-,[3] sometimes in conjunction with the suffix -e: 1. from verbs: nouns denoting a protracted activity; often pejorative (productive): das Gelaufe *running about, bustle*, das Geschwätz(e) *idle talk, gossiping* 2. from nouns: collectives, with Umlaut where possible: das Geäst *branches*, das Gebirge 3. many nouns outside 1. and 2.; cf. 27.
Miß- 1. opposite: der Mißerfolg 2. pejorative: der Mißbrauch *misuse, abuse*. (Main stress on Miß- exc. die Mißártung and die Mißhándlung; but see also 691 N.ii).
Mit- 1. being together: der Mitreisende 2. co-operation: der Mitarbeiter 3. contemporariness: die Mitwelt.
Rück- is the prefix normally used with nouns corresponding to the verbal prefix zurück-: die Rückfahrt, der Rückstoßantrieb *jet-propulsion* (zurückstoßen). Note: 1. some nouns have the prefix Zurück-, e.g. die Zurückhaltung *restraint* 2. with some nouns Rück- is a contraction of 'der Rücken', e.g. die Rückwand *back wall*.
Un-, from nouns only: 1. opposite: die Unruhe 2. an undesirable deviation: der Unmensch *hard-hearted wretch* 3. with nouns denoting quantity, it has a magnifying and/or pejorative effect: eine Unsumme *a vast sum*.
Ur-, from nouns only, denotes origin and beginnings (in OHG ur=aus

---

[1] cf. Fleischer, op. cit., pp. 166 f.
[2] cf. Fleischer, op. cit., pp. 64, 161 ff.
[3] For the gender and plural of Ge- nouns, see 27.

out of, from) (productive): die Uraufführung *first performance,* der Ur(ur)großvater, Urtierchen *protozoa.*
Wohl- denotes the good or agreeable: der Wohltäter, der Wohlklang *pleasing sound, euphony.*

(b) 3 noun prefixes which are themselves nouns (productive):[1] **Grund-** foundation, basis: der Grundgedanke; **Haupt-** head: der Hauptangeklagte; **Spitzen-** (die Spitze *peak*): die Spitzenbelastung *peak-load* (electr.).

(c) Many of the separable and all the variable prefixes treated under the formation of verbs also appear attached to nouns; these are mainly nouns formed from the corresponding verb, e.g. der Abflug, die Darstellung, die Voraussage, but in many cases these prefixes are attached to nouns with no verbal counterpart, e.g. der Abgott *idol,* der Ausweg, die Nachsilbe, Überstunden, die Umgegend.

717. Compound nouns are formed by joining together two or more words, the last being a noun; this process, not limited to nouns, is an extremely common, productive and distinctive feature of the German language. The first word of a compound noun or adjective carries the main stress and in most cases defines the sense of the second.

The first word of a compound noun may be:

a noun (the commonest type)	die Haarbürste	*hair-brush*
an adjective	der Edelstein	*gem*
a superlative	der Kleinstbildfilm	*sub-miniature film*
a participle	der Gebrauchtwagen	*second-hand car*
a numeral[2]	der Dreifuß	*tripod*
a verbal stem	der Hörsaal	*lecture theatre*
a preposition	die Untertasse	*saucer*
an adverb	die Jetztzeit	*the present day*

718. Where the first word is a noun, some compounds are formed with, and others without, a linking letter or syllable. The following are the only serviceable rules for these links:[3]

-s is regularly attached to the following:
 i the masc. or neut. endings -ing (der Heringssalat), -ling (meine Lieblingsfarbe), -tum (die Altertumskunde).
 ii infinitives used as neut. nouns: die Lebensversicherung.
 iii the fem. endings -heit (Sicherheitsmaßnahmen), -keit (Müdigkeitserscheinungen), -schaft (die Gesellschaftslehre), -ung (die Meinungsumfrage *opinion poll*), -ion (die Präzisionsarbeit), -tät (die Universitätsbibliothek).
 iv in most compounds of the fem. words Geschichte, Hilfe, Liebe: das Geschichtsbuch, das Hilfsmittel *remedy,* der Liebesbrief.
Group 7 nouns and substantival adjectives have the link -n or -en: die Heldentat, das Fremdenzimmer.

---

[1] cf. Fleischer, op. cit., pp. 201 f.
[2] Zwei- has the form Zwie- in certain compounds; see 728(d).
[3] cf. Du. Gram. 3790, 3805.

-n is the commonest link for fem. nouns in -e: der Scheibenwischer, die Straßenecke; Schule is a common exception: das Schulbuch.

719. Further miscellaneous examples of compound nouns

der Bergfrühling *spring in the mountains* (taken from a letter)
der Feinschmecker *gourmet*
Madames Goldplombenlächeln (V. Baum) *Madame's smile with its gleam of gold fillings*
das Kernwaffenversuchsverbot *nuclear test ban*
der Schwarzhörer *owner of an unlicensed wireless set*
das Spritzschweißen *spray welding*
die Tiefkühltruhe *deep freeze*
die Vorfreude *pleasure of anticipation*

J. THE FORMATION OF ADJECTIVES AND ADVERBS

720. Adjectives are formed from verbs, nouns, adjectives and adverbs by means of a suffix

(a)

-artig (productive): resembling, of the type indicated: bösartig *ill-natured*; *malignant* (disease), vogelartig *bird-like*.

-bar: common and productive, particularly with verbs; = Engl. -able: erreichbar *attainable*, zusammenklappbar *collapsible*. See also -lich i below.

-haft: mainly from nouns: greisenhaft *senile*, tierhaft *animal-like*.

-ig: common and productive; often causes Umlaut; mainly denotes qualities: günstig *favourable*, holperig *bumpy*, dortig *of that place, there*: das dortige Museum. See also -lich N.3.

-isch (productive):
i it forms adjectives from proper names (homerisch: see also 734) and from geographical names (europäisch, französisch; frankfurterisch: see 116(d)N.v).
ii it forms numerous other adjectives, preponderantly from nouns and applicable to persons, often pejorative and often with Umlaut: bäuerisch *boorish* (contrast bäuerlich *rustic*), modisch, närrisch, wählerisch *fastidious*.
iii it is the commonest suffix for adjectives based on foreign words: buddhistisch, klimatologisch, musikalisch.

-lich (often with Umlaut):
i from verbs: here -lich frequently = -able (like -bar), especially negatively: unbeschreiblich, unvermeidlich (or: unvermeidbar); there may be a difference in meaning, e.g. sträflich *criminal, unpardonable*; strafbar *punishable* (by law).
ii from nouns (productive): schiedsrichterlich *by arbitration*, tödlich.
iii from adjectives: generally a weakened or derived sense of the attribute in question: rötlich *reddish*, kleinlich *petty*.
Note:
1. After en, t (or d) is inserted before -lich: öffentlich *public*, morgendlich *matutinal*.

2. From e.g. ärgerlich, there developed the extended suffix -erlich: leserlich *legible*, weinerlich *lachrymose*.

3. Distinguish 'mein dreiwöchiger Urlaub, ein dreiwöchiges Kind' from 'unsere dreiwöchentliche Konferenz' our (*regular*) *three-weekly conference*; cf. -stündig/-stündlich etc.

-los (productive) = Engl. -less: funktionslos, rauchlos.

-mäßig (productive):
i in accordance with, as demanded by: gewohnheitsmäßig *habitual*, planmäßig. (Here **-gemäß** is sometimes an alternative for -mäßig, e.g. ordnungsgemäß, plangemäß; normal usage generally makes no semantic distinction and prefers -mäßig.)
ii with regard to: die verkehrsmäßige Wichtigkeit der Stadt.
iii resembling the type indicated: der lehrbuchmäßige Stil.

-n, -en, -ern: adjectives denoting materials: golden, hölzern, seiden. In general, compound nouns are preferred: eine Holzbrücke, ein Seidenkleid, though not with gold and silver: eine goldene Uhr.

-sam: furchtsam *timid*, gemeinsam (*in*) *common*, sparsam *thrifty*.

(b) 9 adjectival suffixes which are themselves adjectives (productive):
-arm poor in: ein getreidearmes Land *a country growing little grain*.
-fähig capable of: konkurrenzfähig *competitive*.
-fertig ready for: reisefertig *ready to set out*.
-frei free from: eine atomwaffenfreie Zone *a nuclear free zone*.
-gerecht: lit. just; here: in accordance with: altersgerechte Wohnungen *dwellings suitable for old people*.
-reich rich in: ein fischreicher Teich, einflußreich.
-voll full of: geheimnisvoll *mysterious*.
-wert worth: lesenswert, sehenswert.
-würdig worthy of: abbauwürdig *ready for demolition*, sehenswürdig.

721. Adjectives are formed, mainly from adjectives, by means of a prefix. (These prefixes always carry the main stress.)

erz-: intensifying; limited in use: erzdumm *extremely stupid*, erzkatholisch.
grund-: intensifying; limited in use: grundfalsch *radically wrong*.
miß-: mißmutig *ill-humoured*, mißtönend *out of tune*, *discordant*, mißtrauisch, mißverständlich *misleading*, *ambiguous*.
un-: normally it negates a meaning and produces the opposite: unartig *naughty*; where the adj. has an independent opposite (e.g. klug: dumm, schön: häßlich), the form with un- is less radical or less literal in meaning: unklug *unwise*, unschön *dubious*, *reprehensible* (action).
N.B. unheimlich *uncanny*, unmutig (elev.) *annoyed*, unscheinbar *plain-looking*, unwillig (elev.) 1. *angry* 2. *unwilling*.
ur- 1. origin and beginnings: urgermanisch *from oldest Germanic times* 2. intensification: urgemütlich *extremely cosy*, urkomisch.
wohl-: mainly with participles: wohlschmeckend, wohlverdient.

722. Compound adjectives are formed by joining together two or more words, the last being an adj. (cf. beginning of 717). In some cases the second word does not exist as an independent adjective, e.g. blauäugig, eintönig, gegenseitig.

The first word of a compound adjective may be:

a noun	pflichttreu	*dutiful*
an adjective	kleinlaut	*meek, subdued*
a numeral[1]	dreijährig	*lasting 3 years; 3 years old*
a verbal stem	kauflustig	*keen to buy*
a preposition	unterirdisch	*subterranean*
an adverb	frühreif	*precocious*

723. **Where the first word is a noun, the compound is frequently formed with a linking letter or syllable**, e.g. geisteskrank, menschenähnlich. The only worthwhile rules are that, as in the case of compound nouns, where the first word is a noun ending in -heit, -keit, -schaft, -ung, -ion, -tät, an s is added (e.g. gesundheitsschädlich) and where the first word is a fem. noun in -e, -n is the commonest link: krisenfest, sonnengereift, BUT e.g. hilfsbereit, sprachempfindlich.

724. **Further examples of compound adjectives** (The second word is often a participle, as in the 2nd and 5th examples.)

gebrauchstüchtige Anzüge *hard-wearing suits* (from Du. Gram. 3955)
hochglanzpoliert *with high-gloss finish*
scheinheilig *sanctimonious*
todunglücklich *desperately unhappy*
zweckentsprechend *appropriate, expedient*
diebesselige Kirschensommer (H. Hesse) *blissful summers of cherry stealing*
ein greisenbrüchiges 'Grüß Gott, Herr Doktor' (H. Broch) '*Good day, doctor*', *in a croaky senile voice*

725. **Hyphenating two adjectives**, whose association is not current enough to justify a single compound word, e.g. eine schaurig-schöne Erzählung (from Du. Gram. 2195) *a gruesome and beautiful tale* (contrast: ein naßkalter Herbsttag); this effective type of compound adjective is difficult to render adequately in English.[2] Cf. end of 119: 3rd literary example.

726. **Adverbs may be formed by means of suffixes:** erstens, meistens, hoffentlich, blindlings, rechts, vorwärts. There are also **many compound adverbs:** bergauf, diesmal, geradeaus, *straight ahead*, unterwegs, vorgestern, wortwörtlich *word for word*.

---

[1] zwei- has the form zwie- in certain compounds; see 728(d).
[2] cf. D. V. White: Words and Notions in German (*Modern Languages* Sept. 1964).

XVIII ORTHOGRAPHY

A. MISCELLANEOUS ORTHOGRAPHICAL POINTS

727. (a) **Points treated elsewhere**: plur. in -n or -en? 17 iv; masc. and neut. gen. sing.: -es or -s? 45; masc. and neut. dat. sing.: add e? 47; adjectives ending in -el, -en, -er when inflected: 92(b), 103, 190(c), and possess. pron. unserer, euerer: 161(a)N.iii; verbs in -eln and -ern: 340(g).

(b) **The e of el in nouns with the suffix -ung formed from verbs in -eln is dropped in many words**, in both speech and writing, e.g. die Sammlung, die Wandlung, die Entwick(e)lung.

The corresponding e of er is more frequently retained: die Neuerung, die Wanderung, die Verbess(e)rung.

For analogous adjectives (e.g. neb(e)lig) and possess. pronouns (e.g. der uns(e)rige) see 103(d)N.iii, 161(b)N.ii and (c)N.ii.

(c) **Nouns in -ee and -ie** do not add an e in forming the plur., even where the plur. is pronounced as an additional syllable, e.g.
der See *lake*, die Seen (pron. See-en)
die Industrie, die Industrien (pron. Industrie-en)
das Knie, die Knie (pron. Knie-e or Knie) (cf. the verb knien (pron. knie-en or knien), kniend, sie knien, knie!)

(d) **Nouns containing a double vowel** drop one vowel where their plural form or a derivative has Umlaut: der Saal, die Säle; das Paar, das Pärchen; das Boot, das Bötchen.

(e) One of **a potential sequence of 3 identical consonants** in a compound word is dropped before a vowel: das Bettuch, stillegen *to close down* e.g. a factory, BUT: der Fetttropfen.

(f) **An optional e occurs at the end of**: **14 adjectives**: 104; **16 adverbs**: 104 N.i and ii, 277, and, colloquially, fest(e), sacht(e), vorn(e); **some nouns**, the e or its absence being here often dialectal or archaic, e.g. der Bursch(e), das Geklirr(e), das Geschwätz(e) (and others in Ge-), der Hirt(e), der Ochs(e), der Schütz(e), die Stirn(e), die Tür(e).

728. (a) **f or ph?** ph is yielding, or has yielded, to f in the following words and their derivatives (and in a number of less common analogous words):

das Autograf (autografieren etc.), das Foto (der Fotograf etc.), die Grafik *graphic arts*, das Mikrofon, die Sinfonie, der Stenograf, das Telefon, der Telegraf. Distinguish: die Fantasie *fantasia*, die Phantasie *imagination*.

(b) **-eur or -ör?** French loan-words in -eur retain that spelling (e.g. der Chauffeur, der Ingenieur) exc. der Likör and der Frisör (commoner than the older Friseur).

(c) **ss or ß?** (It is the predominant usage, in both writing and printing, to make this distinction; if a typewriter lacks the ß symbol, ss may be used instead.)

RULE: ss is only used to denote the voiceless 's' sound between vowels if the preceding one is short; all diphthongs count as long vowels.

EXAMPLES: der Fluß, die Flüsse; der Fuß, die Füße; die Masse *mass*, die Maße *measurements*; wir lassen, ihr laßt, ich lass' ihn kommen, laß ihn kommen! wässerig, wäßrig; beißen, gebissen; die Schlußsitzung, russisch.

EXCEPTIONS:

i compound words, e.g. das Meßamt *celebration of mass*, mißachten *to disdain, despise*, flußabwärts *downstream*, weissagen *to foretell*.

ii a few proper names end in -ss: Günter Grass, Theodor Heuss, Ricard Strauss (BUT: Johann Strauß), Carl Zeiss (whence: das Zeissglas *binoculars*).

(d) **Zwei- or Zwie-?**
Zwie-, an old variant of zwei, occurs at the beginning of the following, and of a few less common words:

der Zwieback *rusk*, das Zwiegespräch *dialogue, colloquy*, das Zwielicht *twilight*, der Zwiespalt, die Zwietracht *discord, dissension*, zwiespältig *discordant, conflicting*
Contrast: der Zweisitzer, die Zweiteilung, zweideutig, zweimotorig etc. etc.

729. (a) **die Stadt, die Statt, die Stätte**

i die Stadt (⁼e) *town, city*: die Hauptstadt, die Stadtmitte, der Städter *townsman*.

ii die Statt *place, stead*: only used in set phrases, e.g.
an Vaters Statt, an Kindes Statt annehmen *to adopt* (*a child*), an Eides Statt *in lieu of oath*.
cf. (an)statt+gen., stattfinden, Statthalter *representative, governor*, die Werkstatt (plur. Werkstätten) *workshop*.

iii die Stätte *place, abode* (elev.) e.g. eine bleibende/heilige/liebgewordene Stätte.
cf. die Brandstätte *scene of a fire*, die Gaststätte *restaurant*, die Werkstätte (-n) *place of work, workshop*.

(b) **der Tod** *death*: **tot** *dead*. **Compounds:**
der Todfeind, todblaß, todmüde, todsicher, tödlich.
sich tot-arbeiten, sich tot-lachen, tot-schießen, totgeboren *stillborn*, die Totgeburt.

B. CAPITALS AND SMALL LETTERS

730. Basic rule: all nouns are written with a capital (der Sack, beim Lesen, das Für und Wider, eine Drei, ein Drittel), while all other parts of speech are written with a small letter, unless they open a new sentence.

731. Miscellaneous exceptions and special cases

(a) **Nouns used as separable prefixes** have a small letter, e.g. acht-geben, teil-nehmen; but see 712(a)(b).

(b) **Personal pronouns and possess. adjectives and pronouns**:
i the polite you (your): Sie (Ihr).
ii in a letter, Du (Dein), Ihr (Euer), Deinetwegen etc. are written with a capital.
iii Er, Dein, Sein may have a capital when referring to the Deity, but this is less regular than in English usage.

(c) **Indeclinable adjectives in -er** formed from the names of towns have a capital: die Berliner Straßen.

(d) **Adjectives forming part of geographical or established names** have a capital: das Schwarze Meer, das Neue Testament, das Auswärtige Amt *Foreign Office*, die Ewige Stadt (Rome), die Französische Revolution.
Note:
der Eiserne Vorhang, BUT: der kalte Krieg
das Goldene Kalb, BUT: die goldene Hochzeit
das Schwarze Brett *notice-board*, BUT: der schwarze Markt

(e) For the **titles of books, poems etc.**, see 55.

(f) **Note the use of small letters in the following miscellaneous items**:
außer acht lassen *to leave out of account*; sich in acht nehmen *to take care*; in bezug auf *with regard to*; ein bißchen; es tut mir leid; ein paar *a few* (BUT: ein Paar *a pair*); er hatte recht/unrecht; es ist schade; er ist schuld daran (BUT: es ist seine Schuld); ich lerne schwimmen (or: (das) Schwimmen)

732. Adjectives and participles used as nouns normally have a capital: see 106 ff. and cf. die Seinen *his people*; du mußt das Deinige tun *you must do your share*. The neut. adj. has a capital in nichts Neues, alles Neue and analogous phrases (see 111).

EXCEPTIONS:
(a) Substantival adjectives are written with a small letter in many set phrases: see 110.
(b) Distinguish: Es ist das richtige (=richtig), ihm alles zu sagen; tue das Richtige!   Es ist das beste (=am besten), wenn wir ihm alles sagen; es ist das Beste, was ich je gegessen habe (and analogous instances).
(c) The indefinite adjectives (listed in 112(b)) have a small letter, even when used substantivally, e.g. nichts anderes, ich habe noch einiges zu tun, alles übrige, viele sind dagegen.

Main deviations:
i The following have a capital after nichts etc. and alles etc. (see 111):
ähnlich, bestimmt, derartig, gewiß, weiter, e.g. nichts Ähnliches,
alles Weitere.
ii die Folgenden *those who followed*
iii Weiteres (das Weitere) *further details*
(d) All the miscellaneous adjectives and pronouns treated in 187–239
always have a small letter, with the exceptions given before 187.

733. deutsch or Deutsch?[1]

with a small letter:
i when used adjectivally (das deutsche Volk, eine deutsche Stadt)
except in official names ((die) Deutsche Bundesbahn (DB)).
ii when it is the equivalent of an adverb phrase:
Der Botschafter hat mit dem Außenminister deutsch gesprochen.
Das Buch ist auch deutsch (or: in Deutsch) erschienen.
Er denkt sehr deutsch.
Wenn ich deutsch reden soll, . . . *If I'm to speak plainly,* . . .
iii after auf: Wie sagt man das auf deutsch? auf gut deutsch *to put it
plainly.*

with a capital, when used substantivally:
Wir haben Deutsch in der Schule.
Er spricht (kann, lehrt, lernt, liest, versteht) (kein, gut) Deutsch.
Er kann kein Wort Deutsch; sein Deutsch ist schlecht; das ist gutes
Deutsch; im heutigen Deutsch.
ein Deutscher, eine Deutsche, die/wir Deutschen.
Er hat das Buch aus dem Deutschen ins Französische übersetzt.

**734. Adjectives formed from proper names (by means of the suffix
-isch (-sch)):**
i they have a capital when they denote the creator or possessor, a small
letter when they denote 'in the manner of'.
ii they frequently have the suffix -sch when used attributively and -isch
when used predicatively or adverbially.

die Shakespearischen[2] Lustspiele, eine Wagnersche Oper, die Bismarcksche
Politik, das Müllersche Grundstück.
Der Humor in dieser Szene ist fast shakespearisch; er versuchte, wagner-
isch zu komponieren; die platonische Liebe.

735. Numerals
i For hundert and tausend, see 245.
ii **Ordinals** are written with a small letter with the following main
exceptions:
Er ist der Erste in der Klasse; der Erste unter Gleichen; Wilhelm der
Erste; die Erste Hilfe; der Erste Weltkrieg; er kommt am Ersten (des
Monats) zurück; ein Dritter *a third party, outsider.*

---

[1] mutatis mutandis, this paragraph applies to all national adjectives: französisch, nor-
wegisch etc.
[2] Names in -e generally drop the e and add -isch.

iii Fractions are written with a capital: zwei Drittel: see 250. Two exceptions: dreiviertel is almost always written as one word with a small letter; halb almost always has a small letter: see 251.

736. **Time phrases**, being the equivalents of adverbs, are in general written with small letters unless a preposition, article, adjective or numeral stresses the fact that a noun is involved.

Thus: sonntags, gestern abend, monatelang.
BUT: am Sonntag, eines Abends, drei Monate lang, letzten Mittwoch.

Main exceptions: i Er arbeitete Tag und Nacht.
ii Er kommt Mittwoch zurück; er kommt Weihnachten.
iii Er kommt Anfang/Mitte/Ende Mai zurück.
iv seit langem, seit/vor kurzem.

C. ONE WORD OR TWO?[1]

737. **Miscellaneous cases**

(a) **Cases treated elsewhere**: irgend 207(h); soviel, zu wenig etc. 235; Mal 254 f.; sep. prefix or independent adv. (or infin. or noun)? 689(b), 693 (mit-), 707 f., 710, 712(e)–(h).

(b) **noun object + pres. part.**: grauenerregend *horrifying*. Some further instances where this combination has established itself as a unit and is generally written as one word:
aufsehenerregend *sensational*, bahnbrechend *pioneering, epoch-making*, herzerquickend *heart-warming*, vertrauenerweckend or vielversprechend *promising*, zeitraubend.

Generic compounds of this type are always written as one word: blutstillende Watte *styptic cotton-wool*.

(c) **noun + pres. or past part. with suppressed prepositional link**: this combination is always written as one word, e.g. staubbedeckt (= mit Staub bedeckt), freudestrahlend *beaming with joy*.

(d) **Distinguish**:

sobald *as soon as* (conj.)	so bald *so soon*
solange *as long as* (conj.)	so lange *for such a long time*
sooft *as often as, whenever* (conj.)	so oft *so often*
wieweit *how far, to what extent*	wie weit *how far, what distance*
woanders *elsewhere*	wo anders? *where else?*
womöglich *possibly, perhaps*	wo möglich *if possible* (coll.)

Note: 'so daß' is always written as two words.

738. **Adverb + Adjective or Participle**: many short and common adverbs (unless they are limited by an adverb of degree) are compounded with adjectives and participles used attributively, but not when they are used predicatively:
eine leichtverdauliche Speise *an easily digestible dish*

---

[1] based on *Duden-Taschenbücher 3*, pp. 130 ff.; the examples in 737(b)(c)(d) and 738 are mainly selected from the lists there given.

BUT: eine sehr leicht verdauliche Speise.
Diese Speise ist leicht verdaulich.

Compare:
blankpoliert, blaugestreift, engbefreundet, ernstgemeint, fettgedruckt *in bold type*, gleichgesinnt *like-minded*, gutbezahlt, halboffen, hochbegabt, neugeboren, obenerwähnt, schwerbeschädigt[1] *badly damaged*.

Note:
i Adverbs which are **not** compounded include eben and soeben *just (now)*, fast, gerade, kaum: das soeben erschienene Buch.
ii Generic and figurative compounds of this type are always written as one word:
Der Mann ist schwerbeschädigt;[1] cf. minderbegabt *backward, handicapped*, reinwollen *pure wool*.
Seine Reden sind oft etwas hochtrabend (*pompous*); cf. weitblickend *far-sighted*.
iii 'nicht' is compounded in generic compounds used attributively: nichtamtlich *unofficial*, nichtrostend, nichtübertragbar *non-transferable*, BUT: Diese Karte ist nicht übertragbar.

D. THE USE OF THE HYPHEN

739. Miscellaneous uses[2]

(a) occasionally, to break up unwieldy compound words, e.g. der Provinzial-Marktregulierungskommission gegenüber (G. Grass).

(b) in ad hoc combinations, e.g. Schließlich taten sich die Protest-Demonstranten mit den Ostermarschierern zusammen (*Zeit*).

(c) to link the words of an elaborated substantival infinitive, e.g. die unaufdringliche Eleganz des Immer-aus-dem-Ei-gepellt-Seins (*Zeit*) *the unobtrusive elegance of being perpetually spick and span*.

(d) Where two or more compound nouns, adjectives, adverbs or verbs, generally joined by 'und' or 'oder', have their final component in common, the repetition of the latter is often avoided by means of a hyphen:

Funk-, Fernseh- und Filmautoren (E. Kreuder)	*writers of radio, television and film scripts*
genuß- und ergebnisreiche Tage	*enjoyable and fruitful days*
ein- und aussteigen	*to get in and out*
Compare:	
Geld- und andere Sorgen	*financial and other worries*
nicht alle Fach- und praktischen Ärzte	*not all specialists and general practitioners*

(e) to avoid a sequence of 3 identical vowels in a substantival compound: die Tee-Ernte *tea-harvest*, BUT: schneeerhellt *lit up by the snow* (participial compound).

---

[1] applied to a car, schwerbeschädigt is purely descriptive; applied to a person, it is generic and officialese: *seriously disabled*.
[2] see also 725.

740. Hyphenation at the end of a line

(a) Compound words are divided up into their component parts: Apfel-baum, ent-erben, nach-geben.

(b) For all other words a serviceable rule is to divide them according to the syllables that result from saying them slowly: Glä-ser, Ka-tho-lik, Näch-te, Trans-port.

(c) Some special points:
    i a single vowel is never divided off, e.g. Ahorn, Klaue.
    ii double consonants should be hyphenated after the first consonant: Bet-ten, rol-len, flüs-sig; ß (or ss written in place of ß) is regarded as a single consonant: Fü-ße, sto-ßen.
    iii where one of a potential sequence of 3 identical consonants is dropped in forming a compound (see 727(e)), it reappears when hyphenated: Bett-tuch, still-legen.
    iv st is not divided in simple words, e.g. Fen-ster, Gä-ste, BUT: aus-teilen, Donners-tag.
    v ck is hyphenated as k-k: drucken: druk-ken; lecker: lek-ker; Stockung: Stok-kung.

741. The chief remaining uses (and non-uses) of the hyphen are shown by the following examples, almost all taken from Duden-Taschenbücher 3, pp. 158 ff.:

die H-Bombe, die U-Bahn, der I-Punkt, der K.-o.-Schlag, C-Dur *C major*, O-beinig *bandy-legged*

die 1000-Jahr-Feier (BUT: die Tausendjahrfeier), eine 10-Pfennig-Briefmarke, die 4 × 400-Meter-Staffel (*relay*)

die römisch-katholische Kirche, deutsch-amerikanische Beziehungen (*relations*)

Ost-West-Gespräche, Hals-Nasen-Ohren-Arzt, Erste-Hilfe-Ausrüstung *first-aid equipment*

das Schiller-Museum, ein Bach-Konzert, die Nixon-Mannschaft *President Nixon's team*, die Dresdner-Bank-Aktien (*shares*), BUT: der Dieselmotor, Röntgenstrahlen *X-rays*, das Schillertheater

die Bahnhofstraße, die Goethestraße, die Münchener Straße, die Richard-Wagner-Straße; Sankt Peter (St. Peter), die Sankt-Peter-Kirche (die St.-Peter-Kirche)

der Rheinwein, das Nildelta, Großbritannien, Kleinasien *Asia Minor*, Westdeutschland (BUT: West-Berlin), der Dortmund-Ems-Kanal, Nordrhein-Westfalen (one of the 11 West German 'Länder'), Hamburg-Altona (a part of Hamburg), Dresden-Nord, Bad Ems.

E. THE USE OF THE APOSTROPHE[1]

742. The apostrophe is used to indicate the omission of letters and words in colloquial or dialectal pronunciation and sometimes in poetic style (e.g. ird'sche Güter).

---

[1] see also 51(g).

Ihm geht's gut. Siehst du's? Ja, ich seh's. Ich hab's gesehen.
Hast du's Paket? Ich hab' meinem Bruder's Geld gegeben. Ich hab'm
Lehrer geholfen. So'n Blödsinn! 'n richtiger Grabstein? Wie auf'm
Friedhof? (Th. Valentin) (cf. 638 N.vi)
Seine Freud' war groß (BUT: (in) Freud und Leid: fixed phrase). Nach
wen'gen Wochen; die Leut'; der Käs'.
Ich kauf' noch was. Ich möcht' dir helfen. Hätt' ich das gewußt, . . .
'n Abend! (=Guten Abend!) Was 'ne Frau! (H. Fallada) (=Was für
eine Frau!) Was schreibst'n da? (J. Rehn) (=Was schreibst du denn
da?) Is' gut (=es ist gut *right you are*).

Note: Omissions of the following three types are accepted as constituting
alternative forms and no apostrophe is needed:
i the e of -en after a verbal stem ending in a vowel or a vowel + h: sie
schrein, wir haben gesehn.
ii the e of the imperative sing.: Komm her! Schlaf gut!
iii the e of el, en, er occurring in the middle of a word: ich segle, neblig;
seltner; unsre, der Wandrer.

XIX PUNCTUATION RULES

Note:
i Most cases in which German and English practice is the same
have been omitted.
ii For the punctuation of a postal address, see 260.

A. THE COMMA

743. (a) **Two sentences joined by 'und' or 'oder'**: comma before 'und' or
'oder' if the second sentence has its own subject-word: Mein Vater
arbeitet im Garten, oder er macht einen Spaziergang.
Exc. if something other than the subject, standing at the beginning of
the first sentence, causes inversion in both: see 645(a), examples 3–5.

(b) **Always put a comma before aber, sondern, allein** *but,* **doch** *yet,*
nevertheless, **jedoch** *yet, however,* **vielmehr** *rather, on the contrary*: Er
ist nicht sehr intelligent, aber fleißig.
Exc. when aber (meaning 'however') and jedoch occur in the middle
of the sentence: Er aber/jedoch ist ein Deutscher.

(c) **No comma with entweder . . . oder, weder . . . noch, sowohl . . .
als auch, sowie (auch)** (unless they connect clauses):
Weder er noch sie hat mich gesehen.
Schmidt sowie auch Müller fehlten heute.
Note: 'und/oder' is used, though less than English 'and/or'.

(d) **Divide off all subordinate clauses with commas,** including noun
clauses without 'daß': Er sagte, er käme bald zurück.[1]
Exc. No comma after the first of two sub. cl. joined by und or oder.

(e) **Compound conjunctions and conjunctional phrases**
i Where they are felt to form a single unit, they have a comma in front,
e.g. Er war hinausgegangen, ohne daß ich es merkte. Cf. als daß
(see 469(a)), anstatt daß, außer daß, außer wenn, besonders wenn,
gerade als, insofern als, je nachdem ob/wie/wann etc., kaum daß
(but see 531(d)), selbst wenn, BUT: dadurch, daß (cf. 452).

---

[1] Note position of comma in e.g. Er starb, zwei Jahre nachdem er Deutschland verlassen
hatte.

ii The remainder are of two kinds:

1. prep.+def. art.+noun+daß: these have a comma before daß.
Ich will nach Bonn fahren in der Hoffnung, daß ich ihn sprechen kann.
Cf. im Falle, daß; unter der Bedingung, daß; unter der Voraussetzung, daß *on the assumption that.*

2. participle or miscellaneous phrase+conjunction: these have a comma in front and also before the conjunction.
Ich bin um sechs Uhr zurück, vorausgesetzt, daß alles gut geht. Ich freue mich über seinen Erfolg, um so mehr, als er völlig unerwartet kam.
Cf. abgesehen davon, daß; angenommen, daß; ausgenommen, wenn *except if*; es sei denn, daß *unless*; gesetzt, daß *supposing that.*

(f) **Infinitive phrases**
i **zu+infin., with nothing else**, is not divided off:
Ich hoffte zu gewinnen.
Except:
1. when there is more than one such phrase: Ich hoffte, zu reiten und zu schwimmen.
2. when it forms the complement: Mein Ziel war, zu gewinnen.
3. when it is a perf. or passive infin.: Sie glaubten, gesiegt zu haben. Er verlangte (*demanded*), bezahlt zu werden.

ii **zu+infin. with at least one other word** is divided off:
Ich bat ihn, mir zu helfen. Er kam, um zu arbeiten.
Except:
1. when the infin. phr. stands alone as the subject:
So etwas zu erlauben ist unerhört.
(BUT: So etwas zu erlauben, das ist unerhört.)
2. when the infin. phr. is enclosed by a compound tense or a sub. cl.:
Ich habe ihm zu helfen versprochen.
Ich weiß, daß er sein Geschäft zu verkaufen versucht.
3. when the infin. phr. is not self-contained:
Das will ich dir zu erklären versuchen.
(BUT: Ich will versuchen, dir das zu erklären.)
4. after brauchen, haben, pflegen *to be accustomed to*, scheinen, sein, vermögen *to be able to*, wissen *to know how to* (cf. 434 (c)):
Ich brauche heute nicht ins Geschäft zu gehen.
Du hast dir jetzt die Hände zu waschen.
So ein Transistor ist in London (leicht) zu bekommen.

iii **an infin. phrase without 'zu'** is not divided off:
Ich muß spätestens um acht Uhr im Büro sein.

(g) **Divide off participial, adjectival and absolute phrases with commas:**
Später wanderte er, ein altes Lied summend, durch den Garten.
Bald darauf verließ er, blaß vor Wut, das Zimmer.
Die Hände in den Taschen, kam er auf mich zu.

(h) **Adverb phrases and qualifying words and expressions are not normally divided off** (But see 642(c)):
An diesem schönen Nachmittag ging er wie gewöhnlich spazieren.
Bitte bringen Sie mir wenn möglich eine Zeitung.
Erstaunlicherweise war er im großen und ganzen zufrieden.

(i) **Two or more adjectives** are divided off by commas if they are of equal status (put differently: if they could be joined by 'und'): gute, billige Äpfel, BUT: gute englische Äpfel; 'englische Äpfel' forms one concept. Some German authors eschew commas in any list of adjectives.

(j) **Comma and semi-colon**: Germans (including German authors) frequently put a comma between two main clauses, where English usage would put a semi-colon. In many instances this is not officially correct, but in some it is due to Germans' regarding as a conjunction what in English is classified as an adverb or adverbial phrase, e.g. insofern *to that extent*, stattdessen *instead*, trotzdem *in spite of this*, unterdessen *meanwhile*. E.g. Gehe in die Stadt und kaufe Mehl, unterdessen heize ich schon den Backofen an (Schulz-Griesbach, op. cit., G 510).

B. PUNCTUATION MARKS OTHER THAN THE COMMA

744. (a) **The semi-colon**: see 743(j).

(b) **The colon**: when direct speech is introduced by a preceding verb of saying, a colon is used: Dann sagte er: 'Ich kann es nicht.'

(c) **Inverted commas** ('...' or ‚...'): with titles they are placed thus: Goethes Gedicht 'Der Erlkönig', BUT: in der letzten Strophe des 'Erlkönigs'.

(d) **The exclamation mark** is used in the following cases:
  i after interjections and exclamations: see 639 ff.
  ii after imperatives: Seid vorsichtig, Kinder! BUT: after completely unemphatic imperatives, a full stop or comma may be used: 'Geben Sie mir bitte die Zeitung', sagte er.
  iii after most substitutes for the imperative: see 459.
  iv after the optative subjunctive: see 476.
  v after the words of address at the beginning of a letter: Lieber Hans! Sehr geehrter Herr Dr. Müller![1] (cf. 673) (Some Germans prefer a comma.)
  vi more frequently than in English in public notices (Kein Zutritt!) and in letters (Ich bin gespannt auf seine Reaktion! Von meinem Fenster aus sehe ich schon den ersten Schnee auf den Bergen!)

(e) **The use of the full stop in abbreviations**
  i If an abbreviation is pronounced in the form of actual words, the letters forming it are followed by a full stop: d.h. (das heißt) ev. (evangelisch) s.o. (siehe oben!) z.B. (zum Beispiel). N.B. usw. (und so weiter)

  ii If an abbreviation is pronounced (a) as individual letters or (β) as a new word constituted by those letters, no full stops:
  (a) DGB (Deutscher Gewerkschaftsbund *German Trades Union Federation*), LKW (Lastkraftwagen *motor-lorry*), USA

---

[1] These two letters might respectively end: Herzliche Grüße, auch an Deine Schwester, Dein Karl. Mit vorzüglicher Hochachtung (verbleibe ich) Ihr (sehr) ergebener Karl Kramer.

(β) NATO, Degussa (Deutsche Gold- und Silberscheideanstalt *German Gold and Silver Refinery*)

iii No full stop after A (Ampere) C (Celsius) cm (Zentimeter) DM (Deutsche Mark) ff (fortissimo) g (Gramm) l (Liter) s (Sekunde) SW (Südwesten) and analogous abbreviations.

C. PUNCTUATION IN NUMERALS

745. (a) Millions and thousands are indicated by a gap, not by a comma:
3 835 500   10 000 (BUT: 9000)
(b) Ordinals are indicated by a full stop: am 3. Mai; Heinrich III.; am Hofe Ludwigs XIV.
(c) A decimal point is indicated by a comma: 8,5 Kilometer
(d) See also 257.

INDEX

Note:
1. A hyphen denotes a prefix or suffix.
2. Numbers refer to paragraphs, not pages.
3. In the case of some words and phrases (e.g. some misc. adjectives, adverbs, verbs) either the English or the German form is given, but not both; where both are given, fuller references follow the German form.

AUTOPIA
THE FUTURE
OF CARS

'Entertaining, thought-provoking and well researched, *Autopia* is an essential read for anyone interested in the future of cars.'

Jason Dawe, former presenter of *Top Gear* and motoring journalist

'A riveting and quirky look at the latest in car technology. Perfect for geeks, petrolheads and geeky petrolheads.'

Rick Edwards, presenter of *!mpossible*

Jon Bentley is a presenter on Channel 5's *The Gadget Show*. He was the producer and executive producer of *Top Gear* for many years and has a bend named after him on the programme's test track. He is a committed car enthusiast and has written for multiple car publications.

AUTOPIA
THE FUTURE OF CARS

JON BENTLEY

Atlantic Books
London

First published in hardback in Great Britain in 2019 by
Atlantic Books, an imprint of Atlantic Books Ltd.

1 2 3 4 5 6 7 8 9

A CIP catalogue record for this book is available from the British Library.

Hardback ISBN: 978 1 78649 634 8
E-Book ISBN: 978 1 78649 636 2

Printed and bound in Great Britain by Clays Ltd, Elcograf S.p.A.

Atlantic Books
An Imprint of Atlantic Books Ltd
Ormond House
26–27 Boswell Street
London
WC1N 3JZ

www.atlantic-books.co.uk

CONTENTS

INTRODUCTION

WHY THE CAR MATTERS

Since its invention nearly 130 years ago the car has been an extraordinary global success story, extending its influence over most of the planet and transforming vast tranches of human life. There are now about 1.3 billion of them scurrying round the world's roads. By 2035 there'll likely be more than 2 billion – a growth rate comfortably exceeding that of the human population. The car has revolutionised patterns of human settlement, reshaped the geography of cities and countryside and transformed the working lives of hundreds of millions of people.

Cars are so much more than a means of getting from A to B. From the beginning to the end of our lives, they're a powerful psychological force. A few weeks after my seventeenth birthday, I passed my driving test and experienced that amazing sense of freedom that only the car can give. Suddenly I had the means to go wherever I wanted with minimal effort. Like countless drivers before and after me, I embraced an explosion of new opportunities for employment, travel and (yes) romance.

People may say that taking your driving test is no longer the universal rite of passage that it used to be back then in the late 1970s, but I can vividly recall my seventeen-year-old daughter on her return from her first fully independent drive saying it was the most liberating thing she'd ever done. More soberingly, I can remember the look of crestfallen disappointment on my late mother's face when I told her she should give up driving on account of her all-consuming Alzheimer's. That was the end of the road in more ways than one.

As objects go, cars have an incredible capacity to inspire loyalty and affection in their owners. They can rival our pet cat or dog because, like our favourite animal companions, they also have their own loveable quirks. There's the noise of the engine, the sensation of acceleration, the rich variety of dynamic experiences through steering, cornering and handling characteristics plus the tactile sensations of the controls, the ways the doors open and shut, the weight and feel of throttle and clutch. All of these create the potential for a truly satisfying relationship between driver and machine.

Your choice of motor says a lot about you. For a nineties sales rep, embroiled in British company-car culture, fretting over whether the badge on the boot-lid was an L or a GL was practically part of the job description. Boy racers of the era agonised in meticulous detail over the specs of a VW Golf GTI versus a Peugeot 205 GTi. But the psychology isn't solely an individual affair. There's an intense social dimension to car ownership. Banger racers, Vintage Sports-Car Club members, muscle-car enthusiasts and Austin Allegro owners are all part of a developing network of driving tribes. People make friends all over the world through their ownership of a particular type of car.

The last fifty years have witnessed the golden age of the car, with the once-spluttering invention dominating the globe and shaping all our lives. But is this set to change? Along with its power to transform the world for the better, mass car owner-ship has also had a profoundly negative legacy. Doctors talk of how emergency departments took on a whole new level of gruesome in the 1960s. Previously quiet Saturday nights became bloodfests. Pollution and resource depletion became a concern shortly afterwards and, in recent years, the internal combustion engine has been pilloried for its contributions to climate change. A whole catalogue of lesser problems include ever more congestion, road rage, the loss of rural idylls to commuting and tourism and, let's not forget, the increasing nightmare of finding anywhere to park.

Rather than representing freedom and opportunity, are cars going to become an expensive anachronism that take up too much of our money and time? Are they a burden in an age when urban populations are far more concentrated?

There is reason to hope that all is not lost. Most cars today still have four wheels and run on fossil fuels, but that doesn't mean that we haven't already seen incredible breakthroughs in speed, safety, efficiency and – of course – gadgetry. And, while the technology has remained fundamentally the same for decades, industry insiders insist that we are on the cusp of a revolution.

I'm writing this book to explore such innovations and see where they might lead in the years to come. From self-driving trucks to cars that can see round corners, I'll examine the mind-blowing challenge of successfully designing artificial intelligence to take the place of human drivers. I'll explore the options available for powering the cars of the future and question whether electric cars will ever get over their bugbears of range anxiety and sluggish charging. I'll ask whether hydrogen will at last realise its potential and whether diesel really deserves to be demonised.

By talking to designers young and old, I'll discover the ways in which future cars will retain their allure – and their speed. I'll ask whether cars will continue to get safer or if increased technology will make the car into an unpredictable lethal weapon as hackers bypass their often shamefully lax security. If the car embarks on a radical new career of change, what will happen to all the existing ones – not least those classic cars lovingly cherished by millions of enthusiasts? Finally, I'll consider some of the more unlikely future scenarios for personal transport and if the car will remain relevant in the face of fierce potential competition.

I've been fortunate to spend my whole working life engaged with my two childhood obsessions – cars and technology. I worked with the iconic TV series *Top Gear* for fifteen years, many of those as its producer. Red-letter days came thick and fast. I can remember getting 190 mph out of a Porsche 959 on the autobahn entirely legally near Stuttgart, driving my first 911 – my first Ferrari – and my first drives in a whole spectrum of iconic classics, like an XK120, D-Type and Aston Martin DB4 and 6. And there was the time I drove Alan Clark up and down the Italian Alps in his Rolls-Royce Silver Ghost.

As well as my car passion I can barely recall a time when I wasn't fascinated by gadgetry and technology. I used to build radios, mend TVs and practise old-fashioned analogue photography, including developing and printing, and I have dabbled with computers for as long as they've been around. In recent years I have presented *The Gadget Show*, the UK's most popular consumer-technology programme.

Dr Ian Robertson, BMW's global sales chief, said in June 2017 that 'The car industry has done the same thing for over a hundred years. In the next five to seven years the car will change enormously. We're at the tipping point in an industry worth $2 trillion a year.' It's an incredibly exciting time, but also a crucial one. Avid customers no longer queue round the block for a fresh model, like they did in the 1960s with a Ford Mustang. Instead, they are far more likely to camp outside an Apple store, waiting for the latest iPhone. If the car is to stay relevant, it needs to evolve.

'Connected', 'autonomous' and 'zero emission' are the industry buzzwords right now. According to a designer I spoke to from Jaguar Land Rover, every single one of the future cars in their studios is battery-powered and self-driving. But are our favourite brands on the right track? Or will our love of being behind the wheel win out? Will we really have the patience with battery-powered cars? Certainly it's hard to see us giving up on cars as a whole but, in a world of rapid technological change, it feels like it's time for the car industry to catch up. Let's start with perhaps the most talked about and the most ambitious of the predicted changes: autonomy – or the car that drives itself.

ONE

CONNECTED AND AUTONOMOUS

the Rise of the Robot Cars

The bright-red Golf GTI weaved in and out of cones at the very limits of its grip. We took the sharp corner ahead and I was thrown to the left as the driver took a perfect racing line and began to accelerate out of the turn. I was being hurled round the test track at VW's rather remote facility in Wolfsburg and feeling in awe of the test driver's remarkable command of the course.

What made it more impressive was that the driver wasn't even human. In fact, there was no visible driver at all. The steering wheel, accelerator and brake were all magically moving entirely of their own accord. This wasn't even a Google car: it was 2006, when autonomous aspirations were yet to hit the mainstream. You can understand why I found the effect so stunning.

9

Car automation has a surprisingly long history. For decades, scientists have sought to slash the death toll on our roads by replacing the fallible human driver with a more capable technological alternative. Until recently such aspirations were confined to science fiction, their real-world potential thwarted by practicalities of technology and cost. But now, thanks to recent improvements in computer power, artificial intelligence, machine learning and sensor technologies, the impossible is becoming possible.

The driverless journey started with a radio-controlled car that hit the streets of New York in 1925. Inventor Francis Houdina fitted a brand-new Chandler with a radio receiver and 'apparatus' attached to the steering column. This turned in response to signals from a radio transmitter in a car following behind. According to a contemporary report in the *New York Times*, the car drove 'as if a phantom hand were at the wheel'.

The initial unveiling didn't go well. After making wildly uncertain progress down Broadway, the car narrowly missed a fire engine and crashed into a car full of news cameras recording the whole operation. Police instructed Houdina to abort the experiment. Even more bizarrely, the similarly named Harry Houdini became irritated by Houdina's efforts and accused him of 'using his name unlawfully in the conduct of business'. The famous magician broke into the Houdina Radio Control Co. and vandalised the place – a misdemeanour for which he was later summoned to court.

The automation journey stuttered on with 'magic motorways', which were first shown at General Motors' 'Futurama'

The autonomy spectrum

There are six levels of automation as defined by the Society of Automotive Engineers:

Level 0 No automation.

Level 1 The most basic level of automation, whereby just one function of the driving process is taken over. The car might have lane centring or adaptive cruise control but not both.

Level 2 In which multiple functions are controlled – both lane centring and adaptive cruise control, for example.

Level 3 So-called 'conditional automation', where the car can take control of safety-critical functions but still needs a driver to be permanently paying attention in case intervention is necessary. A Level 3 car might take over driving in a low-speed traffic jam, for instance.

Level 4 Whereby cars are autonomous but only in controlled areas – say, a robotaxi operating on a housing estate. Level 4 cars do not need steering wheels or pedals. (Some wags have suggested that horses are a Level 4 autonomous vehicle.)

Level 5 The 'fully autonomous' stage. The car can take over completely and doesn't require special lane markings or any other dedicated infrastructure; it really can self-drive anywhere, and the 'driver' can go to sleep or do anything they wish.

exhibit at the 1939 World's Fair in New York. A brainchild of designer Norman Bel Geddes, the concept featured electro-magnetic propulsion and guidance systems built into the road. Embedded circuits in the road were also behind experiments to guide cars by the American electronics company RCA. It started with model cars in 1953 and graduated to real ones in 1958. Sensors in the front bumpers picked up signals from a buried cable that provided information on roadworks and stalled cars ahead; the system would apply the brakes or change lanes as required. The company thought self-driving cars would be widespread on highways by 1975. The British government's Road Research Laboratory (later the Transport Research Laboratory, or TRL) came up with a hands-free Citroën DS prototype a year or two later that worked in a similar way – and it too predicted that by the 1970s all motorways would feature a lane offering hands-free driving. Like many who followed, its claims were wildly optimistic.

The first real stand-alone autonomous vehicle appeared in Japan in 1977, but it was far from being really roadworthy. Instead of buried electronics it relied on a huge computer that occupied most of the dashboard and the passenger footwell. Using information gleaned about its environment from inbuilt cameras, it could follow white lines on the tarmac – though only at a rather pedestrian 20 mph. Nevertheless, this was one of the first vehicles to move beyond level 0 on today's autonomy spectrum, as defined by the American organisa-tion SAE International, formerly known as the Society of Automotive Engineers.

German aerospace engineer Ernst Dickmanns upped the levels of speed and artificial intelligence with the help of a boxy Mercedes van. The VaMoRs prototype was tested successfully in 1986 and drove itself at 60 mph on the autobahn a year later. It led the pan-European research organisation EUREKA to launch the painfully named PROgraMme for European Traffic of Highest Efficiency and Unprecedented Safety, or PROMETHEUS project. With a significant injection of €749 million, researchers at the University of Munich developed camera technology, software and computer processing that culminated in two impressive robot vehicles: VaMP and VITA-2, both based on the Mercedes S-Class. In 1994, these piloted themselves accurately through traffic along a 600-mile stretch of highway near Paris at up to 80 mph. A year later, they clocked up 108 mph on a journey from Munich to Copenhagen that included a 98-mile stretch without human assistance.

Many manufacturers started developing limited autonomous features around this time, but they were strictly aimed at driver assistance and certainly couldn't contend with the vast range of hazards we encounter all the time on the road. This would soon change when a new player entered the game: the US military. At the dawn of the twenty-first century, they sponsored the DARPA Grand Challenges, in which a $1 million prize was promised to the team of engineers whose vehicle could navigate itself fastest around a 150-mile obstacle course. Although no vehicles finished the inaugural event in 2004, it generated hype and helped spur innovation. Five vehicles finished the next year's challenge, with a team from Stanford nabbing the $2 million prize.

The Stanford team caught the eye of a certain technology company called Google and the rest is history. In 2010, Google announced that it had been secretly developing and testing a self-driving car system with the aim of cutting the number of car crashes in half. The project, which would later be renamed Waymo, was headed by Sebastian Thrun, director of the Stanford Artificial Intelligence Laboratory, and its goal was to launch a vehicle commercially by 2020.

Six Toyota Priuses and an Audi TT comprised the initial test fleet. Equipped with sensors, cameras, lasers, a special radar and GPS technology, they were completely interactive with their environment rather than restricted to a prescribed test route. The system could detect hazards and identify objects like people, bicycles and other cars at distances of several hundred metres. A test driver was always in the car to take over if necessary.

Google's involvement prompted an explosion of interest in the subject. Investment by established brands in the technology and automotive industries ballooned, along with a bevy of new start-ups. According to American think tank The Brookings Institution, $80 billion was spent on self-driving car attempts between 2014 and 2017. This may prove to be a giant capitalist mistake that'll make the South Sea Bubble, tulip mania and the subprime mortgage meltdown seem positively rational by comparison.

As usual, the targets of when full-scale autonomy would really be achieved were often overly ambitious. It becomes easier to see why when you appreciate how these wonders of technology are actually supposed to work.

Sensing the road

This brave new world of genuinely intelligent cars requires a diverse array of hardware with which the car tries to gain an accurate perception of its environment.

The most expensive, spectacular and distinctive sensors on a self-driving car are LiDAR, which stands for Light Detection and Ranging, usually housed in a roof pod. These systems bounce low-powered invisible laser beams off objects to create extremely detailed and accurate 3D maps of their surroundings. Their field of view can be up to 360 degrees and, because powerful lasers are used, LiDAR has the advantage of working in any lighting conditions.

Scientists have been using lasers to measure distances since the 1960s, when a team from the Massachusetts Institute of Technology (MIT) accurately logged the distance to the moon by measuring how long the light took to travel there and back. Its pioneering use in cars began with an experiment carried out in 2007 by an audio-equipment company called Velodyne. Five vehicles equipped with the company's revolutionary new sensor successfully navigated a simulated urban environment.

Around 2016, LiDAR could cost around $75,000 per car. As of 2019 this sum has fallen to around $7,500 for a top-of-the-range unit. That needs to fall further and Ford is targeting approximately $500 as a cost for the component in the future. At present, most cars use one LiDAR unit, which creates a 360-degree map by either rotating the whole assembly of lasers or by using rapidly spinning mirrors. Many researchers think a key requirement of lowering the cost will be to create solid-state designs with few or no moving parts, eliminating the need for such spinning mechanisms.

Mirrors could possibly be eliminated by so-called phased arrays, which use a row of laser emitters. If they all emit in sync the laser travels in a straight line, but by adjusting the timing of the signals the beam can shift from left to right. Flash LiDAR is another possibility. This operates more like a camera. A single laser beam is diffused to illuminate an entire scene in an instant.

Laser-powered eyes on the road. LiDAR sensors are getting smaller and cheaper.

A grid of tiny sensors then captures the light bouncing back from various directions. It's good because it captures the entire scene in one moment, but it currently results in more noise and less accurate measurement.

There are other stumbling blocks. Once most cars on the road have LiDAR they could soon start interfering with each other. Systems normally fire their lasers in a straight line and use a super accurate clock. They could be easily upset by lasers on other cars operating in the same range. Similarly, sceptics worry about the ability of the system to cope in awful weather. Lastly, to avoid eye damage, the lasers are fairly weak and currently limited in range to about 150 metres. For a car to accelerate and join a stream of fast-moving traffic, the laser range needs to be at least 300 metres. LiDAR manufacturers are working on increasing the laser frequency to allow stronger output with a beam that is further from the visible light range. As the systems improve, it is likely other shortcomings will be dealt with too. The technology already functions decently in snow and rain, and it is getting better at avoiding interference.

While LiDAR allows the car to 'see' over short distances, a different solution is needed for longer distances. This is where radar comes in. Many new cars already have radar sensors, used for adaptive cruise control, blind-spot protection and automatic emergency-braking systems. Their field of view is about 10 degrees and they're relatively cheap at between £80 and £120 per sensor.

Traditionally radar's main advantage is the ability to perceive distance and velocity. It can measure speed from a long way away and it's a well-proven technology. Radar can even see round things. Its wavelengths are relatively long so there's significant diffraction and forward reflection – you can 'see' objects behind other ones. On YouTube there's a video, taken inside a car driving along, which shows radar in action when the car's automatic emergency-braking system suddenly activates and the brakes are applied. The view ahead is showing nothing out of the ordinary; but half a second later the car in front rear-ends the car ahead of it. The car's radar was able to see that the (optically hidden) car two cars ahead had braked suddenly, and then braked hard itself to avoid a crash.

Radar's big disadvantage, and why it needs to be supplemented by other sensors, is that it can't perceive detail. Everything's just a blob. It's no good at distinguishing between a pedestrian and a cyclist even though it can tell whether they're moving or stationary. A Waymo's LiDAR, on the other hand, can not only tell the difference but can also tell which way the pedestrian or cyclist is facing. Ultrasonic sensors are used to measure the position of objects very close to the vehicle too. We're accustomed to them in those bleeping parking sensors.

They were invented in the 1970s and the first volume production car they appeared on was the 2003 Toyota Prius. Their range might be a mere 10 metres or so, but they are very cheap and provide extra essential information in low-speed manoeuvring and about adjacent traffic.

High-resolution video cameras are an important part of a self-driving car's equipment. They are used to recognise things like traffic lights, road markings and street signs – objects that offer visual clues but no depth information. Cameras can also detect colour, which LiDAR can't, and they're better at discerning differences in texture. When in stereo they can also help calculate an object's distance – although this effect diminishes the further away something is, which limits the technique's usefulness in high-speed driving. They are relatively cheap at around £150 per car but they are greatly affected by prevailing light conditions and visibility. Infrared can help here to some extent.

You might think that GPS would also be critical for getting around. However, it is normally accurate to only a few metres and not consistently so, with the signal being easily interrupted by tall buildings and tunnels; its role in the autonomous car is therefore somewhat limited. It can, however, be useful in combination with other sensors. MIT, for example, has built a self-driving Prius that manages its way round back roads pretty well using just GPS, LiDAR and accelerometers.

The brain of the car

Of course, all these sensors would be useless without something to interpret their data. Processing the vast quantity of incoming information – and processing it sharpish – requires a very powerful computer with far more heft than the average PC. Even current cars like Waymos are thought to generate up to 150 gigabytes of data every 30 seconds. That's enough to fill many laptop hard drives and is equivalent to 19 terabytes per hour. The cars also need to store these colossal quantities of information in case of later enquiries, crashes and disputes. This takes its toll on energy consumption, with the typical prototype needing 5,000 watts of power – or about the same as forty typical desktop PCs. That's enough to have a serious hit on fuel consumption or battery range. Imagine switching off the self-driving to conserve the battery and get you to your destination. That wouldn't feel like progress.

There's a lot of effort going into making processors that are more suited to the demands of the self-driving car. Google has developed new chips especially designed for self-driving tasks, called Tensor Processing Units. They fire up only those bits of the chip necessary for a given task, which allows more operations per second and better power efficiency. They're suited to machine learning of many kinds because they can handle a lot of relatively low-power processing tasks at once.

Nvidia, which is best known for making graphics cards on computers, has come up with a chip called Xavier. It allows 30 trillion operations per second (about 500 times more than a decent laptop) on a chip that consumes just 30 watts of power. It packs an amazingly powerful and efficient punch, and it's the most complex system on a chip ever created, with an 8-core CPU and 512-core GPU, a deep learning accelerator, computer vision accelerators, and 8K video processors. 'We're bringing supercomputing from the data centre into the car,' says the bloke leading their automotive work, Danny Shapiro. Still, there's a long way to go until the systems are sufficiently energy- (and cost-) efficient for the mainstream. And you can have the most powerful computers in the world, but without the right software they are just expensive black boxes.

Artificial intelligence

If you thought the hardware was complicated, the software needed to make self-driving cars an everyday reality is hundreds of times more brain-defyingly baffling. This is possibly the greatest test of artificial intelligence the world has ever seen.

The idea is the car takes the various bits of information from all the sensors, and combines them to determine where it is, exactly what surrounds it and how those surroundings will change – and then plots a course of action through the space. This all has to be done within milliseconds and to unfailingly high levels of accuracy.

The car uses a technology called deep learning. I'm oversimplifying, but essentially the on-board computer turns all the information from the sensors into a vast matrix containing billions of bits of digital information. It then searches for known patterns within the data, which it can use to select the right behaviours. This is sometimes termed a neural network. Once patterns and necessary behaviours are detected and decided upon, this is translated into physical form through the accelerator, brakes and steering, as well as by using other systems like the lights and even the horn.

⚙ Extra intelligence

Self-driving isn't the only way in which cars will become brainier.

In a straight rip-off from mobile phones, facial recognition could soon be the way you unlock and start your car. Another phone feature coming to your car is a voice assistant. Siri, Alexa and the like will get much better at playing your music and answering life's pressing questions. Electric-car users will increasingly be able to choose what noise their car makes – a sort of ring-tone selection for cars. BMW has already recruited *Blade Runner 2049* composer Hans Zimmer to provide an attractive tone to warn pedestrians of its near-silent cars' presence.

Your new motor will soon be clever enough to receive your deliveries wherever you are. Services will be able to unlock it and leave parcels or even your cleaned laundry inside.

Self-parking will come well before self-driving. Summoning your car a few metres by an app on your smartphone or letting it take over parallel-parking tasks will soon seem very old school. Instead your car will know in advance where available spaces are and navigate itself around a car park to park itself. Then you'll be able to retrieve it automatically when required.

Sound management will get better, with improvements in noise cancellation and vocal enhancement tailored to different seats in the car so you can talk to fellow

passengers more easily. Furthermore, increasing propor-
tions of the interior will be plastered with screens so you
can customise it with your favourite dashboard style or
interior graphics. Augmented reality displays will help
streamline GPS guidance and put useful instructions on
your windscreen.

In short, the car operates by detecting patterns in data and responding to them. It's the same sort of technology that's helped to predict things ranging from earthquakes to heart disease and has developed the capacity to analyse cancer scans, identify eye disease and muscle damage – all more quickly and accurately than human doctors. It's also proved very useful, if not creepily disturbing, in facial recognition. Episodes like the recording of biometric information about concert-goers when they snap themselves in selfie booths and people being mistakenly arrested for shoplifting merely because they share similar features with criminals have brought facial recognition into some disrepute, and show how deep learning can fall short.

Identifying patterns on the road is far more demanding in terms of the variety of things that need to be recognised and the short time available to do so. Creating software that then knows how to respond to these perceived environments is even more of a nightmare. The most obvious way the car is taught how to behave is through 'behavioural cloning' – accumulating data from how (decent) human drivers behave. Then the system can practice and learn, improving its own driving as it gets better at making decisions itself, while being watched by a real driver in case things go wrong – which they will.

At its most basic, a system might recognise an open road from vast experience of seeing pictures of a clear road ahead, translating that into an action to accelerate up to a predetermined speed limit. At the more challenging end of the scale, it has to cope with a busy, previously un-tackled junction, packed with other cars, trucks, pedestrians and cyclists. It has to predict how they're all going to behave and respond accordingly.

Sebastian Thrun thinks accurate perception is the most difficult challenge. In the early days of Google's autonomous-vehicle project, he recalls, 'our perception module could not distinguish a plastic bag from a flying child'. As already indicated, it's getting better. At a Google conference in 2018, Waymo showed examples of a pedestrian carrying a door-sized plank of wood, a construction worker poking halfway out of a manhole cover and even people in inflatable dinosaur costumes. In each case the pedestrian's profile was obscured but the Waymo car correctly identified them as pedestrians.

There are issues with any deep-learning system. In effect, every situation it faces will need to have been experienced before in some way; otherwise it won't know how to react. One problem is termed 'overfitting'. The system can draw correlations between totally irrelevant attributes. One could imagine trying to predict the score of a dice depending upon the time of day or even its colour. An artificial-intelligence program will always try to construct a hypothesis as to why the scores are occurring based on whatever factors it has at its disposal.

The problem gets worse if more factors are being considered. Imagine I turn left – the system may intuit that I did so because I'm 200 metres from a cyclist and I happen to have done similar several times before when I'm in this part of town at this time of day. This is all a gross oversimplification, but it helps to illustrate the scale of the AI challenges in relation to driving when there are so many variables.

'Underfitting' is the opposite. The AI system can't always capture the correlations we want it to. For example, it might not know where the edge of the road is or perhaps it can't deduce from the laser and camera data that a pedestrian or cyclist is ahead. The usual way to avoid underfitting is to feed the system more data or to give it more experience of correlation between the AI system and the real world. Self-driving car companies have thousands of people manually tagging images with useful information to help avoid underfitting, supplementing neural networks with known real-world data.

'Generalisation' is another problem. If we know what a mouse looks like and what a gerbil looks like, humans can interpret a hamster as something between the two – another mammalian rodent. Artificial intelligence finds this difficult. It struggles to take what it already 'knows' and come up with something different that's sensible. It either doesn't recognise the new object at all or it creates constantly varying descriptions. This is why chatbots really aren't very good at speaking yet. They don't give you the impression they're understanding anything; they're just repeating things they've heard before where they gauge it to be appropriate.

Watching AI at work. The Nvidia chips generate multicoloured oblongs or other confidence-inspiring highlights as they identify familiar shapes like cars, people and bicycles.

Self-driving car software is what AI experts call a 'black box' system. You know what the inputs are. You know what the outputs are. But how the system derives the outputs from the inputs is a mystery. We don't really understand how the algorithms work or how cars 'think'. Nvidia has attempted to visualise this in a self-driving context by highlighting the parts of the image from a car's sensors that are involved in decision-making. Reassuringly the results show that the chips are focusing on the edges of roads, lane markings and parked cars – exactly the things that human drivers would be attending to.

'What's revolutionary about this is that we never directly told the network to care about these things,' Urs Muller, chief architect of Nvidia's self-driving cars, wrote in a blog post.

It isn't a complete explanation of how a neural network reasons, but it's a first step. As Muller says: 'I can't explain everything I need the car to do, but I can show it, and now it can show me what it learned.' There's a strong argument that visualisation should be displayed to passengers in self-driving cars so they can appreciate how the machine is thinking, building confidence in the system.

On top of the neural network, the software suite of a self-driving car normally includes high-definition mapping that needs to be continuously updated over the air. These maps are down to centimetre accuracy (on lane markings, for example), are 3D and have many different layers, including those for real-time activity like traffic lights and so-called 'semantic' features such as road signs.

Who are the main players?

The widespread adoption of self-driving cars in the real world always seems to be tantalisingly close yet just out of reach – like hoverboards and BabelFish-esque real-time translation devices. In 2015, Elon Musk predicted that his company would be selling fully autonomous Teslas by 2018. It wasn't. NuTonomy's plans for driverless taxis in Singapore by 2019 didn't work out either, though trials have begun. GM's steering-wheel-free, fully autonomous production car was due to hit the market in 2019. At the time of writing it hasn't appeared.

Google formed the parent company Alphabet in 2015 and rebranded the Waymo subsidiary the following year. Waymo is widely considered to be way ahead in the self-driving car race, leading by measures such as miles driven autonomously and how many miles its cars cover between 'engagements' when a safety driver in the car is forced to take over control. Some of the most telling statistics come from the California Department of Motor Vehicles (DMV), reflecting the concentration of tech companies and self-driving vehicle experimentation in the state. Waymo declared that its vehicles travelled an average of 11,018 miles between engagements in California in 2018 and celebrated 10 million miles travelled in total by its cars, over a million of which were in 2018 alone.

Since 2015, respected research outfit Navigant has been analysing the sector according to ten criteria: vision, go-to market strategy, partners, production strategy, technology, sales, marketing and distribution, product capability, product quality and reliability, product portfolio and staying power. They put Waymo on top too.

Rather than selling cars to owners, Waymo sees its future in robotaxis. It's more profitable to spread the extortionate cost of the self-driving equipment over cars that are used more intensively. After brief flirtations with creating its own vehicles, Waymo now doesn't bother building cars. It leaves that up to the likes of Jaguar, from whom it's getting 20,000 I-Paces to be delivered from 2020 onwards, and Chrysler, who is in process of supplying 62,000 Pacifica Minivans. Effectively they're treating car companies as suppliers whose kit they add value to through their self-driving conversion.

Analysts rate Waymo as worth between $175 billion and $250 billion – more than Ford, GM, Fiat-Chrysler, Honda and Tesla combined – and think that the major car companies will all be asking it for help in years to come as they strive to make their products autonomous. But traditional car companies are also fighting back by partnering up like never before, both between themselves and with technology companies. They're also madly acquiring start-ups with particular self-driving expertise. The sector has reached fever pitch in terms of new entrants, acquisitions and deals.

Number two in the global self-driving stakes is General Motors. With a distance between engagements of 5,205 miles in 2018, it's some way behind Waymo in the DMV statistics. During that year it travelled nearly half a million miles autonomously in California, meaning that Waymo and GM together accounted for 86 per cent of the autonomous miles completed in the state. GM is a serious contender thanks to, in this case, purchase rather than partnership. It bought 2013 start-up Cruise Automation in 2016 for a reported $1 billion.

Like Waymo, General Motors is concentrating on robotaxis rather than individually owned or leased cars. It won't sell as many but, like Waymo, it thinks it'll make more money out of them than conventional cars. At present a car company earns only one cent from every mile the car travels. When it's in charge of a robotaxi it's earning over twenty times as much. Little wonder that the self-driving division is responsible for a third of the current stock-market value of GM. Unlike Waymo, GM has a factory ready to make all the Chevy Bolt taxis required, which are undergoing tests mainly in San Francisco with additional work in Arizona and Michigan.

Among other deals, Volkswagen has teamed up with Ford who in turn is investing $1 billion in a software company called Argo AI; Daimler is working with a range of tech companies, including Nvidia; and former bankrupt GM parts outfit Delphi has become another major player in the field, buying software makers and driverless car company NuTonomy. The tech giants in China are also muscling in on the action.

Pure tech companies getting a foothold include Apple, who started testing its self-driving cars on public roads in 2017, again in California. It's involvement in the area has naturally encouraged wags to envision their cars made out of aluminium with rounded corners, with proprietary charging plugs no one else uses, non-replaceable batteries and using only the company's own roads unless you buy an expensive dongle. Oh, and obviously they'll get thinner every year. Groan.

The reality is that Apple seems to be lagging behind the competition, with its cars requiring intervention every 1.15 miles, though the company claims it uses a different measurement technique and the figures aren't directly comparable. In 2019 Apple bought drive.ai, a struggling start-up developing self-driving artificial intelligence that could potentially be fitted to any vehicle.

Uber is one company that ranks highly in terms of the public's perception of self-driving cars but badly in terms of

China

China's President Xi is super-keen to make artificial intelligence a vital component of the country's economic roadmap. To that end both start-ups and established Chinese tech giants are part of the action. Despite the ever-escalating trade war between China and the US, it's a process that seems to span the two countries with close links and interdependencies between them. Offices in Silicon Valley send skills back to China, where until recently self-driving car tests on public roads were banned.

Now tests in China are gathering pace. In a process that mirrors the Google-Waymo dominance, Baidu, the operator of China's largest online search engine, completed the country's first autonomous-driving road test based on a 5G network environment, in Beijing on 22 March 2018, using open-source, autonomous-control software called Apollo. Online retailer Alibaba and tech company Tencent are also developing platforms for self-driving vehicles while partnering with vehicle manufacturers.

Among vehicle manufacturers, Shanghai-based Nio is developing a self-driving car called Eve, while Byton is developing its autonomous K-Byte model with self-driving software provided by Aurora, a company started by the former head of Google's autonomous car programme. Most Chinese companies are aiming only at Level 4 rather than Level 5 autonomy, which may reveal where the world's biggest car market thinks self-driving technology is ultimately heading.

the intervention rate. Human-driver assistance was required every 0.35 miles in 2018. Maybe the extra $1 billion investment the floated company has secured from Toyota and Saudi Arabia will help improve things as it strives to develop an autonomous taxi fleet on land and maybe even in the air.

However, some question if miles travelled between interventions is the right measure of success. Professor Paul Jennings of Warwick University suggests that complex cases are best addressed in simulators or through augmented reality. 'You could condense lots and lots of edge cases in a simulator and get a much better idea of the competence of your system,' he says. With a simulator, a system could be more easily exposed to rare and difficult driving conditions like dazzle from sunlight and water on flooded roads.

One company that does use extensive simulator testing, but doesn't figure in the DMV rankings at all, is Tesla. Tesla's Autopilot system was first fitted to the Model S in 2014, though so far it's really been a driver aid rather than a full self-driving system, offering lane guidance, adaptive cruise control, self-parking and the ability to automatically change lanes and send the car to and recall it from a garage or parking spot.

However, the company has long expressed its intention to offer full self-driving at a future time, acknowledging that legal, regulatory and technical hurdles must be overcome first. Indeed, many owners paid in advance to be supplied with this upgrade when it becomes available. Unsurprisingly, there has been some discontent among those who suspect that day may never come.

Tesla has a different approach to other outfits in the game

in that its systems are almost totally reliant upon software and cameras. Elon Musk doesn't include LiDAR on any of his cars; he thinks it's too expensive and bulky. He also notes that human beings and animals navigate using their eyes, which are the biological equivalent of cameras. According to him, given low prices and ever increasing resolution, optical cameras are sufficient when supplemented by sufficient AI (plus radar and ultrasonic sensors).

'Eyes are basically just cameras. All creatures on Earth navigate with cameras. A fish eagle can see a fish from far away and take into account the refractive index of the water, dive down and get the fish from far away. There's no question that with image-recognition neural nets and cameras, you can be superhuman at driving with just cameras,' Musk said.

The company is accumulating its AI in the form of vast quantities of data about actual driving behaviour. As a Tesla user you're given the option of operating in 'shadow mode'. When you're in it the car isn't taking any action but registers when it would have taken action. If the car is in an accident the company can see if the autonomous mode would have prevented it. The car is also uploading data from its cameras.

Information recorded by your car's sensors gets uploaded to the company and they use it to help make better self-driving AI in the future. Tesla owners report that their cars can regularly upload over 100MB of data a day. This sounds much less than Google's cars but it's often geared to particular requests. When Tesla identifies something it needs more information on, it can request that the cars look out for it and upload relevant data. It can request images of, say, bikes mounted on cars if it is thought that they might confuse the autopilot, so that they can train the system on extra data. The paths taken by human drivers in various situations can be watched in order to analyse what cars are doing before a particular type of event and see whether patterns can be perceived. Unlike virtually every other company in the field, Tesla is keen to offer self-driving abilities on real cars you and I could buy or lease.

How far have we got to go?

On average, a vehicle in the UK would have to travel about 200 million miles before being involved in a fatal accident. That gives some idea of the scale of the safety proofing required by autonomous systems. And even if they do match human drivers, that level will still be way short of what is needed to ensure widespread acceptance.

Some researchers have attempted to do the maths. Tasha Keeney of ARK Investment has suggested that a self-driving car will need to offer 'expected failures' – where the car comes to a halt because it recognises that it can't proceed and signals to the human driver to take over – no more than once every 50,000 miles. That's about how often people break down in the US, apparently, though my personal experience of break-downs is much better. 'Unexpected failures', meanwhile – where the system doesn't recognise something is going wrong and continues to drive on without any signal for help – will apparently be tolerated every 240,000 miles. That's about how often drivers in the US have a scrape of any severity in their cars. It all seems a bit optimistic to me. I think the public and legislators will demand higher standards.

Even Google's own people are cautious. Too many surprising things happen in the driving environment for deep learning to perform well when left unsupervised. DeepMind founder Demis Hassabis has cautioned against self-driving car trials on public roads; he thinks they need to get better in private first. Certainly Waymo has encountered multiple issues with trials of its self-driving taxi service in Phoenix, despite being limited to areas of the city that are almost ideal for self-driving.

An Uber-beater? A Waymo robotaxi pounds the streets of Chandler, Arizona, where the company has launched the world's first commercial driverless taxi service.

The cars tend to stop longer at intersections than human drivers, stop suddenly without warning, have trouble merging into heavy traffic, stick too literally to traffic laws and even fail to recognise red and green lights. According to a report in *The Information*, they're consequently hated by local residents. Playing chicken with self-driving cars has surfaced as a sport for the naughty (and not just teenagers). And Waymo's cars are already the focus of callous recreation. One driver from Chandler, Arizona, admitted hating the cars so much that he tried to run them off the road in his Jeep Wrangler. In one incident he drove head on into a robotaxi that just stopped in time. He said he 'finds it entertaining to brake hard' in front of them. His wife told the *New York Times* that it all started when their young son was almost hit by one of the Waymo cars. It could be a new form of road rage. People have even been witnessed throwing rocks at Waymos, slashing their tyres when they're stopped and even pointing their guns at them and their occupants.

Pedestrians' interaction with normal cars is already to some extent a bravery contest. Each crossing involves a pedestrian calculating the risks between crossing the road as quickly as possible and the chance of being hit. Drivers also have to decide whether to slow down and let the pedestrian cross or keep driving on. In heavy traffic a driver is more likely to yield. Different cultures have different behaviours: compare central Rome versus an English village, for example.

One solution might be to have cars that communicate with other road users. To this end drive.ai displayed messages on its van taxis. For instance, if one of the company's cars stopped for a pedestrian on a crossing, the message 'Waiting for You' flashed up on a screen, along with a graphic of a person crossing the road. Jaguar has shown a car with eyes that interact with pedestrians to show they've been spotted. Cars may need a whole new system of commonly understood lights and gestures just like the ones we already recognise, such as bright red lights for braking and flashing orange ones for the intention to make a turn. How about purple ones for dithering self-driving cars that aren't quite sure what to do next? Judging by the Phoenix experience, though, the cars may need something more radical. At the very least, legislation will need to be tightened so that the cars are not bullied in their moments of indecision.

It should by now be obvious that full automation may still be decades away. However, Level 4 automation, where cars are operating in a well-defined, controlled environment, seems much more achievable. They'll have more in common with driverless public transport than conventional cars. For example, low-speed pods already marketed by companies like Coventry-based Aurrigo and the French company Navya operate as shuttle buses at airports and in retirement communities and universities, with customers sometimes hailing them by app. They're also proving popular in city centres for the 'last mile' of transport to a destination. Navya's latest Autonom cab is already being used in trials in Las Vegas, at the University of Michigan, and in over a dozen other locations round the globe. Unlike Waymo, Navya does not operate the vehicles itself but sells them to other service providers; the current cost of an

Autonom is €250,000. Shuttles like these may well get people accustomed to self-driving vehicles. In the near future, you're much more likely to encounter one of these than a fully fledged autonomous car.

The connected car

Fully developed robo-rides may remain on a distant horizon, but cars are going to become much smarter in other ways too. Using Wi-Fi and 5G they'll start talking to each other more and to the surrounding infrastructure. We're already used to cars being connected to the internet. This is usually achieved via the infotainment systems and our smartphones. Technologies like Apple CarPlay, Android Auto and manufacturers' own systems give real time navigation and internet-based media. Apps can tell us remotely whether an electric car is charged and even switch on the heating.

Vehicle-to-vehicle (V2V) technology goes further. It lets cars broadcast their position, speed, steering-wheel position, braking status and other data to vehicles within a few hundred meters. One use of this technology is platooning. This is where cars or, more typically, trucks link together into a sort of road train. Thanks to communication between the vehicles, some in the train can be driverless – rather like a railway carriage. Drivers in all but the lead vehicle do not need to pay attention to the road, and the vehicles can drive closer together. Because electronic communication is near-instant, they don't need the normal reaction time to operate brakes and they occupy less road space. This, in turn, achieves better fuel economy thanks to less air resistance. Platooning technology could conceivably be retrofitted to existing vehicles, though lead drivers might need additional licences because of the responsibilities involved.

It's feasible already, and companies like Mercedes and Volvo have demonstrated working platoons of trucks. It's even been shown that vehicles can join and leave a platoon with ease. Trials will, however, be necessary to iron out problems and ensure public acceptance. For example, could other cars be prevented from joining or leaving a motorway if there's a long chain of platooning vehicles effectively blocking the exit?

Another potential use of V2V technology is in transmitting information to help others avoid a crash – maybe via a seat vibration or, one imagines, a loud vocal alarm. The cars use the pooled information to build up a comprehensive picture of the events taking place round them, revealing potential dangers that even the most assiduous and alert driver – or the very best sensor systems – would fail to detect or anticipate. Car-to-car communication would also help solve the problem that sensors can't generally see through obstacles.

In live demonstrations on test tracks, cars are shown slowing down to avoid cars out of direct sight that go on to drive through red lights. Similarly cars can adapt their speed to avoid having to stop at traffic lights. Whether they'll easily be able to achieve the same dexterity in more complex scenarios is debatable.

The US National Highway Traffic Safety Administration and the University of Michigan have done a great deal to

⚙ The truck in front

Fully self-driving cars continue to prove elusive but the truck without a driver is already here. In February 2018, one designed by Starsky Robotics completed a seven-mile journey at 25 mph on public roads without a single human in the cab. In June 2019, one of its Volvo articulated eighteen-wheelers travelled 9.4 miles along Florida's Turnpike, successfully navigating a rest area, merging on to the highway, changing lanes and maintaining a speed of 55 mph. The secret of these trucks' success is that they can be controlled remotely from HQ in Jacksonville. Though 85 per cent of the trip is done fully driverless, difficult manoeuvres are performed by human drivers sat in an office with a steering wheel looking at screens showing feeds from the truck's six cameras, rather like a video game but for real.

In the US as in much of the developed world there's a huge shortage of people willing to be truck drivers and there's a great incentive to make remote-control trucking work. While there are many other start-ups in the field, it looks like Starsky is ahead for the moment. This truck system would work for driverless taxis only if you were happy to pay a premium to be piloted around by someone sat at a games console somewhere else.

show how valuable car-to-car communication could be in the town of Ann Arbor, Michigan. Between 2012 and 2014, they equipped nearly 3,000 cars with experimental transmitters. After studying communication records for the cars, NHTSA researchers concluded that the technology could prevent more than half a million accidents and more than a thousand fatalities in the United States every year. John Maddox, a program director at the University of Michigan's Transportation Research Institute, reckons that on its own this technology has the potential to transform the way we drive.

The technology could, for example, route information between vehicles and bridges, toll booths, construction signs and other roadside infrastructure. There could even be special lanes where autonomous vehicles are allowed to travel really fast because they're able to share information about incoming and outgoing traffic at great speed, and road signs may become unnecessary because they're fully digitised. On the negative side, though, we may end up with 5G masts every 300 or 400 metres along major roads and only slightly fewer on rural routes. The technology is viable only with a basic minimum infrastructure and a lot of roadworks. More devastatingly, it offers the authorities a previously undreamed of scope for interfering with our driving, in terms of continuously monitoring speed and lane discipline and dishing out penalties and pay-as-you go driving charges in the process. Drivers' costs may spiral with monthly statements, like deranged telephone bills. In the event of a crash your car will automatically shop you to your insurance company.

Brain-to-vehicle technology, or B2V, is an even more ambitious endeavour. It uses electroencephalography to pick up the driver's brainwaves using a cap on the head. I first saw such a device at the technology show CeBit in Hamburg around 2006. I was impressed that someone could use thought to alter a computer mouse and (rather laboriously) type out a message. Since then, it's been refined (a bit) and is used in video games and modern prosthetic limbs.

Nissan has been pioneering B2V use in cars, where it could potentially allow the vehicle to detect your mood as you get in and adjust the climate and entertainment systems to suit. More usefully, the company claims, it will be able to read the driver's reactions to what's happening on the road ahead and translate them into the required action fractions of a second sooner, helping to make driving more relaxing and to avoid accidents. Say the system detects that the driver is about to turn the wheel. Driver-assist systems in the car can begin the action more quickly, maybe 0.2 to 0.5 seconds faster than the driver on their own. Brain-to-vehicle technology will also work to detect when the driver is about to suffer from a bout of road rage and instruct the car's autonomous controls to take over. No more red mist in all its unsavoury permutations.

Given the way we react against technologies that require headgear (think of the failure of 3D glasses and Google Glass), I suspect the equipment will have to be a great deal less obtrusive than the electrode-encrusted shower caps that currently feature in tests. It's safe to say it's in an early stage of development; Nissan estimates it's at least five to ten years away, but as usual

Will 5G really make a difference?

Given the flaky quality of many mobile-phone conversations, you could be forgiven for thinking that the last thing you'd put your faith in for anything safety critical, like driving, is a mobile phone network. But 5G could make a huge contribution to the development of autonomous and connected cars.

It's much faster. All networks suffer from latency – the time it takes for a command to be translated into action. With 3G it's typically 200 milliseconds; with 4G it's around 100 milliseconds. But with 5G it's only 5 milliseconds. So 5G devices, whether they're cars, traffic signs or even bicycles, can communicate with each other in an instant. A driver left to their own devices typically takes between 250 and 500 milliseconds to react.

It can support a far greater number of devices – a million in a square kilometre. With 4G it's nearer 60,000. What's more, those devices can be travelling at up to about 220 mph. In one recent test a McLaren was going at 160 mph round a track and retained a rock-solid 5G connection with a data rate of up to 20 gigabits a second. Breathtaking performance figures.

However, it doesn't always need a network connection: though not ideal, 5G does support devices talking to each other without one.

this is probably wildly ambitious. The safety implications of malfunctions are frightening and there will need to be measures to ensure that other body parts don't generate interfering signals. However, the driver's brain could eventually be recruited to form yet another part of the intelligent car.

What does it all mean?

When autonomous cars eventually arrive, one of our most visible and widely used technologies will undergo a huge transformation. As a result, there is endless speculation about its consequences. The biggest positive, of course, will be a reduction in the number of accidents on the road. Stephen Hamilton, a Cambridge lawyer with a specialty in autonomous cars, suggests 99.7 per cent of road casualties could be avoided in the future. Millions of lives will be saved and millions more people will escape injury. This will lead to a reduction in the amount of healthcare resources required to deal with car crashes and in police time devoted to traffic.

Cars will be lighter and more fuel-efficient if they don't have to withstand crashing, as there will be no need for heavy, energy-absorbing safety structures. Wearing a seat belt will be a practice strictly reserved for the eccentrically pessimistic. Insurance costs will decline rapidly. Autonomy should help efficiency in other ways too. Most autonomous vehicles will not be owned but instead rented out to drivers by the hour; cars therefore won't spend so much time idle and won't spend so much time parked. Parking is a dominant land use in many cities, and self-driving cars might even scoot out of densely populated areas on the relatively rare occasions they're not being used.

Dieter Helm of Oxford University thinks the 'density of use' in cities will increase significantly and quickly. Multistorey car parks could be redeveloped into housing. Even domestic garages and driveways could be turned to alternative uses: expect a lot more man caves across the country. City and suburban streets will also be reclaimed. There will no longer be a need for half their width to be devoted to almost permanently parked cars. Fewer road signs and less road paint will make the cityscape more attractive. Cyclists and other road users will feel safer, and this could encourage further reliance on healthier forms of transport. For the increasing number of people who really are too old to drive regularly (some of them much younger than the famously tenacious Prince Philip), there will be a whole new freedom. The same is true of children and teenagers (and their long-suffering parents, who will no longer have to ferry them everywhere).

An autonomous driver will use energy more efficiently than a human one and won't show a heavy right foot. All these efficiencies will slash the cost of getting about. In March 2017, Barclays estimated that the total costs of car travel will fall from between $1 and $1.60 a mile to just 8 cents thanks to autonomy. Self-driving cars should also provide more efficient links to public transport networks, filling in the blank spots between stations. Out-of-town pubs and restaurants could see an increase in trade as there's no need for drivers to remain sober or for groups to have designated drivers.

Traditional petrolheads may even begin to love self-driving. It could be an enthusiast's dream. Pop the Caterham or the Aston into the pod and get transported to the circuit, or the countryside driving park with its perfect bends and no speed limit; get rid of the boring journey in between, and spend the time on the way being entertained or doing something useful rather than getting frustrated by traffic jams and speed-limited tedium. It's a win all round.

On the negative side, the biggest issue might prove to be the uncertain future facing people who drive for a living. By some measures driving jobs are the biggest sector of the global employment market. Others argue that the efficiency claims are exaggerated. Professor David Begg, an expert in sustainable transport, thinks that cars take up too much space in relation to the number of people they carry, whether they're self-driving or not. Just imagine everyone exiting from an underground station in their own self-driving car – it would be chaos. Central London, for example, already seems packed with fleets of Toyota Priuses thanks to the Uber boom.

More comfortable private journeys with less stress could also prompt people to commute from further afield, generating still more congestion. Might health and fitness actually decline as it becomes easier to make short journeys by hopping in a shared car rather than walking or cycling? And all these cars driving themselves in circles between tasks is in itself a pollution issue.

The technology could also increase a sense of inequality, as it won't be rolled out everywhere at once but instead in limited 'urban islands'. There could be wealthy, safe, automated areas enjoying the benefits of efficient, safe and clean cars, while poorer, more dangerous zones still rely on unpredictable human-controlled cars.

Then there's the housing market and house design. Could your car be transformed into an additional room of your house, or a sort of personal roaming hotel room that ferries you to work? If houses and cars combine, what parts of a country like the UK will be devoted to them and what areas will be saved from the ensuing environmental blight? Areas with industrial parks may become vast parking lots for self-driving mobile homes.

Whatever happens, it isn't going to happen as quickly as the most excited pundits suggest. Self-driving aspirations will continue to collapse and artificial intelligence could well prove unable to cope with the randomness of the open road, with its unpredictable variety and bustle. Cars piloted by drivers are likely to have a fairly long future ahead, albeit one assisted by the connected car's safety-conscious driving aids. I wouldn't normally be so presumptuous as to dole out financial advice but on this I'm fairly certain – if anyone suggests you invest in an exciting autonomous car start-up I'd steer well clear.

TWO

SPARKING INNOVATION

Alternative Power and the Future of the Internal Combustion Engine

At the start of the twenty-first century it looked like the car would continue to be powered the way it had been for the previous 100 years: namely, by oil and the internal combustion engine. In spite of decades of rumours to the contrary, we had plenty of the black stuff and extra reserves were being found all the time. Thanks to a combination of legislation and improvements in vehicles, emissions were getting better too. Likewise, helped by the phase-out of coal for industry and domestic heating, at least in mature economies, our air was getting steadily cleaner. Good news all round.

Even global-warming worries were being calmed by the increasing use of diesel engines. By offering a 16 per cent improvement in efficiency on average over their petrol counterparts they were helping the industry to meet new CO_2 goals. And the assumption was that, by dint of technical advances, the traditional diesel problems of dangerous particulates and nitrogen oxides would soon be things of the past.

But then some developments came along to disrupt this comfortable status quo. Wannabe Bond-villain Elon Musk seized on the fact that lithium-ion batteries – which powered laptops, phones and other gadgets – now made electric power feasible for mass-market cars. Nissan made the first tentative forays into the market with the Altra, launched in Los Angeles in December 1997. But, despite a claimed 140-mile range, the batteries had a limited shelf life and the cars sank without trace. Musk's zeal was something altogether different. He was hugely influential in advancing the idea that the battery-electric vehicle (BEV) might become a credible alternative to those fuelled by petrol.

The original 2008 Tesla Roadster was far from perfect but its perky performance, dynamic handling and lithium-ion batteries combined to smash our preconceptions about electric cars.

Musk believed that tackling the market step by step could transform a notoriously conservative industry. First, he made an electric car on a tiny scale for practice. This was the sporty Lotus Elise-based Roadster, which deliberately went against the traditional economical, box-like, electric-car stereotype and demonstrated that electric cars could be a hoot to drive too. Then he made a luxury saloon to take advantage of the electric car's innate speed and disguise its high cost. After that, he expanded into other areas of the market first by building an SUV, and then by creating a lower-priced, compact executive car. Even better, he made sure his new customers had access to the required electricity. Tesla cunningly provided a network of its own high-speed superchargers in key locations. Initially these were even free for all customers to use.

At the same time as Tesla was taking an industry by storm, health organisations were becoming more vocal in highlighting links between pollution and death rates. Premature deaths and disease were being increasingly linked with pollutants like particulates and nitrogen oxides. Traditional cars and commercial vehicles were seen as a significant part of the malaise. The World Health Organisation declared in 2017 that 92 per cent of the world population and 96 per cent of those living in cities are breathing 'unsafe' air and set a series of target limits – for example, 10 micrograms per cubic metre for particulates smaller than 2.5 microns. Such targets focus minds, especially when they are routinely missed. In 2016, Beijing had an average of 85 micrograms and Delhi a shocking 122. London and Los Angeles were dramatically cleaner, though still above the limit.

Diesels also turned out to be much filthier than promised. A combination of lax testing regimes, the widespread gaming of emissions tests and manufacturer dishonesty exploded with the 2015 Volkswagen Dieselgate scandal. This, along with air-pollution figures and the threat of fines and legal action, prompted politicians worldwide to announce low-emission zones and propose bans on many diesel-engine cars. Madrid, Paris, Athens and Mexico City all announced that they were going to ban all diesels by 2025, while many German cities have already banned older, more polluting diesels.

The threat of global warming meant that the pressures on the industry weren't (and aren't) going away either. In fact, with the new shift away from diesel to petrol, they were increasing, and targets like the EU's promised 66 g/km of CO_2 (which is now tougher still) were becoming harder to meet. Equivalent targets in China and the US were also becoming more stringent. In the US, California and eight other states have a zero-emissions mandate; car manufacturers must sell a certain number of zero-emission vehicles in order to be allowed to sell the rest of their cars. In short, if you're serious about making and selling cars today, CO_2 emissions cannot be ignored.

Anti-internal-combustion-engine sentiment has spread through world politics like wildfire. Norway claimed it was going to ban the sale of new internal-combustion-engine cars as soon as 2025. The UK and France opted for 2040. Such aspirations aren't necessarily unrealistic. There's abundant energy landing on the earth every day (solar eclipses permitting). It's just a matter of harnessing, storing and converting it in a way that doesn't cause local and global pollution. There have long been alternatives to mainstream power. But the cheap dominance of the internal combustion engine stopped them taking off. The question is whether the proposed replacements are ready for the big time.

Electric dreams (and nightmares)

The obvious route to salvation is to follow in Musk's footsteps. A new assumption has rapidly emerged that future cars will increasingly be powered by batteries alone. Governments effectively said to car manufacturers: if Tesla can do it why can't you? And an aura of evangelism of the kind you see at Apple product launches started to surround the industry.

As Ian Foley of Equipmake, who designs and manufactures high-performance electric motors, observes: 'If you look at what Musk has done it's very hard to knock the guy because he has almost single-handedly transformed an industry. I was a huge sceptic. I think the tipping point was when he announced the Model 3 and raked in more than $300 million of cash deposits in a week when no one had seen the car. That's what shocked the car industry and made them say, "Crikey, we'd better do something here."'

But there are also hurdles to overcome. These are the same failings that have traditionally limited the appeal of battery vehicles: limited range, slow charging, heavy weight and high cost.

Electric cars are more expensive than their petrol equivalents and still nothing like as useful. In 2018 I spent a week or so with a 40 kWh Nissan Leaf and by the time I gave it back I'd dubbed it the Nissan Stress, such was my range anxiety. I just couldn't get where I wanted to go without worrying. I needed significantly more range and, crucially, the means for faster charging. At a normal person's motorway speeds I found I could travel little more than 100 to 110 miles, not the claimed 150 (why *is* the motor industry forever committed to that gap between actual and claimed figures?). The fastest charger it would accept – 50 kilowatts – could charge it in around an hour, reaching about 80 per cent in 40 minutes. So, not hopeless, but any long motorway journey would be a real chore. On even a fast domestic charger, though, it was a new level of slow. Seven hours for a full charge! As transport delays go, that's worse than the longest airport security queue and slowest rail replacement bus service combined.

All too often the roadside chargers were out of order, or operating on a network that I wasn't signed up to. Even worse, they were rarely plentiful enough that you could leave your car on the charger overnight without fear of breaking new charging-etiquette laws. Would other owners be angry about you hogging the thing? I would get to the hotel after a long day, put the car on charge and, *Oh no…* I couldn't have a couple of drinks at the bar because I'd need to shuffle the car round the car park in an hour's time, taking it off the charger and moving it to a standard space. And it's not just a matter of manners. There can be hard cash involved. Tesla threatens you with 'idle fees' if you leave your car hooked up to one of its chargers after your battery is full – up to 70p a minute in the UK at the time of writing.

The batteries are the main villains behind all these drawbacks.

The limits of lithium

The batteries in cars are typically packs of hundreds or thousands of individual cells that look rather like an oversized pack of AA batteries you might pick up from the supermarket. Combined, they might provide a premium electric car with 90 kWh of battery capacity, about enough to propel the car for 200 miles or so on a motorway. To go the same distance with a combustion engine takes roughly 22 litres of diesel or 25 litres of petrol. But, whereas the diesel fuel weighs 4.25 kilos – a figure that goes down as you burn it – that battery pack weighs a mighty 700 kilos, or only slightly less than an entire Mk1 Golf. An electric car is therefore likely to be at least 20 per cent heavier than a petrol equivalent. The longer the range, the bigger the battery and the greater the difference in weight and extra energy required to lug it round.

This isn't likely to change dramatically any time soon. Lithium ion was the big revolution in batteries but they're now a long way down their development path. You can work out the theoretical energy density of a perfect lithium-ion battery by considering the electric chemistry of the elements. It's only about double the best batteries today. And you'll only get that

Charging ahead

Alternative batteries that have the potential to make a substantial difference are still years away, but there are labs full of scientists hoping for a breakthrough.

Solid-state batteries, where the liquid electrolyte is replaced by a solid material, are the closest to fruition. The earliest they'll arrive is the mid-to-late 2020s. Dyson and Toyota, among others, are working on them. They should offer greater capacity, faster charging, longer life in terms of charge cycles and the ability to be moulded into the shape of the car body. The solid electrolyte should also be more fire resistant and work over a wider temperature range.

Lithium-air batteries are closer to fuel cells than batteries and promise huge energy density and thousands of miles of range, but experimental designs have tended to get clogged up as the lithium ions combine with carbon dioxide and water vapour in the air, leading to a very limited shelf life.

The glass battery may sound ridiculous but it's the brain-child of John Goodenough, the inventor of lithium-ion batteries, so must be taken seriously. Now in his nineties, Goodenough says they have prototypes made of just salt and sodium with no combustible or rare earth materials. He claims they have an energy density many times that of current lithium-ion batteries, improved cycle life and much shorter charging times. Other scientists are sceptical.

Supercapacitors can absorb and release power extremely quickly and, unlike batteries, there's no theoretical limit to the amount of power they can store for a given weight. The trouble is that their energy density is currently pretty rubbish, at less than a quarter of lithium-ion batteries. Breakthroughs are on the horizon, though. British company Super Dielectrics Ltd, in partnership with the Universities of Bristol and Surrey, is exploring the potential of using polymers like those in disposable contact lenses to create next-generation storage supercapacitors that will match or exceed existing batteries in energy density. The much-hyped super-material graphene, with its huge surface area, also has the potential to form the structure of future game-changing supercapacitors.

if it has 100 per cent efficiency and zero packaging weight – neither of which we'll ever achieve.

Incremental improvements will come from things like better cooling, but there won't be a revolution and alternative technologies are still years away. Wolfgang Ziebart, who oversaw Jaguar's Tesla-rivalling I-Pace program, cautions against believing battery hype. 'You read every month that someone has invented something great and revolutionised everything. What we have experienced over the last ten years is basically an increase in energy capacity of about 5 per cent per year... and a decrease in the price of the cell of about 10 to 12 per cent a year. Knowing now what's in the pipeline for the next five years I think this is going to continue. But I think we will stick to the current battery technology in principle.'

Whatever the battery technology, you still have to get the power to the car and the physics makes replicating the petrol-station experience impossible. You need to put around 3 megawatts of electricity into a car to have that two-minute fill, but a 3-megawatt cable would be impossibly heavy to pick up; getting such power to the station and coping with the heat generated are also near insurmountable obstacles.

Seasoned petrolheads, like me, are inclined to question how green electric vehicles really are anyway. Heavier than equivalent combustion-engine cars, they produce more particulates from their tyres and brakes. Then there's all the CO_2 embedded in the production of their battery packs, whose raw materials come from people working in miserable conditions in unstable countries like the Democratic Republic of the Congo and Bolivia. Politicians could be about to ban environmentally benign small petrol cars but welcome particulate and CO_2 profligate, politically destabilising battery-powered behemoths with open arms.

Recycling is a big issue with batteries. Lithium is only a small part of a battery and traditionally it hasn't been economic to recycle it. The battery tends to be broken down to form a sort of grease and then incinerated to separate the different metals, but this wastes a lot of the lithium. And as if all that wasn't enough there is still a lack of confidence that battery packs will last the life of the car, which is a worry if you're thinking of buying rather than leasing.

Positive thinking

There are obvious advantages to electric power, though. An electric vehicle powered by a pure electric motor is around 85 per cent efficient at turning electricity into motion and could quite easily get to 90 per cent. By contrast, an internal combustion engine will never get beyond 50 per cent efficiency. The best at the moment are probably about 35 to 40 per cent; the worst convert only 25 per cent of the energy in fuel into motion, wasting the rest as heat. A typical petrol car has to dissipate 100 kW of heat from the engine – hence the grilles and inlets that adorn virtually all cars today. This is terribly inefficient.

Battery cars, with no gearbox and fewer moving parts, are simpler to build and to maintain. They're quiet and smooth compared to internal-combustion-engine cars and often dazzlingly fast, especially when accelerating at lower speeds. I was given the chance to drive Tesla's Model S and Model X shortly after launch. Naturally the press office always supply the fastest version and I can vividly recall the eyeball-stretching acceleration in Tesla's aptly named 'Ludicrous Mode'. By the standards of petrol cars this performance comes tantalisingly cheap. At the time of writing, the bog-standard £77,200 Model S does 0–60 in 3.7 seconds. The performance model with the Ludicrous option costs a mere £14,600 more and, at 2.4 seconds for 0–60, is one of the fastest-accelerating cars in the world. Porsche's list price for the 911 GT3 RS is half as much again and it only manages the sprint in 3 seconds.

Renewable energy is becoming more common and cheaper, so much more of our electricity from our national grid is being classified as zero carbon. That's starting to remove one of the traditional objections to electric cars – that you're just transferring the global warming and other pollution from the car to the power station. And that trend will grow: on a windy, sunny summer's day, well over 50 per cent of UK electricity can be generated renewably. By 2030, it's estimated that renewables will comprise over two thirds of the UK's energy. Similar trends hold throughout the world.

All this makes it very hard to compare the overall environmental impact of battery-powered and conventional cars. MIT has said that an electric Tesla Model S P100D saloon produces more carbon dioxide, at 226 g/km, than a small petrol car such as the Mitsubishi Mirage, which is responsible for 192 g/km. But this is an unfair comparison of a very small petrol car with a large battery one, and assumes that the cars are driven in the Midwestern US, where the electricity grid is carbon intensive. Overall, in most of the developed world, the lifetime CO_2 emissions for an EV – including the global mining and manufacturing, and the electricity to run it – are estimated to be roughly half what they are from a conventional car.

Erik Fairbairn is founder and chief executive of Pod Point, one of Britain's leading suppliers of electric-vehicle charging points, with headquarters in Clerkenwell, London. An entrepreneur by inclination, he ran a supercar club for a while, before having an environmental epiphany. They've rolled out over 70,000 chargers since 2009, nearly a fifth of them in electric vehicle-mad Norway. Their offices are a mixture of the traditional and trendy, with conventional desks and what can only be described as an upmarket shed for meetings. Somewhat to my surprise, I found him agreeing with me about some of the shortcomings of battery power.

'The reason that electric vehicles are only between 2 per cent and 3 per cent of the market today is mainly because the ones that are at a sensible price point don't have enough range. Most people are looking for a car that does 200 or 250 miles on a charge. That's when you're beginning to cover 99 per cent of all the activities that people do.'

He thinks that those marginal improvements in battery power and cost will soon add up to a tipping point. Electric cars are already cheaper to make. They're also cheaper to fuel, at around a tenth of the cost per mile. When the battery costs have come down to the point where the whole car is the same price as a petrol equivalent and gives 250 miles, then 'people will seriously start to engage with electric vehicles'. Fairbairn predicts that costs will continue their downward course. Having been the expensive short-range option, the electric car would then become cheaper to buy and run than its petrol counterparts.

At this point depreciation – another electric-car bugbear – would cease to be a problem. At present, electric cars can depreciate heavily, in spite of healthy new demand, because new ones have much better range. You don't want the old car with a miserably sized battery now there's a new one that goes at least half as far again on a single charge. According to Fairbairn, 'battery packs for most reasonably large cars will plateau around the 90 to 100 kWh mark'. Petrol cars might then begin to depreciate faster themselves as they dwindle in number and face imminent bans. There may even be social pressures in the mix. 'Your peer group questions your decision not to go electric. It's like passive smoking. Your friends and colleagues will know that there's a perfectly decent electric equivalent to the internal combustion engine – which doesn't damage the air.'

As for charging, he doesn't think we need to replicate the petrol-station experience. Electricity is everywhere already. We just need to make sure it flows into your car whenever it's parked. For most people this is probably at home so that's where most charging will happen. In the UK, 7 kW power is the maximum – slightly more power than two kettles. Germans, with their three-phase domestic supplies, tend to opt for a higher 11 kW standard. Either way, a 250-mile range car can be charged overnight… just.

Early electric-car adoption will be driven by people with the luxury of garages and off-street parking. In the UK that's about 60 per cent of households, representing 75 per cent of vehicle owners. Fairbairn thinks it's only when electric-car adoption gets to 10 per cent overall that cities might be persuaded to invest in on-street charging points. These will be installed on the principle that there will be facilities to charge your car wherever you can park, and it won't need to be at high speed. At private establishments, the charging rate and capacity will vary according to the 'dwell time'. With hotels, you're there all night so slow charging is fine; but you might be at a supermarket for only an hour, or at a zoo for five hours, so chargers at such places will need to be faster. Owners of shops and attractions will plan accordingly and may try to attract you with the offer of free power.

On longer journeys you will still want a full charge quickly. Suitably fast chargers are more expensive to install and are likely to be much more expensive to use. The hope is that you'll find the ten or fifteen minutes it takes for an expensive fast boost to get you home on the motorway quite acceptable on the rare occasions you have to do it.

The most powerful chargers are likely to top out at 350 kW, the charging rate used by the IONITY network, which was founded by BMW, Daimler, Ford and the Volkswagen Group, with plans to install stations every 75 miles on average on Europe's main highways. A charger this powerful will add about 240 miles to the reserves of a high-performance electric car in less than half an hour. To avoid compatibility nightmares they're using the Combined Charging Standard (CCS), increasingly adopted by virtually all manufacturers. The network's also compatible with the slower maximum charging rates that will still be used on smaller cars.

Such chargers could become the norm in countries where long-distance road travel is more frequent, like the US or Australia. However, even with the prospect of fast chargers the Australian Prime Minister Scott Morrison has expressed doubts about electric cars: namely that they won't have the range to take his country's families to their favourite holiday

⚙ Electric dead ends

Charging electric vehicles is a hassle that needs to be resolved and to that end a number of innovative suggestions have been made. Not all of them are practical (or sensible).

Wireless charging has taken the mobile-phone world by storm. But it is relatively inefficient, especially as power levels increase. Slow charging an accurately positioned car might be just feasible at 3 kW, but wireless on-the-move charging is scuppered by the air gap and the need to switch between many cars using a given stretch of road. You simply can't get enough juice into the car, and that's before taking into account the cost of ripping up roads and installing the infrastructure. Scalextric-type slots for private cars are little better; you can transmit the power but it's very restrictive. The whole point of a car is you can go anywhere you want.

Swapping a discharged battery for a fully charged one can take as little as two minutes. It works for forklift trucks, which are used intensively in a confined space. However, it's just too expensive to keep duplicates of a car's most expensive component on standby in a network of swapping stations.

Solar panels seem like a good idea. One of the world's most famous solar-powered car races has been taking place since 1987 between Darwin and Adelaide, right through the heart of Australia. However, cars that manage to complete the 1,864 miles resemble king-size beds of solar panels on wheels with a tiny bubble for the driver's head to poke through. There's now a 'cruiser' class for slightly more practical machines. The five-seat Stella Vie from the Eindhoven University of Technology won it in 2017 at an average speed of 43 mph.

But few places are as sunny as Australia and it's generally more effective to have batteries charged by static solar panels, which can be angled towards the sun. Small solar panels are appearing on car roofs and bonnets but they only supplement more powerful charging methods. Leaving your solar-panelled car in the sun for a day will probably only get you a mile or two's worth of charge.

destinations, and that purchase prices are too high to meet his political opposition's target to increase their uptake to 50 per cent of all new-car sales by 2030. This would, he thinks, spell curtains for the country's gas-guzzling 4x4s and herald 'the end of the weekend'.

It does all sound to me like it will create a huge amount of roadworks. But even if we get to the stage where you can charge your car wherever you park it, will the power infrastructure be able to cope? There were nearly 32 million cars on Britain's roads in 2018. Imagine them all charging at the same time. It would be like half-time tea breaks in the World Cup but thousands of times worse. There's only enough capacity to charge about a million and a half cars if you try to charge them at peak times – like 6.30 on a winter's evening, when people are coming home from work, switching on the heating and cooking supper. But when you consider capacity across the grid over twenty-four hours, the system could probably cope.

Success will be down to the management of power through smart charging systems. Apps will enable charging to be scheduled during the night when there's less demand and when cheaper electricity is an incentive. On shared public systems or in office car parks the charging posts themselves can talk to each other to spread the load. App-controlled overrides would be possible if you needed to get going in a hurry, at an extra cost.

Erik Fairbairn sees battery-car sales becoming the majority by the mid-2020s and rising to 90 per cent of European new-car sales by the end of the decade. Most in the European industry are far more cautious, though, estimating that a third of the market will be plug-in by 2030. Wolfgang Ziebart reckons that battery-electric vehicles will achieve a 10 per cent share in Europe by 2025, up from 1.4 per cent in 2017. He thinks the share will be a little less in the US, but rather more in techno-logically keen countries like China.

I would bet on the more conservative projections. Even after hearing from a true battery-car enthusiast I couldn't completely shift my feeling that for many drivers there'll still be too much range anxiety and loitering at charging points. Fortunately there are other technologies brewing that will better suit their needs.

Hydrogen

Hydrogen has long been touted as the ideal future power source for cars, because its only by-product is water rather than carbon dioxide or other nasties. While it can be burned directly in an internal combustion engine, that's not the most efficient way of using it. The preferred route is to use a fuel cell. Hydrogen goes into it and reacts with oxygen to produce electricity and water in the presence of a catalyst, typically platinum. The electricity gets stored in batteries (or sometimes supercapacitors) and drives an electric motor as in a battery-electric vehicle. There's no air pollution and, if you can generate the hydrogen using renewable energy, no global warming either. Unlike battery cars, there's no range anxiety. You can refill a hydrogen car nearly as quickly as a petrol one. It sounds like the perfect power source.

It's therefore both surprising and depressing that people who like battery-electric cars often seem to hate hydrogen. Rather like the argument between nuclear power and renewable energy, it generates heated debate among those who largely have similar aims. To me it brings to mind a famous scene in Monty Python's *Life of Brian*. The hapless Brian mistakes the activists of the anti-Roman People's Front of Judea for the activists of the Judean People's Front. Reg, the leader of the People's Front, is not pleased: 'The only people we hate more than the Romans are the f***ing Judean People's Front.'

Elon Musk himself is one such hydrogen sceptic. Here's a typical rant: 'I just think hydrogen fuel cells are extremely silly... It's just very difficult to make hydrogen and store it and use it in a car. Hydrogen is an energy-storage mechanism; it's not a source of energy. You have to get that hydrogen from somewhere. If you get that hydrogen from water... electrolysis is extremely inefficient as an energy process.'

He goes on to say that 'Hydrogen has very low density, it's a pernicious molecule. It likes to get all over the place. You get metal embrittlement from hydrogen, you get hydrogen leaks, it's an invisible gas, you can't even tell that it's leaking; it's extremely flammable when it does and it has an invisible flame. If you're going to pick an energy-storage mechanism, hydrogen is an extremely dumb one to pick.' Doing the rounds on the internet is a diagram that explains what he means. Once you take into account generating the hydrogen from water and storing it, electric vehicles appear much more efficient. With them you're looking at keeping 69 per cent of your original energy at the wheel compared to only 19 per cent with hydrogen.

In addition to issues of efficiency, safety and transport there's the problem of very little existing hydrogen infrastructure. In the UK, for example, there are only nine filling stations and they're concentrated in and around London. On top of this, the fuel cells themselves are incredibly expensive and most hydrogen production in the world currently comes not from renewable electricity and electrolysis but from natural gas, via a process called reforming. This involves exposing the

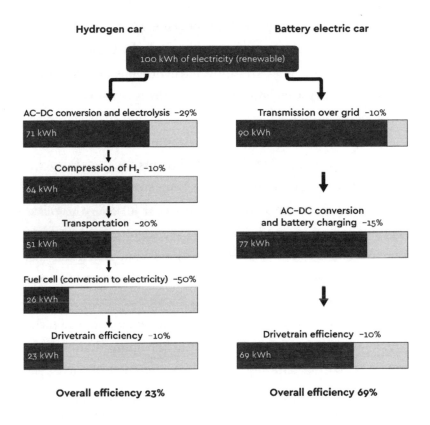

Hydrogen versus batteries – where the energy goes.

gas to high-temperature steam, which causes it to separate into carbon monoxide and hydrogen. The carbon monoxide itself is then reacted with water to produce more hydrogen and carbon dioxide. Obviously the process doesn't do much to help reduce CO_2 emissions.

On the positive side hydrogen is, by weight, the most energy-dense material on the planet, and it's everywhere – in water. Some of the biggest players in the car world think that any difficulty you can name with hydrogen is surmountable and that once you overcome them it has an unrivalled ability to fuel the world's sustainable-transport needs. Toyota, Hyundai and Honda all back the technology and Daimler has now revived its hydrogen plans too.

The car manufacturer that's been most enthusiastic for the longest time is Toyota. It started its hydrogen-car experiments as long ago as 1992 and has been steadily working on eliminating hydrogen's drawbacks as a vehicle fuel. As with its hybrids, the company has taken a very long view. The thinking is that it takes forty years to develop an automotive technology from the drawing board to the mass market. There could be a tortoise-versus-hare battle going on. Musk is getting to market quickly with his flashy batteries but Toyota's slower, more methodical approach, though it may at first appear lumbering, might actually become dominant and achieve better results in the end.

I spoke to Jon Hunt, Toyota's alternative-fuels manager in the UK. He points out that his company was searching for an energy-dense battery long before it made cars, in the days when its primary business was making weaving looms.

'Back in the 1920s, Sakichi Toyoda, who was the grandfather of the company, thought electrification would be the best route for looms and offered a prize of a million yen for whoever could come up with a battery that was the equivalent of petrol in terms of energy density. Nobody's managed to win the prize. The chemistry of batteries means it's impossible to get the energy you get in the equivalent litre of petrol or diesel.'

Though Toyota does build battery vehicles, it's concentrated its efforts on hybrid technology – and its hydrogen fuel cell research started as a spin-off from that. The fuel powers electric motors directly, while batteries or supercapacitors are on hand to store any energy recovered during deceleration and provide extra power while accelerating. In effect Toyota took its hybrid powertrain and mated it with a fuel cell. The first commercial car was the limited production Mirai of 2015. *Mirai* is Japanese for 'future'.

There are various types of hydrogen fuel cells used in cars. Toyota chose a so-called 'proton-exchange membrane' because it's lighter than other types, though it does require precious metals as a catalyst – in this case platinum again. The design was improved by making it virtually maintenance free, apart from the occasional filter replacement and water top-up. The company is gradually reducing the amount of platinum required – it's now only marginally more than in many conventional cars' exhaust systems and it's also completely recyclable. Newer cells used by Mercedes and Hyundai have also further reduced platinum usage and there's a lot of work going on into using alternative, non-precious metals as well.

The biggest challenge with hydrogen isn't really the fuel cell, though. It's the fuel storage. Hydrogen has a curious property whereby it can diffuse into metal structures and cause all kinds of problems. The metal becomes more brittle, which means that conventional fuel tanks would need to be far too heavy and costly. They'd also need frequent replacement as the compression and decompression of hydrogen during filling and emptying causes expansion and contraction of the metal.

Toyota's solution was to develop a carbon-fibre tank with an inert glass liner that can contract and expand without any fatigue. It is light and cheap to make in volume.

With safety concerns about hydrogen refuelling, Toyota then helped develop an international standard to refill cars with a universal high-pressure gas nozzle and a standardised connector. It's a contrast to the bewildering variety of plugs and connectors that complicate life for battery-car users. The fuel itself is also standard, unlike electricity with its different voltages and different outputs.

When I drove a Mirai I found it surprisingly normal. It feels like a very competent electric car. It's quiet, accelerates smoothly and feels brisker than its 0–60 time of 10.5 seconds would suggest. The fuel cell takes up some luggage and passenger space but it's still reasonably roomy and comfortable for four. The range is 300 miles and the cost per tank is comparable with petrol. At the end of a journey a tiny splash of clean water dribbles out of a hole under the boot floor – this is its only emission.

At present the price is a not insignificant £66,000. Jon Hunt anticipates that that will fall by 20–25 per cent per generation, as with hybrids. The drivetrain's the same as in a current hybrid, so a similar cost already. The costs of the fuel cell and tank will fall too as they enter mass production in Japan – from its current cottage-scale 3,000 a year to the tens of thousands. 'I think the third-generation car will probably be mass market in pricing,' says Hunt; it is slated to arrive around the late 2020s.

Public hydrogen-fuelling stations currently cost about four times as much to build as their petrol and diesel equivalents – another considerable obstacle to widespread adoption. But even a skeletal network would be a start. The UK H_2 mobility team at Toyota, tasked with investigating just such things, estimates that you can get away with just sixty-five stations on the main arterial routes, but that for greater convenience you need a maximum of twenty-five to thirty minutes' journey time between stations, which equates to a figure of 1,100. That's still much less than the 8,000 or so fuel stations the UK has currently. Building such a network will take lots of time and money, but it will need to happen if a solution is to be found for the chicken-and-egg problem that always seems to plague discussions about hydrogen. Why would you build the filling stations if there are no cars, and why would you buy a car if there are no stations?

The incentive to make this massive investment increases when you look at hydrogen's potential to provide fuel right across the economy. This is a fuel that can power industry, homes and transport in all its modes. The Hydrogen Council, initiated in Davos in 2017, is a global group of CEOs committed to developing a hydrogen society. Representing over thirty companies, they've come to the realisation that it's not sustainable to maintain our current energy distribution and production. When you look at industrial, transport and domestic uses there's a synergy you can achieve with hydrogen that you can't with anything else.

Heavy transport would make the transition first because the

weight problems of batteries are vastly more severe with heavy trucks and long journeys. You need tonnes of batteries, days of recharging – and all those batteries really eat into your payload. In the US, Coca-Cola, Walmart, Amazon and others have made significant investment in fuel-cell forklift systems that use hydrogen generated on site, leading towards a sustainable zero-emission energy-production system that will power their factories and take them completely off grid. Giant US brewing outfit Anheuser Busch is going further and looks set to deploy huge hydrogen-powered interstate haulage trucks, made by a company called Nikola.

Nikola is building a network of 700 fuelling stations in the US and the order book for its trucks grows by the day. Some London buses and German trains already run on hydrogen fuel-cell power – further examples of how commercial vehicles are forging the foundations of hydrogen-powered transport.

As for worries about efficiency, in many parts of the world the percentages highlighted by Elon Musk aren't really an issue. In Orkney, just off the mainland UK, the prodigious tidal and wind energy infrastructure frequently generates more electricity than the local grid can accept. There's now an electrolysis machine to use some of the surplus to convert water into hydrogen that's then used as a substitute for fossil fuels. Elsewhere, there's a strong economic case for putting free, surplus energy to use in the production of hydrogen that can then be sold on. As more national grids are powered by renewable energy, efficiency will become less relevant.

One radical hydrogen car coming to market is the Rasa. Surprisingly, this revolutionary vehicle isn't being manufactured in Stuttgart, Tokyo or even California. It comes from Llandrindod Wells, Wales. Rather than converting the architecture of a conventional vehicle to hydrogen power, a company called Riversimple, headed by Hugo Spowers, is completely rethinking the car and its ownership experience around the current limitations and opportunities presented by the hydrogen fuel cell.

Spowers seeks to eliminate the environmental impact of personal transport. 'We can have sustainable cars but not if we blunder along blindly just making things a little less bad. Elimination, not reduction, has to be our goal. Being less unsustainable is still not sustainable.'

He was inspired by the work of American physicist Amory Lovins of the Rocky Mountain Institute, who invented the term 'hypercar' in the 1990s – long before it was used to refer

The hydrogen-fuelled Riversimple Rasa is an instructive exercise in reducing the car's environmental impact.

to super-powerful luxury sports cars. Lovins's vision was for a vehicle that has little or no environmental impact; this would be achieved by making it out of ultra-lightweight materials and powering it by a renewable, sustainable and non-polluting source of energy. The Rasa is the closest I've ever seen to anyone making this dream a commercial reality.

Weight is the first priority. Making the car as light as possible means that a lower-powered fuel cell can be used. The cost of lower-power fuel cells is much lower than higher-powered ones because the precious metal plates have a much smaller surface area. (This is unlike petrol engines, where the production costs can be quite similar for different power outputs.) The Rasa's body is made from carbon fibre. At 580 kg it's half the weight of a conventional small hatchback and lighter than the battery packs fitted to some electric cars. It's so light that the hydrogen fuel cell needs to generate only a tenth of the power of the engine in a normal car, around 11 bhp. Although carbon fibre is relatively expensive – the 39 kg of the material in each Rasa costs about £2,000 more than a body made of steel – the benefits in reduced weight more than offset the additional cost in the longer term.

Whereas the hydrogen-powered Toyotas and Hyundais have a weighty bank of batteries charged by the hydrogen fuel cell, and a conventional electric motor, the Rasa has a miniature electric motor in each wheel, which makes the car effectively four-wheel-drive. Most of the Rasa's power is 'live' electricity, generated by the fuel cell, but it also recovers electric power from braking. It does this more efficiently than most battery and hybrid cars. Normal braking power is achieved by running the electric motors in reverse; the electricity generated is then stored in supercapacitors rather than batteries. Because these store energy as electricity, rather than in chemical form, they can hold and release power more quickly, which aids acceleration and efficiency. While a Prius recovers around 10 per cent of the kinetic energy involved in braking, the Rasa recovers 50 per cent. The supercapacitors are also constantly charged by a trickle of electricity from the fuel cell, so there is extra power on hand if needed. Spowers explains his sums:

'In a normal car the engine is sized for maximum acceleration, which you only use for less than 10 per cent of the time. When you're cruising on a motorway a typical car uses only 15 to 20 per cent of its peak power so it means that the engine is 80 per cent redundant for 90 per cent of its life. What we've done is sized our fuel cell for that 20 per cent, not the 100 per cent, and relied on the supercapacitors for the other 80 per cent when you want to accelerate.'

Aerodynamics is also vital. The car has a classic teardrop shape with surprisingly high ground clearance. As a car moves, the air is sheared between the stationary ground and the moving floor of the car. So, the further you can get the two surfaces apart the better. The inspiration here is work done by Dr Alberto Morelli in the 1970s and seen in the Californian-built Aptera. This wingless aircraft was not a practical real-world car, but the Rasa takes some of its elements – the high ground clearance, the use of teardrop and elliptical shapes – to achieve low drag.

In spite of all the weight-saving and technological wizardry, there's no way the Rasa could be sold profitably in a conventional ownership model. Because it is built by a low-volume specialist car manufacturer, it would cost about three times as much as normal cars. Spowers's solution is to sell the car as a service for a specified period, typically one to three years. The package includes maintenance, tyres, fuel and insurance. There's a fixed-price element and a mileage rate.

By looking at costs from manufacture to end of life, Spowers reckons he's in a position to tackle ordinary cars in terms of value for money. Conventional car manufacturers make most of their money by selling the car and a few branded parts in the early years of a car's life, so they need you to buy a new replacement as soon as reasonably possible; this business model does of course encourage built-in obsolescence. With the Rasa, Riversimple pay for all costs and are therefore incentivised to keep their investment going as long as they can. The result is much less wasteful.

Gull-wing doors add a touch of glamour, the suspension's been designed by former motor racing engineers, and 0–60 acceleration takes a respectable 10 seconds. But 60 mph is also the maximum speed, to save energy, which would be rather tiresome on long journeys. Over 2,000 people have expressed an interest in taking part in the initial trial of 20 cars. I was fortunate enough to meet some of them at the launch in Abergavenny. There was a palpable Welsh enthusiasm in the air. Some were keen to swap their second car for a Rasa. Most seemed happy with the rental of £370 a month and an 18p mileage charge to cover fuel and other consumables.

The car is a technological tour de force and the company could well have a future marketing its technology. As proof of concept, I hope the Rasa succeeds; but I fear the car itself may struggle. It's competing in the area of the market where cheap battery cars are most likely to be successful. And overall, I'm still left with the impression that the internal combustion engines won't be comprehensively bested for some time yet – either in terms of practically or enjoyment. But how can they be cleaned up?

Hybrids

Happily for those of us who still enjoy the roar of an internal combustion engine, cars have continued to become massively cleaner in terms of local emissions and they are more efficient too. Furthermore, while they still emit CO_2, they contribute less to global emissions than you might think.

The main way in which the internal combustion is now being goaded to a greener future is by combining it with battery power. Though car manufacturers and politicians are saying they'll eliminate the internal combustion engine from the streets, read the caveats and they're often restricting the cull to new vehicles powered solely by petrol or diesel. The venerable technology will still have a major role in a hybrid system or as an additional motor.

For an increasing number of drivers in the next decade or so the car of choice is going to be a petrol hybrid. Though hybrid

How bad are cars really?

You might think that cars are the main contributor to carbon emissions but you'd be wrong. According to the US Environmental Protection Agency just 6 per cent of green-house-gas emissions are down to cars and vans globally, although they contribute more in certain countries (with 19 per cent in the US). Nevertheless, electricity, heating, agriculture and industry are all much bigger villains.

Similarly, some of the limits laid down by the World Health Organization and others may need a reality check. Cooking a Christmas dinner can raise particulate matter in your home to twenty times WHO limits for more than eight hours, according to research carried out by the University of Colorado, Boulder; meanwhile Germany's Fraunhofer Institute has highlighted limit-busting levels of NOx when you light up your gas hob. Researchers have found particulate pollution in London's tube stations is up to thirty times higher than beside the city's busy roads.

The late Tony Frew, who until recently advised the UK government on the medical effects of air pollution, suggested we balance the risks against the benefits. He agreed that high levels of pollution in places like Beijing or Delhi should be addressed. But he questioned how much political and financial effort should be expended to bring places like London, LA or Nairobi – all of which have much lower levels of pollution – below WHO guidelines.

'If you got rid of all the transport in London you might be able to reduce the particle concentration by about 2 micrograms per cubic metre,' he said. 'At the moment for millennials, median life expectancy is into the mid-nineties. If you get rid of that pollution and nothing else happens you might live [one month longer]. We have to ask ourselves whether that extra month is a worthwhile benefit in return for not having any cars or any public transport or any delivery vehicles.'

Sir David Spiegelhalter of the Winton Centre for Risk and Evidence Communication at the University of Cambridge says: 'There are huge uncertainties surrounding all the measures of impacts of air pollution, with inadequate knowledge replaced by substantial doses of expert judgement. These uncertainties should be better reflected in the public debates.'

technology has been around for years in one form or another – the first diesel-electric trains appeared as early as the 1920s – hybrid technology really got going with the launch of the Toyota Prius in Japan in 1997.

The Prius is still the most popular form of hybrid car, what's commonly termed a 'full' hybrid: in this case, a petrol engine combined with an electric motor, with each being powerful enough to drive the car. A sophisticated control unit distributes the power seamlessly from each power source to the wheels via an automatic transmission. Toyota has sold over 6 million of them and you've probably driven or at least travelled in one. In London, for example, they are ubiquitous as the choice of Uber drivers. Of course, Toyota is not alone in manufacturing full hybrids; they are also produced by Audi, BMW, Citroën, Land Rover, Lexus, Mercedes, Peugeot, Porsche and Volkswagen, amongst others.

Using two engines where one would do may seem obviously inefficient but it does have advantages. The idea is that each engine is used where it is most efficient. Electric power is better when setting off, or in stop–start driving at low speeds, as it exploits the abundant torque (best thought of as the twisting effect) of the electric motor. The petrol engine provides more power and is therefore better suited to relatively high-speed cruising. When maximum power is needed, both engines can be used together – meaning that the petrol engine can be slightly smaller for a given level of performance. Crucially, like battery and hydrogen cars, the full hybrid also harvests some of the energy that would otherwise be lost in braking and uses it to recharge the batteries.

The petrol engine tends to take over at about 25 mph. They operate together only when maximum acceleration is required. (You can see this in a graphic on the dashboard, but in my experience the novelty wears off quickly.) Batteries in most hybrids are smaller than those in full-time electric cars. The range in electric-only operation is usually just a mile or two, as the cars are not designed to be used in this way. They've already started to rival the economy of diesels and should soon be able to offer similar performance – in particular better acceleration – as they become the norm for medium-size everyday cars upwards.

Smaller cars will increasingly be so-called 'mild' hybrids. Here a relatively small conventional engine uses an electric motor, mounted 'in parallel' between the engine and gearbox, to give extra help when required. The big difference is that the electric motor is not capable of powering the car on its own. The batteries regenerate when the car's driving normally and provide small but significant assistance with launching off from rest. Again the idea is that you can have a smaller, more economical petrol motor for a car of a given size, and hence greater economy. Mild hybrids will deliver a 10 or 20 per cent improvement in fuel efficiency for a petrol engine and enable them to more effectively take the place of diesels. Such technology will certainly take over from small, high-revving turbocharged engines, which produce unacceptable levels of nitrogen oxide and aren't anything like as economical in real life as they are in the test lab.

'Plug-in' hybrids are closest to pure electric cars. As well as being boosted by the engine and braking while on the move, these cars can be plugged into the mains to charge the batteries for longer battery-only journeys. The batteries are typically larger than in a full hybrid and in some models can give a range of about 30 or 50 miles of electric driving. Mitsubishi's Outlander plug-in hybrid has proved particularly popular in Europe. Increasingly, on new models, you'll be able to use the engine to charge the batteries as well. So for a long journey between two urban areas you can start off on battery only, switch over to combustion on the motorway and recharge at the same time so your battery is full when you reach your urban destination for no tailpipe-emission travel there.

It's often been hard to justify the extra expense of buying a hybrid because the fuel-consumption benefits are marginal. But combustion-engine cars are necessarily becoming more complicated just to pass tightening emissions tests, so over the course of time the cost differential will likely disappear. Nevertheless, as with many car statistics, hybrids' advertised fuel efficiencies can be misleading. Furthermore, with some of them you can actually end up with worse fuel consumption if you don't plug them in or if you use them almost entirely on motorway journeys – essentially you're running a normal combustion-engine car and just lugging around a heavy payload of batteries.

Take that hugely popular Mitsubishi Outlander. In 2018, it was the UK's most popular plug-in hybrid. Its official fuel-economy figure is a staggering 131 mpg and its official CO_2 emissions are a mere 46 g per 100 km, making it exempt from the London Congestion Charge and subject to tax benefits. But this really is playing the system.

These positive figures are based on a test cycle that starts with a fully charged battery when the Outlander can travel only about 28 miles on battery power alone. Then the petrol powertrain kicks in and the Outlander becomes a large petrol car carrying around a couple of heavy electric motors and a battery. In reality it would be a truly eco-friendly car only if you did short journeys (under 28 miles) and charged the batteries in between. How many people do that?

The emissions expert Nick Molden recognises the hybrid's capacity to be a goodie-two-shoes and a very naughty boy. 'Even to say "hybrid" you have to be careful because it covers a multitude of sins. The Prius is probably the best in class. The fourth generation of Prius is an incredibly clever vehicle. [Toyota] created a 10 per cent fuel-economy jump in one generation. From what I understand, for every turn of the engine they decide if it is more efficient to fire the engine, or use a bit of electricity. The devil's in the detail. What is the exact nature of your hybrid technology? It's becoming like internal combustion engines. You get good ones and bad ones. We should judge hybrids at the model level rather than at the generic "if it's a hybrid it must be good".'

If all this talk of carbon emissions and efficiency is sounding rather dull, don't worry. There is a special form of hybrid that deserves a category all by itself – the hybrid hypercar. The first was the Porsche 918 Spyder. It produced a stupendous 887 horsepower through a combination of a 4.6-litre V8 petrol engine and two electric motors. Porsche quoted a 0–60 time of 2.5 seconds, the price was £624,000 and it could do 214 mph. And yet, according to official figures, when it launched in 2014 it was so economical that it was exempt from the London Congestion Charge. The battery-only top speed was 100 mph.

Others followed at similarly eye-watering prices: the McLaren P1 at £866,000 with 727 bhp, and the Ferrari LaFerrari at £1,150,000 with 950 bhp. The hybrid-hypercar concept is now being taken to further extremes. The 1,035 bhp, £1.75

million McLaren Speedtail has a V8 petrol engine – but a staggering 309 of those bhp will come from its electric motor, even though it can't power the car on its own. The dramatic extended rear bodywork is to promote aerodynamic efficiency at its 250 mph maximum speed. Aston Martin offers the 1,160 bhp, £2.5 million Valkyrie: 1,000 bhp from a naturally aspirated 6.5-litre V12 combined with 160 bhp from an electric motor.

Most ambitiously, the 1,000-plus bhp Mercedes-AMG One aims to bring Formula One hybrid technology to the road. The rear wheels are driven by a turbocharged 1.6-litre petrol V6 with direct injection and 11,000 rpm. There are four electric motors. Two drive the front wheels plus there's a motor directly linked to the crankshaft to boost acceleration and another built into the turbocharger to reduce lag. The engine is consequently highly efficient, but has to be dismantled and rebuilt after about 30,000 miles to check the integrity of the components. The 275 cars being built at a cost of £1.9 million each have all been sold already. Mercedes received over 1,000 orders but have restricted production to keep the car exclusive.

Falling in love again with diesel… maybe for a bit

But do we need hybrids at all? In the short term, the miserly motorist's best friend diesel may well have a comeback. Finally, after years of false promises, the fuel is now much cleaner. It seems that Dieselgate spurred manufacturers on to almost eliminate its issues. As we wait for battery-powered and

Dieselgate

As soon as governments began vehicle-emissions tests, car manufacturers started cheating them. However, the 2015 Volkswagen Dieselgate scandal made previous incidents look like petty crime. VW were in a major push to sell diesels in the US and trumpeting the cars' low emissions, which were miraculously achieved without costly and inconvenient tanks of exhaust treatment liquid.

In reality they'd rigged as many as 11 million diesel cars globally with 'defeat devices' – cheat software that detected when they were being tested under laboratory conditions and reduced emissions accordingly. Out in the real world, the pollution controls were turned down or switched off and NO$_x$ levels soared as high as forty times the legal limit.

When this was discovered by researchers examining the differences between laboratory tests and real-world emissions, the consequences were huge. In the US, VW agreed to buy back or fix 475,000 cars, owners getting compensation of up to $10,000 each. Seven employees have been sentenced, including executive Oliver Schmidt, who was given seven years and a $400,000 fine after admitting that he helped the firm evade clean-air laws. It has cost the company over $30 billion and rising.

More widely the saga exposed widespread gaming of tests by manufacturers. Pollution has been much higher than it should have been in many countries and nobody believes car-industry pollution figures any more. Ironically, the scandal may have been the final push needed to clean up the notoriously dirty fuel.

hydrogen-fuelled cars to become mainstream, diesel cars will help minimise the environmental impact of keeping us moving thanks to their relatively low CO2 levels that in many cases outperform petrol hybrids altogether.

Making (rather than faking) diesels cleaner has made them more expensive and more complicated. As well as particulate filters the latest diesel-engine models have tanks of exhaust fluid, a colourless, non-toxic mixture of urea and de-ionised water, often termed AdBlue. Tiny amounts of this are injected into the flow of exhaust gases and at high temperature a chemical reaction takes place that turns the harmful nitrogen oxides into harmless nitrogen and water.

It works. Under real driving conditions NOx is down as low as 20 milligrams per km. The regulated level is 80. Even the last generation of vehicles were regularly putting out 800. What's more, Loughborough University claim they've discovered a technological breakthrough that will get diesel NOx down to 13 milligrams per km. Arguably, they don't even need to.

While 20 milligrams isn't zero, we're at the point where there are other, much bigger problems in terms of urban pollution – like wood-burning stoves, construction equipment, domestic heating and cooking, and even the modest candle.

A modern diesel produces less particulate matter than a battery-electric car, which is typically heavier and creates more dust from tyre and brake wear. The particulate filters are now so good that when the car is driving through a polluted urban area it sucks in more particulates than it emits, capturing them in the car. The air coming out of the tailpipe is cleaner than the air going in. Nick Molden calls this 'net negative emissions'. In contrast, the electric vehicle with no tailpipe and no filters has no such cleaning effect. These new cleaner diesels even produce fewer harmful particulates than the latest petrol cars.

The problem is what to do with older, more polluting diesels. In Europe the new standards include on road testing but apply only to model approvals from 1 September 2017 and to all new registrations from 1 September 2019. The diesel clean-up has only just started.

The previous standard, which applied from 2014, incorporated some good and some very bad cars. The combination of a lax testing regime and manufacturers' willingness to bend the rules meant that in Europe, although no one actually broke the law, some cars were massively over-emitting. These 'Euro 6' diesels currently attract no extra charge in London's Ultra-Low Emission Zone and German cities haven't banned them. But if the air stays dirty they won't stay on the road for long and many people will be incensed. Nick Molden reckons that manufacturers may start feeling obliged to protect their reputations by offering big incentives for owners of new-ish but dirty diesels to swap them for something cleaner.

These newfangled diesels will also need to be carefully maintained. To get these cars so clean involves an array of complex systems. It only requires one bit to break down and the car goes back to being like a cigar smoker in a pub. A more detailed MOT test may need to be introduced. So-called plume chasing might also be proposed. Police patrol vehicles would pull in behind cars and physically detect what comes out of the tailpipe while you're driving; it takes around 30 seconds. They'll be a bit like speed cops but sniffing tailpipes rather than checking radar guns.

Fuels of the future

Other fuels can make internal combustion engines more environmentally friendly too. One ambitious idea is synthetic fuels. These would use CO_2 captured from the air, which would then be combined with hydrogen created by renewable electricity. Giant processing plants would be erected in parts of the world with surplus solar energy that could be used in the conversion. Big fans draw in the ambient air across plastic corrugated sheets coated with potassium hydroxide to extract the CO_2. A typical plant should be able to extract about a million tonnes a year. This is equivalent to the CO_2 produced by about a quarter of a million cars.

Deserts would be ideal locations. Professor Jamie Turner from the Department of Mechanical Engineering at Bath University's Powertrain and Vehicle Research Centre thinks that 770 square miles of the Sahara could supply Europe's entire transportation needs. Although synthetic fuel would release carbon dioxide on combustion it would be a closed loop, because the fuel is derived from CO_2 already in the air.

The principal problem is that the process is very inefficient. Because hydrogen needs to be generated from water and because the carbon is captured from the air, the current overall efficiency is just 15 per cent. Consequently costs per litre could be several times higher than conventional fuels, even when producing at scale.

Wolfgang Ziebart tells me that 'Synthetic fuels will be required where energy density is the most important thing.' He has little doubt that aeroplanes will be using synthetic fuel in the future as it has the highest amount of energy per kilogramme. Mazda is trying to make synthetic fuels biologically in a laboratory, as a way of reducing costs, but has so far succeeded in doing so only at a miniature scale.

Liquefied petroleum gas (LPG) or autogas could also bridge the gap before hydrogen and electric become widespread. The fuel has been around since the late 1920s. It is produced as a by-product of natural-gas processing and is currently used to power just 3 per cent of the world's cars but is very popular in certain countries. In Armenia 20 to 30 per cent of the car fleet runs on it. In Turkey it's 10 per cent. Poland, Italy and Japan are all large markets. It's estimated that here in the UK some 170,000 cars have been converted to run on LPG. And with 1,400 stations selling it the infrastructure is already there, so filling up isn't a problem.

Most petrol engines can be converted and independent tests have shown that CO_2 emissions are 20 per cent less than petrol on average. However there are good reasons why it may never make the mainstream. Cars while they're warming up still run better on unleaded, so the original fuel tank and fuel system need to be retained. A typical car uses a tank of unleaded to every five of autogas. The size of the extra fuel tank encroaches on luggage and conversions aren't particularly cheap at around £2,000. It can take over 30,000 miles of running to get the money back. LPG is also heavier than air and tends to settle in low spots. For this reason it's regarded as an explosion hazard and is banned in many car parks and in the Channel Tunnel – so make sure you take the ferry and let's hope it doesn't go up in flames.

Natural gas also has its drawbacks. It's an energy source that's in great supply at the moment thanks to shale-gas discovery and exploitation. According to NGV Global, who collects statistics on such things, there will be 30 million gas vehicles by 2024. Large trucks can use liquefied natural gas (LNG), which isn't likely to be getting into your car's fuel tank unless you live somewhere very cold. This is a cryogenic liquid, formed when natural gas is chilled to around -160°C depending upon composition. Compressed natural gas (CNG) is more practical for cars. It can be stored on a vehicle in high-pressure tanks and CNG cars have typically between 60 and 80 per cent of the CO_2 emissions of petrol cars plus they emit much less NOx. But they need bulkier fuel tanks and they take slightly longer to fill. Gas cars could be part of the short-term bridge to an all-electric future but in most countries they're unlikely to be a significant long-term solution.

The nuclear options

For every sane solution to the problem of emissions there are several outlandish ones too. Let's talk nuclear. Each kilogramme of enriched uranium is equivalent in energy terms to 2,700 tons of coal. So, nuclear cars could render altogether obsolete the whole idea of refuelling. A reactor of the right size to power your mum's Audi would need more enriched uranium only every five or ten years and there would also be no exhaust fumes. On the other hand, it would be difficult to switch off – perhaps requiring some way of siphoning off the energy to the national grid. And there's also the slight problem that the radiation emitted would likely kill the driver, passengers and any nearby bystanders. An aircraft carrier or large submarine is big enough to carry the required radiation shielding. With current technology, a car is not.

There were a few brave (or foolhardy) attempts at nuclear-powered concept cars in the 1950s and 1960s, though working prototypes were never built. The 1957 Ford Nucleon, for example, featured an interchangeable reactor that owners would swap every 5,000 miles and included the option to choose from different performance levels. France in 1958 saw both the Arbel Symétric and Simca Fulgur. Ford tried again in 1962 with the spectacular six-wheeled Seattle-ite XXI, but the interactive computer navigation and modular design were more accurate indicators of the future than its interchangeable fission powerplant. Perhaps the most optimistic concept from the atomic age is the Studebaker-Packard Astral. As well as being nuclear powered, it would balance on one wheel thanks to gyroscope technology and feature a force field to protect it against collisions.

The notion of the nuclear automobile occasionally resurfaces. Cadillac did a World Thorium Fuel or WTF (ho-ho) concept in 2009 featuring 100-year refuelling intervals of the thorium core; one gram yields the energy equivalent to 7,500 gallons of gasoline when excited by lasers. The fuel may have

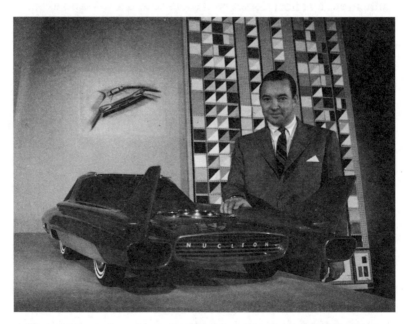

William Clay Ford Senior, grandson of motor pioneer Henry, with Ford's 1957 vision for the atomic age, the Nucleon.

some future in power generation, but for the usual safety reasons it looks unlikely to be included in cars for the foreseeable future. Cadillac really designed it as a tongue-in-cheek fantasy, but the razor-sharp concept still looks incredible today and features six mini-wheels within each tyre.

At the moment, the only future for nuclear-powered cars is in fiction and games. The 1957 Nucleon is the inspiration for atomic cars in the *Fallout* video-game franchise, which has a variety of nuclear cars in its digital fleet. When shot at they explode in a mushroom cloud.

If nuclear is too far-fetched as a zero-emission option, what about air? It sounds reassuringly wholesome and is not actually as ridiculous as you might suppose. Air-powered trams were successful in parts of France in the nineteenth century, operating reliably for decades. Back in 2009 on *The Gadget Show* we filmed a car that ran on compressed air. It did only 30 mph but the claimed range was a passable 65 miles and there were no emissions to accompany the amusing noise it made, which was rather like a sort of hydraulic sewing machine. The styling wasn't exactly inspiring: the car resembled something between a slug and a snail. It had portholes instead of side windows, and it carried only one person – the driver – in what looked like a rather vulnerable position at the front. Nevertheless, its inventor, Guy Nègre, and his son, Cyril, had high hopes for the Airpod – as they'd christened their device, years before Apple used the same term for wireless earphones. Unfortunately, however, like most forays in the field, it's been dogged by technical difficulties and false starts.

Nègre's car stores its compressed air in a tank at high pressure and it powers a piston engine. However, the pistons are driven not by an ignited fuel-air mixture but by the expansion of compressed air, in a similar manner to the expansion of steam in a steam engine. Refuelling could potentially take place in a few minutes; there are no emissions and there's no need for a cooling system, spark plugs, starter motor or an exhaust. The car can even recapture some energy while braking, like electric cars, by compressing and storing air.

There are a few technical shortcomings, though. You need energy to compress air in the first place. And you also need energy to cool the air while compression takes place. This, together with low energy density, reduces the overall efficiency to around 30 per cent. Expressed in terms of energy per litre of space, the energy density is about one tenth of a typical lithium-ion battery, which is in turn, as mentioned above, less than a tenth of gasoline. Also, when it decompresses, the air gets very cold and it can literally freeze up the engine. In a dystopian world of global-warming apocalypse, it could at least form a ready-made air-conditioning system.

Guy Nègre licensed the technology in 2007 to the Indian giant Tata, which also owns Jaguar Land Rover. Photos have appeared of a multi-passenger taxi model. So far neither model has made it into production and the same seems to be the case with the restyled AIRPod 2.0, featured on a website operated by a US company called Zero Pollution Motors. Guy died in June 2016 aged seventy-five but his son continues his work.

Powering the future

Longer term, I think it is fair to say that we will increasingly move to batteries and hydrogen but that petrol and diesel cars will continue to justify their existence. We've been used to personal transport based on oil but the future will be based on diversity. We're going to have a greater variety of propellants: very clean internal-combustion engines, various degrees of hybridisation, battery-electric vehicles and fuel cell electric vehicles. These technologies will compete with each other in terms of efficiency and pollution reduction. With luck we'll have good unbiased information and let the market work rather than have governments dictating that 'it's got to be batteries' or imagining that simply throwing prohibitions around will be the only stimulus required. Instead, here's hoping that governments will adopt a more positive approach of intelligent regulation and help to drive synergies between industries, as in the case of hydrogen power. A blinkered 'give it up' message likely won't work.

Whatever the headlines, road vehicles are responsible for a smaller and smaller proportion of air-quality problems. According to Nick Molden: 'If we were to wind forward ten years from now, and if no other policies were put in place for cars, you'd find that cars were a pretty small proportion of urban particulates and NOx. They have had a dodgy record over the last fifteen years of failed regulation but they've finally fixed it for the very latest versions.'

Cleaner combustion engines and an increasing proportion

of zero-emission vehicles will start to challenge the automatic assumption that carbon emissions are caused by cars too. Authorities and industries will have to shift focus to address the other factors lying behind air-quality and carbon-emission problems.

THREE

DESIGNING THE FUTURE

How the Shape of Cars will Change

The car is the most significant and influential expression of industrial culture the world has ever known – even more so than the now ubiquitous iPhone. Back in the 1980s, the design guru Stephen Bayley – perhaps best known for resigning in a huff as creative director of London's Millennium Dome after a disagreement with Peter Mandelson – suggested that were Michelangelo alive today he wouldn't be wasting his time creating marble sculptures for tombs in the Vatican, but would be in Detroit working in brown modelling clay to create the modern world's true modern art form: the motor car.

Top of the tree in terms of manufacturing sophistication for more than a century, cars are the most complex mass-produced industrial products in the world. Each one has around 10,000 components, yet normally works perfectly for years on end – often while being mercilessly thrashed in the hardest and most arduous of environments. At their best, the standards of design that cars embody are impeccable, with interiors as good as product design anywhere and exteriors that can attain the sculptural qualities of fine art. Car technology and engineering are not only incredibly complex; they're also surprisingly affordable – cars are assembled to precise quality standards, hundreds of thousands of times over, to a price that, in the developed world at least, most people can easily afford.

Cars have, over the years, become vastly more varied, with new genres and niches appearing all the time. Sports cars first arrived during the Edwardian era, with the 'Prince Henry' Vauxhall, so-called because it was specifically designed to compete in a 1,200-mile-long 1910 motor trial named in honour of Prince Henry of Prussia, Queen Victoria's grandson. Civilian off-roaders bounded into view after the Second World War in the shape of the Land Rover and Jeep. Grand tourers, hot hatches, supercars, estate cars, people carriers, sports utility vehicles and crossovers between all of them have added to the daunting array of aesthetic choices open to today's car buyers.

On the way, some true design icons have been created. The 1959 Cadillac and the 1961 Jaguar E-Type are internationally recognised emblems of industrial creativity. Some of the most charismatic supercars ever designed soon followed – cars like Tom Tjaarda's Ferrari 365 California, Marcello Gandini's Lamborghini Miura or his iconic Maserati Khamsin. And star cars still emerge from creative designers today. The Alfa Romeo 4C, the Jaguar F-Type and the Ferrari 458 are just a few exemplary contemporary designs that look set to take their places on the automotive wall of everlasting fame.

Car-making culture has spread round much of the world, from Europe and America through Japan and South Korea to India and China. And with it there has been the rise of the car brand. Bristling with styling cues and a heritage that makes each one distinct, car marques are some of the most carefully honed, promoted and valuable properties in capitalism. Each has a meticulously defined style and appeals to a defined tribe of consumers, wannabe consumers and pure enthusiasts.

Conceptual art

Most full-scale future-gazing is done by manufacturers themselves with their concept cars. They perform various roles. One is pure fantasy. The heyday of American and European concept cars was probably the period from 1950 to 1975. Inspired by the Space Age, creations like the 1961 Ford Gyron – a dart-shaped two-wheeler that used gyroscopes to stay upright – weren't serious projects but they looked fantastic. The jet-inspired Oldsmobile Golden Rocket from 1956 and the GM Firebird III from 1959 are even more outrageous, both products of the aero-obsessed fertile brain of General Motors' styling chief Harley Earl. His rival at Chrysler, Virgil Exner, produced equally stunning visions, such as the 1956 Diablo or 1960 Plymouth XNR.

There's also a whole genre of spectacular fantasy supercars that were always too thin, pointy, impractical or fragile to quite make it into production. Consider the almost flat

Ford's 1961 vision of the future, the Gyron, was a balancing act: a two-wheeled dart kept upright by gyroscopic stabilisers.

1970 Ferrari 512S Modulo or the frangibly greenhouse-like 1967 Lamborghini Marzal. The definitive example of the breed is probably the still-stunning 1970 Gandini-styled Lancia Stratos Zero, which appeared in Michael Jackson's 1988 film *Moonwalker*.

The purpose of other concepts is to test out public reaction before cars hit the market, or to allow manufacturers to assess the reception given to styling themes before gambling the company's future on them. The BMW i concepts helped to prepare the public for the expensive move the company made in the direction of electrification. Another BMW, the Gina, which was created by the legendary designer Chris Bangle in 2001, used cloth bodywork that could be morphed into various shapes, transforming the car. (If you need a spoiler, for example, you can grow one.) Bangle claimed that his experience working on the Gina enabled him to massively and confidently extend the range of shapes that steel could be pressed into.

Some concept cars are surprisingly close to future production cars and generate interest in them. For example, the 1995 Audi TT prototype almost precisely predicted the real car apart from the rear windows; the Lamborghini 350 GTV mirrored the 350 GT; and the Jaguar CX-16 and CX-17 concepts closely foreshadowed the F-Type and F-Pace respectively.

A sprinkling of futuristic design surfaces in films and TV. *Minority Report* from 2002, for instance – that most polished of prophetic movies – includes a rather neat fuel-cell-powered self-driving 'Lexus 2054' with advanced biometric security features like eye and fingerprint recognition. The film's fast-moving living rooms on wheels that race down highways and climb walls look surprisingly like current autonomous concepts such as the Renault EZ-GO, albeit somewhat more sprightly. Not all futuristic movie cars are so inviting, though. They may be distinctive with projecting, spidery front wheels and vertical-take-off capabilities but I doubt you'd fancy a future where most cars are as gawky as the 'Spinner' cop cars in the original *Blade Runner*.

Film product placement is seen by some manufacturers as an opportunity to align their brand with a positive-looking future. For the 2019 animated Will Smith movie *Spies in Disguise*, Audi struck a deal with its distributors, Twentieth Century Fox, to feature the RSQ e-tron concept car used by spy character Lance Sterling. Naturally, it is fully autonomous when required and

Futuristic cars from the movies

A Clockwork Orange (1971)

The Durango 95 was a real car that looked outlandish enough for Stanley Kubrick's dystopian vision of the future. A mid-engined car created to explore the 'extremes of styling' by Dennis and Peter Adams in 1969, it's really called the Adams Probe 16. The car still exists and is so low it's almost impossible to drive. You can get in through the roof.

Minority Report (2002)

John Anderton – played by Tom Cruise – has the Lexus 2054 built round him in an automated factory. It's self-driving when desired, with hydrogen power, biometric security and voice control. Electronic rear-view cameras instead of mirrors were a novelty back in 2002 but are now relatively common.

I, Robot (2004)

Audi developed the gorgeous RSQ especially for the film. Top features include automation and wheels that are capable of moving in any direction. Many of the styling cues appeared on the next generation Audi TT.

Tron: Legacy (2010)

Created by German car designer turned 'automotive futurist' Daniel Simon, the Light Runner looks like a cross between a Formula One car and an off-roader. It could morph from a grid-runner into an all-terrain vehicle on demand. It's unlikely that the light-missile launcher would make it into a production motor.

Blade Runner 2049 (2017)

The flying police cars of the future are an update on the cars Syd Mead designed for the original film, and feature vertical takeoff, autonomous driving and detachable, gesture-controlled surveillance drones. The Peugeot badge might seem an odd choice for an American-made movie, but the company is eyeing a return to the US market and the movie's producers had high hopes for the film in China, where Peugeot-badged cars sell well.

features a holographic speedometer. It follows on from the company's successful involvement with *I, Robot* and *Iron Man*.

Will the future kill off our design heritage?

All these prototypes have helped to create a magnificent legacy of design culture around the car. But is this under threat? Some of the developments revolutionising the car industry today can be seen as good news. Electric cars, with their more flexibly shaped and compact powertrains, could free designers from a whole host of constraints and in turn stimulate more distinctive styling. But new trends also suggest trouble ahead. Car sharing and the rise of mobility as a service, rather than as a pure physical product, may require car makers to think more like airlines than like aeroplane manufacturers. Efficiency and comfort rather than looks may determine profit margins. And the autonomous future doesn't seem a great omen for good design if current driverless car prototypes are anything to go by. They're a rather depressing prospect, all too frequently blob-like pods with less allure than an airport shuttle. Just look at the slipper-like Waymo Firefly or the GATEway vehicles pottering around Greenwich in London. The average washing machine boasts a more assertive and exciting countenance.

For some this won't matter. When you're renting a shared autonomous car, its styling will be as irrelevant as the look of an Airbus or Boeing plane is to most flyers. What is crucial is the service you get from the airline or, in this case, the outfit that maintains the car and provides the much-needed mobility. The pride of ownership and self-identification with those carefully crafted car marques will be history. BMWs, for example, were once the Ultimate Driving Machines but if you're no longer driving or owning one you'll need something else to secure the brand's future.

In search of that alternative, and a future where we are all spared the fate of a miserably bland roadscape, I visited two of Britain's leading educational institutions, Coventry University and the Royal College of Art in London's Kensington. Between them they're responsible for training a massive proportion of the world's top car designers.

I wanted to see what these up-and-coming designers, and some of their tutors, had in mind for our motoring futures. If they were thinking positively then I could relax, confident that car design would continue to amaze and delight. If they had given in to the defeatism of pod-like anonymity then I would have to go into mourning as we'd be doomed to a future of lowest common denominators.

Coventry and the RCA don't have quite the monopoly on car design they once did. When I filmed an item on how to be a car designer for *Top Gear* back in the 1990s they were practically the only game in town. Now there are thriving courses elsewhere too, such as at the Strate School of Design in Paris and at the Umeå Institute of Design in Sweden. But taking an undergraduate transport course at Coventry and progressing – if you're lucky and skilled enough – to the postgraduate course at the RCA is still a route of choice into the profession.

The RCA's Vehicle Design course was renamed Intelligent Mobility in 2019, perhaps in recognition of the car's changing morphology. There are only twenty or so places available on it each year and it boasts a long list of influential alumni, including the current design chiefs of more than a dozen of the world's car companies. For starters there's Julian Thomson, design director of Jaguar (who replaced Ian Callum, another distinguished RCA graduate); Marek Reichman, design director of Aston Martin; and Peter Horbury, the man who reinvented Volvo in the 1990s and who's now design boss of car giant Geely in China. The heads of four out of five of Geely's design studios are graduates of Coventry.

Considering they're temples dedicated to the discipline of design, both courses are housed in surprisingly unattractive buildings. At Coventry they're in a concrete tower block next to the Ring Road; the RCA is a slightly more prepossessing concrete building in the shadow of the Royal Albert Hall.

To me the most difficult challenge is how anyone can get excited about designing cars we don't even drive. But it's not one that seems to worry today's students on either course; in fact I was struck by their zealous anticipation of an autonomous future and readiness to embrace new opportunities.

Driverless cars can be more 'architectural' – so enthused graduate Sam Philpott, whose Haven concept was inspired by the feeling of calm he experiences while relaxing in a window seat at home. The Haven is a vision of an urban vehicle for young people looking to reduce their stress levels; this would be privately owned but shareable by invitation.

A mindful window on the restless city and a study in mobile architecture, Sam Philpott with his Haven.

It looks rather attractive in spite of a distinctly rectilinear silhouette. A slope in the lower section is sufficient to express movement, Philpott thinks, and I am inclined to agree. It's a kind of blend between vehicle and building design. It also exemplifies the way autonomy will shift the design emphasis on to cars' interiors. Going driverless frees up the inside space in so many ways. At its most obvious, there's no need for a steering wheel and no requirement for a view of the road ahead. There's also no longer that sense of a hierarchy in the car, with the driver 'in control'. Philpott sees the Haven as having two different types of space: one for 'mindfulness' and another for 'interaction' with people invited in to share the environment. It even comes with its own sort of dating app, where passengers can be selected to interact with on stress-reducing urban meanderings.

This wasn't the only concept that explored the role of the car as an escape from the pressures of the modern world. Others I encountered included one that featured a meditation room made out of wood; one that featured plants and the sound of trickling water; and even one – perhaps for the more paranoid traveller – that was shielded against all radio communication.

Some designers even see the car as a fully fledged mobile room that when you're not making journeys in it becomes part of your house. The most ambitious car I saw, if indeed it can be called a car at all, was Sebastian Rokeberg's Polestar PS10. Don't let the Volvo sub-brand fool you – this is as much a house as a car.

Rokeberg's vision is a compact two-storey, luxuriously equipped home. It's about the size of two London double-deckers parked next to each other and can be part of a high rise or located independently in a remote landscape. Part of the living-room furniture is also a car interior – the 'interior module'. This includes three seats in different states of recline, a fridge with two compartments at different temperatures, footrests and tables. When you want to travel, you stay in your seat while the floor of the living room slides away and the module descends to meet a fully charged electric platform that contains the wheels, powertrain and batteries.

A section of the floor slides back above you to become the car's roof, which is supported magnetically to give an entirely open experience; if you don't fancy that, or the weather's not playing ball, interactive display screens roll up to shield you from the outside environment. The roof also contains the autonomous driving equipment. When you return home the process is reversed and the module resumes its role as part of your living room.

The interior module can be separated from the platform at certain hubs, too – at, say, restaurants or shopping areas; places where you can interact with others. It can also move round the house to take advantage of sunlight; to this end a maglev staircase can move out of the way as required. This may sound like something from *Wall-E* but the design is very tastefully done, honest. If it ever works!

Several of the nascent designers thought we could instigate a relationship with our driverless cars by emphasising all the things we like about cars that aren't the actual business of driving – such as a sense of your own space, or the physical sensation of movement and control. This might involve physically moving your seat or cockpit about to exaggerate sensations of cornering and acceleration, much like a fairground car-racing simulator. Or perhaps introducing virtual reality via headsets or screens, so that you can be in reality stuck in traffic at 30 mph but feeling like you're on an open country road doing 130. Air can even be harnessed to create passion by channelling it directly into the cabin to create a feeling of speed when you're not travelling that fast.

In place of the charismatic noise of the internal combustion engine, Irene Chiu advocates personalised soundscapes for autonomous-vehicle interiors: a car that creates its own audio experience. She'd made a highly engaging video of what a future trip in a self-driving Bentley might sound like. After a quick calibration to the driver's ears the car starts off in town, where some of the jarring noises are filtered out. As it powers through a winter landscape that looks distinctly Nordic, the natural sounds of that environment are magnified – including that of a sika deer crossing the car's path (of course, being perfectly automated, the car deftly avoids the obstacle). As night descends and the northern lights appear, the car creates eerily celestial music to enhance your journey.

You could choose to hear more or less of the ambient sound according to your mood, and you'd still be able to listen to music or the radio if desired. I presume the car would need a noise-cancelling system like that used in headphones, or like the in-car version that those with long memories might remember was pioneered by Lotus back in the 1990s. Chiu envisages conductive sound through the seats as a way of enhancing the travel experience for deaf passengers.

Another suggestion to enliven the autonomy is to combine it with some sort of vestigial driving experience in the same vehicle. But I'm not convinced. The notion of a dedicated driver zone in an otherwise autonomous car seems too wasteful of space and resources. I think you're more likely to have a different car that you rent for a track-day experience than you are to spend the extra cash on a car that can do both.

And in any case such designs appear to make the car far too large for ever more crowded road conditions.

None of the designs seemed to have the fluidity of film cars in this respect. In *I, Robot* Will Smith's Audi R8-inspired hybrid switches quickly and elegantly from self-driving to driver mode with a smooth extending steering column. I think it's one of those transformations that will always look better in the movies with a wealth of CGI at their disposal.

To share or not to share?

Autonomy brings with it the question of whether future vehicles will be shared or owned, or a mix of the two. For many drivers, sharing will be a horrific prospect. One of the traditional joys of the car is that you're in your own private space in a crowded world, with your own media and even to some extent your own climate, a locale shared only with those to whom you've given express permission. A shared car has more in common with public transport: dirt, inconvenience and the great unwashed threaten at every turn.

Whether you'll accept sharing will depend upon where you live and how old you are. In America autonomous vehicles look far more likely to be private and personally owned. In Paris the authorities have already decreed that all autonomous vehicles must be shareable by law: self-driving cars will be required to scurry away by themselves to be used by someone else.

According to one Coventry student, Denny Julian Deemin, Generation Zs (born between the mid-1990s and mid-2000s) will still want their own cars but Generation Alphas (born since 2005) will want a simpler lifestyle without the bother of ownership. When buying cars, particularly used ones, I've always found the hassles of dealing with insurance, registration documents, finance and provenance checks rather onerous, so I can to an extent empathise with Denny's generation Alphas. However, I wouldn't yet be ready to go as far as abandoning car ownership altogether.

Idealists as they are inclined to be, the students saw lots of advantages in sharing. Some notions were more like small-scale buses, trains or shops on wheels. Concepts included a massage parlour, a sort of mobile-games console pod for entertainment, a doctor's surgery and the inevitable pub. To ease the potential pain, technology will help you decide who to share with – like having the equivalent of Tinder to suggest compatible travelling companions. As most of us like listening to music in our cars, Or Shacar from the RCA proposes sorting your fellow occupants by Spotify playlist so at least you'll be listening to the same tunes.

Another idea is cars that are a mix of shared and private spaces. These could be useful for people who don't want to share but who need to when they travel into city centres where single-occupancy vehicles have been banned. Just like swarms in nature, these autonomous vehicles could be continually changing in size and configuration. RCA graduate Yang Liu envisages a car with several distinct sections that can operate either independently or together. A front section is for group sharing; and I rather liked the way Liu's seats were composed of separate inflatable sections so they could adapt to different sizes of passenger or deflate completely to carry someone in a wheelchair. The back of the car has an individual area with greater privacy, while at the very back are three smaller autonomous pods – two of these can either travel with the car or break away for local deliveries, while a third provides charging and cleaning on the move so the whole system never needs to stop except to load and unload.

It's an exhausting concept just to think about, a world of endlessly varying perpetual mobility and autonomy within autonomy, but Liu is adamant it's efficient, making the best use of road space, time and energy.

Other shared-use concepts are more like hire cars. You still have your own space but you're renting it. Fukhita Wong from Coventry has created the Snooze, an autonomous mobile hotel that promises to combine the comfort of a conventional hotel room with the convenience of a taxi, bookable through an app that would hopefully offer guidance on where to park to avoid the noise of passing traffic. You can also use it to travel as you sleep in an individual incarnation of the train sleeper car.

A benefit of shared autonomy that for some may help in the pill swallowing is that there'll be no need to choose a car that can do everything – one that's equally at home on the urban commute as on holiday. There can be specialised cars developed for every conceivable role, potentially leading to more interesting designs. You can have different cars for different purposes delivered to your door.

RCA student Anand Askinar's Fractal is a shared vehicle specifically designed for families with a single young child or baby. It's a mobile space that will appear at your home on demand and can be configured as required. You can switch between a 'care mode', with a crib between the seats, and 'share mode', where you're chatting and interacting with an older child. The concept includes a buggy, which is separately autonomous if you want it to be, and a digital screen in the roof offers entertainment. As your family expands, or when you have visitors, you will presumably be able to choose from more commodious Fractals. However, having your precious offspring speeding along the motorway in an autonomous buggy in the company of trucks, buses and other vehicles would of course take parental anxiety to a whole new level.

Maybe you'll just carry round your own intelligent steering wheel. That's the idea behind Jaguar's Future-Type concept, first shown in 2017. You summon up different Future-Types depending on your transport needs, slotting the wheel into each vehicle. When you're taking the kids to school, for example, you might choose one with '2+1 Social Seating' so you can chat face-to-face while the car autonomously drives you there, using its 'Sayer' AI (named after the designer of the E-Type, Malcolm Sayer). Keeping all options open, Jaguar also envisages you perhaps owning a Future-Type as well and using your steering wheel for actual driving.

For me, some of the most exciting and romantic shared-vehicle concepts are the ones aiming to take the place of your holiday hire car by forming their own mobile tourism experience. RCA student Stavros Mavrakis has created the Zephyr. It has no relation to classic Fords with the same name, though it does have the same mythological and poetic-sounding inspiration: the Greek god of the west wind.

The Zephyr is designed to help you experience the Cyclades islands without the hassle of driving yourself round the narrow roads. There are design themes that echo the geometry and colours of local architecture; and local materials like rattan, a palm that can be woven into fabric, cover the cushions while the seats are finished with cork. The body shape is inspired by local boats and, in a chillingly modern twist, the hull is made from a composite material derived from ocean waste.

'You're not just being transported; you're absorbing the experience of the region by using this car. It's the key part of an experiential adventure,' enthuses Mavrakis. With the help of his VR headset I was able to imagine the relaxing autonomous experience of being transported around an idyllic island. The view of the local sand and boulders would be framed by my land yacht's hull, while I rested my feet on a rattan cushion and immersed myself in ancient mythology. As all this goes on, the built-in turbine would be harnessing the very wind after which my craft was named to charge the batteries ready for my odyssey to continue. Perhaps the remaining seven of the eight Greek wind gods could inspire different, equally characterful tourist conveyances.

Luca Robert Barberis's Infiniti concept is an autonomous-car subscription service specifically designed for tourism. The only thing you own is a custom-made suitcase that fits into a slot in the bonnet. The car is low and muscular; it's like the best classic sports cars from the front, while from the rear it has the elegance of a traditional coupé. From the top there's a teardrop profile with crease lines and roof graphics to emphasise the dynamism. It has real glass rather than screens, so you can see the actual view, but augmented reality tells you more about what you're seeing. Barberis, who's from the US, thinks too many of his country-folk are geographically ignorant and wants to change this. 'You come back from your vacation a better-informed person.'

This service would be at the premium end of the vacation market. There'll still be a role for carefully nurtured upmarket brands in an autonomous world but it'll be geared to a high-end service. According to Professor Dale Harrow, who's head of the Intelligent Mobility Design Programme at the Royal College of Art in London, 'It's not just about materiality; it becomes the whole experience of the journey from the moment you leave your home to when you arrive somewhere, including how the vehicle presents itself to you at one end and how you say goodbye to it.'

Harry Wilson, a Coventry student, told me about his project called the Usu, where you subscribe to an upmarket brand that would become a sort of universal global taxi service giving you access to a fleet of identical autonomous cars. Whether you're in London, Shanghai, New York or Singapore you'd interact with the (inevitable) app on your phone and configure the car as you wanted it before you arrived. When you reach your departure point the car's already there with seats and lighting set to your preferences and your choice of entertainment playing. If you're an international business traveller and you left this car at Heathrow, you'd get an identical car coming round to collect you in Shanghai and drive you around the city.

As someone who has long been annoyed by the appalling service offered by airport hire-car companies, with their penchant for giving you a car of the wrong size, renting the one you booked to someone else and charging mind-blowing excess payments, this would be an understandably appealing service in the autonomous era. Autonomy of course is a long way off. Before we get there, the rise of electric cars is the most important development.

Should electric cars look different?

An immediate issue is what electric cars should look like. David Browne, who was director of the Coventry course for two decades, questioned whether there will be a distinct design language for electric vehicles, noting that cars like the Honda Insight, with its teardrop shape and enclosed rear-wheel arches, the original Nissan Leaf, and the BMW i3 and i8 have made a stab at creating a new look for electric cars. 'What I liked about the original Honda Insight, and now like about the i3 and i8, is that they didn't take their conventional car and put a bunch of batteries in. They're engineered to be what they are. The Insight was aerodynamically efficient and used exotic materials to keep the weight down. The i3 and i8 were designed to be electric and not spin-offs from any other BMW. The production and the mechanics are different, as is the styling.'

At the RCA, student Bin Sun from China sees the Insight and the BMWs as exceptions to the rule and set himself the task of creating a new design language for electric vehicles. 'At the moment the electric car mainly looks the same as an ordinary car. Aggressive. A fake grille. Angry eyes. But I believe we have some unconscious feeling about electric power. Petrol power is furious and sometimes even dangerous. Electric energy is purer and safer. It's more rational and peaceful. When someone drives an electric vehicle they say how quiet it is. My main attention is to express those feelings.'

I suggest that people also often say how quickly an electric car accelerates, so it's not all about a new humility, but have to concede he has a point. When I drove a 2018 Nissan Leaf for a short period I couldn't help noticing that many people expressed their disappointment to me that an electric car looked very much like any other car.

Bin describes his concept as looking more digital, with a central bar round the car and small grilles where the parts of the car that are being cooled, like the batteries, are located. The surfaces and graphics are designed to communicate what he calls a more rational line, with larger radius curves to promote a feeling of calmness. A spectacular pair of gullwing doors adds some glamour.

Dongwon Lee came up with a suggestion for Tesla, a company admired for its technical expertise by the students but less for its design, which was considered rather bland. His Project Berry is mixture of the nostalgic and the fantastical. It's part car, part spacecraft, a sort of concept car for space exploration.

Addicted to space himself, Dongwon thinks Tesla should let some of Elon Musk's SpaceX project genes loose in their cars. His one-seater was inspired by 1960s concept cars. 'Space was fresh and new. It was the age of spaceships, with thoughts of people moving to space, and space movies like *2001*. Design in the sixties had space-orientated shapes, whether in cars like the GM Firebird or furniture like Eero Aarnio's ball chair. They're soft. Each part is interconnected and seamless. My rear lights and front lights are linked in one circle, for example.'

Fancy a trip to Mars? Electric cars like Dongwon Lee's 'Project Berry' could revive the space vibe.

The car has the look of a personal USS *Enterprise* about it. I wondered about the large overhang at the back but that's apparently space-inspired too, from the tails of comets and the shape of Saturn's rings. It's a bit like a Harley Earl or Virgil Exner concept for the twenty-first century.

Honda looks set to continue the electric differentiation with its Urban EV and Sports EV concepts, which have a sort of innocent and wide-eyed, circular-headlamped and round-bumpered look. But other manufacturers are committed to a more conservative approach. Tesla says it'll keep its styling conventional to maximise market appeal. BMW has expressed a desire to make its new electric cars more like its conventional models, while VW's electric I.D. concepts look very conventional apart from their full-width LED lights and sliding doors (which apparently won't make it into production anyway on cost grounds). In the short term I think conservatism will win out and we'll see electric cars merging with the mainstream. But, in the longer term, brands are always going to be looking for new ways to stand out.

The future of status

Status and the car have always been closely linked. Not for nothing does the famous car stylist Chris Bangle, who was responsible for reinventing the look of BMW in the 1990s with his flame-edge effect, call the car an avatar. It's a reflection of yourself: you buy it and you become it.

For the first few years that cars existed, the status attached merely to owning one meant that it didn't really matter what they looked like. But it didn't take long for prestige cars to appear. The human desire to look different and be seen above one's peers in the pecking order quickly extended to motoring. A 1904 Mercedes was a vastly more prestigious device than a De Dion-Bouton of the same year. In 1906 the new Rolls-Royce Silver Ghost was justifiably marketed as 'The Best Car in the World' and created an ultimate status symbol in the process.

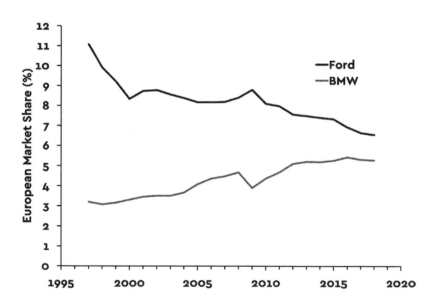

Keeping up appearances: over recent years luxury brands have boomed.

By the 1920s the likes of Delage and Delahaye in France, and Duesenberg, Cadillac and Pierce-Arrow in the USA, were producing superbly crafted and glamorous conveyances out of the very highest-quality materials. And if that wasn't enough, you could buy the chassis and commission a coachbuilder to create something even more extravagantly individual.

Style spread downmarket in the 1930s, with streamlining applied to more affordable cars from the Lincoln Zephyr to the Flying Standard. In the 1960s, marketing departments refined the buying process by multiplying the options available to ordinary car buyers. The 1964 Ford Mustang was available in a groundbreaking number of variations. Ford brought the trend to Britain with the 1969 Capri, which featured twenty-one different engine and trim combinations and was sold as 'The Car You Always Promised Yourself'.

Everybody wants status. Helped by leasing deals, sales of upmarket brands have boomed at the expense of the mid-market. These days the top-ten sales charts in countries like the UK are more likely to include BMWs and Mercedes than they are Ford Mondeos. More luxury cars are sold than ever. Look how sales of Ford-badged cars in Europe have declined over recent decades, while those of BMW and Porsche have soared. It's the same story in the US.

Status will become easier to attain thanks to new technologies like scanning and 3D printing, which will facilitate the bespoke manufacture of cars. They will foster a revival of small-scale production and even the individually commissioned car. Coventry 3D printing company Vital Auto already prints complete headlamp assemblies for the NIO EP9 supercar, which is assembled in China. The company sees huge potential for 3D parts for cars with small production runs of between one and a thousand per year.

This rebirth of bespoke will be helped by the move to electric platforms and the 'skateboard' chassis. This is a compact floorpan that incorporates all the batteries and powertrain and unsurprisingly looks rather reminiscent of a (very large) skateboard. It will be relatively easy to create custom designs on this simple, common chassis. Semi-autonomous crash-avoidance features like the automatic emergency braking already seen on current mass-produced cars will also help to keep the car safe without the need for expensive crash testing and the associated complex body structures.

Brian Clough is a former senior lecturer at Coventry and now a freelance designer who is keen on the potential for customisation. 'It's a throwback to the days of Mulliner Park Ward and other coachbuilders, where people put bodywork on a chassis. We might see a democratisation of bespoke. You and I could sit down at a tablet and agree a design on Alias modelling software and produce a 3D model within a week, in the way you hire an interior designer to decorate your house. You'll sit there with a designer and design a car to suit you, they'll make a little car model for you to evaluate and a month later you'll have the full-size one sitting on your drive. The only limit is your imagination.'

New kids on the block

Creating more upmarket, individual cars may become easier but the old brands aren't going to have it all their own way. A new force in the market is China. At 23 million units a year it is already the biggest car producer in the world. Its factories crank out more cars than the EU, or the USA and Japan combined. It has 70 different car manufacturers and a bewildering variety of its own brands, though many of the cars sold there still have Western badges on the bonnet. They are produced under joint arrangements with the Western companies that helped establish the industry in the 1980s, but that are not presently allowed to produce cars there in their own right, either for the domestic market or for export.

There have been some issues with Chinese models, ahem... 'taking inspiration' from other well-known car designs, most notably the BMW X5 (Shuanghuan SCEO), Porsche Macan (Zotye SR9) and Range Rover Evoque (Landwind X7). Perhaps more surprisingly, other targets have included the likes of the Daewoo Matiz (Chery QQ), the Smart Fortwo (Shuanghuan Noble) and even a Mercedes-Benz CLK front bolted on to a Renault Megane rear (the BYD F8 Coupe). Slightly less comprehensive imitations include the Mini knock-off Lifan 320 and the Renault Twizy-esque Rayttle E28. You can even buy kits to replace the badges on your Chinese copies to make them look even more like the original.

Spot the difference

Chinese imitation

Original

Zotye SR9

Porsche Macan

Landwind X7

Range Rover Evoque

Shuanghuan Noble

Smart Fortwo

Such misbehaviour will have to stop if the Chinese companies are to sell their cars globally, and do for cars what Huawei, Oppo and Xiaomi have achieved with smartphones. But, there are already signs that the Chinese courts are enforcing intellectual-property rights more aggressively. In addition, car manufacturers will need to improve quality – which has so far fallen well short of the standards reached by their counterparts in the telecoms industry.

Nevertheless, we'll be seeing and hearing a lot more from the big Chinese car manufacturers in the near future. Geely's prestige brand Lynk & Co is leading the way with exports and will be one of the first lines to make it into Europe and North America. Geely already exports to South America, Russia and the Middle East under its own nameplate and looks set to exploit its control of UK sports-car manufacturer Lotus by broadening the range of cars carrying the racing brand. The Geely Icon, first seen at Beijing Motor Show 2018 and based on the XC40 made by Volvo, may be produced in Europe.

New names in the West will also include Hongqi, best known for producing China's state luxury limousines but now promoting its GT Concept, a coupé somewhere between Bentley and Aston Martin in style. Dongfeng has shown some very handsome sports-car concepts, while XPeng concentrate on battery EVs. BYD is another big name that looks set to start exporting soon. The company has hired an ex-Audi designer Wolfgang Egger and unsurprisingly produced some rather Audi-like concepts. Qoros and Changan do more conventional-looking SUVs and aim to sell in the West in the near future;

and at the more prestigious end of the battery-electric market the NIO EP9 electric supercar scored one of the fastest times up the hill at the 2018 Goodwood Festival of Speed.

Africa will also become much more important. As things stand, it's the only major continent on earth without a substantial car industry. By 2030, however, it is expected to be the fastest-growing car market in the world and will create another location for manufacturing. The 'digitisation' of production will make the location of factories and their role as important national icons less important than the software making the car and controlling its production. According to Brian Clough, 'Now, you can almost open a factory anywhere. It's not as difficult as it was in the days of the Hillman Imp and the Vauxhall Viva to take production somewhere else. As in the aircraft industry, you don't have to make the part in a particular factory anymore; you just send over the data.'

It's a development that has parallels in the RCA and Coventry students' own model-making. Virtually all the projects are built as scale models just under a metre in length. Traditionally students have produced these themselves using clay, a skill that has been one of the definitive talents of a car designer and one that's in demand from other industries as well for the sculpting expertise it represents. While Coventry's students were still creating their own clay models, in London this was the exception rather than the rule, with designs taking place mainly on the computer and the file sent elsewhere (usually China) for 3D printing into a resin model. 'Made in China. Designed here, though,' noted David Browne.

The old meets the new

Clay is unlikely to die away, though its demise in this role was thought inevitable until recently. Some students said they emphatically preferred working in clay and couldn't truly work with shapes on screen. As Brian Clough confirmed, 'Renault was one of the companies trying to get rid of clay modelling entirely. And make it all digital.' But it changed its mind. 'There are still lots of companies that want to stick with clay models because the way you perceive a three-dimensional object is different from the way you see it on screen, even using the best VR systems. Clay modelling isn't dead yet.'

The best of both worlds is to have both clay and digital. There's no doubt that looking at a 6x6-metre Powerwall – a high-definition video display made seamlessly of other large displays – through 3D glasses gives you a very realistic view of a new design, and one you can refine, tweak and re-colour in a fraction of the time it takes to craft another clay model. But clay itself is delightfully tactile and there's nothing like the realism it engenders and the relationship it creates with a design, which can be developed and refined as it's shaped.

A reverence for the past is likely to be important in car styling too. In the 1990s and early 2000s, cars like the Beetle, the Fiat 500 and above all the Mini all nodded significantly to their ancestors. The trend will embrace more recent cars. Even companies that would never have considered retro styling have started to plunder their past. At the Paris Motor Show in

2018 Peugeot showed their E-Legend, a brilliantly handsome reimagining of the 1960s Peugeot 504 Coupé by the company's chief designer Gilles Vidal. It's a car that the firm's CEO, Jean-Phillipe Imparato, says he would love to put into production after 2020.

Cars from Japan in particular are receiving much more retro attention, as the old ones become more fashionable. Student Seok Hyun Kim, for example, wants to revive the 1967 Mazda Cosmo in his Cosmo Revival 2027 concept. 'The original car challenged convention, with its strikingly individual styling and its rotary engine,' he says. 'The successor will carry on the spiritual heritage.' He envisages it lending its model name to a new premium electric sub-brand for the company. As well as echoing the old car's styling his car will continue to be technologically innovative, as demonstrated by its hydrogen-fuelled rotary-electric powertrain.

Even the truly kitsch will get a look in. Paul Busuego's Cadillac Emperado concept is an enormous luxury car with styling inspired by 1970s Cadillac Fleetwood formal limousines, including their rich burgundy interiors. It has a hugely long wheelbase to maximise passenger space, a built-in bar, which works like a Sushi conveyor belt, and champagne flutes laid out as a sort of V8 facsimile under the bonnet at the front. 'It's an extravagant and ostentatious way of displaying your wealth, more old-school American luxury than how many gadgets you can stuff in your car.'

Rather than fretting about rights and licensing, car companies usually welcome students using their brands in design exercises. They're intrigued to discover what creative young people, unconstrained by the quotidian formalities of corporate cultures, think about their cars' future. They even offer to help the students develop their ideas. These days, though, it's usual for students to ask the companies for permission first to avoid any potential legal tussles.

Sometimes there are more formal collaborations between design courses and car companies' design departments. In 2018 Bentley, for example, challenged second-year post-graduate students at the RCA to develop concepts around 'the meaning of future British luxury in the year 2050'.

Bentley's design director Stefan Sielaff, himself an alumnus of the RCA course, explained the company's motives. 'We are looking for ideas and concepts that could potentially lead us in new and interesting directions, using the perspective of these digital natives – from all over the world – to see things differently… the taste makers in training, if you will.'

As well as an appreciation of the old, new materials will undoubtedly become more common in car design. Carbon fibre and lightweighting will be crucial. Safety and equipment demands have meant that cars haven't enjoyed the 'dematerialisation' of other industries' products. Beer cans have fallen in weight over the years. They were 73 g in 1950 and 21 g in 1972 and are only 13 g today, according to Kevin Kelly's book *The Inevitable*. But cars haven't. A 1922 Austin Seven weighs 320 kg. A 1974 VW Golf weighs 790 kg. A 2019 basic Golf is 1,245 kg. If cars are to maintain large ranges and run on electric batteries, they will have to get lighter in the future.

Car interiors will also transform as a result of the increased focus on autonomy. There is likely to be a shift away from wood and leather as the go-to choices to represent luxury. It's already causing some friction in the world of established car manufacturers. In particular there was a ding-dong between Lagonda and Bentley after the 2018 Geneva Motor Show.

Aston Martin, whose luxury-focused Lagonda brand had remained dormant for years, revealed its Vision Concept, a Rolls-Royce-sized, all-electric, aerodynamic limousine to be produced in its new Welsh facility from 2021. The dramatic body was styled by studio head Marek Reichman. There were promised self-driving features, a retractable steering wheel and 360-degree spinning seats. This was to be expected; although Aston Martins should always be driven, the Lagonda brand is more at home with the notion of autonomy.

But more controversial was the interior, imagined with the help of English furniture designer David Linley. He'd blended

Silk, ceramics, cashmere and hand-woven wool seats redefine luxury in the Lagonda Vision.

ultra-modern materials with the traditional. The modern included carbon fibre on the trim panels and ceramic tiles that open and close to alter the ventilation and adjust the volume of the music. The traditional element comprised hand-woven cashmere upholstery and silk carpets. There was no wood and leather to be seen.

Reichman, himself an RCA alumnus, has been quoted getting a dig in at his luxury competitors. 'Rolls-Royce and Bentley are Ancient Greece today. I worked on the original Phantom. The brief was Buckingham Palace on wheels. It was important to do that to establish it. But the world has changed and the royals have changed [too].'

The chief executive of Rolls-Royce Motor Cars, Torsten Müller-Ötvös, hit back saying that the sports-car maker had 'zero clue' about attracting rich motorists and that 'they really don't understand our segment, they really don't understand the customers'. He was 'sorry to be so blunt'.

Such squabbles aside, another aspect of car interiors that is likely to transform in the future – and this is one that I'm particularly partial to, as a presenter on *The Gadget Show* – is the technology inside.

Gadgets!

No new motor-show concept car is complete without the ever-increasing scope of touchscreens. Buyers are certainly swayed by 'infotainment'. In a study based on 2015 data,

McKinsey found that 37 per cent of car users would switch from their current car make to another if it was the only one to offer full access to apps, data and media. Meanwhile 32 per cent of respondents would be willing to pay for these features on a subscription basis. The passion varies between territories. In China 60 per cent would switch manufacturers to gain connectivity features whereas the figure in Germany was 20 per cent. The younger you are and the more urban your abode, the more likely you are to make the switch. It should be a big deal for car manufacturers. Most customers are aware of, but seemingly not worried by, data-privacy implications of people having their driving data. However, McKinsey found that people were more relaxed if the apps involved relate directly to driving.

In terms of who controls this area there's going to be an interesting battle between car manufacturers, tech companies and maybe some altogether new players. At the moment bringing your own phone into a car and using Apple CarPlay or Android Auto is far better than trying to wade through car manufacturers' built-in infotainment systems. These are often confusing, difficult and costly to update. Also, given that the media is likely already on your phone anyway, it can be far too slow to load.

However, the 'bring your own device' model may prove inadequate in a world of more sophisticated connected car features. I suspect manufacturers will group together and offer certain features in conjunction with technology companies, forming a few competing car-related ecosystems, much as Google's Android operating system supplies several different phone manufacturers. These will encompass new features like real-time parking information, self-parking facilities and even collision avoidance. Developing applications for such ecosystems may prove as attractive to car manufacturers as it is for existing mobile platforms, giving car users access to the work of hundreds of thousands of motivated software creators.

I already want a sort of multi-window approach in Android Auto or Apple CarPlay so I can have Spotify or a podcasts app open on one screen and Google Maps or Waze on another, while a further screen is devoted to the manufacturer's in-car offerings such as terrestrial radio or the heating system. Indeed, one could almost imagine every surface in a car's interior being a screen, some of them interactive, so that while you're watching it, it'll be watching you for any commands, or to monitor your health or attention levels.

You may not even need to touch the screens. Augmented-reality systems might work with your smart contact lenses so that you can swipe through your heating controls with a gesture rather than have to make smudgy dabs on a screen.

The RCA's Professor Dale Harrow thinks that the future may well see a backlash against all this in-car technology. 'There's a lot of debate going on about the amount of information presented to you in cars. One thought is that a deep digital detox is required. You maybe should keep the car as a clean space. We're seeing lots of screens appearing – but the opposite of that is to leave them out and make it a very calming space.'

It will still be (mostly) about styling

Whether they're manufacturers' concept cars or student designs, the most memorable models that I've seen are the ones with that most traditional quality: kerb appeal. Perhaps above all else, car design is still about that emotional draw of a wonderful shape – a matter of surfaces and shapes and how light falls on them. As Coventry's design-course director Aamer Mahmud put it, 'It's got to be something that's so beautiful that people can't resist having it.' For me, three of the students' designs particularly embodied such values.

Arash Shahbaz's engaging update on the concept of an MGB mixes the modern and traditional in unexpected ways.

Arash Shahbaz has transported the MGB into the twenty-first century with a blend of tradition and modernity.

The shape of the car is cutting-edge modern, with a residual wraparound windshield, yet it manages to evoke the volume, proportion and stance of the MG original and even hint strongly at its two-slot radiator grille. And, remarkably, it would use bold, dominant leather straps to fasten the bonnet and echo earlier MGs from the 1930s. There would be no self-driving kit here. Power would come from four separate electric motors with full independent torque vectoring, so it's designed with both the road and the track in mind.

Shyamal Kansara showed me his Eclipsx. With wheels at an extreme camber and highly aerodynamic bodywork based round a flipped-over aeroplane wing it would, he claims, be as frisky as a fighter jet yet generate between 6 g and 7 g of downforce for extreme cornering – significantly larger forces than a current F1 car at maximum speed. It's a mesmerising-looking shape, though the tyre wear has yet to be estimated and may prove an issue. So far, the scale-model toy version he's built shows its agility. It can certainly turn on the spot; and he thinks that as well as performance applications it could help the elderly get into more ordinary cars by flattening the wheel arches, and also inform more efficient bus designs.

Christopher Saetrang's reimagining of an Alfa Romeo, the Milano 2027, is technologically advanced yet packed with heritage, showing influences from open-wheeled Alfas of the 1930s with their 'narrow grilles and open wheels', while keeping elements of the delightfully pretty 1960s Spider Duetto with its boat-like rear body shape. Any shortage of power encountered when putting his chosen MV Agusta motorcycle engine in a car body has been overcome by supplementing the petrol power with electric motors and supercapacitors. Everything from the bumpers to the roof – and even larger parts of the bodywork – would be fully customisable to maximise customer choice and also generate extra income for the company. There's a Formula One-style legs-in-the-air driving position but a sliding seat mechanism ensures that the car is still easy to get in and out of, in order to avoid alienating older buyers.

These three cars, all beautiful and desirable but incorporating massively different levels of technology, make you confident that the best days of car design are anything but over, and there's a good chance we'll see a truly exciting and engaging visual feast on the road ahead.

FOUR

SPEEDING AHEAD

the Future of Performance Cars and Motorsport

In a quote that surely applies more to the car than to any other means of transport, Aldous Huxley once famously said: 'Speed, it seems to me, provides the one genuinely modern pleasure.' Certainly the car's capacity to offer that thrilling sensation, magically under the driver's control, has proved more seductive than any of its other features.

But for every Toad who loves nothing more than driving fast on the road, captivated by the blur of foliage and tarmac being sucked past the windows, there is a nannying puritan who regards speed as the ultimate form of selfish waste and a pointless danger to others. Here, prejudice meets genuine concern and it's not always easy to separate the two.

Such naysayers haven't stopped the fastest cars becoming ever faster. In 1949, the Jaguar XK120 held the production-car speed

Fastest production road cars since 1949

Year	Car	Top Recorded Speed
1949	Jaguar XK120	125 mph
1955	Mercedes-Benz 300SL	151 mph
1959	Aston Martin DB4 GT	152 mph
1963	Iso Grifo GL 365	161 mph
1965	AC Cobra MkIII 427	165 mph
1967	Lamborghini Miura P400	171 mph
1968	Ferrari 365 GTB/4 Daytona	174 mph
1969	Lamborghini Miura P400S	179 mph
1982	Lamborghini Countach LP500 S	182 mph
1983	Ruf BTR	190 mph
1986	Porsche 959	198 mph
1987	Ruf CTR	213 mph
1993	McLaren F1	221 mph
2004	Koenigsegg CCR	241 mph
2005	Bugatti Veyron EB 16.4	254 mph
2007	SSC Ultimate Aero TT	256 mph
2010	Bugatti Veyron 16.4 Super Sport	258 mph
2017	Koenigsegg Agera RS	278 mph

Christofer Sætrang's Milano 2027 reimagines an Alfa Romeo sports car with supercapacitors and a motorcycle engine.

A vision of extreme agility with extraordinary wheels. Shyamal Kansara's Eclipsx racer.

Bringing a sense of exploration to tourism, Stavros Mavrakis's Zephyr is the gateway to a self-driving romantic Greek island experience.

Instead of retrofitting kit to an existing production car Google designed their own third-generation self-driver in 2014. The egg-like shape and Smart car size aimed to make the technology friendly.

Automation need not be boring. Steered by AI and inspired by Tron, the Robocar is the world's first driverless racing car.

Hyped-up Hybrid. The Mercedes-AMG One is a £2 million, 1,000-plus bhp, Formula One car for the road.

Brainpower on your windscreen. Technology company WayRay develops holographic augmented-reality to help you to find the best racing line... and somewhere to park.

The perpetual dream of the flying car gets an image boost in the shape of the Terrafugia TF-X. Hybrid power, autonomous flight and vertical take-off and landing are all promised within a decade.

Renault's Symbioz Concept is car as home extension: an autonomous lounge on wheels with matching furniture. Renault regards traditional clay modelling as a vital part of its design process.

BMW's plug-in hybrid Vision M NEXT concept is distinctively futuristic while fully exploiting the company's rich design heritage. You can choose autonomous 'ease' mode or 'boost' for hands-on driver control with 592 bhp on tap.

record at 124.6 mph. By 1968 the Ferrari 365 GTB/4 Daytona achieved 174 mph (I can recall being very excited by this as a seven-year-old). The McLaren F1 scored 221 mph in 1993 and held the record for eleven years. Manufacturers have seriously pushed limits in their efforts to outdo each other in flat-out speed, and these record-breaking cars represent some of the finest achievements the world of motoring has to offer.

The latest high-performance 'supercars' and 'hypercars' are the fastest yet. The new American outfit Hennessey Special Vehicles unveiled its upcoming Venom F5 in Las Vegas in 2017. With its bespoke 7.6-litre twin-turbocharged V8 engine it's aiming to achieve 301 mph and 0–186 mph in under 10 seconds and 0–249 mph in under 20 seconds. The production run is to be limited to 24 and buyers will, apparently, be 'hand-picked'.

Providing you can stump up the asking price there are more cars than ever capable of hitting 200 mph, including convertibles like the Lamborghini Huracan, Ferrari 488 and McLaren 570s Spider, and even four-seaters like the Ferrari GTC4 Lusso, the Aston Martin Rapide and the Bentley Flying Spur. For those with an eye for a bargain the £89,900 BMW Alpina B5 can also hit 205 mph.

The Koenigsegg Agera RS holds the title of world's fastest road car at the time of writing. The Swedish manufacturer's one-off £1.5 million car clocked up 277.87 mph on a two-way run on a closed public road in Las Vegas in 2018. The technology is conventional but powerful: the RS's 5.0 litre turbocharged V8 produces a fearsome 1,341 bhp.

The popularity of supercars and hypercars – or whatever you

call these elite expressions of sculptural beauty and blistering power – is surging (among certain very well-heeled drivers at least). Bolstered by rising income inequality, the growth of new wealthy classes round the world and their seemingly insatiable desire to own something fast, supercar sales have soared in recent years. But can these vehicles survive an age where environmental and safety concerns seem to get more pressing by the day, and where any sort of wanton performance and speed is frowned upon?

In search of some answers I drove down to see Simon Saunders of Ariel. The firm took its current name in 1999, after a pioneering bicycle and motorcycle manufacturing company created by James Starley in Coventry in 1870. It's most famous for its highly individual, extremely lightweight exoskeletal sports car, the Atom. It's one of the fastest-accelerating cars in the world and a special V8 in 2012 could reach a top speed of 168 mph. Ariel also produces an off-road buggy based on the same design principles as the Atom, called the Nomad, and a 'naked' exoskeletal motorcycle called the Ace.

Those of a cruelly critical disposition have likened driving Ariel cars to driving a piece of scaffolding, but I've always found them tremendously exciting as both driver and passenger. Ariel operates from a small factory that appears to be literally bursting at the seams, located in Crewkerne, Somerset, many miles away from Britain's traditional motorsport corridor. The place looks like a large brick farmhouse built round a court-yard. I inspected the bright, well-disciplined manufacturing room, where one individual is responsible for building each car and bike from start to finish and puts their name on the completed vehicle. The atmosphere of quiet dedication there was impressive.

The company is about to launch its own supercar, named the HIPERCAR, which in a semi-acronymic way stands for 'high-performance carbon reduction' – an absurdly sensible name considering it's styled to look like some form of automotive sci-fi fantasy. Saunders is immediately aware of the strange contradictions inherent in the supercar breed.

'It's a bizarre product. They tend to get driven round relatively slowly with the odd traffic-light Grand Prix, making a lot of noise. We had someone here from America the other day, and he asked where he could go to see lots of interesting cars. And I said that your best bet is probably Mayfair. You'll see everything. A Bugatti; every kind of Lamborghini; all the Ferraris, Bentleys, Rolls-Royces. In this country most supercars are in London. I'm sure [the concentration of ownership] is the same round the world. In the US a lot of them are in Beverly Hills. It needs to look sensational, make the right noise and be fast away from the traffic lights.'

But it's also vitally important that it can perform quickly round the track, at least in theory. It's all about bragging rights, top speeds and lap times.

'As a supercar manufacturer, you are ranked by your performance. We will want our cars tested on a track by journalists and test drivers, whether it's *Autocar* or *Top Gear*. We can't say we're not going to do that: a "we don't do track times" attitude. You'll just get a "couldn't do it" rating.'

Saunders worries that eventually the bubble will burst. People will ultimately realize that there's hardly anywhere that these cars can be used to their full potential. 'Take the Bugatti Chiron. It does, what, 250 mph. But has any Bugatti owner actually done 250 mph? Where would you do it? It's a technical achievement. You have to take your hat off to these people. But people don't use it for that. They use it for driving round town, showing off and having a nice car.'

He's concerned that people will lose interest, especially as many supercars are, he feels, quite boring to drive at low speeds.

'We had a test day a few days ago and sampled a lot of supercars. Sounds like a hard day out! But everyone came back so disappointed. Ferraris and Lamborghinis have become better cars in that they're actually more reliable and easier to drive. Your average Ferrari has been designed, wind-tunnelled, engineered and tested at Fiorano. It'll do a fast lap time at Dunsfold, in the hands of a racing driver or a journalist, but they can be a bit soulless. People say the same about 911s. A new 911 is a fantastically fast car. But getting into an old one – people get excited about that. It's a strange world, the supercar world.'

There's a difficult balance to strike between comfort, raw power and safety. Take the legendary 1992 McLaren F1, which was the most sensational car of that decade and perhaps of all time. A true icon, designed by Peter Stevens and Gordon Murray under the leadership of Ron Dennis; just 106 cars were produced. Ownership of this seminal car, which currently is valued at about £20 million, grants you access to one of the most exclusive automobile clubs in the world, second only to having a Ferrari 250 GTO in your garage.

TV presenter Tiff Needell tells me more. 'It had 600 horse-power, which, with no computers involved, is huge power – as Rowan Atkinson proved. It's got no traction control and 600 bhp is too much for an average driver on public roads.' He's referring to the *Mr Bean* actor-comedian twice crashing his much-loved burgundy model, which on the second occasion needed over £1 million of repairs. That is quite some insurance claim. Despite such misfortunes, he still reportedly sold it for almost $12,000,000 in 2015, substantially more than the sum he paid for it.

Now, supercars have become much more sensible. 'All they're doing is giving you huger and huger headline horse-powers,' says Tiff, 'and then giving you bigger and bigger computers to make sure you never have that power. So, when you open the throttle you don't get 1,500 horsepower, you get about 200. They can't be let loose without traction control or else they'd all be in the ditches. You'd have more fun in a Mazda MX-5 or Caterham 7.'

The supercar grows up

I can recall driving supercars myself for the first time in the 1980s. They'd looked brilliant in magazines and as posters on my bedroom wall, but the reality was often a disappointment. A Lamborghini Countach springs to mind. It was bright red and borrowed for filming a test against the Ferrari Testarossa. The scissor doors were scene-stealingly gorgeous and the noise of the 4.8-litre V12 thrilling, but the crude build and seats reminded me more of a kit car than the apex of automotive engineering. It seemed to require two feet and two hands just to depress the clutch and operate the gear lever. I was thoroughly exhausted by the time I'd arrived on location. The Testarossa was rather better, incidentally, and a foretaste of how supercars would develop. Although wide for its day, it offered impressive visibility, comfortable seats and surprising refinement. You could go for a long drive without fear of nervous exhaustion and actually enjoy being in command of its delightfully musical flat-12 engine.

One man who agrees with me is Dan Parry-Williams, the director of engineering design at McLaren Automotive. This is the sister company of McLaren Racing, one of the world's oldest and most successful Formula One teams. It built on the influence of the McLaren F1 and launched a new series of supercars starting with the 12C in 2011.

'If you go back to the old Lamborghinis they were difficult to get in and out of; you couldn't see where you were going. You certainly couldn't see where you'd been. Broadly speaking they were uncomfortable and intimidating. I don't want to single out Lamborghini but that was the general sense of what you'd expect in a supercar. The cars would get horribly out of shape and scare the living daylights out of you. There was a sense that they weren't accomplished track cars and they were very compromised road cars.'

McLaren's probably done more than any other to make supercars more accessible and enjoyable as a day-to-day driving experience while retaining their competence and speed on the track. To Parry-Williams, the way to avoid a future decline in interest due to the cars being boring at everyday speeds is to engineer in more low-speed tactile feel and involvement.

'We need to jealously guard the characteristics that people like about our cars. Our cars are about driving pleasure and experiencing what [our customers] might call engagement. They're having an exciting drive in the car because we've worked hard on all touch points, whether it's the calibration of the throttle, the brake feel, the steering feel in terms of speed and lateral acceleration build-up, the vibration in the cabin, the noise quality inside the car as well as outside, or the gearshift calibration. All these things are carefully designed and tuned so that the response of the car is proportional to what you're putting in – if you want to drive the car harder your experience is more rewarding as a result. We have to make sure we safeguard that as we move into a new era where maybe we haven't got the traditional soundtrack of a multi-cylinder big engine.'

I first visited their stunning Norman Foster-designed curved glass lakeside headquarters in Woking when it opened back in 2005.Production is now set to expand to 6,000 cars a year and the company has announced that it'll be close to 100 per cent hybrid, with eighteen new models announced before 2025. Only a very few ultimate niche vehicles will be non-hybrid.

Parry-Williams thinks that electrification and using light-weight materials will most probably ensure the supercar's survival in a potentially hostile world. The two technologies will keep those all-important lap times and performance figures improving, while the environmental credentials continue to increase as well.

'We're wholeheartedly embracing hybrid technology. We've been open about our pathway towards electrification and the number of cars that will be electrified in our future lineup. That's very much the core of our strategy.'

As for their lightweight credentials, the company has a new composite-materials centre in Sheffield; and they have tremendous experience in the field, having made over 15,000 so-called MonoCells since 2010. This is the F1-inspired carbon-fibre tub, in which the driver and passenger sit, that forms the primary structure of all McLaren's road cars. They've been developing the technology to be able to produce higher volumes at more affordable prices. This will mean they can make a larger portion of their cars out of the material. They are also trying to simplify the cars, so that they can make them out of fewer parts. For example, if they can replace a roof structure that was formerly made out of twenty parts with just two complex carbon-fibre mouldings, it would be substantially cheaper, better quality, lighter and easier to assemble. They're even pioneering the use of recycled composite materials that can be used in some areas of the cars.

Short circuits – can supercars become fully electric?

The main cloud on this horizon is rapid change in some countries that might make hybrids illegal. This is a problem because the power-to-weight ratio will suffer. Teslas have brilliant 0–60 times of around 2.5 seconds in their fastest models and YouTube is full of videos of them beating Ferrari 458s and Porsche 911 Turbo Ss but they can't sustain them on a track day. The batteries overheat. Weight and the sheer demands of the track make pure electric supercars if not impossible then pretty frustrating for their owners.

'What Tesla have done fundamentally is that they've specified an energy cell and pushed it much harder for very short periods of time.' Nick Carpenter of Delta Motorsport tells me. 'So, your 0–60 run is way beyond the spec-sheet capability of that cell. But what they've understood is that you can push that cell for very limited periods of time, a few seconds. When you floor it in a Model S you get to 60 in 2.5 seconds but you're never going to do more than 4 or 5 seconds before you reach your speed limit and beyond so you ease off.'

If you want something purely electric you have to accept a few knocks to the performance or the staying power. Aston Martin's first all-electric car, the Rapide E, has a top speed of 155 mph and a relatively leisurely 0–60 mph time of just under 4 seconds. The company has fitted a comparatively small 65 kWh battery, presumably to help keep weight down, though this limits the range to around 200 miles. Porsche appears to be prioritising endurance over headline-grabbing acceleration figures with its first fully electric car, the Taycan. Ferrari is only just starting to explore a pure electric car.

Croatian company Rimac and Tesla are throwing bigger and bigger batteries at the problem. Rimac's powertrain is included in the £2 million Pininfarina Battista, which debuted at the Geneva Show in 2019, promising sub-2-second 0–62 mph times, a 217 mph top speed and 1,900 horsepower from its 120 kWh battery pack. Tesla's Roadster 2.0 is set to have a 200 kWh battery and offer similar acceleration and a top speed of over 250 mph, with a range of over 600 miles at highway speeds. Rimac claim that their 1,914 horsepower C Two, with slightly more power than the Battista, will lap the Nürburgring twice without any loss of speed. Whether these cars really will deliver this stunning performance lap after lap without overheating is yet to be proven.

At Ariel, Simon Saunders hopes the politicians won't demand pure electric for the sake of it. His HIPERCAR uses inboard electric motors with a range-extending turbine engine charging the battery. The engine is used only to top up the battery, rather like the petrol engine on the original BMW i3, but is vastly more powerful. It boasts 1,180 bhp, can achieve 0–60 mph acceleration in 2.4 seconds and 0–100 mph in 3.8 seconds. It will offer low levels of pollution and high levels of economy, and the ability to keep driving all day if you want to.

'A turbine which will be running at 120,000 rpm is very, very efficient once it's up to speed,' says Saunders. 'And, once it gets going, it's almost emission free. Delta Motorsport are working with Johnson Matthey to make the start-up procedure as clean as possible. There's a certain amount of emissions in the start-up but not much. The range extender is very, very, very low emissions. Our calculations show that we can go for 500 miles on a 30-litre tank of fuel.'

Ripping up the supercar rulebook – Ariel's gas-turbine-electric 1180 horsepower HIPERCAR.

Turbine cars are nothing new of course. Rover built a prototype called JET1 in 1950 that went on to record 152 mph over a flying kilometre at Jabbeke in Belgium in 1952. Chrysler lent a limited run of fifty experimental cars to potential customers in the 1960s. They offered a spectacular soundtrack but proved thirsty and suffered from terrible lag on acceleration as the turbine gained speed. Their exhausts also tended to singe pedestrians' legs. Making the turbine part of a hybrid powertrain means it can operate at maximum efficiency, helping to keep heat within the system, while battery power can be used to compensate for any lag.

A turbine is also much lighter than batteries would be to achieve the equivalent power. 'Added lightness' was the 1950s catchphrase of the remarkable Colin Chapman, who invented the rear-engine racing car and produced remarkable classics like the original Lotus Elan and Lotus Seven. 'It's more true than ever today,' says Saunders. 'It's not necessarily the cheapest way, but certainly the easiest way to improve performance, fuel economy and so on is to make vehicles lighter.' The company has even experimented with creating titanium components – a monumental headache, as titanium can be engineered only in a chemically inactive atmosphere. This can involve an airtight tent full of argon with people reaching in through sealed sleeves; most annoying if a tool needs to be retrieved from outside, as the tent would need to be purged of oxygen once more.

Certainly as it stands, zero emissions for the sake of it may well compromise the sheer unassailable stamina that is the raison d'être of supercars. And then we'd have to make do with survivors from what will be seen as a golden age of performance road cars. Whatever happens to the power source, though, changes elsewhere in the car industry will definitely have their effect at the fast end too.

Supercars and future tech

With supercars so eye-wateringly expensive, Parry-Williams at McLaren Automotive thinks we could see a move to car sharing rather than ownership. 'You won't necessarily have to own the vehicle to get your hands on one. It'll show up when you want it and you won't have to worry about it when you're not using it.'

Professor Dale Harrow from the Royal College of Art sees the potential for supercar ownership of the future to go in two different directions. On the one hand, a company might produce a series of cars that are used exclusively on race tracks – so, more like owning a luxury yacht or a racehorse. On the other hand, it might create a whole service experience with hotels and resorts where the car can be driven in a unique environment.

McLaren is already offering its wealthy customers a broad range of holidays and other adventures, whether driving through the Italian mountains or on historic race tracks like Hockenheim. As of October 2018, its website featured this enticing invitation: 'Winter may be fast approaching, but our programme of events isn't cooling off just yet. Whether you put yourself in the hot seat at the legendary Kyalami circuit as part of our Epic 9-day driving tour across South Africa, or join us 200 miles north of the Arctic Circle for an exhilarating experience on the ice – ensure your winter is truly epic.'

The supercar club is a thriving international phenomenon that looks set to flourish. You pay a subscription and indulge in events where you can take cars to the limit. If (like most of us) you can't afford to buy your own, you can share one of the club's garage of exotica. Britain's Auto Vivendi has a fleet that includes a rotating selection of Lamborghinis, Ferraris, Aston Martins and McLarens. Membership fees to drive them are between £12,500 and £33,500 per year – which doesn't seem so extortionate when you consider that a major service for a Lamborghini costs around £4,000 and a set of tyres about £3,000.

Freedom Supercars in the US offers a similar deal but the really exclusive clubs, like the Supercar Owners Circle, set up by Swiss brothers Florian and Stefan Lemberger, require you to own your car. Membership is restricted to those with a collection considered worthy, probably valued at more than £5 million. You get access to bespoke track days, fast-track passes to the latest cars from select manufacturers and excursions like Alpine trips over specially closed roads. It's a sort of Davos on Tour for the world's elite car owners.

Brands will increasingly broaden out to offer more than just the car itself; ownership appeal will be as much about shared experience as it is performance. This will be especially true in the supercar sector. Aston Martin are also keen to offer hotels,

Merch too far?

How far can you extend a brand? Ferrari knows no shame, it seems. Its first branded amusement park opened in Abu Dhabi in 2010, with Portaventura following in 2017. More are planned for Spain, China and the US. Then there's the Ferrari-branded Segway that, at $10,000, was nearly twice the price of the original and made you look twice as ridiculous. The bright-red branded Acer netbook wasn't much better. It was one of the slower computers you could buy at the time, even with the vroom sound effect on start-up.

Overpriced and poorly specified mountain bikes are another speciality with luxury car brands but there are also plenty of exceptions. The 2011 £12,000 Specialized S-Works McLaren Venge justifiably laid claim to being the fastest road bike in the world at the time and the 2012 £25,000 Aston Martin One-77, with its sophisticated on-board computer, body measurement and touch-screen, was widely regarded by pundits as the most advanced bike in the world when launched.

Perhaps the ultimate brand extension is the merchandise associated with the £2.5 million Bugatti Chiron. I'm not talking about the £3,000 leather jacket, or the £400,000 Jacob & Co watch, but the Niniette 66 yacht, priced at $4m and including a hot tub, a fire pit and a champagne bar. Buyers beware however. There is rumoured to be a longer 80-foot model on the drawing board, and you wouldn't want to be trumped.

yachts and other luxury experiences. It makes a welcome change from most off-topic brand extensions by car companies, which have long been rather poor quality. But for these more ambitious augmentations to work companies will have to take them very seriously.

Autonomy is a development that will mix very well with supercars and speed. Many manufacturers are already considering the inclusion of in-car expert electronic driving tutors – something like KITT in *Knight Rider*. Heads-up displays will communicate with the driver on how to corner, suggesting lines through a bend; like a video game, but for real. The idea that a virtual Lewis Hamilton could teach you how to drive on a race track is going to be really compelling for the person who owns that Mercedes.

Porsche CEO Oliver Blume is on record as looking forward to the day when you can compare your own driving abilities with a Formula One driver. If you find out you're ten seconds slower than Mark Webber round a track, the onboard system would analyse why by looking at your braking, racing lines, etc. It's a mixed- or augmented-reality driving format, with information added in your field of view as a driver. This information will be filtered, so you receive only what you need, and on both road and track it will assist with driver skills, keep you out of trouble and help you get the most from the car while keeping you safe.

The high cost of supercars increases the likelihood of their manufacturers having the margins to introduce new assisted-driving technologies. Saunders suggested that high-end manufacturers might develop the new technology, get the patents and then sell it to the volume manufacturer, who would later use it in such high volumes that the cost would go down. Volkswagen have already shown a virtual race trainer based on a Golf. You can use it to get a handicap for your driving talent: as in the sport of golf, you get a par for the course, here set by an AI driver, which you have to try to match or surpass.

Racing

The visceral draw of speed is not only for the driver. From the car's early days, speed has also been savoured by spectators vicariously revelling in the thrill and danger of competition. Across the world, racing has created its own hallowed temples of speed, from Bonneville and Brooklands to Indianapolis and the Nürburgring. Race-car technology has also helped to develop more quotidian road models. As the technological demands of motorsport depend on efficiency and constant progress, developments in tyre technology, braking, hybridisation and aerodynamics often first appear on the track.

It's certainly a big industry. Formula One, traditionally the pinnacle of the sport, was sold to Liberty Media in 2017 for $4.6 billion and claims over 490 million viewers worldwide. And the taste for watching cars go round and round in circles is being particularly keenly adopted by emerging economies. Brazil is F1's biggest market, with 115 million viewers, and new circuits like Hanoi in Vietnam are part of an expanded calendar. In

Britain alone the industry is estimated to be worth £10 billion to the economy.

Will the industry go through the same upheavals that the road-car industry is currently experiencing? How will it be affected by electrification, autonomy and the explosion of environmental concerns? For some, the future survival of the sport depends upon embracing electrification. And this is on a total basis, not just the hybridisation seen in Formula One's energy-recovery systems. But if electric supercars are difficult to produce, the demands of track racing are even greater. A spike of power for road use lasts a few seconds but in racing it is sustained for lap after lap after lap. Batteries drain incredibly quickly and overheat fast. If you need ten times the power, you've got ten times the current. As the heat generated is proportional to the square of the current, you've then got 100 times the heat. If you don't want everything to melt, thermal management is a big issue.

In spite of this, Formula E, the all-electric racing formula operated by the world motorsport governing body, the Fédération Internationale de l'Automobile (FIA), is leading the way. Conceived in 2011 and with the first championship starting in Beijing in September 2014, it claims it's 'reinventing racing for the 21st century'. It's cunningly devised. They've gone for city race tracks, like Paris, Hong Kong, Monaco and New York, because that's potentially the biggest market for electric cars. While working hard to ensure that the 335 bhp cars have attractive styling, they've kept the bodywork and chassis stock so they can stop teams spending a fortune fiddling about with aerodynamics and the suspension. They've also compelled all teams to use the same battery. This stops any one of the teams doing an exclusive deal with whoever's battery technology is currently judged to be best.

Consequently, by international motorsport standards, it's relatively cheap. Formula E costs about $40 million per team per year, which is a fifth of the cost of Formula One, but it already attracts half the global audience. Not surprisingly this is proving an appealing option for car manufacturers keen to establish their electric credentials. Formula E's second-generation car appeared for the 2018–19 season and is raced by manufacturers including Mercedes (with Venturi), Audi, Porsche, BMW, Jaguar, Nissan, DS-Citroën (with Techeetah) and Mahindra as well as new Chinese EV manufacturer NIO. All this manufacturer interest in Formula E will undoubtedly enhance the image of electric vehicles.

Phil Charles is the technical manager of the Jaguar Formula E team. The team operates from the Williams Formula 1 team's headquarters near Didcot in Oxfordshire. The building contains the largest private collection of Formula One cars in the world, all squeaky clean, polished to perfection and dramatically displayed. I strolled round them with Charles, who studied automotive design at Loughborough prior to specialising in vehicle dynamics and aerodynamics. He worked with the Renault F1 team and Toro Rosso before taking up the Formula E challenge.

The cars in the museum represent an era where the most competitive developments were in aerodynamics – bodywork tweaks to smooth airflow round brake ducts or enhance ground force, for example. With Formula E, the competition is all about how to manage the available energy from the supplied battery through the motor, the inverter and the gearbox – the bits they've allowed teams to play with. The progress has been so quick that the championship has advanced from drivers having to change to a second fully charged car during the 45-minute race to one where a single car can keep going for almost the same duration.

'In Formula One I was employing people who were vehicle dynamicists and aerodynamicists,' says Charles. 'Here I'm employing mathematicians. Because they're doing a lot of work on the energy side – to be really clever with the energy.' The result seems to be that drivers are in constant communication with the wider team during races. One aspect of this driving teamwork is 'energy cycling', or how to conserve energy round a lap. The power has to be 'scheduled' to eke out its full potential.

'In the Formula E car we tend to accelerate, accelerate and accelerate and then get to a certain point on the straight where we lift and coast so you cut the power and pull the regen paddle. That point is particular to how you do that straight in the fastest way you can with a given amount of energy. We work all this out. We give Mitch [Evans, one of their drivers] lights and beeps and some of it is automated for him. We can't do it live for him but the car is programmed to help him.'

It's the same on the bends. 'Let's say, for example, that for a low-speed corner we make the car balanced so that it rotates itself. He turns the steering and the car turns easily. If it understeers and he has to use the throttle to turn the car, then he's burning energy to turn the car. It's simple but the way we balance the car around him helps him save energy. That's kind of key. A tyre slide somewhere along the line will cost you energy. The maths guys we are using to look at the energy cycle are also looking at how Mitch is driving all the time.'

I wondered if this all made the cars more boring to drive. I spoke to Mitch Evans, who is from New Zealand, started with GP3 and who was, at sixteen, the youngest person ever to win a Grand Prix. He confirmed that the required driving style was rather different, and that he found it more difficult to detect wheel spin in an electric powertrain, but if he had any complaints he wasn't admitting to them.

TV presenter Tiff Needell was less equivocal. 'The throttle response isn't so good. Though you have all this peak torque from zero, you're stuck with one level of torque whatever your throttle position. People rave about the torque but you don't want a lot at times because it breaks traction. So unless you have traction control you get very embarrassed very easily.'

Whatever the truth about the driving experience, it is certainly a fact that electric racing is continuing the trend – which is occurring in conventional racing too – that the driver is becoming more of an operator, rather than solely responsible for their own decisions.

Another concern I had at Didcot was whether the model of motorsport using closely controlled formulae could prevent useful innovation, both for the sport and the much-vaunted crossover between racing cars and road cars. It tends to favour incremental optimisation and little tweaks. Greater freedom in what the teams can do might yield more interesting and radical progress. Formula E, for example, demands a single rear-mounted motor driving the rear wheels through a gearbox. It therefore rules out experiments with developments like motors in wheels and the more sophisticated approach to torque vectoring this allows.

Torque vectoring refers to technology that can vary the amount of torque sent by a power unit to each individual wheel. This can be used to help a car corner, accelerate and brake more effectively. With a central battery and a power unit in each wheel, designers can control the power distribution by computer, substituting a cable for heavy driveshafts and gearboxes. There would be a huge incentive for Formula E teams to develop this technology, if only the Formula were less prescriptive. Phil looks forward to a more varied future when such things are possible, maybe with the next generation of the car in 2025.

Finally, there is the elephant in the Formula E room; the most obvious question for someone coming from Formula One to Formula E, and a key one for the future of electric motorsport: what about the lack of noise? For Phil Charles (rather predictably) it is not a major issue. 'When you go to a Formula One garage and hear the noise, that hits you in the face. But when you're tuning in on TV you're not getting that aspect. I want to see the [Formula E] championship maintain really good racing. Because if you're able to overtake it's really entertaining. And when you actually get people there and they see that the cars actually look pretty quick, they're going round tight and twisty circuits, they're overtaking each other, and they have crashes and dings as they're trying to do it, then the noise gets forgotten because it's so exciting anyway. Formula One noise isn't pretty – it's more of a kick-in-the-nuts-type noise, and personally I don't miss it.'

Electric sprints

While endurance racing and all but the shortest of rallies look like nonstarters for electric power as it stands, Formula E's success has inspired suggestions for other forms of electric motorsport, particularly those that require short, powerful sprints. These include rallycross, hill climbing and, most intriguingly, the land speed record.

The current holder of the outright World Land Speed Record is Thrust SSC, a twin turbofan jet-powered car that achieved 763.035 mph – 1227.985 km/h – over one mile in October 1997 driven by RAF pilot Andy Green. This was the first supersonic record with the car cum rocket reaching a scorching Mach 1.016. Its successor has been relaunched, under new management, as Bloodhound SR, and is aiming for 1,000 mph.

There are many and varied land speed records and electric cars are already holders of some, but they're some way off the outright pace. The current electric land speed record of 341.4 mph was set by the Venturi Buckeye Bullet 3 (VBB-3) on the

⚙ Esports

Removing the noise from motorsport is one thing, but what about removing the whole car? Esports – multiplayer video games played competitively for the benefit of spectators – will become ever more closely entwined with motorsport. Though slow to take off compared to first-person shooters, battle-arena and strategy games, race-car esport is now becoming an ever more important part of what, by 2022, should be a $2 billion industry with over 600 million viewers.

No other esport so closely parallels the real thing, and in some ways it's better. With no risk of personal injury and shattering priceless carbon fibre, the racing can be closer and riskier – and driving skills can be honed over hours of virtual practice. The drivers aren't hidden in their cockpits and you get to see them hard at work. In the future, sponsors may even defect to esports events to reach a younger audience.

Whatever your preferred game, there's an esports championship to go with it, including Gran Turismo Sport, Forza Motorsport and rFactor. Meanwhile real race formulae are branching out into esports, from NASCAR to Formula One. F1 esports has four qualifying rounds, organised in tandem with real races, culminating in a stage where the esports F1 teams – versions of real ones – pick their drivers for the final. The winner of F1 esports gained a real drive with Mercedes for the first time in 2018, and a cut of the $200,000 prize fund.

With the colossal cost of entering real motorsport a major handicap to discovering future Ayrton Sennas and Jack Brabhams, esports could solve a talent shortage as the new grassroots of motorsport. You'll progress from one to the other. You'll just need the price of a game (and usually steering wheels and pedals) to take part rather than the usual arm, leg or kidney.

Feet up and flat out as the 2018 F1 Esports series gets underway at the Gfinity Arena in London.

Bonneville Speedway on 19 September 2016. Developed by a team of students from Ohio University, it is four-wheel drive and highly streamlined with an extremely low drag coefficient. The car uses two motors and can vary its power split between front and rear axles, usually favouring the front to avoid 300 mph powerslides. The main problem for electric land speed record cars is finding somewhere to run them. Thrust SSC strutted its stuff in a South African desert which provides plenty of room, while the sandy surface isn't a problem for its jet power source. But electric cars are dependent on putting their power down through rubber tyres and they need a higher friction surface. Amazingly this, more than anything else, may stop electric land speed record cars reaching the very highest levels of performance.

Rallycross may embrace electric motors in the relatively near future. It's long been one of the most spectacular and spectator-friendly motorsports. You can see the whole course from one vantage point, the races are short, overtaking is constant and there's plenty of body contact. I can vividly remember watching races broadcast by the BBC from Lydden Hill as a child in the 1960s with somersaulting Mini Coopers and Hillman Imps battling it out with Escorts and Cortinas. The top cars are now four-wheel drive. The new electric ones on the drawing board will be based on a carbon-fibre chassis supplied by longstanding French motorsport company Oreca and using Williams-developed batteries. Rather like Formula E, the batteries and chassis are standardised while manufacturers will be allowed to develop their own drivetrains around two 250 kW electric motors, which together will produce the equivalent of 670 bhp. Volkswagen, Audi and Peugeot are said to be keen to support the sport's move to electric propulsion. Independents will be allowed to develop their own drivetrains and bodies from an FIA-approved base design. Not all manufacturers are keen to embrace the switch, however, and it seems that the

Frenchman Romain Dumas smashes all records up the epic Pikes Peak Hillclimb in his all-electric Volkswagen I.D. R.

electric championship due to start in 2021 will have a slightly lower status than the petrol-powered one that will continue to run alongside it.

For inspiration and a reminder of how electric cars can lead the way, one needs to look to another field of motorsport where they are proving their prowess and popularity: hill climbing. Pikes Peak is a brilliantly mad event that takes place every year on the 14,115-foot mountain in the Rockies, North America. A twelve-mile-long road with sheer drops climbs right to the top. It's a thrilling and dangerous course for a hill climb, even though it's now fully tarmacked and the cars go one at a time rather than in groups.

In 2018, Volkswagen proved electric propulsion's potential when double Le Mans winner and former World Endurance

Champion Romain Dumas raced the company's all-electric I.D. R up the hill, not only smashing the record for electric cars but also besting Sebastien Loeb's long-standing record, set in 2013 in a Peugeot 208 T16. Loeb's time was 8:13.878. Dumas and the VW I.D. R finished the course in 7:57.148, despite a track that was slightly damp in places. An advantage of electric cars is that whereas combustion engines lose performance as they climb and the air thins, electric motors are consistent in their power output whatever the altitude. They can also exploit the fact that the thinning air offers less aerodynamic resistance.

Unlike Formula E or Rallycross, the hill climb is lightly regulated – and VW could let loose their design creativity. They maximised downforce through aerodynamics and took advantage of the relatively short course and relatively low speeds by keeping the batteries in the 670 bhp car small to save weight. They also used carefully designed air flow to cool them. It's now thought that it will be hard for a combustion-engined car to beat VW's record in the climb, such was their expertise in balancing the car's aerodynamics, cooling flow, battery size, weight distribution and power delivery. VW even compensated for the quietness of the car by installing a hooter.

Autonomous racers

Some people see not only a future for electric power in racing but a role for autonomy too. Roborace is a company that was founded by Russian smartphone entrepreneur Denis Sverdlov in 2015. It specialises in developing autonomous racing cars. I met its strategy officer, Bryan Balcombe, at the Goodwood Festival of Speed, where his company's Robocar became the first-ever fully autonomous car to ascend the venue's famous hill climb. He had the studied, calm good nature and open smile of a man who's relaxed in the face of often hostile criticism. His background is conventional motorsport and he's served sixteen years in Formula One as a systems engineer.

The Robocar was designed by Daniel Simon, who also created the vehicles for the film *Tron: Legacy*. It's about the same size as an F1 car, has a 540 kWh battery and four separate 135 kW motors. Costing around £1 million to build, it has a claimed maximum speed of 195 mph. Its autonomous technology is similar to those of its road-driving cousins and the intention is to set up a 'driver's championship'. As Bryan explains, 'We have radar, LiDAR, sonar, machine-vision cameras, GPS and inertia sensors and slip-angle sensors [as well as] all the normal motorsport sensors that you'd have on a car such as tyre temperatures, tyre pressures, suspension movement and everything to do with the powertrain. So, all of the data is provided to the AI driving software and the teams work on providing the best AI driver.'

The traditional motorsport influence is evident in the standardised elements of the car. 'We run a standardised hardware platform so all the vehicles are identical. At the moment all the sensing and communications are identical and the teams just write the software. In terms of their freedom they can write whatever software they want in whatever way they want. They just have to pass a driver-licensing test before they're able to compete.'

Bryan envisages teams of autonomous cars competing against each other. 'All the sensor data is identical so you have a fair starting point. What sensors do you choose to use? How do you weight those? What computer algorithms do you have attached to them? Those are the decisions that need to be made for you to perceive your environment. That's the challenge number one. Challenge two is once you know where you are in the world and what the other objects are, what's your driving or racing line that you're going to take? Your trajectory. That's a really challenging task in itself.

'That's really how we point the competition. Perception is one level. And above that is the driving task, which is what as humans we want to see. Racing interaction: two cars at least interacting with each other.'

The cars learn the tracks where they race in slow motion and have to pass a qualification process in what they call a DevBot vehicle, a version of the race car that can also be human-controlled. 'We need to do that from a safety perspective and also from an entertainment and performance perspective. We want to know that these AI drivers are good-quality drivers.

'At the moment we find the AI software is 10 per cent or 20 per cent below where a human driver is. Most of that is because of the safety margin, which in our public demonstrations we've been willing to take. We leave a 1-metre safety margin to the wall at Formula E tracks, whereas a driver will nudge up against the wall if they're on the limit. We don't ride the kerbs when we go through chicanes, but a driver will and there's a lot of time to be made in those areas.'

Goodwood provided some AI challenges. The car is usually raced at Formula E events where the track has concrete walls either side. The car can detect where it is in relation to vertical surfaces rather more easily than the edges of the Goodwood track, which are grass.

'When you're trying to use LiDAR on a horizontal surface it's difficult to differentiate because there's no height variation. So the only way to do that is looking at machine vision and looking at the difference between road surface and grass, which is called image segmentation.'

Fortunately they'd already done work with grass using hyper-spectral cameras that are now being used in agriculture to look at crops. They use infrared and other ranges of light beyond human vision and can take account of the way grass changes colour, height and surface characteristics depending upon the time of year and the weather conditions. But, even so, I remain sceptical.

I think it's hard to envisage this form of autonomous motor-sport having much appeal unless it becomes a sort of *Robot Wars*-style crashfest and I can't see the serious governing bodies of motorsport sanctioning that. But Bryan was obviously not perturbed by regulatory hurdles and even had another, rather more extreme-sounding suggestion that involved mixing autonomous or highly assisted race cars with actual road traffic and encouraging no-holds-barred racing, all on real roads, among everyday cars, buses and trucks, driven by the likes of you and me.

'If motorsport's going to play a role in developing Level 5 autonomy for the road – vehicles that can go anywhere; any situations, any roads – that technology has got to grow beyond the race track. It's got to start looking at other types

✦ Vrrrrrrrrr!

Formula One may boast the biggest global audience of any motor sport but there's a constant worry that not enough young spectators are attracted to the sport. It's a problem usually blamed on racing being too boring. Cars go round in processionary circles and the circuits conspire to prevent overtaking. Far from gladiatorial combat, miniscule iterative engineering provides the edge. Sometimes the most interesting thing about the sport seems to be the politics.

Maybe the answer lies with technology, including virtual and augmented reality. Youngsters who aren't attracted to the sport could be put behind the wheel feeling the forces, the vibration and the noise through a combination of headsets, exoskeletons and haptic smart clothing. Sensors on the driver would transmit the sensations they feel to the audience. Spectators would be able to see the instrumentation, touch the controls and sense the airflow round the car. Even the driver's brain signals could be read and communicated to viewers at home, who would also be able to customise their cars, get a fully immersive view of the race and have the option of competing against the real drivers.

of formats, challenges and competitions that really develop the software that's required. That would mean looking at real road environments filled with traffic and having cars racing through that traffic environment. A completely different type of motorsport than we've ever seen before.'

In the meantime, driver assistance is already happening in some branches of the sport. Bryan tells me that 'assisted driving is almost creeping into Le Mans at the moment. In the GT class of racing you have a radar system and a camera system, looking rearward and automatically identifying the cars that are coming past you with a range of about 250 metres, giving the driver information about when to let a car past that isn't a competitor. In a way that's an assistance technology like an advanced rear-view mirror, if you like. It doesn't control the vehicle. If it started to control it we'd say that was augmented. Then you have both the human and the machine trying to control the output of the car.'

Future racing technology will be about more than electrification and autonomy. There's a whole host of other innovations that will smarten up the sport. Augmented and virtual reality will link audience and driver to provide new levels of spectator involvement. The use of more advanced composites and new wonder materials like graphene and carbon nanotubes will also open new avenues to explore. Bodywork will change its shape on command and self-repair. Tyres will morph too. Hankook has shown a prototype tyre that broadens out on corners, exposing an aerodynamic insert that boosts ground force but then slims down on the straights for lower wind resistance.

Others reject any suggestion of a techno-utopian view of motorsport. Maybe we should just revel in the petrol-head gloriousness of traditional motorsport as the only place in the world you can still go to hear the sounds, smells and raw competition of petrol engines thundering round a track – an antidote to the boredom of an autonomous and electric world. That's certainly Tiff Needell's view.

'Motorsport will eventually realise it can't be the science lab anymore because science has overtaken us. The more the world goes autonomous and electric, as it inevitably will, the more motorsport will be petrol and entertainment and hopefully we'll just have wild motorsport for things you never see on the roads. Like NASCAR. They've got 300 quarter-mile dirt ovals with racers going round every night of the week. In American motorsport they're still using 1950s cars pretty much. No driver aids. Just big, rorty V8s howling round in any sort of big old chassis you want. We'll be like the gladiators of Roman days – entertainment that's enjoyable for both driver and spectator.'

There's no room for autonomy in Tiff's view of the world. Nor for that matter in Ross Brawn's. He's the new boss of Liberty's Formula One empire who's revising the championship in 2021 with entertainment in mind. Quoted at the Ferrari exhibition at the Design Museum, London, in 2018, he said:

'I think the change in transportation is a fascinating area. We are challenged in Formula One as to how much relevance we should have and we believe our fans and our enthusiasts enjoy a certain aspect of Formula One, and we can't necessarily maintain that or create it if we go an electric-car route, or even

So much more than a black circle – Hankook's prototype racing tyre that maximises downforce and minimises air resistance.

an autonomous-car route. The last thing we need is autonomous cars in Formula One, because the driver is the gladiator, the driver is the hero, and the one we want for people to really engage with.'

But might this petrol-head's dream be impossible because of an environmental backlash against traditional motor sport – with all those resources devoted to going nowhere, all that degradation in air quality?

Fuelling waste or driving innovation?

Racing cars are typically designed to be fast, not to meet emissions and environmental regulations. The smell of burning race fuel has often been quoted as part of the appeal of motorsport events but will we soon start worrying about breathing it in? Then there's all the tyre and brake dust. At the Goodwood Festival of Speed in 2018, I even found myself worrying for the first time in my life about what I was inhaling while watching some drift cars shredding their tyres in the cause of entertainment. Attitudes may be changing without us old guard realising it.

Evidence of direct pollution is limited because, for some reason, people don't seem to put up air-quality measuring stations near motorsport venues. However, it's certainly true that Formula One cars used to be gas-guzzlers. Back in 2007, each race car emitted around 1.5 kg of CO_2 for every kilometre it drove, or about nine times that of a family car, but they've since become more economical. Race fuel has become more like standard petrol. Early fuels were reputedly so potent that the engines had to be washed in ordinary petrol at the end of the race to stop the fuel from corroding them. They contained a huge array of chemicals and additives, featuring large quantities of benzene, alcohol and aviation fuel.

Studies of a race in Montreal noted that race days tended to coincide with high pollution levels, particularly if it was a day when there was a thermal inversion. But most of the nasties were the result of general traffic and fireworks displays rather than the race itself. And there was another vital statistic noted: that one private jet flying in for the race emitted more toxins than all of the race cars *combined with* the emissions from the cars of all the spectators travelling to the event, which rather puts things into perspective.

A study of the Grand Prix of Baltimore – an IndyCar Series race held on a street circuit in Baltimore, Maryland, between 2011 and 2013 – concluded that the racing had very little environmental impact and race days had less pollution than usual because more roads were closed, reducing the normal social, commuter and commercial traffic. It's certainly true that the pollution caused by motorsport is almost entirely down to teams lugging their equipment round the world and fans travelling to the circuits. The actual racing constitutes just 0.3 per cent of Formula One's emissions while teams do 100,000 miles a year in planes to test cars and compete. But, then again, air miles are a consequence of many sports, not just motorsport – and indeed of any gathering that brings people in from all over the world, even committees on climate change. Ironically, cycle racing has a huge environmental effect due to the travelling demands of teams, equipment, spectators and the media, even though the racers themselves are obviously, in a narrow sense, zero emission. Also, with cycling there's not even the corollary benefit that technologies on the track can yield improvements on the road.

Greenpeace has previously tried to disrupt Formula One events in its habitual way – climbing on buildings with banners and suchlike. But the anger has normally been directed against corporate sponsors – for example Shell and their Arctic drilling plans – rather than the sport itself. In fact the charity has made very encouraging comments about Formula One. Its former executive director Kumi Naidoo was an ardent devotee, praising its 'technology, sportsmanship and innovation'. Individual teams have also tried hard to become more environmentally conscious. McLaren for example became carbon neutral in 2011, largely through controlling its emissions but also with some amount of offsetting. It recycles two thirds of what it throws away and sends zero waste to landfill.

So, motorsport looks like it's going to generate no more environmental angst than any other global sport with roving teams and mass audiences. However, to keep appealing to a wide audience, it is going to need to embrace both its noisy petrol-head traditions and an exciting technology-packed future. The gladiatorial glories of the past will live on while technology, from electrification and esports to radical design and virtual reality, will make it more immediate to a wider audience while re-establishing the positive link between race-car and road-car development. Once again, bleeding-edge development on the track will drive progress on the street.

FIVE

HACKERS AND CRASH-TEST DUMMIES

Safety and the Age of Automation

If you ever find yourself in a procrastination cycle watching YouTube, it won't be long before you encounter a 'Bad Drivers' compilation. Whether it's percussive parking, road rage or dysfunctional driving, these videos make clear that for every careful driving instructor there's a plethora of road users who should never be allowed behind the wheel. Road crashes now kill 1.35 million people a year globally. And, despite driving authorities and the industry working hard to improve road safety, particularly in more developed countries, the sheer success of the car has meant that this annual global death toll has continued to rise.

The first recorded fatality caused by an automobile was in Ireland, in 1869, when Mary Ward was thrown from an

⚙ Ugly ducklings

The 1950s saw a bizarre collection of concept cars designed in the US to signal a new era of safe driving. What they lacked in practically, they often made up for in their monstrosity. The most spectacular was the 1957 Aurora, built by Father Alfred A. Juliano, a Catholic priest. The nose was designed to be a padded scoop to catch errant pedestrians and provide crush space. The windscreen swelled out miles in front of the driver so their head didn't hit it in a collision. There were side-impact bars, a built-in roll cage, seat belts and a padded instrument panel.

Slightly more conventionally shaped but no less innovative is the 1957 safety car conceived by Cornell University and insurance company Liberty Mutual. Seat belts, nets to help prevent whiplash and extensive padding were all features that would be adopted by later production cars. More unusually there was no steering wheel to impale the driver but two sliding levers surrounded by cushioning material.

Frustrated car designer Father Alfred Juliano wanted to build the world's safest car, but instead his Aurora achieved global automotive fame for its sheer ugliness.

experimental steam car and fell under its wheels. In 1895, there were only two cars in the US state of Ohio, yet they still reportedly managed to run into each other. So far this century, more than 650,000 people have been killed on the roads in the US alone. Sadly, when humans and cars meet, bad things can happen. Consequently, from the outset, the evolution of the car has moved in step with technology designed to prevent its devastation.

Safety statistics must always be interpreted with care, but deaths and serious injuries have often trended downwards in wealthier countries. The UK, for example, currently has some of the safest roads in the world. Measured by road deaths per 100,000 population, it was behind only Micronesia and Sweden according to the World Health Organisation in 2015. I sometimes wonder if this is because the traffic is becoming so bad it's just getting hard to reach potentially fatal speeds. But the research says otherwise.

Cars have unquestionably become safer but it's been a slow process, punctuated by many odd inventions along the way. You can trace the history by browsing the plentiful range of car-crash YouTube videos, as referred to above. Crashes are often the best way of testing safety features and quite coincidentally seem to be endlessly popular as well. When I started producing *Fifth Gear*, one of Channel 5's demands was that we incorporated plenty of crashes into the show. This apparently wasn't just for the wanton destruction; they had to be car crashes that illustrated something in particular. We worked hard to come up with various scenarios: big cars into large cars; new cars into old cars; truck sideswipes – a problem on British motorways, where left-hand-drive trucks change lane and collide with cars in their blind spot. We also investigated the dangers of unrestrained boot luggage, along with killer road signs, kerbs and lampposts that might squash your car or catapult it on a spectacularly dangerous trajectory. We used remote car radio control but with full-sized cars, all developed by an enthusiastic team at Cranfield University.

The allure of twisted metal can almost border on fetishism, as demonstrated by movies such as *Crash* or those odd sixties American rock songs like 'Dead Man's Curve' with macabre themes derived from real-life collisions. Then there's the mystique that surrounds celebrity car deaths. Albert Camus was famously killed in his publisher Michel Gallimard's Facel Vega in 1960, when it hit a tree in Villeblevin, France. Isadora Duncan's silk scarf entangled itself around the axle and open-spoked wheels of her mechanic lover's Amilcar CGSS near Nice on the French Riviera in 1927. She was pulled from the car and broke her neck. Marc Bolan's fabled demise was in a Mini 1275 GT, driven by American singer Gloria Jones, which hurtled into a tree on Barnes Common in 1977 and killed him instantly.

And yet, beyond all the mayhem and morbid fascination, car crashes can be incredibly useful. The car industry has learned from them and safety has vastly improved as a result. First there was the emphasis on structural integrity: if your car could survive being chucked off a cliff and drive off again this was deemed excellent. Then seat belts appeared and brave stunt drivers could perform repeated barrel rolls in what would now be regarded as 1950s classics. The next developments were crumple zones and safety cages; cars became tougher in the middle to protect the occupants, and softer at the extremities to cushion the initial force of an impact. Prototype and production-car crash tests have become a staple for upholding safety standards.

Legislation will continue to get tougher but a big incentive for improvement comes from consumers themselves – people will continue to demand cars that are safer. The importance of the market can be traced back to the work of American consumer campaigner Ralph Nader and his infamous book *Unsafe at Any Speed*. Here he criticised cars like the Chevrolet Corvair with its swing axle rear suspension and rear-mounted engine that made the car spin with remarkably little provocation. He exposed cars with interiors full of sharp edges into which occupants were impaled during impacts – somewhat like mediaeval battle implements. Thanks to his work the US became the world leader in automotive safety. A framework of federal crash-test standards followed and the National Highway Safety Bureau announced its Experimental Safety Vehicle (ESV) project, to encourage the development of safer cars by 1980.

The initial results weren't necessarily attractive, mainly thanks to their enthusiastic use of rubber. One thinks of Volvos with their chunky bumpers or the Fiat ESV 1500 prototype of 1973, a miniature car with massive black growths disguising the bodywork. Joan Claybrook, a former colleague of Ralph Nader, began independent crash tests of cars on the US market in 1979.

They don't make them like they used to. Euro NCAP tests show you'd be killed or seriously injured in a 1997 Rover 100 (left) but likely to get away with minor bruises in a 2017 Honda Jazz (right) in the same 40 mph smash.

Called the New Car Assessment Programme (NCAP), it was the first-ever consumer safety rating system for cars. It harnessed the power of consumer information to accelerate safety. The programme generated instant media interest and manufacturers soon started to compete to make their cars safer. They'd proved the power of the market could improve crashworthiness standards.

In contrast to America, European countries initially relied on more forgiving crash tests; in the UK these demanded merely that the steering wheel moved less than 6 inches when the car hit a block of concrete at 30 mph. There was little incentive to make cars safer or to include better bodywork or airbags, for example. But by the mid-1990s over 45,000 people were being killed annually in road crashes across the EU. And attitudes were changing – led by the UK.

The Berkshire-based Transport Research Laboratory (TRL) was established by the UK government as a centre for road research in 1933 and eventually privatised in 1996. It had long campaigned for a tougher frontal crash test combining a higher speed of 40 mph with an offset barrier that concentrated the forces of the crash on less of the car's structure. Car manufacturers kept up a steady resistance to improving standards but with Department of Transport pressure, together with support from the Swedish government and the FIA, the TRL launched a project known as Euro NCAP. The first results were launched in February 1997 and aroused strong interest from the media. One of the cars tested, the Rover 100, collapsed completely and became an icon of the inadequacy of prevailing safety design.

Cars were awarded between one and five stars, with the Rover 100 unsurprisingly scoring just one star. Accompanying detailed reports specified the forces on the various parts of the test dummies used to represent car occupants and pedestrians. According to David Ward, a crashworthiness expert, 'the industry even tried to restrain their own competitive instincts and agreed not promote Euro NCAP results in their own marketing at all. This "gentleman's agreement" collapsed in a matter of weeks as more successful manufacturers couldn't resist boasting about a good rating!'

It's a competitive force that's resulted in stronger car structures, vastly better restraint and airbag systems and much improved pedestrian protection. Features such as electronic stability control (ESC) have been included in the assessment programme as well.

This is where computers detect skidding and loss of steering control. The system brakes wheels individually to help the driver regain stability, a technology compulsory on all new cars in the EU since 2014 and the US since 2012. Another area is the development of autonomous emergency braking (AEB), where cars detect objects in the vehicle's path and apply the brakes automatically if the driver hasn't spotted them.

David Ward claims that the combination of EU legislation and Euro NCAP crash ratings has saved around 78,000 lives since 1997. Today, 25,000 and not 45,000 people a year die in road crashes across the EU, which now has the safest road network in the world.

Safety gadgets of the future

Such improvements are only the beginning. To find out what novelties we're likely to see in coming years, I spoke to Matthew Avery of Thatcham Research, the centre established by the UK's motor-insurance industry in 1969 with the specific aim of reducing the cost of insurance.

He predicts that increasing numbers of sensors will soon be fitted to most new cars to detect vehicles you could collide with and even warn you about vehicles crossing your path. 'The next thing we're doing for Euro NCAP is Turn Across Path. A few cars, for example some Volvos, will already detect cars coming in the other direction and prevent you moving into the path of the other vehicle. The car uses the same sensors as it's using for emergency braking.'

Avery believes that a large proportion of deaths and serious injuries could be prevented by this technology,

⚙ Smart materials

Making cars safer has traditionally meant making them heavier, but this won't be true in the future. Materials will be more advanced, with greater use of aluminium, magnesium and composites arranged in ways to channel energies in a crash but without the extra lard.

More intriguingly, materials will also be smart and be able to change their state. One example of this is Google's sticky bonnet, or as they call it 'an adhesive vehicle front end for mitigation of secondary pedestrian impact'. Normally the bonnet has a conventional paint finish; but should the car strike a pedestrian the impact makes the surface adhesive. Basically, the person sticks to the bonnet instead of bouncing off and getting run over.

Apple has patented a shape-shifting car seat that can warn you of trouble ahead. New materials promise to be able to detect an impact and stiffen in a controlled fashion to absorb it. They'll be lighter and occupy less space, but be more effective at controlling a collision and preventing forces being transmitted to car occupants.

New materials may revolutionise roads too. Highways England is about to start trials of a new technology that allows sunflower oil to repair roads. The technique has been successfully tested by Dr Alvaro Garcia at the University of Nottingham, who was inspired by a Spanish edition of the television programme *Masterchef*. A contestant used spheres of jellified liquid in their cooking, which popped open and burst in the mouth, releasing their flavour – a technique known as spherification. In a brainwave of lateral thinking Garcia realised that capsules of oil could be placed in asphalt used for surfacing roads in order that when the roads start to crack the capsules would break open and release the oil within, softening the road around it. This helps the asphalt 'stick' back together, effectively filling in cracks and making roads self-heal.

including what crash investigators call Looked but Failed to See (LBFTS) incidents. This is where a driver, for example, wants to overtake and looks for traffic ahead but isn't actually concentrating. Their brain deceives them into thinking all is clear and they pull out on to the opposite side of the road. But all isn't clear.

'We can then start to do junctions as well. We're looking to introduce it into Euro NCAP 2020.' Cars will start looking sideways with special sensors fitted for the job. They'll be able to detect and alert drivers to avoid errant motorcycles or children about to run across your path. They'll help prevent the sorts of horrifying crash seen in the 1970s Think Once, Think Twice, Think Bike campaign (see YouTube again). Rear sensors will also be included in the testing around this time. These will have an extended range to alert you to fast moving traffic steaming up behind when you're about to overtake. Autonomous Emergency Steering (AES) will go beyond current lane guidance, with its gentle 'nudges' on the wheel to keep you on track, and adopt a more assertive attitude, steering away from potential impacts.

The arsenal of airbags is set to expand even further in the near future. At present, side impact tests are focused on minimising the forces endured by the dummy sitting in the side of the car hit by the test barrier. Beefed-up body structures and airbags are designed to protect that occupant. But a third of casualties in side impacts are sitting on the opposite side of the car to the one that's been hit. For example, car occupants may collide with each other, banging their heads together. More airbags help to compartmentalise the car and assist in preventing grisly human-on-human carnage.

The Euro NCAP test will also start to pay attention to a tricky issue known as 'compatibility'. When cars are crashed into a static barrier – as is the case in most crash tests – they are really replicating a collision with another identical car. The reality is very different. Big SUVs hit small hatchbacks, sports cars slide under people carriers and, at the most extreme end, tiny city cars get squashed by trucks. As the car fleet is getting more diverse the compatibility problem gets worse. More extreme differences in weight and vehicle heights make it highly unlikely that crumple zones will crumple equally or that the 'right' parts of two cars' structures will coincide in a crash.

The result is an automotive arms race where responsible parents or those with a keen survival instinct buy the biggest vehicle they can. Volvo have been keen to point out that nobody's been killed in one of their jumbo-sized XC90s in the UK since the model was launched in 2002 – an achievement of invincibility that the model shares with the equally vast Audi Q7. But who knows how many superminis they've flattened.

Matthew Avery talked through how cars will change to compensate. 'It means you've got to make the Fiesta a bit stiffer and bit stronger and the Range Rover a bit weaker and softer so that the Range Rover is doing some of the work for the Fiesta.' The test will also encourage more uniform car structures with fewer aggressive hard areas that punch through other cars' bodywork in a crash.

Increasingly cars' restraint systems will be expected to adapt to different weights and heights of driver too. The sylph-like will have different airbag firing patterns to the big and burly. Older people currently have a poorer survival rate in crashes because they're literally more fragile than younger drivers. Seat belts for more mature drivers may need to be triggered more gently while smart materials that change their shape, strength or stiffness in response to a specific stimulus will also play a part in safety enhancement.

Euro NCAP is looking to prevent unattended children (and presumably pets) dying of heatstroke in cars by incorporating systems that monitor the temperature in the car and ventilate it automatically when necessary. Busy parents can apparently forget they've left their offspring locked in the car; and, as temperatures can reach 47°C inside when it's just 22°C outside, death occurs in minutes. Though not a huge killer, an average of thirty-six children die every year in the US this way and many more across the world.

Death rates are often much higher on the roads outside Western developed economies. This is consequent to multiple causes. In Thailand, where the death rate is ten times higher than it is in the UK, the large number of mopeds and motor-bikes are a major factor. Elsewhere driving tests, road design and attitudes to risk are responsible. However, the statistics also reflect the fact that car manufacturers have tended to palm off older and less sophisticated designs on poorer countries – frequently charging top dollar in the process. Even where vehicles have been specifically designed for these markets they've been very poor in terms of crashworthiness. However, a Global NCAP program is now underway, devised and promoted by UK charity the Towards Zero Foundation, which campaigns for a world free from road fatalities. The program's mission is to bring European and US standards to the rest of the world, by naming and shaming manufacturers whose cars aren't up to scratch – the Rover 100 effect gone global.

In one round of tests in May 2016, all five India-made models achieved a zero-star rating – the Renault Kwid, Maruti Suzuki Celerio, Maruti Suzuki Eeco, Mahindra Scorpio and Hyundai Eon. But it looks like such shaming is having an effect. In 2018, the Tata Nexon became the first car made in and sold to the Indian market to achieve the Global NCAP's five-star crash-test rating.

Outside the orbit of NCAP, there are other safety devel-opments expected. Car responsiveness and crashworthiness may have improved over the years, but it's become weirdly hard to actually see the road outside the car. If you throw yourself back in time and consider a boxy family car from the 1970s and 1980s, something like a Mk1 Golf or an Audi 80, you're immediately struck by the greenhouse-sized windows and your ability to see every corner of the car. It's amazingly easy to place on the road and park. But curvier, more aerodynamic bodywork with higher waistlines has reduced the glass area of more recent models. Similarly, the easiest way to meet demands for more crashworthy bodywork has been to thicken pillars, which has worsened visibility.

The Royal Society for the Prevention of Accidents in the UK thinks the problem is so bad that it has called for special driver training to deal with it. Cameras and screens might help, as well as transparent pillars with a lattice structure providing the strength. Volvo (who else?) showed such a prototype system as long ago as 2001 in its Safety Concept Car. Jaguar Land Rover and Bentley have used screens in the pillars as a more expensive and technologically sophisticated solution.

Meanwhile the HGV market, which is perceived as having a bigger and more urgent problem with visibility – sometimes resulting in collisions with vulnerable road users like pedestrians and cyclists – may lead the way in terms of legislation. In 2016, the London Mayor, Sadiq Khan, launched the world's first Direct Vision Standard (DVS) for HGVs. It rates what a driver can see through the cab's windows (not reliant upon screens, mirrors or cameras). If the plans are adopted, vehicles not meeting the required standard won't get an HGV Safety Permit and won't be allowed on London's roads. Similar standards are now being discussed across Europe as part of the European Commission's review of the General Safety Regulation. These are indeed positive advances, but it's no use having a better view of the road if you're looking at your phone.

Distraction driving

In several developed countries, road casualties have bottomed out and even started to rise again. As ever with car crashes, nobody's exactly sure why. However, the consensus is that it's down to our lack of concentration – and distractions. Whether it's the use of smartphones or dashboards practically built out of multiple touchscreens, there is more opportunity than ever to lose focus while driving.

Most of the evidence for distraction of professional drivers comes from naturalistic studies of HGV drivers in the USA, where researchers observe real behaviour while interfering with it as little as possible. One study reported that drivers were performing tasks unrelated to driving during 56.5 per cent of safety critical events. Also, drivers texting while driving were twenty-three times more likely to be involved in a safety-critical event than drivers who did not. However, drivers who talked on a mobile phone while driving were no more likely to be involved in a safety-critical event than those who did not. This would appear to give credence to the idea that it's looking down and interacting with a screen or keyboard that causes the most heinous levels of distraction, while holding a conversation with someone else seems relatively fine.

More careful analysis is required. There's long been quite a bit of uncertainty on the topic. Take road-safety charity Brake, which has come up with some rather odd suggestions over the years – including the idea of forcing newbie drivers to avoid motorways because of their higher speeds, despite the fact that they are far safer than other roads. Brake regards listening to music while you're driving as a no-no because it means you're using some of your brain capacity for listening. I think that's ridiculously puritanical and scientists seem to agree. The University of Groningen in 2013 suggested that, overall, listening to music while driving has very little effect on driving performance. Indeed, any effects that were measured turned out to be positive. Apparently music can help drivers to concentrate, particularly on long, monotonous roads. Personally I'm convinced I drive better while listening to the radio and I shall continue to inflict BBC Radio 3 on my passengers as an aid to my concentration.

There are a number of possible solutions to our distraction epidemic. These might include increased use of heads-up displays or wearables that reduce the need for manual interaction and therefore keep eyes on roads. Voice control sounds like another obvious fix but current evidence suggests it may be distracting in itself – maybe because voice control is so flaky. Another option is driver monitoring, whereby cameras keep an eye on our driving by recording our hand and eye positions. For example, some Volvos (them again...) display a coffee cup when driving becomes a bit erratic, which indicates that the driver should take a break. Cars could similarly use cameras to monitor whether the driver appears fully awake; if you look like you're getting drowsy or distracted an alarm would prompt you to get back in the loop. Some Cadillacs already warn you if they detect you're not paying attention.

From governments the usual response to all safety concerns is to lower speed limits and find more ways to enforce them. The European Commission has proposed that all new cars will need to have intelligent speed-assistance systems from 2022. These will inform drivers of speed limits and use the cars' cruise control to adapt to them. They would rely on optical observation of road signs and GPS and would enforce speed limits by slowing cars automatically.

GPS-based systems have been trialled for decades but have frequently proven useless because of inaccuracies inherent in the technology. For example, you might be stuck at 30 mph when joining a motorway because the system thinks you're on a parallel road with a 30 mph limit. Reducing a driver's options can be a dangerous game. There are also occasions where a quick burst of speed is necessary– like overtaking a long truck.

The autonomy question

The discussion so far has focussed on the incremental improvements in design and technology that have been happening for decades. However, when full automation finally arrives, all our safety fears may be answered in one fell swoop. Without human error casualties on the road will diminish to near zero – or so the theory goes.

In the meantime, we will have a range of semi-autonomous systems that might actually be more deadly than no driving assistance at all. Because drivers think they can relax and look

Lower speed limits – help or hindrance?

In France, road deaths fell to a low of 3,268 in 2013 but then started to rise again, reaching 3,469 in 2016. In 2016, 55 per cent of fatalities were on rural two-lane roads. So they decided to lower the limit on single-carriageway roads from 90 km/h to 80 km/h for a two-year trial period from 1 July 2018. The government was quick to credit the move with lowering deaths again (to 3,259). But road deaths actually started to fall at the start of 2018 before the speed-limit reduction was introduced. So, did the slow-down really address the problem or was it just a coincidence? Whichever is true, the policy emerged as one of the initial major grievances of France's *gilets jaunes* or yellow-vest movement.

In Denmark a similar speed-limit trial was reversed in 2017 because higher speed limits actually meant fewer accidents, maybe because people felt less need to overtake. Speed limits were also increased on certain motorway stretches and this also resulted in fewer fatalities on those stretches of road. The slowest drivers increased their speeds, but interestingly the fastest 15 per cent drove 1 km/h slower on average. The traffic flows better too.

In the United States speed limits on interstate highways have risen in recent years and researchers from the Insurance Institute for Highway Safety found that for every 5 mph increase in a highway's speed limit, roadway fatalities rose 8.5 per cent. The debate will continue.

away from the road, they can be lulled into a false sense of security. Tesla, for example, has been accused of using language that might encourage owners of their cars to think of the vehicles as self-driving when they're not.

In May 2016, Joshua Brown was driving his Tesla in so-called Autopilot mode in Florida, USA, and was killed when the car failed to distinguish between the bright sky and a large white eighteen-wheel truck and trailer crossing the highway. A report into the crash by the NHTSA was definitive: 'All evidence and data gathered concluded that the driver neglected to maintain complete control of the Tesla leading up to the crash.' Other crashes have followed, including those where telemetery recovered from the car shows that drivers weren't holding the wheel in the vital seconds or minutes leading up to impact. In some cases, drivers have admitted to having been engrossed in their phone or another task.

Arguably the most serious and pernicious form of distracted driving is with Level 3 autonomous vehicles. These are cars that can drive themselves but the driver must be prepared to intervene if the car signals it can no longer cope. Most of the time the car will run fine on its own – and that is where the ultimate problem lies. As Matthew Avery tells me, 'The danger is that people won't understand the limitations of the system. They'll say, "I can go to sleep and do so-and-so." If you know the car's going to steer for you, you'll get on with your email admin.' In other words, the more you experience the car taking control the more your confidence in it grows.

With fully self-driving cars the issue is often mixing human drivers with cautious autonomous technology on the same road. In February 2016, a Google Lexus SUV was driving itself down El Camino Real in Mountain View when it encountered some sandbags surrounding a storm drain blocking its path. It paused and then proceeded to move over a lane to pass them. A bus driver behind wasn't expecting the manoeuvre and collided with the automated car. The Google test driver thought the bus driver had spotted the car and would slow to allow it into the lane.

The first pedestrian to be killed by a self-driving car was Elaine Herzberg in March 2018. An experimental Uber vehicle,

An Uber self-driving car after a collision in 2017. Self-driving cars will have to be many times safer than human drivers to gain widespread acceptance.

operating in autonomous mode, struck and killed her while she was wheeling her bicycle across a four-lane road in Tempe, Arizona. Preliminary investigations suggested that the car's autonomous systems had detected Elaine six seconds before the crash but classified her as an unknown object. Only after several seconds delay was she categorised as a bicycle with an unpredictable path. Then, just 1.3 seconds before the crash, the car decided emergency braking was required. The car's automatic braking system, however, had been disabled to avoid erratic behaviour while under computer control.

Though there was a human driver on board to take over in emergencies, she was looking down at a display and failed to brake in time.

The incident caused a flurry of negative publicity and Uber paused their self-driving testing for nine months, before resuming in December 2018. However, self-driving tests have continued to increase in number and scale. Waymo has even begun testing without a safety driver behind the wheel in both California and Arizona. The vehicles may not be perfect but they are already pretty safe, with a lower at-fault accident rate than cars driven by humans alone.

The hacking threat

As more intelligent cars (hopefully) reduce collisions, they also introduce new dangers. Not least of all, there is the risk of hackers using vehicles as deadly weapons. This threat has already made it into mainstream movies like *Fast and Furious 8*, where thousands of self-driving cars are shown rampaging through New York, cascading out of control from multistorey car parks and hemming in the film's heroes.

At a technology show in 2006 I saw that Microsoft was promoting a new collaboration with Alfa Romeo to bring their Windows operating system to cars. The platform featured now-familiar developments such as Bluetooth phone connectivity, USB sockets for playing media and accessing files, and voice activation for weather forecasts. As well as these benefits it also seemed to bring potentially alarming aspects of the Windows experience into the car: viruses, the Blue Screen of Death and a reputation for hanging, freezing and software crashes, for example.

I can recall asking car companies and Microsoft at the time whether the dashboard version of Windows was fully isolated from safety-critical functions like braking, steering and throttle control. I was assured there was absolutely no inter-connection. That may have been true then but it certainly isn't now. In 2015, two cybersecurity researchers, Charlie Miller and Chris Valasek, hacked into a Jeep Cherokee remotely using the car's Uconnect communication, navigation and entertainment system. The system proved to have no firewall or any other security that you might take for granted on your home computer so the researchers, once they'd got hold of the car's unique IP address, were able to take limited control of the car's self-parking system, operating its steering, engine and brakes.

An ethical hacker holds a circuit board from a Tesla. He'll try to reveal vulnerabilities and penetrate its security, finding what they call in the trade the 'attack surface'.

I went to visit Ken Munro of Pen Test Partners, an organisation employing several of the UK's leading ethical hackers – people who use their computer skills not to create criminal havoc but to expose weaknesses in systems for the common good. Ken is particularly passionate about car security and when I arrived the team was surrounded by a scattered assortment of Tesla parts. They were wielding oscilloscopes, laptops and other sundry gadgets. One person was hard at work attaching minute wires to a circuit board that would normally live in the Tesla's instrument panel, trying to find where electronic signals were unencrypted and what they could reveal about the car's security.

Historically the car industry has tended to regard security as a physical matter – best addressed by fitting tougher keys and locks. But with increasing numbers of in-car systems, protection against hacking is just as important. Munro takes a dim view of the industry's recent track record and cites what is known in the trade as the Megamos transponder hack. A group of researchers at Birmingham University and Radboud University at Nijmegen in the Netherlands discovered how to beat the transponder in the locking system fitted to a whole range of VW group cars, effectively leaving the vehicles with no security at all.

'When the researchers told VW about the problem and how to solve it, rather than VW engaging, talking to them and discussing with them, they slapped a non-disclosure agreement on them: a court injunction forbidding them from talking about it,' Munro says. VW chose to keep quiet and not issue a public recall. Instead they updated the cars quietly when they came in for service – a sort of soft-recall process that took about two years. During that time thousands and thousands of cars remained vulnerable.

Regarding the Jeep hack, Munro was scathing of how the company attempted to solve the issue: 'The "solution" was to post USB sticks to customers... By establishing the principle of sending USB sticks to an owner and the owner then updating it you're exposing them [to further threats]. All it would take was for a scammer to do exactly the same and no doubt one of them would have seen the exact syntax and format of the letter that came with the USB key. Owners could then be posted rogue updates and happily install them on to their vehicles.'

Hackers call the sum of the ways to get into a software environment the 'attack surface'. Such surfaces of most modern cars are both vulnerable and growing. Part of the problem is that the electronics of even new cars date from a bygone age. They're based round something known as the Controller Area Network or CAN bus. It was developed by Bosch in the 1980s and first appeared in a production car with the 1991 Mercedes S-Class W140. It's a messaging system that links together all the electronic-control units in a vehicle – the controls for everything from the engine management and the audio system to the power windows, lights and lane assist. It's robust and reliable but was developed in the pre-internet era and can be vulnerable to attack. Its central role means that the potential number of systems at risk in any hacking attempt is vast. The increasing number of cars that have the capability to phone home and connect to the internet only adds to the worries.

The E-call system was made compulsory in April 2018 on all cars sold in the European Union. It requires a cellular internet connection to let emergency services know a car's location in the event of a crash or other emergency. Penetrate the system and you can wreak havoc. In the case of an electric vehicle, even turning on the heating overnight could run down the batteries. Or, worse, you could inflict alarm and loss of control by suddenly turning on the sound system full blast when a driver is on the motorway. The opportunities for chaos are legion.

So far the Tesla model of security and updates seems to be the best. The security-conscious connected car can be updated remotely without trips to the dealer. Munro tells me that 'software updates can solve almost all security problems. Not all but most. That's where having a really robust over-the-air update platform is important. That's what most manufacturers are trying to do right now, so that when they do find a problem, instead of it being a multiple-thousand car recall which will cost millions and millions of pounds, they just push out a piece of software overnight.'

Car builders in the future will have to ensure they don't underestimate criminal resourcefulness and expertise, as they have in the past. In recent years, the whole keyless-entry saga has been one example of a woeful miscalculation. The problem caused a 20 to 30 per cent increase in car thefts in a matter of years. In the West Midlands area of the UK alone car thefts jumped from 5,344 in 2015 to 9,451 in 2017. Thieves can intercept the signal being generated by the key and boost it to gain access to the car and drive it away, even when the key is inside a house and a car is on the road outside.

According to Munro, 'People were aware of the problem about eight or ten years ago and the automotive industry was, as far as I'm aware, informed about it; but, because it was a very technically advanced hack, it was thought to be beyond the wherewithal of the average vehicle thief. The problem is that it doesn't take long for somebody to realise there's a market in this and automate the process.'

Attitudes in the automotive sector are slowly changing. Manufacturers are realising the huge costs involved if something goes wrong and they have to recall cars. But, as with all the Windows XP computers still in use today, it will be the older cars that are most at risk. What's even scarier is that when vulnerabilities are found they could apply to huge numbers of cars. Ken Munro asks me to imagine a vulnerability in all Range Rovers that could be exploited to make every one of them on the road turn left at the same time. It's a sobering thought indeed.

Even if hackers don't take control of your car they could try to extract some money by penetrating the infotainment system and installing ransomware. Imagine the first thing you see on a busy morning when you're in a rush to drive to the station is the satnav popping up with a message saying you can't start your car until you pay twenty quid. If the price tag was low enough and you needed to get somewhere urgently, you might well pay up. And the price would be higher next time.

Manufacturers may use network security as a further justification for forcing owners to use their dealers for servicing and repairs, rather like the ongoing iPhone saga where third-party screen repairs can stop the phone working after software updates. Only manufacturer-approved options will be allowed to be installed and we may see the end of common OBD (On Board Diagnostic) ports that allow independent garages to carry out repairs. Even dealers may not be secure enough to

⚙ Electric fireballs?

Tesla may have the best approach to online security but does electric power bring its own safety risks? Recalls for faulty batteries are a frequent occurrence in the gadget world. Samsung's Note 7 saga in 2016, with its unnerving catalogue of overheating and exploding phones, is one of the most notorious. The phones were recalled – twice in some cases – highlighting the potential fire danger of lithium-ion (li-ion) batteries.

Li-ion batteries in cars can suffer the same so-called thermal runaway, but their capacity is typically 8,000 times bigger than those in phones. They also suffer increased risks of impact damage. As the number of battery-powered vehicles increases, could there be a massive highway explosion waiting to happen? In a word, no.

In fact, electric cars could be less likely to catch fire than petrol-powered ones. Petrol is a risky material in itself and in the US there are about 174,000 car fires a year – equivalent to 55 fires per billion miles driven. Electric-car fires are relatively uncommon so far because there aren't many such vehicles on the road. Nonetheless, the latest estimates suggest that electric cars suffer fires at just a tenth of that rate.

The batteries are much better protected than the ones in a phone by firewalls and cooling jackets. Li-ion fires start slower than petrol ones, so there's more chance to get clear of a car in a crash. On the negative side, battery fires take longer to put out, can start days after a crash and can even reignite. When cutting bodywork to get someone out of an EV it's also vital to avoid high-voltage cables. Orange colour coding of anything over 60 volts helps prevent a very nasty shock.

be entrusted with the cryptographic keys that more complex connected cars will require. These may need to be kept at a company's HQ.

Fully autonomous vehicles will be much more vulnerable than cars today. The trouble with them from a safety and security aspect is their dependence upon arrays of sensors and vehicle signals that are so easily jammed. Signals without a physical connection can always be intercepted and wiped out by a criminal. Anything that requires vehicle-to-vehicle communications, such as platooning – where vehicles automatically follow one another in convoy – has safety vulnerabilities for which there is at present no known solution. In general, mass automation will bring with it a host of options for the tech-savvy terrorist.

And there's all that data to worry about

The threats from more intelligent cars don't have to result in huge crashes to be devastating. The vast volumes of data that vehicles are accumulating about their owners is another looming threat. For some high-profile users this could be a real security risk in itself. Even if your only issue is a colourful private life, a data leak might cause serious embarrassment. How secure are the car maker's data centres?

Current cars store quite a bit of data already, from phone contacts to satnav destinations. While this can be useful to potential future owners – a car's claimed low mileage might be questionable if the satnav shows regular trips to foreign holiday resorts, for instance – the present belief is that such data should be expunged from the car on sale. But routinely it isn't. Future owners connecting a car to an app or an online account can often see a whole litany of information. Former owners who stay logged in can also determine the current owner's whereabouts and journey history.

In Europe, the authorities are now wading into this emerging legal fog with GDPR, or General Data Protection Regulation legislation. This broadly prevents things being recorded. But it also conflicts with black-box legislation, which is set to mandate that all cars record their location, speed and state of various systems as they travel round.

As the stored data grows, questions arise as to who owns it – the manufacturer, the authorities or the user? The anonymity of data can easily be reversed by revealing locations and searches. It's going to be a pain if we have to agree permissions before every journey, even down to an individual-passenger level. I'm already sick of accepting cookies online. These requirements may be well-meaning but can be a right hassle if they're not properly thought through.

The incentive will grow for the individual user to hack their connected car to their advantage. At its simplest they'll want to jam or remove their black-box data or speed control. As autonomy becomes more commonplace there's the prospect that intelligent mobility systems will route self-driving vehicles in a way to collectively maximise traffic flow. But an individual user may find their car is taking a couple of minutes longer on a particular route. Rather like today's drivers chipping their engine control units (ECUs) to get a performance boost, clever users of the future might chip their cars not to follow the herd. When engineers started fitting big rubber bumpers to cars half a century ago, none of them would have imagined that data privacy and hacking might become the key issues in future car safety. It's a brave new world that might lead some to seek refuge in the more comforting one of old, familiar classics instead.

SIX

THE FUTURE OF THE PAST

Classic Cars and Enthusiast Drivers

Being nuts about old cars usually seems to mean getting together in a club with like-minded enthusiasts who share the goal of preserving them. The first outfit in the world dedicated to keeping classics alive was the Veteran Car Club (VCC), created in 1930 in the Ship Hotel, Brighton, and still in existence today. Its original aim was to conserve cars made up to the end of 1904, which were eligible for the annual London to Brighton Emancipation Run. This had begun in 1896 to celebrate an increase in the speed limit for so-called self-propelled vehicles to a heady 14 mph from a quite literally pedestrian 4 mph in the country and 2 mph in town. Later the club extended its scope to include 'Edwardian' cars made before 1919, as members became concerned that cars like Ford

211

Model Ts and Rolls-Royce Silver Ghosts were being scrapped at an alarming rate.

In 1934, a few years after the VCC was formed, the Vintage Sports Car Club was created, specialising in sporting cars manufactured before 1930. According to the mythology that's developed round its genesis, a group of enthusiasts were concerned that newfangled mass-produced cars were taking over from handcrafted traditional sports cars, which were considered to possess an artisanal beauty and mechanical directness. Or, in the words of Sam Clutton, who edited the VSCC's magazine, traditional cars created 'an intimacy between car and driver which is fostered by absolute positive and accurate steering, a close-ratio gearbox, aided only by a clutch stop and controlled by a sturdy vertical lever, and the (all-in-a-piece) roadholding that was characteristic of the best vintage years'. Although some of these vintage sports cars might have been only five years old in 1934, they needed urgent preservation before their joys were lost.

The club's still going today, with 7,500 members, and like the VCC now incorporates slightly more modern machinery as well. There is an alternative explanation for the club's formation that's based more on pecuniary matters than purity of design. Namely, the members feared that their cheap, old, second-hand sports cars could no longer compete with modern ones in races, so they needed to form a special club for their sluggish old bangers to do battle on equal terms. Nevertheless, it is the more romantic story that has stood the test of time.

Somebody loves them. The Reverend Colin Corke with his cherished Austin Allegro 1750 SS, finding pride and enjoyment in cars other people may not.

Every decade brings forth a crowd of passionate, misty-eyed enthusiasts wanting to forever preserve the cars' glories. I can recall there being a boom in interest in so-called classic cars during the 1980s, when drivers started appreciating just how magnificent some of the models produced in the fifties and sixties were – from Austin-Healeys and MGs through to Gullwing Mercedes and Jaguar Mk 2s. Now we have a 'modern classics' movement bent on preserving motors from the 1980s, the 1990s and later. And who can blame them. It's a bit of a golden age for me, including as it does the likes of Lotus Carltons, Golf GTIs, Lancia Delta Integrales, BMW M3s, Subaru Imprezas and Alfa SZs. I could name a hundred more I'd love to drive again tomorrow.

With the exception of the darkest days of winter, the British year has an astonishing variety of car events to fuel this passion. There are thousands if not tens of thousands of them, ranging from car tours and drive-it days to village fêtes and shows. There are social occasions that celebrate thoroughbreds, like the Goodwood Revival and the Festival of Speed, and the magnificent Silverstone Classic, where multimillion-pound cars are enthusiastically hammered flat-out round famous racing circuits while attendees dress in period garb. And it's not all top-end stuff. There's the rather politically incorrectly named Japfest, which celebrates recent classics from Japan, and there's my own favourite car show, the Festival of the Unexceptional, where cherished examples of the everyday cars of yesteryear are honoured, including those that were frankly a bit crap when still new. Recent winners have included a mint Nissan Sunny and an immaculate Austin Allegro 1750 SS, owned by a Birmingham vicar who once had twenty of the things.

Many of these events are anything but small-scale affairs. Over 350,000 people visit the Goodwood gatherings and classic cars have a huge following. In the UK alone there are over a million vehicles over thirty years old registered with the DVLA; and, according to a 2016 report by the Federation of British Historic Vehicle Clubs, an umbrella organisation for Britain's 400-plus old-vehicle associations, 8.2 million people in Britain are interested in historic vehicles. Historic cars are seen as part of Britain's heritage by 23 million people and the associated business employs 35,000 people and is estimated to be worth £5.5 billion to the economy.

There is similar enthusiasm elsewhere in the world. The Woodward Dream Cruise, held on the third Saturday in August in Detroit, is billed as the world's largest one-day classic-car event attracting 1.5 million people and up to 50,000 cars from around the globe. The emphasis is on muscle cars, street rods and American classics from the 1950s to the 1990s. Whole districts are turned into a dramatic historic carscape, like a giant *American Graffiti* scene made real. The Monterey Car Week is another top contender for every classic car enthusiast's bucket list. The Californian town hosts dozens of classic-car shows, culminating in the Pebble Beach Concours d'Elegance featuring 200 of the finest and most valuable cars in the world and an auction worth hundreds of millions of dollars.

Could the rapid change afoot in the motoring world threaten all of this? Well, arguably, it might if it makes owning and using a historic car more inconvenient.

Taking the MG for a spin

One of the most remarkable things about old cars is that they're so practical and easy to use. You can drive a 110-year-old Clément-Bayard on the same roads as a brand-new car and fill it up at the same fuel stations. The infrastructure is all still there. Slightly newer cars can even mix it perfectly easily with modern traffic. I can well remember the first time I drove a Rolls-Royce Silver Ghost and how straightforward and sprightly it was once I'd mastered the steering-wheel controls for hand throttle, ignition advance and mixture strength.

Most things in the heritage world aren't so refreshingly practical. Aeroplanes get grounded for safety reasons. Old electronics don't work, and are unfathomably difficult to repair. I can recall visiting the Victoria and Albert Museum a few years ago to assess the design of a computer with Kieran Long, who was in charge of the museum's digital collection at the time. Though many of the objects he was curating were less than twenty years old they had usually lost all their functionality, which he found hugely frustrating.

Most obviously disruptive of all is the fear that old cars will be regarded as too polluting for modern use. Old ordinary cars are set to get banned or heavily discouraged through taxes from city centres, so why not classics? We're used to having our roads open to all, but certain ages and classes of vehicle are increasingly likely to be excluded. Will this change our relationship with classic cars?

It probably depends on how tough councils are with the old stuff. Dutch cities initially seemed set on making no exemptions for historic vehicles in their city-centre, low-emissions zones. Earnest Dutch politicians regard all this very seriously – they don't want their good work on pollution reduction undermined by an army of classic-car enthusiasts. This has not necessarily gone down well. When a blanket ban on older petrol and diesel cars was proposed in Rotterdam there were mass classic-car protests that paralysed the city for a day in

Classic-car drivers on a protest ride in Rotterdam. They won't be a pushover for politicians touting disproportionately severe bans on historic cars in cities.

both 2016 and 2017. They worked. A historic vehicle exemption has now been allowed.

In Britain it looks like we may avoid such draconian measures and the associated protests. Britain's classic-car interest is centred around its plentiful old-vehicle clubs and the Federation of British Historic Vehicle Clubs is very proactive in looking after their interests. Contrary to what you might expect, this isn't an outfit dominated by enthusiasts with beards, tweed suits and a penchant for real ale. Their committee may be largely composed of gentlemen of a certain age but their number includes several ex-FTSE 100 board members who know their way around the corridors of power in Westminster and lobby very effectively if a threat looms on the horizon.

When I visited the Federation's communications director, Geoff Lancaster, at his Lincolnshire home I found him in his garage, actively maintaining his Formula Ford racing car and his classic Maserati. The Federation has successfully argued that historic vehicles should be exempt from the Ultra Low Emission Zones in London.

'Our argument was that the percentage of historic vehicles in a given area is extremely small,' says Lancaster. 'If every single historic vehicle which is registered within the postcode area of your emissions zone were to come out on the same day the additional load on the emissions in that area would still be immeasurably tiny. It's a disproportionate action not to exempt historic vehicles. They provide much more heritage value to the public than any damage they could conceivably cause.'

I noted his use of the term 'historic', which refers to cars above a certain age. The more commonly used term 'classic' is meaningless when it comes to serious matters like legislation. 'Classic means nothing at all in our world. It's the same as beauty. It's in the eye of the beholder. There's no definition. It's your opinion. Personal taste,' says Lancaster. There is some debate about how old 'historic' is, however. The EU's definition is thirty or more years old. The UK government, on the other hand, is adopting a requirement of forty years and older.

'London's an interesting precedent because it doesn't mean everywhere's going to do it. Basically the government has delegated how low emission zones are going to be regulated to a local level. But every time one comes up, we're going to be lobbying with local authorities. And we're going to use exactly the same argument.'

In 2017, the then Secretary of State for Transport Chris Grayling said that there were many big transport problems facing the UK, 'but classic vehicles are not one of them'. He pledged that while he was Transport Secretary he would not do anything to undermine owners 'getting out on the roads and enjoying using their classic cars'. Hopefully his successors will share this rational and wise view (probably, in many people's eyes, one of the few rational positions he has held). There are positive signs elsewhere in the world too. Paris was originally due for a ban, but now anything older than thirty years counts as historic there and will be allowed to be used, even after the 2024 diesel and 2030 petrol-car bans in the city.

Out of gas?

One practical issue that may become more irritating for classic-car owners in the future is the availability of fuel. So far fuel issues have been minor. The switch to unleaded was a problem for old cars in the 1990s but that's largely been dealt with by using additives or making engine modifications. There are also still a handful of stations in Britain that pump old-fashioned leaded fuel (at about £2 a litre). More recently the addition of ethanol to petrol has caused problems. It can attack the copper fuel tanks and soldered joints of certain veteran cars, but this problem is usually sufficiently minor to be solved by selecting super-unleaded fuel with its lower ethanol content.

Fuel could be a much bigger inconvenience if we're all running on batteries or hydrogen; there'll no longer be any handy roadside filling stations for your traditional motor. There will still be companies who'll deliver anything you like in a drum to your door, such as high-octane race fuel for your historic racer, or 'motor spirit' for your 1885 Benz with a surface carburettor that relies upon the volatile fuel's rapid rate of evaporation. But all this is possible only at considerable financial cost and barely practical if you're planning on using a historic vehicle regularly.

Such developments may end up sorting out the expensive classics from everyday ones. The owner of a pedigree Aston Martin or Bentley is likely to have the means to trailer a car to somewhere they can drive it in private and with supplies of fuel shipped in. But an everyday MG driver might find the requirement to have fuel delivered to keep in the garden or garage quite a disincentive to historic-vehicle ownership.

In a rather negative scenario the classic car of the future could be like the horse of today. Once a daily form of transport enjoyed by the masses, it may soon be a recreation enjoyed by only a tiny minority. It would no longer be used regularly on the road, but would instead be towed to the race circuit or leisure park by a modern or autonomous vehicle to be used by its relatively wealthy owner before being taken back to its cosseted home.

If petrol does become a rarely used specialist product, a more positive possibility is that concerns over pollution will evaporate along with any suggestion that we might eventually run out. In this respect the relationship between fossil fuels and cars reminds me of the one between silver and photography.

Back in the 1980s, as photography became more popular, there was a real fear that we'd run out of the precious metal, which plays a vital role in making traditional photographic films and light-sensitive papers. Instead digital photography became universal and film enthusiasts can now pursue their thriving niche without any fear of depleting global resources.

We might see more classics being converted to battery power. In the 1997 movie *Gattaca*, set in a future world where human genetic modification is the norm, people drive round in classics converted to use turbine-driven electric power. And a very splendid range of classics they are too, ranging from a Studebaker Avanti and Citroën DS Décapotable to a Rover P6 and a Buick Riviera. We're not at the stage of turbine conversions just yet, but battery conversions of classics are already quite common and could become more widespread in the future.

In the real world the development has always intrigued yet disturbed me – my normal enthusiasm for classics has crashed head-on with my passion for new technology. A very large part of the appeal of classic-ownership experience is that characterful mechanical engine, with its sound, feel and performance curve unique to each car, often mated to a manual gearbox for the satisfaction of gear changing and control. The whine of an electric motor and the gear-free transmission threatens to neuter and enfeeble the classic-car experience.

When my fellow *Gadget Show* presenter Jason Bradbury bought a DeLorean and announced his intention not only to convert it to full *Back to the Future* time-machine spec, with date displays, flux capacitor and all, but also to replace its (albeit rather feeble) Peugeot-Renault-Volvo V6 with an electric motor and batteries, I tried to dissuade him from the whole project.

Early conversions tended to use basic lead acid batteries giving short ranges of fifty or sixty miles and limited performance. But the motors have become faster and the battery technology more advanced, and a growing number of cars are being converted. The torque advantage of an electric motor has even been translated into drag-racing prowess.

A French firm called Ian Motion has begun converting classic Minis to lithium-ion power with a range of about 100 miles and a price ticket of around £35,000. In California, a company called Zelectric converts classic Porsches and VWs using lithium-ion batteries to give a similar range starting at $56,000. The VW Camper is in some ways the ideal conversion candidate. It's relatively plentiful so you're not doing anything sacrilegious to a slice of automotive heritage, and it didn't have a particularly brilliant engine in the first place. The performance improvement is vast and by careful placement of the batteries you even improve the somewhat wayward handling. Heating is taken care of with a supplementary electric-powered ceramic unit – though camping trips would have to be planned round your charging programme!

A key question in an electric-classic conversion is whether to keep the original gearbox. Enthusiast Steve Labib of Jozztek converted a Mazda MX-5 into a 350 horsepower car. 'With the torque these motors provide, there was no point driving it in

It's a drag

American electric-car gurus Mitch Medford and John Wayland have a passion for converting classics with electric powertrains. Their creations have posted frankly terrifying stats in drag races, far exceeding their petrol performances. The numbers speak for themselves, beating the acceleration of the fastest production cars available today. You can find them on YouTube.

	Standing quarter-mile	Terminal speed	0–60 mph
1968 Ford Mustang V8 289 3-speed manual (petrol)	16.3 sec	85 mph	8 sec
1968 Ford Mustang (Electric Conversion – Zombie 222)	10.24 sec	140.8 mph	1.94 sec
1972 Datsun 1200 Export Saloon (petrol)	19.1 sec	70 mph	14.5 sec
1972 Datsun 1200 (Electric Conversion – White Zombie)	10.4 sec	117 mph	1.8 sec

anything but fourth gear and it would spin its wheels in third. I really wish I'd taken the gearbox out, then put the motor in the gearbox hole and left the whole under-bonnet area empty.' He thinks old classics are easier to convert. 'On modern cars it's hard to make things like the antilock brakes or any of the electrical systems work without the engine in there. On an old car you find the power lead and connect it to an auxiliary battery and all the electrics work.'

I wouldn't be surprised if volume-production electric kits, which will bring the costs down, are developed for common classics like Morris Minors, MX-5s and MGBs. Sensitive cyborg-like conversions are already a small but significant part of the classic-car world and look set to become more popular in the future. This may be just as well, as the skills necessary to repair classics might begin to die out.

Where's my wrench?

Modern car-mechanic training schemes reflect the modern maintenance world, where you're as likely to be chasing fault codes on a laptop as you are to be dealing with greasy metal parts. With electrification and fuel-cell vehicles, not to mention increasing automation, the gap between some classics and modern cars is set to become even wider.

'A lot of skills are in danger of being lost – mainly through natural wastage.' says Geoff Lancaster.

'In the next ten years there aren't sufficient trained people coming through the system to replace those that'll be lost in the next ten years. We're not talking about people with sophisticated skills, like trimmers and English wheel operators [a device that helps shape complex sheet metal panels by hand]. Just basic mechanics. Take a kid going the Light Vehicle Apprenticeship, which is what the current franchises put their trainees through; you will not find the word "carburettor" anywhere.

'We're trying to replace the people being lost to retirement. We've started a historic-vehicle apprenticeship, which basically teaches all the traditional skills. And a lot of kids are leaving the Light Vehicle course to do ours. They do a year of Light Vehicle and some say they've never touched a car in all that time. They've looked at laptops and analysed diagnostic programs but what they actually want to do is pick up some spanners and get oily.'

The Federation's permanent training workshop has been up and running for the last four years at Bicester Heritage. The place is a fascinating microcosm of the future of classic cars – and maybe the future of enthusiast driving of the non-classic variety as well. Founded in 2013, it's based at a 350-acre former WW2 RAF Bomber Training Station, a location reeking of heritage and history before you even see an old car. It's a sort of classic-car hub that's already home to thirty specialist businesses and a track for driving a classic; soon there'll be a hotel and classic-car resort too. According to their website: 'The unique ecosystem of businesses acts as a "marina-like" cluster, promoting skills and expertise, employment, qualified customer footfall, shared business incubation and aggregate growth. Collectively, Bicester Heritage is all about driving the future of the past.' To me it looks like they're well on course to giving the past a thoroughly healthy future.

New skills will be always be needed. The classic-car passion is a moving target. Younger enthusiasts are interested in younger, more technological cars. A 1980s MG Maestro and its talking dashboard may not require the same skills as the immediate post-war classic MG TC. Talking dashboards were a quite a faddish technological dead end that appeared on a few models in the mid-1980s. The Maestro's was the most famous in Britain, fitted to the top-of-the-range MG and Vanden Plas versions of this Golf-size car that first appeared in 1983. Desperate to give the rather conservative design a technological edge, they ordered suppliers Smiths and Lucas to develop a digital dashboard complete with voice synthesiser. The result has a thirty-two-word vocabulary, recorded in fifteen languages, warning of potential troubles like 'high engine temperature' or 'battery not charging'. It also gave oral explanations for the display on the also newfangled trip computer, with phrases such as 'average fuel consumption' and 'trip distance'. A rotary volume-control knob is attached and the voice was provided by New Zealand-born actress Nicolette McKenzie, who had recently appeared in the BBC soap *Triangle*, set on a North Sea ferry.

Some of the earliest hybrids will soon be old enough for historic status and the best of them – like the Honda Insight, with its function-over-form clever design – are already in the frame to be future classics. Then there's the newer VW XL1, a tiny diesel hybrid that I remember felt almost like a Morgan 3-Wheeler when I briefly drove one round the roundabouts of Milton Keynes. Who knows, even the Toyota Prius, which has been hugely significant commercially yet never desirable from a driving perspective, might one day be considered a classic.

Future classics

Guessing correctly which cars are going to be future classics can be hugely profitable. But while it can yield a far better return on your investment than putting the money in the bank, it can be tricky to separate the winners from the losers.

Big middle-of-the-road saloons or humdrum hatchbacks aren't likely to be good bets. Relatively rare, high-power versions of models that look great and drive well are better choices. Convertibles often appreciate more than hardtops. Cars of the 1990s and early 2000s that are transitioning to become affordable modern classics include the Alfa GTV V6, Renault Clio V6 Sport, Jaguar XKR Supercharged and Nissan 350Z.

More expensive opportunities include the Porsche Boxster Spyder and recent stars like the BMW 1M Coupé. Some cars, like the Alpine A110, are so good you might want simply to buy them new and hold on to them. With others it's better to wait for that point where their value reaches rock-bottom and purchase a low-mileage, unmolested example just as all the rotten ones are heading for the scrapper. It's a tactic that's worked well in recent years with fast Fords and may do the same for a whole new generation of Focus RSs.

But are modern cars with all their ECUs and a whole host of other electronic equipment too sophisticated to keep alive as classics in the future? What about something as complex as a Mercedes S-Class? When it's pushing thirty, how are you going to keep ahead of failures in an equipment list that includes a perfumer, a 3D camera that links with the suspension, an ionised air-filtration system and seats that give a hot-stone massage? One car that regularly crops up on lists of potential future classics is the Audi TT. How easy are they to keep on the road as they enter the springtime of their glorious classic afterlife? I seem to remember that the TT, like the Triumph Stag, wasn't exactly a paragon of reliability in the early days. If anything they appear to be getting less demanding with age. According to Neil Crayford of Norfolk Performance Car Sales, a TT specialist, the only modern problem they have is a failure of the dashboard pod. This was also a common problem when the cars were new. But whereas an Audi dealer would have charged a small fortune to repair it back in the day, they can now be repaired for £120.

Perhaps I shouldn't be surprised. In my experience few people can be bothered to diagnose and repair a faulty control board on a kaput tumble dryer or oven, yet with cars the same components form a much smaller portion of the total value of the machine so there's much more incentive to find a solution. Whatever goes wrong, if there's a will to keep a classic car going, there'll be a way to do it.

Even airbags don't appear to be a problem. As the materials are tightly packed away from light they don't seem to deteriorate and cause problems. This is a hypothesis backed up by a US Insurance Institute for Highway Safety crash test in 1993 with a 1973 Chevrolet Impala, one of the first cars equipped with airbags. Though the car had done over 100,000 miles, and the radio and clock weren't functional, the airbags worked perfectly.

Can you still get the parts?

Parts availability is always a big worry for classic owners but if anything that's likely to improve in the future. For a start, if the car's manufacturer survives, they'll be taking more of an interest in bits for their old cars. Manufacturers are increasingly realising the profit potential in their heritage vehicles and the trend is likely to continue. You can, for example, get most of the parts for a 1950s Gullwing Mercedes from your local dealer, even including the seat upholstery.

In some cases manufacturers are actually still making complete heritage cars. Jaguar's Continuation series of lovingly re-crafted classic Jaguars is astonishing in its quality and attention to detail. The Jaguar Classic workshop has recreated six 'missing' E-Type Lightweights that were never produced back in the 1960s and nine £1 million Jaguar XKSS models that were originally lost in a Coventry factory fire in 1957, and is in the process of building twenty-five Le Mans-winning D-Types that complete the intended original production of 100 cars. Here, everything from the wheels and the gauges to the rivets and

The six £1 million E-Type Lightweight Continuation models built by Jaguar's Classic division are a magnificent time-shift legend within a legend.

the carburettors are as good as the original, and the cars take 10,000 hours of labour to make.

Usually such replicas aren't road legal because, as new cars, they would need to conform to the same current regulations as other new cars. But it's not cut and dried. Jaguar's six missing E-Types, for instance, have the potential to be fully road legal because they had originally been issued chassis numbers back in the 1960s but were deliberately sold in racing specification to encourage use on the track. Individuals building their own replicas in the UK can obtain 'Individual Vehicle Approval' for their creations. Though the four-hour test is tough it does not mandate crash testing, and the emissions requirements are those for the age of the engine fitted rather than for current ones.

With those cars that aren't deemed road legal, the fact that they have to be transported to tracks for use tends to increase the possibility of a future rich-versus-poor classic-car divide.

Porsche now makes parts for a huge variety of its old cars and is expanding its catalogue with 300 new components every year. Even arguably less prestigious models like the 924 Turbo are included. As Ed Myland from the Porsche 924 Turbo Owners Club told me: 'We're so lucky that Porsche is now supporting the car so much – there are 4,200 bits you can just go into a Porsche dealer and get.' The other way in which parts availability is improving is through 3D printing. This is bringing the price down and making an increased range of components readily obtainable. Again I found evidence at Bicester Heritage, where a company called Retrotech is dedicated to using the technique to help with the restoration of historic vehicles.

'Recent advances in laser scanning, together with digitally enabled manufacturing methods such as 3D printing and multi-axis machining, have greatly reduced lead times and tooling costs for one-off and short-run components,' says Retrotech chairman Francis Galashan. 'Parts that previously would have taken months of painstaking work by skilled pattern-makers can now be digitised within hours, then manufactured directly from a 3D model with big savings.' The company has helped make inlet manifolds for Metro 6R4 rally cars, exhaust manifolds for 1960s Sunbeam Tigers, brake parts for pre-war Alvises and a whole range of engine parts for vintage Bentleys, including the blocks themselves.

Even at an amateur level, the 3D printer is paying dividends. Ed Myland told me more: 'We have a couple of specialists in the club who are working on remaking parts, which is fantastic. The 924 Turbos have these special grilles on the bonnet which were fitted to nothing else; when they come on eBay they're invariably in very poor condition and going for £80 each. They're completely unavailable new so we're getting those 3D printed. Headlight washers are becoming difficult to obtain so they're being 3D printed as well. Even for pattern-making, if we're getting any metal parts cast, we'll use the tech where we can.'

It's possible that 3D printing could even ease the pressure on classics being crashed for entertainment. One of the more depressing aspects of seeing a historic car in a movie or TV series is that it's likely to meet some terrible fate. Think of Thelma and Louise's Ford Thunderbird, or the 1969 Mercedes 280 SE cabriolet in *The Hangover*. This is destruction you don't get with historic houses or paintings. In some ways the more expensive fare isn't the problem. There are numerous Lamborghini Countaches still in working order, so it arguably doesn't particularly matter as much when one gets destroyed in the making of *The Wolf of Wall Street*. Director Martin Scorsese wanted to use a real car rather than a model for more authentic bodywork damage in the crash sequences.

But often a lower proportion of the ordinary cars made survive so a film can have a more devastating effect on the remaining population. The Black Beauty car used by the Green Hornet in the 2011 film of the same name was based on a mid-sixties Chrysler Imperial, an ordinary car and a sort of American Austin Westminster. The production used twenty-nine vehicles, the vast majority of which did not survive the various stunts and action sequences. The producers of *The Fast and Furious* franchise are also often criticised for the number of classic vehicles they destroy in their action-packed movies.

The 2012 Bond film *Skyfall*, however, avoided having to harm a real Aston Martin DB5 by 3D printing several replicas at one-third scale. They were each assembled from eighteen components to give realistic door- and bonnet-opening functionality. One hopes to see such techniques more widely adopted in the future as charismatic classics get in shorter supply. If they ever remake the first *Godfather* movie, the pretty 1946 Alfa Romeo 6C driven by Michael Corleone in Sicily that gets blown up along with his bride won't be genuine, just a replica. With current values well over £100,000 there may be no choice in that.

The $100 million car

The most valuable classic car in the world – a Ferrari 250 GTO with racing history – changed hands privately for $70 million in June 2018. While a private purchase saves on auctioneers' fees, nobody would describe that as small change. A whole industry is making a very tidy income on the back of this particular asset class and it surely can't be long before we see a car hitting $100 million. Values have traditionally gone

The top ten most expensive classic cars sold at auction*

*Adjusted for inflation at 2018 prices

26/08/2018	1962 Ferrari 250 GTO	$48.4 million
14/08/2014	1962 Ferrari 250 GTO	$38.1 million
05/02/2016	1957 Ferrari 335S	$37.3 million
12/07/2013	1954 Mercedes-Benz W196	$31.8 million
10/12/2015	1956 Ferrari 290 MM	$29.6 million
17/08/2013	1967 Ferrari GTS/4 NART Spider	$29.6 million
16/08/2014	1964 Ferrari 275 GTB/C Speciale	$27.9 million
19/08/2017	1956 Aston Martin DBR1	$23 million
25/08/2018	1935 Duesenberg SSJ	£22 million
19/08/2016	1955 Jaguar D-Type	$21.8 million

up and down as investors have entered and left the market in response to returns available elsewhere in the economy. Likewise, trends for individual models vary as tastes change. But over the whole market, prices have increased hugely in recent years. The Hagerty 'Blue Chip' Index averages the values of twenty-five of the most sought-after cars of the post-war era. It's seen prices increase nearly five-fold from January 2007 to January 2019.

One driver of such price appreciation is a newly powerful international force in the market: China. As Geoff Lancaster says, 'The Chinese love brands, and have an affinity for high-end historic vehicles.' He once asked the chairman of the Chinese equivalent organisation over. 'We took him to Prescott and let him drive a 1920s Bugatti Brescia up the hill. He was literally speechless for half an hour afterwards; it was the pinnacle of his experience. He'd probably never been near anything like that, let alone actually driving it. And at such an iconic location. We also took him to a Bentley Drivers Club meeting and he drove a 4-litre Blower Bentley that one of the members had brought. If he could have imported it, he would have got his cheque book out there and then.'

At present, the Chinese government doesn't allow the importation of historic vehicles. According to Lancaster, 'The rich Chinese guys all keep their cars in either New York, Paris or London. Some are in the city and others are in hangars with lots of Carcoons [the trade lingo for a plastic tent intended to protect your car while simultaneously ensuring adequate airflow]. They fly in on their Lear Jets; the car's already warmed up for them and they take it off on a scenic tour. They bring it back on Sunday afternoon, it goes back in the Carcoon and they fly back home.

'There's quite a bit of politics in the world classic-car movement. We were invited to go to China for a convention to convince their central committee. We made a presentation about the importance of heritage to the economy to try to convince them to liberalise the importation of historic vehicles.

Don't expect it to change overnight, because it takes decades rather than years, but they reckon, in the next ten years, it'll be liberalised and prices will go through the roof. There's such a pent-up demand and a huge purchasing power bottled up by legislation. Container ships will be thick with E-Types and Bentleys.'

The dark flip side to such burgeoning demand is that it means more incentive to manufacture fakes. Authenticity has long been a problem in the car world but with new markets it will get even worse, becoming more than ever like the art market. For example, take the MG Magnette K3, a short-chassis variant of the car that achieved great success in racing in the 1930s, driven by the likes of Captain George Eyston, Count Lurani, Tazio Nuvolari, Sir Tim Birkin, Whitney Straight and 'Hammy' Hamilton. Many ordinary K1 and K2 Magnettes were made into K3 replicas but their history is often confused.

Geoff Lancaster tells me that this can become tricky when the Federation of British Historic Vehicle Clubs has to rule on dating and provenance. One extreme position is where three people with three different cars are all asking the DVLA for an original historic number plate. All three of them can demonstrate that at least a proportion of the parts on their car are from the original but, over time, someone has turned one car into three cars. It's impossible to decide which car is the real deal.

There's long been a similar problem with Mk1 Ford Cortinas, whereby ordinary ones are tarted up and passed off as the Lotus high-performance variant – which featured a tuned twin-cam engine developed by Lotus, a vastly improved suspension, an interior bristling with extra dials, a repositioned gearshift and a wood-rimmed steering wheel. Increasing values means that the problem now affects a wider range of historic cars. Even the once humble Ford Escort is subject to the same treatment. There's growing demand for people who know their way round the intricate details that sort out the fake from the fortune.

As David Brown from Ford performance-car specialists RO Performance of Bury told me, 'If someone can find a two-door Escort shell they'll try and turn it into something better.' 'Something better' might mean the Mexico model, which had a 1,600 cc crossflow engine instead of the ordinary 1,100 cc and 1,300 cc motors, and was built to celebrate the model's greatest sporting victory in the 1970 London to Mexico World Cup Rally. You have to be a purist to know where the subtle changes are as they turn a five-grand car into one worth up to £50,000.

There are also genuine, openly manufactured replicas. Pur Sang is an Argentinian company that exhibits at the Goodwood Revival and manufactures replica Alfa 8Cs and Bugatti Type 35s. These are very, very accurate copies. They've got the patina as well. Pur Sang isn't passing them off as genuine but there's always the possibility that subsequent owners will. If the Chinese market restrictions come off, prices will go up, making the incentive to produce replicas even more irresistible. Given the Chinese fondness for making copies of ordinary modern cars, one wonders whether the classic-replica industry is about to get a kick-start.

Will classic cars be listed?

Discussions of art and provenance make one ponder this question. It's a difficult problem because, unlike buildings or works of art, cars are manufactured objects and not individual items. The Fédération Internationale des Véhicules Anciens (FIVA) is lobbying UNESCO for World Heritage status for classic cars. Geoff Lancaster says that 'through FIVA we've been trying for the last decade to get historic vehicles recognised as moving heritage in much the same way as they recognise ships and steam trains. There are hoops you've got to jump through. It's not a fast-moving organisation but the first thing you've got to do is declare a charter which defines what a heritage vehicle is, what condition it should be in and shouldn't be in. So we created a thing which was sent to UNESCO a couple of years ago called the Charter of Turin. Basically it's a manual of what constitutes a heritage vehicle.'

It's similar to the nonbinding but widely accepted Venice, Barcelona and Riga charters, which set standards for the definition, maintenance and preservation of historically significant buildings, watercraft and rail vehicles. The Turin Charter aims to 'support and encourage the preservation and responsible use of historic vehicles as an important part of our technical and cultural heritage'.

The definition UNESCO accepted is any vehicle capable of running on the highway under any form of motive power, including motorcycles but not bicycles. It's helpfully broad,

A work of art. The original Ford Mustang from the film *Bullitt* is on America's National Historic Vehicle Register.

including categories for cars, light commercial vehicles, trucks, ex-military vehicles and agricultural vehicles (perhaps surprisingly one of the biggest sectors of collected historic vehicles). Any that are thirty years old or more meet the definition.

In America, the Historic Vehicle Association is developing a National Historic Vehicle Register to carefully and accurately document America's most historically significant automobiles, motorcycles, trucks and commercial vehicles. In March 2013, it began collaborating with the US Department of the Interior to create a permanent archive of significant historic automobiles within the Library of Congress. There are so far only twenty-two vehicles that have achieved the accolade of a place on the register. They include the original 1947 Tucker 48 'Tin Goose' prototype, the 1968 Mustang that appeared in *Bullitt* and the 1938 Buick Y-Job, one of the first concept cars created by General Motors under the direction of their first design chief, Harley Earl.

Not all cars on the register are US built. There's also a 1954 Mercedes-Benz 300 SL W198 Gullwing Coupé. Apparently it's there because it was the first foreign mass-produced automobile built for and launched in America, and this particular one was owned by Briggs S. Cunningham, a prominent American businessman who achieved international success in automobile and yacht racing. It's also the first production car to use fuel injection and features a lightweight tubular space-frame chassis, an advanced aerodynamic body design and, of course, its distinctive 'gullwing' doors. Perhaps more surprisingly the register includes the 1985 Ferrari 250 GT California Spyder replica that appeared in the film *Ferris Bueller's Day Off*. This listing is based on 'its association with an important person and events in American history and culture'.

Are everyday classics the most endangered?

Most of the listings and talk of cultural heritage affect more expensive cars – the elite of the classic-car world. Lower down, the biggest danger might be a lack of interest. Is it the everyday classic that's most in danger?

One fear is that driving and car ownership as a whole will cease to be part of culture for younger drivers and potential classic-car owners. Cars may become inconvenient to keep in metropolitan areas and the classic car may become victim to this just like any other car. If you own a small hatchback, you can easily imagine driving a brand-new Ferrari. Will that still be the case in a world where the everyday experience of mobility is as a rented service? Will classic cars be seen as closer to motorbike riding or skydiving or hang gliding: something that's still pretty accessible but nevertheless a specialist activity?

Rob Symonds of the Morris Register encapsulates the challenge. 'The problem with classic cars in general is that you tend to warm to the classic cars you grew up with. I was a chemistry teacher at King Edward's School in Birmingham. I was there for forty-three years; I retired last year. I was into Morris 8s as a student. Younger generations are into the Escorts of the seventies, that sort of thing. Our membership increases year on year, which is not what a lot of clubs can say. But it's the demographics that are worrying. The average age of the membership must be solidly over sixty, and lots of our members are now in their seventies and eighties and they're going to the great car park in the sky.'

Some car clubs are attempting to reach out to younger owners by offering to lend one of their member's cars for a year, for free. The Morris Register decided to buy a car especially for the purpose and included free insurance as well. The club advertised the offer in various classic-car magazines. According to Symonds, 'It was like a lonely-hearts ad. Pre-war car seeks driver for a summer of love. Unfortunately we were a bit underwhelmed by the response. Maybe it's just too good to be true and that frightens people off.'

In the end the club selected a woman who lived in Derbyshire and taught art in Nottingham. She was very enthusiastic, apparently, and 'the fact she's a woman is a bit of a bonus as it is essentially a male hobby'. The trouble was that this 'young' driver was actually forty-four, which was older than they wanted. 'We hope there's some sort of equilibrium,' says Symonds, 'but the fact is it's getting harder and harder to get young people interested.'

Maybe he shouldn't fret. One conversation heartened me more than ever about the future of classic cars. The club that started it all, the Veteran Car Club, is still going strong. I spoke to its secretary, Stephen Curry, and he dispelled one worry immediately. 'I don't think there are many people alive who knew our sort of cars when they were new.' So much for people only loving the old cars of their youth, then. 'The old-car world has a life of its own.'

He did note a trend towards trailering cars to quiet areas of road where they can be enjoyed away from dense traffic. This process tends to favour smaller cars, which are easier to ferry about. So lightness is now prioritised over the need to keep up with modern traffic.

'Amongst American cars Model Ts were always looked down upon and people would go for Buicks and Cadillacs and things like that,' says Curry. 'Nowadays Model Ts are very sought after because they're light. You can easily put one on a trailer and tow it behind a normal car. Put a big old car on a trailer and try towing it behind a Land Rover and you find that it's even beyond the weight limit of that.'

The lesson from the VCC is that that the future of old cars is bright. 'There's still a demand, there is still an active membership. You could probably do an event with the Veteran Car Club somewhere in the country practically every weekend of the year. We're widespread and we're very strong.'

Personally, I think the future of the past, the destiny of our motoring heritage, is an area we have little need to worry about. A combination of leagues of enthusiasts, the rise of electric and hydrogen everyday cars easing the pressure on fuels and emissions, and the mainstream availability of new technologies like laser scanning and 3D printing all means our heritage will be savoured and appreciated well into the foreseeable future.

IS THE CAR DEAD?

We've seen how the car has been shocked out of its complacent stupor with better, cleaner power, added safety and ballooning intelligence-boosting convenience and comfort while cutting the casualty count. It's not the all-encompassing overnight revolution many had hoped for but it will nevertheless steadily transform our cars while retaining the joy of driving, keeping our ever-growing motoring heritage in rude health and satisfying our urge to race and compete. But could something more radical take the car's place? Some of the alternatives sound rather exhilarating.

In a sci-fi-and-superhero world there'd be no need for cars. We'd all use jetpacks. Yves Rossy showed the way. The veteran Swiss ex-jetfighter pilot turned 'Jetman' straps two carbon wings and four small jet engines to his body before swooping over the English Channel, looping-the-loop over the Grand Canyon or soaring over Burj Khalifa in Dubai. It's a trifle inconvenient that he has to throw himself out of a plane to get started but there's no denying his breathtakingly spectacular achievements.

He's not the only advocate of personal jet power. JetPack Aviation's $340,000 JB11, a pack with six kerosene-powered turbojet engines, more usefully takes off from the ground and it's claimed is capable of reaching 15,000 feet and 120 mph. Four of the engines are used to fly with two in reserve for emergencies. I found watching David Mayman fly up the hill with one at the Goodwood Festival of Speed in 2018 a genuinely thrilling experience.

Richard Browning, dubbed the 'Real-Life Iron Man', is another jetpack showman, from Salisbury in England. When I met him I was delighted to discover he's also a car lover with a 4.5 litre TVR Cerbera he uses for trials, drag racing and hill climbs. His rig has two micro-turbines belted to his back and two tied to each arm. My fellow *Gadget Show* presenter Ortis Deley was fortunate enough to try it. He found it frustratingly difficult. 'It's a weird feeling of lightness because you've never been lifted in that way before. It's not like being lifted under your arms. It's quite intuitive in the sense that you put your arms back to go forward. But I didn't get off the ground.'

That need for large amounts of operator skill and training, plus the vast cost and high noise levels, are sure to keep jetpack use restricted to the extremely wealthy in search of a few minutes of exhilaration. There are many other perpetually enduring fantasies that are never going to replace cars for very good reasons.

One of the most consistent – and consistently unattainable – dreams of personal transport is the flying car, the ultimate transport hybrid. Fiction and fantasy are full of them. A

London Transport poster of 1926, picturing the city as it would be in 2026, foresaw a sky full of car-like flying objects. Other examples are the Spinner police cars in *Blade Runner*, the Jetsons' Hovercar, Bruce Willis's flying taxi in *The Fifth Element*, Doc's DeLorean in *Back to the Future II* or even Chitty Chitty Bang Bang.

Even before these fantasy visions people were trying to build real flying cars. The 1917 Curtiss Autoplane is widely considered the first attempt. It featured large, non-folding but fully detachable wings (from a Curtiss Triplane) that proved rather too heavy and aerodynamically challenging for the 100 horsepower engine. The vehicle made a few short hops but never flew reliably. Other historic examples from the 1930s and 1940s include the Arrowbile, the ConvAirCar and the Airphibian.

More recently, five MIT graduates started Terrafugia in 2006 and commenced development of their Transition, with a price tag of around $280,000. At the time of writing none has been delivered to customers – not entirely surprising, given that it more closely resembles an awkwardly folding plane than it does a car. Nevertheless, the company, now part of the Chinese Geely Group, has already announced its successor, the TF-X, which is expected to debut in 2023. This looks like a far slicker piece of kit, at least based on the available 3D-rendered YouTube video.

So, the frightening expense of flying cars is prohibitive but they've also failed to get going because they're surprisingly inconvenient. Take-off normally requires a runway, which is rarely at hand. They also demand far too much skill from the driver – you need a pilot's licence on top of your normal driving licence. Above all they've tended to be a bit rubbish at being both a car and a plane. A car has to be strongly built for refinement and crash resistance, with large tyres to aid road holding. A plane needs to be light, with tiny wheels, and to get off the ground has traditionally required bulky wings, which rather get in the way when negotiating terrestrial traffic. The aerodynamics of the two are dissimilar and even the ideal drive systems for rotors and road wheels are vastly different. It's predictably almost impossible to design a single vehicle that's good at both.

The future of personal flying transport now looks more likely to be small electric vertical take-off and landing (eVTOL) craft and passenger drones. If anything, using the term 'flying car' puts you in danger of being perceived as a dinosaur. Uber, for example, has NASA on board to help develop its flying taxi, which you'll summon via an app and which will allegedly fly between the tops of tall buildings. Dallas and Dubai are set to get the first examples of this novelty.

Passenger drones won't be beating the morning rush hour for a while. Batteries aren't yet powerful enough for passenger-drone use. According to Uber, an air taxi will require batteries yielding at least 400 Watt-hours per kg but Tesla's most powerful batteries delivered just 250 in 2018. Another drawback is that drones take up far too much air space. Imagine everyone leaving an office block and hopping into their drone. The sky would be black with a dense swarm of buzzing activity. Also yet to be tested is whether the sensation of being whisked around in a drone is too close to a manic rollercoaster ride to be acceptable as transport.

The hyperloop is another idea that won't be threatening the survival of the car. The term was created by our old friend Elon Musk in 2013 while he was launching a competition to create a low-pressure tube that will enable passenger pods to zoom from San Francisco to Los Angeles in 35 minutes at 760 mph.

The concept itself is nothing new. British inventor and engineer George Medhurst took out a patent for trains operating in airless pipes in 1799. At the time they were more poetically described as 'atmospheric railways'. More recently there have been numerous plans for magnetically levitating trains in vacuum tubes. So far they've mostly been grounded at the pipedream stage by the cost of building a lengthy maglev system and the logistical difficulties of maintaining a near or absolute vacuum over long distances.

In Musk's twenty-first century version the air in the tube is at low pressure rather than in an actual vacuum, making the system less vulnerable to leaks. By virtually eliminating air resistance and the friction of wheels, high speeds can be achieved relatively efficiently. The tubes would be 6 feet in diameter and pods containing twenty-eight passengers would depart every thirty seconds.

Keeping air out of the tube is still a huge challenge. From Los Angeles to San Francisco the volume is 2 million cubic metres over 373 miles. The largest vacuum chamber in the world at present has just 1.5 per cent of this volume and requires enormous amounts of structural reinforcement. The steel tubes would need to withstand 10 tons of pressure per square metre and resist expansion and contraction with changes in temperature. Just one failure in a tube risks depressurising the whole system, potentially causing pods to brake suddenly from high speed as a wall of air enters the system.

If a pod gets stuck the ensuing pod will need the ability to make an emergency stop, so the distance between pods needs to be vast, limiting capacity. A slight failure in a pod's structure would cause the occupants to be exposed to a fatal lack of pressure – a death rather like being thrown out into deep space without a suit.

To cap it all, the nausea may be insurmountable. The hyperloop pods won't be doing a constant speed in a straight line. They'll be going uphill and downhill, round obstacles and doing stop-starts at stations. G loadings seven times higher than the limits within which Japan's Shinkansen bullet train operates have been suggested. The proposed $7.5 billion cost of the LA to San Francisco hyperloop seems short of a nought or two, or maybe even three. As vanity projects, perhaps, some hyperloops may be built but they'll rival trains and planes, not cars.

At the opposite extreme, there has been a naïve hope that, in urban areas at least, we'll all be whizzing around on miniature electric scooters. From personal experience I have to say these things have such miniscule wheels that they get caught in the tiniest potholes, launching you headfirst into oncoming traffic. Nevertheless, Silicon Valley has been enthusiastic and the most famous start-ups, Bird and Lime, have been valued in the billions of dollars. The idea is that apps track scooters' location and who's using them so you just pick one up and go, and teams of roaming personnel will find them when the batteries are flat and whisk them off for recharging. Supported initially by brainlessly optimistic politicians, they've become renowned for creating urban litter with abandoned devices – and for a series of nasty crashes.

A day after they were made legal in the Swedish city of Helsingborg, a rider was killed and the Swedish transport authorities immediately called for the devices to be banned. In Portland, Oregon, e-scooters are involved in accidents forty-four times as often as motorbikes, while in Austin, Texas, one in three users are injured on their first trip.

When it comes down to it, there is nothing that can compete with the convenience and cost-effectiveness of the car. The idea of travelling round in a box with (usually) four wheels on the ground isn't going away. Though city centres will become even more car-hostile and congestion may continue to get worse as the car remains a victim of its own success, there is nothing to indicate its imminent demise.

The dream of an autonomous, connected, shared and zero-emission future will live on but don't believe all the hype. We're not on the verge of a sudden and dramatic revolution. Instead, we'll see a more diverse and gradual evolution of the car.

The furthest away from manifestation is the nirvana of autonomy. The dream of a luxury transport capsule that appears at your house and scoots you off quickly to your desti-nation, disappearing from view at the end of your journey, is a long way off. Artificial intelligence simply doesn't seem capable of providing it yet, at least without massive investment in infrastructure. A world of exciting targets has become one of missed deadlines. While automated pods look destined to be a slow form of transport in very controlled spaces, it will be some time before they make tentative steps further afield with special lanes on motorways and dedicated zones in towns and cities.

Zero-emissions, or something close to it, is a dream that we will attain earlier. Battery-electric cars will be most successful at either extreme of the car market. Some drivers will keep an additional electric city car for popping into or around town, while the rip-roaring acceleration of all-electric hyper-cars will appeal to rich ex-petrolheads who'll be queuing up and endlessly debating the merits of superstars like the Tesla Roadster 2 (1.9 seconds 0–60 mph) and Rimac C Two (1.85 seconds 0–60 mph).

Don't expect the roads to be entirely dominated by the whine of battery-powered electric motors, or whatever alternative soundtracks have been installed to help you hear their approach. Internal-combustion-engine cars in the form of cleaned-up diesel and hybridised petrol models will continue being the mainstay of personal transport for at least the next couple of decades, and becoming more and more efficient at powering lighter cars made of more advanced materials. The lightweighting expertise of the likes of McLaren, with its clever composite confections, will spread down to a wider market. In the longer term hydrogen will join batteries to make an anxiety- and carbon-free choice for all types of driver. Meanwhile, our cars will continue to become more connected, contributing enormously to safer driving and, hopefully, increasing speeds again.

Car use and buying patterns won't change overnight either. Americans will still buy pickup trucks. We'll continue to dream of faster and faster cars and make more and more gorgeous designs. The future will have its own Lamborghini Miuras, Jaguar E-Types, Aston Martin DB4 GT Zagatos and, for that matter, Minis and 2CVs. Expressions of individuality and customisation will soar, aided by 3D printing. Our love of speed won't be put back into the box. Young people won't give up on driving, however much older people might wish them to. Indeed the very promotion or subsidy of car sharing, and attempts to cut car ownership by nanny-ish planning and punitive taxation, might actually make owning a car seem even more desirable and prestigious.

When Nikita Khrushchev, leader of the Soviet Union, visited the United States in 1959 he was appalled by the numbers of cars. 'In our country cars will be used more rationally than in America,' he declared. 'Taxi pools will be widely developed where people will obtain cars when they need them. Why would one rack one's brains over where to put the car, why be bothered with it?' This taxi-sharing model of personal transport never took off. Every Russian wanted a car of their own and spent years and years saving up for a rotten Lada or similar piece of junk.

There is a revolution ahead but it's not the autonomous and electric tunnel vision one might expect. The future is one of more intelligent, more diverse driving experiences. We'll embrace a much wider range of cars in the future and use more rather than fewer of them. We might cherish something historic and have the option to exercise and maintain it on a heritage campus, use a battery-EV for urban trips, and take something more autonomous with a hybrid or hydrogen power unit for longer journeys. We'll pay subscriptions to motorsport driving-experience parks where AI and VR offers unparalleled instruction on how to drive better, and witness new, more exciting and more involving forms of motorsport. We'll continue to experience the sensual delight of tyres straining against tarmac and cars like Lotus Elises, Porsche 911s and Ariel Atoms with chassis expressly designed to capture the sheer pleasure and dynamic thrill of tackling the twisting blacktop.

Perhaps a more gradual process is a blessing in disguise. We like to be in control. Cars give us ecstatic thrills while we sit down in a comfortable environment and listen to the entertainment of our choice. They represent freedom combined with some of the best tactile pleasures and sensations that life can offer. They're not going away anytime soon.

IMAGE CREDITS

Main Text

© Wikimedia Images, pages 16, 126 (top left, middle left, bottom left)

© Nvidia, page 26

© Waymo, page 35

© Tesla Motors Inc, page 50

© Laura McFarlane, page 69

© Riversimple, page 75

© Getty Images, pages 94, 102, 165, 167

© Jon Bentley, pages 108, 120, 122, 136, 201, 213

© Aston Martin, page 132

© Porsche, page 126 (top right)

© Land Rover, page 126 (middle right)

© Daimler, page 126 (bottom right)

© Ariel Motor Company, page 151

© Hankook Tires, page 175

© NCAP, page 184

© AP Images, page 198

© www.andysaunders.net, page 180

© Gert van der Ende, page 217

© Jaguar, page 230

© Ford, page 239

© McLaren, chapter opening illustration

Plate Section

Page 1 (both images): © Christofer Sætrang

Page 2 (top): © Shyamal Kansara

Page 2 (bottom): © Stavros Mavrakis

Page 3 (both images): © Getty Images

Page 4 (both images): © Mercedes

Page 5 (both images): © WayRay

Page 6 (both images): © Terrafugia

Page 7 (both images): © Renault

Page 8 (both images): © BMW

INDEX

Page numbers in *italic* indicate illustrations

257